MASTERPLOTS II

POETRY SERIES

MASTERPLOTS II

POETRY
SERIES
SUPPLEMENT

8
Fre-Poem

Editors

JOHN WILSON   **PHILIP K. JASON**

Project Editor
MCCREA ADAMS

SALEM PRESS

Pasadena, California   Hackensack, New Jersey

Editor in Chief: Dawn P. Dawson
Managing Editor: Christina J. Moose
Project Editor: McCrea Adams   *Production Editor:* Yasmine A. Cordoba
Acquisitions Editor: Mark Rehn   *Manuscript Editor:* Douglas Long
Research Supervisor: Jeffry Jensen   *Research Assistant:* Jun Ohnuki

Library of Congress Cataloging-in-Publication Data
Masterplots II. Poetry series. Supplement / edited by John Wilson
and Philip K. Jason.
    p.   cm.
Includes bibliographical references and indexes.
        1. Poetry—Themes, motives. I. Wilson, John, 1948-   .
II. Jason, Philip K., 1941-   .
PN1110.5.M37   1992
809.1—dc20   91-44341
Supplement   CIP
ISBN 0-89356-625-X (set)
ISBN 0-89356-627-6 (volume 8)

First Printing

PRINTED IN THE UNITED STATES OF AMERICA

LIST OF TITLES IN VOLUME 8

MASTERPLOTS II

POETRY SERIES

FRENCH AND ENGLISH

Author: Leonard Cohen (1934-   )
Type of poem: Satire
First published: 1978, as "Our Government-in-Exile," in *Death of a Lady's Man*; as "French and English" in *Stranger Music*, 1993

The Poem

"French and English" comprises fifty lines of mostly satirical free verse. In this poem Leonard Cohen attacks extremists in the political and linguistic dispute that began to intensify in Quebec during the early 1960's. No explicit mention is made of this most distinctive of Canadian provinces in the poem, but Cohen grew up there in the 1950's and 1960's. His primary residence is now near Los Angeles, but he still maintains a home in Montreal. His own experiences in Quebec are clearly the inspiration for this poem. It is an attempt to shock, shame, and insult fanatics on both sides, encouraging everyone involved to find a peaceful solution to the escalating conflict.

French Canadians and the language that they speak are subjected to rhetorical scorn in the first sixteen lines. For example, the extremely abstract thinking of French philosophers such as René Descartes is mocked as "inflamed ideas" and as "a theoretical approach/ to common body functions" caused by the French language. The domination of Quebec society before the 1960's by the Roman Catholic Church is burlesqued by the reference to "a tacky priesthood devoted to the salvation/ of a failed erection." Even the stereotype of poor dental care in Quebec is flung into the reader's face. Quebeçois "pepsis" are ridiculed for drinking too much soda pop, causing the "rotten teeth of French." Effective expression of the glorious goal of independence for Quebec is thus overwhelmed by bad teeth and halitosis.

The next fourteen-line segment of the poem is devoted to English, described as a "sterilized swine of a language that has no genitals." Scatological images and references proliferate, identifying English-speaking people with "peepee and kaka and nothing else." The stereotype of English culture as particularly reserved is lampooned by the implication that the English are hesitant to French kiss because they "are frightened by saliva." As a final insult to conclude the stanza, the English are castigated as being "German with a licence to kill."

The satirical assault on both French- and English-speaking Canadians continues in the third section of the poem. Together they are referred to as "boobies of the north" and "dead-hearted turds of particular speech." However, an optimistic alternative is also invoked. The speaker proposes the possibility of communication beyond the built-in prejudices of any language and of salvation beyond politics. This positive alternative is sketched in a series of striking sexual, musical, and religious images. The poet suggests that kneeling "between the legs of the moon" and performing a sort of mystical cunnilingus is a better use for the human tongue than speaking either French or English. Escaping the respective chauvinisms that are paralyzing Quebec, both francophone and anglophone extremists are invited to lift their voices musically, "like the wind harps you were meant to be." Both sides could then awake into a "state of common grace."

Forms and Devices

The speaker of this poem assumes the first-person point of view, using the personal pronoun "I" throughout. The poem doubtless expresses Leonard Cohen's attitudes and feelings toward the conflict that is its subject. However, Cohen is speaking as it were through an angry puppet: he has adopted an extremely aggressive persona in order to dramatize his theme effectively. The persona of the speaker in "French and English" employs the rhetorical technique of hyperbole. He rants and raves in wild exaggeration, understood as such, in order to depict clearly the warped extremes each side tends to mirror in the other. He subverts the appeal and dissipates the hatred of French and English fanatics by turning them into ridiculous caricatures.

The primary rhetorical mode employed in this poem is satire. Satire was allegedly invented by the Greek cynic Menippus, whose works are lost. Since then it has been written in many formal variations, but the common element in all of them is attack. Public institutions, political parties, fashionable attitudes, even prominent individuals are held up for intense criticism in this way. Perhaps the best-known example of satire in English literature is "A Modest Proposal" by Jonathan Swift. In this parody of a political editorial, Swift proposed a radical solution to the problem of poverty in eighteenth century Ireland. His proposal was to sell the infants of poor Irish people to be cooked and eaten as an exotic delicacy for the tables of the ruling class. His point was to attack the callous attitude of certain people toward the suffering of those less fortunate than themselves.

The structure of "French and English" is based on the dialectical method originating with the Greek philosopher Socrates and developed more systematically in the nineteenth century by Georg Wilhelm Friedrich Hegel and Karl Marx. The three stanzas of the poem correspond to the three stages in the dialectical evolution of an idea: the thesis, antithesis, and synthesis. The first stanza caricatures the attitude of the ruling class in Quebec. (Historically, English dominance dates from the defeat of the French by the English on the Plains of Abraham near Quebec City in 1759.) By virtue of their military dominance and the cooperation of the Roman Catholic Church, the English ruling class was able to prosper disproportionately.

The second stanza caricatures the antithetical reaction of the French majority, which intensified dramatically in the 1960's. The power vacuum left by the declining influence of the Church and the global devolution of the British Empire has been filled to a great extent by the independence movement in Quebec politics. This movement arose in opposition to the thesis of the status quo. The synthesis in dialectical theory is created from the struggle between the thesis and the antithesis. The third stanza of "French and English" calls for a positive and peaceful resolution to the conflict. Such a possibility is imagined through the power of music, love, and spiritual awareness.

Themes and Meanings

This poem focuses on the impasse of linguistic and cultural misunderstanding in Canada. Hugh MacLennan coined the expression "two solitudes" in his 1945 novel of the same title to refer to the psychological distance between the English and French communities. Though this problem, satirically described in parts 1 and 2, has become extremely political, the solution to it evoked in part 3 is not.

Parts 1 and 2 begin respectively with the same line, the last word only being changed: "I think you are fools to speak French/English." Cohen seems to be implying that all people are fools when they depend on the formal peculiarities of any language. No language is adequate, by itself, to effect the miracle of human communication. Words are dead and useless unless they are animated by music, love, and spirit. The third stanza also begins with two practically identical lines, "I hate you but it is not in English/ I love you but it is not in French." The poet is saying that the particular sound and/or written form of a word are incidental to its real significance. Both love and hate are essentially expressed by a language of the heart, which all people share.

Leonard Cohen is better known as a songwriter and singer than as a poet, and his reputation demonstrates his commitment to the musical element in language. His tunes are a protest against the "flat rhythms" of English. Without music, language becomes a trap, and "the lovers die in all your songs." The reader is invited to escape from the trap with the help of "other voices" in order to find a common "mother tongue/ and be awakened by a virgin." The reference to oral sex ten lines earlier is still fresh in the reader's mind when it is extended, transformed, and combined in this line with an image of spiritual reawakening or rebirth. The radical juxtaposition and intertwining of sexual and spiritual images in the third stanza is typical of Cohen's writing. Sexual communication and spiritual awareness are understood as two inseparable aspects of love.

Fanatical French and English partisans in Quebec are attacked in this poem from the point of view of the fundamental force of life, sex, which requires no particular language. They are also attacked from the point of view of the enlightened spirit that can transcend ordinary language. Though Cohen is Jewish and has studied Zen Buddhism for many years, the references here are mainly to the spiritual tradition of Christianity. The poem concludes with the image of prisoners of "particular speech" being resurrected by the intercession of a virgin, presumably Mary. The possibility of political and linguistic peace in Quebec is thereby affirmed as a potential benefit flowing from the "grace" of God.

Steven Lehman

THE GIFT

Author: Jean Burden (1914-   )
Type of poem: Lyric
First published: 1992, in *Taking Light from Each Other*

The Poem

"The Gift" is a twenty-eight-line poem written in free verse. Under the title, Jean Burden dedicates the poem "for Cristy." Writing in the first person, Burden reveals the nature of the gift in the first two lines: "You gave me the socks/ off your feet." Possessing a wry wit, Burden parodies the expression "the shirt off your back" with these opening lines. Although Cristy's age and relationship to the poet are never precisely identified, it seems clear that Cristy is much younger than Burden and that they must be very close friends. In reality, Cristy was a young woman in her twenties and nearly forty years younger than the poet at the time of the poem's writing. Written in 1976, "The Gift" is one of a number of poems that Burden composed while staying at the MacDowell Colony, a colony for artists located in Peterborough, New Hampshire.

The socks, "dark blue, striped in red and white,/ with embroidered clocks of cats," are given to the poet in a restaurant. Cristy states matter-of-factly, "'Of course you must have them.'" The waitress in the poem is startled by the sight of Cristy removing her socks; "Demure/ in Japanese kimono," she "almost spilled the tea" when Cristy strips "to pink toes." After being given the colorful socks, Burden says, she placed them "in a napkin/ and stuffed them in my Gucci bag." She and Cristy then left the restaurant and "squeaked up Park Avenue." With the identification of Park Avenue, it is clear that Burden and Cristy are in New York City. As they walk, Cristy is wearing her "leather boots" with "sockless feet," and the poet, in contrast, feels "embarrassingly/ over-shod."

Reflecting on how generous Cristy was and how the poet desires to balance the scales, Burden comments, "I never gave you anything/ as right as that/ except once—a fossil polished/ by the sea." Since Cristy has been such a loyal friend and given up even the socks off her feet, Burden understandably wants to do right by her friend. Cristy lets it be known that the socks cost only forty-nine cents. Burden plays on this fact by concluding the poem with the lines "Nothing comes out even./ The stone was free." Without bombast, she has employed subtle humor to talk about the real value of any gift. The appropriateness of a gift is not contingent on its monetary value. It is indeed, as the saying goes, the thought that counts.

Forms and Devices

In numerous other poems Burden has shown herself to be adept at using common speech in original ways. In "The Gift" the poet addresses the reader in a direct manner rather than employing a persona to express some experience that is not her own. What transpires in the poem is Burden's own experience. Cristy is a real person, and she did give the poet her socks in a New York restaurant. Although "The Gift" is written in free verse, there is nonetheless a subtle lyrical rhythm in the poem. The lines of the poem are condensed. Burden is a master of the delicate observation, of creating a well-modulated poem through spare and understated images. Without relying on cliché or worn-out phrases, she uses common language to create fresh images. Although Robert Frost once described writing free verse as "playing tennis without a net," there is a need for discipline in free verse just as there is in any other poetic form. Burden uses precise language to convey sights and sounds. One of the sound devices that Burden employs is alliteration, the repetition of initial consonant sounds of words that are in close proximity. In "The Gift" there are *s* sounds with such words as "socks," "striped," "staid," "stripping," "spilled," "stuffed," "squeaked," "said," and "stone." While in untrained hands alliteration can be over used and thus awkward or ponderous, Burden drops in the appropriate sound precisely where needed.

In her 1966 essay collection *Journey Toward Poetry*, Burden speaks about the need for poems to possess simplicity without being simpleminded, to be stripped of artifice, and to speak in a straightforward manner. As the poetry editor of *Yankee* magazine, beginning in 1955, and a veteran poetry teacher, Burden believes strongly that a poem should be filled with the poet's vision. When a specific event is related honestly and freshly, it can become an experience with which the reader can identify. While "The Gift" may seem slight and does not demand to be seen as a "consequential" poem, its value grows through its quiet use of humor. The idea that humor or wit is employed only by poets who are writing lightweight poems is a severe underestimation of the value of humor in contemporary poetry. Humor is a very human response to many monumental concerns, and it can provide a fresh viewpoint to an age-old problem. In "The Gift" Burden uses a quirky and amusing experience to speak about friendship, sacrifice, and obligation to those one loves.

Themes and Meanings

Although written in 1976, "The Gift" was not collected until 1992 with the publication of Burden's second poetry collection, *Taking Light from Each Other*. Her first collection, *Naked as the Glass*, was published in 1963. *Taking Light from Each Other* is divided into five sections, and "The Gift" is included in the fourth section of the book. As with other poems of the section, it celebrates the value of interpersonal relationships with pointed observation and cunning wit. No matter how serious the topic, Burden never loses sight of the playful ordering of words. She approaches the favor that Cristy did for her without sentimentality. Although unorthodox, the giving of socks is a magnificent gesture of friendship. A true friend will make a sacrifice even in a public place where it could be awkward or embarrassing. While Cristy feels no qualms in giving up her socks, the poet puts them away in a bag. The reader has a sense that these are two unique individuals who express themselves in their own personal ways. Burden recognizes what has been done for her and regrets that she has not done more for her good and loyal friend.

The cost of the socks was forty-nine cents, almost nothing, but in comparison with a stone that was free, they were expensive. As Burden states, "Nothing comes out even." Between friends and between lovers, good deeds cannot be balanced in a ledger. It is self-evident that people who are close will want to help each other when the need arises, and Burden uses one humorous incident to make this larger point. As with many of her poems in *Taking Light from Each Other*, Burden has written freshly, lovingly, humorously, and convincingly about the complexities of human relationships.

Jeffry Jensen

GIRL POWDERING HER NECK

Author: Cathy Song (1955-   )
Type of poem: Lyric
First published: 1983, in *Picture Bride*

The Poem

"Girl Powdering Her Neck" is a free-verse lyric poem written in short lines of varying length divided into seven stanzas, also of varying lengths. The title and descriptive subtitle ("from a ukiyo-e print by Utamaro") refer to the Japanese artist Kitagawa Utamaro (1753-1806), the most well-known of many Japanese printmakers working in the ukiyo-e tradition who produced sensitive studies of a privileged class of highly cultivated and well-respected courtesans (among other subjects). The Japanese word *ukiyo-e*, commonly translated as "pictures of the floating world," suggests the transitory nature of beauty. Like the wood-block print that the poem's third-person narrator is describing and interpreting, the poem is a close-up view of a woman preparing herself, as she does daily, to be the object of a transitory but beautiful encounter.

The first two stanzas describe the setting in which this woman (or "girl," according to the title) is depicted, but because the setting has already been presented by Utamaro, what the narrator offers is essentially an art critic's view of a fine print. For example, the opening lines—"The light is the inside/ sheen of an oyster shell"—ask the reader to imagine the quality of light in the print as much as in an actual scene, a double pleasure. Yet the poem is more than an art critic's adventurous use of form; the narrator is as entranced by the story this scene suggests as the artist must have been, as can be seen in the poem's interpretation of the oyster-sheen quality of the light as "moisture from a bath." One part of the poem seems to imagine what is beyond Utamaro's print; outside "the rice-paper doors" of the room in which the woman kneels, this being a traditional Japanese house, she has left her slippers. Because everyone in this culture took off their shoes before entering a house or a room off a balcony (as the room in the poem probably is), this intimate detail portrays the woman as utterly human, ordinary, needful of slippers—hardly the intensely seductive and fragile creature she is about to turn herself into for her day's work. Again, in the last two stanzas of the poem, the narrator imagines the woman as human, as perhaps longing for some break in the facade that she creates daily.

From the setting the narrator moves in the second stanza to the woman herself, briefly describing the color of her hair. The third stanza provides evidence of the woman's occupation as a courtesan, with the phrase "the ritual/ wheel of the body" hinting at the countless days begun with the same ritual application of powder used to whiten and smooth, to make "translucent skins" with many delicate layers of powder. The implications of the double entendre of the next line, that "She practices pleasure," are made clear in the closing lines of the stanza, in which the narrator looks ahead to the movement "some other hand will trace" upon the woman's face, following, as the verb "trace" suggests, her very movements.

The fine kimono, draped open at the shoulders so that the woman can powder her neck without spoiling the silk, is described in stanza 5. From the woman's shoulders and neck the narrator's attention turns to her face reflected in the mirror, a familiar device of ukiyo-e prints that allows the artist to portray two views of a woman's beauty. The narrator compares the mirror to "a winter pond" in which the woman's face can be seen "rising to meet itself." The stanza's comparisons of the woman's shoulder to a snow-covered hill and her face to a reflection in a pond suggest cool appraisal of her beauty, which is indeed what the woman herself bestows upon her reflected beauty in the sixth stanza, where her "eyes narrow/ in a moment of self-scrutiny." The final image of the poem of two chrysanthemums touching and drifting apart "in the middle of a lake" is a metaphoric echo of the woman's futilely parting her lips in the previous stanza, "as if desiring to disturb/ the placid plum face."

Forms and Devices

The poem is rich in visual imagery. The second stanza's deliberately unconventional comparison of the color of the woman's hair—"black/ with hints of red"—to "the color of seaweed/ spread over rocks" picks up the hint of ocean and water imagery begun in the opening stanza's comparison of the scene's light to the "sheen of an oyster shell." This imagery is continued in the fifth stanza with the comparison of the woman's mirror to "a winter pond" and in the last stanza's comparison of her face itself to a still lake. The "floating world" to which this woman belongs, as suggested by this imagery, is not only a quality of experience that she can provide but also an essential part of her own character or person. She exists as part of the natural world, a positive force in it as well as a creature trapped by it.

The richest image comes in the implied metaphor that ends the poem. The striking placement of this metaphor in its own, final stanza creates the same effect as can be achieved in haiku, in which a single image reverberates with meaning barely suggested by a previous line. While more than one interpretation of the metaphor is possible, one possibility is that the two drifting chrysanthemums floating in a lake are the just-parted "berry-stained lips" in the woman's still, white face. The aimless passivity of the flowers' movement echoes the woman's own absolute silence, in itself a part of the stylized "mask of beauty" that she wears, as another, smaller metaphor, "the symmetry of silence," suggests.

The lining of the free verse is fairly simple, with line breaks coming at points suggested by naturally occurring breaks in grammatical units, such as before similes, as in the lines "She dips a corner of her sleeve/ like a brush into water," before prepositional phrases, as in "Her hair is black/ with hints of red," or after verbs:

> The eyes narrow
> in a moment of self-scrutiny.
> The mouth parts
> as if desiring to disturb
> the placid plum face.

Slightly more complex lining is found in stanza 4, with "Morning begins the ritual/ wheel of the body," but this is almost the only instance of an unexpected disruption of a syntactical unit. The effect of this steady pulsing rhythm is to echo the poem's theme, that almost nothing unexpected will ever occur in the ritualized form of beauty this woman inhabits.

Themes and Meanings

"Girl Powdering Her Neck" is both about the girl of the title and Utamaro's depiction of her. As in poems by William Carlos Williams, Cathy Song "reads" the work of a visual artist and finds meaning in it, leading the reader to see beyond the surface of the beauty the print depicts. The "peach-dyed kimono/ patterned with maple leaves/ drifting across the silk" is a lovely image whose surface is so perfect there seems to be no need to look beyond it. Yet Cathy Song offers an interpretation of this beauty that is at odds with its pure serenity. By gazing long enough at the woman preparing to powder her neck, some idea about what is going on in the woman's mind surfaces: She may have something to say but does not. She is so thoroughly masked by the powder, the berry-stain, even the lovely kimono that no disruption of the beautiful surface that she has created can be allowed—either by the conventions of the culture that invented her beauty or by herself, who lives and fulfills those conventions. She thinks ("The eyes narrow/ in a moment of self-scrutiny"), but her lips "do not speak."

Another theme of the poem may be that beauty is as rigorous, demanding, and confining as it is beautiful, but it is not so thoroughly masklike as to forbid any glimpse into the human being behind the facade. Cathy Song brings the humanity of the girl powdering her neck alive by recognizing in Utamaro's print Utamaro's recognition of that humanity. The poem is a tribute both to this girl and those who lived lives like hers and to Utamaro, for his insight into the nature of their beauty.

Lisa A. Seale

GIRLFRIEND

Author: Alan Shapiro (1952-   )
Type of poem: Narrative
First published: 1996, in *Mixed Company*

The Poem

"Girlfriend" is a medium-length free-verse poem with eighty lines divided into three stanzas of twenty-five, twenty-one, and thirty-four lines. The lines of the poem are short: Most of them vary from four to six syllables in length, although some lines have as many as nine syllables. In the first stanza, it almost appears that longer, decasyllabic lines have been divided in half in order to make up two lines of Shapiro's poem. The title suggests that the poem will focus upon a memory or anecdote about a girlfriend from the speaker's past. The poem is written in the first person, and the voice of the poem's speaker, like most of the other poems in *Mixed Company* (1996), greatly resembles the voice of the poet as he remembers people and events from childhood and adolescence.

The speaker in "Girlfriend" is an adult male who is looking back fondly, yet ironically, at a relationship that he now calls "The perfect match." The girlfriend, who is unnamed, is slightly more sexually experienced than the young speaker. The speaker recognizes that her experience and knowledge are what attracted him to her. She was able to instruct him as a "school marm" might. Shapiro's speaker shows no regret for this lost love. Instead of lamenting the absence of the girlfriend, the speaker views her merely as someone who guided him through one rite of passage that is associated with coming-of-age.

The second stanza begins with an address to readers that reminds them of their place as observers and informs them that passing time has not allowed the speaker enough distance to judge this story objectively. This stanza also reinforces the analogy to the teacher-student relationship. The speaker remembers being an earnest student, not in order to please his girlfriend but in order to avoid embarrassment. Shapiro's speaker has an awkward moment of self-awareness when he remembers being lost in his own thoughts: He was so caught up in his own pleasure during intercourse that he was oblivious to the reactions of his girlfriend. He was so absorbed in his own thoughts that he found this intimate moment to be another "way of being left/ alone."

The third and final stanza begins with the end of intercourse and the girlfriend excusing herself. The young speaker is left alone and is wholly overwhelmed by his own thoughts. He is so absorbed in his self-awareness that he reimagines the act that they have just completed over and over in his head. He finds that the reimagination of the sex is better than the sex actually was. He is brought out of his own thoughts by the sound of his girlfriend giggling on the phone in the next room, presumably talking to one of her girlfriends about his poor performance. The poem concludes with the adult speaker stating how her voice continues to haunt him: Whenever he feels too self-confident, it always serves to humble him.

Forms and Devices

Shapiro's diction and syntax often mimic the rhythms of plain, colloquial speech. This is the literary convention that readers will immediately notice as they read this poem. Readers who are familiar with the Romantic tradition in English literature will recognize an adherence to William Wordsworth's instruction in the preface to *Lyrical Ballads* (1800) about how "the language of a large portion of every good poem, even of the most elevated character, must necessarily, except with reference to the metre, in no respect differ from that of good prose."

Although "Girlfriend" resembles the language of prose, that does not mean that it is prose. Shapiro's own comments on James McMichael's "Four Good Things" (1980) in *In Praise of the Impure* (1993) can also be used as an apt description of "Girlfriend": It "seems like poetry on the verge of speech and speech on the verge of poetry." Within this free-verse poem, there are passages in which Shapiro employs a loose iambic meter that makes the reader aware of a heightening formality within the speaker's voice. Most noticeable is the address to the reader in the second stanza. The first two lines of the second stanza ("You'd be, of course,/ a better judge of this"), if combined into one line, would read as iambic pentameter. Allowing meter to enter the poem at this time forces the reader into an awareness that this poem is not a story and that it is instead a crafted and sculpted lyric poem that merely resembles a story. It also creates an odd tension between the speaker and the reader. At the moment that the conversational language of this poem becomes more formal, the speaker invites the reader into the poem to be an observer who should assess the motivations of the poem's characters.

The speaker's conversational voice resembles that of a storyteller who brings all of his experience and personality into the retelling of a personal anecdote, which allows the reader to recognize the poem as the product of a particular individual who speaks from a particular historical moment. The voice of the speaker allows the reader to learn about the narrative in a way that makes the narrative itself seem secondary to the way that it is told. Indeed, one important aspect of this poem is the way that the details come back to the speaker willfully. The speaker always remains in full control of the story that he is telling the reader. There is little free association or wordplay in Shapiro's poem. Instead, the poem is a thoughtful and sober retelling of a memory that often returns to haunt the adult speaker.

There is a sculpted and almost minimalistic quality to the detail; readers know much less about this drama than Shapiro must know. One never learns the girl's name or what she looks like. There is no discussion of the relationship before or after this moment. There is little to prove that the girl exists anywhere in the world outside of this brief drama. Also missing are clues about the poem's location. The spareness of details reminds one that this drama exists in the speaker's consciousness more than it exists in the physical world.

Themes and Meanings

"Girlfriend" is a poem about memory. The speaker is committed to exploring the past and examining how his past actions are revised by his memory. This speaker does not express a desire to change any of the details of this drama about the loss of virginity. Instead, he hopes to come to an understanding of how this one small incident from the past helps make him the person that he is today. Therefore, the work of a poetic project such as this is never finished; it is ongoing because any one person's life has too much complexity to be resolved in one poem. In many of Shapiro's poems, past interacts with present as he engages in his quest to understand all the complex factors that have contributed to his becoming the person that he is today. Thus, the drama that the speaker in "Girlfriend" reveals is more than an anecdotal remembrance of something that once took place. It takes on a dimension of heroic proportions when one recognizes that the adult speaker is wrestling with all of his personal history.

There is also an instructive quality to such a confession. Without telling its readers that similar explorations are necessary in order to understand all the history that goes into the creation of each person's self, it displays a person engaged in such exploration. Readers will realize that if they are to understand themselves they must also engage in a similar exploration of their past experiences and actions. One's whole life is constantly reexamined and explored in order to understand one's experience. Poets such as Robert Lowell, Anne Sexton, and W. D. Snodgrass are famous early examples of the confessional tradition in American poetry.

The poem is notable for what it discovers about the self. Instead of being able to look at this somewhat humiliating experience and laugh at it, the speaker admits that the girl's giggling still haunts him and that he cannot escape the burden of this memory. In this brief drama, the older and experienced speaker remembers one incident that led to his loss of innocence. The loss of innocence that occurs is not necessarily the loss of sexual innocence. Instead, it is the loss of solipsism. The young, virginal speaker was not at all concerned with the pleasure or desire of his partner. In his unwise and innocent state, he was only concerned with his own pleasure. His memory of this experience reminds him that he cannot return to such solipsism, that her reliable "tune/ of scorn" will not allow it. This constant reminder forces the speaker to be wiser. He will always remember the possible pitfalls when he might "grow too free/ in pleasure." This memory of his girlfriend's scorn is an inescapable reminder of the young, overly self-aware, pathetic young boy that he once was. It is the act of remembering this drama that keeps the adult speaker from returning to his youthful, unwise solipsism.

Jeffrey Greer

THE GLASS ESSAY

Author: Anne Carson (1950-   )
Type of poem: Poetic sequence
First published: 1995, in *Glass, Irony, and God*

The Poem

"The Glass Essay" is an ambitious, inventive, thirty-eight-page series of interrelated poetic montages and meditations on the loss of love. This central theme is developed using three interwoven sets of images: memories of the life and works of nineteenth century English novelist Emily Brontë, memories of the author's family, and visions concerning the nature of poetry. Using short prose passages, triplet line structure, one-word subheadings, and short sentences floating in white space, Anne Carson intermingles dreams, memories, family portraits, and quotations from Brontë's letters and diary papers to explore the nature of gender, the artistry of writing, and, most importantly, the painful feelings in the aftermath of lost love. With these juxtaposed streams emphasizing the place of the mind and body in human relationships, the poem begins and ends with two perspectives on the female body, the central image of the poem.

The poem begins at four o'clock in the morning in a dream, followed by the poem's first glass or mirror image: "my face in the bathroom mirror/ has white streaks down it." The setting then moves to the house of the poet's mother where the three central women of the poem—the poet, her mother, and Brontë—are compared and contrasted, showing three generational perspectives regarding self-identity and relationships with men. Carson begins weaving her tropes by stating that visits with her mother make her fear that she is becoming Brontë, and she compares her kitchen to the moors in Brontë's novel *Wuthering Heights* (1847). Kitchen imagery—the dining table, food in the refrigerator, the mother eating toast—represent conventional expectations of women. The narrator's mother believes modern bathing suits arouse men, dislikes feminists, and tells her daughter that she should have worked more on her relationships with men, particularly the poet's five-year affair with the principal lover of her past named Law. This criticism prompts the poet into a meditation on Brontë's interest in "watching" from the cliffs on the moors and feeling imprisoned in a world of men. Brontë, the daughter of a clergyman trapped by strict Victorian conventions, walks the moor, has no friends, has no sexual life, cannot earn her own living, and thus writes poetry about prisons from her "invisible cage." The narrator connects her own life with Brontë's biography and fictional characters, observing that during the long period of grief after the loss of love, her body's needs are also a prison. The poet realizes that resolving these needs will be a major part of her healing process.

The poet sees mirroring characteristics that she shares with Heathcliffe, the male protagonist of *Wuthering Heights*, who is also tormented by his perceived loss of love. The poet recalls the scene in the novel in which Heathcliffe overhears a conversation in the kitchen but only hears the first half of his lover's sentence. Had he not run away, he would have heard her desire for him instead of living a half-life as a "pain devil." This fragmented communication is echoed in the poet's life when she goes to the hospital to visit her aging father who can no longer speak full sentences. She recalls previous uncertain meanings when her parents were younger and they exchanged sexual innuendoes beyond their then eleven-year-old daughter's comprehension. Throughout the poem, fragments and unclear meanings are a central motif demonstrated in Carson's images and line structure.

Carson develops her major points, remembering the thirteen pictures of female nudes in Law's house that become artistic muses in separate, numbered sections of the poem. Carson first attempts to perceive the female body intellectually as art, but she then decides that Brontë wrote art she "could neither contain nor control." This lack of control is seen as the link between art and romantic love that leads to loss and despair.

In a pivotal scene, the poem shifts back in time with descriptions of the last meeting between the poet and Law where he tells the writer he no longer desires her. In a last attempt to arouse him, the poet offers him her nude back, his favorite part of her body. Law moves on top of her and the poet realizes "Everything I know about love and its necessities/ I learned in that one moment." Thrusting her "burning red backside like a baboon/ at a man who no longer cherished me," the narrator describes images of coldness, winter, and cruelty. She compares Law with Heathcliffe and juxtaposes images of light and dark, saying she prefers the light of sexless day. Recalling the pictures of nudes, she focuses on nude "#1," a "Woman Caught in a Cage of Thorns." She describes Charlotte Brontë's conventional responses to her sister Emily's poems and compares her own self-expectations with those of the nineteenth century. This connection again becomes personal when the poet returns to the setting of her mother's kitchen where the two women argue about the responsibility of women arousing male sexual desires and the poet realizes her mother is afraid. The poet points to generational differences in their perspectives. Then, in a hospital, "where distinctions blur," the narrator visits her mentally ill father who is strapped to the wall, representing the other side of the glass or mirror. In the guise of her father, males are seen to be equally subject to imprisonment and mental anguish but for different reasons from those suffered by women.

Forms and Devices

In her narrative, Carson uses a number of common poetic techniques such as the repetition of words to emphasize dramatic moments. Many "broken moments" are intentional fragments meant to illustrate "half-lives" as "half-finished sentences." Carson's original imagery and mix of tones and styles move the poem from one theme to another in shifts that keep her three narratives easily understandable. Simultaneously, her images reinforce each other, repeating and underlining her points. For example, transparent images—primarily glass, mirrors, and ice—are both metaphors and euphemisms for sex and interpersonal communications and also serve as vivid, strongly drawn, and primarily quiet settings. Descriptions of the settings illustrate both external and emotional states. Wintery images of ice and cold underscore the poet's feelings of loss and reinforce her glass imagery. Near the poem's opening, Carson states, "It is as if we have all been lowered into an atmosphere of glass./ Now and then a remark trails through the glass." These fragmentary remarks evoke responses from different levels of the poet's consciousness, linking perspectives with experience. These glass images move from weather and the natural world to psychological states, allowing the poet to evaluate moments in her life from an emotional distance as in the lines "the video tape jerks to a halt/ like a glass slide under a drop of blood." Her "atmosphere of glass" is later juxtaposed with Brontë's "electric atmosphere" in which women wrestle with the "pain devil" of love.

Carson also makes use of colors and juxtapositions of light and dark. "Strings of lights" and lamps illuminate dark rooms, blue and black colors are repeated in various settings, and painful memories take place in cold, wintry settings that emphasize the darkness of feelings of loss. She observes that her mother and Law both prefer the dark. Her mother is angry over the poet's unwillingness to close shades and her preference for the morning sun. Carson's use of cool colors, particularly blue, contributes to the tone, mood, and imagery of the poem: Her aloof ex-lover Law lives in a "high blue room," time is described as "blue and green lozenges," and ice pokes through the "blue hole at the top of the sky." Gold is another repeated symbol of irony, including "gold milk," a "gold toothpick," and the "Golden Mile," the name of the chronic wing of the hospital where the poet's father is confined.

Several sets of images unify the different narratives, including visions of the body that begin and end the poem and are recurring images throughout. For example, when Law announces he no longer desires the poet, she realizes "There was no area of my mind/ not appalled by this action, no part of my body/ that could have done otherwise." The poem's final lines return to the author's body, nude "#13" now transformed into a vision:

> trying to stand against winds so terrible that the
> flesh was blowing off the bones.
> And there was no pain.
> The wind
> was cleansing the bones.
> They stood forth silver and necessary.
> It was not my body, not a woman's body, it was the
> body of us all.
> It walked out of the light.

By making her body a symbol of universal pain (literally stripped to the bone), Carson makes her breakup with Law a shared event with her readers, and she counsels them on how to deal with loss. Her reconciliation with loss allows her to create a distance from the pain in the mind, to put feelings in artistic and intellectual terms, and to examine loss and relieve its power.

Themes and Meanings

While most readers of "The Glass Essay" interpret it as primarily a statement of feminist anger against men, Carson's last stanzas broaden her theme of loss and love. Her use of Brontë's work points to a gender-based comment on the separation of the woman artist from cultural conventions and demonstrates the contrasting desires of the body and the intellect. In the opening of the poem, Carson states the importance of her internal conflict, but to "talk of mind and body" begs a series of questions particularly relating to the soul. "Soul is what I kept watch on all that night" and soul is "trapped in glass," she says, seeing family members forced to "tilt" to survive. Surviving and resolving loss take the soul through painful moments, forcing individuals to deal with the necessities of mind and body: "Soul is the place,/ stretched like a surface of millstone grit between body/ and mind,/ where such necessity grinds itself out." As with much of her other poetic work that explores the nature of eros and loss, bodies and boundaries, Carson sees religion as part of the struggle to achieve resolution. The moment of her breakup with Law is centered "between heaven and hell"; the poet connects this to her thoughts on Brontë and states that "one way to put off loneliness is to interpose god." Carson notes that Brontë's poems speak to a biblical, patriarchal "Thou," which prompts the poet to meditate and to chant Latin prayers. However, emulating Brontë, who "has gone beyond religion," Carson says she simply needs someone to talk to at night without "the terrible sex price."

The flesh as prison of mind and body is a dominant theme, from beginning to end a central conflict in the author's identity. At one point, the narrator's psychiatrist asks why she keeps dwelling on the terrible nudes in Law's rooms, but the poet has no answer. Later, reflecting on the first picture, the poet declares that speaking of nudes will perhaps make her points clearer, and she uses the heavily symbolic portraits to examine female psychological states. The grotesque, tortured pictures continually portray women as wounded victims in a series of surreal settings open to a wide variety of interpretations. For example, nude "#3" depicts a woman who is trying to pull out a "single great thorn implanted in her forehead." Nude "#4" shows a woman "on a blasted landscape" with her head covered by a contorting contraption. Women's lives are then symbolized by a white room without planes, angles, or curves (images of order reflecting male "law"). Other nudes return to vivid torture images: green thorns poking through a woman's heart with blood in the air and women under pressure of "bluish-black water." The repeated thorn imagery can be seen in both biblical and Freudian terms, while other images evoke sexual connotations. Nude "#13," which resembles nude "#1," brings the cycle full circle. She is the body stripped of its flesh, the poet herself coming out of the light.

Issues of identity and self-definition, forged in anger, are reflected throughout the poem: The poet sees women shaped by themselves and men linked in the sex acts she resents. "Girls are cruelest to themselves," she asserts, especially virgins such as Brontë, "who remained a girl all her life despite her body as a woman." Love changes girls to women, creating "animal hunger" that leads to "anger dreams" following the loss of love. The narrator believes "anger could be a kind of vocation for women."

This anger comes from the imprisoning "ropes and thorns" of male desires. Only loneliness allows "true creation" for women, and the poet ultimately declares, "I am my own nude and nudes have a difficult sexual destiny." To reach this destiny, a woman travels "From love to anger to this cold marrow,/ from fire to shelter to fire." Concluding "The Glass Essay," Carson discards mortal boundaries and ultimately finds resolution in rejection of gender and the body, peeling away layers of human conditions. Only after being cleansed to the bone can the poet walk out alone from the light in an artistic vision that transcends the needs of the body, images of the body, and mental interpretations of the body.

Wesley Britton

GOLD AND BLACK

Author: Michael Ondaatje (1943-   )
Type of poem: Lyric
First published: 1973; collected in *There's a Trick with a Knife I'm Learning to Do*, 1979

The Poem

"Gold and Black" is a short poem in free verse, its twelve lines divided into three stanzas. The title suggests color; its function is to show the color of the bees as well as the light images in the poem: the black night and the gold light. The first two stanzas are written in the first person. In the third stanza, the poem shifts to the third person, which adds a generality to its theme. There are times when a poet uses the first person to speak through a persona, as in a dramatic monologue, but here no distinction is implied between Michael Ondaatje the poet and the speaker of the poem. Yet, as Douglas Barbour writes in *Michael Ondaatje* (1993), "The 'I' that writes in these seemingly 'confessional' poems is purely inscribed, exists in each poem as a subject but alters his subjectivity from poem to poem." The "I" of "Gold and Black" can be seen as a character rather than the poet himself. A lyrical poem is about a subject, contains little narrative content, and addresses the reader directly.

"Gold and Black" begins with a metaphor for a nightmare, something that readers can readily understand. Just as a nightmare comes at night and disturbs the sleeper, so do the bees in the poem "pluck my head away." As the nightmare surrounds him, "Vague thousands drift" over him and "leave brain naked stark as liver." The nightmare, portrayed with the image of the bees, removes integral parts of his identity and creates a kind of spoiling of his thoughts. As the tone here is haunting and frightening, the image of the bees attacking the sleeper and taking away "atoms of flesh" is representative of the speaker's helplessness regarding his own nightmares, products of his unconscious.

In the second stanza, another person, Kim, is introduced; she is outside the speaker and outside the nightmare. The poet is no longer haunted by his nightmare but is instead affected by his lover, who is turning beside him: She "cracks me open like a lightbulb," he says. This action can be seen as Kim breaking the speaker into darkness as the nightmare flies away. As the poet takes readers out of the nightmare of the speaker, he takes them to the external forces in the speaker's world. His lover, too, is "In the black" but seems unaffected by her own nightmares. She is, rather, "a geiger counter" gauging his.

The third stanza shifts to a third-person point of view and describes "the dreamer" from a distance, as opposed to inside his own mind. This shift from the extremely personal first-person point of view to the generalization of the third-person point of view suggests that the problem of nightmarish hidden thoughts is everyone's problem. The shift also implies a universality in the loss of control in a nightmare, and ultimately in the unconscious. As this stanza concludes the poem, the reader is left with the image of "the dreamer in his riot cell," which suggests entrapment in a chaotic stage of sleep.

Forms and Devices

Metaphors are abundant in Ondaatje's work. He works with wondrous imagery and sometimes violent action, which both balance and reflect off each other. The people who inhabit his poems are often verging on madness and trying to deal with the violence and beauty of their worlds. With "Gold and Black," Ondaatje takes the ordinary state of sleep and creates a world of horror and loss of control over the speaker's thoughts, which buzz around him like bees and take parts of him with them.

A metaphor is a direct comparison between two dissimilar things, and "Gold and Black" is a series of images that are compared with one another. Most of the metaphors are implicit—the comparisons are not completely spelled out. For example, the poet never explicitly compares the nightmare to the "gold and black slashed bees," yet the context of the poem clearly suggests the comparison. The metaphors that the poet employs are both surprising (the bees taking the speaker's flesh away) and awesome (the dreamer trapped in the "riot cell" of his own mind), and they work to create the fantastic and private world of the speaker. They aim at mystery rather than explicitness, just as dreams often do.

The metaphors in "Gold and Black" move from the mind of the speaker to his external world and finally to the universal. This pattern is established in stanza 1, where "the gold and black slashed bees come/ pluck my head away." Although at first the image suggests external forces acting on the dreamer, it becomes clear that the bees are internal, as they "drift/ leave brain naked stark as liver." The last line of stanza 1 completes the pattern of the internal, creating a metaphor for the thoughts of the dreamer as rotten meat. Stanza 2 introduces Kim, who is outside of the speaker's mind (and nightmare), and takes the reader from the internal world of the dreamer: "She cracks me open like a lightbulb." The simili indicates that Kim has woken the speaker. She has cracked open the speaker's mind, the bees have flown away, and there is darkness in his mind where there was light.

The sleeper and Kim are surrounded by darkness, and the light in the speaker's unconscious has been put out. Stanza 3 depicts "the dreamer" from outside. The description of the subconscious as a "riot cell" depicts the loss of control in the realm of the subconscious as well as the confines of the "cell," or mind, that encompasses the thoughts. In several poems Ondaatje uses images of animals alongside images of the unconscious, particularly in the section "Rat Jelly" in *There's a Trick with a Knife I'm Learning to Do*. "Near Elginburg," "Spider Blues," and "The Gate in His Head" are other examples of this technique.

Themes and Meanings

"Gold and Black" is a poem about the unconscious, which is portrayed through nightmares and dreams. In one sense, the sleeper's underlying thoughts control the sleeper—as dreams and nightmares are seldom controlled—and illuminate hidden fears and desires of which the dreamer may or may not be aware. When we sleep, the subconscious surfaces and sheds lights on our innermost thoughts. The idea of being surrounded by darkness in order to see innermost thoughts has been explored by many poets. Ondaatje takes a somewhat unusual approach, however, in that here the light illuminates horror and violence, as opposed to beauty and truth, and it leaves the dreamer feeling helpless against his innermost fears. The shift to the third person at the end of the poem suggests, but does not definitively conclude, that all people are prisoners in their unconscious minds.

"Gold and Black" is also about isolation. The dreamer, in his nightmare, is isolated from the world and his loved ones. He must face his unconscious alone. Communication with the outside world is impossible within the nightmare, but as a loved one turns and wakes the dreamer, the nightmare goes dark, the light in the unconscious now out. "Gold and Black" takes the reader into the chaotic world of the senses and illustrates the difficulty that a suffering individual has in communicating his fears to the outside world—and even to himself.

Paula M. Martin

THE GOLD CELL

Author: Sharon Olds (1942-   )
Type of work: Book of poems
First published: 1987

The Poems

Sharon Olds is among the most highly regarded contemporary American poets. Her work has been described as "haunting" and "striking," and the novelist Michael Ondaatje has said that it is "pure fire in the hands." Like the poet's earlier books *Satan Says* (1980) and *The Dead and the Living* (1984), Olds's third collection, *The Gold Cell*, makes aspects of everyday life—news items, childhood, family, and sexuality—its subject matter. Olds tells her audiences at poetry readings that she did not publish her poetry until late in life (she was thirty-seven years old when her first book was published) because she did not know whether she wanted to make her work public. She also says that when she decided to publish, she considered using a pseudonym. This hesitation to publish may have had something to do with Olds's tendency to blur the lines between the public and the private, for it is never quite clear where she draws the line between what she calls "the paper world and the flesh world."

As a result, many of Olds's readers view her books as "poetic memoirs," comparing her to confessional poets such as Anne Sexton and Sylvia Plath. Historically, American poets have argued that to assume too much of a connection between a poem's speaker and its writer is to commit a "biographical fallacy," though some contemporary American poets, perhaps influenced by a growing tendency in the United States to view public exposure of the private self as emotionally healthy and socially productive, admit to writing highly autobiographical pieces (Linda McCarriston, for example). Olds has been unwilling to publicly discuss the connections between her private life and her poetry, though, so readers must encounter Olds's poems on more universal grounds, taking them as one poet's attempt to see the world clearly and to represent it accurately. In an interview with Patricia Kirkpatrick, Olds says, "We need to know how bad we are, and how good we are, what we are really like, how destructive we are, and that all this often shows up in families." When Olds writes about the difficult aspects of human nature, then, she invites her readers to confront those realities with her, to know that these are the circumstances not only of individual lives but also of life in general.

Olds has been described as a poet of the landscape of time, and *The Gold Cell* traverses that landscape. The book has four parts: The first part is concerned with the relationship of the poet to the world in which she lives, the second focuses on childhood, the third deals with life beyond childhood, and the fourth is about the relationships between parents and children. Among the most frequently discussed poems in the first section are "On the Subway" and "The Girl." In their own ways, these two poems are at once disturbing and redemptive. In "On the Subway," the speaker encounters a black man on the subway and is forced to acknowledge her own racist assumptions. She says, "white skin makes my life, this/ life he could break so easily, the way I/ think his back is being broken." "The Girl" is about a twelve-year-old girl who is raped and left for dead, then must go on with her life: "she does a cartwheel, the splits, she shakes the/ shredded pom-poms in her fists," knowing "what all of us want never to know."

"I Go Back to May 1937," in part 2 of *The Gold Cell*, is about the speaker's desire to communicate with her parents before their marriage to warn them, "you are going to do things/ you cannot imagine you would ever do,/ you are going to do bad things to children,/ you are going to suffer in ways you never heard of,/ you are going to want to die." Initially, the speaker, who has the 20/20 vision of hindsight, wishes she could collapse time in order to influence her life and the lives of her parents; she wants to save herself and her parents by warning them that they are going to make terrible mistakes. In the end, however, the poem declares, "Do what you are going to do, and I will tell about it." In the course of the poem, the speaker—clearly a writer—decides to speak about her life, to answer it in her own words rather than wish it away. This poem's primary goal is to tell about the world as the poet sees it. Olds says that the poet has only what she knows and that the poet's unique experiences are central to her work. The question both the reader and the poet must ask is, "What can this poem tell?"

The title of the book is directly connected to the overriding themes in *The Gold Cell*. The book's cover art, which illustrates the title, is an adaptation of figure 14 from *The Collected Works of C. G. Jung* (1959). The figure is a gold ball surrounded by a snake, and Jung identifies it as an "Indian picture of *Shiva-bindu*, the unexpected point." Jung explains, "The god rests in the point. Hence, the snake signifies extension, the mother of Becoming, the creation of the world of forms." The Hindu god Shiva is the primordial state and the snake encircles that state, indicating both the containment and the continuity of creation and life. Therefore, all life forms connect, and life itself connects with the concept of god and with its own beginnings or source. This reference to creation, and particularly to the feminine aspects of creation, plays itself out in virtually every poem in the book; each of the poems works to examine and elucidate both life's cyclical nature (the connection of every moment to the previous and to the next) and the connections among lives.

Forms and Devices

In *The Gold Cell*, as in most of Olds's work, the metaphor represents the poet's vision and thinking. In interviews, Olds expresses concern with seeing accurately; her poems reveal her commitment to this goal, for their vision is unflinching. Part of what Olds wants readers to see has to do with the connections between endings and beginnings. "Summer Solstice, New York City" has as its narrative core the story of a man threatening to commit suicide by jumping off a building and his interactions with the people who convince him not to jump. However, the poem's metaphors reveal one of its philosophical points: that life's beginning and its end are inextricably tied. That tie becomes apparent when the title, in which the summer solstice represents birth and renewal, comes together with the poem's first image: a suicidal man walking across the roof of a building, then standing with "one leg over the complex green tin cornice." Within the poem, Olds describes the bulletproof vest one "cop" puts on as a "black shell around his own life,/ life of his children's father," an image that illustrates that the police officer, in the middle of his life, is aware of the impact his death would have on the lives of his children who have just begun their lives. Olds describes the net meant to catch the man if he does jump as a sheet "prepared to receive at a birth" and the burning ends of the cigarettes that the man and the police officers smoke as "tiny campfires we lit at night/ back at the beginning of the world." Though the man finally chooses life, the poem is about the possibility of his death. When Olds ends by connecting the image of the men smoking and the image of campfires at the beginning of the world, she implies that there is a connection between the beginning of all time and the beginning created when the man chooses not to jump. One life, the poem seems to imply, can represent all life.

In "Alcatraz," the prison, famous for its remote location and for its reputation as inescapable, becomes a metaphor for a child's shame and for the intense power parents have over their children's sense of self. The connections between humans and other animals and between the manufactured and natural worlds are established as the metaphor deepens; the prison becomes "white as a white/ shark in the shark-rich Bay," and its bars are like the shark's "milk-white ribs." The child sees herself as a shameful creature who will be swallowed whole by the prison shark. She believes she will be trapped there forever with "men" like her "who had/ spilled their milk one time too many,/ not been able to curb their thoughts." "Alcatraz" draws a connection not only between the child's life and that of other animals but also between the female child and the adult men who inhabit the prison when the speaker proclaims, "When I was a girl, I knew I was a man/ because they might send me to Alcatraz/ and only men went to Alcatraz."

If the metaphor reveals to readers the way Olds sees and thinks, then the poetic line helps readers hear how she speaks. Like most American poets writing in free verse during the latter half of the twentieth century, Olds has expressed great concern for the poetic line. Olds is known for her run-on sentences broken into lines and for lines that end in articles and conjunctions. In the Kirkpatrick interview, she publicly analyzes her use of the poetic line in *The Gold Cell:* "As for ending lines on *of the*, I think I did that too much in *The Gold Cell*, so much that the poems as written lack the musical form I hear in them." In spite of the poet's criticism of her own work, the lines as she writes them serve an important function. In "Looking at My Father," for instance, the second sentence spans sixteen-and-a-half lines. There are, in those sixteen lines, fifteen commas, two semicolons, and one colon. The combination of a run-on construction and lines that end in articles and conjunctions lends a breathlessness to the poem that expresses the difficult moment when a child both recognizes the failings of her father and acknowledges her connection to and affection for him.

Themes and Meanings

Olds is known for her frank discussions of sex and sexuality, and poems such as "First Sex," which appears in *The Gold Cell*, illustrate that she sees sexual issues as inextricably tied to other issues related to the human condition. She says, "I'm just interested in human stuff like hate, love, sexual love and sex. I don't see why not." "First Sex" focuses, as the title implies, on the speaker's first sexual experience. It begins with the speaker's confession, "I knew little, and what I knew/ I did not believe—they had lied to me," then goes on to describe in vivid detail a sexual encounter. "First Sex" embodies both the excitement of sex and the youth of its characters in phrases such as "his face cocked back as if in terror" and "sweat/ jumping out of his pores like sudden/ trails." As is the case with many of Olds's poems about sex, "First Sex" is a poem with a punch line, for in the end the speaker proclaims, "I signed on for the duration."

After the first printing of *The Gold Cell*, Olds revised several poems. These revisions seem to be designed to clarify images or reflect the poet's further thinking about an issue. The most significant revisions occur in the poem called "What if God" in which she modifies an entire metaphor. Between the original and final versions of the poem, Olds clarifies the mother's role, changing the lines "when my mother/ came into my bed" to "when my mother/ came into my room, at night, to lie down on me/ and pray and cry" and "like a/ tongue of lava from the top of the mountain" to "like lava from the top of the mountain." Olds says that she made these revisions because readers were interpreting the poem as a piece about the sexual abuse of a female child by her mother, a reading she had not intended. She says that she had not realized her metaphor could be read so literally but that when readers pointed the reading out to her she felt it important to clarify the image.

The revision of the metaphor necessitated a revision of the entire poem, and changes that occur toward the end are perhaps more significant than the changes to the original metaphor. In the first version, the speaker asks, "did He/ wash His hands of me as I washed my/ hands of Him," but in the final version she says, "He/ washed his hands of me as I washed my/ hands of Him." In the first version there is a possibility for hope that God has not abandoned the child, but in the final version that hope is eradicated. In the next two lines, the speaker asks (in both versions), "Is there a God in the house?/ Is there a God in the house?" In the first version of the poem, in which the possibility of heavenly intervention to help the child exists, these are hopeful cries, but in the second version, in which there is no hope of such intervention, they are the futile cries of a helpless child. While Olds removes the disturbing images of the sexual abuse of a child from the poem, the final version is ultimately more hopeless than the original.

Michelle Gibson

GRAVELLY RUN

Author: A. R. Ammons (1926-   )
Type of poem: Lyric
First published: 1960; collected in *Corsons Inlet: A Book of Poems*, 1965

The Poem

"Gravelly Run" is a thirty-line free-verse lyric divided into six stanzas in which the speaker meditates on a small stream, questioning the connection between the world of human thought and the world of nature. The poem is characterized by a struggle between the highly abstract thought processes of the speaker and the concrete imagery of the stream. The poem opens with the speaker wrestling with a problem. The first line sounds as if the speaker has already been pondering the problem for a while. "I don't know," he says, indicating the tentative nature of what follows. The speaker proposes to himself that it is "sufficient" to concentrate only on the natural world, thus losing self-consciousness in nature, in "stones and trees."

In the second stanza, the poet explores the reasons for losing oneself in nature. He says that it is not as important "to know the self" in an absolute sense as it is to know the self as nature ("galaxy and cedar cone") knows it. This second way of knowing the self does not take in the notion of time, the notion that people are born and must one day die. Rather, the "galaxy and cedar cone" approach the self as it is at any given moment, without the intrusion of past or future.

Having come to this conclusion, the speaker turns to the scene at hand, the stream named in the title of the poem, which flows from a swamp and down to a highway bridge, washing the water plants along the way.

At this point, the speaker looks at the banks of the stream, where holly and cedars grow, both trees laden with religious symbolism. The grove of cedars, with their long, "gothic-clustered" trunks, makes the speaker think that they could inspire religious thought in even the coldest heart ("winter bones"). He looks at the trees and tries to evoke that religious sense, but it does not come. There is no revelation. Each distinct object, each tree, each holly leaf remains separate. The natural objects will not be transformed into something spiritual.

In the final stanza, the speaker comes to grips with the realization that the natural world is not a harbor for human emotions or thoughts. He realizes that no systems of thought ("philosophies") can be based on nature, that God does not exist in the holly. The objects of nature, he realizes, are not conscious ("the sunlight has never/ heard of trees"). Therefore, the speaker now sees that the "surrendered self," the self that lost itself among the "stones and trees" in the first stanza, is among "unwelcoming forms" that do not recognize it. The self is therefore a stranger in the natural world, and, since the natural world is not a place for philosophies to be built, the self must take up its burdens (which philosophies might solve) and take them back "down the road" (a human-made object) to civilization.

Forms and Devices

The major device in "Gravelly Run" is the play between abstract and concrete language. The poem itself is about a struggle between the speaker's human self-consciousness and the utter lack of consciousness on the part of the natural world.

The first three lines of the poem contain no concrete visual imagery: The language is abstract, reflecting the speaker's interior monologue. In these lines, the speaker advances the poem, developing his thoughts. Lines 4-6, however, contain only visual imagery. Whereas the first three lines are full of verbs ("know," "seems," "see," "hear," "coming," "going"), the second half of stanza 1 contains none ("bending" acts as an adjective). The language also slows the poem. The repetition of the preposition "of" and the increased number of hard stresses slows readers down, forcing them to dwell on the imagery.

In stanza 2, the poet reverts to the abstract. Lines 7 and 8 are dense and difficult to sort out. Line 8 repeats many of the words used in line 7, and the key word, "know," appears three times. This spare vocabulary forces the reader to go back over the lines to make sense of them. Even readers who know the poem well often stumble over line 8. In contrast, line 9 is effortlessly clear because it refers only to readily comprehensible, concrete objects. In effect, the reader moves from the cramped, restricted space of the mind into the vast reaches of nature. Furthermore, the rhyme of "known" with "cone" gives the lines a feeling of completion. Furthermore, the repetition of "it" (referring to the self) at the end of lines 10 and 11 brings the interior monologue to a close.

Another prominent device in the poem is the use of alliteration. In stanza 3, Ammons uses alliteration and half-rhymes to give the passage the feeling of a meandering stream. The *s*'s and *w*'s in line 12 move the poem along, while "comes," with the *m* and *s* (pronounced as a *z*) causes the reader to pause momentarily. The reader is then hung up again on "Run" in the next line, which forms a half-rhyme with "comes." The *ng*'s and *l*'s in the next line-and-a-half again move the poem forward like liquid. Ultimately, the stanza comes to a halt at the harsh sound of the human-made object, the "bridge."

A third device Ammons uses to great effect in the poem is punctuation. The poem consists of a single sentence broken into sections by colons. Ammons uses the single sentence because the poem elucidates a single thought: The natural and the human are distinct. However, the dominant form of punctuation in the poem is the colon: The poem contains ten of them. There is one at the end of each of the first five stanzas, and there are five in the last stanza. The colons in the poem function as semicolons, linking closely related independent clauses. The semicolon suggests connection, and Ammons's poem is about the separateness of things, and so he uses a colon, an element of punctuation that marks boundaries and separated elements such as hours, minutes, and seconds, leaving "each thing in its entity."

Themes and Meanings

"Gravelly Run" is a poem about the relationship of the world of human thought to the world of nature. American nature writing has long been concerned with this connection. What is the place of the human in the natural world? One of the great paradoxes of this issue is the desire on the part of some writers to be lost in nature, to shed the concerns and consciousness of the human world for the immediacy of the natural world. Transcendentalist thinker and poet Ralph Waldo Emerson sought exactly this kind of experience in nature, describing himself in this state as "a transparent eyeball. . . . [T]he currents of the Universal Being circulate through me; I am part or particle of God." Yet, there is a contradiction in Emerson's transcendence: Any attempt to make the natural world carry the intellectual freight of human consciousness obscures the natural world. Thus, people who attempt to lose themselves in nature are merely imposing human meaning on nature.

Like Henry David Thoreau, Emerson's literary heir, Ammons has had a lifelong interest in science. As a result, he views the natural world with the precision of a naturalist and consistently refuses to anthropomorphize nature. Yet, like Thoreau, Ammons is powerfully drawn to the beauty of nature, which must remain always before him like some Eden. "Gravelly Run" enacts this struggle. The speaker desires to be lost in the natural world, to lose consciousness, yet that very desire is itself an act of consciousness. The run, coming out of the dark mystery of the swamp and flowing through the banks of holly and cedar toward the highway bridge, seems to offer a place of refuge, a place of spirituality. In the end, however, the natural world remains beyond human thought. Ammons is too much aware of the complexity of the natural world to simplify it into symbols of human consciousness. Each thing, each tree, bush, and rock, remains sealed in "the air's glass/ jail"; Ammons cannot reduce the objects simply to serve the human desire for spirituality. Ammons recognizes that philosophies may not be grounded in natural facts. The only proper ground for philosophy is human ground, and so the speaker is told to "hoist [his] burdens," and "get on down" that other gravelly run, the road.

Andrew C. Higgins

THE GREAT BLUE HERON

Author: Carolyn Kizer (1925-   )
Type of poem: Elegy
First published: 1958; collected in *The Ungrateful Garden*, 1961

The Poem

Carolyn Kizer first published "The Great Blue Heron" in *Poetry* magazine as a poem of fifty-five lines and three irregular stanzas. When it was later reprinted in *Mermaids in the Basement*, she split the middle section, creating a fourth stanza. She has dedicated the poem to "M.A.K." These initials and the dates that follow them, as well as the content of the poem, confirm that this is an elegy, a long, sustained poem of mourning, for her mother, Mabel Ashley Kizer, who died in 1955 in her seventy-fifth year. The tone is serious and melancholy. The speaker in this first-person poem seems to be Kizer herself, as references to "my mother" also suggest. The youthful vision of the heron may likewise be autobiographical.

In the first stanza of the poem, the speaker remembers the day when, as a child on the beach near the family's vacation home "Some fifteen summers ago," she saw a solitary great blue heron standing "Poised in the dusty light" and was struck by this prophetic apparition. Her startled response, "Heron, whose ghost are you?" indicates the intensity of this experience. Her body reacted as if in physical shock as she stood in "the sudden chill of the burned." Even though the child raced to find her mother in the house and bring her back to the beach, "the spectral bird" had vanished from sight. The mother, however, called her attention to the heron in soundless flight above the trees, afloat on "vast, unmoving" wings ("ashen things") that the child beheld as "A pair of broken arms/ That were not made for flight."

Although the child speaker grieved for the loss of the bird, she could not quite comprehend what she had lost. Like little Margaret, who weeps for the falling leaves in Gerard Manley Hopkins's famous poem "Spring and Fall: To a Young Child," the child's heart had intuitively grasped the meaning of an omen that her mind could not yet accept, even as she was aware that her mother understood. The mute vision of the heron is a central metaphor for the child's dawning perception of mortality, to be confirmed in the poem's final lines.

In the last stanza, the adult speaker addresses the heron directly. Now that the years have passed, now that many Fourth of July rockets and pinwheels have fizzled and burned out and the summer house itself has burned to the ground, "Now," she says, "there is only you." Why has the memory of the heron followed her? The somber vision of that moment fifteen years ago has haunted her until this day when, "like gray smoke, a vapor," or "A handful of paper ashes," her mother too has disappeared. It is clear to the adult that the silent heron prefigured death and that the death to come was her mother's. The poem travels from the child's vision to the mother's indirect vision and ultimately to the speaker's mournful recognition.

Forms and Devices

Critic Elizabeth B. House has observed that Kizer uses form in this poem in order to distance herself from the raw pain of her mother's death. Although this relatively early poem may appear to be composed in free verse, it is actually in a form, as is most of her early work. The meter is accentual (of a type sometimes known as "loose iambic"), with the two-syllable iamb as its basic metrical foot. Each line consists of three distinct stresses or beats, with a varying number of unaccented syllables. Both the meter and the device of repetition give the poem an aura of inevitability.

Kizer makes use of repetition through occasional end rhyme and slant or imperfect rhyme, as well as through consonance and assonance (repeated consonant and vowel sounds). Perhaps most significant is her emphasis on key words such as "shadow" and "heavy," which help to establish the poem's mood and tone. First the child feels a premonition like the "sudden chill of the burned"; later the summer house has "burned." She watches the heron "drifting/ Over the highest pines" with its "ashen" wings, and fifteen years later the "ashes" of the mother "drift away." These words were carefully chosen for their connotations, their emotional impact upon the reader, as have such shaded words as "bleaker," "tattered," "ragged," and "decayed."

Kizer's vivid visual imagery is noteworthy. Her contrast of the implied colors of summer and fire with the complete absence of color identified with the heron creates a dramatic tension within the poem. The glow of a past that cannot be recaptured—the warm, bright Fourth of July images of "smokes and fires/ And beach-lights and water-glow/ reflecting pin-wheel and flare"—fades to bleakest ash. That once brilliant, light-drenched past is contradicted by the flat shadow of the heron in its "dusty light." The dark shape of the bird drifting in the sky is echoed by the drab, intangible qualities of gray smoke and vapor.

The great blue heron obviously becomes something more than a bird. It is otherworldly, passionless, almost mechanical in its movements. It appears and vanishes in ominous silence. The fact of its gloomy presence is warning enough. "What scissors cut him out?" asks the child, perhaps echoing William Blake's question of "The Tiger": "What immortal hand or eye/ Could frame thy fearful symmetry?" The poet offers no answer.

Themes and Meanings

Love and death are both major themes in Kizer's work, appearing in multiple variations, but here they are combined in a single poem. "The Great Blue Heron" not only confronts the hard fact of death (specifically of the mother, but by implication of all humankind) but also seems to ask, What is the meaning of death—and, perhaps, of life?

Certainly the poet mourns for her mother, and in that sense this is also a poem of love. Mabel Ashley Kizer was a most uncommon woman for her time. She held two degrees in biology, taught at Mills College and headed the biology department at San Francisco State College, was a radical political activist and organizer, and did not marry until her mid-forties. In "A Muse," the second prose section of her Pulitzer

Prize-winning collection Yin (1984), Kizer credits her mother as the source of inspiration for her writing. She notes with deep affection and respect that her "serious life as a poet" began after her mother's death in 1955: "I wrote the poems for her. I still do." Other portraits of her mother appear in the poems "The Blessing," "The Intruder," and "A Long Line of Doctors."

In addition, this poem is an elegy, a serious meditation on the vanishing past and the despoiling of nature: "The pines and driftwood" have been "cleared/ From that bare strip of shore." Kizer's reverence for nature comes partly from her love of its beauty, which was encouraged by her mother; it was also influenced by her love for Chinese poetry, which again was nourished by her mother, who would read to her from translations of Chinese poets by Arthur Waley. In Chinese poetry, images taken from nature, rather than those from religion or myth, predominate.

In her essay "Western Space," Kizer points out some of the differences between poets such as herself who hail from the American West (specifically, Washington State), as opposed to poets from the East. Characteristically "there is something about our great spaces . . . that makes us feel small, and fragile, and mortal," she writes. "To live in the midst of this [natural beauty] is to live . . . like a fallen angel who sees paradise taken from him piece by piece." She suggests that the destruction of nature's beauty has created in western poets "the impulse to conserve, to memorialize what is lost, to elegize what is dying before our eyes." A reader can sense this concern as well in the speaker's awareness of her changing landscape.

Ironically the heron, which in ancient Egypt was believed to be a sacred bird that housed the soul and symbolized the generation of life, serves here as death's indifferent and inexorable messenger. Yet the heron is clearly part of the living world of nature. Perhaps the symbol of the heron has been used to reconcile the opposites of life and death as they coexist in the great cycle of nature. The poem's speaker, whether she realizes this truth or not, remains heavy-hearted in her grief.

Joanne McCarthy

GREEN CATEGORIES

Author: R. S. Thomas (1913-   )
Type of poem: Meditation
First published: 1958, in *Poetry for Supper*

The Poem

"Green Categories" is one of R. S. Thomas's more complex poems, drawing in part on the ideas of the German philosopher Immanuel Kant that are developed in *Kritik der reinen Vernunft* (1781; *Critique of Pure Reason*, 1838). Thomas blends language and concepts from Kant's work with images of the Welsh countryside, a device that simultaneously raises questions about Kant's ideas and provides a larger context for the representation of a Welsh farmer, Iago Prytherch. The title reflects this blend: "Green" describes the countryside, while "Categories" refers specifically to Kant's divisions of forms of pure understanding.

Stylistically, the poem is not particularly complicated: It consists of two stanzas, a long first one and a shorter second one. It is written in the second person and addressed to Prytherch, who is a character in several of Thomas's other poems, including "Iago Prytherch," "Lament for Prytherch," and "Invasion on the Farm." Thomas introduces Kant in the first line, writing, "You never heard of Kant, did you, Prytherch?" He goes on in the stanza to speculate upon what Kant might have thought of Prytherch's life and draws distinctions between Kant's logic and abstract ideas and Prytherch's life on the farm, a life tied to the natural world and concrete objects. Slightly more than halfway through the first stanza, Thomas takes two of Kant's concepts, space and time, and gives an alternate definition for them in Prytherch's life. He justifies his definition by then asking "how else" Prytherch could live as he does and as the men before him did. The stanza ends as it begins: with a question. However, both questions are rhetorical; the speaker is using them to make assertions about Prytherch's life.

The second stanza is significantly shorter. It begins with a contrast, indicating that Prytherch and Kant would have given pause to each other, then concludes by saying that they "could have been at one." While each one's logic and mind could not stand up to the other's, the two men do share a kind of faith.

Perhaps because of the use of Kant's ideas and terminology, Thomas keeps the rest of the poem structurally simple. He uses no rhyme and, as is typical of his work, does not rely heavily on metaphors or elaborate images, using, instead, simple and plain words. This simplicity of language does not, however, keep the poem from being a difficult one to understand; even a reader who is well versed in Kant's philosophy will probably have to puzzle out what Thomas means by "faith." At the same time, though, the reader can connect to the concrete images of objects belonging to Prytherch's world and, in comparing them to the abstract terms referring to Kant, think about different ways of being. One need not understand Kant to see that the poem contrasts a life shaped by inner logic and mental properties with one formed by external forces upon the body; furthermore, one need not understand Kant to try to find connections between these two lives.

Forms and Devices

Thomas does not use many of the traditional forms or devices associated with poetry in the poem: It has no obvious rhyme or meter, and there are only a few metaphors. Several of them are used to describe the landscape: "the dark moor exerts/ Its pressure," "the moor's deep tides," and the "moor's/ Constant aggression." These representations of the land as a heavy, moving, dangerous force bring home the difficulty of Prytherch's life and its close connections to the natural world. Thomas's other metaphors reinforce this theme: A "green calendar" suggests that Prytherch lives according to the seasons rather than by the arbitrary dates delineated in a calendar, and the phrase "cold wind/ Of genius" reminds the reader of the hostile forces of nature that Prytherch encounters, even while it deepens the contrast between him and Kant.

One of the more interesting stylistic devices in the poem is the linguistic shift between certainty and uncertainty. The first stanza contains three questions, and, while the first and last are actually assertions in question form, the second one, beginning "What would he have said," is a question for the reader to consider. Prytherch, never having heard of Kant, could not speculate on what Kant might say to his life, but Thomas is asking the reader to engage in such speculation: Although the poem is written in the second person to Prytherch, the language requires readers to take parts of the poem as addressed to themselves. The speaker then returns to a descriptive voice, stating as fact that "Here all is sure." This certainty continues through the first stanza, even with the question at the end. The second stanza, however, moves from what is to what is possible, stating that "His logic would have failed" and that "you could have been at one." While neither of these are speculative in the same way that the poem's second question is—indeed, both assert that, given certain conditions, such would have happened—they do ask the reader to imagine a contrary-to-fact situation: a meeting between the philosopher and the Welsh farmer. Thomas moves back and forth in the poem from defining a situation to inviting the reader to reflect on that situation, a move that is, in some ways, parallel to the difference between Prytherch's life of the body and Kant's life of the mind.

Themes and Meanings

Several of the terms in the poem are taken specifically from Kant's work: categories, antinomies, space and time, and mathematics. In *Critique of Pure Reason*, Kant defines the categories as "concepts of synthesis that the understanding contains within itself *a priori*." The categories, which include such thing as "Unity," "Reality," and "Possibility-Impossibility," are ways in which the understanding synthesizes or groups its ideas and which have not been taught to the understanding; they are known intuitively, without benefit of experience. The antinomies consist of the conflicts between different ideas in transcendental philosophy that cannot be proved or disproved experientially; they transcend all experiences. Kant's first conflict, for example, is between the thesis that the world has a beginning in time and the antithetical statement that it has none: Space and time are not concepts that can be derived from experience but are rather a priori concepts upon which a person's intuitions are based (space underlies outer intuitions and time underlies inner ones). Mathematics is an example of a form of synthetic knowledge derived from the a priori knowledge of space and time.

In the poem, Thomas is juxtaposing Kant's ideas of a knowledge that is not based on experience or empirical data with Prytherch's understanding. Prytherch comprehends and understands the world through his experiences, through the flesh, through the things of the natural world around him. When the speaker says, "Space and time/ Are not the mathematics that your will/ Imposes, but a green calendar/ Your heart observes," the distinction being made is between Kant's ideas of space and time as something that leads to a pure science (such as mathematics) and Prytherch's experience of space and time as connected to the physical earth and the seasons. Prytherch's knowledge comes not from intuition but from experience.

In the last stanza, Thomas claims that Kant's logic could not continue in the face of Prytherch's relationship with the world, even while Prytherch's mind would be unable to comprehend Kant's. The speaker does find a connection between them, however, in the faith that they share "over a star's blue fire." What he means by "faith" is not clear; one strong possibility, however, is that both men have a faith in existence itself. While Kant's logic is indeed "remote" to Prytherch's world, it is founded on the idea that one does exist. Space and time are intuitive concepts, and the world's beginning cannot be substantiated through any experience, but the antinomy does not deny the world's existence itself. Thomas imagines Prytherch and Kant together at night with the hostile moor outside, a condition that would make each man aware of his own existence and his desire to continue to exist. Beneath intuition, beneath experience, there is the enduring faith that one is and things are. "Green Categories" uses Prytherch's life to point out the remoteness of Kant's philosophy from everyday experiences, but it does not validate Prytherch's life as the best way to exist either. Instead, the poem moves beyond asking how one knows the world to affirming that one is in the world.

Elisabeth Anne Leonard

THE HABIT OF MOVEMENT

Author: Judith Ortiz Cofer (1952-   )
Type of poem: Lyric
First published: 1987, in *Triple Crown: Chicano, Puerto Rican, and Cuban-American Poetry*

The Poem

"The Habit of Movement" is a short poem of twenty lines divided into two stanzas. It is written in free verse, a style that does not adhere to any regular meter or rhyme scheme. The lines are irregular, some as long as thirteen syllables and others as short as six. The poem is categorized as a lyric because of its subjective, emotional, and personal qualities. Although the poet herself is the speaker of the poem, she uses the first-person plural pronoun "we" as she refers to herself as part of a family.

Judith Ortiz Cofer was born in Hormigueros, Puerto Rico, which served as the archetype for Salud, the imaginary town in her first novel, *The Line of the Sun* (1989), nominated for the Pulitzer Prize in 1990. The title of the poem "The Habit of Movement" refers to the family's practice of moving back and forth between Puerto Rico and Paterson, New Jersey, because of her father's Navy career. Jesús Ortiz Lugo was first stationed in Brooklyn Navy Yard and was then assigned to other places around the world. Because the family was forced to move so often, they never established roots in any one place. This poem reflects Ortiz Cofer's struggle to make a place for herself out of a childhood spent traveling back and forth between cultures. However, the poet moves beyond her own experience as a Puerto Rican immigrant who grew up bilingual and bicultural to voice the collective experience of the Puerto Rican community.

In the first stanza, Ortiz Cofer shows the problems that frequent movement causes the family: loss of identity, a sense of rootlessness, and an inability to feel at home in either culture. Eventually, she and her family lose the will to become part of the new community and accept the transient state that keeps them no more grounded than the library books they borrow and return "hardly handled."

In the second stanza, the meaning shifts and Ortiz Cofer uses the habit of movement as a symbol of safety. Moving from place to place keeps the poet and her family insulated and safe as they continue to relocate without becoming attached to or feeling a part of any particular place. Since they never stay in one place long enough to establish roots, they are also free of any responsibility to a community. The poem reflects Cofer's ambiguous attitude toward a life spent traveling between the United States and Puerto Rico as the family struggles to make a home in the new environment. As a writer, she seeks to create a history for herself out of the cultural ambiguity of a childhood divided between two cultures.

Forms and Devices

By using the pronoun "we" throughout the poem, Ortiz Cofer is able to show her deeply personal attitude toward the nomadic life while, at the same time, giving voice to other immigrants with similar backgrounds. The first-person plural form allows her not only to refer to herself and her own family but also to move outward to include other immigrants struggling to find identity in a foreign setting. The metaphors reinforce the sense of restlessness, of not being grounded in one country or one culture. She compares her family to "balloons set adrift" who have lost their "will to connect." When she says her family "carried the idea of home on [their] backs," she calls up images of refugees fleeing with bundles of their belongings tied to their backs. To show the depth of her feelings of isolation and dispossession, she compares "the blank stare of undraped windows" to "the eyes of the unmourned dead." As the family moves on, this habit of movement not only keeps them isolated but also keeps them safe like "a train in motion" that "nothing could touch."

Instead of a rhyme scheme or regular metrical pattern, Cofer uses other poetic devices as a way of providing a sense of unity in the poem. Here, alliteration, rather than rhyme, is the chief means of repetition. When she suggests that her family's lives are of no more importance than the books they borrow from the library, she uses alliteration to emphasize the comparison: "books borrowed" and "hardly handled." Alliteration also serves as a unifying agent in the repetition of the *c* sound in the following lines: "we lost our will to connect,/ and stopped collecting anything heavier/ to carry than a wish." Through her choice of words, Cofer shows the contrast between the tropics and the new world: The family was "nurtured" in the "lethargy" of the tropics. In the new world, with its "wide sky" and libraries as foreign as Greek temples, the family drifts until they lose the will to connect. She juxtaposes the idea of a rich, full life with her feeling of displacement in the seemingly contradictory phrase, "we grew rich in dispossession."

Themes and Meanings

"The Habit of Movement" is a poem about the difficulties involved in the painful assimilation into another culture. Ortiz Cofer shows the stages along the way as she and her family move away from one culture but are not yet absorbed into another. Ortiz Cofer says she is "a composite of two worlds." Since she speaks English with a Spanish accent and Spanish with an American accent, she feels that she has never completely belonged in either culture. She writes in English, the language of her schooling, but thinks of Spanish as her cultural and subconscious language. She is a mixture of both worlds, constantly straddling two cultures. She has spent too much time in the United States to think of leaving, but she says she becomes melancholy at times as she continues to yearn for Puerto Rico.

In "The Habit of Movement," the poet provides a mental picture of the dichotomy of the immigrant experience. Ortiz Cofer has said that "every time I write a story where Puerto Ricans live their hard lives in the United States, I am saying, look, this is what is happening to all of us. I am giving you a mental picture of it, not a sermon." In this poem, she shows the ambiguous state of immigrants who no longer feel at home in their old culture but are not part of the new one. The images that she uses to illustrate this struggle begin with a feeling of nostalgia for the homeland that nurtured her and quickly move to the feeling of being adrift in a nomadic lifestyle. By using sensuous imagery, she involves the reader in the experience, comparing her family to "red balloons set adrift/ over the wide sky of this new land." Her poetic imagery appeals to the visual sense, and the vivid, concrete details help create the tone and meaning.

To show how little each new place means to her, Ortiz Cofer uses the image of "the blank stare of undraped windows." This failure to connect with new places has an advantage in that the family members never experience a sense of loss when they leave. Again, the poet shows the ambiguity: Her family does not belong to the community, but this same sense of alienation protects them from pain when they leave. As they move, they leave behind places that hold no meaning for them. They never stay long enough in any one place to "learn the secret ways of wood and stone" or become familiar enough to call it home.

The poet's family has lost the feeling of warmth and safety that their home in Puerto Rico had provided. As they drift from one place to the next, the "lethargy" of the life in the tropics gives way to a loss of "the will to connect." Yet the nomadic life offers another type of safety: The constant movement that isolates the family from others also keeps it united. The poet is not alone in this isolation because she is part of a family as well as part of a community of immigrants who share her experience. The poem ends with the image of a train in motion as Ortiz Cofer, knowing the family will continue to move, accepts the safety their habit of movement provides.

Judith Barton Williamson

HALF-HANGED MARY

Author: Margaret Atwood (1939-   )
Type of poem: Narrative
First published: 1995, in *Morning in the Burned House*

The Poem

"Half-Hanged Mary" is a medium-length narrative poem in free verse that has ten sections, each containing one to five stanzas. In it, Atwood reconstructs the hanging of Mary Webster, a woman accused of witchcraft in Massachusetts in the 1680's. Webster was hanged but did not die; thus the title of the poem.

The poem is written in the first person: Mary tells her own story. The ten sections of the poem are titled by time. The first, "7 p.m.," tells of the hour in the evening when authorities come for Mary while she is milking the cows. Her crimes, she deduces, include living alone, owning her "weedy farm," knowing a cure for warts, and, most of all, being a woman: having "breasts/ and a sweet pear hidden in my body." Her specific examples show how well she understands her situation. The times are ripe for witch-hunts, and any woman a bit out of the ordinary is vulnerable. "Rumour," she tells her reader, was "hunting for some neck to land on."

At "8 p.m.," the time of the second section, Mary is hanged. She describes the excitement of the men who hang her; they are excited "by their show of hate" and by "their own evil." At "9 p.m.," she describes the women who watch. She understands that they cannot help her, for they, too, are vulnerable just by being women. Should they choose to help or even acknowledge her, they might be the next to be accused. At "10 p.m.," Mary addresses God. She suggests that now she and God can continue to quarrel about free will, obviously an important subject to her. She searches for some reason for her suffering, and she finds God indifferent to her plight.

At "12 midnight," Mary fights against death. It waits for her and tempts her. She knows that giving in to death means giving up the pain, but it also means "To give up my own words for myself,/ my own refusals." Staying alive is an assertion of her own personhood, of her refusal to accept the allegations and punishment of her society, and she is determined to hold out for as long as she can. The focus of her fight is against oblivion, and this fight carries her through the night. At "2 a.m.," she feebly cries out, a cry that mostly means "not yet." At "3 a.m.," her strength is ebbing, and she feels as if she is drowning. She reiterates her innocence and refuses to give in. By "6 a.m.," although she is still technically alive, she feels that she has already died once, and, in fact, she has.

At "8 a.m.," the townspeople come to cut down the corpse. However, Mary is not dead, and the law prohibits another attempt at killing her. Her tenacity is a mixed blessing, however, for the citizens are more certain of her dark powers now that she has escaped death, and, in her struggle, she has lost much of her own self: "Before, I was not a witch./ But now I am one."

The final section, titled "Later," substantiates these two lines. Now people stay out of her way. Now she can say and do anything without fear. Now she is truly an outcast, surviving on berries, flowers, dung, and mice. She has, in fact, become crazy from the same experience that has made her free. Absolutely mistreated and misunderstood, she speaks "in tongues." The townsfolk have created the witch that they wanted.

Forms and Devices

Margaret Atwood's poems are loaded with imagery, and, in "Half-Hanged Mary," the imagery often disturbs. Atwood forces the reader into what contemporary poet Adrienne Rich calls "re-vision": "seeing with fresh eyes" in order the break the hold of tradition over us. Her images grab and surprise the reader and insist upon the reader's reassessment of expectations. Some of the images depend primarily on visual surprise. The rope is put around Mary's neck and she is yanked skyward: "Up I go like a windfall in reverse,/ a blackened apple stuck back onto the tree." She later compares her hanging self to "a turkey's wattles." Death is "like a crow/ waiting for my squeezed beet/ of a heart to burst/ so he can eat my eyes." These similes present fresh, startling pictures that require a moment for the reader to take in.

Often, single words or simple phrases form the image. When Mary speaks of the women watching her, she uses synecdoche (the use of a part to represent the whole) to freeze the image. It is the "bonnets," "dark skirts," and "upturned faces" who come to stare. Her images often shock. An aborted baby is "flushed" from the mother. Mary looks down into "eyeholes/ and nostrils" from above. Atwood's angels do not sing, but "caw." This raw imagery pervades the poem, intruding on the reader's sensibilities like static on the radio.

The unexpected word or combination of words creates not ambiguity but clarity. By the last section of the poem, "Later," Mary's lunacy or witchness seems certifiable. She skitters and mumbles, "mouth full of juicy adjectives/ and purple berries." As she scavenges for food because her position and means of self-support are gone, she speaks without fear: "I can now say anything I can say." Yet, in reality, she is voiceless. First, nobody listens to her. Even worse, she has less ability to speak, as indicated by the second "can" in the quote above. She is now limited by her own emotional demise, and the words Atwood uses for her speech are "mumbling," "boil," and "unravels"; she speaks in tongues to the owls.

Throughout the poem, Atwood emphasizes the irony of Mary's situation, often expressing her cynicism in sarcastic renderings of common phrases. In describing herself, Mary mentions her breasts and ovaries, then says that "Whenever there's talk of demons/ these come in handy."

She understands that the women cannot come to her aid because "Birds/ of a feather burn together" and because "Lord/ knows there isn't much/ to go around." She starts a conversation with God because she has "some time to kill," but she later finds him absent from the sky. "Wrong address," she says, "I've been out there." By the end of the night, she is "At the end of [her] rope," and, when she is cut down and gives the onlookers a "filthy grin," she speaks to her reader: "You can imagine how that went over."

The tone of these expressions clearly shows Atwood's attitude toward the whole hanging affair. Seemingly light statements are steeped in sarcasm and thus hang in the air in judgment of the society that does kill the original Mary and reincarnates her as a witch and lunatic.

Themes and Meanings

Atwood revisits a witch hanging, an incident familiar in American history, and forces the readers to revise their understanding of the event by giving us the story through the eyes of the accused. Atwood is a feminist who is deeply interested in women's rights and in the plight of women who are held subservient in a male-run society. Her novel *The Handmaid's Tale* (1985) portrays a futuristic society where the men in power control women as completely as Mary Webster's seventeenth century Puritan society controlled her. "Half-Hanged Mary,' like much of Atwood's other work, is a political statement.

Telling her own story and expressing her own feelings, Mary challenges many assumptions about the events she narrates. One assumption is that she is, in fact, a witch. The reader sees her as bright (she understands her situation fully), responsible (she cares for herself and others in her town), and strong (she outlasts her own hanging). Her treatment is based primarily on fear. The men fear Mary, her independence, and her powers, and they also fear their own act of violence. When she refuses to die, they fear Mary even more. The women fear connection with Mary because they know that only the slightest circumstances separate them from her: In the most basic way, they are connected because they are women and, as women, they are controlled by men. When Mary looks to her God for help, she only finds indifference. Having practiced faith, charity, and hope, she expects some compassion and understanding. Just as she is shown none from the villagers, she is shown none by God.

Though the hanging does not kill her physically, it does kill her emotionally. The woman who rises from the ground after she is cut down is, in fact, a lunatic—a madwoman. The free will she has questioned God about—a free will that society did not allow her in her first life—is now hers. As long as she stays clear of the society that shuns her, she can, and must, do as she will, using her own resources. But her resources are tremendously limited now—compare the woman struggling to stay alive in earlier stanzas with the woman eating dung in the final section. Mary Webster is, in fact, not alive, as she acknowledges near the end when she asks, "Who else has been dead twice?" Without her sanity, she has been made less than human, and the punishment of her judges is final and terrible.

Janine Rider

HAPPINESS

Author: Jane Kenyon (1947-1995)
Type of poem: Meditation
First published: 1995; collected in *Otherwise: New and Selected Poems*, 1996

The Poem

"Happiness" is a short poem in free verse. Its thirty-one lines are arranged in five symmetrical stanzas containing four, eight, seven, eight, and four lines respectively. The last is a quasi stanza, emanating from a dropped line in the previous stanza. Dramatic intensity builds and then subsides; the central stanza is the keystone, carrying the poem's rhythmic and thematic weight. The lines of the first and last stanzas are similar in length and meter, with three or four stresses per line. The three middle stanzas are more irregular, containing lines with five stresses and ending on shortened lines. The final words of the middle stanzas—"alone," "despair," and "night"—precede an emptiness both visual and aural.

The poem is meditative. The "you" of the poem addresses both the general audience and the individual reader. As the poem progresses, it becomes increasingly evident that the "you" also includes the speaker and that the poem is born of the speaker's suffering. The first two stanzas introduce the two driving forces of the poem: parable and paradox. The parable of the prodigal son, as related in the New Testament, tells of a young man who squanders his inheritance in another country. Contrite and destitute, he returns to his father, seeking forgiveness and shelter. The father not only forgives the son but also honors him with finery and a feast. The parable of the prodigal son is presented in the poem virtually intact, dense with words that evoke the Scripture from which it comes—"dust," "forgive," "feast," "garment." The parable becomes a metaphor for the unpredictable extravagance of happiness. However, the return of happiness causes the speaker to "weep night and day"—and therein lies a paradox. The poem, unlike the parable, is spoken from the perspective of the one abandoned, and the effusive generosity of the welcome is unmistakably linked to the pain of the abandonment.

The central stanza introduces another metaphor for happiness, "the uncle you never knew about," who singlemindedly and with great effort seeks out a soul in extremis. In a curious twist, the act of finding suddenly becomes reciprocal. In the first stanza, it is happiness that is lost and then found; in the third stanza, it is the speaker. The prodigal who was found and feasted becomes the uncle who "finds you asleep mid-afternoon/ as you so often are during the unmerciful/ hours of your despair."

The entire fourth stanza is a litany of others who are found by happiness, representing all ages, genders, and classes. Moral judgment is suspended; in a nod to the first line of the poem, "no accounting" is necessary. Happiness, like the proverbial rain, falls upon the just and unjust: a monk, a lover, and a laborer; a man, a woman, and a child; a drunk and a pusher—even a dog. The final stanza is both a visual and a thematic extension of the one before it. The blessed litany continues but now includes inanimate objects: rocks, rain, and a wineglass. At the poem's end, careful layering of images and skillful matching of form to meaning have imbued these things with life and significance.

Forms and Devices

All of the poem's structural elements—rhythm and meter, grammar and syntax, sound and image—serve and preserve its larger themes by a fine manipulation of contrasts and ambiguities. The dactylic waltz rhythm initiated by the title continues throughout, interspersed with hard-hitting iambs that ground the poem and echo a heartbeat heard in solitude. The silences speak as well: The foreshortened last lines of the three middle stanzas and the spaces that follow them are the formal equivalent of existential isolation.

The poem rides on marvelous extended sentences, the clauses rolling after each other like waves toward a shore. The first, third, and fifth stanzas are each one long sentence. The intervening stanzas, ever graceful, also contain jetties that break up the waves. The speaker's question, "How can you not forgive?" and the litany of the forgiven stand out sharply against the flowing tide around them. An uneasy ambiguity surfaces on this syntactical sea in the form of negatives imbedded in phrases that first appear positive: "There's just no accounting for happiness" hints at indiscriminateness; "And how can you not forgive?" begs the question; "an occasion/ you could not imagine" and "you weep . . ./ to know that you were not abandoned" point to a terrible siege of despair. All these statements are found in the first two stanzas. At the extremity of hopelessness, revealed by the juxtaposition of the words "No, happiness" in the pivotal third stanza, help arrives. Contrasting images abound: happiness and weeping, fortune and dust, night and day, losing and finding, solitude and union. Even the prosaic grocery clerk who works the midnight shift is a foil for the prodigal who squanders a fortune.

Perhaps the poem's best example of structure serving meaning is demonstrated by the recurring images of solitude. Over and over, happiness is given and received in solitude. The uncle comes alone and flies a single-engine plane. Each recipient—from the monk to the wineglass—is named in the singular and, at first glance, so too is the "you" of the poem: "happiness saved its most extreme form/ for you alone." However, the ambiguity of the pronoun "you"—its function as either singular or plural— intimates a movement away from isolation and toward a fragile commonality.

Themes and Meanings

From first line to last, "Happiness" is disturbing. The metaphor of the prodigal son is immediately unsettling. The biblical prodigal is a rather callow and wayward young man who was driven back to the comforts of home by hunger and hard labor. This is not a very flattering picture of happiness. The speaker's response—"And how can you not forgive?"—is also problematic. The question simultaneously suggests two possible responses—forgiving without question and choosing not to forgive. Yet the speaker, like the father in the parable, is also a prodigal, lavishing a welcome on wayward happiness: "You make a feast in honor of what/ was lost, and take from its place the finest/ garment."

The metaphor of the uncle contains an ominous undercurrent as well. On the one hand, this intrepid relative echoes the Good Shepherd of the New Testament, who braves the wilderness in order to find one lost lamb. On the other hand, the questions lurk: Where has he been until now? What does he want? Why would he go to all this trouble? Is he looking for a share of the inheritance as the speaker dies of despair? Happiness's "most extreme form" may, after all, be death, release from a body that is weary of life, "the wineglass, weary of holding wine." The poet Galway Kinnell employs a similar image in "The Striped Snake and the Goldfinch" (*Imperfect Thirst*, 1994): Wine fills "the upper bell of the glass/ that will hold the last hour we have to live." Although Kenyon wrote "Happiness" before she knew of the leukemia that killed her at the age of forty-eight, she fought depression all her life—a battle that shadows and deepens her poetry.

In "Happiness," Kenyon exquisitely describes the human condition. Happiness is neither deserved nor permanent. It is given indiscriminately, not possessed deliberately. At the beginning and the end of happiness there is loss—the loss that recognizes its appearance and the loss that follows its departure. However, those somber brackets lend it meaning and value. "Happiness" also touches delicately upon last things. Coexisting with the "perpetual shade" of death is the mystery that even inanimate entities—a boulder, rain, a wineglass, a despairing soul "asleep mid-afternoon"—can receive the unexpected blessing that renews life and suggests the possibility of an afterlife.

Kinnell's lovely poem "How Could You Not" (1995), written in Kenyon's memory, draws on the devices and themes of "Happiness" and ends thus: "How could you not rise and go, with all that light/ at the window . . . and the sound,/ coming or going, hard to say, of a single-engine/ plane in the distance that no one else hears?" "Happiness" is a rare look into the poetic imagination that sees what others do not, that breathes life into words and significance into life. The "feast in honor of what was lost" and the "finest garment" that honors the return of happiness are also "happiness" itself. The prodigal has become a poem. That is its ultimate paradox and its ultimate gift.

Louise Grieco

HARLEM SHADOWS

Author: Claude McKay (1889-1948)
Type of work: Book of poems
First published: 1922

The Poems

With the publication of *Songs of Jamaica* and *Constab Ballads* (both 1912), Claude McKay achieved immediate recognition in Jamaica as a poet of some consequence, especially in the use of dialect, and he was considered a local equivalent of Robert Burns, the Scottish Romantic poet. However, upon his migration to the United States he abandoned dialect, and in *Spring in New Hampshire and Other Poems* (1920) he showed his ability to experiment with rhythm, rhyme, meter, and even poetic structure.

The extent of his willingness and ability to explore new poetic techniques is revealed in *Harlem Shadows*: In the "Author's Word" prefatory to the poems, McKay notes that he adhered to many older poetic traditions (such as the sonnet form) while trying to achieve "directness, truthfulness and naturalness of expression instead of an enameled originality." In 1922 Harcourt, Brace issued both *Harlem Shadows* and Virginia Woolf's *Mrs. Dalloway*, a combination suggesting that the prestigious New York publishing house perceived McKay as a significant and potentially major new voice in contemporary writing. The collection was well received by readers and critics.

Harlem Shadows, a collection of seventy-four poems, brought together what were thought to be the best poems that McKay had written since his arrival in the United States, many of which had appeared in such periodicals as *Seven Arts*, *Pearson's*, the *Liberator*, and the *Cambridge Magazine*. It had an introduction by Max Eastman, the left-wing mentor of many young writers, and consequently achieved some cachet in literary circles. Eastman observed that McKay's poems had an obvious quality, "the pure, clear arrow-like transference of his emotion into our breast, without any but the inevitable words." He continued by saying that this was what John Keats sought to cherish when he said that poetry should be "great and unobtrusive, a thing which enters into the soul and does not startle or amaze with itself but with its subject." This endorsement and comparison was extraordinary yet justified.

The poems can be divided into three groups of about equal number: those about nature (many of which are nostalgic reminiscences of Jamaica); those about love, affection, and attachment to persons; and those that deal in some way with race. Seriousness—even despondency—is a pervasive mood. After such titles as *Songs of Jamaica* and *Spring in New Hampshire*, which exude a bright, happy spirit or tone, *Harlem Shadows* intimates an almost binary polarity; the connotations of the two words are (for both black and white readers) generally negative, bringing to mind overcrowded and dilapidated tenements, unemployed or underemployed menials; and pervasive social problems (including prostitution, gangsterism, illegitimacy, gambling, and drug addition) existing in the shadow of New York, with its consumerism, wealth, and bright lights.

There is nothing comparable to the optimism and positive outlook implied by the songs and spring of his earlier titles, even though some of the poems are about red flowers, jasmines, and homing swallows. "Wild May" is "weighted down with fetters" and "the victim of grim care"; "A Memory of June" recalls that love is fugitive; even "The Easter Flower" bemoans "this foreign Easter damp and chilly." Other poems that indicate the prevailing tone and attitude of the collection are "In Bondage," "Futility," "Through Agony," "Enslaved," and "Polarity." The poems that have retained their interest for readers, critics, and anthologists are the obviously polemical poems, those that concern race: "Harlem Shadows," "The White City," "If We Must Die," "The Lynching," "America," and "The Harlem Dancer," which remarkably combines lyricism and social protest within the confines of the sonnet form.

While "Harlem Shadows" is affecting in its condemnation of a society that obliges "little dark girls . . . in slippered feet" to engage in prostitution and thus to live lives "Of poverty, dishonor and disgrace," its concluding couplet is almost anticlimactic in moving the focus from the "dusky, half-clad girls of tired feet" to the poet himself ("Ah, heart of me"). The mixture of language registers, exclamations, and changing metonymies diffuses the focus. In "The White City" the passion is forceful, unmuted, pellucid: "I muse my life-long hatred," "this dark Passion . . . fills my every mood," "I hate," yet "I bear it nobly as I live my part." Though readers might be offended by the poet's confession, nonetheless they must admire his candor and forthrightness.

"If We Must Die," indubitably McKay's most popular poem among some radical groups, is commendable for its "transference of his emotion into our breast," as Eastman observed. Yet it is not without its weaknesses: Would any black orator of the period have used the exhortation "O kinsmen"? Or "let us show us brave"? Nonetheless, the poem is an exceptionally powerful rallying cry.

"The Lynching," which depicts one of the most deplorable practices of southern racism, has exceptional power, which derives from the juxtaposition of "a bright and solitary star" and "the swinging char" and from the representative community crowd of women and children watching "the ghastly body swaying in the sun." None of the women shows sorrow in her steely eyes, "And little lads, lynchers that were to be,/ Danced round the dreadful thing in fiendish glee." This concluding couplet is moving in its simplicity: The black man has been reduced to a thing, and the racial, communal hate will become a social norm. Yet in spite of the terrors and torments of life in the United States, McKay says, in "America," "I love this cultured hell that tests my youth."

Forms and Devices

Whereas McKay's dialect poetry required copious annotations to explain to non-West Indians the meanings of words and the significance of allusions, the poems in *Harlem Shadows* did not. Whereas the earlier verses were mainly written in iambic trimeters and tetrameters, the New York volume is almost all in tetrameters and pentameters—though not exclusively in iambic or trochaic rhythms. So unconventional were some to Max Eastman that in his introductory essay he noted that "One or two of the rhythms I confess I am not able to apprehend at all." He could have been alluding to these lines from "When Dawn Comes to the City": "But I would be on the island of the sea,/ In the heart of the island of the sea." Or he could have been referring to these from "Exhortation: Summer, 1919" (a year of American race riots): "In the East the clouds grow crimson with the new/ dawn that is breaking,/ And its golden glory fills the western skies." These rhythmic variations were not even then unusual, however: Walt Whitman, Gerard Manley Hopkins, and others had already experimented with half-stresses and outriders in their attempts to capture the essence of speech rhythms.

In fact, in the earlier *Songs of Jamaica* and *Constab Ballads* McKay had taken numerous liberties with standard syllabic (or quantitative) verse and had incorporated numerous modifications of the rather static ballad meter of iambic tetrameters and trimeters in alternation. In *Harlem Shadows* he continued this independent approach to conventional form, even to the point of modifying the sonnet structure to suit his needs, so that in neither the ballad nor the lyric was he a slavish observer of traditions. Some of his sonnets are Elizabethan, some are Italian, some are Wordsworthian. However, it must be conceded that the Elizabethan sonnet form seemed most congenial to him and that most of his best and most memorable poems are in this style. Within the sonnet form McKay generally observed proper rhyme; nonetheless, he is not averse to rhyming "over" with "lover," "souls" with "ghouls," and "love" with "move," a technique often referred to as a visual or eye rhyme.

Generally in the nonsonnet lyrics McKay favored the four-line stanza and most frequently employed closed couplets; however, "A Prayer" is composed in the form of five couplets of seven-beat lines, and "Harlem Shadows" itself is in six-line stanzas of iambic pentameters in which almost all the lines are run-on.

One of McKay's strengths as a poet is his use of a wide range of imagery. Visual imagery predominates, though appeals to the other senses are also common. The very titles of the poems are at times forcefully visual: "The Easter Flower," "Flame-Heart," "The Night Fire," "Birds of Prey," and "A Red Flower." In some poems, olfactory imagery is primary, as in "Jasmines," "Subway Wind," and "The Easter Flower." Kinesthetic imagery is also encountered: "Homing Swallows," "The Tired Worker," and "The Harlem Dancer" employ this device effectively.

While a few of the poems in *Harlem Shadows* can be considered love lyrics ("La Paloma in London," "Tormented," "One Year After," and "A Memory of June," for example), most are poems of place or of protest. In the former category are those that are purely celebratory ("Spring in New Hampshire" and "Summer Morn in New Hampshire" as well as "Winter in the Country" and "Flame-Heart") and those that are reminiscent, such as "The Tropics in New York," in which the sight of Caribbean produce in a New York store window makes the poet "hungry for the old, familiar ways."

The propaganda or protest poems indicate a sea change in the poet's social and political thinking following his emigration from Jamaica a decade earlier. Gone are the flippant, cordial protestations about discriminations; they have been replaced by penetrating analyses of inequalities, injustices, and humiliations, which are laid bare in "The Barrier," in which McKay states without equivocation:

> I must not see upon your face
> Love's softly glowing spark;
> For there's the barrier of race,
> You're fair and I am dark.

The opening poem in *Harlem Shadows* celebrates Easter, with its "lilac-tinted Easter lily/ Soft-scented in the air" and "its perfumed power." The second one contrasts the "cheerless frozen spots" of New York with the "birds' glad song," the "flowering lanes" and the "vivid, silver-flecked blue sky" of the West Indies. The third poem, "America," introduces the McKay of the Left, of social awareness, of political proclivities. He is no longer the youthful singer of tropical beauties or personal attachments: He is now a fully committed critic of racial discrimination and social injustice. But a certain ambivalence can be discerned beginning with the fourth line:

> Although she feeds me bread of bitterness,
> And sinks into my throat her tiger's tooth,
> Stealing my breath of life, I will confess
> I love this cultured hell that tests my youth!

This ambivalence is also to be found in "The White City," wherein he acknowledges the "life-long hate" that he bears "nobly as I live my part"; he has to make his "heaven in the white world's hell"—"because I hate."

The other deeply passionate poems of protest are equally affective: The reader cannot but be moved by the repetition of such words as "hate," "lynching," "fiery," "fighting," "tears," "dead," and "dying" that permeate them like punctuation marks. Some readers do not respond positively to McKay's lines in "If We Must Die" that propose that, "Though far outnumbered, let us show us brave,/ And for their thousand blows deal one death-blow!" However, their power is attested by the fact that Winston Churchill, the British prime minister during World War II, quoted them to incite his countrymen to rally to defeat Hitlerite Germany.

Themes and Meanings

Harlem Shadows is fundamentally Claude McKay's philosophy of life, even though it was published when he was in his early thirties and had not experienced his infatuation and subsequent disillusionment with communism, had not seen his fame (and subsequent eclipse) as a writer of novels and short stories, and had not suffered poverty, disease, calumny, and ostracism by former friends and colleagues—particularly after espousing Catholicism.

The collection juxtaposes his delight in natural beauty, whether witnessed in individuals, flora, or fauna (and regardless of whether it is to be discovered in the country or the cities) and his despair in discovering the discrimination against the poor, the dark-skinned, and the immigrant in a society that professes itself to be open, nondiscriminatory, and egalitarian. All these negative characteristics of American society he inveighs against, yet not so offensively as to alienate sympathetic liberal or progressive whites. He is aware of and celebrates the achievements of modern American capitalist society, yet he fervently believes that it can be amended to the end of offering all people better lives.

Whites are seen to be in the sun; blacks are presented as in the shadows, both literally—in the crowded streets and buildings of the North—and figuratively. McKay proposes that no group can grow culturally, socially, intellectually, and economically if perpetually assigned to the umbral regions, the Harlems of the nation. While some of his language of protest might seem to be political harangue, it is really not violent in its intent: It is designed to arouse, to foster critical thinking rather than revolt or violence. *Harlem Shadows* is a noteworthy testament to the serious side of the Roaring Twenties that were just under way and also to the Harlem Renaissance.

A.L. McLeod

HAY FEVER

Author: A. D. Hope (1907-   )
Type of poem: Meditation
First published: 1973; collected in *A Late Picking: Poems, 1965-1974*, 1975

The Poem

"Hay Fever" was written in the author's maturity, though not in his old age. It demonstrates that A. D. Hope, although he is sometimes considered primarily an imitator of eighteenth century poetic technique and a facile satirist, is also an innovator in structure and a lyricist at heart. While he is perhaps indebted to Alexander Pope and Jonathan Swift in attitude, he is not in method, for he takes numerous liberties in both structure and content that they would not have approved. In place of regular stanzas, the closed couplet, and iambic pentameter, Hope freely intermixes stanza and line lengths and uses iambs, dactyls, trochees, and anapests in lines that vary in length from tetrameters to alexandrines; further, he makes use of both single and double rhyme in alternating lines or in lines widely separated; the four stanzas of this poem are in eleven, thirteen, eight, and eleven lines. In fact, this poem shows Hope in a somewhat uncharacteristic light, for he is generally observant of the niceties of Augustan poetic technique.

The poem opens with the general observation that "Time," personified as the grim reaper with scythe in hand (a commonplace in art of the Western world as well as in end-of-the-year cartoons), is a mature, skilled workman who is ever alert and at his task of claiming lives, usually without discrimination. The poet expresses his relief that it is not yet his turn to die (though he is "Waiting my turn as he swings"), and then he recalls how he himself learned to use the scythe to harvest lucerne (the Australian term for alfalfa) and hay in his early adolescence. As the neophyte, he took the last position in the row of harvesters, in case he could not keep up with the others or made poor strokes, which could be corrected on the next sweep. This recollection of a youthful apprenticeship conjures up an analogy: The poet sees himself "As though I were Time himself."

The poem proceeds with detailed recollections of the long-ago summer in Tasmania (the small, southernmost state of Australia) when the neighbors of his father, a Presbyterian minister who owned a small farm, came to harvest his crops and brought with them a scythe with which the young man could learn the skill and thus be inducted to the world of farm men. There is a catalog of the grasses, flowers, and weeds that are cut simultaneously during the harvest—an indication that the good and the bad are harvested indiscriminately, a sort of paradigm of life itself. The catalog is more than a Whitmanesque list; it also reveals a fond recognition of the "still dewey stalks" that, personified, "nod, tremble, and tilt aside." Then, almost inadvertently, the boy sees a dandelion "cast up a golden eye" at browsing cows, but the boy does not consider the cows' hay-breath "the smell of death" as the dandelions do.

In the third stanza, as in the first, the point of view moves from that of the omniscient observer to the first person; the boy has become as proficient a harvester as his associates, but he has a poetic response to his task that the others lack: He notes "the sigh/ Of the dying grass like an animal breathing," identifying with the Other, the object of his scythe. This returns him to the question—both literal and philosophical—"How long can I hold out yet?" The concluding stanza reveals the persona noting the passage of time ("obsolete" scythes have been replaced by harvesting machines). He acknowledges that he has metaphorically "made hay" but has stored consoling memories against the inevitable scythe-stroke of Time; he will "lie still in well-cured hay."

Forms and Devices

The principal poetic device in "Hay Fever" is the analogy between Time as a reaper and the poet himself as first a literal wielder of a scythe and then as a reaper of the joys of life, "stacked high," though intermixed with "a thistle or two . . . for the prick of remorse." Other figures and tropes abound: Personification is used to make Time more forceful, as when he "takes a pace forward" and swings "from the hip" like a masterful harvester. It is used again in reference to the still, dewy stalks that "nod, tremble and tilt aside" and the dandelion that "casts up a golden eye"; the dying grass sighs, the steel scythe sings. Time drives a harvester.

Metaphors are used throughout the poem. Almost every line uses them, from the initial image of Time's scythe being honed fine to the last line's image of lying still in well-cured hay and drifting into sleep (death). Other effective devices are the similitude of a barn stacked high with "good, dry mow" and a brain full of pleasant remembrances, and the statement, "I am running with, flooding with, sweat"—an illustration of hyperbole, which occurs sparingly. There are also a few similes of merit: the sigh of dying grass like animal breathing, and romping like a boy in the heap of harvest.

As in much of Hope's poetry there is evidence that he values those compositional elements that were especially prized in the eighteenth century and that he, as a professor of English, taught: parallelisms, balanced statements, antitheses, trials, and double elements. Accordingly, one reads "new to the game and young at the skill," "Out of the lucerne patch and into the hay," and "in his hay, in my day," among the balanced items. There is an abundance of dyads: "Crumples and falls," "lucerne and poppies," "place and pace," "arrows and bow," "the grass and the flowers." Effective triads include "By the sound of the scythes, by the swish and ripple, the sigh/ Of the dying grass," which also illustrate the author's penchant for alliteration, particularly sibilance.

In his imagery, Hope makes frequent use of compound adjectives to gain specificity: The dock is red-stemmed, the milk thistle is hollow-stalk, and the oats are self-sown. Not all of the imagery is visual; some is olfactory ("the sweet hay-breath") and some is auditory ("thin steel crunch" and "the sound of the scythes"). Hope also makes use of kinetic imagery, as in "I snag on a fat-hen clump" and "I set the blade into the grass."

One characteristic of Hope's poetry that has frequently been noted is his use of declamation, of unmodified statements. Here one sees ample evidence of this in "the men are here// They have brought a scythe for me. I hold it with pride.// I set the blade into the grass." Related to declamation as a development device is the inclusion of apothegms, or aphorisms, such as "It is good for a man when he comes to the end of his course/ In the barn of his brain to be able to romp like a boy" and "Time drives a harvester now: he does not depend on the weather." The effect of these aphorisms is to endow the poet with a philosophic disposition and acuity.

The mere inclusion of these poetic devices would be insufficient to grant merit, but the long, run-on lines and the almost imperceptible shifts in point of view make it appear that they are organic rather than applied like decorations. That is, the poem's success is in part the result of the rich texture of the prose itself and in part its philosophic content and its stanzaic form. The almost casual, conversational tone, atypical of Hope, adds to the poem's charm.

Themes and Meanings

In "Hay Fever" Hope addresses an issue that has challenged almost all poets of stature: As we age, we wonder when we will die and whether we have had sufficient satisfaction in life to "go gentle into that good night," as Dylan Thomas phrased it. Hope's conclusion is that, though he has "made hay" (or sown his wild oats) in his day, has good and bad memories, successes and failures to acknowledge, life has been good to him and he can leave this world in a state of satisfaction—or even reverie—as he recounts the good times and perhaps forgets the bad.

This summation and evaluation would not have been possible without the recollection of his adolescent participation in haying on his father's farm, which proved to be an induction into the adult world, an initiation that brought him face to face with the similarity between his cutting down everything in his path, whether good or bad, decorative or essential, and death. All are taken, regardless of merit, it seems, and there is no reprieve or deferment when Time "takes a pace forward, swings from the hips" (almost as if in obedience to an instructor).

Because Hope spent his adult life as a teacher and then a professor of English, he was adept at explication and the use of analogy; "Hay Fever" invites his readers to see the analogy that he offers and then offer their own explications, though his concluding three lines are clearly intended to direct them to certain conclusions.

The poem's title, which might well mislead potential readers into believing that the common allergy is the subject of the poem, comports with Hope's practice of being ambiguous at times. Haying can cause discomfort in people who suffer from allergies, causing tears and sweat, but for him haying caused sweat and tears from physical exhaustion. Moreover, the remembrance of those days—and the contemplation of death—may produce some tears of regret and the sweat that comes from apprehension. "How long can I hold out yet?" he asks, and the answer is implicit: until Time, with his scythe or harvester, comes along. "Hay Fever," like the other poems in *A Late Picking* (the title refers to the final harvest of grapes for wine, which are somewhat riper and sweeter than the main vintage) is fuller-bodied, sweeter, and more satisfying than many of Hope's earlier poems, and it appeals to the connoisseur rather than the beginner.

A. L. McLeod

HEART'S LIMBO

Author: Carolyn Kizer (1925-   )
Type of poem: Lyric
First published: 1971; collected in *The Nearness of You*, 1986

The Poem

"Heart's Limbo" is written in six free-verse stanzas of varying length. As is typical of a dramatic monologue, the poem's speaker ("I") addresses a silent listener, presumably a potential lover, and through her words reveals her innermost self. From her choice of language ("rolls ready to brown 'n' serve,/ the concentrated juice"), the speaker appears to be a woman, although she may not necessarily be Carolyn Kizer. She may be a persona, a voice created by the poet.

In Christian tradition, the word "limbo" refers to a place in the afterlife, somewhere between heaven and hell, which is set aside for the innocent souls of the unbaptized. Here the "limbo" of the title carries the more general meaning of a place or state of confinement or neglect, a place where nothing happens. In the poem's central metaphor, the speaker's "maimed" heart has been placed in limbo (literally, in a freezer) for safekeeping and is now being thawed for use.

The poem begins as the speaker tells her listener that she had placed her heart, like a piece of meat, in the frozen food section of her refrigerator to prevent it from spoiling. She has had to remind herself not to snack on it ("It wasn't raspberry yoghurt") and not to give it to the cat by mistake—in other words, to take special care with it. It is not like the other food in her refrigerator. Although she continues to refer to the heart as an object, the rest of the poem makes evident that the heart symbolizes her ability to love.

Someone has come into her life, even though she is not ready: "Suddenly I needed my heart in a hurry." She offers her heart, her frozen love in its "crystal sheath," in its half-thawed, incomplete state, and the prospective lover is not put off by it: "You didn't even wash its blood from your fingertips." He (or possibly she, as the person's gender is not specified) is "not even visibly frightened/ when it began to throb with love." The fifth stanza reveals the speaker's fear. In a series of vivid similes, she compares her heart to an injured animal, a smooth-skinned but treacherous snake, and a defenseless baby bird. The heart is savage, dangerous, yet helpless, even as it lies imprisoned and protected in the warmth of the lover's hands.

The final stanza shifts to a positive note, as the speaker urges her new lover to heal her damaged heart with gentleness and asks in turn for the lover's own heart. It is clear that previous relationships have hurt this woman and that she is now willing to take a great risk in order to encounter love again.

Forms and Devices

When it was initially published in *Poetry* magazine, "Heart's Limbo" consisted of forty-one lines in eight stanzas. Kizer extensively revised the end of the poem before its inclusion in *The Nearness of You*, where she replaced the final three stanzas with a new, succinct quatrain and reduced the number of lines to thirty. Each version ends with a satisfying couplet, one of only two examples of perfect end rhyme in the poem.

Kizer originally began her career as a formalist poet, basing her early poems on strict classical and older Chinese models. In later poems such as this one, she seems to prefer irregular breath lines to the more uniform line created by regular meter and patterned syllables. Yet even though this poem is written in free verse, the iambic foot predominates, which is appropriate for a poem about a heart. The two-syllable iamb, with its accent on the second syllable, has often been identified as a rhythmic echo of a beating heart. In one instance Kizer begins a line with a trochee ("Quicken"), thus shifting the accent to the first syllable and reversing the pattern of the iambs that surround it: "Quicken its beat with your caresses." This shift emphasizes the change in heart rhythm that is being described. When rhyme appears, it is largely incidental, occurring primarily within the lines and emphasized by repeated phrases: "I had to remember not to diet on it./ . . . / I had to remember not to thaw and fry it."

The image of the frozen heart, that icy organ in stasis, is underscored by words that emphasize its chill: "crystal," "cold and dripping," "numbed." Personified, it appears as a lifeless creature, "not breathing" until the lover's touch restores it. As the heart revives, it begins to "throb" until its final transformation, lying in "your warm fingers' cage." Poet and editor A. Poulin, Jr., has called attention to the "emotional impact" of Kizer's work, "enhanced by her unique intellectual wit and hearty, often stinging, sense of humor," or what Kizer herself has called "the shield of bitter laughter." The image of a wounded heart lying numb among the unbaked rolls and cans of frozen juice is in a sense comic, but her sly humor also serves a serious purpose, to mask and lessen pain.

Kizer employs a related device, her characteristic irony, to highlight the incongruity of everyday household phrases such as "brown 'n' serve" or "ran out of tuna," as they are placed side by side with more elegant metaphors such as "smooth as a young stone-bathing serpent." One moment the heart is plunged "deep/ among the ice-cubes," and in the next it rests "in its crystal sheath, not breathing," as the language ricochets from the mundane to the (almost) sublime. Through it all, the reader is aware of the speaker's pain.

Themes and Meanings

Certainly "Heart's Limbo" is a poem about the central importance of love in human life, but it seems to focus more on vulnerability—both the risk and pain of love in addition to the intense human need for it. Kizer writes in "A Month in Summer," a long poem that chronicles the end of a love affair, that for her one of the endearing qualities of male Japanese poets is their "overwhelming impulse, when/ faced with hurt or conflict, to stay in bed under/ the covers!" They too understand vulnerability.

Any reader who is familiar with "Pro Femina," Kizer's widely known feminist poem about the status of women, may not at first think of her as a writer who is sensitive to the delicacy of love. However, love has always been one of her primary themes, beginning with her poem "Lovemusic," published in *The New Yorker* when she was only seventeen. Several of the love poems in her first book, *The Ungrateful Garden* (1961), are filled with lush opulence, images from classical mythology, or the paradoxes and metaphysical concerns that are vaguely reminiscent of English poet John Donne. On the other hand, "Heart's Limbo," with its contemporary, bloody images, offers an abrupt contrast to the more mannered poems.

She has written of love in its various guises, including sensuous poems of physical love such as "The Light" and bleak poems of lost love such as "A Widow in Wintertime," where the yowl of mating cats reminds the widow of the fierce animal pleasures to which she "would not return" although she has obviously not forgotten them. Kizer has composed several other poems that might also be identified as love poems and dedicated them to close male and female friends. Still other frequently anthologized poems such as "The Blessing" and "The Great Blue Heron" address the bond that connects mother and daughter. Finally, characteristic of the witty and outspoken author of "Pro Femina" are the tough, ambivalent love-hate poems such as "Bitch," in which she reveals her doggy self.

In her later work Kizer presents the subject of love directly and without sentimentality. In "Afternoon Happiness," a poem that describes the joy of a happy marriage, she asks, "So how does the poem play/ Without the paraphernalia of betrayal and loss?" She concludes that, in order to be successful, a good love poem must draw on pain rather than happiness as its source. In "Heart's Limbo," which is laden with domestic details such as rolls in the freezer, Kizer opens the poem to the universal experience of love in all its complexity. Her writing is clearly not limited to the lives of women but rather includes them in her observation of the full human condition. Poulin, who published her Pulitzer Prize-winning collection *Yin* in 1984, contends that, "without sacrificing their feminist edge, Kizer's poems are powerful, myth-making hymns" of celebration.

Joanne McCarthy

HERE, BUT UNABLE TO ANSWER

Author: Richard Hugo (1923-1982)
Type of poem: Elegy
First published: 1982; collected in *Making Certain It Goes On: The Collected Poems of Richard Hugo*, 1984

The Poem

Richard Hugo's "Here, But Unable to Answer" consists of four symmetrically arranged stanzas of seven, ten, ten, and seven lines (a total of thirty-four lines), written in unrhymed, accented lines that approximate iambic pentameter. As its dedication implies, the poem is an elegy mourning the death of Herbert Hugo, the poet's father (actually his stepfather). The title echoes a response that is sometimes given during roll call in the military when an individual, ill or indisposed in some way, is for all other purposes present and accounted for. Its use here is ironic, for the father is dead and thus truly unable to answer, even though he is still present symbolically in the speaker's heart.

The speaker in the poem addresses the father directly, as if the father could still hear him. Several details indicate that Hugo himself is this speaker: the dedication, the term "Father," the autobiographical references to Hugo's lonely childhood with his grandparents ("I alone/ with two old people"), with whom he lived while his father, a Navy man, sailed the world, and glimpses of his own career as an Army Air Corps bombardier in World War II, "praying the final bomb run out."

The poem begins at early dawn. "Eight bells" mark the end of the night watch (four A.M.) as "first light" illuminates the father's face. Hugo imagines him in command on the bridge of his ship, a powerful, almost godlike figure whose "voice rolls back the wind" and whose eyes light up the ship's compass. In the second stanza, however, the poet momentarily seems to take on some of that power. Had the father been lost at sea, Hugo vows he would have rescued him by tearing away the clouds to reveal the north star by which he might safely navigate homeward. They would then have sailed off together. Yet the poet immediately contrasts that dream with the reality of his desolate childhood.

In the third stanza, Hugo reveals that, during the war, more than physical distance separated the two men. In spite of the father's desire to serve in combat, he was assigned to pilot new ships from the shipyards, whereas the son became an unwilling hero who bombed the enemy and returned home after the war, "these hands still trembling with sky." Hugo remarks that their war will go down in history as the last war worth dying for, a comment often made about World War II.

As the poem shifts to the present in the final stanza, the father has died and lies buried "too close" to a modern highway, but the poet still envisions him on the bridge of his ship, a mythic figure "naming/ wisely every star again, your voice enormous/ with the power of moon, of tide." He assures his father that he has become strong enough to assume control of his life: "I seldom/ sail off course. I swim a silent green."

He is guided even when asleep by the father's compass, although the father himself is gone. Here the poet seems to experience a symbolic and benign union with the father, one they could not share in life.

Forms and Devices

Hugo's poetic form owes much to the tradition of Anglo-Saxon poetry. While fellow poet and critic Dave Smith has called attention to "the mighty tug of his cadences," which is present in nearly all of his work, Hugo's use of formal meter is seldom strict. In "Here, But Unable to Answer," he employs a characteristic five-beat line that falls somewhere between the purely accentual meter of Anglo-Saxon poetry and a looser version of unrhymed iambic pentameter, or blank verse, the traditional meter that has been called the most natural rhythm in English.

Typically his metrical pattern will vary, influenced, he once said, by the shifting riffs of American swing and jazz. These lines, for example, contain anywhere from six to thirteen syllables, with three to seven stresses. However, in his well-known and widely imitated syllabic "Letter" poems, published in *31 Letters and 13 Dreams* (1977), he created a precise line of fourteen syllables.

Hugo is essentially a poet of sound. He employs repetition as a frequent device. Like the Anglo-Saxon poets, he favors a heavy emphasis on consonance and assonance (the repetition of consonant and vowel sounds) and, to a lesser degree, alliteration (the repetition of beginning sounds), to unify his lines: "*A* small *d*awn, *s*ailor. Fir*st* ligh*t* glin*ts*." He often repeats syllables, whole words, and even phrases, as he does in "Eight *bells*. You *bell*ow orders" and "Even in *war* we lived a *war* apart." Still another type of repetition may be found in the final lines of the poem's first and fourth stanzas, where five words or their variants are echoed: "Your *eyes light* numbers *on the compass* green" and "When *I* dream, *the compass lights* stay *on*." Seldom does he employ end rhyme in his work, creating instead a more subtle internal rhyme:

> Father, now you're buried much too close for me
> to a busy highway, I still see you up there
> on the bridge, night sky wide open . . .

Like the English Romantic poet William Wordsworth, Hugo seems to favor the rhythms of natural speech, although his choice of words is less mellifluous and more direct. He prefers one- and two-syllable words derived from the Anglo-Saxon language to the more ornate, multisyllabic Latinate terms. As Smith has pointed out, "He is, in words, and has always been a meat and potatoes man."

Themes and Meanings

An overriding theme of "Here, But Unable to Answer" is the concept of loss or abandonment, as seen through what poet Marvin Bell has called "the vengeance of time [and] the clarity of failure." The poet mourns not only the loss of the father through death but the loss of a father who was absent in life as well. This idea of loss is pervasive in Hugo's poetry, whether of a lost era or a past that never was, whether of the faded dreams of "Degrees of Gray in Philipsburg" or the collapsing buildings of a "Montana Ranch Abandoned," two of Hugo's best-known poems.

Here he adopts a typical stance, that of a solitary figure with a desire for connection who views past and present with what critic Frederick Garber has identified as a "stereoscopic vision" of what is and was or, more often, what was not but should have been. In this poem, Hugo views the father in his imagination not from memory but on the bridge of his ship. The father stands alone, as does the poet, who envisions a powerful union between them: "what a team/ and never to be." This statement embodies a kind of wishful thinking. The bond between solitary father and isolated son in this poem is a yearned-for relationship rather than a real one. In truth, they have always been separated.

A related theme, again very typical of Hugo's work, is the undercurrent of personal guilt, as if the poet somehow bears responsibility for the physical and emotional distance between the two men. His tone is melancholy and even apologetic. The phrase "Me and my unwanted self" expresses a clear discomfort with his own identity. The poet urges his father to "forgive the bad nerves I brought home," as if the post-traumatic stress caused by his experiences as a bombardier in the war were something for which he was personally responsible. Even in his final vision of the father, there is a stab of regret for a relationship, a love, never fully realized.

The outer landscape of Hugo's poem mirrors the inner psychological landscape of the speaker. The scene is one of vast space and isolation. At the beginning of the poem, dawn is breaking over the ocean; at the end the dead father, who in reality is buried on land, remains alone on the bridge under a night sky studded with distant stars. This is the landscape of solitude, of sea and sky. The poet remains a contemplative observer throughout, his voice thick with sorrow. Even though he expresses his grief and admiration for the father, they do not touch. There is never a physical connection between them.

Close friend and poet James Wright has written of Hugo's work, "The absence of outcry seems . . . deeply significant. It suggests the spiritual silence at the heart of the poet's imagination." Indeed, one often encounters in Hugo's poetry a quiet loneliness, a reaching out, and here it is very appropriate as he mourns the death of his father.

Joanne McCarthy

THE HILLS

Author: Guillaume Apollinaire (Guillaume Albert Wladimir Alexandre de Kostro-witzky, 1880-1918)
Type of poem: Lyric
First published: 1918, as "Les Collines" in *Calligrammes*; English translation collected in *Calligrammes*, 1980

The Poem

"The Hills" is a poem in blank verse divided into forty-four stanzas of five lines each. The title is a metaphor that will continue throughout the poem, thus giving coherence to a long sequence of apparently disparate images. The hills suggest altitude and, implicitly, the possibility of a better vision: One can have a better perspective and see farther from the top of a promontory. This elevated position becomes the equivalent of foresight and superior knowledge.

Like traditional lyric poetry, "The Hills" is written mainly in the first person, but, in the original French version, poet Guillaume Apollinaire sometimes uses the second-person singular (*tu*) when addressing his old self in order to make a clear distinction between his old nature and his new one, between past and future. He also uses the second-person plural (*vous*) when he addresses the whole of mankind in a prophetic voice.

The poem begins with an image that could be related to Apollinaire's experience in World War I: two planes involved in combat over Paris. However, one of the planes symbolizes the poet's childhood and youth, and it is brought down by the other one, which symbolizes the future. This metaphoric victory of the future over the past announces a new era of unlimited knowledge and magic, where poets can perceive, as if from the top of a hill, things that had not been seen before and where they can announce "Billions of prodigies" to come.

Each of the following stanzas contains a prophecy, a memory, or a dreamlike image that implicitly continues the oscillation between future and past. The origin of these images is not observation but rather something that may evoke psychoanalysis: the productive "Depths of consciousness" to be explored in a near future. It is from these "abysses" that the poet-prophets emerge like hills and bring a different type of knowledge of the world that is as precise and valid as scientific knowledge. In a reversed time perspective specific to many poems by Apollinaire, this new predicted era is actually "coming back," as if the future has already happened. The world is cyclic: "Here nothing ends nothing begins" and the "Helpful spirits" of the ancestors mingle among the new generations.

The poet talks about his own role as a prophet and his ability to remember and foresee at the same time. The instrument of his magic tricks is language, that "talisman . . ./ Dead and yet subtler than life." Language has a history and therefore has its roots in the past, but it also belongs to the fugitive present of the utterance and to the future by the poetic legacy of innovation. As a prophet, the poet can levitate and raise himself above "all natural things." Like a shaman, he can explore realms that nobody else has ever imagined. He can view his past, and poetry becomes a way by which the poet can freely contemplate himself, split into a subject and an object, author and matter of the poem: "it is I/ Who am the flute I play."

All these trancelike images end when the poet is reunited with himself as he hears his "footsteps coming back." He sits at his desk to write about his experiences of travel in time, and each stanza represents disparate images meant to break any connection with tradition, literary convention, or prosaic semantics: The orange tastes like a fireworks display, a maître d'hôtel pours unreal champagne for his dead customers, and a chauffeur discovers new universes around every corner. The poem ends with a complex image of a multilayered world, like a rose whose hidden essence needs to be discovered.

Forms and Devices

Although it has no punctuation, "The Hills" may seem more traditional than other poems published by Apollinaire in *Calligrammes* because of its regular stanzas. (*Calligrammes* is famous for its poems that are shaped like objects such as cigars, trees, guitars, and the Eiffel Tower.) In spite of its regular pattern, however, "The Hills" experiments with new poetic language and imagery. Each stanza contains a global and instantaneous image of the world. The poem is made of several such independent frames that succeed each other in an order that seems arbitrary; it is actually the result of a different temporal perspective that is specific to a poetic vision that covers present, past, and future in one glance. The poet uses the future tense to mark his prophetic tone ("A time will come for suffering" or "Man will become a god"), and he alternates it with both the past tense, which indicates a return in time, and the present tense, which he uses to describe himself experiencing the future he predicts.

Many critics have contrasted the Apollinaire of *Calligrammes* to the Apollinaire of *Alcools* (1913; *Alcohols*, 1964) and other early works in prose and verse, stating that the war experience marked a turning point in the writer's style and themes. However, the unique graphic arrangement of some poems in *Calligrammes* should not prevent readers from seeing the continuation of certain images and themes throughout his work. Thus many of the metaphors in "The Hills" can be better understood when placed in the context of other poems or writings in prose. For instance, the whole sequence describing Italy in stanzas 21-23 is a literary allusion to Apollinaire's short story "Giovani Moroni," in which Rome during carnival represents a powerful childhood memory. The "dead talisman" in this poem is a metaphor for language, as is the "dead purple" in the earlier collection entitled *Le Bestiaire* (1911; *Bestiary*, 1978). Even the image of the dual or split persona appears in the poem "Cortège" (*Alcools*), in which the poet is described as waiting to meet himself and calling his own name as if calling a friend's name.

What is definitely new in this poem, however, is the sequence of dismantled visual fragments evocative of cubist or Dadaist painting. The images are decomposed, and their separate elements are juxtaposed: The still life in stanza 37, for example, gathers different and unrelated objects (a hat, fruit, gloves) on a table. The dreamlike sequences (stanzas 37 and 38) anticipate the incongruous associations in surrealist art. Apollinaire, after all, is said to have invented the word "surrealism" and also wrote the first surrealist play, *Les Mamalles de Tirésias* (1917; *The Breasts of Tiresias*, 1961). These elements allow the reader to establish a connection between Apollinaire's poetry, his art criticism, his aesthetic vision, and even his relationship with contemporary artists such as Pablo Picasso and Marcel Duchamp.

Themes and Meanings

"The Hills" is considered to be one of Apollinaire's poetic testaments (a quote from it is engraved on the poet's tombstone) in which he develops his vision of the future of art and literature. In this poem, he predicts a new kind of aesthetic ideal, superior to the traditional one that "arose from symmetry." This idea of new aesthetic creation is expressed in an allusion to a Greek myth. In stanza 8, when he foresees that "Sea-foam would once more be mother," the poet refers to Venus, the goddess of beauty born from the sea foam, and he announces the advent of a new type of beauty.

Apollinaire refers to another Greek myth when defining his vision of the poet's new mission. For him, the poet is also similar to a magician or a prophet gifted with almost supernatural powers. In this definition, the reader can identify the mythical figure of Orpheus who, in Greek mythology, was a poet, musician, and prophet with magical powers. His art could charm the most ferocious beasts and bring peace and harmony. He traveled to the underworld to bring his wife, Eurydice, back from the dead. This myth is one of Apollinaire's favorites, and, in "The Hills," the imagery of travel in time and space, beyond life and death, can be interpreted as a modern replica to Orpheus's journey.

In Apollinaire's interpretation, the myth of Orpheus also incarnates the idea of the poet as a martyr and of poetry as a sacred and sacrificial gesture (Orpheus, who appears in many of Apollinaire's poems and stories, is killed and torn to pieces by bacchantes who do not understand his art). "A time will come for suffering," the poet predicts in stanza 25, and this theme of poetry as suffering and martyrdom is continued throughout the poem in images inspired also by Christian parables and medieval legends. In "The Hills," the poet's words become vegetal: They are "sweet fruits" and "grain" (in stanzas 27 and 28) that can be shared and eaten. The suffering (converted into vegetal food) is always mentioned in relation to the goodness of heart (in stanzas 24, 25, and 35, for example), so it appears like a deeply humanitarian sacrifice. The image of the poet-martyr sacrificing himself for mankind and offering himself to be eaten as fruit or grain is derived from the Eucharist (in which Christ symbolically offers his body to be eaten).

The presence of numerous archetypes, timeless stories, and myths in Apollinaire's poetry may seem surprising when one considers that he was trying to promote what he called "a new lyricism" and a "new spirit." However, his temporal perspective explains this intermingling of ancient figures (references to myths and legends) and modern descriptive elements (such as airplanes, car drivers, and elevators): In "The Hills," Apollinaire expresses his belief that the poet must include in his view both tradition and innovation. The past and the ancestors must somehow be permanently present in an artist's life. Thus, the new aesthetic ideal that he predicts is not the destruction of older models but rather the continuation of a heritage.

Anca Mitroi Sprenger

THE HIND AND THE PANTHER

Author: John Dryden (1631-1700)
Type of poem: Narrative
First published: 1687

The Poem

   The Hind and the Panther is a long poem in three parts totaling 2,592 lines. In this poem, John Dryden employs his favorite verse form, the heroic couplet. Taken as a whole, *The Hind and the Panther* is an allegorical and argumentative treatment of the religious conflicts that took place in England during the reign of King James II. More specifically, the poem is a defense of the Catholic faith and of Dryden's conversion to Catholicism in 1685. The hind of the poem's title is an allegorical deer representing the Catholic church, while the panther represents the Anglican church.

   In part 1 of *The Hind and the Panther*, Dryden introduces the various religious factions of his time as allegorical beasts. Thus, the bear represents religious independents, the hare represents Quakers, the ape represents atheists, the boar represents Baptists, the fox represents Unitarians, and the wolf represents Presbyterians. The fox and the wolf are described with special satiric intensity. Also in part 1, Dryden includes a moving and beautifully expressed confession of his own religious faith. Part 1 concludes with a meeting between the Catholic hind and the Anglican panther, which sets the stage for part 2.

   Part 2 is essentially a vigorous debate between the hind and the panther in which the main differences between Catholicism and Anglicanism are argued in verse of great power and discursive clarity. The issues discussed include church authority, biblical interpretation, the value of Catholic oral tradition, the Catholic doctrine of infallibility, and the 1673 Test Act, which prevented Catholics from being appointed to important state positions. Consistent with the general purpose of the poem, the Catholic positions are expressed with overwhelmingly persuasive force.

   Part 3 continues the debate between the hind and the panther but deals less with doctrine than with the political future of Catholics in England. The panther tells an animal fable dealing with swallows and martins in which the swallows, representing Catholics in general, and the martins, representing the Catholic clergy, are fooled by mild weather into delaying migration until they are destroyed by the coming of winter. This fable within a fable not only expresses Anglican antipathy toward the Catholics but also serves as Dryden's warning to his fellow Catholics that they should not depend too much on King James's pro-Catholic policies. By way of answer to the panther, the hind tells her own fable of the pigeons and the buzzard in which she warns of the dangers to the Anglican church if the Anglicans ally themselves too closely with the sectarian supporters of the anti-Catholic Test Act. Following this fable, the poem ends with a beautiful passage that suggests the divine nature and the glorious future of the Catholic church.

Forms and Devices

Dryden's most obvious literary technique in *The Hind and the Panther* is the allegorical animal fable. Not only is the poem as a whole an animal fable, but part 3 also presents two distinct animal fables within the larger fable. As Dryden makes clear at the beginning of part 3, he is very much aware of the tradition of the animal fable, which goes back to ancient times. By using the fable, he is able to deal with very controversial and potentially explosive religious and political matters with humor, detachment, clarity, and simplicity. His use of the animal fable gives *The Hind and the Panther* a lightness and playfulness that the reader might not expect from the poem's serious subject matter.

Dryden balances the lightness of his fable with another literary technique that is important in both *The Hind and the Panther* and his poetry in general. Dryden was a great master of the verse essay. There are few poets in all of world literature who can equal his ability to reason and debate within the restrictions and formal demands of verse structure. Thus, especially in part 2, the debate between the hind and the panther regarding complex religious issues is handled with a precision, force, logic, and polish that are uniquely Drydenian. Much of the success of *The Hind and the Panther* stems from Dryden's remarkable combination of fabulistic charm and discursive strength.

Dryden's poetry as a whole is famous for its satire, and satire is, predictably, an important element in *The Hind and the Panther*. In part 1, Dryden sharply satirizes religious sectarianism in general and Unitarianism and Presbyterianism in particular. Moreover, the history of Anglicanism, the contradictions of the Church of England, and the political effects of radical Protestantism are handled with flashing ridicule.

Dryden's imagery is also important in *The Hind and the Panther*, especially imagery associated with light. Light is most often used to describe the purity and truth of Catholicism. Thus, the Catholic church is "a blaze of glory that forbids the sight," while the Anglican church is seen as a moon that reflects the higher light of Catholicism: "The rays she borrow'd from a better star." Dryden also uses a wide variety of imagery to clarify arguments or to sharpen satiric points. Thus, he communicates the doctrinal instability of Anglicanism with a simple but effective image: "Her wild belief on ev'ry wave is toss'd." In discussing the intellectual darkness of radical sectarianism, Dryden reduces the followers of such sects to blind insects. They are "such souls as shards produce, such beetle things/ As only buzz to heav'n with ev'ning wings." His wonderfully diminishing imagery also describes the origins of Calvinism on the shores of Lake Geneva near the Alps: "What tho' your native kennel still be small,/ Bounded betwixt a puddle and a wall."

Finally, Dryden's complete mastery of the neoclassical heroic couplet is crucial to *The Hind and the Panther*. His handling of narrative, argument, and satire in the poem depends on the compression and energy of his couplets. As an example, note how Dryden uses rhythm, parallel structure, and alliteration within the heroic couplet to define the weakness of the Anglican church surrounded by sectarian enemies: "Rul'd while she rules, and losing ev'ry hour/ Her wretched remnants of precarious pow'r."

Themes and Meanings

In his formative years, Dryden saw the chaos and destruction brought by a religiously inspired civil war in England. Most of Dryden's major poems, including *Absalom and Achitophel* (1681-1682), *Mac Flecknoe* (1682), and *Religio Laici* (1682), deal with his search for an authority and a coherent tradition that could stand against anarchy and the destructive power of radical individualism. *The Hind and the Panther* is Dryden's longest and most ambitious treatment of this theme. His fear of and scorn for the radical individualism that leads to extreme sectarianism is evident throughout the poem. In part 1, the sectarian animals (the wolf, the fox, the hare, and the boar) are all satiric portraits revealing the dangers of "private reason." For Dryden, all religious sects are tainted by pride, arrogance, confusion, violence, and a generally rebellious spirit. This sectarian rebelliousness has dangerous political and religious implications. Also for Dryden, sectarian belief in the efficacy of reason presents a fundamental and profound problem. In Dryden's view, the very essence of religion is that it deals with things beyond reason. Reason is valuable in those areas where it is appropriate, but it is helpless and misleading in the higher sphere of divinity: "Let Reason then at her own quarry fly,/ But how can finite grasp Infinity?"

In part 2 of *The Hind and the Panther*, Dryden sees the Anglican church as the least tainted of non-Catholic faiths. It is "least deform'd, because reform'd the least." Still, with great argumentative and poetic skill, Dryden expresses what he sees as the essential faults of the Anglican hind: It has no real apostolic authority, it is the dubious result of English political history, it is inconsistent and wavering in its basic doctrine, and it relies on a belief in individual biblical interpretation that can only produce chaos. In part 3, Dryden goes on to emphasize what he sees as the Anglican church's destructive willingness to enter into unscrupulous political alliances.

Since, for Dryden, no church based on "private reason" and sectarianism can provide a true authority and a valid tradition, it is in the Catholic church that he finds what he calls the "one central principle of unity." For Dryden, the Catholic church is "Entire, one solid shining diamond." It has the majesty of the bride of Christ. It is an authoritative and unwavering source of doctrine. It has a unity, a sanctity, a universality, and a claim to apostolic succession that form a telling contrast to the intellectual and spiritual chaos which, for Dryden, marked the English religious sects of the late seventeenth century. Certainly, from one point of view, Dryden's poem is a brilliantly versified defense of Catholicism. It is, however, something more: the dramatization of a powerful mind's search for certainty in a world of political and religious confusion.

Phillip B. Anderson

HIS SHIELD

Author: Marianne Moore (1887-1972)
Type of poem: Lyric
First published: 1951, in *Collected Poems*

The Poem

"His Shield" is a thirty-three-line poem in five stanzas, with an end-line rhyming scheme. Moore chose the title "His Shield" (originally "The Magic Shield") in an attempt to explain the life of Presbyter John, a legendary Christian of medieval times from Asia or Africa who was said to wear a salamander's skin for protection, thus shielding him from heat, fire, and other natural phenomena. Making the name "John" doubly interesting is the fact that her own father was named John, as was her grandfather, who was himself a "Presbyter": He was a Presbyterian minister in St. Louis, Missouri, where Moore was born in 1887.

Moore's poetry has been compared to the poetry of John Donne and, like Donne's poetry, is often called "metaphysical" because she uses images from nature and expands them by using metaphors. The central metaphor of nature's protective devices is used throughout "His Shield." In the first stanza Moore immediately mentions a number of animals, including the hedgehog, porcupine, and rhinoceros, that wear some sort of protection on their bodies. Her point is that many animals are prepared for life as they might be prepared for war; life is so dangerous that animals must evolve shields to battle the elements, as well as other animals, every day: "everything is battle-dressed."

In the second stanza Moore recognizes that human beings have very little protection in life, and she turns to the legendary Presbyter John for a clue as to how to save herself from the dangerous elements that might bombard her skin. She decides to use salamander skin, which supposedly has asbestoslike qualities, to shield her from fire and the sun. If John could protect himself in Africa with salamander skin, she too can become "asbestos-eyed asbestos-eared" to "withstand fire" and avoid drowning.

Attending to the Presbyter John legend in greater detail in stanza 3, Moore states that in Africa, where Presbyter John might have lived in perhaps the twelfth century, the land was rich with gold and rubies, yet no one valued these items greatly. No one was envious or greedy. Presbyter John was able to gird himself even more effectively than with salamander skin: He donned a coat of humility that deflected all jealousy and harm.

Stanza 4 explains that a shield of humility, similar perhaps to that used by Presbyter John, could provide protection for the leader of the African country of Ethiopia in the 1940's (the time when the poem was written). This dimension of the poem is difficult to grasp from the text alone, but Moore provided some explanation in other writings and interviews. Haile Selassie (also called the "Lion of Judah") was the emperor of Ethiopia, which was being besieged by Italy during World War II. Perhaps, Moore suggests, Selassie and Ethiopia could remain free without actually being free. Surrounded by his enemies, Selassie is advised to stay humble, avoid greed, avoid pomp, and avoid provoking the enemy.

In the final stanza Moore gives direct advice to readers on how they might avoid battles in their own lives. "Become dinosaur-/ skulled" and "ironshod," she suggests. More important, along with this armor, readers are urged to "be/ dull. Don't be envied." In other words, they should not be pompous, should not appear proud and haughty. People should stop counting their money and counting their victories. They should put aside their "measuring-rod" for sizing up their enemies and their friends. Remaining humble and avoiding confrontations is the way to survival.

Forms and Devices

Marianne Moore often used works of art, photographs, or newspaper articles to trigger ideas for poems. In addition, common animals such as porcupines, elephants, swans, and snakes often inspired her. As Patricia C. Willis explains in her book *Marianne Moore: Vision into Verse* (1987), "His Shield" was inspired by an article in *The New York Times* entitled "Rare Animal Freak Is Echidna in Zoo." Moore read and clipped the article, and later she combined what she had read with a book she had been reading about Haile Selassie. This book also included the legend of Presbyter John. The newspaper article described the echidna as an animal with "spines as defense armor." Moore added to this the idea of Presbyter John living his life in humility and the World War II theme of protection for Ethiopia, where Haile Selassie was facing the enemy in a battle for freedom.

Thus Moore began with an animal and built a metaphor that is challenging for the reader to decipher. The echidna, an Australian animal, is somewhat like a porcupine except that it hatches its young from eggs and then raises them in a kangaroolike pouch. The echidna is a very obscure creature to use as the central metaphor in a poem. Moore explained the problem of challenging the reader, yet being understood, when she said to Donald Hall (*A Marianne Moore Reader*, 1961), "I think the most difficult thing for me is to be satisfactorily lucid, yet have enough implication in it to suit myself."

The problems in understanding "His Shield" are not resolved once one can picture the echidna. One must also be able to picture a religious man living centuries ago in Africa, perhaps Ethiopia, preaching the gospel and wearing the skin of the salamander (another unusual animal) to protect himself from the heat. There is also the problem of understanding the situation in 1944 Ethiopia, where Haile Selassie was in reality battling his Italian enemies, using weapons and armor to save his country. In a sense, Moore's poem seems to be written to the world at large in 1944. The poem is sufficiently ambiguous that the reader wonders exactly what Moore intends. Is "His Shield" an antiwar poem? Is Moore advocating that Selassie become humble to avoid death? Should he and Ethiopia put down their armor and rely only on being humble and "dull"?

Themes and Meanings

"His Shield" uses nature as a model, as a provoking influence, to guide humans to make the right decisions. Moore suggests that people can find metaphors—and answers—for human problems by studying nature carefully. However, she goes beyond the physical to the metaphorical and the psychological. Perhaps, she muses, people can use a state of mind—in this case, humility—to foil their enemies. They can be "dull," paradoxically relinquishing their freedom to keep it alive. They can become "dinosaur-skulled" to protect the brain and can use the brain to be humble.

Moore's themes, though they typically start with a simple, obscure image, grow until they encompass a way of life, a way of living, that can protect and enlighten. Moore gave a hint at the meaning of "His Shield" when she spoke of humility in a speech she gave at the Grolier Club in 1948:

> Humility, indeed, is armor, for it realizes that it is impossible to be original, in the sense of doing something that has never been thought of before. Originality is in any case a by-product of sincerity . . . of feeling that is honest and accordingly rejects anything that might cloud the impression.

"His Shield" could also be described as a sort of "metaphysical satire." If satire pokes fun at the pompous, if it shows that a common way of dealing with life is false or egotistical, then "His Shield" is satirizing those who rely on weapons, verbal darts, and other offensive tactics to dominate others. Whether in actual warfare or in coffeehouse conversation, Moore admonishes people to put away armor, greed, and envy and to replace these ineffective tools with a humble approach. After all, since there is nothing new in nature, humans have little that is new. Therefore, perhaps they should stop measuring one another for greatness in life or imagination. Instead, Moore would have people put away their "measuring-rod" in order to be safe and free.

Larry Rochelle

A HISTORY OF CIVILIZATION

Author: Albert Goldbarth (1948-   )
Type of poem: Lyric
First published: 1981; collected in *Original Light: New and Selected Poems, 1973-1983*, 1983

The Poem

Reading "A History of Civilization" is somewhat like opening a box within a box within a box. The poem consists of four six-line stanzas organized so that each stanza focuses on a particular place and each place suggests a particular past. Each of the first three stanzas ends on the open phrase "In back," thus sending the reader quickly into the next stanza. For all its brevity, "A History of Civilization" does not quite fit the definition of a lyric. The reader does not "overhear" a speaker, but is treated to a complex layering of scenes.

The poem opens in the present, in a "dating bar" where everything is a bit suggestive. All the details evoke the contemporary—silk blouses, sweet brie. In back of the dating bar is the "last one-family grocer's," with its strings of vegetables, coffee, kidney beans. The lush details of the store—the "millet barrel" and the cash register "as intricate as a Sicilian shrine"—seem to be of another era. The woman here is proud of her clean linen apron rather than a silk blouse.

In back of the grocery is a room with a fireplace where a ring of "somber-gabardined grandpas" play dominoes: "Even their/ coughs, their phlegms, are in an older language." This scene evokes America's immigrant past. The final stanza takes place "in back/ of the back room" where rutting cats are eyeing other cats, spraying the sacks and baskets with their scent. Here, in the animal world, it's mating season too. "The dust motes drift, the continents." Time moves inexorably on, and very little has changed over the "history of civilization." All species must reproduce themselves in order to move into the future, and the poem concludes, "In the fern bar a hand tries a knee, as if unplanned."

Although the poem presents these rooms as opening into each other, as though they were linked in physical space, the subtle shifts in vocabulary hint that they may inhabit a continuum in time, as though there were only one room that has gone through the transformation from storage vault to "back room" to grocery to dating bar, following the needs of the new generations. Either "reading" is acceptable, since history is not only a series of successive events but also a fluid connection *between* events—a layering of time and place and interpretation.

The title of the poem makes large claims, but the details of the poem are so particular—and sometimes humorous—that the reader understands that the title is at least partly tongue-in-cheek. Take any place and peel back the layers, the poem seems to say, and you will find just such a "history." The progress of the human race depends on rooms such as these. "A History of Civilization" honors the daily lives of ordinary people even as it pokes some fun at the concepts of "history" and "civilization."

Forms and Devices

The most notable device in "A History of Civilization" is the use of subtle shifts in tone and language. Goldbarth not only lingers lovingly on the details of each specific place but also looks at each scene with a slightly altered eye. In the dating bar, sexual innuendo is extended to inanimate objects; the ferns are seen as "spore-studded/ elopement ladders." There is a sardonic eye that equates "slices of smiles" with "slices of sweet brie." Even the atmosphere of the bar ("dark and its many white wedges") is reduced to pockets of light where the single people can eye one another. In the grocery, however, Goldbarth illuminates the past, as though it were imperative to "fix" it in memory. His adjectives and similes make the objects almost palpable. The coffee barrel has a "cordovan sheen," and the millet scoops "stand at attention." "Sheen" extends to the woman polishing the cash register until "sheen" elides to "shrine."

The next stanza finds its core in the repeated imagery of insubstantiality. The old men doze and wake in "fitful starts" by a "guttering" fire. Their beards "flicker" in the light. In the shimmer of such vocabulary, the people appear and fade, half-seen, nearly legend. There is an almost formal tone as the poet pays homage to their simplicity. The vocabulary and tone of the final stanza returns to the informal, almost hip, language of the opening. (Both stanzas have to do with sexuality and procreation, the first of humans, the last of cats.) Cats "eye" cats, and everything "comes down to a few/ sure moves." There are "sure moves" in language, too, as Goldbarth deftly describes an era in a few chosen words.

"A History of Civilization" relies heavily on alliteration and assonance. "Two top buttons" emphasizes the letter *t*, and "white wedges" and "flicker like filaments" are other obvious examples of these techniques. Goldbarth also carefully orchestrates his phrases more subtly to take advantage of consonants, as in the parallel sounds of "coffee barrel" and "kidney beans" or the elegance of "unlit lengths." Vowels are given similar importance, starting with the short *a* of "back," which is echoed throughout. The short *u* of "rut" and "estrus" weds them in sound as well as sense. But the *tour de force* of assonance remains the "register as intricate as a Sicilian shrine." The shift from a hard to a soft *c* and the repeated *n* make the tongue "polish" the phrase just as the woman lingers over her dusting.

There is a ghost of meter behind this poem—"In the dating bar, the potted ferns lean down" has more than a hint of iambic pentameter, and this rhythm is repeated just often enough to remind the reader of its presence. Never singsong, the poem builds toward the metrical authority of its most important sentence: "The dust motes drift, the continents."

Themes and Meanings

Albert Goldbarth's poems are spun from an encyclopedic mind that engages odd snippets of information as well as the whole of scientific treatises. The "larger" issues have been Goldbarth's themes, but he treats them in unique, even spectacular ways. Funny, ironic, bitter, hilarious, irreverent, sexy, serious—this list of adjectives could apply to almost every one of his poems. "A History of Civilization" is a relatively early poem. It is less experimental, more traditional, than Goldbarth's later poems. Yet through its title and its complex structure, it predicts the poet who went on to write books with such titles as *Heaven and Earth: A Cosmology* (1991) and *Across the Layers: Poems Old and New* (1993) and to win the National Book Critics Circle Award. Goldbarth's style developed into one of excess—excessively long sentences packed with an excess of fact, speculation, memory, data of all kinds. Images and incidents fuse, break apart, then connect again. Everything is part of a larger chaos that, in the end, belongs to an even larger order.

When it is like the short journey of the dust mote or the more dramatic shifting of tectonic plates, the life of any individual is insignificant when measured against eternity. History, however, creates a context and reveals significance. "A History of Civilization" peels back layers of remembered time to uncover the basic values of America, to shine the spotlight briefly on the hard work of the immigrant family before the poem veers off (or back) to the one procreative force that shapes animals and humans alike. Lives are composed of an amalgam of history, coincidence, and imagination; we go on layering the quotidian until the past becomes so distant it needs to be reinvented.

When Goldbarth introduces the old men playing dominoes, firelight flickering on their beards "like filaments still waiting for the bulb or the phone to be invented," he describes the scene with the benefit of hindsight, naming the technology that will pull them into the present even as it thrusts the scene into the past. But Goldbarth looks through both ends of the telescope at once. The rooms become a palimpsest, time superimposed on place, until they fuse into one story. Thus, in the way of all "stories," history is being made this evening in the dating bar.

In the poem's final line, "In the fern bar a hand tries a knee, as if unplanned," the "as if" is important. It knows something of human nature. The planning is part of the age-old ritual of courtship that keeps the world spinning. This final line is also the moment when the reader becomes aware of the speaker as a shaping presence. More than an omniscient author, he is someone with a wry commentary, a point of view. If a cosmology implies a philosophy, Goldbarth's might be simply this: In a universe so vast, we have each other.

Judith Kitchen

HOME BURIAL

Author: Robert Frost (1874-1963)
Type of poem: Narrative
First published: 1914, in *North of Boston*

The Poem

"Home Burial," a dramatic narrative largely in the form of dialogue, has 116 lines in informal blank verse. The setting is a windowed stairway in a rural home in which an unnamed farmer and his wife Amy live. The immediate intent of the title is made clear when the reader learns that the husband has recently buried their first-born child, a boy, in his family graveyard behind the house. The title can also be taken to suggest that the parents so fundamentally disagree about how to mourn that their "home" life is in mortal jeopardy—in danger of being buried. Further, Amy, because of her introspective grieving, risks burying both her marriage and her sanity.

The husband enters the stairway from below and sees her before she sees him, because she is wrapped up in herself. He tardily observes that she has been looking out the stairway window at the graveyard, already containing four of "my people" and "the child's mound." She doubts that he ever noticed the graveyard from that window and cries out for him to stop talking. Avoiding his touch, she shrinks past him down the stairs. When he asks why a man cannot speak of his "lost" child, she counters first by saying "Not you!" and then by doubting that any man can. She abruptly announces that she must get some air. He tells her not to take her grief to "someone else this time," sits so as not to seem domineering, and, calling her "dear," says he wishes to ask her something. When she replies that he does not know how to ask, he requests her "help," grows bitter at her silence, and generalizes: Men must give up some manliness when married, and further, two who love should to be able to discuss anything. He wants to be allowed into her grief, which he thinks she is "overdo[ing] . . . a little," and hints that their love could produce a child to replace the dead one, whose "memory might be satisfied" by now.

Her rejoinder that he is "sneering" makes him upbraid and half-threaten her and ask why he cannot talk about "his own" dead child. This provokes her longest speech, briefly interrupted by his comment that he feels so "cursed" that he should laugh. The essence of her complaint is that he does not know how to speak, that she could not even recognize him when he dug the grave so energetically that he made "the gravel leap and leap," and that his voice then was too "rumbling" when he commented that foggy and rainy weather will rot good birch fences. Concluding that he cannot care, she in turn generalizes: Friends grieve for another's loss so little that they should not bother "at all," and when a person "is sick to death" he "is alone, and he dies more alone." Even when survivors attend a burial they are busy thinking of their own lives and actions. She calls the world evil and adds that she will not have grief this way if she "can change it."

He mistakenly feels that she has said her say, will stay now, and should close the door. She blurts out that he thinks "the talk is all" and that she must "go—/ Somewhere out of this house." He demands to know where and vows to "bring you back by force."

Forms and Devices

"Home Burial" achieves tension first of all through its use of unpretentious wording in blank verse, a poetic form with a tradition going back centuries, to tell a tragic domestic story in an homely locale. More obvious tension results from the fact that Amy and her husband have no meeting of either heads or hearts. He speaks fifty-eight lines, many of which are incomplete, while she speaks forty-five such lines. In contrast to the rhetoric of William Shakespeare's flowing blank-verse dialogue, Frost's is full of rushes, interruptions, and pauses. Amy tells her husband to stop talking thus: "Don't, Don't, Don't, Don't." Frost called this burst the best part of the poem. The husband puts too much faith in words, saying at one point, "There, you have said it all and you feel better." In Amy's reply—"oh, you think the talk is all"—that "oh," which Frost also said he liked, is more effective than a dozen words.

Much remains unarticulated. Frost never tells readers the husband's name, what the house looks like inside or out, how long ago the child died, or where Amy plans to go as she leaves. The poem is partly about the ineffectiveness of words. When the husband says that he must laugh because he is cursed, Amy does not even hear him but chooses to quote—and misunderstand—his earlier talk about wet days and birch fences.

Frost freights his sparse words with much meaning, often subtle, sometimes symbolic. When he talks of rotting birch wood, Amy says only that his comment has nothing to do with their child's body when it was "in the darkened parlour." The astute reader, however, will connect wood rot with human decomposition. When the husband compares the graveyard to a bedroom in size, he is being harmlessly literal. The reader, however, will think that Amy is recalling with displeasure the bedroom in which their child was conceived. When the husband pleads, "Let me into your grief," there is another sexual overtone of which he is not conscious. The stairway should be a place where the two might walk together, connecting levels of shared living; instead, it is merely a stage where body language reinforces the poem's words. Amy silently spies on her husband through the window instead of calling and waving to him. He climbs the stairs until his nearness makes her "cower . . . under him," at which he promises not to "come down the stairs." Frost intends a pun when the husband complains that his words to Amy "are nearly always an offence." Truly the two are fenced apart, by words and acts.

Amy's most effective verbal barrage, loaded with *l* alliteration, is her description of her husband's fiercely digging the grave with the leaping, leaping gravel "roll(ing) back down the mound beside the hole." Surely Frost wants the reader to connect this up-and-down motion with sexual activity but also, and more important, with the birth-life-adulthood-love-death cycle of humankind.

Themes and Meanings

Frost's primary concern in "Home Burial" is to present modes of grief and communication. The Frosts' first child, a son, died in 1900 at the age of four. Their grief, which permanently wrenched their long marriage, took conflicting forms, during which his wife, unlike the more talkative Frost, bottled up her grief and called the world evil exactly as Amy does. Frost, who gave innumerable public and private readings of his poetry, never included "Home Burial," explaining that it was too sad.

Amy and her husband are disastrously contrasting spouses. She is masochistic and rebellious. When she says, "I won't have grief so/ If I can change it. Oh, I won't, I won't!," she risks losing not only husband but reason itself. He moves coarsely from trying to question her to protesting and threatening. He never explains his sense of loss or his mode of grieving and never tells her that his commonplace talk and actions might represent a flinching from heartbreak. He never says that when he buried their baby he wished she had been standing beside him. Amy too misses a change to replace discord with harmony, by not helping him frame the question he wants to ask; instead she stifles him by saying that neither he nor "any man" can speak acceptably to her. Never once do they speak of "our" child.

They communicate by body language more expressively than by words. At first she is at the top of the stairs, and he is at the bottom. After they have reversed positions of seeming dominance, he sits—but with his chin in "his fists," not his hands. When he generalizes about off-limit topics between couples, her only response is to "move . . . the latch" of the door. Her intention is to get out of the house. It, along with her husband in it, is smothering her. Frost offers two messages in "Home Burial," one for pessimists such as himself, another for optimists. Its action exposes barriers to communication even among people "wonted" to intimacy. On the other hand, the dreadful aftermath of such barriers should encourage readers of good will to speak from the heart, listen, and be sympathetic.

Robert L. Gale

HOME COURSE IN RELIGION

Author: Gary Soto (1952-   )
Type of poem: Narrative
First published: 1991, in *Home Course in Religion*

The Poem

"Home Course in Religion," a long narrative poem, does not adhere to a specific rhyme or rhythm scheme. Instead, this prose poem relies on a variety of structural devices to provide unity. As with many of his other poems, Gary Soto is more concerned with creating and conveying an image with short, tight lines and direct, succinct diction than he is with rhyme and rhythm. For example, Soto consistently juxtaposes two seemingly ordinary, terse words (such as "Top Ramen" and "cereal bowl") that together reinforce the reality of the persona's poverty, a poverty that influences his every action: "I was living on Top Ramen and cold cereal." The socioeconomic concept of poverty and its resulting oppressiveness is pervasive in the poem. Building on this sense of poverty, the poem, written in the first person, allows Soto to create a persona whose view of the world and whose experiences are very similar to his. Thus, the poet speaks directly to and intimately with the audience, conveying an experience that is immediate and authentic.

The poem universalizes the archetypal journey of an eighteen-year-old college student as he struggles to find the "quiddity," or essence, of his life. As the title "Home Course in Religion" implies, the student undertakes his introspective journey by turning to religion. He begins by reading "a really long book" that *"ought to be read by anyone/ Who has had a formal or home-study course in metaphysics."* Unable to understand the convoluted images, he turns to other sources such as the Bible and *The Problem of Evil*. Although "much clearer," neither source alleviates his sense of separateness; rather, both books further obfuscate his search.

Throughout the poem, the young man's attempts to find answers through prescribed religion are thwarted. He then turns to other venues: politics, society, and education. For example, when he and his roommates discuss former U.S. president Richard Nixon's Watergate debacle and try to make sense of it, their ability to communicate with one another is impeded by a language barrier: "none of us understood what the other/ Was saying." In college, his teachers lecture about "pumice" and the "Papuan people," and, even though he takes notes, he is more intent on watching the teacher sweat—perhaps implying the nonrelevance of the subject matter. None of these institutions provides him with answers or helps him reconcile the ideal of the American dream with the reality of his world of "cracker crumbs" and the jar of peanut butter he regards as a "present" that he and his girlfriend used on their "last three crackers."

The poem concludes with the gradual, and sometimes painful, disintegration of the young man's belief in organized religion and institutions and with the deep personal sense of disorientation that results from his discovery. His three-day journey leads him to a rather dark, almost nihilistic, epiphany: "I realized I might be in the wrong line of belief." This statement conveys a sense of growth and maturation; he realizes prescriptive religion can neither abate his suffering nor ease his socioeconomic hunger. He is now a stronger person because he knows that he will have to survive on his own.

Forms and Devices

Soto defines himself as "an imagist, one who tries to provide a stark, quick image." His definition could well apply to the prominent images and metaphors he creates in "Home Course in Religion." Although he employs biblical allusions, ambiguities as a rhetorical device, and irony, Soto relies on central images and metaphors to convey the physical, psychological, and spiritual hunger of the young man.

Soto directly addresses the physical hunger the young man and his brother experience as they exist on Top Ramen, crackers, and cold cereal, which he eats in his Top Ramen bowl. Occasionally, the brothers are treated to "oranges that rolled our way" or peanut butter that the narrator's girlfriend gives them. Soto's continued, matter-of-fact references to these images resonates and heightens their emotional impact. By understating the multifaceted deficiency, the author explicitly conveys a deep sense of hunger that is reinforced when he says, *"People with big cars don't know how much it hurts."* This hunger precipitates the young man's spiritual quest as a means of abating, or at least understanding, his pain and suffering; therefore, he begins reading religious books.

After trying to understand the content of one of his religion books, the young man plays basketball to "get the air" back into his brain. At first, the image of "air" conveys a positive, vibrant, life-affirming quality. When juxtaposed with reading a religion book, however, the connotation becomes subtly negative. Once again, after reading ten pages in another book that seems clearer (*"Costly grace . . ./ . . . comes as a word of/ Forgiveness to the broken spirit/ And the contrite heart"*), the "good air" leaves him and he falls asleep. The metaphorical suggestion in both examples is implicit: Prescribed religion cannot alleviate his suffering if the messages it conveys are too esoteric or too difficult to understand.

Nonetheless, the young man continues to search for a sense of reassurance through religion by reading about a "French mystic." Instead of providing him with insight and hope, however, he learns that she talked "in weird/ Ways and no longer reached people with her thoughts." Later, he reads another numbing text and again falls asleep. Once again, his efforts to understand his plight are thwarted. Ironically, on the second day of his journey, he learns "more about life" from a karate instructor in physical education class than he does with the help of a book: *"Pain doesn't exist . . ./ . . . Pain is in the mind./ The mind is the spiritual nature/ That follows your body."* He learns that he must control his pain and that pain is part of the human condition.

Metaphorically, by juxtaposing the images of "good air" leaving the brain or falling asleep with religious texts, the author conveys a sense of the young man's alienation that is reinforced throughout the poem. Whether reading the Bible or *The Problem of*

Evil, the young man experiences the same dullness in his senses. His vitality and energy are seen when he talks to and jokes with his roommates and when he makes love to his girlfriend. Again, when he plays basketball and returns home, "sweaty in every hole," he feels revived and alive. In contrast to the deterioration of his vitality or life force when he delves into religious dogma, all of these interpersonal activities reaffirm his existence, evidence that neither his physical nor his spiritual hunger have been alleviated.

Themes and Meanings

"Home Course in Religion" is a poem about hunger (literally and figuratively) and the human pain or suffering that is a prerequisite to growth. In the poem, Soto explores the motif of hunger and universalizes one man's search for spiritual meaning in a world that seems devoid of spirituality.

Soto addresses the issues of hunger and poverty in several of his poems. The poem "Salt," in *Where The Sparrows Work Hard* (1987), poignantly describes two young boys whose hunger destroys their energy, even their will to live. "The Wound," in *Tale of Sunlight* (1978), focuses on the pain and anguish one young child endures as a result of his abject poverty. Although not directly stated, the boy suffers from a disease endemic to the impoverished. While hunger in both "The Wound" and "Home Course in Religion" begins as actual physical deprivation, it becomes a catalyst to attain a deeper understanding, a metaphysical explanation for the persona's pain.

The young man's quest in "Home Course in Religion" is complicated by his increasing involvement with his girlfriend. As his physical attraction to her intensifies, so too do his feelings of guilt and its accompanying remorse. One evening after his girlfriend leaves, he prays in his room, then crosses himself with his "fingertips\ Pushed into [his] flesh." His sense of guilt leads him to punish himself masochistically for what he perceives to be sins of the flesh. As he searches for answers to his conflicting feelings in a religious book, he falls asleep.

On the third and final day of his journey, the young man once again tries to sort through another book, but the "good air" leaves his brain, and he falls asleep. When his girlfriend arrives, she wakes him, literally and metaphorically, from his slumber. During the course of the evening, they become physically intimate, an intimacy that leads him to a deeper understanding of himself: People feel lonely "because they don't know themselves." By becoming sexually involved with her, he begins to acknowledge his need for life-affirming vitality. His immediate reaction to the sexual contact is similar to their first physical experience: He begins to feel "ashamed." His need to expiate his guilt drives him again to the Bible and to his futile search for divine affirmation. However, the sense of shame escalates when he realizes that the same hand that touched her turns the pages of the Bible. Out of a sense of remorse, he washes his hand, an act of physical, emotional, and spiritual purification. After performing this act, he begins to contemplate the evening during a "cat-and-dog storm" and realizes that he "might be in the wrong line of belief." This simple understatement symbolically underscores his epiphany, and the "line" he refers to implies a simultaneous movement away from systematic, organized religious dogma and toward more subtle, subjective, and life-affirming personal insights.

Sharon K. Wilson

HOMECOMING

Author: Friedrich Hölderlin (1770-1843)
Type of poem: Elegy
First published: 1802, as "Heimkunft. An die Verwandten"; English translation
collected in *Friedrich Hölderlin: Some Poems and Fragments*, 1966

The Poem

"Homecoming" is the last of Friedrich Hölderlin's eight elegies. It consists of six
stanzas of eighteen lines each, for a total of fifty-four elegiac distichs. The poem
begins with unqualified expressions of joy in the sight and sounds of a world
disclosing itself in its pristine relation. It then moves to a somberness still marked by
joy but wrought with care: The poet must care, if others cannot, about apprehending
the divine source of joyousness and finding names for the High Ones to supersede the
outworn terms that have lost the glory of radiant holiness. The naming of God, in the
deity's disclosure of himself, is a participation in creation as a constant reality. The
poet, still joyous in his ability to address the higher powers (the great Father and the
angels), confronts incipient despair at the apparent impossibility of new efficacious
naming.

The first stanza picks up the ambiguity of the poem's dedication, "An die Verwandten," which might be dedicating the poem to relatives to whom the poet is
returning or simply to like-minded persons whom the poet is addressing. It exhibits
creation as gloriously fraught with inherently resolved contradictions: bright night
under a cloud; a cloud in the act of composing the poetic lines that the poet is
composing about the cloud; a *gähnende* valley (a valley that is gaping or yawning as
it comes awake and that is swallowing—presumably swallowing the night covered by
the cloud in infantile self-sustenance). The stanza begins, "There inside the Alps it is
still bright night, and the cloud, composing/ Joyousness, covers it within the yawning
valley." The darkness is bright within a yawning (deep) valley that is waking with a
yawn and gapingly devouring the night, covered by a cloud that is creating, as a writer
creates, joyousness. The joyous pangs of beginning then issue from a young-looking,
roaring and rushing Chaos, shaking in joyousness and reveling in bacchanalian
discord, as dawn, like a newly born universe, moves toward order and temporality.

Above this terrestrial upheaval there is, in the second stanza, a silvery silence in
which, paradoxically, roses bloom in the snow of the mountain peaks. Above the snow,
and above the light itself, dwells the pure, blissfully silent radiance of God dispensing
beams of joyousness and perpetually creating life and the accoutrements of happiness.
The vision of God is followed in the third stanza by assertions that whatever poets
meditate upon or put into poetry is of concern or value to angels and God. Poetry, then,
is a joyous acknowledgment of divinity's constant gift, and it is directed not to
recipients but to the agency of donation. The acknowledgment includes, paradoxically, an apostrophe to the poet's fellow country-dwellers, reminding them that what

he is experiencing is theirs to experience, if only through his relation of his vision to the Spirit providing that vision.

The fourth and fifth stanzas elaborate upon the homeland, the clear view or fully subjective experience of which is Spirit's unfolding itself to the viewer. Specific parts of the German Fatherland are identified by name: Lindau, the Rhine, and the tree-filled valleys of the Neckar. Here the note of care enters into the poet's joy at his vision of God, which is a full and clear experience of universal reality's unfolding itself to him. The poet senses that the unfolding is in process but that the process will not be completed. To this sense of incompletion is added his care that his compatriots, who feel the joy of their homeland do not know that they feel it. Consequently they do not fulfill the provisions of their destiny. The best thing, the discovery—actually the recovery—under the holy rainbow of peace, of their native truth, is reserved from—or reserved for and yet kept from—the young and the old.

The conclusion of the fifth stanza moves into the beginning of the sixth as an invocation of the angels. The elegy concludes with the recognition that deity must be named: The outworn names have become names of names, mere words, and the poet must—but knows that he cannot—name afresh the divinity that constantly creates afresh and must always be named afresh.

Forms and Devices

Hölderlin applies the literary devices of ambiguity and paradox to an inversion of the biblical experience of Saul of Tarsus on the road to Damascus. Saul, leaving his home, was blinded by the divine light and was changed by his audience with God into Paul, God's emissary to those whom he must persuade to eschew their earthly homes. The poet in "Homecoming" is enlightened by the darkness and is restored by his audience with God to appreciation of the joys of his homeland at the same time that he is tentatively saddened by the impossibility of relating this vision and its significance to those whom he must nonetheless encourage to fulfill themselves in their earthly homes.

Inversion is also extended to the effective use of indirection—that is, achieving a goal by distancing oneself from it. Hölderlin's poet is seeing his home not as he had seen it while he lived there but in an entirely fresh Chaos of joyousness occasioned by his having been away from it. This achievement through indirection is analogous to the experiences of other characters in literature: Odysseus gets home by being kept away from it, Parzival finds the Grail by departing from the castle in which it is housed, Dante gets to the Blissful Mountain by going through the Inferno, Franz Kafka's K gets closer to the Castle when he is moving away from it than he does by heading straight for it, and Pär Lagerkvist's Tobias sustains his pilgrimage to the Holy Land by choosing to sail on a pirate ship going in a direction opposite to that of a Pilgrim ship.

Even the development of reference and allusion entails an inverseness that informs readers by disorienting them. The first stanza, for example, includes both direct references and allusions to Greek and Roman myth. Subsequent stanzas depart from such mythic terms in favor of general references to God, Spirit, and angels, alluding to the passage from classical antiquity to the Judeo-Christian middle ages and then to the modern age. However, they invert the Christian movement from earth to heaven so as to posit heaven's potential disclosure of itself constantly to earth-dwellers who can apprehend heaven within the truth of home. The subjective return to the home is an almost complete removal of the anxieties and uncertainties and uneasiness of human life.

This passage, or progression, is narratively enforced by the cabalistic device of beginning each of the six stanzas with a key word: "Inside" (*Drinn*), "Quiet" (*Ruhig*), "Much" (*Vieles*), "Definitely" (*Freilich*), "There" (*Dort*), and "Angels" (*Engel*). This succession provides a sense that there is great restfulness within oneself and that there are certainly angels outside oneself. The body of the poem intones the potentiality of the angels' provision of this great peace.

Themes and Meanings

"Homecoming" is a profound meditation upon the nature, or essence, or home. The blessings of home are brightness, friendliness, the experience of belonging, a sense of rightness, and ultimately a communion with the divinity who confers the blessings.

Martin Heidegger has provided a cogent essay on the meanings inherent in "Homecoming"; it was published as "Heimkunft / An die Verwandten" in *Erläuterungen zu Hölderlins Dichtung* (1944; a translation of the essay as "Remembrance of the Poet," along with its foreword, "Prefatory Remark to a Repetition of the Address," appears in the collection *Existence and Being*, 1949): "The innermost essence of home is already the destiny of a Providence, or as we call it: History. Nevertheless, in the dispensation of Providence, the essence is not yet completely handed over." It is reserved, given to be discovered but kept back from all. Heidegger identifies the reserved as that which introduces care (*Sorge*) into joyousness. He observes that the poem ends with a recognition that the poet must dispel care by caring rightly, not as he may wish or choose to care. He emphasizes the fact that the last word of the poem is 'a "blunt not"' (*nicht*).

Following Heidegger's lead, one could add that *nicht* is an element of the *Sorge* theme as it develops from the expression of joyousness. *Nicht* is absent from the first two stanzas; it then appears once in each of the next three stanzas and five times, in all, in the last stanza. The increasing note of negativity serves as a check on the joyousness that the poet feels. Words denoting joy appear fourteen times in the poem, five times in the sixth stanza, and are missing only from the fourth stanza—which does, however, include the word "happy" in modification of Lindau, the locale of the homecoming.

Heidegger selected Hölderlin's poetry as the prime example of his notion that poetry alone is receptive of Being's reserved unfolding of itself. Poetry, he says, is not about homecoming: poetry is the actual homecoming. The homecoming is serenification, the return to the serenity of Being. The unfolding of this serenity is best and most nearly fully experienced in one's existential home, where long residence effectively inhibits one's ability to achieve the experience. Distancing oneself from home ultimately serves to sharpen the ability to experience serenity upon returning or drawing near to home once again. The sensibility of the poet, exclusively, is attuned to the joyousness of homecoming and its attendant quality of care.

Roy Arthur Swanson

HOMILY

Author: Jim Harrison (1937-   )
Type of poem: Satire
First published: 1985, in *The Theory and Practice of Rivers*

The Poem

"Homily" is a free-verse poem written in thirty-five lines with no stanza breaks. The construction of the poem is free from most formal conventions of poetry, including patterned rhyme, rhythm, and meter. Its organization follows the develop- ment of the poem's content, which is aptly described by its title. The term "homily" refers to a sermon often delivered in church to a congregation. The subject of the sermon is often designed to instruct or enlighten the audience for moral or spiritual improvement. In "Homily," Harrison offers his readers a list of "do's and don'ts" that escalates through the vices of indulgence in wine, song, pornography, and lust, culminating in the dissolution of the subject as he is torn apart by his desires. Though the persona of this poem could be said to speak to its readers (its congregation), the speaker in "Homily" also appears to be speaking only to himself, as if the reader were listening to someone talking alone in an attempt to find a balanced and moderate middle road in life.

The poem begins with a statement of "simple rules to live within." The first image is related to writing with one pen in the morning and another at night. Soon the poem's imagery moves to the kinds of indulgences that traditional church homilies often spoke against: "avoid blue food and ten-ounce shots/ of whiskey . . .// . . . don't read/ dirty magazines in front of stewardesses." The catalog of images includes a number of activities that might prove hazardous to one's physical health; other images relate to one's positive mental health. A few of the images are based on stereotypical words of common sense, such as "don't point a gun at yourself" and "don't use gas for starter fluid." The reader is reminded that a balanced life is not as easy as simple choices between right and wrong. Harrison asks, "who can/ choose between the animal in the road/ and the ditch?" These lines suggest that at times the choices one faces may not offer easy alternatives or clear avenues to a decision. Further, the lines imply a situation where the only offered alternatives are to do harm to another (the animal in the road) or to do harm to oneself by avoiding harming the other.

As the poem continues, images become more peculiar and inventive. The catalog of images focuses on the subject of love: self-love, love of another, infatuation, and fantasy. The climax of the poem is the admonition not to "fall in love/ with two at once." In the final set of lines, the reader is asked to look down upon the person who is now part of a threesome, "though one might be elsewhere." The person looked down upon from above tears himself apart and whirls in a circle: "he whirls so hard everything he *is* flies off." Because of this indulgence, this lack of moderation, the subject crumbles, only to experience the same fate again: "He crumples as paper but rises daily from the dead."

Forms and Devices

One of the significant features that individualizes Harrison's poetry in comparison to so many of his contemporaries is the lack of consideration he gives to formal constraint. His poems often encapsulate wild flights of the imagination and surreal images that lack any definite closure and that do not demonstrate the least hint that any of the language was constructed in advance. Even when he has written in form, Harrison has most often employed the ghazal, a short series of couplets that allows a "metaphorical leap" from couplet to couplet, thus offering the kind of freedom within the form that Harrison continually appears to seek. He has stated that his tendencies "run hotly to the impure, the inclusive, as the realm of poetry."

"Homily" demonstrates Harrison's exuberance and wit as well as his facilities with language. The main device Harrison relies on to create the poem is the blazon, the catalog of images related to a single idea. The blazon supports Harrison's desire for inclusiveness and helps to develop the tone of dark humor that the poem suggests. The poem is a satire of the homily, a form delivered over many years in church services that, in the cleanest and most socially acceptable language possible, warned church-goers of their potential for sin. Harrison's images warn against excess, but the images are so stark, so free of self-consciousness, that the reader can respond to the honesty and authenticity of the lines.

Harrison employs a number of the more common literary devices, including an early pun on the word "snipe" and a late series of similes that concretize the ways in which one might "fall" in love. Harrison's similes offer heterogeneous comparisons and unusual connections between images whose disparate natures create a high level of energy. There is also a natural cadence to the lines despite the lack of a patterned rhythm or meter. The sound cadences resemble those of speech, as the poem attempts to replicate the building intensity of an orally delivered homily. The sentence patterns employed in the poem are similar, usually consisting of imperatives that, because of their identical structure, create a rhythmic cadence. Though the poem is constructed in lines, conventional patterns of sentence structure and punctuation are used. The opening lines build with images in the longest sentence of the poem, quickening the pace of the reading. After the opening ten lines, sentence lengths vary but are generally relatively short as the poet's admonitions become more unusual and complex. In addition, the use of comparable phrases embedded within sentences of the poem supports the flowing cadence of the homily.

Themes and Meanings

"Homily" is concerned with the continuing challenge to find balance in life in the face of numerous seductions. Instead of the traditional, socially accepted language and subject matter offered in the church tradition, Harrison uses graphic images of temptations and behaviors that create humor on the surface of the piece. Underlying these comedic aspects, however, Harrison suggests the complexity involved in at-tempting to live a moderate life.

The poem begins with the relatively easy "rules to live within." These rules become habits that allow for a structured life. In addition to practicing certain kinds of habitual behavior, the speaker of the poem offers a few of the more obvious rules related to dangerous behavior, variations on the clichés most young people are told as they are growing up. The poem creates humor by employing more distinctive images of those things to avoid, including "blue food and ten-ounce shots/ of whiskey." The theme of the poem moves from a foundation of the basic principles of practicing positive behavior as an outcome of good habits and avoiding negative behavior by practicing common sense.

As the poem continues to develop, Harrison complicates the theme by introducing choices that are less easily defined and less easy to make. The poem moves to those experiences that are healthy and positive at a certain level but become increasingly dangerous with excess. The poet insists that dangers are not always a result of the kind of choice that has been made; they are sometimes a result of the degree to which one engages in these behaviors. Food is a life-giving necessity at one level and an unhealthy danger if consumed in overabundance. The imagination is a wonderful invention, but fleeing from real experience to a solely imagined life leads to misery. After the right choices are made, one must be on guard against excess to live a balanced life.

The continuing tension between the free will of choices and the fatalism of what happens builds to an extended set of images related to the dangers of love. One of the images warns not to fall in love "with photos of ladies in magazines," which suggests the harm of investing emotion in appearances. A series of images cautions not to fall in love so intensely as to be swept off one's feet. Each of the images shows the damage that results from this excess born innocently from the heart. The final stage of development related to this theme issues from the admonition against falling in love "with two at once." This excess is described with language that shows the individual "spinning" and "whirling," resulting in disintegration. The loss of self resulting from this experience is enacted repeatedly as the person "rises daily from the dead" only to travel the same circle to his or her own deterioration. The poem ends its series of warnings with this image of annihilation. The reader can then leave the poem in fear, though resolved to avoid these temptations. The satire of the traditional homily is complete.

Robert Haight

THE HORSES

Author: Edwin Muir (1887-1959)
Type of poem: Narrative
First published: 1956, in *One Foot in Eden*

The Poem

Edwin Muir's "The Horses," a free-verse narrative poem of fifty-three lines, opens to the reader a future that may have seemed all too possible at the time of its composition in the 1950's. In the opening lines, "Barely a twelvemonth after/ The seven days war that put the world to sleep," Muir ushers the reader out of the realm of the everyday. Brief wars have occurred in the past, but have such wars put the entire world to sleep? The notion seems outrageous. Yet that sense of outrage in itself helps to color the passages that follow and put them into perspective. The reader learns, line by line, that things in the world have gone seriously awry. Technology has reached an impasse. "On the second day," Muir's narrator says, in chronicling the war, "The radios failed; we turned the knobs; no answer." The nature of the calamity comes gradually clear. "On the third day a warship passed us, heading north,/ Dead bodies piled on the deck. On the sixth day/ A plane plunged over us into the sea. Thereafter/ Nothing." An enormous but quiet disaster has overcome the world. In a dreamlike state, the weapons of war appear to the survivors less as machines than as mysterious signs of new times. When the warship appears, no pursuing ships follow. No enemy planes land to disgorge conquerors. The survivors of the "seven days war" emerge into a world in which only defeat is visible. They see no victors. From these cues, readers of Muir's poem may guess he is imagining the aftermath of atomic war, the one kind of conflict that might "put the world to sleep."

Muir's vision is by no means lacking in hope. Readers know from the beginning that some have survived. The survivors even thrive in an odd way: They remember certain ways of the past and return to a preindustrial level of coping. They learn again to produce food from the earth with their own hands. The horses of the title unexpectedly intrude upon the lives of these postapocalypse people. They initially possess a fearsome aspect, being "strange" and making their appearance with a haunting and "distant tapping on the road,/ A deepening drumming; it stopped, went on again/ And at the corner changed to hollow thunder./ We saw the heads/ Like a wild wave charging and were afraid."

The survivors know their forefathers had abandoned these horses in favor of tractors, which makes the unasked-for reappearance all the more unsettling. The animals return to the farms as if the "long-lost archaic companionship" between horses and the workers of the land is to be restored. The reestablishment of this relationship marks the return of natural order to the world. The horses also signal the return of validating emotional life. "That free servitude can still pierce our hearts," Muir's narrator says. "Our life is changed; their coming our beginning."

Forms and Devices

While "The Horses" is a speculative poem in that Muir uses a poetic narrative form to speculate into the future from an existing situation in the world, the poem may also be read as a conceit or an extended metaphor. The future world that has been brought to stillness and silence by technology may be none other than the contemporary world in which humans have become so divorced from their "natural," or at least traditional, modes of living that they are no longer fully in touch with their own true nature. Rather than being a future danger, the rift between humankind and the world has already grown wide.

Muir uses the narrative to take a hopeful view of the situation. By having the horses return to the farmers of their own volition, he suggests that humans may look to the world itself for the closing of the rift. A natural order may reestablish itself, even at a time when people appear unwilling to make the effort on their own. The narrator of the poem makes clear the attitude of the survivors toward the horses: "We did not dare go near them." The horses, nevertheless, offer their "free servitude," which allows the survivors to then rediscover their own place in nature. Muir gives depth and resonance to his free-verse lines with a series of intertwined repetitions and contrasts. Using the same adjective in the first three occurrences of "horses" in the poem, Muir emphasizes the dilemma of the survivors through a subtle oxymoron: The very animals that should have been most familiar to the farmers have instead become "strange" to them. Muir refers to the state of the world and, by inference, to the state of the survivors by speaking of the war "that put the world to sleep" and of nations "lying asleep." That it is an unnatural sleep Muir suggests obliquely: The poet refers to "days" and "noon" in speaking of the aftermath of war. It is a daytime sleep in which the nations are plunged. If the war was indeed atomic in nature, this daytime sleep would have been brought on not only by the artificial sun of the atom bomb but also by the figurative "light of reason" of science.

In contrast, when evening comes to the survivors, they confront an odd spectacle. The once-useful tractors now "lie about our fields; at evening/ They look like dank sea-monsters couched and waiting." The approach of true sleep casts a mythological shadow over the machines. Evening also brings the horses and gives them similar shading: "Now they were strange to us/ As fabulous steeds set on an ancient shield/ Or illustrations in a book of knights." The parallel Muir draws between different animals at the plough also underlines a contrast. "We make our oxen drag our rusty ploughs," the narrator initially says. The horses then return. "Since then," the narrator says, "they have pulled our ploughs and borne our loads." Muir distinguishes the unwilling and forced relationship between farmer and land in the first line from the willing and unforced relationship in the latter by speaking immediately afterward of the "free servitude" offered by the horses. The farmers need no longer "make" nature do their will. Muir also links the changes brought on by war and those brought on by the horses through parallel phrases: "it was so still/ We listened to our breathing and were afraid," the narrator says of the first days of the war. After the farmers hear the approaching horses, they "saw the heads/ Like a wild wave charging and were afraid." First, unusual silence brings fear. In striking contrast, the noise of life does the same.

Themes and Meanings

In its imagery and its contained events, "The Horses" focuses upon communication, both failed and successful. At least initially, silence represents the former. The war itself starts with stillness and silence without the violence and clangor normally associated with major conflicts. Its first result, moreover, is added silence: The radios fall quiet. The passage of the warship and the falling of the plane seem noiseless events in Muir's emotionally muted, or numbed, lines. By the time the horses arrive, the survivors have already made a "covenant with silence" and have reached the point of preferring that the radios do not speak again. Muir conveys the anxiety with which they regard the notion of working radios and, by extension, the return of the techno-logical world in emphatic lines of repetition: "But now if they should speak,/ If on a sudden they should speak again,/ If on the stroke of noon a voice should speak,/ We would not listen." No sounds are mentioned in the poem before the arrival of the horses except for a few words, presumably spoken by one farmer to another. The words relate to the return to soil. People are returning to the soil as farmers, and their old machinery is doing likewise in a more literal way: "'They'll moulder away and be like other loam,'" one says of the old tractors. Sound returns forcefully with the horses, beginning with an insistent tapping, followed by drumming and then the "hollow thunder" of their hooves.

In discriminating between the failed and the successful, Muir suggests there may be two kinds of communication. One kind, which relates to intellectual and technical knowledge, is represented by the radios, now fallen silent. This kind of speaking, and this kind of knowledge, has let down the survivors. War has transformed it to silence. The second kind, relating to the communication between people and their world, is, ironically, also represented by silence, even though it is ushered in by the stamping of hooves. The farmers do not, and cannot, speak with the strange horses, after all. The ancient relationship between humankind and horses restores itself without words. A new silence replaces the old. In this silence, however, the people are no longer alone.

Mark Rich

HOUSE ON A CLIFF

Author: Louis MacNeice (1907-1963)
Type of poem: Lyric
First published: 1955; collected in *Visitations*, 1957

The Poem

"House on a Cliff" is a sixteen-line poem in flexible iambic pentameter rhymed *abcb* and divided into three stanzas of four lines each. The title sets the scene and, to a certain extent, the mood as it creates an image of a life lived in a precarious place exposed to the elements. The poem is written in the third person, and the narrator is seemingly omniscient, moving quickly and repeatedly from descriptions of the interior of a house and its inhabitant to descriptions of the night outside and back again.

"House on a Cliff" begins indoors, where the poet notes "the tang of a tiny oil lamp," a detail that gives the impression of a confined, stifling space. The scene then switches immediately to a view of the "waste of sea" outside. This formal procedure of alternating between descriptions of the interior of the house and the outside environment will be followed throughout the rest of the poem. The stanza continues with a mention of the wind before concluding indoors with images of emotional frigidity: "the locked heart and the lost key."

The alternation of outdoors and indoors continues in the second stanza, which begins with a depiction of the inhospitable elements outside. There is, however, an important difference in this stanza: A character, the inhabitant of the house, is introduced. From this point on, this man, rather than the physical setting, is the focus of the indoor sections of the poem. The description of him in this stanza—"The strong man pained to find his red blood cools"—implies that he is aging and growing less vigorous. He is also very much aware of the ticking clock. However, the clock does not really grow "louder, faster" as the poem says it does; rather, this description is an indication of the man's preoccupation with time. The stanza ends outdoors with "the silent moon," another symbol of time.

The final stanza begins, "Indoors ancestral curse-cum-blessing," a phrase that characterizes the situation of the man mentioned in the previous stanza. The poet, by his use of the Latin preposition *cum* (together with), suggests that the man is both cursed and blessed by all the things—biological and cultural—he has inherited from his ancestors. When the perspective switches back to the outdoors, the reader is presented with a picture of the "empty bowl of heaven, the empty deep." The moon was out in the previous stanza, so the heavens cannot be literally "empty" nor does empty seem a plausible description of the sea, with all of its creatures. The poet means that the sky and sea are empty because they are missing the god or gods once thought to dwell there. The last two lines of the poem bring the reader back to the inhabitant of the house, who has fallen asleep. The man, described as "purposeful," "talks at cross/ Purposes, to himself, in a broken sleep." When two people are talking at cross purposes, they have somehow misunderstood each other. The poem ends, therefore, with the image of a man troubled by his lack of self-understanding.

Forms and Devices

In "House on a Cliff," Louis MacNeice is able to convey a sophisticated worldview in a very few lines, chiefly because of his use of form. The most striking formal device in the poem is the way the poet switches back and forth between "indoors" and "outdoors," consistently using these two words as signposts for the reader. It is not unlike the quick cuts a film director might use. This technique, combined with the metaphors it allows the poet to pair, ensures that the reader will find parallels and relationships between the two environments. The poem's short length makes it ideal for this technique. If it was any shorter, the poet would not have sufficient space for the picture he wants to paint; if it was any longer, the constant alternation would grow tiresome.

The correspondence between indoors and outdoors is not always as simple as in the first two lines, where the "tiny oil lamp" is paired with "the winking signal." Indeed, if the relationships between the indoor and outdoor sections were always this close, the poem would seem too neat. MacNeice sidesteps this danger by making the pairings that follow less closely related. What is the reader to make, for example, of "the locked heart" and "the lost key" being compared to "the chill, the void, the siren"? The first is much more obviously a metaphor. The second, aside from an allusion contained in the word "siren," which could be either a warning sound or a creature from Greek myth who lures sailors to their deaths, could be a straightforward naturalistic description. The poet, by placing them side by side, compels the reader to search for resemblances. "The chill, the void, the siren" become, in this context, a counterpart to the stunted emotional life being lived in the house.

MacNeice, like his contemporary and friend W. H. Auden, was a master of traditional forms and an expert at using meter, rhyme, alliteration, and assonance in such a way that they reinforce meaning. The last line of the first stanza is a good example of this: The crowding together of strong stresses, combined with alliteration and assonance—"the locked heart and the lost key"—creates a feeling of tension that reinforces the sense of the words. Another example is the second line of the second stanza, where the use of one-syllable, strongly stressed words in "The strong man pained to find his red blood cools" causes the line to move very slowly, thus complementing this description of the man's ebbing vitality. The reader should not take this sort of analysis to extremes. Meter cannot be expected to match meaning perfectly in every case, and there are other effects in the poem that are more or less ornamental. Taken as a whole, however, "House on a Cliff" is a fine example of how a poet can use meter to convey a message more effectively.

Themes and Meanings

"House on a Cliff" is a poem about the human condition and, more specifically, the perceptions of that condition in the twentieth century. MacNeice came of age as a poet in the 1930's when the ideas of thinkers such as Charles Darwin, Sigmund Freud, and Karl Marx were beginning to gain widespread acceptance. Darwin, with his book *On the Origin of Species by Means of Natural Selection*, published in 1859, had undermined faith in the biblical account of creation. Freud had posited the existence of the unconscious, a part of the mind ruled largely by drives for sex and power. Marx, in *Das Kapital* (1867, 1885, 1894; translated 1886, 1907, 1909) and *Manifest der Kommunistischen Partei* (1848; *The Communist Manifesto*, 1850) had described a purely materialistic world in which change was driven by struggle between different economic classes. MacNeice realized the importance of these thinkers for his own time. In an earlier poem, "Autumn Journal," he called Marx and Freud "The figureheads of our transition."

By the time "House on a Cliff" was written, the universe in which many had come to believe was both much older and much larger than previously thought. Suddenly, many people doubted that God had created the universe or, if He had, that He had much to do with its day-to-day operation. Doubts about the existence of God crop up in a number of other poems by MacNeice, such as "The Blasphemies" and "London Rain." The outdoor portions of "House on a Cliff," with their descriptions of vast, empty spaces, of the "waste of sea" and "the empty bowl of heaven," exemplify the bleakness MacNeice saw as inherent in this new view of the universe. The indoor portions symbolize a human civilization that, though it may afford a certain amount of shelter and comfort, is still a very fragile thing. It is important to note also that the man, while sheltered, is unhappy and alone. There are many problems society cannot cure and some it may well make worse.

The view of human nature had also changed considerably. Darwin's idea that human beings were, in some fashion, descended from lower animals was a considerable blow to the ego. In addition, Freud's theories of the unconscious made the ancient Greek admonition to "know thyself" seem far more difficult. The contents of the unconscious were either those drives that society required be kept in check or incidents in childhood that were simply too painful for the conscious mind to remember. These drives and memories were thought, however, to reveal themselves in dreams. The man in "House on a Cliff," as he "talks at cross/ Purposes, to himself, in a broken sleep," provides readers with a concrete picture of this newer, more conflicted picture of human nature. This is not to say that such a bleak view of human life must necessarily follow from the conclusions of Darwin, Marx, and Freud. Some poets have been inspired by what they see as humankind's new freedom from divine interference. Wallace Stevens's poem "Sunday Morning," for example, invests the idea of a godless world with considerable grandeur. MacNeice, however, was never able to share this optimism uncritically.

Bill Coyle

HOUSEBOAT DAYS

Author: John Ashbery (1927-   )
Type of poem: Lyric
First published: 1976; collected in *Houseboat Days*, 1977

The Poem

"Houseboat Days" is a free-verse lyric divided into two irregular stanzas, one of thirty-nine lines and one of twenty-nine. The title "Houseboat Days" comes from a 1929 *National Geographic* article by Florence H. Morden, "Houseboat Days in the Vale of Kashmir," a phrase that seems to mingle the exotic with the ordinary.

"Houseboat Days" begins with an unattributed quotation, shifting abruptly from someone speaking, apparently in the immediate present, to a sentence placing that immediacy in the past on "that day." "Day" echoes the title and signals time as a subject of the poem. With the verb "walk," the poem moves into a new present. The setting, where blue hills are visible from a vantage point "along the shore," gives readers an anchor as they bob along among sentences and phrases that appear not to make much sense. John Ashbery likes to link abstract and concrete terms in humorous and disorienting combinations.

In the first stanza, the pain, "like an explosion in the brain," gives way to banal clichés: "life is various./ Life is beautiful." Then Ashbery makes the mock portentous observation that one who reads that cliché wisdom "Knows what he wants, and what will befall." The second stanza comes back to pain, implied in the "Pinpricks of rain" falling again. The constantly oscillating mind is in danger of letting the rain wash away that moving houseboat window in the first stanza through which varied and beautiful life is visible. The meditation on pain tries to move toward hope, but it is only "The picture of hope a dying man" cannot have. Now the poem/houseboat floats toward evening and sleep, making it clearer that the poem's overall shape is that of a houseboat day, from memories of breakfast china to the "pressure of sleep." The day is summed up this way: "mornings of assent/ Indifferent noons leading to the ripple of the question/ Of late afternoon projected into evening."

The ending leaves the reader with a slightly more comforting conundrum than pain and its automatic cancellation and return. Instead, the poet reassurances the reader that "a little simple arithmetic tells you that to be with you/ In this passage, this movement, is what the instance costs." This self-referring statement is blurred by uncertainty about who is to be with whom. However, that statement is followed by a peaceful specific metaphor, "A sail out of some afternoon, beyond amazement." This elegant and "astonished" mood of peace is "not tampered with" by the gathering rain (or pain). Just as earlier pain carried its own cancellation, this peaceful mood now "protects/ Its own darkness." The poem closes with the teacups with which it began, the point of departure for each houseboat day.

Forms and Devices

Ashbery's free verse pushes toward the limits of prose. Deliberately avoiding both blank verse and the carefully measured lines of free verse, Ashbery seems to break his lines haphazardly, as if he were more concerned with the rhythms of his sentences and paragraphs than with the effects of pauses at the ends of lines. Thus the line breaks and the syntax of a sentence are sometimes at cross purposes. However, Ashbery wants to challenge readers' expectations and explore the effects of conflicting and well as complementary relationships between poetic measure and sentence sense.

"Houseboat Days" is more about imagination than about consciousness in general. Abstract language makes up most of the first stanza, from "The mind" to "And then it . . . happens." The passage says that insincere "reasoning on behalf of one's/ Sincere convictions" leads to pain, whether the convictions themselves are true or false. Although pain immediately gives way to "triumph over pain," the triumph is paradoxical, "pain/ . . . created just so as to deny its own existence." The word "pain," which rhymes with "brain" in one of the poem's few end rhymes, is repeated four times. Readers are then reminded of it again by "train" in the penultimate line of the first stanza and by "rain" in the opening line of the second stanza. Thus pain is played with, mocked and made light of, but it remains the poem's strongest emotional reference.

Not only does the poem begin with an unattributed quotation clearly indicated as a quotation, but it also includes actual transcriptions of the words of Walter Pater, not set off by quotation marks but identified with "he said." The pedantic-sounding passage in the first stanza, beginning with "that insincerity of reasoning" and ending with "At times," is taken verbatim from Pater's *Plato and Platonism* (1910). Another passage later in the same stanza also comes word for word from the same source. Ashbery's appropriation of these passages gives him an opportunity to gently mock abstract diction while, at the same time, using it for his own purposes, significantly changing the contexts from the originals. It also allows him to absorb into his poem all kinds of language, from the colloquial "Poking ahead" to the foreign "trouvailles" (French for the noun "find," including godsends and windfalls.)

This inclusiveness, as well as the long lines, suggests a generosity of spirit, a willingness to accept anything. Ashbery, however, leaves out a great deal, carefully avoiding any details readers can clearly identify as personal or confessional and refusing to give readers specific information about places, times, and characters. As with Ashbery's grammatical manipulation of tenses, this disorienting approach detaches the poem from conventional time and space.

Themes and Meanings

The fact that Ashbery chose the title of this poem as the title of the collection in which it first appeared suggests the importance of the poem to the body of Ashbery's work. Ashbery is well known for assigning whimsical titles to his poems, titles that have nothing obvious to do with the poem. However, this poem is, in a sense, about what its title says: days spent in a dwelling that moves with time. A synopsis of the poem might make it sound more weighty and melancholy than it is. In fact, the tone of the poem is often quite light as Ashbery takes such serious subjects as pain and the nature of time and space and parodies the language poets and others might use to talk about them.

Ashbery is concerned with the passage of time and the way memory and perception bounce back and forth in the mind to give people a sense of what they call reality. In "Houseboat Days," reality is the interchange between perception and the world and, within perception, between sensing, thinking, and feeling. Odd though the poem's opening is, it is an opening, for the quotation ends with the word "began," and, as the first stanza ends, Ashbery brings readers back to the vague "beginning, where/ We must stay, in motion," flashing light into the "house" of consciousness (imagination) within, with its memories and associations. Ashbery's transcription of mental associations at first makes "Houseboat Days" jumpy and incoherent. Out of the seemingly random associations, however, Ashbery develops an abstract coherence metaphorically similar to a houseboat day, moving and standing still, rocking on gentle waters.

Uncertainties of time and place put the reader "beyond amazement." In fact, "Houseboat Days" is full of evasions and deflections. Pronoun shifts, quotations that are not obviously quoted, and quotations in unidentified voices all put readers in a realm that challenges their normal expectations of time and space. One cannot tell exactly to whom events are happening or when they are happening. Even in relation to each other, time references shift suddenly back and forth. The vague pronoun references in the first stanza refer to unspecified situations and people to suggest vague generalizations about life and consciousness. These vagaries are given weight and specificity by lively back and forth movement into and out of specifics.

A key generalization in the first part of the poem is the sentence beginning, "The mind/ Is so hospitable, taking in everything." Cut free of the conventions of narrative or lyric verse, Ashbery's poetry has a certain exhilarating freedom and seems almost infinitely open to interpretation. In a sense, Ashbery has deconstructed his own work and left it to readers and critics to put the pieces back together, however they see fit.

Thomas Lisk

THE HUNTING OF THE HARE

Author: Margaret Cavendish, Duchess of Newcastle (1624?-1674)
Type of poem: Satire
First published: 1653, in *Poems and Fancies*

The Poem

Margaret Cavendish's poem begins in a field where a small hare, Wat, lies close to the ground between two ridges of plowed earth. The poet notes that Wat always faces the wind, which would otherwise blow under his fur and make him cold. Wat rests in the field all day. At sunset he begins wandering, which he continues to do until dawn. Huntsmen and dogs discover Wat, who begins to runs away. As the dogs bark, Wat becomes terrified and believes that every shadow is a dog. After running a distance, he lies under a clod of earth in a sandpit. Soon he hears the huntsmen's horns and the dogs' barking, and he begins to run once more, this time so quickly that he scarcely treads the ground. Wat runs into a thick wood and hides under a broken bough, frightened by every leaf that is shaken by the wind. Hoping to deceive the dogs, he runs into unenclosed fields. While the dogs search for his scent, Wat, being weary, slows down. Sitting on his hind legs, he rubs the dust and sweat from his face with his forefeet. He then licks his feet and cleans his ears so well that no one could tell he had been hunted.

Wat sees the hounds and is again terrified. His fear gives him the strength to move more quickly. Ironically, he has never felt stronger than during this time of crisis. The poet notes that spirits often seek to guard the heart from death but that death eventually wins. The hounds approach Wat quickly. Just as the hare resigns himself to his fate, the winds take pity on him and blow his scent away. The dogs scatter, each searching bits of grass or tracts of land. Soon the dogs' work, which the poet compares to witchcraft, brings them back on task. When one dog discovers Wat's scent, the horns sound and the other dogs follow. The poet now provides an extended analogy comparing the barking dogs to members of a choir. The large slow dogs are the basses; the swift hounds are the tenors. Beagles sing treble, and the horns keep time as the hunters shout for joy. The hunters, seeming valiant, spur their horses, swim rivers, leap ditches, and endanger themselves only to see the hare, who has died with weeping eyes. The hunters begin rejoicing "as if the devil they did prisoner take."

The poet now satirizes hunting, noting that the sport is not valiant. Although men think that hunting provides good exercise, the poet argues that men are cruel when they kill harmless creatures which are imagined to be dangerous game. Hunters, the poet continues, destroy God's creation for sport, and in so doing make their stomachs "graves" for the murdered animals. The poet states that, although men believe themselves to be gentle, they are actually the cruelest creatures. Proud men, Cavendish concludes, believe that they possess a godlike entitlement and that all creatures were made for them to tyrannize.

Forms and Devices

"The Hunting of the Hare" is written in rhymed lines of iambic pentameter, or heroic couplets, which would become the most important verse form of Restoration and eighteenth century poetry. Cavendish uses this form and several poetic devices and conventions to create a sustained effect, one that shows the cruelty and sense-lessness of hunting.

Early in the poem Cavendish anthropomorphizes (gives human characteristics to) the hare, first by naming him and then by assigning to him human emotions. When first startled from his hiding place, Wat hopes to outrun the dogs and is then "struck with terror and with fear" as the dogs pursue him. By making the hare appear human, Cavendish accentuates the drama of the hunt and enhances her appeal to the reader's emotions. She furthers her intention by manipulating the rhythm and sounds of her lines. Describing the dogs' pursuit, for example, she reverses the iambic rhythm and offers trochaic lines: "But they by nature have so quick a scent/ That by their nose they trace what way he went." These lines re-create the bouncing and running of the dogs, which is accentuated by the tapping *t* sound. In contrast to these fast-paced lines, the poet offers slow lines to describe the hare: "Then Wat was struck with terror and with fear,/ Thinks every shadow still the dogs they were." In this couplet the repeated *s* sound, the *oz* sound in "was," the *ur* in "terror" and "were," and a pause all cause the lines to drag, while the jumbled syntax of "still the dogs they were" gives the line an almost nightmarish quality of paralysis.

Later the poet accentuates the barbarity of the hunt by allowing nature to function on behalf of the hare. After running through field, wood, and plain, the exhausted Wat is momentarily saved by the winds that "did pity poor Wat's case." Here the poet is using a poetic trope later critics would call the pathetic fallacy: assigning human sympathies to the natural world. Feeling pity for Wat's fate, nature tries to prevent the unnaturalness of the dogs' pursuit. After Wat is killed, the poet depicts the sense-lessness of the hunt. The huntsmen endanger their lives only to recover the pathetic hare. By showing the ridiculousness of the hunters risking their lives for so inconse-quential a prize, Cavendish introduces to her poem a mock-heroic quality. Cavendish, like John Dryden and Alexander Pope, uses the mock heroic, which treats trivial issues with exaggerated seriousness, to ridicule human folly. Finding the poor hare, the hunters appear silly and deluded: "Men hooping loud such acclamations make/ As if the devil they did prisoner take,/ When they do but a shiftless creature kill." Near the end of the poem, Cavendish uses metaphor to heighten her message. The hunters' stomachs become "graves" which hold the "murthered bodies" of the prey. This metaphor prepares the reader for the poem's unsettling conclusion, in which Cavendish exposes the unnaturalness of the hunters' pride.

Themes and Meanings

"The Hunting of the Hare" explores several issues that are important to under-standing Cavendish's poetry. Early in the poem the narrator describes how the hare lies close to the ground and faces the wind in order to stay warm. Cavendish had a keen interest in natural history. Herself an amateur scientist, she used her poetry as a vehicle for scientific speculation. As the critic Steven Max Miller has noted, her poetry "abounds with a sense . . . of wonder and delight in nature," and it sometimes questions "whether animals might know more natural science than man is capable of learning" (*Dictionary of Literary Biography* 43). Not only does the hare shield himself from the wind, he also executes a thoughtful initial escape from the dogs. Until his death, Wat appears to have an acute perception of his surroundings.

The poem is also, of course, an antihunting statement, one of the earliest in the language. Cavendish depicts the hare's death as a result of unnecessary cruelty. The hunters have no reason to kill the innocent creature except "for sport, or recreation's sake," and Cavendish makes clear that in indulging their desires they commit the equivalent of a crime. Earlier poems, such as Sir John Denham's *Cooper's Hill* (1642), used the hunt as a metaphor for man's political intrigues. Alexander Pope's *Windsor Forest* (1713), published sixty years after Cavendish's poem, explores the ambivalence and responsibility that accompany the "pleasing Toils" of the hunt. With its exaggerated pathos, Cavendish's poem is unique for its time, standing as seventeenth century England's strongest poetic condemnation of blood sport.

Cavendish condemns more than hunting, however; she also attacks the pride that causes individuals to engage in such activities. Near the end of the poem, the narrator reveals that hunters believe that God provided them with a "godlike nature" and that and that all creatures were made for man's domination. Believing in their own superiority, the hunters become morally inferior to the animals they hunt. In satirizing the hunters' pride, Cavendish anticipates a central theme of Restoration and eighteenth century poetry. Disrupting an implied natural order, the hunters become the embodiment of pride as understood by poets such as Pope, who wrote, "In Pride . . . our error lies;/ All quit their sphere, and rush into the skies. / . . . And who but wishes to invert the laws/ Of ORDER, sins against th' Eternal Cause" (Pope's *Essay on Man*).

Christopher D. Johnson

I BRING AN UNACCUSTOMED WINE

Author: Emily Dickinson (1830-1886)
Type of poem: Meditation
First published: 1891, in *Poems: Second Series*; collected in *The Poems of Emily Dickinson*, 1955

The Poem

Typical of Emily Dickinson's terse, succinct poems that have a way of exploding with meaning, "I bring an unaccustomed wine" delivers its impact in twenty-two lines divided into seven stanzas, the first of four lines, the subsequent ones of three lines each. Dickinson frequently uses alcoholic metaphors—wine, beer, liquor—in her poems, not to celebrate drinking but to convey cryptic messages to her readers. In her poem "I taste a liquor never brewed," for example, the liquor she refers to is honey, liquor to the bees that gather the pollen to make honey.

In "I bring an unaccustomed wine," the wine referred to is an elixir of sorts, a potion to wet dry, unkissed lips. The "lips long parching," however, are not her own but are next to hers, giving a passionate overtone to the first verse. She summons the lips to drink, which can be taken to mean that she longs for them to kiss her lips. This poem is among Dickinson's "I/eye" poems. In letters that she wrote during this period in her poetic development, Dickinson revealed that she was experimenting with these words. Note that not only does the poem begin with the word "I" but that also in the first two lines alone the letter "i" appears in "bring," "wine," "lips," and "parching." Save for her letters indicating her conscious experimentation with "I," one might think simply that many two-line segments of poetry or prose could contain the letter five times. The evidence gleaned from her letters is that Dickinson's incorporation of this single letter was calculated and deliberate.

As the poem proceeds, the "I" in the poem turns "my brimming eyes away," suggesting tears and a denial of love. But although her eyes are turned away, the speaker returns the next hour to look. By stanza 3, the speaker is hugging the glass that holds the wine. She calls the glass "tardy," meaning that the salvation that the wine would have brought—metaphorically a kiss and even more broadly, love—has been delayed to the point that it is no longer likely to occur. The final line of this stanza suggests that the lips are cold, that either the object of the speaker's love or the love itself is now dead.

The following verse reveals clearly that it is the love rather than the object of that love that is dead, because the speaker asserts that she cannot hope to "warm/ The bosoms where the frost has lain/ Ages beneath the mould—." Here the word "mould" suggests "mound," although it serves a dual purpose in invoking images of the disintegration of organic matter as well as that of a form that is used to shape pliable materials.

The speaker goes on to imply that the possibility of some other love entering her life might have existed but that this has not happened. During her lifetime, Dickinson lived through the painful losses of many people she loved dearly; from the isolation of her secluded room, she loved many people who were unavailable to her. But in the next to last stanza, she implies that her love is still available, her thirst still unslaked, leading into the last stanza in which she proffers the hope, but not the guarantee, of an eternity, of final salvation.

Forms and Devices

Emily Dickinson's poems are usually less than a page long and consist most frequently of short stanzas, often no more than three or four lines long. This poem is typical in this respect. It is also typical in that just as the poet has achieved the conventional rhyme of "wine" and "mine" in the first stanza, she departs from conventional rhyme by introducing the word "drink," which certainly does not rhyme either with "parching" (line 2) or with the last word in the second stanza, "look," although here the *k* sound gives Dickinson the poetic link she requires.

In stanzas 3 and 4, the last word of each stanza, "Cold" and "mould," rhymes perfectly. Dickinson again uses rhyme whimsically with her choice of the final words in stanzas 5, 6, and 7, where she suggests rhyme by choosing "speak" and "slake" but then returns to conventional rhyme with "slake" and "awake."

An examination of Dickinson's poetic manuscripts, presented in striking detail in Thomas H. Johnson's edition, *The Poems of Emily Dickinson, Including Variant Readings Critically Compared with All Known Manuscripts*, published by the Harvard University Press in a three-volume edition in 1955, reveals that the poet often obliterated a word that rhymed perfectly, preferring another word that suggested only the slightest similarity, as seen in the linking *k* sounds of "drink" and "look" in stanzas 1 and 2, of "warm" and "lain" in stanza four, and of "cup" and "drop" in stanza 6. She selected her words with the conscious intent, as both her revisions and her letters indicate, to heighten her reader's attention, of keeping her writing from becoming pedestrianly sing-songy.

For the same reasons, she also frequently disturbed regular meter, as she does in the last line of stanza 3 in this poem, which reads, "Are so superfluous Cold—." A more regular and conventional meter would have been achieved by using "superfluously" rather than "superfluous," a much more usual choice because the word in question is an adverb of manner and such words often end in "-ly."

The imagery in "I bring an unaccustomed wine" is highly visual, with words that overlap other words, such as the lips that are "crackling with fever" in the second stanza. Not only do readers receive the impression of lips that are hot and dry, but the work "crackling" also is so similar to "cracking" that one involuntarily concocts a double visual image upon reading it. Although she wrote under the Victorian constraints that characterized her day, Dickinson was a highly passionate, albeit sexually frustrated, woman. Her use of the word "bosoms" in the fourth stanza ties in with her choice of "cup" in the sixth stanza rather than "glass," as used previously in the third stanza. In her refined and indirect way, she here expresses the unfulfilled passion that dogged her solitary, puritanical existence.

The "drink/thirst" metaphor in this poem extends far beyond its literal meaning, although the literal meaning is credible, as the meaning of any successful metaphor must be. The thirst Dickinson refers to is a longing, a restrained passion; on a metaphysical level it may be seen as a thirst for the eternal life that many religions promise. Dickinson did not dogmatically regard eternal life as a certainty but only as a possibility, as she makes clear in her last stanza. The wine to which she refers is clearly the wine of salvation, but it exists as a hope, a mere possibility.

Themes and Meanings

In "I bring an unaccustomed wine," Emily Dickinson is concerned both with unfulfilled love and with questions of eternity. The first concern is exemplified well in the early stanzas of this poem, but as Dickinson moves into the poem, beginning as early as the fourth stanza, she begins to consider questions regarding death and immortality, subjects with which she deals extensively throughout the corpus of her writing.

Despite having been raised in a conventionally Christian home as a member of a socially prominent New England family, Dickinson was far from a blind follower of Christian theology. Throughout her life she harbored a profound skepticism. She hoped that the Christian promises with which she had been raised were valid, but she did not presume to assert categorically that they were. The poem also deals with unrequited love and with loss, but just as Dickinson has not foreclosed the possibility of an eternal existence, neither has she foreclosed the possibility that love may still come.

The "I" in Emily Dickinson's poems is more often a universalized "I" than a first-person reference to the poet herself. Her natural modesty would have forbidden her to use the personal "I" to the extent that she uses that pronoun in her poems. In most of the poems, a universal voice interacts with the reader, which is one of the distinguishing traits of Emily Dickinson's poetry.

In this respect, although her poems are far removed stylistically from those of Walt Whitman, she bears a similarity to him. In both poets, some inexperienced readers may be irritated by the seeming egoism of the poet, but in neither poet is the surface egoism a personalized egoism. Rather, this seeming egoism is a device used thematically to develop a relationship among the poet, the reader, and the substance of what is being written about.

This is not to suggest that the poems of either Dickinson or Whitman are not informed by their personal experiences. Such experiences are basic to most writing. The competent writer, as in the case of these two significant American poets, moves from the specifically personal to the universal.

R. Baird Shuman

I HAVE A RENDEZVOUS WITH DEATH

Author: Alan Seeger (1888-1916)
Type of poem: Elegy
First published: 1916, in *Poems*

The Poem

A short elegy in iambic pentameter, "I Have a Rendezvous with Death" has three stanzas of six, eight, and ten lines that employ irregular rhyme. Elegy is a lyric poetic form that traditionally takes as its subject a meditation on death or other similarly grave theme. In its classical form, in both Latin and Greek poetry, the elegy was distinguished more for its use of the elegiac meter, the dactylic hexameter—an accented syllable followed by two unaccented syllables—than for its subject matter. The elegy has been a popular form throughout the English poetic tradition. Geoffrey Chaucer, John Donne, Thomas Gray, and Alfred, Lord Tennyson all wrote in the conventional form. Elizabethan poets often used the elegy for love poems which they called "complaints." A typical example in American poetry can be found in Walt Whitman's "When Lilacs Last in the Dooryard Bloom'd."

In "I Have a Rendezvous with Death" the American poet Alan Seeger modernized the elegy by employing an iambic meter that gives his poem a more regular, even cadence and by emphasizing the theme of impending death. Not occasioned by the death of someone else, as elegies generally are, Seeger's poem meditates on his own possible death during World War I, when he was serving on the Western Front. In fact, Seeger was killed in action in the war at the Battle of the Somme.

An atypical lyric on the war, "I Have a Rendezvous with Death" alludes to the realities of the war only sparingly in phrases such as "disputed barricade," "some scarred slope," and "some flaming town." The poem's title announces its theme of death, while suggesting, through its use of the word "rendezvous," that the poet is heading toward his meeting with death involuntarily. "Rendezvous" suggests a prearranged coming together at a particular time and place. In this context it implies a deliberate or willed connection with death, which reinforces the root meaning of the word, derived from Old French for "presenting oneself." Seeger's use of the word also echoes his reasons for joining the army in the first place: He wished to stand up and be counted in the struggle against the cultural darkness that German military expansion represented to him and the Allies during the early years of the conflict.

The poem opens with Seeger contemplating his death in the springtime—a particularly jarring note because spring is normally associated with the renewal of life after the "death" of winter. The second stanza reverses this disjunctive note as the poet hints that his journey into death's "dark land" with the "closing of his eyes" and quenching of his breath might be avoided and that he may yet once again experience the seasonal return of life and "meadow-flowers."

The third stanza begins with a conventional comparison between death and sleep by contrasting "blissful sleep" with its dear "hushed awakenings" to the finality of death from which no one awakens. However, the elegy concludes with the poet's reiteration that his death comes, not unexpectedly, but as a result of his "pledged word," the word of a soldier who has volunteered to embrace death as a part of his profession. It is a rendezvous that the poet-soldier will not fail to keep: As spring "trips north again this year," at midnight in some burning town he may meet his end.

Forms and Devices

The presence of death in the poem is softened by the recurring references in each stanza to springtime and the life-giving urges that spring evokes. The poet says that the season will bring back "blue days and fair" with "rustling shade," "apple-blossoms," and "meadow flowers." Reminiscent of Geoffrey Chaucer's description of spring in his prologue to *The Canterbury Tales* (1387-1400), Seeger's poem also "throbs," pulses, and breathes with the reawakening of life's urges. Its references to spring—a time the poet may well not live to see—add an especially poignant note to the possibility of his dying.

The poem's personification of death also contributes to its touching mood by emphasizing both the acceptance and tenderness of death. Its second stanza describes meeting death in terms almost of friendship. Death will take the poet by the hand and lead him into his "dark land." It is an image suggesting a gentle, coaxing death, not one that arrives violently or unannounced. Such imagery evokes Seeger's traditional grounding in the classics. This poem reminds one of the cicerone, or guide, in Dante's *Inferno* (c. 1320) who shepherds his charge through the mazes of the underworld, instructing him at every turn. In Seeger's poem, however, the guide will not lead him safely through the pitfalls of Hell and out again but will close the poet's eyes and quench his breath. Here death is gentle but also insistent, and the journey he presages is terminal.

In the third stanza, Seeger introduces sleep imagery—using a traditional trope of death as a "little" sleep, comparing and contrasting to the finality of death. He does this by employing a seductive and inviting sexual imagery. Sleep is described as "deep/ Pillowed in silk" and "scented down." In this "sleep," "Love throbs" and pulse is "nigh to pulse, and breath to breath," and awakenings are "hushed" and "dear." The Association of love with death is deeply rooted in the traditions of poetry. With its conceit of a "rendezvous," which also has overtones of a meeting of lovers, this poem's connection of love and death becomes all the more suggestive. Such comparisons join with the final couplet of the poem in which the poet uses the term "pledge," another word often applied to meetings between lovers, that additionally expands the meaning of the poem.

Themes and Meanings

"I Have a Rendezvous with Death" is a young soldier's poem about facing the very real possibility of his own death. To any soldier who fought during World War I the possibility of dying in combat was especially real. The casualty figures for combatants in that war were staggering. Alan Seeger happened to be living in London at the outbreak of the war in August, 1914. During the late summer of that year the realities of the conflict were perhaps more urgent for him than for most Americans. He enlisted in the Foreign Legion of France because of an urgent sense of duty to the cultural values and traditions he had learned to embrace. In this respect he truly represented the idealism that motivated so many to volunteer for the war effort. His enlistment in the Foreign Legion was also necessary because the United States was not yet an active participant in the conflict. His eager involvement in the war further illuminates the pledge he mentions in the last couplet of the poem and to which he wished to remain true.

Seeger's idealism contributes to the tone of the poem, in which the poet does not shirk from his rendezvous with death but actually welcomes it. His idealism also may account for the absence of the more unpleasant aspects of the war's horrors in the poem, the grisly details of which characterize the better known war poetry of such British poets as Rupert Brooke, Wilfred Owen, and Sigfried Sassoon. Furthermore, Seeger's idealism helps to explain his place as the most famous of America's war poets. Wealthy, young, and full of promise, he became a symbol for the United States of the selfless sacrifice that the war called forth in the name of all that was thought worthy in the Western civilization which was being destroyed by German military aggression. In contrast to the later American writings about war by such authors as Ernest Hemingway, John Dos Passos, E. E. Cummings, and Laurence Stallings, Seeger's patriotism appears as an anomaly.

The equanimity with which Alan Seeger could write about his own mortality and the haunting gentleness of his most famous poem have made "I Have a Rendezvous with Death" one of the more telling literary expressions from what was then known as the Great War. It also assured this young and sensitive poet a small but secure place among the writers of elegies in the English language.

Charles L. P. Silet

I KNEW A WOMAN

Author: Theodore Roethke (1908-1963)
Type of poem: Lyric
First published: 1954; collected in *Words for the Wind*, 1958

The Poem

"I Knew a Woman" (along with fifteen other short lyrics) appeared in a section of *Words for the Wind* entitled "Love Poems." This poem was apparently written about the time of Theodore Roethke's marriage to Beatrice O'Connell (a former student of his), and its speaker is a man very much in love and awed by the beauty of the woman he admires so profoundly. The poem concentrates on the erotic and physical but deals also with larger philosophical issues. Its tone is a subtle mix of the comic and the serious.

The poem's metrical pattern is consistently iambic pentameter, but its stanza form is somewhat unusual. Each of the four stanzas consists of seven lines, and the typical rhyme scheme is *ababccc*. Actually the first four lines contain no rhyme at all, but later lines (except for line 21) follow this scheme precisely. This movement from complete lack of rhyme to a very regular rhyme scheme parallels the growing harmony between the two lovers.

Since the poem's first line uses a past-tense verb and refers to bones, some readers have assumed that the central female character is now dead. Such a conclusion is questionable. In this case the verb "knew" surely alludes (in the biblical sense) to specific episodes of sexual intimacy and not necessarily to a relationship that has ended completely. Furthermore, the assertion that the woman was "lovely in her bones" may actually be extravagant praise of her enduring beauty. Such beauty is not only skin deep, and it will abide even if she is, in due time, reduced to a skeleton. Thus the poem is a grand eulogy rather than an elegy.

In its high praise of a beloved woman, the poem recalls numerous English sonnets in the Petrarchan tradition by such authors as Sir Thomas Wyatt, Henry Howard (the earl of Surrey), and Sir Philip Sidney. (In fact, according to lines 5-6 these "English poets who grew up on Greek" might be worthy of singing the "choice virtues" of Roethke's lady.) Just as those poems cataloged the physical traits attributed to the ideal woman (eyes bright as the sun, lips red as rubies, hair shining like gold, cheeks like roses, and so on), Roethke's speaker lists comparable qualities in the one he loves. In stanza 1, for example, this woman's voice is as harmonious as the song of birds, and she moves about with dazzling grace.

Even so, the woman's beauty and erotic allure are not the only subjects of the poem. In stanzas 2 and 3 she becomes also a skilled teacher, schooling the speaker in the ways of love. These lessons in worldly love lead, in stanza 4, to cosmic insights. Through his relationship with this remarkable woman, who lives in total harmony with the natural world, he acquires more profound knowledge about the cycles of life and his own role in a mysterious universe.

Forms and Devices

Roethke's metaphors are rapidly changing and, in some cases, subject to diverse interpretations. In their complexity and extravagance they are akin to the conceits of John Donne and other metaphysical poets. In stanza 2, for example, several capitalized terms ("Turn," "Counter-turn," "Stand," and "Touch") establish a sustained comparison. These terms describe the content of the speaker's lessons in love, and figuratively they suggest movements or positions in a carefully choreographed dance. Dancing is a recurring image in many of Roethke's poems (see, for example, "Four for Sir John Davies"). Here the various stages of the dance imply a graceful movement through seduction to lovemaking.

While Roethke compares lovemaking to dancing, he simultaneously suggests another conceit. The capitalized words denoting dance positions are also technical terms from the sport of coursing, or hunting with hounds. In Roethke's complex metaphor the seductive woman is both the dog trainer and the object of the hunt. She strokes the speaker's chin as the keeper of the hounds might pet a favorite dog. She coyly orchestrates the chase by indicating changes in the direction ("Turn" and "Counter-turn") taken by the hound. In hunting, the term "Stand" denotes the rigid posture of the hound as it locates and points out the quarry, and here the term is also a humorous indication of the speaker's readiness for lovemaking. The term "Touch" denotes the initial contact between hound and quarry, and Roethke uses it to suggest the imminent union of the two lovers. Finally, the speaker nibbles meekly from the woman's hand. Just as a faithful dog might gain a treat from its trainer, the man receives the rewards of love. At several points Roethke's hunting metaphor is sexually suggestive, but its ingenuity prevents it from becoming especially bawdy.

To describe the actual lovemaking, Roethke abandons the hunting conceit and shifts abruptly to an earthy agricultural metaphor. Figuratively the two lovers are now engaged in making hay. The sickle is frequently a grim image associated with death, but here it suggests exuberant life—the woman's erotic power over everything in her path and also perhaps the enticing curves of her body. "Coming behind," the speaker enthusiastically rakes the mown grass. Here the term "rake" is a triple pun—agricultural implement, dissolute male, and (recalling the earlier coursing metaphor) a dog's action of following a trail by keeping its nose to the ground. Mowing, especially in Scottish dialect, is a slang term for sexual intercourse, and Roethke slyly reinforces this double meaning in a later poem entitled "Reply to a Lady Editor." That poem is a comic response to the literary editor of Harper's Bazaar who had liked "I Knew a Woman" but apparently failed to comprehend its sexual implications. In the later poem Roethke incorporates more Scottish dialect by calling Cupid a "braw laddie-buck."

Along with extravagant metaphors Roethke uses a number of paradoxical statements. Amid energetic sexual activity he observes in the "several parts" of his partner "a pure repose." Indeed, in line 21 ("She moved in circles, and those circles moved"), he suggests that she is like the *primum mobile*. In the old Ptolemaic astronomy the *primum mobile* was the outermost sphere of the universe, which contained all lesser orbits of heavenly bodies and whose revolution was the source of all other celestial movement. By implication then, the woman in the poem is the powerful cause of dramatic action but at the same time she remains the basis of order and stability.

Themes and Meanings

The paradox of the *primum mobile* prepares for a more solemn consideration of the poem's themes in stanza 4. The speaker's union with a remarkable woman is both the means to and a symbol of a higher union. Ultimately carnal knowledge becomes elevated to philosophic insight.

Several of Roethke's love poems portray women as instruments of illumination and salvation. For example, in "The Voice" (placed immediately after "I Knew a Woman" in the *Words for the Wind* collection) the woman is not even present physically. Nevertheless, simply hearing her voice lifts the poet above the level of awareness afforded to most mortals. In "Light Listened" the female character is again a teacher, and when she sings, even the light pays careful attention. In this exaggerated claim that the woman controls light, Roethke implies that she is a crucial source of illumination.

In "I Knew a Woman," just as the act of love fuses the physical and the spiritual, it leads the speaker on to other important harmonies. Well taught by the woman, he is now able to reconcile the temporal and the eternal, tyranny and freedom. By referring to seed, grass, and hay in line 22, the speaker acknowledges the inevitable cycle of birth, life, and death. He is a slave to this grand movement through time just as he is a "martyr" to the alluring motion of the woman who acts as a sickle. In this realization his mood is not mere resignation but eager acquiescence. In slavishly following behind another person, he sacrifices autonomy but gains a larger freedom. In accepting his mortality, he acquires the power to live more fully.

In his newly enlightened state the speaker measures "time by how a body sways." Presumably this body is that of the woman he loves rather than a clock pendulum or a planet in orbit. In short, the woman has completely displaced traditional methods of measuring time. All such conventional guides seem trivial compared to his new source of order and direction.

Two more paradoxical statements in the final stanza reinforce the speaker's bold assertions. In line 25 he affirms that the woman "cast a shadow white as stone." Ordinarily shadows are dark and insubstantial, but this one is strangely bathed in light and solid as a rock. In line 27 he speaks of "old bones" that are alive to continue learning. Though skeletons usually suggest death, these bones are vital and energetic. Having made his peace with mortality, the speaker is now animated by the energy of love.

Albert E. Wilhelm

I LIE HERE IN A STRANGE GIRL'S APARTMENT

Author: Richard Brautigan (1935-1984)
Type of poem: Meditation
First published: 1968, in *The Pill versus the Springhill Mine Disaster*

The Poem

Like almost all of Richard Brautigan's poems, "I Lie Here in a Strange Girl's Apartment" is short (three stanzas, fourteen lines) and written in free verse. The title, which is also the first line, not only provides the setting of the poem but also suggests the dynamic that is the subject of the narrator's meditation: the narrator as he sees himself in uncomfortable relation to this "strange" woman. The language of the poem, characteristic of Brautigan's style, is colloquial and deceptively direct—though the final stanza makes it clear that the author's appreciation of the abstract and surreal should not be underestimated, as it tends to vastly complicate otherwise simple images.

The structure of the poem appeals to a kind of minimalism that introduces only what is necessary in order for the payload of the poet's meaning to be delivered to the reader in the most direct, significant, and unburdened fashion. In the first stanza, the narrator presents himself as a man lying (presumably in bed) in the apartment of a woman who is "unhappy." As he watches her move "about the place," he reveals that she has both a sunburn and a poison oak rash. The curious similarity between these two ailments makes it unclear whether she is unhappy because she is afflicted with this double irritation or whether her unhappiness is being characterized by Brautigan's use of the metaphor of the skin conditions. She is clearly uncomfortable. Her unease, Brautigan seems to be suggesting, is akin to the itching experienced with a sunburn or poison oak. She is, as the saying goes, uncomfortable in her own skin. This unease is given greater specificity by the final, more explicit metaphor that closes the first stanza and points to the emotional and psychological breach between the narrator and the woman, who appears to him "distant" and "solemn."

The second stanza implicates the very language of the poem in the ambiguity that characterizes the relationship between the narrator and the woman. The woman's actions are described in both ambiguous terms ("She opens and closes things") and specific terms ("She turns the water on"). But these rather quotidian images give way to the broad and almost overwhelming metaphor of the final stanza, wherein the sounds the woman is making as she moves around the apartment are likened to a distant city populated with people of its own. The enormity of the metaphor for what are the relatively minor sounds of movement in a small apartment suggests that the narrator is at once fixated on the movements of the woman (thus their seeming huge) yet inevitably alienated from them (thus their seeming distant). Indeed, the final metaphor seems to take on a life of its own, dominating the reader's memory of the poem by the vastness of its scope. We are left, finally, with not simply the narrator's fixation with this woman but with the image of an entire city of people whose "eyes are filled with the sounds/ of what she is doing."

Forms and Devices

As with many of his contemporaries, Brautigan playfully explores the disparity between poetic devices (such as metaphor) and minimalist description (which eschews such poetic devices) by abutting the two in the same poem. The colorless second stanza avoids poetic imagery altogether, refusing to make the woman's actions any more vivid to the reader. Brautigan resists poeticizing his subject, employing a dull repetition to reinforce the quotidian aspect of the scene: "She turns the water on,/ and she turns the water off." The metaphor of the third stanza, however, achieves an almost absurd extreme of poetic artifice—especially in comparison to the previous stanza. Here Brautigan employs a metaphor that is so broad, so indulgent in its poetic license, that the reader is apt to forget what, exactly, the metaphor refers to by the end of the stanza. Indeed, the final line has the air of a reminder, returning us to the woman whom we may have let slip from our focus: "Their eyes are filled with the sounds/ of what she is doing." By presenting the reader with two distinct reading experiences—one completely unqualified by metaphor, and the other overwhelmed by it—Brautigan calls into question the uses of the poetic device itself.

Even if the final stanza were to stand on its own, we could not help but notice that Brautigan exerts an extreme degree of pressure on the final metaphorical device. Whereas a metaphor is meant to qualify or elucidate the less obvious layers of significance behind any given object, Brautigan's metaphor goes beyond its object. The metaphor of the city, by employing much more specific and vivid imagery than any found elsewhere in the poem, usurps and dwarfs the significance of the woman's movements by drawing all poetic attention to itself. At first, we are told simply that the sounds are so far away that they could be in a different city—a simple enough statement, mildly evoking the unprepossessing image of a city. Many poets would end the metaphor here. However, Brautigan goes on to populate and describe the city, telling us that it is dusk and that people are staring out of their windows in the city. This image removes us from the initial image of the woman moving around the apartment because we are hard-pressed to understand just exactly how her sounds are *similar* to a city filled with people at dusk. Furthermore, when the connection between the metaphor and its subject is so abstract as to be lost, then the metaphor breaks free of its subject and becomes a subject of its own.

This self-conscious use of poetic devices is characteristic of Brautigan's literary era, the eve of postmodernism, in which writers were less interested in using literary devices invisibly to draw in a reader than they were in focusing the reader's attention on the *process* of the writing itself. A poem that is seemingly "about" a woman in a room turns out, at the end, to be "about" the poetic device of metaphor, its uses, and its abuses.

Themes and Meanings

As with many instances of postmodern literature, this poem blurs the distinction between its "devices" and its "themes." By the end of the poem, the devices *become* the theme; the metaphor, its function, its purpose, its value as a mode of expression, and its effect when taken to its extreme—all of these issues become relevant to Brautigan as a theme of metaphoricity. By giving us an example of how a metaphor can get out of control if not used with care, he gives us both an invitation and an admonition. We are invited to revel in the free-form playground of poetic language and succumb to the temptation of poetry's extremes—and we are warned that if we do so we may lose sight of perhaps more "real" concerns. These other usurped concerns in the poem involve the narrator's relationship with the woman in the apartment.

Brautigan uses language and metaphoricity to emphasize the strained relation between the concrete specificities of the apartment around him and the ambiguous distance he feels between himself and the woman. The narrator feels at once intimate with this woman—even if by simple proximity, one human being to another—yet he is also anxious about the alienation he feels from this "strange girl." He seems, on the one hand, infatuated by the absolute particulars he can glean from the situation: her movements, her discomfort, her sounds, the fact that he is given the opportunity to observe it all so closely. Even though the repetition of her turning the water on and off reinforces the movement's rote plainness (as discussed above), the simple fact of such a mundane action being afforded two whole lines in a short fourteen-line poem validates the action and gives it an magnitude it would not otherwise have. The focus of two lines on her turning the faucet on and off reveals the (appreciative) scrutiny with which he observes her.

On the other hand, the narrator is forced to reconcile the fact that he is a stranger in her daily life; he must come to grips with the fact that as close as he may be in proximity to the movements he so reveres, they are nonetheless foreign to him. Although in intimate quarters, he is so alienated from the sounds of her daily movements that they seem far off. The final image of the poem is a melancholy but reconciled one, as the narrator determines to observe her affectionately even if he must do so from a great distance. Her actions may belong to a different world than his own, they may be so far away as to be in a different city, but whatever city she lives in, all the eyes of that city are fixed on "what she is doing."

Joshua Alden Gaylord

I, MENCIUS, PUPIL OF THE MASTER . . .

Author: Charles Olson (1910-1970)
Type of poem: Dramatic monologue
First published: 1954; collected in *The Distances*, 1960

The Poem

"I, Mencius, Pupil of the Master . . ." is a long, open-form poem in three major sections containing twenty-five stanzas. The entire poem comprises eighty-four lines of various length. Understanding the title is crucial in detecting the voice, theme, and tone of this challenging poem. Assuming the persona of an earlier poet is a technique that Charles Olson, one of contemporary America's first postmodernist poets, used throughout his controversial career. In this poem, he speaks through the persona of Mencius (372-289 B.C.), a devoted follower of the great Chinese philosopher Confucius (551-479 B.C.) and author of *The Book of History*, in which he set out the Confucian rules for a "benevolent government." First and foremost, great rulers must be men of virtue.

In the voice of Mencius, Olson scolds his poetic master, Ezra Pound. The occasion for Olson's outrage was the publication of Pound's translation of one of the most venerated books of Chinese poetry, *The Book of Odes* (poetry written between 1000 and 700 B.C.). Confucius himself had gathered the 305 poems that made up *The Book of Odes*. What provoked Olson's anger was that Pound translated them into ballads, an archaic form of English poetry in regular meter, rhyme, and stanzaic form. Ironically, it had been Ezra Pound himself who helped formulate the rules for a fresh kind of poetry called Imagism, rejecting what he considered the worn-out poetic tradition of Victorian and early twentieth century English poetry.

One of the tenets of Imagism required that a poem's rhythm be based "in the sequence of the musical phrase, not in the sequence of the metronome." Pound also laid down directives for using rhythm: "Don't chop your stuff into separate iambs. Don't make each line stop dead at the end, and then begin every next line with a heave." Pound had derived the clarity of Imagist poetry from Chinese and Japanese art and poetry, and when his translation of ancient Chinese poetry into the rigid structures of traditional English ballads appeared, Olson was incredulous. Olson embodied that rigidity in the image of Pittsburgh, the seat of the American steel industry and, more specifically, in the rails of the railroads which covered and violated the American landscape. Olson compares the "clank" of the locomotives' wheels to the "clank" of the regular rhythms, rhymes, and couplets of an exhausted literary tradition: "We do not see/ ballads."

Forms and Devices

The major structural device Olson uses throughout the poem is juxtaposition. In all three parts he juxtaposes the fallen world of technological violation (such as the steel mills of Pittsburgh and the Bremerton Shipyards) to the clarity of the world of James

Whistler, whose paintings had been affected by Japanese and Chinese art and whose influence had spread to Pound himself: "Whistler, be with America/ at this hour." Olson also juxtaposes the image of the whorehouse (the product of an inhumane industrial system) to the palace, representing the innocent world of Mencius. Pound's balladizing of *The Chinese Odes* was mere "decoration" rather than "presenting the image accurately," which was the chief aim of the Imagist poets. Olson also juxtaposes the open structure of part 3, with images positioned all over the page, to some of the closed, clotted stanzas of parts 1 and 2.

In the seventh stanza of part 1, Olson replaces the word "clank" with "Noise!" and then scolds his master Pound for betraying his original project:

> . . . he
> who taught us all
> that no line must sleep,
> that as the line goes so goes
> the Nation! that the Master
> should now be embraced by the demon
> he drove off! O Ruler.

Olson puns on the word "lines," referring to the poetic line, which Pound had emancipated from traditional restrictions and then returned to its former constraints in his translation of *The Odes of Confucius*. Olson demonstrates the power of presenting the image accurately in the second half of part 1: "that what the eye sees,/ that in the East the sun untangles itself/ from among branches." Olson had learned from Pound, his master, that the greatest accomplishment of Imagist poetry was to give the reader a direct and sensuous experience of reality.

Olson also used the poetic device of apostrophe to address Walt Whitman, the great American bard who broke all the rules:

> o Whitman,
> let us keep our trade with you when
> the Distributor
> who couldn't go beyond wood,
> apparently,
> has gone out of business.

Olson criticizes Pound for forgetting what he had learned from Whitman's use of free verse and for not being able to move beyond the Sacred Wood, the central metaphor of Pound's early book of literary essays, *The Spirit of Romance* (1910). That book placed the beginning of European civilization in the pastoral works of ancient Greece and Rome, a view Olson found too limited in scope.

Part 3 begins with the pronoun "we," referring to those poets of Olson's circle who refused to revert to the regressive pastoralism of romantic ballads: "We'll to these woods/ no more, where we were used/ to get so much." Olson then brings in the image of the dance, a favorite of Pound's, and refers to his former master as "Old Bones."

"[D]o not try to dance," he advises, "the Charleston/ is still for us." In other words, the old traditional dances are no longer relevant (they are literally "still") for the genuinely new poetry and its practitioners. Pound had become an "Old Bones" or mere observer of the emerging poetics of process which he began and to which he had led Olson: "we are the process/ and our feet," feet here meaning an open-form poetry that does not confine poetic feet to the rules of regular rhyme and rhythm. Olson separates himself and his fellow poets from old forms: "We do not march"—"march" referring both to rigid rhythms and to moving in lockstep without imagination. Words such as "roads," "rails," "march," "clank," "noise," "ruler," and "ballads" become cumulative metaphors for an over-industrialized, life-denying culture built on dead traditions that impede the growth of new poetry.

Themes and Meanings

"I, Mencius, Pupil of the Master . . ." is from *The Distances* (1960), Charles Olson's first major collection of poems. Many of the poems in this collection deal with one of Olson's major themes throughout his writing career; the distance or alienation of human beings from anything that comes between them and their direct experience of reality. Olson's most beloved quotation was from Heraclitus, the pre-Socratic Greek philosopher: "Man is estranged from that with which he is most familiar." That is the major theme of "I, Mencius, Pupil of the Master. . . " Furthermore, Olson's greatest inspiration was Ezra Pound, whose early poetry cleansed the English language of empty abstractions. Pound's dictum "Go in fear of abstractions!" helped formulate the rules for Imagism which, when followed, would give modern poetry the clear, revelatory quality of Chinese and Japanese poetry and art. "Images in verse are not mere decoration, but the very essence of an intuitive language," asserted one of the other founders of Imagism, T. E. Hulme. Hulme also wrote that the best poetry "endeavors to arrest you, and to make you continuously see a physical thing, to prevent you gliding through an abstract process."

This poem expresses Olson's outrage that his old mentor had rejected the very rules that he helped formulate and violated the clarity and simplicity of the venerable *Odes of Confucius* by reducing them to "coolie verse." That, for Olson, was a sacrilegious act and returned poetry to the "clank" and "noise" of old, depleted forms. Olson's use of the persona and voice of Mencius gives the poem even greater thematic impact and underscores Olson's sense of betrayal.

According to Olson, Pound, by joining with the reactionary enemies of art and poetry, shared the same mentality that created the dark satanic mills (to echo William Blake's phrase) of Pittsburgh Steel and the Bremerton Shipyards. Pound had produced "the dross of verse." In returning to an enervated tradition, Pound had betrayed his original definition of virtue: to restore human beings to that with which they are most familiar, their own sense of themselves responding to the vividness of a life of the senses and, thus, an intensification of objective reality. The second word in the poem, and the most important, is "dross," which literally means the waste product on the surface of molten steel but also echoes Pound's use of it in his most famous poem,

Pisan Canto 81: "What thou lovest well remains, the rest is dross/ What thou lovest well shall not be reft from thee/ What thou lovest well is thy true heritage." By alluding to one of Pound's most famous lines, Olson shows how far he had fallen from his earlier position as the major defender and practitioner of a new kind of poetry intended to restore poetry to the freshness of original perception, unencumbered by the useless "decoration" of dead forms.

Patrick Meanor

I SAW IN LOUISIANA A LIVE-OAK GROWING

Author: Walt Whitman (1819-1892)
Type of poem: Lyric
First published: 1860, as "Calamus.20," in *Leaves of Grass*, 3d ed.; 1867, as "I Saw in Louisiana a Live-Oak Growing," in *Leaves of Grass*, 4th ed.

The Poem

"I Saw in Louisiana a Live-Oak Growing" is a short lyric poem made up of thirteen lines of free verse (verse written in no traditional meter). The speaker of the poem may be identified with the poet or at least with "Walt Whitman," as the reader comes to know him in *Leaves of Grass*, the book in which this poem appears. The poem begins with a memory: The poet remembers the live oak tree he saw standing by itself in Louisiana, whose "rude" and "lusty" look reminded the poet of himself. In one important respect, however, the tree was very different from the poet, for the tree was "uttering joyous leaves" even though it stood without another of its kind (a "companion") nearby, and this is something that the poet knew he could never do. That the tree was in Louisiana may have some autobiographical significance: Whitman, who lived most of his life in New York and New Jersey, spent some time in Louisiana. In any case, the live oak flourishes in Louisiana, and the geographical reference grounds the poem in fact. The poet is speaking of a real tree he actually saw rather than of a metaphor for his feelings.

In speaking of the tree as "uttering" its leaves, Whitman uses a word that is perfectly appropriate on a literal level. In this context, "utter" can simply mean to "put forth" or "sprout." However, since the word is more commonly used to describe human speech and since Whitman habitually refers to his poems as "leaves" (as in the title *Leaves of Grass*), the word implies more. The tree that "utters . . . leaves" is an image not only of the man but also of the poet. The poet tells the reader that he broke a twig from the tree and that he now keeps the twig, with a little moss tied around it, in his room, where it remains a curious token. Its purpose is not to remind him of his friends because, he tells us, he thinks of little else. Rather, it stands for manly love or the love of man for man. Yet the phrase is ambiguous. A reader might take "manly love" to mean the love a man may feel for a woman. Whitman probably accepted, even intended, the ambiguity.

The poem's last lines return to the theme of the opening. In this restatement, the live oak's isolation is still more strongly emphasized: "solitary/ in a wide flat space." The phrase "friends and lovers," uniting two forms of human relationship in one grammatical unit, appears for the first time. Furthermore, the poet is again in awe at the memory of the tree "uttering joyous leaves" in its isolation. The poet's response is reaffirmed in the last line of the poem: "I know very well I could not." For the poet, then, it is in the presence of companions, friends, and lovers that he finds the inspiration to utter his leaves; for the man, to be isolated from those he loves would cause him pain beyond his powers of expression.

Forms and Devices

Whitman was a pioneer in the development of free verse, but, as any experienced reader knows, successful free verse is never really free. Free of meter (the regular distribution of stresses across a line that dominated English verse from the Renaissance to Whitman's time and beyond), free verse must find its own principles of rhythm. A number of qualities contribute to the overall rhythm of Whitman's verse. Two of these are line length and syntax. Using the syllable as the unit of measurement, the reader can find in the poem a rhythm of expansion and contraction. The first line is shorter than any other line except for the last. The longest lines, the fifth and sixth, are followed by three relatively short lines of fifteen syllables each. Line 10 expands to twenty syllables, line 11 to twenty-five. Line 12 contracts to seventeen syllables, leading to the eight syllables of the eloquently concise last line.

Syntax also contributes to rhythm. Each line is capable of standing alone as at least a complete sentence, and line 11 could be written as two sentences. Yet only line 11 ends with a full stop of any kind, and the first period appears only at the end of the poem. The result is a rhythmically significant tension between sense and sound as the punctuation forbids the major pause at the end of the line that the sense would seem to call for. Syntactical subtleties also produce effects beyond the rhythmic. An air of straightforward simplicity is suggested by the repeated use of the simple past tense in the early lines of the poem. Yet the subjects of these verbs shift from "it," a pronoun whose antecedent is "live-oak," through "moss" and "its look" to "I," defining the progression of the poet's thought. Furthermore, while the last lines restate the theme of the opening, what had been in the past ("stood") is now in the present ("glistens"). An experience of the past transcends temporal categories to live in the present of the poet's, as well as the reader's, imagination.

Themes and Meanings

What one takes to be the meaning of this poem depends, in part, on context. To a reader not otherwise familiar with Whitman's work, it seems to be a reflection on the relation of the natural and human, with a special bearing on the artistic. While the tree utters its leaves regardless of the absence of companions, the human consciousness requires human companionship to inspire it to creativity. Readers who are familiar with *Leaves of Grass*, however, and specifically with "Calamus," the section (or "cluster") of the book in which the poem is found, will be aware of further implications. "Calamus" immediately follows "Children of Adam," a cluster dealing with what Whitman calls "amativeness" or the love between men and women. The organizing theme of "Calamus" is "adhesiveness" or male comradeship. Readers are increasingly inclined to read "Calamus" as an expression of the poet's homoerotic inclinations, but it seems that few of Whitman's contemporaries read it that way. To most of its nineteenth century readers, "Calamus" moved beyond the sexual concerns of "Children of Adam." In fact, some readers were scandalized by "Children of Adam," but "Calamus" seems to have raised scarcely an eyebrow during Whitman's lifetime. While later critics are prepared to ridicule the naïveté and bad faith of nineteenth century readers, those are the readers Whitman knew. If one attempts to read these poems as one of Whitman's contemporaries might have, the emphasis on relationships between men is not necessarily homosexual. For these readers, relationships between men are simply not sexual. Thus, these poems are about the spiritual dimensions of human experience, taking the reader beyond the physical and implying the judgment that the spiritual is "higher" than the physical.

Any interpretation of poetry reflects the worldview of the interpreter. More than a century has passed since Whitman's death, and in that time American culture has come to question hierarchies such as the one valuing the spiritual over the physical; it has also come to place the sexual much closer to the center of human experience than Whitman's contemporaries would have. Whether this has been, on the whole, for better or worse, it may have brought readers closer to the personal feelings and values of Whitman. For more recent readers, the poems of "Calamus" derive much of their emotional energy from the sexual longings of the poet, which seem to have been toward members of his own sex.

The "manly love" of "I Saw in Louisiana a Live-Oak Growing" is thus the love (including, even if not limited to, the sexual) of man for man. No reading that denies that is likely to be accepted today by sophisticated readers. Does this mean that the poem affirms that poetry is based on homosexual love? It seems, rather, to suggest that poetry is inspired by the poet's deepest and most authentic feelings, whatever value the surrounding society may place on those feelings. For Whitman, these are the feelings of a homosexual man, and it is not difficult to see a symbol of male sexuality in the twig around which a little moss is twined. Yet the poem is not, in any reductive sense, about sex; the longing that drives the poem is linked to the artistic creativity of which the poem is an emblem. Further, the authentic feelings of a heterosexual man or of a heterosexual or homosexual woman are equally powerful sources of inspiration. What kills creativity, the poem suggests, is inauthenticity, the denial of oneself and of one's feelings. This, rather than mere physical separation from other people—there is no lover present as the poet speaks—is perhaps, at the deepest level, what would prevent the poet from uttering his leaves.

W. P. Kenney

I THINK CONTINUALLY OF THOSE
WHO WERE TRULY GREAT

Author: Stephen Spender (1909-1995)
Type of poem: Elegy
First published: 1932; collected in *Poems*, 1933

The Poem

"I think continually of those who were truly great" is an untitled poem that first appeared in *New Signatures*, a collection of poetry selected by Michael Roberts to offer an imaginative and intellectual blend that would deal positively with the problems of the twentieth century. This popular collection also represented the works of emerging poets such as W. H. Auden, C. Day Lewis, William Empson, John Lehmann, and Richard Eberhart, who collectively became known, for a time, as *New Signatures* poets. Spender contributed more poems than any of the others, and his seven poems promptly became part of his collected canon.

"I think continually of those who were truly great" is written in free verse with three stanzas containing eight, seven, and eight lines respectively. The meter of the poem is highly varied, containing fine examples of most meters used in English poetry. While this poem settles into no regular meter, line length, or rhyme scheme, it is, nonetheless, highly musical with its syncopated rhythms and sharp images.

The opening line of the poem, which is typically used in place of its omitted title, sets a tone of reminiscing about the great; the verb "were" signals that those the poet admires are already dead. The second line declares that these noteworthy souls were born to greatness, having existed before birth and having had a history of the greatness they would realize in life on earth. The language is almost Neoplatonic as the poet discusses how these individuals have come from the light and are going back to the light or "Spirit." Plato's philosophy of learning maintained that education was a process of remembering what one already knows. Great people, as described in this poem, are those whose recollection of the lofty state from which they have come is fresh and vital like spring blossoms.

The second stanza continues this definition of greatness as a process of remembering not only human ancestry but also the spiritual ancestry dating before the creation of the Earth as humans know it. In one sense, the poem seems to be advocating a kind of reincarnation, but, in another sense, the poem is discussing the power of getting in touch with the ancient roots of culture that form the lifeblood of most great poetry. To continue this tradition introduced by great people, the poet encourages people to never forget these individuals and "Never to allow gradually the traffic to smother/ With noise and fog, the flowering of the Spirit."

The final stanza declares that creation itself celebrates the names of the great. This creation is alive and well aware of the noteworthy souls. The final four lines of the poem state elegantly how the great are "those who in their lives fought for life." Such souls who keep the value and purpose of life in their hearts leave their signature across the sky like a vivid sunset that one can never forget. Those who have been true to the best in life are destined to be remembered well.

Forms and Devices

"I think continually of those who were truly great" is a fine example of the *New Signatures* era of poetry. The style of the poem shows the influence of T. S. Eliot (whom Spender respected and admired), especially in its use of a highly imagistic, free-verse form. Those of Spender's own generation, such as Auden and Lewis, also influenced Spender to hold a very optimistic view of what humanity could accomplish in life. While the *New Signatures* poets often, in keeping with Marxist ideals, railed against capitalism and championed the common laborer, Spender seems to set aside this agenda for a moment. What remains of this cultural development among the poets is a sense of enthusiasm about the potential of individuals for achieving greatness.

The images in this poem are primarily tied to life and inspiration. In the ancient Greek tradition, inspiration was the product of the gods breathing new life into the writer, performer, or speaker. The phrase "lips, still touched with fire" reminds one of Isaiah 6, in which the prophet's lips are cleansed by the touch of a coal from the altar, leaving the prophet with inspiration to go forth and speak purely for God. Images of light and singing are also connected with inspiration. For the ancient Greeks, from which this elegiac form is derived, all forms of poetry and most parts of their plays were to be sung. Singing was considered the natural medium of inspiration, especially for the poet.

The images in the second stanza contrast with those in the first and third stanzas by being more visceral and earthy. Images such as "blood," "rocks," "grave evening," "noise," and "fog" are reminders of the frailty and struggle of life against impending death. Great people are those who face great challenges well. The images in the third stanza are also earthy, but they move one's view upward toward the sun. The elements of these bodily souls dissolve into light as they leave their honorable signature on the very air other people breathe. The phrase "vivid air" in the last line is another reminder that creation itself is vitally alive to the greatness of humanity and can be played like a harp humming with the song of life. The motifs of travel in the closing lines also remind readers that life is a pilgrimage. While this journey through life is terribly brief, it does tell much about one's basic inclinations and sets an angle of travel into eternity. The great not only aim high, they aim truly at their point of origin, which is also their point of destiny.

Themes and Meanings

"I think continually of those who were truly great" springs from an era of great enthusiasm for the potential of people to change their world. The Marxist dogmas that many of the idealistic upper middle class English people adopted were, in many ways, a well-intentioned effort to improve the state of the poor and underprivileged. Spender gave up his affiliation to Marxist ideologies after seeing the inconsistencies of the communist leaders in the Spanish Civil War. Spender was also to lose some of his naïve optimism about life after he witnessed the protracted suffering and death of his sister Margaret, who died of cancer on Christmas day, 1945. His "Elegy for Margaret" is much more somber than this earlier elegy, yet the sense of triumph is still evident, and the sense that this life is only a phase of one's total existence is still very strong.

The exact philosophy that undergirds this poem is ambiguous. One can find evidence of strong Christian convictions as well as views that are more Eastern or Hindu in their mystical view of life. As critic Sanford Sternlicht has noted, throughout his life, Spender remained "unsure of, and ambivalent toward, philosophy, aesthetics, religion, politics, and sexuality." This ambivalence helps explain why this poem does not fit firmly into any given philosophical or religious agenda. Spender is speaking of the universal yearnings of the soul and of the sense that all of humanity is connected to the past in some profound way, whether spiritually, genetically, or psychologically.

Regardless of how one assesses the religious and philosophical dimensions of this poem, Spender has achieved an extraordinary statement of hope about the potential of human beings to live significant, great lives. Such a statement is all the more surprising when one realizes that it came out of the era of the Great Depression and not long before Europeans knew they would soon be engulfed in another world war. Somehow, Spender has been able to take the images that have often been used in elegies and employ them with a fresh turn of phrasing that makes of these images a brilliant statement against death, which often seems to dwarf the value and significance of life. The poet seems to understand that the spiritual dimension of who people are is more significant than the mortal body. This view strongly contrasts with the Marxist view of life as being materialistic and existing exclusively on this side of death.

Compared to Spender's other poems from this era, "I think continually of those who were truly great" stands out as one of his best works. Some of his early poems, such as "Beethoven's Death Mask" and "The Express," also achieve a degree of aptness in phrasing and imagery, but most are very romantic and sometimes sentimental, the product of seeing the trials of life from a distance. These early successes show that Spender was a fine poet in the making who was moving toward the sun of his greatness. In 1971, he was awarded the Queen's Gold Medal for Poetry; in 1979, he was made an honorary fellow of University College, Oxford; and, in 1982, he was knighted—a fitting crown to his own noble career as a poet and critic.

Daven M. Kari

I WASH THE SHIRT

Author: Anna Świr (Anna Świrszczyńska, 1909-1984)
Type of poem: Lyric
First published: 1985, as "Piorę koszulę," in *Cierpienie i radość;* English translation
collected in Talking to My Body, 1996

The Poem

"I Wash the Shirt" is a prose poem composed of nineteen lines that vary greatly in length. It is a very short work, but, like many of Anna Świr's poems, it is rooted deeply in her private life. The author describes washing the shirt of her recently deceased father, a task so personal that Świr kept the poem to herself for several years; it was only published posthumously by her daughter. Although it can be appreciated on its own, the reader who understands something of Świr's life and circumstances will see more meaning in it than others will. In many of her poems, Świr depicts her father as a strong, gentle man who took pride in his people's culture and who labored continually to depict that heritage in his art despite the lifetime of poverty and struggle he endured to do so. This image is continued in "I Wash the Shirt." He was a painter who specialized in religious and historical themes, and the title refers to Świr washing the shirt he wore while working in his studio. Since he did not wear the shirt outside, he merely asked his daughter to dry it on the wood-burning stove that heated his workshop rather than iron it. For Świr, the shirt has strong associations with her father's daily toil as well as with his passion and pride; even its scent, as she puts it into the wash water, reminds her of him.

Świr compares washing the shirt with the other times she washed her father's clothing, which always smelled of his perspiration. She has performed the same task since girlhood, but while she previously laid the shirt for him to find on the stove, now she simply prepares to put it away. Once it is washed, it no longer conveys the familiar sense of her father's presence, and she realizes that in one more small way she has lost another aspect of him. His paintings will be left, but they are a public and sterile (if beautiful) side of his activity. The living, breathing, perspiring man whose love and effort brought that beauty into existence is gone forever and so is his scent. She also suggests elsewhere that although he labored intensely on his paintings, they could never adequately convey his feelings. In "I Wash the Shirt," death has removed the devoted artist and father, leaving only a shirt and some oil paintings. What could easily be a grotesque meditation on soiled laundry, seemingly inappropriate in the face of death, becomes instead a musing on how irreplaceable Świr's father was, not because of his paintings but because of his unique presence and personality.

Forms and Devices

As in most of her poetry, Świr makes no attempt in "I Wash the Shirt" to sound "poetic." Her translator, Czesław Miłosz, discusses Świr's desire to write poetry in which the ideas would show through clearly, unimpeded by any noticeable attempt at style or verbal sophistication. She specialized in very short works, often termed "miniatures" by critics. These poems, by concentrating the reader's attention on one or two images in only a few lines, strengthen the impact of those images. In "I Wash the Shirt," as in many of her works, Świr succeeds particularly well. Her language is purely conversational, as in the third and fourth lines: "The shirt smells of sweat. I remember/ that sweat from my childhood." Just as the image of a sweaty shirt is neither traditionally poetic nor even aesthetically pleasing, the language also avoids ornamentation and communicates its forceful emotion through simple, almost blunt wording. Because of Świr's approach, the image of the woman washing a shirt as she recalls more than six decades of her father's presence, now lost forever, is haunting.

Such writing depends upon its thought and subject matter (in this case loss and death) for its poetic power, and this strength is particularly found in the novelty of finding the smell of stale clothing a powerful reminder of a beloved parent, the sort of reminder most people are not likely to prize or even to think about until the loved one is gone. In keeping with her concept of poetry, Świr transforms a mundane chore into a moment of profound insight and grief. She smells the scent of the almost obsessive effort that he put into his work rather than the scent of the paintings themselves, which only smell like oil paint. What survives—the paintings—are only artifacts, not part of life. The sweat recalls his spirit, his concentration and patience, and his compulsion to keep the Polish heritage alive. In washing the shirt, she realizes she has lost not only a physical smell but also the sense of her father's presence, the body that produced the perspiration. The simple three- and four-syllable lines ("I destroy it/ forever") evoke the finality of loss more powerfully than most traditionally written laments would. The alteration of her father from living man to mere memory is complete: Although his paintings remain, the sense of his active and moving body, the passion and feeling of the man who sweated while he worked, the influence he had in his daughter's life, and his love are all gone forever.

Themes and Meanings

Świr was affected all her life by the death and destruction she witnessed as a young woman during World War II. For her, life itself, with all its processes, attractive and otherwise, became compelling. Her poetry generally reflects an intense interest in the physical, simple acts of existence such as breathing and walking and in the everyday sights, sounds, and smells of urban streets and crowded apartment buildings. For such a poet, the scent of a deceased man's perspiration can evoke a strong sense of his identity. Świr sometimes uses breathing as a symbol of life, strength, and joy in her poems. In "I Wash the Shirt," however, breathing, coupled with a simple task performed for the last time, evokes grief. For Świr, that scent, so familiar to her from almost seven decades with her father, identifies only one body in the world. Since that body is gone, she feels she destroys a remnant of the man by washing his shirt. Breathing and perspiring are essential functions of human life and are thus tokens of continued living; the poet's father, who no longer lives, neither breathes nor works. Only relatively odorless and inanimate paintings remain of his vision and the struggle he underwent to express it. However much these paintings reflect his love of beauty and of his homeland, they do not have the physical, animal presence his missing body once had, and the poet will never have the comfort of his presence again. In other poems, she writes about how he painted, working painstakingly and correcting himself as he went. This process, with its great self-discipline and perseverance, was the true mark of her father's personality and feelings. It is thus her father's process of painting rather than the paintings themselves that she loves and misses.

Such a theme is typical of Świr's work, and it is true to the experience of many people who lose loved ones. Those who grieve often find that mundane tasks and ordinary objects trigger the deepest feelings of sorrow. In the case of "I Wash the Shirt," Świr's grief is caused by doing a very familiar task that she will never perform again. There will be no point to laying the shirt on top of the wood-burning stove for her father because he will not wear it to work anymore. Just as small, commonplace realizations often evoke the profoundest sadness, a short poem in everyday language suggests Świr's deep loneliness and sadness for her father and the stunning finality of death, which can make even the act of doing laundry seem like another instance of destruction and loss.

Paul James Buczkowski

THE IDEA OF ANCESTRY

Author: Etheridge Knight (1933-1991)
Type of poem: Dramatic monologue
First published: 1968, in *Poems from Prison*

The Poem

"The Idea of Ancestry" is a forty-two-line poem in free verse divided into two parts of three and two stanzas respectively. The title names the subject of the poem—the poet's connection to his family, his birthplace, and his culture. The poem is written in the autobiographical, first-person voice of Knight. In stanza 1 of part 1, the poet describes his cell in prison, the walls covered with "47" photographs of his relatives. He reclines on his bunk and contemplates the pictures, imagining they are alive and looking at him. Pointedly, he reflects that he shares identities with them: "I am all of them, they are all of me." He ends the reflection and the stanza with a statement that presents a radical shift in point of view: "They are thee." "Thee" addresses all the poem's readers, indeed all of humanity.

In stanza 2, the poet inventories the twelve relatives he has been "in love" with, starting with his mother and ending with a seven-year-old niece who sends him letters in prison. One of the aunts he loved went into an asylum. It is not clear if all these relatives are female. In stanza 3, the poet gives an inventory of his male relatives, especially those with whom he shares the same name. He considers, in particular, a fugitive uncle who has, since age fifteen, been conspicuous by his absence. This uncle is missed each year by the family at its reunions, particularly by the poet's ninety-three-year-old grandmother ("my father's mother") who keeps track of everybody's birth and death dates in the "Family Bible."

In the first stanza of part 2, the poet's attention turns from the members of his family to himself as he recalls his beginnings in Mississippi, his grandfathers' graves there, and his return visit the previous year. He says his visit from Los Angeles was almost strengthening enough to allow him to break his drug habit—but not quite. He therefore takes drugs ("caps") and walks barefoot in his grandmother's backyard, flirts with the local women, and has fun until he runs out of narcotics, experiences withdrawal pain, and ends up stealing drugs from a doctor's house ("cracked a croaker's crib for a fix"). In the second stanza of part 2—the poem's final stanza—the poet describes himself again in his prison cell. It is "Fall," the poem's dominant season. He repeats his reference to his forty-seven photographs of "black faces." In stanza 1, "they stare" at him. In this final stanza, he stares back at them. He repeats that he is "all of them, they are all of [him]." Climactically, he also repeats that "they are thee," addressing the reader and perhaps himself, as if talking to himself as people in solitary environments such as prison might. Finally, the poet announces that he has "no sons" to take a place in the world that he shares with the reader ("thee").

Forms and Devices

Knight's poetry is essentially oral. His own voice was a baritone warble, full of water and passion, exactly right for the poetic diction he created. His poems are rich with single-syllable words, and "The Idea of Ancestry" is no exception. Monosyllabic words outnumber polysyllabic words by over four to one through the first four stanzas, an effect that is multiplied until the proportion is ten to one in the final stanza. Monosyllabic words arrest rhythm and are the discourse of the arrested time of the imprisoned poet who is forbidden participation in the flow of his "birthstream"—and thus in history, wherein "ancestry" occurs. The poem's grammar and punctuation are resolutely simple: The poem's lines do not begin with capitalized words; integer numbers—1, 2, and 3, for example—are not spelled out; and words such as "yr," "1st," and "2nd" are adopted, though "year" is also used. Notably, after its use as the principal word in the title, "ancestry" is not among the words used in the poem. Meanwhile, additional oral characteristics of the poem are in keeping with its elemental and emotionally simple meaning. For example, memorized inventories of the contents of one's life are typical of oral culture, and certain kinds of oral poetry are designed to collect and remember the personalities of family members. The poem also inventories the poet's personal experience. He has forty-seven photographs of forty-seven relatives, indexed as "father, mother, grandmothers (1 dead), grand/ fathers (both dead), brothers, sisters, uncles, aunts, cousins (1st & 2nd), nieces, and nephews." He reports having been "in love" with twelve relatives, whom he enumerates. Next he inventories his male relative namesakes— eight of them. In part 2 of the poem, an inventory of ten declarative sentences enumerates the events of his trip to his Mississippi birthplace.

Significantly, the poem's most important figurative language occurs in part 2 of the poem. The first example is its central metaphor, "like a salmon quitting/ the cold ocean—leaping and bucking up his birthstream," which is completed in the last stanza, "a gray stone wall damming my stream, . . . [I] flop on my bunk and stare" (like a fish). The second example employs an oddly esoteric diction in the "electric/ messages" from his home in Mississippi that are "galvanizing" his "genes." The third example is a sampling of a drug addict's jargon: "a monkey on my back" and "I cracked a croaker's crib for a fix." Otherwise, the poem's diction is literal. These details of the poet's simple personal culture are nevertheless divided in the diptych structure of the poem's two parts, hinged like a tabletop photograph frame. The parts are pictures, respectively, of Knight's relatives and of Knight himself. A final feature worth noting about the poem is the average number of syllables in its lines. The first forty-one lines have an average of thirteen syllables. The last line, "to float in the space between," is emphatically truncated, one is tempted to say decapitated, at seven, followed by the endless space beyond the end of the poem, an emptiness in place of the "sons" the poet does not have.

Themes and Meanings

The main meaning of the title "The Idea of Ancestry" can be expressed as an interrogative one: Is there an ancestry—an actual relationship to a prior human family—or is it just an idea, a construct of language, photography, and Scripture? The Bible is an ambivalent referent for African Americans, used as it was to help them cope with slavery and other difficulties. Even so, it presents, with its enumeration of the tribes and families of the Hebrew people, the most famous of all Western civilization's rubrics of homage to ancestry. Meanwhile, it is interesting that Knight does not name the dynastic ancestry celebrated in the Egyptian culture that paralleled the Hebraic one. People of African ancestry can claim an authentic and august pedigree in Egyptian terms, but Knight eschews this. He is without pretension. Instead, he mentions his grandmother five times: She is old, and she has survived long enough to become an ancestor. His grandfathers are both dead. The poem does answer these questions about ancestry, however. Ancestry does exist. The stone wall of the prison dams the poet's "stream," his "birthstream." When it separates him from society, it erases him from history, and therefore he cannot have sons and thus become an ancestor.

The idea of ancestry, therefore, works both ways: The society that put the poet in prison enjoys an ancestry, a historical identity that nourishes and "galvanizes" it. Society denies the dignity of ancestry to the imprisoned poet, whose identity in history is thereby interrupted. Ancestry, however, is collective: "I am all of them" and "they are thee." Therefore, when society erases the poet's identity in history by extinguishing his power to have sons, it diminishes the numbers, of which the poet is one, of its ancestral generation and thereby flaws its unanimity. Thus, the space left by the poet's lost uncle, the space of the prison cell, and "the space between" with which the poem ends represent the loss of personhood, the extinction of freedom, and the end of connection to family, people, and history.

John R. Pfeiffer

THE IMAGE IN LAVA

Author: Felicia Hemans (1793-1835)
Type of poem: Lyric
First published: 1828, in *Records of Woman*

The Poem

"The Image in Lava" is a short poem of eleven four-line stanzas. The title refers to an impression, in volcanic ash and lava, of a woman clasping a baby to her breast that was discovered during the excavation of the ruins of the ancient city of Herculaneum (buried with Pompeii by an eruption of the volcano Mount Vesuvius in A.D. 79). In the first stanza, the speaker of the poem addresses the image directly, asking "What ages have gone by" since the moment when the mother and infant were killed ("the mournful seal was set" in "love and agony"). The next stanza comments on all the empires, with their temples and towers (places of power), that have come and gone since that moment. The speaker thus establishes, early in the poem, one of its central themes—that the human love between mother and child is more lasting than all the powerful institutions humans may build. This contrast is continued in the third stanza with the idea that the image of childhood, despite its fragility, has outlasted the "proud memorials" of the "conquerors of mankind."

The next five stanzas address the infant directly, first asking if it was sleeping when the moment of death came, then setting up the idea that though the fiery death was a "strange, dark fate," it was better to end life at that moment of love than to live to know the pain of separation. That thought leads the speaker to speculate about the mother while still speaking to the child. She asks the child if it was the only "treasure" left to the mother, whether she had been forsaken by all others on whom she had "lavished" her love in vain. The speaker wonders, in the seventh stanza, if all the others the mother had loved and trusted had left her only "thorns on which to lean." If so, the speaker suggests in the eighth stanza, it was better for her also to die clasping her remaining loved one than to continue to live and perhaps lose this last object of her love.

The last three stanzas return to the theme established in the second stanza—the contrast between the love of mother and child and all the power of "cities of renown" that have not lasted as the impression in lava has. The speaker says, in stanza 9, that she would bypass all the relics and ruins of all the impressive buildings left from the "pomps of old" to look at the image of the mother and child; though a "rude" (simple, not magnificent) "monument," it is cast in "affection's mould," that is, created by a mother's love. The tenth stanza addresses "Love, human love!" directly, asking it what allows it to leave its imprint to be preserved when all that the mighty have erected has turned to dust. The speaker answers the question in the concluding stanza, saying that human love is the "earthly glow" of holy love, a representation or a shining through into human existence, of the light of immortal love. Though the mother and child have perished, the imprint left by their love has outlasted all the monuments of power and "given these ashes holiness." "It must, it *must* be so," the poem concludes.

Forms and Devices

The eleven stanzas of the poem are in ballad stanza; that is, the second and fourth lines rhyme, while the first and third do not. Ballad stanza was repopularized in Hemans's time; her contemporaries William Wordsworth and Samuel Taylor Coleridge revived the form, which had been in disuse for some time, in their joint volume of poems *Lyrical Ballads* (1798).

"The Image in Lava" also resembles, in its three-part structure, a form that Wordsworth and Coleridge employed and called a "conversation poem": a description of the scene, a meditation upon the scene, and then a return to the scene. The scene in this case would be the impression of the woman and the infant in lava, described in the first three stanzas; the meditation on the scene would be the middle five stanzas in which the speaker of the poem addresses the infant; and the return to the scene would be the final three stanzas, in which the speaker returns to the image in lava to compare it once again to the relics of the mighty and conclude that it is an earthly image of immortal love. As is traditional with ballads, the meter of the poem is predominantly iambic (an unstressed syllable followed by a stressed syllable); it has three iambic feet in a line (trimeter) except for the third line in each stanza, which has four iambic feet (tetrameter).

The imagery of the poem arises primarily from the contrast between the love of the mother and child and the proud buildings and monuments raised by the mighty as evidence of their earthly power. The poet refers to these structures of "empires" and "mighty cities" as "temple" (church) and "tower" (government) and describes them with words such as "pomp" and "pride," using alliteration in both instances. Childhood, in contrast, is described as "fragile," but the words and images used to describe the child and mother and their love for each other suggest permanence—"image," "print," "monument," and "enshrined." These words suggest the iconic and the representational, especially of holy things, of things that are immortal, so that the impression of the mother and child in the volcanic dust, representing a "woman's heart" and "human love," are icons of divine, immortal love.

This ironic use of the imagery of an image is related to another subtle irony: Though the bodies of mother and child have turned to dust and disappeared while the buildings still stand, the image in dust survives because it is a semblance of divine love, while the buildings, symbols of earthly power, are in ruins, and no trace remains of the mighty who built them. This ironic contrast is also embedded in the imagery of dark and light: The sudden, early death of the mother and child was a "strange, dark fate," but their love was an "earthly glow," an image of the divine brightness.

Themes and Meanings

In "The Image in Lava," Hemans explores, as she does frequently in her work, the conflict between fame, which she sought and succeeded in obtaining in large measure, and the quieter, domestic virtues of family and motherhood. This conflict was especially real to a woman writer in her time, since middle- and upper-class women were discouraged from working outside the home and taught that their proper sphere was caring for a household and a family. Women who sought nondomestic careers were thought of as unwomanly, even when financial necessity forced them to earn money, as was the case with Hemans, a mother of five sons and their sole financial support (her husband separated from the family, never to return). The great nurse Florence Nightingale, who knew Hemans's work and copied one of her poems for a cousin, detailed, in her book *Cassandra* (1852-59), the obstacles faced by women similar to herself who sought self-expression outside the home.

In "The Image in Lava," as elsewhere in her poetry, Hemans supports the cultural expectations of her time by suggesting that motherhood is finer than any of the other achievements to which humans can aspire and more lasting than the monuments they build to their own power and fame. Yet the poem also hints at the price women pay for this sacrifice. When the poem explores the possibility that all the others the mother had lavished her love upon had abandoned her, she acknowledges the sad reality, experienced by both herself and her beloved mother, that women were often left to sustain a household and rear the children alone. Hemans was also aware of the grim reality that many women died early from childbirth and the rigors of child-rearing, and that the infant mortality rate in her time was very high; though the mother and child in the poem die in a volcanic eruption, they image the early death of many nineteenth century women and children.

Indeed, much of the poetry of British (and American) women in the nineteenth century is preoccupied with the early death of women; often, the speaker of the poem is a voice from the grave, and often, too, the concern of the speaker is with remembrance of her after death, as in Emily Brontë's "Remembrance" and Christina Rossetti's "Remember." Hemans, whose poetry predates that of Brontë and Rossetti, helps to establish this motif in women's poetry when she contrasts the enduring impression of the love between mother and child to the ephemeral quality of fame in the world. Also like Rossetti, she finds consolation for womanly suffering in the belief in a divine power; "The Image in Lava" concludes with the insistence ("It must, it *must* be so!") that the sacrificial love of the mother for her child is an image of the divine love, an evidence of eternal love.

June M. Frazer

IN DISTRUST OF MERITS

Author: Marianne Moore (1887-1972)
Type of poem: Lyric
First published: 1944, in *Nevertheless*

The Poem

Marianne Moore's "In Distrust of Merits" is a poem so artfully constructed that although it seems to read like prose, it actually follows a consistent pattern that contains many conventional poetic forms. Each of the eight stanzas comprises ten lines. The first four lines of each stanza form a quatrain in which the second and fourth lines rhyme, while the next two lines are decasyllabic (ten syllables to a line). These lines are followed by another quatrain that differs from the first one in that both alternating lines rhyme. Although Moore imposes this formal pattern of syllabic grouping and internal as well as end rhyme, the rhymes are muted and the lines remain flexible.

The first line of the first stanza immediately sets up a thematic paradox by asking whether those who are prepared ("strengthened") to fight or to die are adequately compensated by the "medals and positioned victories" of war. The paradox continues in the next four lines: The soldiers are fighting a "blind/ man who thinks he sees" and who, because of his moral blindness, is "enslaved" and "harmed." The questioner appeals to nature ("firm stars"—perhaps truth) to guide humankind. This apostrophe includes the need for the individual to "know/ depth": In order to understand what motivates humankind to the violence of war, the speaker must plumb the depths of history and of herself.

The second stanza alludes to the possible causes of war: religious differences (the "star of David" of Judaism and the "star of Bethlehem" of Christianity) and racial differences (the "black imperial lion," a title given to Haile Selassie, Emperor of Ethiopia and one of the first victims of Italian dictator Benito Mussolini's fascist aggression). The third stanza describes the ongoing fighting in terms of a disease that will kill some and not others; however, the paradox "we devour ourselves" moves the guilt from the external enemy to an internal one.

The fourth stanza continues to express the need for people to see themselves and not be like the hypocritical "false comforters" who placed blame on a guiltless Job in the Bible. However, the fifth stanza explains the difficulty of trying to make promises not to discriminate when the speaker is not sure whether or not she is the enemy herself. Because of this quandary, the sixth stanza points out the easier decision to fight the foreign enemy as opposed to the more difficult choice of being patient (fighting oneself?) as a form of defense. Finally, the seventh stanza galvanizes the internal dialogue of the persona by describing the results that war always produces: the pain of the survivors ("The world's an orphans' home"). The speaker must learn the lessons that so many dead and suffering people have paid for. In conclusion, the speaker addresses her own "Hate-hardened heart." The merits of fighting are to be distrusted because battles are not directed against the real problem: the inability of people to acknowledge their own guilt.

Forms and Devices

One of Moore's favorite poetic devices is the paradox. This device of presenting an apparent contradiction that proves to be true after some reflection works well to express the thesis of "In Distrust of Merits." Even the title suggests the author is questioning some concept that the rest of society not only accepts without question but also rewards. For example, the first two lines of the first stanza ("Strengthened to live, strengthened to die for/ medals and positioned victories?") immediately set up a thematic paradox by repeating the same action ("Strengthened") with opposite purposes (to live and to die). Yet the meaning is not contradictory, for soldiers are trained both to fight ("live") and to die in combat. The feeling of contradiction provokes continued dialogue as the speaker tries to make sense of a senseless situation. Some other examples of paradoxes in the poem are "a blind man who/ can see," the "enslaver" who is "enslaved," and the "alive who are dead." Most of these paradoxes are based on the gap between material and spiritual perception. People are more impressed when their senses experience success in battle and war; unfortunately, these tangible senses can veil intangible spiritual truth. In spite of witnessing turmoil, fighting, and death, the persona in this dialogue with self must uncover, chiefly by means of unraveling the paradox, the truth that lies beneath the external causes of war: the guilt of the individual conscience that does not express the ideals in which it intuitively believes.

Moore uses some rather traditional metaphors: "hate's crown," "dust of the earth," "heart of iron," the world as "an orphans' home," and Iscariot's "crime." Critics debate whether frequent use has turned these phrases into trite clichés or whether they are being used because they express certain universal feelings and experiences. Like the apostrophe that expresses hope that the "star of David, star of Bethlehem" and "the black imperial lion/ of the Lord" be "joined at last," the well-known phrases point to thousands of years of conflict that preceded the anti-Semitic attacks and claims of Aryan superiority that provoked World War II, which was in progress at the time of the poem's composition. By using these conventional phrases, the author is perhaps saying that war and suffering will continue until individuals in each generation face their moral responsibility and end the underlying causes of war. Like the use of recognizable symbolic phrases, the repetition of certain words such as "fighting" and "patience" provides both a feeling of intensity and a feeling of longevity. The persona is asking, "When will people see themselves as the solution to the horrors of war?"

Themes and Meanings

Although a photograph of a slain soldier in *Life* magazine sparked the immediate compassion and the reaction Moore expressed in "In Distrust of Merits," the poet, throughout her later years, frequently expressed her concern with moral issues in her poetry. When she was asked how she felt about this frequently anthologized poem, she responded that she believed that it expressed her deep and sincere emotion but that it was perhaps somewhat disjointed in form. However, it seems tenable that the form reflects the speaker's feelings: When personal feelings do not conform with those of people with whom one usually agrees, the normal reaction is to feel cut off or disjointed.

The title expresses the feeling the persona explores in the poem. The word "distrust" sets up a rejection of trust in what is usually considered to have merit. The poem attempts to penetrate the positive veneer of society's merits by looking beneath the surface to the reality. In World War II, for example, leaders such as Adolf Hitler and Mussolini were successful in their bids for power; however, beneath the merit of success lay the suffering Jews and the conquered Ethiopians. Such a "successful" leader is "the blind/ man who thinks he sees." The same description is used in reference to those who give "false comfort" to a "disheartened" Job. These comforters suggest the apparent moral uprightness of those who are more concerned about external rectitude than spiritual integrity. They believe that if Job is suffering, he must have deserved it. The poem suggests such merits also are suspect.

The final expression of distrust is directed at the speaker: "I must/ fight till I have conquered in myself what/ causes war, but I would not believe it." The speaker explicitly identifies her inability to accept personal responsibility. Therefore, she does nothing and betrays herself and humanity ("O Iscariot-like crime!"). The final two lines complete the circle from distrust to trust by affirming the perspective at which the speaker has arrived: "Beauty is everlasting/ and dust is for a time." The merits that the world supports are but transient dust; however, true merit will always last. The word "everlasting" also affirms a central theme of the poem: The situations that are usually identified as leading to war may vary, but the underlying cause, a "Hate-hardened heart," remains constant. Recognition of this cause must precede and support the vow "We'll/ never hate black, white, red, yellow, Jew,/ Gentile, Untouchable."

Throughout the poem, the author points to the need for the individual to make hard personal choices and then to express those choices so that others will feel supported in the choices their consciences make. One way the author expresses this movement from one individual toward other individuals (but not toward the collective society that supports the distrusted merits) is simply to use the first-person singular pronoun ("I"), the third-person singular pronoun ("he"), and the first-person plural pronoun ("we"). The syntax supports Moore's concern that the individuals must announce their beliefs publicly, unlike the cowardly Judas Iscariot who betrayed his friend Jesus.

Agnes A. Shields

IN GOYA'S GREATEST SCENES WE SEEM TO SEE

Author: Lawrence Ferlinghetti (1919-   )
Type of poem: Lyric
First published: 1957; collected in *A Coney Island of the Mind*, 1958

The Poem

Within a few months in 1956, Lawrence Ferlinghetti wrote twenty-nine poems that he envisioned as a unit. In his second book of poetry, *A Coney Island of the Mind*, they appear numbered, without titles. Number 1, "In Goya's greatest scenes we seem to see," is a lyric written in open form, having no regular rhyme, meter, or line length. Placed on the page so as to have a visual effect, the poem has six sections of varying length, ranging from twenty lines to three words. (Anthologies vary in the way they present the poem, not always retaining the original spacing between lines and thereby varying the number of sections.)

The title, taken from the first line of the poem, immediately introduces the first of two topics: works by the Spanish artist Francisco de Goya. The poet directs readers first to Goya's works, which present "'suffering humanity.'" Ferlinghetti then suggests scenes of war through words such as "writhe," "veritable rage," and "adversity." Specifically, the poem alludes to Goya's *Disasters of War*, created in 1810 but not published until 1863, years after his death. This series of sketches depicts the brutality, on the part of both the French and the Spanish, in the Peninsular War (1808-1814). Although Ferlinghetti never names the *Disasters of War*, he uses words to bring Goya's images from those sketches to mind: "bayonets," "landscape of blasted trees," "wings and beaks," "carnivorous cocks," "gibbets," and "cadavers."

The grammar and syntax of the first twenty lines (section 1) reveal three sentences, although the lack of straight margins and terminal punctuation suggest fragmentation rather than grammatical units. (Ferlinghetti uses no punctuation in the poem except for quotation marks and an apostrophe, but capital letters help locate new grammatical units.) The open form and line design contribute to a tone of confusion and isolation that matches the tone of Goya's sketches. The next two sections of the poem, each one line long, provide transition to the second topic: The poet maintains that the suffering humanity of Goya's sketches is still alive more than a century later but is now living in another "landscape" and, as the reader soon learns, on another continent: America. The last three sections of the poem describe these new sufferers and this new landscape.

As with Goya's sufferers, these people are "ranged along the roads" instead of being pictured in their homes or communities; again the landscape is bleak, and again the people are seen as victims of a senseless, predatory power. Yet the images of suffering are very different. Goya's sketches focus on the people, often with no background buildings, objects, or vegetation. When buildings or vegetation are included, their presentation adds to the plight of the people instead of taking the focus away from them. In Ferlinghetti's poem, however, the landscape is central and the people are in the background. They are not physically depicted as in the Goya prints; rather, they are described only as "maimed citizens." The landscape is now bleak, not because it is barren, gray, or war torn, but because it is morally vacuous—"freeways fifty lanes wide" are crowded with "bland billboards" and automobiles. The people are trapped in a world built for machinery and advertising.

Forms and Devices

The poem depends, for its power, on the connection Ferlinghetti makes between the people in Goya's sketches and those of twentieth century America. The allusion to art is not unusual for Ferlinghetti. A painter and art critic himself, he is influenced not only by great works of art but also by painters' techniques. Just as he calls up Goya's sketches through words, Ferlinghetti presents his poem, in part, as a picture. The page is a canvas, and his words and lines are placed for visual effect. The design on the page suggests an unexpected or brutal separation of parts that reinforces his theme. Goya's prints graphically show dismemberment; the poem envisions American culture as an isolating force. What is physical brutality in the Goya section becomes spiritual brutality in the section on America. Even Ferlinghetti's alliteration signals the difference: Goya's sketches link "babies and bayonets" and "cadavers and carnivorous cocks," while the section on America speaks of "bland billboards/ illustrating imbecile illusions" and "a concrete continent." The physical destruction gives way to a spiritual nothingness. Yet despite the move from blood to banality, the poem highlights the continuity between the Spanish and the American scenes through the lack of terminal punctuation; one flows into the other. America has discovered its own form of brutality.

Ferlinghetti repeats key images and grammatical structures from the Goya section of the poem in the America section in order to draw a parallel between the sufferers of early nineteenth century warring Spain and those of twentieth century America. In the Goya section, the sufferers "writhe upon the page"; in the second section, they are "ranged along the roads." First they are "under cement skies," then they are "on a concrete continent." The Spanish scenes include "slippery gibbets,/ cadavers and carnivorous cocks"; the American sufferers see "legionaires/ false windmills and demented roosters." A powerful image in the Goya sketches that Ferlinghetti alludes to is the predatory nature of grotesque birds as a symbol of the death and destruction of war. In the America section of the poem, however, the bird is not "carnivorous" but "demented." Instead of predatory birds, car "engines/ . . . devour America." A poet who enjoys puns and wordplay, Ferlinghetti suggests the irony of the word "freeway." Instead of "tumbrils" (carts carrying revolutionaries to the gallows), "painted cars" on "freeways fifty lanes wide" lead Americans to a barren existence. The poet indicts a society that foregrounds technology and privileges merchandising rather than people. In the second half of the poem, Ferlinghetti indicts the American way of life as being every bit as deadly as war.

Themes and Meanings

"In Goya's greatest scenes we seem to see" alludes to powerful sketches of predatory death in order to highlight the dangers of American society. The poem moves from recalling Goya's well-known and influential criticism of war to the poet's view of what is destroying American society. In linking the two, Ferlinghetti takes a risk. Will the reader accept the view that American life is as destructive as war? Is American society so predatory? The reader must decide whether Ferlinghetti has made his case. By beginning with such powerful images of suffering, the poet must, to be credible, establish the reality of the danger he sees in American society. Ferlinghetti seeks to convince the reader that internal destruction is taking place in America on the same scale as the overt destruction that Goya witnessed in Spain. The brutality of Goya's sketches illustrate a lack of humanity. Likewise, the American culture depicted in the poem suggests a lack of human warmth and contact. The people are far "from home," and they are amassed on "freeways fifty lanes wide." As Goya's sketches downplay any natural growth in the landscape, the Americans live "on a concrete continent." The suggestion is that America is being eaten away from the inside by a dearth of humanity. Materialism and mechanism have replaced human interaction. Ferlinghetti admits the America scene has "fewer tumbrils": The death and destruction are not graphic or immediate or physical. However, the poet claims Americans are being devoured just the same.

Goya's war sketches are all the more powerful because of the frankness about the horrors of war. Goya rejected the conventional view of his time; the sketches refuse to glorify the combatants or the cause but instead zoom in on the brutal acts of war—destruction, rape, death, dismemberment of corpses. The Goya section of the poem builds in intensity with the penultimate line asserting that the suffering is "so bloody real." Like Goya, the poet refuses to take the conventional view: He does not extol the wealth and freedom of America but focuses on the destruction. The climax in the second section depends not so much on building to intensity but on withholding, until the last word of the poem, the new landscape of suffering. It is not until the last word that Ferlinghetti tells his readers, predominantly Americans, that he is speaking of them as the new suffering humanity.

Marion Boyle Petrillo

IN JUST-

Author: E. E. Cummings (1894-1962)
Type of poem: Lyric
First published: 1920; collected in *Tulips and Chimneys*, 1923

The Poem

In only twenty-four lines, E. E. Cummings captures both the feeling and the meaning of spring. Only in spring, or "just" in spring, is the world a kind of wonderful mud bath for children. Spring rains make puddles in which children love to play. Spring is a carnival season—a time to celebrate nature—which accounts for the appearance of the "balloonman," who adds a festive air to the season.

The first stanza and the next line also suggest that adults spring to life "in just," or precisely in, spring. The balloonman may be little and lame, but he is whistling and apparently happy to be out and about. Cummings suggests the enthusiasm of children and the childlike enthusiasms of adults in his first use of the word "wee" in line 5. The word "wide" is expected after "far and," but Cummings changes this clichéd expression to convey the "wee" of the fun that spring represents.

In the second stanza, the childlike speaker of the poem revels in playmates and their games. Playing marbles and pretending to be pirates are examples of the energy and imagination that spring stimulates. The poem itself is a manifestation of vigor; it is at once a description, celebration, and evocation of what spring feels like.

Line 10 suggests that spring turns the world into a splendid playground. The balloonman enters the poem again—this time described as "queer" and "old" but still whistling, as if in spring he forgets his age and his difference from others. In spring, everyone shares the same feelings about being alive and enjoying it. Just as the boys play marbles and pirate games, the girls play hopscotch and jump-rope, and the poem—mimicking their animation—proclaims once again that it is spring.

The innocent games of the children are followed in line 20 and in the last stanza by the antics of the "goat-footed/ balloonMan," who is still whistling "far and wee." In this third appearance, he is no longer lame or old, but spry, having come back to life. The image of the goat suggests nimbleness—one thinks of goats threading their way along mountain passes and rocky cliffs. But goat is also a term that connotes a horny or lecherous man. In other words, in spring the lame old man is aroused sexually, and he recovers some of the same spirit and drive that the children channel into their games.

Forms and Devices

Cummings has been justly praised for his innovative use of typography. Beginning with the poem's title, "in Just-," which begins in the lower case and ends with a hyphen, the poet is evoking a fresh way of rendering the freshness of spring. The season is a part of the unending cycle of nature, and the poem's title is an expression of that ongoing cycle. Spring is both a season and an action (a noun and a verb), and to capitalize it—or to capitalize the first word of the title "in"—would be to make spring as a season and a state of mind conform to typography. Cummings takes the opposite approach, making typography conform to the feeling of being in the season of spring.

Similarly, by ending the title with a hyphen (a punctuation mark that usually connects two words) Cummings is emphasizing that spring is connected not to one word or idea but to many—to a sense of the wide world, of its possibilities. Spring makes people feel expansive and connected to each other and to the rest of the world, the poem implies. Finally, "Just" is capitalized because of the poem's insistence that it is "just" in spring that people feel so in touch with everything.

Note also that there are gaps or spaces between words in lines 2, 5, 13, and 21. These intervals between words are filled, so to speak, with the actions and feelings of the poem, with its springing words that imitate the jumping and playing of the children and the balloonman. The gaps also provide a kind of imaginative ground on which the balloonman is whistling and going about and of the children playing. Giving the words more room also makes the words on the page more prominent, so that the multiple value of each word is more easily recognizable. The spaces between the words make each word more important.

The excitement of spring is also conveyed in the way the poet runs words and names together ("eddieandbill") and in words that the poet coins such as "puddle-wonder-ful." Spring is the season of creation, so the inventiveness of the human imagination also springs to life.

The poem's form and meaning are built on subtle repetitions. The phrase "far and wee," for example, is spaced differently each time it appears (lines 5, 13, and 22-24). The variations suggest individuality. The "wee" which expresses balloonman's excitement is never quite the same; each time it is seen on the page and heard in the imagination a little differently. The horizontal placement of the phrase "far and wee" also changes to the vertical at the end of the poem, so that each word forms a column that is the embodiment of spring's vitality. Cummings was a painter as well as a poet, and the look of his poem is obviously as important to him as what the words say. Finally, notice that at line 21 balloonman changes to "balloonMan," emphasizing his sexuality and the idea that he has been aroused by spring.

Themes and Meanings

A nature poet, Cummings wrote poems that celebrate nature as a cycle of experience. The changes of the seasons provoke changes in human moods. In this poem, spring is presented as a miraculous event. An old, lame balloonman comes to life, whistling and nimbly moving about. It is as if he has discovered his second childhood. But spring also makes him more fully a man—as the last reference to him suggests.

Balloons are associated with parties, carnivals, birthdays, and other special events. Balloons are attractive playthings because they float through the air so effortlessly. They express the human desire to fly, and they lift the spirits. They soar through space just as human feelings do in this poem. That a lame, queer old man should be associated with balloons suggests how powerful the need to play and to imagine is for everyone—not just for the children who play games and splash in mud puddles. Whatever is old, or lame, or queer about human beings is cured "in Just-" spring.

The images of nature in the poem—mud and water—suggest the basic elements of life. Without water, life perishes. Moreover, water mixed with earth—mud—becomes a human construction. It is not only a material children play with but also the stuff from which human beings construct their games and build life for themselves. With the word "mud-luscious" the poet mimics the inventiveness of human beings playing in mud. "Luscious" suggests the sensuality of the mud. Children like it because it can be shaped to their desires, and they enjoy the touch and the feel of it. But so do adult sculptors and artists, who use clay or mud for the material of art. In some creation myths, human beings are made out of mud—from the stuff of the earth and of spring. Given the way Cummings coins words, alters punctuation, and invents his own typography, it would seem that the poem is not only about spring but also about creativity itself and how it springs from the earth.

Line by line, "in Just-" is a feast for the eye and the imagination. Read too quickly, the poem seems simplistic, repeating the same message over and over. But if the poem's rhythm is respected, it becomes a complex of intellect and emotion. The first line, for example, seems to gird itself to spring in the poem's third word—spring. The poem jumps just like "bettyandisbel" do in their games of hopscotch and jump-rope. These games arise out of spring, the poem implies, just as the poem's unique use of vocabulary and typography does.

The second part of the second line, "when the world is mud-," sets up the rest of the poem, which suggests what happens when the world turns to mud in spring. The hyphen after mud also connects the physical element to the human imagination, which comes up with the word luscious in the next line. Indeed, much of the poem moves from the physical world to the human imagination, making the poem and what it describes part of an indivisible whole.

Carl Rollyson

IN MEMORY OF MAJOR ROBERT GREGORY

Author: William Butler Yeats (1865-1939)
Type of poem: Elegy
First published: 1918, as "In Memory of Robert Gregory"; collected as "In Memory of Major Robert Gregory" in *The Wild Swans at Coole*, 1919

The Poem

"In Memory of Major Robert Gregory" is William Butler Yeats's elegy to Robert Gregory, an Irish airman who died in battle during World War I. Written in the first person, it is a poem of twelve stanzas, in octets, which is primarily composed in iambic pentameter but which also includes iambic tetrameter. Gregory was the only son of Lady Augusta Gregory, Yeats's close colleague for two decades. They worked together as pivotal figures in the Irish Literary Revival and were among the founders of Dublin's Abbey Theatre. Over the years, Yeats had relied upon Lady Gregory for financial, intellectual, and emotional support. Coole Park, her country estate in the west of Ireland, had been a second home to Yeats.

Robert Gregory's death in January, 1918, occurred on the eve of the move of Yeats and his wife into their new home, Thoor Ballylee, an old Norman tower not far from the Gregory estate. The death of "my dear friend's dear son" leads the author to reflect upon friends from his past, who, because they are dead, cannot dine and talk together before going up the tower stairs to bed.

The first dead friend he mentions is Lionel Johnson, whom Yeats had known from his earliest days as a writer and who had come to love "learning better than mankind." Another absentee is John Synge, among the greatest of the Irish playwrights; his *Playboy of the Western World* had inflamed literary Dublin when first performed at the Abbey Theatre in 1907. Rather than catering to a romanticized or politically acceptable subject, Synge had chosen "the living world for text," modeling *Playboy of the Western World* from the actual lives of peasants in Ireland's western islands. George Pollexfen, Yeats's uncle and a tie to his own Protestant Irish past, is the third who "cannot sup with us." A horseman when young, Pollexfen had later "grown sluggish and contemplative."

Johnson, Synge, and Pollexfen were significant figures in Yeats's life, but all had been dead for many years, and their "breathless faces seem to look/ Out of some old picture-book." Gregory's death, however, was different, and, coming so suddenly, it was impossible to believe that he "Could share in that discourtesy of death." Gregory would have been the "heartiest welcomer" of Yeats and his wife to their new home because, better than the rest, he knew the tower and its stream, the bridge, the broken trees, the drinking cattle, and the water-hen.

In a reference to the sixteenth century Renaissance figure Philip Sidney, a poet who also died in war and who was elegized by Edmund Spenser, Yeats's Gregory personi-fied the Renaissance man. Like Pollexfen, Gregory, too, was an athletic horseman. He was also a scholar and, of course, a soldier; in the poem, however, he is mainly the artist—a painter and a craftsman—who died in his youthful prime, an event that Yeats indicates should have been no surprise when he asks, "What made us dream that he could comb grey hair?" The poem closes with Yeats reflecting that he had intended to describe some of their dreams and accomplishments, but, in the end, he cannot do so, for Gregory's death has stilled the poet's voice.

Forms and Devices

"In Memory of Major Robert Gregory" has frequently been praised as being among Yeats's greatest poems; some critics claim that it is the first of his poems that exhibits the full range of his poetic voice, a voice that later received the Nobel Prize in Literature. Although the poem's meter varies slightly, the rhyme scheme is regular, with an *ababcddc* pattern throughout. On one level, the poem exhibits a straightforward literalness grounded in the actual lands of western Ireland. When the poet describes Thoor Ballylee, "The tower set on the stream's edge" with its "narrow winding stair" and the "old storm-broken trees/ That cast their shadows upon road and bridge," it is a faithful rendering of the landscape. Gregory was a physical product of those Irish counties, "born/ To cold Clare rock and Galway rock and thorn."

In opposition to the poem's solid physicality, however, is the element of dream, of melancholy memory that infuses the poem and raises it beyond mere description. The opening stanza describes the poet reflecting on the past, remembering those gone— both long gone and recently gone—who cannot join him in the tower for talk and drink: "All, all are in my thoughts to-night being dead." Reflecting on Gregory's promise as an artist, the poet states that "We dreamed that a great painter had been born." Continuing with these dreamlike qualities, Gregory's hair is used in a synecdoche to represent the impossibility of his ever attaining a ripe old age when Yeats asks, "What made us dream that he could comb grey hair?"

In one of the central stanzas of the poem, Yeats divides humankind into two categories: Some plod along over the many years, doing what they must do, while others make their contributions and quickly pass on. In a metaphor, he compares those who "burn damp faggots" to others, such as Gregory, who died in Italian skies at thirty-seven and who "may consume/ The entire combustible world . . ./ As though dried straw, and if we turn about/ The bare chimney is gone black out/ Because the work had finished in that flare." The intensity of their lives is both the compensation for and the cause of its brevity.

Themes and Meanings

As in so much of Yeats's work, one of the themes of "In Memory of Major Robert Gregory" is Yeats himself, the self-reflective artist and the Irishman. The tensions between Yeats (a Protestant Irishman) and the Catholic majority, and between his art and that of those who merely pandered to sentimental and patriotic feelings, existed throughout Yeats's career. The tower of Thoor Ballylee, where he lived beginning in 1918, became a symbol for the artist's isolation and for what might be called high culture in many of his later poems. However, if the tower is the symbol of the artist and his retreat from the mundane world in pursuit of his craft, what does it mean to be an artist in the complete sense, to "Climb up the narrow winding stair"?

His choice of absent associates is revealing. All four—Johnson, Synge, Pollexfen, and Gregory—had been important in his life, but in the poem they also signify something other than their human realities. Johnson, an influence upon Yeats in the 1890's, symbolizes the writer who renounces the real world for what Yeats called "the twilight world," seeking the isolation supposedly required by the true artist. Synge, on the other hand, in his portrayal of the Aran islanders in *The Playboy of the Western World*, reached out and "chose the living world for text// . . . a race/ Passionate and simple like his heart." Yeats's uncle Pollexfen was not primarily a writer, but, in representing the Yeats and Pollexfen families, he symbolizes the passing Protestant Ascendancy which, "Having grown sluggish and contemplative," is giving way to the Catholic majority.

Gregory's portrayal in the elegy is something more and something less than the historical Gregory: He becomes a Platonic figure who reconciles, in the poem, the incomplete personages of Johnson, Synge, and Pollexfen. Gregory, Yeats's Renaissance man, is "Our Sidney," another Philip Sidney, the statesman-diplomat, author of the epic prose romance *Arcadia* (c.1580) and a collection of love sonnets, *Astrophel and Stella* (1591), who also died in his thirties of a fatal battle wound. However, while Gregory exhibited all the qualities of "Soldier, scholar, horseman," in the poet's thoughts it is Gregory as the artist who is worthy of being memorialized, though he died as a soldier and a man of action.

The younger Yeats had been active in radical political movements in Ireland, but over time he had distanced himself from those involvements, coming to defend the contributions that the Protestant Ascendancy were making to Ireland's lasting culture. Yeats was not a soldier, and his life was not "finished in that flare" as was Gregory's. Perhaps this was a cause for regret by Yeats when he wrote his elegy to Gregory, given the bloody sacrifices so many (such as Gregory in World War I and the Irish rebels in the Easter Rising of 1916) had made.

The concluding stanza presents a somber world, "seeing how bitter is that wind/ That shakes the shutter." In nostalgic loss, the poet looks back again to comment on his dead friends and their deeds. However, there is nothing he can say, for "that late death took all my heart for speech." The historical Major Robert Gregory was, perhaps, less of a Renaissance man than the one portrayed in Yeats's eloquent elegy, but the poem is also an elegy to the poet himself, alive but now alone in his tower in the emptier present, "For all that come into my mind are dead."

Eugene Larson

IN MOURNING WISE SINCE DAILY I INCREASE

Author: Sir Thomas Wyatt (1503-1542)
Type of poem: Ballad
First published: 1816, in *The Works of Henry Howard, Earl of Surrey, and of Sir Thomas Wyatt the Elder* (vol. 2)

The Poem

"In mourning wise since daily I increase" is a ballad composed of eight stanzas, with each stanza consisting of two quatrains of generally regular iambic pentameter. Based on a historical incident at the court of the English monarch King Henry VIII, the poem is Sir Thomas Wyatt's meditation on the execution of five men of the court for their alleged adultery with Queen Anne Boleyn.

According to Kenneth Muir's *Sir Thomas Wyatt, Life and Letters* (1963), the five men addressed in the poem were executed on May 17, 1536, for improper sexual relations with Queen Anne. They were Lord Rochford, the queen's brother, who was charged with incest; Sir Henry Norris, Sir Francis Weston, and Sir William Bereton, three court officials charged with adultery with the queen; and Mark Smeaton, a court musician who appears to have confessed under torture and who may have implicated the four others.

The poem is divided into three sections: an opening of two stanzas that establishes the specific situation that has saddened the poet; a central portion of five stanzas in which the executed individuals are directly addressed by the poet, who comments on their virtues and weaknesses; and a concluding single stanza that again returns the poem to consider the general implications of this specific tragedy. Each of the people the poet addresses is given some touch of individuality, which, generally, is the immediate reason to mourn his loss. Rochford had great wit, Norris would be missed by his friends at court, Weston was unmatched "in active things," and Bereton, of whom the poet knows the least, at least had a good reputation. Only Smeaton seems to have been without individual virtue, but he is to be pitied, for he has climbed above his station and "A rotten twig upon so high a tree/ Hath slipped [his] hold."

At the time of the executions, Wyatt was himself imprisoned in the Tower of London, perhaps under suspicion of adultery with the queen but more likely as possibly having knowledge of the alleged crimes. It is possible that while in the tower, Wyatt witnessed the deaths of the five men and, on May 19, the execution of Anne herself. It is certain that the impact of the events is registered in his poem. At the same time, however, while this is a poem triggered by a specific historical event, it is also a meditation on the sense of loss and sadness caused by any human death.

Forms and Devices

The poetic form for "In mourning wise" is that of the ballad, which usually tells a story but, in this case, presents a situation and comments upon it. The traditional ballad is typically presented in a four-line stanza, rhyming *abab*. Wyatt combines two of these stanzas into a single eight-line stanza. The ballad's relatively casual, informal style, which allows the poet to address both the participants in the poem and the reader directly, is especially suitable for the meaning and purpose of "In mourning wise."

The underlying logical scheme for "In mourning wise" is that of classical rhetoric. Specifically, Wyatt has taken the rhetorical tradition of addressing absent individuals as if they were actually present. In this case, these individuals are the reader, to whom Wyatt speaks in the opening and closing of the poem, and the guilty dead, each of whom he addresses in turn. This sort of formal patterning was a tradition from the classical world, and educated courtiers such as Wyatt and his readers would have been intimately familiar with it. It permits him to go from a specific personal and historic situation (the execution of five men while he himself was imprisoned in the Tower of London) to a larger, more embracing consideration: how the death of any human being deprives humankind of their unique talents and personalities and so is a cause for sorrow.

Over this logical framework, the poet has fashioned a linguistic surface to express both his meanings and his feelings. Wyatt, who was known among his contemporaries for improving and regularizing the form of English verse, uses a consistent structure for his poem, with the regularity of the rhyme scheme (*ababcdcd*) matched by the rhythmic pattern of the iambic pentameter lines. Wyatt uses this regularity both to link his work together and as a vehicle to present his narration and description: This is who these men were, and this is why the poet is sad they are gone. Moving beyond that, Wyatt's steady, methodical form can be seen as imposing a sense of inevitability about the events described in the poem.

The poem is further knit together by its use of repetition, especially the phrase "dead and gone," which ends the last line of each stanza except the second, where it is only slightly varied as "bewail the death of some be gone." Since the poem is about a group of executed men, the phrase is tellingly apt, and its repetition should heighten the reader's sense of a series of executions happening one after the other and leaving each victim, in turn, inexorably "dead and gone." By the eighth and final stanza, the hammer strokes of the three short words have impressed more than their literal meaning on the reader. In addition to the repeated use of the phrase, its final word, "gone," is invariably linked by rhyme with either "moan" or "bemoan," thus driving home the mournful, elegiac tone of the work. No matter how any stanza opens, its end always draws the reader back to a sense of sadness and loss because of the inescapable fact of death. Such simplicity and repetition are important sources of the poem's powerful impact on the attentive reader.

Themes and Meanings

The underlying theme of "In mourning wise" is a sense of loss in the face of the death of human beings. Such death may be through official execution, as in the case of the characters in this poem, but, ultimately, all human death is a cause for solemn reflection. Rochford and the others have been executed, Wyatt reflects, but the death they endure through judicial violence is the fate that all human beings inevitably experience as part of the course of nature. Death is death, the poem implies, and while these men have been justly punished for their crimes, still their deaths and the loss that they bring are an occasion for sorrow.

A second, interlocking theme is that the deaths of Rochford and the others were unnecessary, since they were caused by bad judgment on the part of the condemned or perhaps, the poem suggests, through the conspiracies of the Tudor court. In either event, death has come sooner than it would normally. The underlying theme of the poem refers to the wheel of fortune, a commonplace of English Renaissance literature that carries individuals into prominence, fame, and power only to cast them down into obscurity, shame, and impotence. Such has been the fate of the characters in Wyatt's poem and such, the poet well knows from personal experience, could be the fate of any attendant of the Tudor dynasty. The ancient biblical adage "trust not in princes" was never more true than at the court of Henry VIII.

Throughout the poem, Wyatt assumes the role of speaker, first to the reader (or perhaps to himself) and then to each of the condemned men in turn. In doing this, he can examine the impact of each man's particular death upon himself. Some he knows well; others, notably Bereton, he knows less well. Still, the sense of loss seems as keen for the unfamiliar as for the well known. This theme is reinforced by the way that the poem presents it to the reader. Having first announced that he has grown deeper (and perhaps more knowing, given the first line's underlying play on words) in mourning, Wyatt next examines the cause of his sorrow by addressing each of the executed men and praising them for some virtue or gift that has been undone and lost by their crime. He is careful to make no excuses for them. Smeaton, the court musician and commoner who dared sleep with a queen, is addressed with brutal directness: "they death thou hast deserved best." Yet even so, the poet will "moan thee with the rest" because Smeaton too is dead and gone. Indeed, as the final stanza makes clear, it is the loss by death of any individual, just as much as the specific situation of these executions of a few members of court, that evokes the pity and sorrow of the poet and his poem: "Leave sobs therefore, and every Christian heart/ Pray for the souls of those be dead and gone."

Michael Witkoski

IN THE CREVICE OF TIME

Author: Josephine Jacobsen (1908-   )
Type of poem: Lyric
First published: 1968; collected in *The Shade-Seller: New and Selected Poems*, 1974

The Poem

"In the Crevice of Time" is a brief meditative lyric consisting of four stanzas of six lines each. The first stanza makes clear the subject of the poem: poet Josephine Jacobsen's reaction to cave paintings in Spain. Unlike many poems that respond to or are influenced by works of art, this poem provides very little sense of what the cave painting looks like. The first three lines identify an ambiguous prey—"The bison, or tiger, or whatever beast"—and "the twiggy hunter/ with legs and spear." The rest of the poem speculates on the artist who created the painting that has endured so long, preserved "in the crevice of time."

The artist is introduced in the last line of the first stanza as "the hunter-priest" since, in an era so primitive, artistry could hardly have been his main occupation. The second stanza shows that the poet imagines this cave painter as the original artist, the first (or one of the first) to act on an impulse to represent reality. She imagines him struck, in the act of hunting, by the spatial arrangement of animals and hunters; the hunter becomes an observer and art is born as "an offering strange as some new kind of death." The puzzling comparison of art to death grows clearer in the third stanza, where the poet relates the beginning of cave painting to the beginning of the practice of burial—both behaviors said to distinguish humans from their more animalistic ancestors. The death that is related to art, then, is not simply the ending of life but "the knowledge of death." With that knowledge comes a different awareness of time and the beginnings of a new emotion: grief. The poet argues, by imaginative extrapolation, that art, like funeral customs, is a way of preserving human experience against the forces of time and mortality that threaten to turn everything to dust.

The last stanza imagines the cave painter in the act of creation, "scraping the wall." However, the great temporal distance has been bridged: The early human is a "confrère" or brother, and, most importantly, "he is close." The final lines of the poem conclude the meditation on the relationship of funeral customs and art by asserting their common purpose as acts of faith; art is celebrated as a force that can cross "the crevice of time," even providing a bridge between the contemporary and the prehistoric.

Forms and Devices

This poem reads prosaically at first. That is, the diction is simple and speechlike, and, in the first two stanzas, most of the lines are enjambed, which tends to disguise the metrical pattern and rhyme. However, like most modern rhymed poetry, a careful structure undergirds the graceful surface of the poem. The rhyme scheme seems more pronounced in the third stanza, with its end-stopped lines and one extra rhyme. The first and last lines of each stanza rhyme, as do the second and fourth. More importantly, the first/last rhyming words outline significant contrasts that reveal some of the poem's meaning: "beast" and "priest"; "breath" and "death"; "grave" and "gave"; and "wall" and "burial." The contrast between "beast" and "priest" highlights the contrast between primitive and civilized organizations of the human species. "Breath" and "death" suggest the awareness of mortality that shapes human consciousness. "Grave" and "gave" remind the reader that the burial customs of prehistoric people ironically give the contemporary world information about how they lived. The "wall" that is the prehistoric canvas is also part of a tomb or "burial."

Most of the lines in the poem are four-stress lines with ten or eleven syllables, indicating a mix of iambic and anapestic feet. In stanzas 1, 2, and 4, the fifth line is a shorter, three-stress line. The point is that the poem, while not adhering to a rigorously strict metrical pattern, is carved out in roughly regular units of four-stress lines—a loose but recognizable meter. The figurative language stands out against the speech-like or ordinary diction, as in the synecdoches "the million rains of summer" and "the mean mists of winter," both signifying the passing of time. "Blood" and "breath" in line 7 also create a synecdoche for the killing of the hunt. When that same device is carried over into the next line—referring to the hunted animals as "shank," "horn," or "hide"—the figurative language becomes literal. That is, the reader knows that the slain prey will be converted into its parts and used by the hunters as food, tools, and clothing. However, the hunter-priest-cum-artist no longer perceives the prey in that way but as an artistic whole—"the terrible functionless whole." The term "functionless," a surprisingly abstract word in the midst of a concrete stanza, reminds the reader that art is often viewed (and even celebrated) as useless, as not having a practical or survival-oriented function.

The third stanza presents two vivid personifications: "time the wicked thief" and "the prompt monster of foreseeable grief." The first is more familiar, even close to clichéd in its association of time with theft of life and memory. The incarnation of grief as a monster is more original, and the words "prompt" and "foreseeable" stress the immediacy of the mental transformation and its consequences in the moment in which art and awareness of mortality are born as twins.

Alliteration, assonance, and word repetition provide further shape to the poem. The second line packs in three versions of "hunt"; the next line alliterates "spear," "still," and "Spain." The second half of the first stanza repeats *m* sounds prominently and sharpens them with the short *i* assonance of "mists" and "winter." Similar examples appear throughout the poem and testify to how carefully Jacobsen chooses her words. The language is chiseled like the lines of an ancient sculpture. In the third stanza, for example, "grave" echoes "gross," while "gesture" is repeated; "neither," "nor," "news," "no," "need," and "knowledge" alliterate in the space of three lines; and assonance is accented in adjacent words (the short *o* in "prompt monster" and the long *e* in "foreseeable grief").

Themes and Meanings

The encounter with a prehistoric cave painting raises questions in the poet's mind. What inspired the first efforts to record experience in human-created, artificial forms? How did the creation of art change the animal that created it? In using poetry to answer these questions, the writer is responding to one art form with another. Ancient paintings offer a way for the poet to speak about poetry. The painter's tools are visual images—line and shape and color—while the poet's tools are words.

Two words that strain with double meanings help illuminate the poet's purposes. In the last stanza, she remarks that the prehistoric artist is "close." The primary meaning here is "near": Paradoxically, the poet-observer feels a kinship with the long-deceased human artist who painted the cave. However, "close" also suggests "shut" or even "dark and stuffy," secondary meanings that remind the reader that a cave is shut off from outside reality and protected from the erosion of the centuries. In the first stanza, the poet describes the Spanish caves as "still." The primary meaning is "quiet and unmoving," but the meaning of "remaining" or "yet" haunts the poem, since part of the point is that the paintings are "still" there. This double meaning of "still" harks back to the English Romantic poet John Keats, who described an ancient vase as a "still unravished bride of quietness" in "Ode on a Grecian Urn." The line identifies the artifact not only as a bride as yet unravished but also as an unmoving and unchanging work of art that endures the ages. It is hard for a modern poet to reflect on the endurance of a work of art across the ages without evoking Keats's famous poem. Keats, too, saw the endurance of the ancient artifact as a triumph against mortality and as an emblem for his own poetry. Where Jacobsen's poem differs is in reaching back to primitive humankind rather than the highly refined civilization of the Greeks. Keats evokes a distant kinship with the artists and people of ancient Greece. Jacobsen, in reaching further to the cave paintings, is able to raise questions about the very origins of art.

Answering those questions, or at least providing an imaginative hypothesis in response to them, Jacobsen sees the artistic impulse as a desire to communicate beyond the grave. The work of art becomes a monument, something that outlives the artist and thus reflects a conscious awareness of mortality. She suggests that such an awareness of death is cause for celebration, an artistic force that gives birth to history out of the prehistoric. In this grand context, the poet's own work has a place, her own equivalent of the stick figures and hunted bison—the record of feelings, thoughts, and images of a living creature that knows it is going to die and leaves a poem behind.

Christopher Ames

INCANTATA

Author: Paul Muldoon (1951-   )
Type of poem: Elegy
First published: 1994, in *The Annals of Chile*

The Poem

"Incantata," written in memory of the artist Mary Farl Powers, is a nearly perfect synthesis of formal construction and emotional content. Spoken directly to the poet's former lover, the poem is both elegy and celebration. Each of the forty-five eight-line stanzas has the rhyme scheme *aabbcddc*, called a "stadium stanza"—a form invented by Abraham Cowley for elegiac purposes and later adopted by William Butler Yeats. Because of its length (360 lines), "Incantata" can sustain some variation; the lines range from four to seventeen syllables, and there is no regular underlying rhythm.

The first twenty-two stanzas tell the story of the accidental fortunes of a friendship, the shared history, the ways one life enriches another and the ways in which they differ. The poet begins thinking of his dead friend when he is cutting into a potato to make an Incan glyph in the shape of a mouth, and this, in turn, reminds him of the first time he saw her works of art. The mouth itself is significant because the poet is attempting to speak across the boundary of death. The title suggests that this is a kind of incantation, as though he could call her back through verbal ritual. It also suggests a "non-song" (in-cantata), and this association, too, is appropriate, since he cannot seem to find the proper words to express his feelings.

As the poet rushes through specific memories of what appears to have been a stimulating and challenging relationship, he is forced to face again the fact that Mary Powers had refused an operation for her breast cancer, believing that everything in life is predetermined, including her own death. There are moments of humor and moments of poignant loss, the most moving of which is a metaphorical sense that something good must be built from such pain, as when a bird plucks a straw to build a nest in the aftermath of a battle.

The central stanza serves as a hinge; poet and poem alike balk at the visual artist's fierce determination to die because her death is part of the natural "order." It ends in a breakdown of speech itself: "with its '*quaquaqua*', with its 'Quoiquoiquoiquoiquoiquoiquoiquioq'." The nonsensical quotations are direct references to the plays of Samuel Beckett, several of whose characters are mentioned throughout the poem.

The last half of the poem transforms grief into celebration—of life, art, history, and especially the power of friendship to transcend death. In Powers' own theological terms, memory is all that is left of the friendship. The last twenty-two stanzas pick up the idea of memory itself, creating one long list of their shared experiences—all that is left. "That's all that's left of the voice of Enrico Caruso" and "of Sunday afternoons in the Botanic Gardens" and of the sight of a particular road between Leiden and The Hague, and of particular pieces of music and specific places and people, and so on.

The incantatory list accelerates, extending for pages as the memories flood over the poet, culminating with, if not an acceptance of his friend's "fate," an imaginative union of the life and the art.

Forms and Devices

Because "Incantata" employs a regular rhyme scheme, it demonstrates how what is sometimes called the "pressure of form" can help give shape to its subject matter. Muldoon is a master of "slant rhyme" or "half-rhyme," so the sounds are often subtle, even clever. Muldoon's poems are characteristically clever—playing on words, making puns, referring to the works of other writers and even to his own earlier poems. He often rhymes one language with another. This approach is somewhat true of "Incantata," but the tendency to play with words (and with the facts) is somewhat muted because of the passionate and autobiographical nature of his material. The poem was written in a rush of emotion over a period of five days, Muldoon has said, and the feelings are all the more compressed and shaped by the use of the regular, rhymed stanzas.

In the first half of the poem, the rhymes are noticeable but do not dominate; the intimate voice of the writer is so urgent that the reader is more involved in the unfolding narrative of Mary Powers' death. In the second half, however, the reader becomes more and more aware of rhyme and how Muldoon is orchestrating his material. The mixture of philosophy, theology, comedy, literary allusion, pop culture, history, and personal memory creates a collage of unrelated images, thereby making the reader doubly conscious of the way the poet is choosing his words. Sometimes the sounds are compressed:

> of the early-ripening jardonelle, the tumorous jardon,
> > the jargon
> of jays, the jars
> of tomato relish and the jars
> of Victoria plums . . .

Sometimes they are deceptive:

> Of the great big dishes of chicken lo mein and beef chow mein,
> of what's mine is yours and what's yours mine,
> of the oxlips and cowslips
> on the banks of the Liffey at Leixlip
> where the salmon breaks through the either/or neither/nor
> > nether
> reaches despite the temple-veil
> of itself being rent and the penny left out overnight on the rail
> is a sheet of copper when the mail-train has passed over.

The slant rhymes (mein/mine, cowslips/Leixlip, nether/over, and veil/rail) are so surprising that the reader must pause to make sense of it all. Even the clichés are given new contexts: the transformation of the sharing of Chinese food into "what's mine is yours" is comic; the salmon could be expected to break through anything but the "nether reaches"; the penny is returned to its original state by the train. The result is a melding of the literal and the figurative as well as of the private and the actively communal.

The use of private material is also characteristic of Muldoon. Some of his material is merely unfamiliar—foreign words, Irish history, references to specific works of art—but remains in the public domain. Some is intensely private, and Muldoon is willing to keep things secret, hardly minding if his audience does not understand many of his references. Because the poem has many of the "overheard" qualities of a lyric, the reader eavesdrops on a very personal grief—with all the specifics of individual loss. And because the poem consistently employs the device of direct address, referring to Mary as "you" throughout, the poet can be confidential without revealing the private references. One could argue that the poem's stance toward the reader is one of profound indifference. Still, in *Paul Muldoon* (1996), the critic Tim Kendall has suggested that, through the use of this device, "even though the particular significance of these references is never explained, 'Incantata' does convey a shared intimacy which incorporates the reader."

Themes and Meanings

To employ a musical metaphor, "Incantata" is the concerto for which Muldoon had been practicing the scales of form. The poet's considerable technical skill keeps the poem afloat as it makes a space for the grief it embodies. The question that emerges in "Incantata" is what to make of an individual life. If the poet can begin to make sense of the death of his friend, he may be able to come to terms with her philosophy of life. The tension in the poem is enhanced by its form—by the quirky rhymes and the way it seems to slip out from under its own overarching questions—but its source is philosophical, maybe even theological. Mary's philosophy is described as Thomism—that "the things of this world sing out in a great oratorio"—but a Thomism "tempered by" Jean-Paul Sartre and Samuel Beckett. So even as Muldoon tries to honor her sense that death is preordained, he is angry at it (and her?), saddened by loss, and frustrated by his failure to find a meaning in the void.

The result is a tacit resistance; even as Muldoon pays lip service to Mary Powers' assertions that nothing is random, he provides a seemingly random set of memories. In the first half, he announces his desire to "body out your disembodied *vox/ clamantis in deserto*," to let his potato-mouth speak "unencumbered." In the second half, he abandons the potato-mouth (reduced to "quaquaqua") in favor of his own embodied voice. In doing so, he illuminates Powers' life in rich detail.

The final three stanzas are not end-stopped, but spill into each other in a frenzy, a furious desire to pull her back from her beliefs, to find buried in the Irish language and folklore the one herb that would cure her, to speak across the barrier of death and have her respond. Because these stanzas are syntactically complex, framed in the negative, the final image is actually positive; the reader watches Powers reach out her ink-stained hands to take Muldoon's "hands stained with ink." The power of the written word has transcended death, however briefly. Finally, "Incantata" is life-affirming. It makes of personal grief an "oratorio."

Judith Kitchen

INNOCENCE

Author: Thomas Traherne (c. 1637-1674)
Type of poem: Lyric
First published: 1903, in *The Poetical Works of Thomas Traherne*

The Poem

"Innocence" is a medium-length poem with sixty lines divided into five parts, each containing three rhyming four-line stanzas (quatrains). It follows an intricate metrical pattern and rhyme scheme. The first three lines of the beginning stanza of each part are in iambic pentameter, while the shorter fourth line is in iambic tetrameter. These first stanzas rhyme *aabb*. The second stanzas in each of the five parts of the poem are entirely in iambic tetrameter and rhyme *abab* (words such as "love" and "remove," which occur in the second stanza of part 2, were pronounced so that they rhymed in the seventeenth century). The first, third, and fourth lines of the third stanzas of each part of "Innocence" are in iambic tetrameter, with the second lines being in iambic trimeter. They also rhyme *abab*.

"Innocence" is the fourth poem in a sequence of thirty-seven, known as the Dobell poems in honor of the man who first published the manuscript containing them. In the preceding three poems, Traherne describes how new and marvelous everything seemed in infancy and childhood, in the Edenlike world that God had prepared for him. In "Innocence" he elaborates upon what most thrilled him as a child—as he states in part 1, that "I felt no Stain, nor Spot of Sin." The title thus refers to the state of innocence that the speaker enjoyed then and to which he desires to return now as an adult. Speaking from the authority of personal experience, the poet expresses wonder at the completely natural and spontaneous state of joy he experienced in his childhood. All he can remember of that blessed state is its sweet simplicity and light, " A Joyfull Sence and Puritie."

In part 2 Traherne goes on to explain that even though he was only a child, he recognized that this pure joy originated within himself, not outside from material things. His inner joy was so complete and full that he was able to appreciate the objects that surrounded him entirely in themselves without becoming dependent upon them for his happiness: "that which takes [Objects] from the Ey/ Of others, offerd them to me." To him alone they seemed perpetually fresh and new.

In part 3 Traherne adds a moral dimension to this experience. He asserts that it was characterized by an immunity to polluting influences such as greed, anger, and pride: "No Fraud nor Anger in me movd/ No Malice Jealousie or Spite;/ All that I saw I truly lovd./ Contentment only and Delight." His sense of his own natural goodness and the delight it engendered inspires him to "daily Kneel" for a return to that blessed state of life.

He then declares, in part 4, that whether his powerful childhood experience was the product of pure nature uncorrupted by human "Custom," or a miracle whereby God removed the stain of original sin from his soul, or the fortuitous experience of one shining day, its beauty and meaning still thrill him. He concludes, in part 5, that his innocence was akin to Adam's experience in Eden before the Fall. He envisions his childhood self, in fact, as "A little Adam in a Sphere/ of Joys!" This innocence is, he exclaims, a foretaste of heaven. It is important to note, however, that this Edenic state, which is "beyond all Bound and Price," is characterized by both a self-sufficient inner happiness and by sensory delights. Traherne's paradise does not deny the senses but rather encompasses both the inner and outer faculties.

That Traherne was orphaned at an early age adds poignancy to the poem. "Innocence," however, does not sentimentalize childhood as some fleetingly charming state of life. It rather argues that the same pure inner awareness which sparkles in childhood is available to adults as well. All in all, the poem serves as a compelling illustration of Christ's teaching that "Whosoever shall not receive the kingdom of God as a little child shall in no wise enter therein" (Luke 18:17).

Forms and Devices

Traherne is one of the so-called Metaphysical poets, a loose grouping of seventeenth century poets who imitated the dazzling poetic innovations of John Donne. Donne's poetry, a poetry of aspiration, was noted for its exuberant rhythms, striking verbal displays, surprising imagery, and artistic intelligence. For Donne, a poem was "a naked thinking heart"—it was an expression of an intense fusion of thought and feeling. Traherne's poem exhibits the energy and flair of Metaphysical poetry generally. It makes a convincing presentation, through universal light/dark metaphors, penetrating paradoxes, and bold imagery, of a more holistic state of being.

Light imagery is present in parts 1, 4, and 5 and is associated with the felicitous state of childhood innocence. Light is both the literal light that shone in Eden and the symbolic light of pure goodness, in contrast to the darkness of guilt and evil. Paradoxically, this benign light filled even the night time, for Traherne says that "the very Night to me was bright." It is as if his mind was fully enlivened by blissful awareness even when sleeping. Perhaps the most stunning image in the poem is that of the boy in the bubble, the "Adam in a Sphere/ Of Joys." The picture of a little Adam floating joyously in a soap-bubble conveys memorably the sense of wonder and freedom that epitomize Traherne's conception of childhood.

An underlying paradox in the poem is parallel with an idea expressed by a later poet, William Wordsworth, namely that "The Child is father of the Man." The belief that childhood is spiritually superior to adulthood is recurrent in Traherne's poetry and prose. That Traherne, an Anglican clergyman (he was the private chaplain to the Lord High Keeper of the Royal Seal, Sir Orlando Bridgeman), yearns with all his heart to "becom a Child again" may sound at first illogical, but Traherne makes a convincing imaginative case for the sublimity of childhood innocence.

One of Traherne's most characteristic techniques, the cataloging device, is apparent in part 3. Here he enumerates the bad inclinations that he did not feel as a child— avarice, pride, lust, strife, fraud, anger, malice, jealousy, and spite. Traherne's catalog suggests an encyclopedic approach to experience, not unlike that of a scientist

drawing up a comprehensive list of observed phenomena. Traherne was knowledgeable about the science of his day and was particularly interested in the writings of
Francis Bacon, the leading English empiricist of the early seventeenth century. His
frequent use in his poetry and prose of such catalogs reflects Bacon's influence.

Traherne's signature exclamation points are not extravagantly sprinkled throughout
this poem; rather, they appear only twice in part 3 and once in part 5. In the hands of
a lesser poet, they could come across as gimmicky overdramatization, but Traherne's
sparing and appropriate use of them at just the right moments in "Innocence"—when
he is full of the memory of the original joy of his childhood and when he concludes
that this innocence was an "Antepast" (or foretaste) of the heaven to come—lends an
infectious quality to the poem.

Themes and Meanings

The poem argues that the innocence which typifies childhood is an actual state of
pure awareness that is recoverable in adulthood. It is, according to Traherne, the basis
of both a full inner spiritual life and of a glorious and free enjoyment of the world.
The mind in this state of felicity is fully awake, self-sufficient, and naturally tending
to good. It is, in short, a state of awareness having primordial Edenic overtones.

In addition to the felicity theme, the concept known as the "pre-existence doctrine"
is strongly implied by Traherne's poem. This idea, that children may recall their
previous unclouded existence in heaven, also occurs in "The Retreate," a poem by
another Metaphysical poet, Henry Vaughan. Vaughan, interestingly, was initially
thought to be the author of the first anonymous Traherne poetry manuscript that was
found in the late nineteenth century, but Dobell corrected this misattribution. Traherne, like Vaughan, reflects the stress that Anglicanism placed on an idealized
childhood characterized by original innocence. This concept stands in contrast to the
view of the Puritans of the time that children were wicked creatures who inherited
original sin, though they could be morally transformed.

James J. Balakier

IT IS DEEP

Author: Carolyn M. Rodgers (1945-   )
Type of poem: Lyric
First published: 1969, in *Songs of a Black Bird*

The Poem

"It Is Deep" is a short dramatic monologue of free verse divided into five stanzas of irregular length. The title, beginning with the indefinite pronoun "it," suggests the slang meaning of "deep": a highly abstract, intellectually profound idea lying beneath layers of superficial meanings. In Carolyn M. Rodgers's poem, the superficial layers stem from the conflicting realities that typically exist between a mother and her adult daughter as the daughter asserts her independence and individuality.

The poet, commenting on her mother's recent visit, notes how different her and her mother's views are on issues of religion, politics, and lifestyle. This difference is particularly noted in their attitudes toward racism. The poet regards her mother, "religiously girdled in her god," as having endured racial oppression by a delusion of heavenly deliverance and meek acquiescence. The poet, however, rebels against racism by stripping the "god" myth away and engaging in revolutionary rejection of the political ideology and lifestyles of white America. The opening of the poem makes the point that the mother, in her dogged role of "religious-negro," cannot appreciate the daughter's racial progress. Thus, when the daughter refuses to use the "witch cord" and gets her telephone disconnected, the mother can only suppose "that her 'baby' was starving" for lack of money to pay bills and buy food. The mother, "gruff and tight-lipped/ and scared," comes to the rescue—uninvited and barely tolerated by the daughter.

The mother's presence only reminds the daughter how little attention her mother pays to things important to her daughter. The mother does not know who "the grand le-roi (al)" is, and she has not seen her daughter's book of poems, which the speaker interprets as a denial of the relevance of black liberation and concludes how much, in "any impression," her mother "would not be/ considered 'relevant' or 'Black.'" However, upon recalling the painful memories of her mother's humiliating encounters with racism, the daughter begins to empathize with her mother's perspective and feels compassion rather than contempt for her mother who is, nonetheless, "here now, not able to understand, what she had/ been forced to deny, still—."

The poet tells of her mother's visit in the first person. With this point of view, the poet/narrator requires only that the reader listen to her complaint about her mother's intrusion. As the conversation recounts this visit, the reader inevitably shares in the poet's discovery of the more profound meaning of the event. "It Is Deep" begins as a simple retelling of the mother's visit, and, as the daughter tells the story, the reader hears not only the details of the visit but also the poet's self-righteous judgment of her mother. Initially, the daughter regards her mother as out of sync with the times. However, by the time she arrives at the end of the conversation, she realizes that there is a connection, after all, between her mother's world and her own. The last stanza and the subtitle, "(don't ever forget the bridge/ that you crossed over on)," express that connection.

Forms and Devices

The language of Rodgers's poem is rich in its imagery and use of black speech forms. The poet's use of rhythmic speech lends cultural authority to her voice as she speaks the language of black culture with all of its irony, humor, and depth. Characteristic of black speech are its complex linguistic forms, the repetition of which create a musical, polyrhythmic style much like that of rap music. Several of Rodgers's descriptions hinge on long phrases consisting of heavily subordinated and embedded sentence elements. For example, the first stanza consists of two long, complex phrases that introduce the main clause, which begins in the next stanza. Rodgers frequently violates conventional syntax to push the rhythm of her words forward. In the line "blew through my door warm wind from the south/ concern making her gruff and tight-lipped," Rodgers juxtaposes the sentence's obvious subject, "My mother," with the "warm wind from the south," leaving the reader to judge whether the mother or the wind blew through the door. Rodgers's irony is that the southern wind intruding through the door is both a real breeze and her mother, who represents the passé lifestyle of the old South with its stereotypically submissive "religious-negro." The inconsistency of conventional punctuation between these complex sentences creates an ambiguity of subject and action, oddly resulting in the poem's structural coherence. This coherence justifies the narrative pattern as the poet develops and reveals a perspective that, in the end, allows her to resolve the ideological conflict with her mother through love.

Along with the rhythm created by carefully crafted sentences, Rodgers uses the conventional devices of alliterative and figurative language. Many of her phrases depend on the colorful imagery of slang for their simple, yet vividly concrete, images: The telephone is a "witch cord" and a "talk box"; "the cheap j-boss" is her mother's Jewish employer; and her mother "slip[s] on some love" and "[lays] on [her] bell like a truck," while the mother gets upset when the daughter talks "about Black as anything/ other than something ugly to kill it befo it grows." The reference to contemporary poet LeRoi Jones (Amiri Baraka) as "the grand le-roi (al) cat on the wall" plays with both the French term *le roi* ("the king") and the jive word "cat" from the Beat generation. The ultimate wordplay, however, is on the word "disconnected," which is explained as being the result of "non-payment of bills." The mother presses fifty dollars into her daughter's hand to pay for her daughter's food and utilities—to get her nourished and reconnected. Likewise, the daughter, seemingly disconnected from her mother's past, gets reconnected to her in the end: Through the mother's past struggles, the daughter receives spiritual nourishment and pays the necessary dues to get reconnected to her cultural past.

Themes and Meanings

Rodgers, a member of the Black Arts movement of the 1960's, often writes about black women seeking their cultural identity. "It Is Deep" is about identity and appreciation for one's roots, a sense of self deeply rooted in family history, loyalty, and circumstance. This is a theme that can be found in Rodgers's companion poem, "Jesus Was Crucified or, It Must Be Deep," which also mentions the persona of the "religious-negro," her mother's arduously long hours in the "white mans factori," and her mother's belief that her daughter is influenced by communists.

The mother in "Jesus Was Crucified," like the mother of "It Is Deep," is a woman who has lived a hard and disappointing life. She is a mother who has no time for causes other than survival and seeing to it that her child gets a better chance. This is a mother who holds tenaciously to her past for all that it was and was not, who, despite her own financial struggles, can find fifty dollars to give to her daughter, and who has invested all the struggles and tears of her past into a better future for her child. Though the mother fails to recognize that the daughter does, in fact, have a better future, the daughter does not fail to recognize that her "better chance" is derived from her mother's life struggles.

The central symbol of that connection to the past is the "sturdy Black bridge" mentioned at the poem's end. Despite the daughter's caustic remarks about her mother's religious delusions ("girdled in/ her god") and her mother's submission to oppression ("what she had/ been forced to deny"), the poet can still admire her mother's pride in having "waded through a storm." The mother shows a comparable contempt for her daughter's lifestyle. She disapproves of her daughter's racially biased politics, her rejection of religion, and her poor management of household and finances. However, none of these differences, including a disconnected telephone, could keep the mother from making the trip down "the stretch of thirty-three blocks," standing in the daughter's room "not loudly condemning that day," and pushing into the daughter's kitchen to check on the food supply. Remembering her mother's tears, the daughter recalls her love and emphatically proclaims that her mother is "obviously/ a sturdy Black bridge that I/ crossed over, on." The comma before the ending preposition emphasizes the daughter's realization that her own passage was made only on her mother's back.

Rodgers's poetic narrative about the conflict between a mother and her adult child was especially timely at its initial publication. The 1960's were a time of great generational conflict and misunderstanding. Rodgers's eloquent use of imagery and language, however, evokes a timeless truth of reconciliation through love and respect for one's roots.

Betty L. Hart

IT WAS MY CHOICE, IT WAS NO CHANCE

Author: Sir Thomas Wyatt (1503-1542)
Type of poem: Ode
First published: Devonshire MS. Add. 17492, in *A Study of Wyatt's Poems*, by A. K. Foxwell, 1911; collected in *Collected Poems of Sir Thomas Wyatt*, 1969

The Poem

Composed of five stanzas with seven lines each, "It was my choice, it was no chance" is one of Sir Thomas Wyatt's poems that was probably written as a song to be accompanied by lute. In many ways a companion piece to the more familiar song "Blame not my lute," "It was my choice, it was no chance" plays on the conventional themes of early Renaissance poetry in England. The persona, a young lover wooing a reluctant mistress, faces the specter of rejection. He carries out his attempts to persuade her to favor his suit with varying degrees of logic and fancy.

In the traditional scenario, the lover usually sees his mistress as a cruel temptress who simultaneously lures and ignores her courtier despite the fact that she has no intentions of returning his affections; furthermore, any dalliance in which she might engage with him will be fraught with inconstancy and infidelity. Wyatt supplies a twist on the usual theme, however, by having fate, rather than the woman herself, present the only real possibility of rejecting his love and, even more significantly, by seeing truth and trust as the only way to achieve a lasting love. In this way, the persona, though he affirms the role of the mistress in his unrequited bondage, softens the "attack" on the mistress and thereby places her at a disadvantage by denying her the possibility of a defensive reaction.

The poem begins with the persona's admission that he has willingly given his heart to his lady. He therefore rationalizes that she will accept his love, which has been patiently waiting in her "hold" for so long. He cannot fathom how she could reject a love so freely given and now, paradoxically, so closely "bound" to her. Only "Fortune," he feels, has the ability to reject his rightful love. This is true only because, as the ancients believed, Fortune becomes jealous of the lovers since their love, no matter how brief, is more powerful than either "right or might." He wonders then what benefit can exist in the rightness of their love if Fortune chooses to frown on them: It will be to no avail.

Questioning this situation, he examines what happens if lovers simply "trust to chance and go by guess" and finds that, if chance does not smile on this kind of lover, his only recourse is to petition "Uncertain hope" for reparation. Others, more skeptical or more naïve, may, on the contrary, assure the lover that he can take his suit to the "higher court" of fantasy where he may make an appeal for his release. Neither of these options is very promising.

However, fantasy, to the persona, indicates the possibility of choice. He can say this with some certainty as he has had personal experience with it: Fantasy stimulated him to fall in love in the first place. He also knows, though, that fantasy breeds a love that is unstable and quickly lost, having no "faster knot." Attempting to maintain a love that must please both changeable "Fancy" and weak "Fortune" is too constraining and unnatural, and it is virtually impossible, so he seeks a surer way, a way that is not doomed to fail. He finds the right way in truth and trust.

Forms and Devices

Composed of plain words and no visual imagery, "It was my choice, it was no chance" definitely fits C. S. Lewis's often quoted description of Wyatt's poetry as "lean and sinewy." While the poem does not contain sensuous imagery, Wyatt does not altogether abandon conventional poetic technique in the poem. He relies on metaphor to carry much of its meaning. The pervasive metaphor of the poem turns on the idea of an imprisoned, "bound" lover who seeks justice: the acceptance of his love that has patiently endured bondage. Wyatt continues this legal metaphor in the third stanza when he speaks of the lover who, having trusted chance, now "may well go sue/ Uncertain hope for his redress" or perhaps "mayst appeal for" his "release/ To fantasy." A brief metaphor, connected with the binding of the lover but unrelated to the legal metaphor, is the slipknot of fanciful love found only in stanza 4. Other words in the poem, such as "choice," "just," "sufferance," "right or might," "power," "abuse," "vaileth," and "prevail," though they are not specifically connected to the metaphor, serve to reinforce the atmosphere of litigation and deliberation. Even the final search for truth echoes the legal terms, since the purpose of every trial supposedly is to find the truth. Here, the truth is what ultimately will free the imprisoned lover. This legal metaphor is particularly apt for a poet who uses logic and rhetorical methods of persuasion to convince his lady: Justice demands that she should love him and thus free him from his state of imprisonment. The metaphor is also particularly appropriate if one considers that the word "court" can mean the court of law in which trials are held, and it can also mean to woo.

Several clues lead scholars to believe that this poem was originally written to be set to music. Frequently anthologized next to a song that has an extant melody, "Blame not my lute," "It was my choice, it was no chance" is structured in much the same way, with the final line of each stanza repeated as the first two or three words of the first line of the next stanza, very much like a refrain. The emphasis on rhyme, as well as the inverted syntax necessitated by that emphasis, may also point to a musical setting for this poem.

The meter, on the other hand, though it does not negate the possibility that the poem was written as a song, is not highly regular as might be expected of a song. This poem appears to be written in what C. S. Lewis called the "native meter" that he felt to be the prevailing meter of fifteenth century poetry rather than the smoother iambic pentameter. Composed predominantly of four stresses per line despite the number of syllables in the line, this type of meter, like verse written during the alliterative revival of the fourteenth century, uses alliteration to mark the stresses and a caesura (a break in the middle of the line) to form word groups. These features are perhaps most clear in the first line of the poem ("It was my choice, it was no chance") with its eight syllables and four stresses: The obvious caesura is indicated by the comma that breaks the line into two repetitive clauses, the only difference between them being the final word of each clause ("choice" and "chance"), which repeat the initial consonant sound.

Themes and Meanings

"It was my choice, it was no chance" is a deceptively simple poem. Perhaps the only certainty about the poem is that it is about a man courting a woman who has not yet returned his advances. Whether the tone of the poem is playful, serious, or cynical, however, is open to debate. The picture the persona draws of the woman he loves is the merest outline. The reader knows that she has held his heart—whether she intended to do so or not is not made clear—for some time without either freeing it or accepting it. The picture the persona draws of himself is, likewise, superficial. Rather than plumbing the depths of his feelings, he makes a relatively objective case before the court of his love.

The real difficulty in interpreting this poem comes with the fourth stanza, in which the persona admits that fantasy first caused him to love. The problem lies in his firm assertion that a love based on fantasy will end as quickly and easily as it began because it has "no faster knot." From this realization, he moves to the further revelation that a love that maintains itself "by change" (a paradox in that maintenance and change are diametrically opposed) cannot endure and that only a love based on truth that leads to trust will triumph. The relationship of these statements to the opening situation is unclear: If he sees his love as based on fantasy (he makes this connection explicit through the use of the word "choice" in the first stanza and "choose" in the fourth), the reader must wonder why he persists in pressing for a love that he knows cannot last. On the other hand, he may see his love as having found a stronger foundation despite the fact that it was founded on such tenuous grounds.

Any interpretation of a Wyatt love poem must mention his purported relationship with Anne Boleyn, the second wife of King Henry VIII. Certain aspects of the poem suggest, but certainly do not confirm, the possibility of such a connection. The references to "one happy hour" that can "prevail" more than "right or might," the power that only "Fortune" has to quash his love, and the legal framing of the entire poem could conceivably allude to this liaison.

Jaquelyn W. Walsh

JAIL POEMS

Author: Bob Kaufman (1925-1986)
Type of poem: Lyric
First published: 1965, in *Solitudes Crowded with Loneliness*

The Poem

"Jail Poems" is a collection of thirty-four numbered lyric strophes (irregular stanzas) that vary in length from one to fourteen lines and function together to convey a series of related though disparate images for the reader. The title of this poem not only sets the mood but also reveals the setting in which the poem is reported to have been written and serves as a recurrent theme throughout. From his perspective inside the jail, the narrator describes the various sensory and reflective perceptions of an inmate, variously turning his eye toward his surroundings, his fellow inmates, the society that put him in jail, and himself.

The first section of the poem describes the narrator's immediate surroundings: what he sees, what he hears, and how he interprets the situations of the other occupants of the jail. The second section is more oriented toward the senses, concentrating on visual imagery at first then moving toward the auditory. The third section takes a philosophical approach, asking "who is not in jail?" and theorizing about the degree to which human beings can "know" things that are outside their own experience. In the fourth section, the narrator speculates about the perceptions of others and questions his own motivations. Thus the poem proceeds, asking difficult questions and then answering them not from the perspective of a "universal truth" but from the unique position of one person in a particular context, the salient feature of which is the jail cell in which the narrator is incarcerated while pondering these issues.

The various sections follow one another as if the reader was following along with the wandering thoughts of the narrator's stream of consciousness. Thus the narrator's discomfort at the death of a "wino" in an adjacent cell (section 5) is followed by focused introspection about the turns of his own life (section 6). Questions about the nature of existence (section 7) are answered with the certainty of sensory perception (sections 8 and 9). As the poem proceeds, the narrator's thoughts become more diffuse and more fragmented until, at the end, they become surreal as the narrator entreats, "Come, help flatten a raindrop." Taken individually, the sections and the lines within them offer a montage of sensory images interspersed with philosophical questions and angry invective. Together, however, the poem paints not just an image of jail life but also an image of a narrator who is separated from society by more than the iron bars that imprison him.

Like many lyric poets, the narrator draws his power from the vividness of personal description. In "Jail Poems," however, there is a tension between the personal nature of the experiences and the necessarily public sphere in which they occur. Perhaps it is because of this tension that the poem vacillates between personal observations specifically made by the narrator and more casual observations that might have been made by a passerby. The former are more numerous, but the narrator seems to be reminding readers that part of the reality of being imprisoned is that one is, at all times, exposed to public view. As the poem progresses, the casual commentary decreases and the observations become more personal and more cryptic until, at the end, the narrator seems to have shut out the outside world altogether and retreated into himself.

Forms and Devices

"Jail Poems," like much of Bob Kaufman's poetry, exemplifies the oral tradition associated with the Beat poets of the 1950's and 1960's, many of whom were influenced by the music of their era, especially jazz. Rhythmic lines such as "Here— me—now—hear—me—now—always here somehow" allow the reader to hear— even feel—the cadence that is present when the words are spoken aloud. Additionally, the nonuniformity of the poem's sections mimics the irregular measures of jazz music, varying between long, drawn-out wailings and short, intense, angry bursts, all of which are held together by the commonality of the unwavering depth of the feelings that inspire them. The Beat poets were reacting against rigid stylistic conventions, eschewing not only regulated rhyme schemes and uniform meter but also formulaic stanzas and consistency of perspective and case. By rejecting the rules of their predecessors, the Beat poets created a style that was fluid and resembled spoken discourse or even thought processes. In fact, Kaufman, who preferred to deliver his poems orally, is said to have resisted their publication, preferring to recite his own poetry (and that of others) from memory whenever the opportunity presented itself.

The Beat poets rejected common formulaic constructions as well, avoiding the binary relationships that are found in other styles of poetry and rejecting simple themes such as male versus female, us versus them, and now versus then in favor of more obscure or complicated depictions that, they asserted, more accurately portray the human condition. Although "Jail Poems" represents the judicial system in a negative way, for instance, it does not portray it as a singular structure, solely responsible for the narrator's misery, that can be readily identified, confronted, and overcome. Rather, Kaufman implies that there are multiple causes of the wretchedness he describes, ranging from the police who "batten down hatches of human souls" to the Muscatel that contributes to "wine-diluted blood."

Surrealist imagery is a third characteristic that "Jail Poems" shares with other examples of Beat poetry. Exemplifying this feature are lines such as "One more day to hell, filled with floating glands," which abuts two or more contrasting, concrete images in such a way that meaning is accentuated by the difficulty of picturing the image itself. Many of the shorter sections (10, 12, 13, and 23 for example) consist entirely of these contrasting images, which heighten the reader's sense of the absurdity of anyone who would condemn the likes of Socrates or turn the American Dream into something that mocks a group of people rather than empowering them. Surrealist imagery expresses visually the same dissonances that loose structure expresses in terms of form.

Themes and Meanings

Everything about "Jail Poems," from its irregular sections, each numbered and kept separate from the other, to the way that the narrator increasingly withdraws into himself, contributes to the overall theme of disfranchisement, a theme that Kaufman addresses often. The collection in which "Jail Poems" appears, *Solitudes Crowded with Loneliness*, begins with a poem entitled "I Have Folded My Sorrows" and proceeds to explore both loneliness and disfranchisement from a number of different angles: from the quiet, solitary isolation of an individual to the collective grief felt by a community when one of its icons passes away. Each of the poems touches a nerve as Kaufman explores grief, disillusionment, and the acute sense of betrayal felt by people whom society excludes or marginalizes. "Jail Poems" contributes to this collage by dramatizing the plight of the disfranchised through a combination of rhythm and imagery; however, because of the complexity with which Kaufman treats his subject even on a thematic level, there are no absolutes.

At random intervals throughout the poem, there are causes for hope such as the "Three long strings of light/ Braided into a ray." Moreover, the poem itself represents an act of expression, an affirmation of self that exists against all odds. Even if, as the narrator asserts, he is writing the poem "For fear of seeing what's outside [his] head," he still admits a desire to eat "a wild poetic loaf of bread," a longing that confirms that even at his worst, the narrator continues to hold on to his artistic desires. The most conspicuous meaning of the poem, however, is much less positive. The final two images are of a man, fumbling on the floor, who was once much more than he is now and a raindrop that will be flattened not by gravity but by a conspiratorial act. Together, these images convey a profound sense of regret that some people are prevented from living up to their potential not because of random happenstance but because forces conspire to limit them. It is these purposeful limitations that Kaufman rails against because, like his contemporaries, he cannot abide rules that make virtual prisoners of those held within their sway. Ultimately, "Jail Poems" is about the need to protest violations of the human spirit. As Kaufman reminds readers, these violations occur not only through physical incarceration but also through sensory deprivation and social isolation.

T. A. Fishman

JANET WAKING

Author: John Crowe Ransom (1888-1974)
Type of poem: Lyric
First published: 1926; collected in *Two Gentlemen in Bonds*, 1927

The Poem

"Janet Waking" is in seven stanzas, four lines each, with the first and fourth lines rhymed and the second and third lines rhymed (*abba* rhyme scheme). The title suggests the coming of age theme that is evident in the poem. As is true of any moment of understanding in the works of John Crowe Ransom, the formal constraint of the tight form reinforces the recognition of people's position in the larger universe: operating within a strict schema and perceiving the abstraction and formlessness of the universe ("far beyond the daughters of men"). The poem is written from the point of view of the father, "Who would have kissed each curl of his shining baby." He is the only adult whose thoughts the reader is given. Beginning as an observation of a beloved child and including the first-person perspective in the final verse paragraph ("Janet implored us"), the poem moves from the intensely personal to the universal.

"Janet Waking" begins with a scene familiar to any parent. Ransom's poem follows the child through her morning rituals. The complication is suggested in the opening lines when the child, thinking of her pet hen, wants "To see how it had kept." The end of the third stanza informs the reader that the hen had died. The centerpiece of the poem is the fourth stanza, in which the bee sting is described, a stanza in which Ransom juxtaposes a "transmogrifying bee" and "Chucky's old bald head," foreshadowing the final change in the poem: The parents' change from seeming all-powerful to being all too weak.

The structure of the poem suggests a brief play in which the opening scene shows the protagonist waking and thinking "about her dainty-feathered hen." The second scene introduces the rest of the characters—the father, mother, and brother. Then, as the setting shifts outside the house to the farmyard, death and danger are revealed in the death of the pet, the tragic force in this brief drama. In drama, the "catastrophe" marks the tragic failure and comes as a natural consequence of the death. In this case the child's innocence and belief die. She no longer believes that her parents are all-powerful because they cannot bring her pet back to life.

The poem's narrative structure leads the reader to experience the frustration and powerlessness of the parent watching the child and being unable to help. The father and child in this small drama are at the mercy of larger forces—forces that they begin to understand through experience.

Forms and Devices

Throughout "Janet Waking," language and situation bespeak the fairy-tale quality of the work. One important device in the poem is allusion. "Beautifully Janet slept" recalls the innocent sleep of Snow White and Rose Red. The child wakes not merely to full sun but to a time that is "deeply morning." "Beautifully" and "deeply" suggest the rhythm and the tone of fairy tales. The fairy-tale motif continues as the father notes that he "would have kissed each curl of his shining baby." Just as the sun sets out on a new day, so does the child of this fairy-tale farm world. The phrase "Running across the world upon the grass" also locates the child in the land of fairy tales. That which intrudes upon her world is "the forgetful kingdom of death." The archaic term "alas" also suggests a past time, a fairy-tale world.

Another important device is juxtaposition. The poem juxtaposes realism with innocence and idealism. To the little girl, the pet is "her dainty-feathered hen." In the father's description, the chicken has an "old bald head." "Janet Waking" also juxtaposes formal diction with simple and direct Anglo-Saxon English. Ransom's choice of "transmogrifying" to describe the bee forces a reader—even a casual reader—to recognize unwitting power. Just as the venom of the bee communicates its rigor, so does the word "transmogrify" communicate the status of the event. The pathos of the unsuspecting victim is heightened by the description of the bee "droning down on Chucky's old bald head." Chucky, bald, is unprotected, vulnerable to the remorseless and methodical bee.

A juxtaposition that further exemplifies the duality of this poem appears in the final two lines of the fifth stanza: "Now the poor comb stood up straight/ But Chucky did not." With humor, Ransom balances the tension and sadness of the poem, again with realism intruding on any romantic description. Ransom shelters the reader from the harshness of death and destruction with his naming the pet "Chucky" and with these final lines of the fifth stanza.

A third device is enclosure. Each of the stanzas rhymes in an *abba* pattern, implying a close relationship between each of the rhymed words, with the closest relationships being those that function as internal couplets. For instance, when in the second stanza Ransom introduces the family in rhyme, lines five and eight rhyme "mother" and "brother"; lines six and seven less exactly rhyme "daddy" and "baby." The mother and brother complete the family, but in this poem they serve merely to enclose what is the closest relationship: the father and daughter. The final stanza serves as another readily accessible example of the relationship between rhyme and meaning. Ransom rhymes "breath" and "death" in the opening and closing of the concluding stanza, enclosing rhymes of "sleep" and "deep." The child's breath itself is ragged and painful, breath with the rhythm of weeping, because she has seen death. The child wants death to be sleep, so the pet will awaken, but the death sleep is too deep. The knowledge that some sleep is not beautiful, that some sleep is deep, the sleep of death, is reflected in the rhyme.

Ransom provides another fine enclosure for the poem itself: "deeply" in line 2 and "deep" in the penultimate line of the poem. Ransom describes a circumstance in which the truth is beyond a reader's understanding, too deep. As Ransom notes, the brown hen has been "translated far beyond the daughters of men" and is therefore beyond the understanding of the child and ultimately of any observer.

Themes and Meanings

Ransom explores change and initiation, drawing attention to the theme in his diction. The first instance appears in the title itself. "Waking" deliberately invokes a time of change, a dawning of consciousness. Rather than a simple return to consciousness, the child awakens to the world, very much as the child in "Jack and the Beanstalk" awakens to full sun and the shadow of the beanstalk, which symbolizes the changed world for Jack. Another word that draws the reader toward change, "transmogrifying," appears in the middle stanza of the poem, centering the poem on transformation. The bee-sting knot itself "Swell[s] with the venom," changing an appearance, realistic once more.

This poem suggests several layers of meaning in the word "waking." At the first level, the child wakes to the meaning of death: Her pet will no longer be in the world with her. At another level the parent wakes to the recognition of helplessness that accompanies all moments of watching a child grow through pain. The child, in fact, cannot "be instructed" but learns on her own; the feeling of uselessness is extremely difficult for many parents to accept. At another level, the speaker recognizes his own similarity to Chucky. If the little girl sees "her dainty-feathered hen" while the father sees "Chucky's old bald head," the reader can be assured that the speaker is aware of who in fact is old and bald. The child, the "shining baby" with curly hair, is analogous to the "dainty-feathered hen" of imagination and innocence. The speaker, helpless at this moment of learning for the child, recognizes that his own bald head is likely to communicate the rigor of mortality.

The poem moves beyond the caring parent and toward existential contemplation in a final transformation, erasure to nothingness: "the forgetful kingdom of death." The word "forgetful" itself suggests the short memory and attention span of a child (realism, once again) as well as the essence of loss and the possibility that all experience and knowledge is ultimately forgotten. The existential question is clearly secondary within "Janet Waking," however, a poem in which family drama provides the framework for Ransom's representation of transformation and growth, making visceral a moment of loving and anguished understanding.

Janet Taylor Palmer

KICKING THE HABIT

Author: Lawson Fusao Inada (1938-   )
Type of poem: Lyric
First published: 1993; collected in *Drawing the Line*, 1997

The Poem

"Kicking the Habit" is a poem of slightly fewer than one hundred lines written in free verse. Most of the lines are relatively short, averaging three to five words. The stanzas are irregular and break every few lines where the voice would normally pause or reach a full stop. Lawson Fusao Inada also indents several sections to indicate vocal emphasis in this poem, which, given its conversational language, was obviously intended to be read aloud. It is also obvious that the poem is meant to be read aloud specifically by the poet himself, who uses the first-person "I" to tell of his experience and frustration with the English language.

The title of the poem suggests a resolution that a person makes to get rid of some annoying, obsessive, or destructive behavior. The phrase is commonly used in connection with smoking cigarettes or consuming alcohol, the goal being to "kick" or overcome a bad habit. Surprisingly, Inada applies the phrase to his habit of speaking English, which readers are to assume has become a bad habit for him: "I was exhausted,/ burned out,/ by the habit./ And I decided to/ kick the habit,/ cold turkey." One of the methods of any poet is to use surprising, even arresting verbal juxtapositions to shape new and memorable images in proving his point, and Inada does that here. He upsets his readers' expectations because he is upset.

From the beginning, Inada brings his readers into the immediacy and frustration that he feels on the particular morning that his poem is set. He has made an urgent and irreversible promise to himself "Late last night" to give up on the English language. This resolve was reached, as a series of seven progressive verbs specifies, after the poet had immersed himself in English thoroughly by "talking," "listening," "thinking," "reading," "remembering," "feeling," and "even driving" in English. He therefore decides to go on an unusual, symbolic journey, pulling himself "off the main highway." After arriving at a place that is completely new, he simply stops. The poet then digresses for several lines to reassure readers and himself that he does not mean to complain; after all, the language that he is intent on giving up is his own "native tongue," and, until last night, he had been "addicted to it" all his life.

After kicking English out of his life, the poet "kicked/ open the door of a cage/ and stepped out from confinement/ into the greater world." It is that greater, larger, and therefore better world that he spends the last half of the poem describing. It is a world of liberation in which nature and humanity of all races are in harmony and real communication, awareness, and empathy are possible. Having happened onto such a new place, having experienced such an elevated realm of sharpened senses and appreciation, the poet is then able to retain some essence of that world and take it with him "on the road of life,/ in the code of life" back to his own place in the universe.

Forms and Devices

The central symbol in Inada's poem is that of a profoundly important journey. This is a significant symbol for a Japanese American writer such as Inada to use. A journey can be undertaken in hope, in the belief that the place of arrival holds the promise of a better life than the life one leaves behind. This was the dream that many Asian immigrants held as they boarded boats bound to America, the Gold Mountain. Though Inada and his parents were born in California—he is thus not a first-generation immigrant but a Sansei, or third-generation resident—some of his writing concerns the history of Japanese people in general and of his grandparents in particular, people who crossed the Pacific Ocean in search of a new life in America. The "greater world" that the narrator perceives and the "'Clackamas, Siskiyou'" that the pine trees utter resonate with the hope and beauty at the end of such a journey, specifically the beauty and peace that Inada found in the landscape of Oregon, where he has made his home since the mid-1960's.

Inada's journey motif is also significant in the sense that some journeys are not willingly undertaken but imposed, and these can be difficult and even harsh. Inada's family undertook this type of relocation three times during the World War II internment of the Japanese living in the United States. "Each camp was different, and the same," Inada says of the three camps in which his family was detained: Fresno Assembly Center (the county fairgrounds), Jerome Camp (an Arkansas swamp in the Mississippi Delta), and Amache Camp (in the Colorado desert). Inada's second collection of poetry, *Legends from Camp* (1992), is loosely based on his childhood impressions of his years in the camps recollected in the adult perceptions of a poet who is also a lover of jazz. The collection in which "Kicking the Habit" appears is Inada's third book of poetry, *Drawing the Line*, which continues the thread of those camp recollections. The title of the book refers to a group of Japanese men in the Heart Mountain internment camp who "drew the line" by resisting the government's order to be drafted into the military and who were thus sent to federal prison. "Kicking the Habit," along with the other poems in this collection, is Inada's way of drawing a personal and ethnic line of his own. It is a statement about what he loves, what he remembers, what place and landscape mean to him, and what it is that has given him hope and has made him wise. Though a journey may be fraught with complexities and surprises, the poem suggests, both the traveling and the arrival significantly shape the poet's identity.

Themes and Meanings

"Kicking the Habit" is protest literature voiced in the most effective way that a poet can utter it. It is a serious statement for a poet, whose business involves writing words, to insist on giving up those words "cold turkey," refusing to use the language anymore. Inada wants readers to think about just how serious the implications are: Poets without words have given up their essences and their identities. Inada knows that this is a metaphor for giving up anything precious and essential, which is basically what the Japanese Americans were forced to do during the internment years of World War II.

They were ordered to relinquish possessions, homes, neighborhoods, and businesses and relocate to barracks in fairgrounds and deserted racetracks. Though Inada's recollections of his camp life in *Legends from Camp* and *Drawing the Line* are told with nostalgia and even warmth rather than overt bitterness or anger, the message is obvious nonetheless: Japanese Americans, Inada and his family among them, were victimized by the U.S. government. He, the poet, will protest this atrocity with an atrocity of his own: giving up his use of the English language.

The poet knows that the problem is that he is a member of a minority race rather than part of the American mainstream: "I pulled off the main highway/ onto a dark country road." He knows he must justify his existence by showing his "passport" to "insects" and his "baggage" to "frogs": "After all, I was a foreigner,/ and had to comply." However, the continual deferring and explaining, the apology for using English, is wearing him out. Therefore, he goes on his own internal journey to get in touch with himself, which results in becoming attuned to a universe of all races and creatures: "Ah, the exquisite seasonings/ of syllables, the consummate consonants, the vigorous/ vowels of varied vocabularies."

The poet's passive method of resistance is to give up his language and then to take it up again after he has been renewed. It is a statement not only of threat and revenge but also of promise because readers find out that the revenge does not last: Having satisfied his need for revenge, having visited that place for a while, the poet has worked through his problem, has been avenged, and has come to a greater, more benevolent, more forgiving place. "Kicking the Habit" is thus a poem of reconciliation and redemption ending with a blessing by the morning sun, which, being "yellow" (usually a derogatory term when applied to Asians and cowards) is also the color of his race, a color he can now acknowledge with pride. The poet has, in effect, turned a negative vision, one that he has harbored and that others have harbored about him and his race, into a positive one.

Jill B. Gidmark

KILLING FLOOR

Author: Ai (1947-   )
Type of poem: Dramatic monologue
First published: 1978; collected in *Killing Floor*, 1979

The Poem

"Killing Floor" is a free-verse monologue that dramatizes three moments in the life of Leon Trotsky. Born Lev Davidovich Bronstein, Trotsky—one of the most important figures of the Bolshevik Revolution of 1917—was assassinated in Mexico in 1940 after being exiled from the Soviet Union. Using violent imagery to establish a context of spiritual and political crisis, Ai constructs a poetic autobiography of Trotsky that exposes the spiritual and psychological dimensions underlying historical fact. Related by Ai's imagined version of Trotsky, the poem's series of nightmares and awakenings leads gradually to the scene of Trotsky's assassination with an ax. Within this context of nightmare, politics, and butchery, "Killing Floor" explores the effects that political and personal sacrifices have on the human soul.

Section 1, entitled "Russia, 1927," introduces the atmosphere of anxiety and violence that gradually permeates the poem. Trotsky, the speaker of the poem, is both Bronstein the private individual and Trotsky the political figure. He awakens "ninety-three million miles" (the distance from the Earth to the Sun) from himself to a swim not in the "azure water of Jordan" but in the "darkened" waters of the Volga. Just as the river Jordan is displaced upon waking by the Volga, the deathlike man with the "spade-shaped hands" is replaced upon waking by Joseph Stalin, the man who exiled Trotsky. Ten years after the revolution, with Communist leader Vladimir Ilich Lenin dead, the Soviet Union is at a crossroads, a choice between the totalitarian road Stalin proposed or the more democratic path advocated by Trotsky. The depravation and violence Stalin would bring to the Soviet Union is foreshadowed in Trotsky's vision:

> but I hear the hosts of a man drowning in water and holiness,
> the castrati voices I can't recognize,
> skating on knives, from trees, from air
> on the thin ice of my last night in Russia.

Stalin whispers in Trotsky's ear the conditions of his exile. The section ends with Trotsky's answer: *"I have only myself. Put me on the train./ I won't look back."*

In the poem's second section, "Mexico, 1940," the submerged violence of section 1 erupts into Trotsky's dreams. Trotsky awakens from a nightmare vision; this awakening amplifies rather than dispels the reader's sense of impending disaster. Ai heightens the dramatic tension of this section by breaking it into two halves. The first half relates the fact that Trotsky has had a dream of murder; the second half depicts in striking imagery the details of this dream. Between the two halves of the section, Ai wedges an expression of calm and serenity: "A marigold in winter." She then closes the section by obliterating this sense of calm removal, returning to the nightmare: "my head fell to one side, hanging only by skin."

"Mexico, August 20, 1940," the third section of the poem, opens with another nightmare but quickly moves the violence into Trotsky's reality. In his nightmare, bullets zigzag up the body of his wife. Trotsky cuts open her gown and attempts to stop the bleeding with his own body. This final nightmare emerges into the reality of the poem. As Trotsky rouges his cheeks and lips at his wife's vanity, he feels "lined and empty." The toll of exile and of continual threat has exhausted him. As he looks into the mirror, he is attacked—not in dream, but in fact:

> He moves from the doorway,
> lifts the pickax
> and strikes the top of my head.
> My brain splits.
> The pickax keeps going
> and when it hits the tile floor,
> it flies from his hands,
> a black dove on whose back I ride

The killing floor of the poem's title resounds with the violence of the fatal blow and the exhilaration of Trotsky's release from the myriad uncertainties of his existence. In the closing lines, the oppositions of identity and perspective that haunt Ai's version of Trotsky are not so much resolved as recognized: "a black dove on whose back I ride,/ two men, one cursing,/ the other blessing all things." In an ambiguous ending, the personal figure (Bronstein) separates from the political one (Trotsky). Ironically, this killing becomes a liberation from duality that frees Trotsky from the burden of nightmarish anxiety. The split between the two halves of himself resolves in a unifying act of purification in the holy river of Trotsky's Jewish ancestors: *Lev Davidovich Bronstein,/ I step from Jordan without you.*"

Forms and Devices

Ai adopts Trotsky as a poetic persona through which she narrates this first-person, three-act drama about the human costs of revolutionary commitment. Emphasizing oppositions between the political and the personal, the public and the private, and dream and reality, this poem portrays the personal crises behind the historical facts of Trotsky's life. The three sections of the poem lead the reader through three stages in Trotsky's journey from exile to assassination. Imparting to history a surrealistic, cinematic context, the poem provides the reader with a narrative of striking images and compelling oppositions. These images and contrasting oppositions, in turn, offer the reader a means to evaluate and appreciate the personal implications of political action.

"Killing Floor" is dominated by the power of Ai's startling images of violence. Recognized and reviled by critics for the visceral power of its imagery, Ai's poetry depicts suffering and survival in sometimes lurid, bloody detail. In very ordinary, very straightforward language, Ai constructs images of violence that capture the reader's attention. Images such as "skating on knives," a head hanging only by a sliver of skin, a bullet-riddled body, and a pickax splitting a brain reflect the unfortunately gruesome facts of life in a violent and cruel society. It would be a mistake, though, to read the violence of "Killing Floor" without also reading its images of beauty. In phrases such as "easing me down into the azure water of Jordan," "water caught in my lashes," and "A river of sighs poured from the cut," Ai offers the reader a respite from the force of blood and violence. She juxtaposes these images of spirituality (baptism, Jordan, dove) and beauty with violent imagery in order to communicate the complex connection between violence and beauty. The alternating rhythm of violence and beauty, nightmare and wakefulness is crucial to the poem's depiction of the divided and hounded life of Trotsky.

Restricted by the historical fact of Trotsky's assassination, the poem's oppositions of imagery and tone serve to enrich the reader's appreciation of the psychological and personal costs Trotsky paid for his commitment to his political beliefs. Juxtapositions of violent and beautiful images—paired with the narration of dream and waking— create a surrealistic atmosphere in which Ai reimagines history. In this atmosphere, the sections of the poem describe the prelude, crisis, and culmination of Trotsky's political and personal drama. By setting up oppositions within the poem (Jordan/ Volga, Russia/Mexico, Bronstein/Trotsky, dream/waking, and marmot/dove), Ai renders history tangible and universal in its human implications.

Themes and Meanings

"Killing Floor" is the title poem of Ai's second collection of poems and represents a departure from the poems of her first collection, *Cruelty* (1973). Published in 1978 and a winner of the Lamont Poetry Selection Award for the best second book by an American poet, *Killing Floor* moves the violent themes of *Cruelty* (monologues delivered by unnamed, ordinary people) into contexts of historical and cultural significance. Ai's straightforward, unadorned language can lead readers to evaluate her poems as merely sensational documents of bloodshed without further meaning. With poems about Trotsky, Mexican revolutionary Emiliano Zapata, film star Marilyn Monroe, and Japanese author Yukio Mishima, *Killing Floor* establishes a larger social context through which readers can interpret Ai's work. Violence in Ai's poetry must be unadorned and direct in order to shock the reader with the bloody contexts of history and of society. "Killing Floor" places the details of Trotsky's life among such imagery in order to situate his life into a more universal dilemma between personal and political choices.

In this process of emotional and psychological reinterpretation of Trotsky, some suggestions of the poet's life arise. For example, the focus on the multiplicity and fluidity of identities of Bronstein/Trotsky connects to the multiplicity of identities Ai herself encompasses. Born Florence Anthony, Ai's poetry reflects the multiple ethnicities of her heritage (Japanese, African American, Choctaw, and Irish) and the anxieties that the world's demand for static identity creates. In this light, one can read the poem as an expression of anxiety over the stricture of social definitions. Identity is too multiple and too persistent to limit itself to rules, even self-imposed ones.

Ai's use of historical and ordinary personas to give voice to her monologues invites comparisons with the monologues of Robert Browning, A. E. Housman, and Sterling Brown. The starkness of her violent imagery, however, is particular to her work. In "Killing Floor," the political life of Trotsky emerges from the Volga and returns, transformed, to the Jordan. Arranged within the concentric boxes of dream and waking, history in "Killing Floor" is fraught with crisis, longing, and violence. Ai ironically humanizes history by her persistent attention to emotional and spiritual identity. By presenting to the reader a rich blend of violence, beauty, nightmare, spirituality, history, and poetry, Ai creates a unique vision of the struggle that rages in life to define and be oneself.

Daniel M. Scott III

KING SAUL AND I

Author: Yehuda Amichai (1924-   )
Type of poem: Lyric
First published: 1958, as "Hapelekh Sha'ūl va'ănī," in *Be-merhak shete tikvot*; English
translation collected in *Selected Poems*, 1968

The Poem

Written in the first person, "King Saul and I" is a poem of fifty-five lines divided
into three sections. As the title suggests, the poem is based on a comparison of the
lives of the legendary King Saul and the author. The tone of the poem indicates that
the poet is speaking directly to the reader, undisguised, in the classic tradition of lyric
poetry.

Section 1 has three stanzas. The first stanza emphasizes the difference between king
and poet in the opening two lines: "They gave him a finger, but he took the whole
hand." By contrast, the poet has been offered "the whole hand" but did not "even take
the little finger." This is followed by a reference to King Saul's "tearing of oxen,"
which refers to the king's action when he needed to raise an army to defend the
Israelites against the Ammonites. He cut up a yoke of oxen and sent the pieces
throughout Israel, threatening to do the same to the oxen of the men who would not
join him. The second stanza has four lines which again emphasize the difference: The
poet's pulse was like "drips from a tap"; the king's, like hammers pounding. The third
stanza states the relationship between the two in a slightly different way. "He was my
big brother," the poet says, and in a homey, familiar image, adds that he got the king's
used clothes.

King Saul is the subject of the second section. The first two-line stanza is a simile,
comparing the king's head to a compass that will always bring him to the "sure north
of his future." The "sure north" refers to the north pole, necessary for navigating
precisely. This section ends with a reference to the asses in the story of King Saul in
the first book of Samuel from the Old Testament. It is typical of Amichai to juxtapose
images from modern life with biblical images, defining the cultural heritage from
which he creates literature. The ass image is continued into the third section of the
poem. When King Saul was looking for his father's lost asses, he inquired of King
Samuel, the prophet, which way he should go. Samuel recognized and embraced him
as a prince of Israel, and Saul gave up his search for the asses. In a bold leap of time
from the Old Testament to the modern era, Amichai writes that he, the poet, has now
found the asses, "But I don't know how to handle them./ They kick me."

Other references to the story of King Saul abound. The third section of the poem
tells of the anointing of Saul, of the people who were below his shoulders when he
came among them, and of his triumph. Yet the poem ends in a series of couplets that
create a mood of resigned weariness, ending with "He is a dead king. I am a tired
man." Glory, power, and victory are associated with Old Testament time, while in
contemporary time the poet leads a weary, diminished life.

Forms and Devices

Yehuda Amichai's career is the longest and most productive in the history of modern Hebrew literature, and he is the most widely read Israeli poet, both in the original Hebrew and in English translation. Although something is always lost in poetic translation, Amichai has a formidable reputation among American readers. He grew up in an Orthodox household but abandoned formal religious practice in his adolescence. He retained his love for the poetry of the Jewish liturgy, which he exploits in his work. "Words are a new beginning with the stones of the past," he said in an address to a writers convention in Jerusalem in 1968: "No matter how small these stones are or how broken they are the new building will be stronger."

Many early biblical documents, such as the Song of Deborah, the Song of Moses, and the Song of Songs, are couched in rhythmic verse, and even the historical prose in the Pentateuch and the stories of Esther and Ruth are close to poetry in their cadenced sentences. The ethical ideas that contribute to Western civilization made their impact because they were written in poetic language. Instead of developing a symmetry of poetic feet, which is the unifying principle of Western poetry, Hebrew poetry developed a symmetry of units called parallelism. There are essentially three types of parallelism: sameness, antithesis (or opposition), and complement. A good example of sameness in the poem is the couplet "My sleep is just/ My dream is my verdict." A solemn sense of justice is suggested in the first line, and the second line, in parallel syntax, reinforces the judgmental quality of his life.

Antithesis is the main device used to organize the poem and create tension. The two opening lines are based on antithesis, and the poem ends with a series of parallel oppositions: "My arms are short, like string too short/ to tie a parcel./ His arms are like the chains in a harbor/ For cargo to be carried across time./ He is a dead king./ I am a tired man." Another interesting use of antithesis describes the poet's life: "I was raised with the straw,/ I fell with heavy seeds." This couplet is also complementary, for although the verbs "raised" and "fell" are antonyms, the second line extends the metaphor in which the poet is a crop growing from the land.

Themes and Meanings

The Israeli writers of Amichai's generation were born between 1915 and 1930. They were either born in Palestine or had immigrated there when very young. They were the first generation to speak Hebrew as their mother tongue, and they were the first to have grown up in the Israeli landscape with its biblical references. Amichai's personality as a poet is a reflection and distillation of this generation, typified by his identification with Israel's historic processes, his argument with Jewish Orthodoxy, and his perspective on contemporary society. He has declared that all poetry is to an extent autobiographical, meaning that it allows insight into the mind and heart of the writer. The lyric "I" that pervades his poetry is a poetic myth of himself, derived not only from his life events but also from biblical motifs, including victories of ancient heroes such as King Saul. The characteristic long runs of metaphors and similes are linked by the spokesman who is at the core of the described experience.

A sense of loss in contemporary life is the mood that dominates "King Saul and I." In addition to individual sets of antithetical lines, the poem as a whole is built on the antithesis between the biblical Saul and "I"; "I" refers to a generalized speaker rather than to a totally individualized one. In every comparison between King Saul and the modern speaker, the speaker is timid, derivative ("I got his used clothes"), and diminished. In this way the poem typifies the social and political disillusionment of Amichai's generation with a state of Israel that had failed to create the agrarian, utopian community for which they had fought.

Amichai's poetry is not strictly chronological. His verse rests on the processes of remembering and forgetting, and through the procedures of memory time becomes an individual, existential, nonhistorical time. The poet is not remembering past events but incorporating them into the desires and disappointments of his present. Time is important in this poem; King Saul's heart is set "like an alarm clock," and "Dead prophets turned time-wheels." Significantly, the asses that King Saul was seeking at the beginning of his own story are still present and have been found by the speaker, although he does not know how to handle them. A bridge is thus created between the past and present.

The dualism so prominent in this poem is characteristic of the body of Amichai's work and points to conflicts in the poet's own autobiography. Personal oppositions are a model for oppositions in the poetry and provide a method of perception which allows a thing and its opposite to be perceived at the same time. The "I" of the poetry speaks from the tension between incompatible poles of his life: past and present, orthodoxy and apostasy; love and death; and two different languages, German and Hebrew. The reference to sleeping and dreaming in "King Saul and I" introduces one more opposition; that of the real and the illusory. In another of Amichai's poems, "This Is the Story of Dust," the poet tells readers that "between my going out in the morning/ and my return in the evening half of what is to happen happens/ and in my sleep, the other half." Amichai's precise imagery is designed to force awareness of the vital contradictions that shape both his life and that of his nation.

Sheila Golburgh Johnson

THE KINGFISHER

Author: Amy Clampitt (1920-1994)
Type of poem: Narrative
First published: 1982; collected in *The Kingfisher*, 1983

The Poem

"The Kingfisher" is divided into seven stanzas, each made up of six lines of approximately the same length. Although it is written in free verse, not in a metrical form, the poem looks more conventional than many other free-verse works, including some in the same collection by Amy Clampitt. It appears even more traditional because each of the first three stanzas is a definite unit, ending with a period; the remainder of the poem consists of double-stanza units, but again, the first stanza in each pair ends with a punctuated pause and the second with a period. Thus the poem is made up of five segments, each distinct in setting, which are arranged chronologically.

Clampitt emphasizes her narrative intent in her notes to "The Kingfisher" when she describes the poem as a "novel trying to work itself into a piece of cloisonné." The subject of this poem, she says, is "an episodic love affair that begins in England and is taken up again in New York City." Although the story is related in the third person, the point of view is that of limited omniscience, for while the author reports the thoughts and feelings of the woman, the reactions of the man are presented as his lover's guesses or assumptions.

The setting of the first stanza and thus of the first episode in this love affair is rural England. In the late spring or the summer of a year marked by especially vociferous nightingales, the two lovers spend an evening going from pub to pub. At some point, too, they walk by the ruins of a convent and see peacocks displaying their feathers. "Months later," the lovers are in a Manhattan pub. They have been attending a symphony concert, and during intermission they have rushed out for refreshments and a discussion of what they have heard. They do not agree, but it does not seem to matter.

The next scene takes place in the Bronx Zoo. Through the headphones provided for visitors, the lovers hear the "bellbird." The man makes a comment that seems to his lover to imply much more than the mere words would indicate. There seems to be increasing tension in the relationship, and the answer on this day is to drink "yet another fifth" of liquor.

In the fourth and fifth stanzas, the lovers are still in New York. On a Sunday morning in November, they stroll through a churchyard in lower Manhattan, near Wall Street, listening to the choirs from nearby churches and looking at a thrush, which has paused there on its way south. Some time later that month the love affair ends. No details are given, only that the breakup was a "cataclysm."

Unfortunately, the relationship did not end neatly. During the years that followed, readers are told in the sixth stanza, there was a great deal of "muted recrimination," until at last the lovers ceased communicating altogether. Long afterward, again in

England, the woman is looking back over the affair, trying to identify the signs of disharmony in every ecstatic encounter. In the last stanza, as urgent as a kingfisher diving upon its prey, the persona summons up her memories. However, she cannot capture her old passion. Her plunge into the past ends in an almost unbearable unhappiness.

Forms and Devices

Like most of Clampitt's work, "The Kingfisher" is crowded with nature imagery, especially references to birds. The poet mentions nightingales and peacocks twice, once in the initial stanza and again when she is summing up the failure of the affair. She also writes about tropical birds in the zoo, including the bellbird, describes a thrush in detail, and concludes by comparing her emotional experiences to the dive of a kingfisher.

Moreover, the symphonic selection about which the lovers disagree is Igor Stravinsky's composition entitled *The Firebird*. In an obvious play on words, the performance is compared to a bird of prey, a "kite." However, since the persona almost immediately refers to her partner's "hauling down" the musical work by his ridicule, it is evident that the poet has switched to another kind of kite, that which is made by human hands and flown for as long as the wind is favorable. Both meanings are applicable to the poem. The bird is linked to the subject of the musical composition and, more subtly, as a bird of prey suggests the developing destructiveness in the relationship; the frailty of the paper creation, its dependence on external forces, including the skill and the will of the person flying it, reminds the reader of the conditional nature of human love.

It has been pointed out that although there are fine examples of visual imagery in her poems, Clampitt draws upon the other senses with equal skill. In "The Kingfisher," she comments on the pheasants' display of feathers and describes both the thrush and the kingfisher in detail. However, there are also many references to sound in the poem, and they are particularly significant in relation to theme. For example, though ordinarily one thinks of nightingales as producing songs of great beauty, Clampitt uses the adjective "loud" in her first mention of them and later seems to blame their noisiness for keeping the lovers awake and for the "frantic" episode which in retrospect has produced more pain than pleasure. Similarly, the sounds made by both the peacocks and the bellbird are characterized as screams, and, again in retrospect, the poet wonders how many sexual encounters have "gone down screaming." Although the birds who seemed to her to be screaming were not indeed suffering, that unusual wording is now more than appropriate as a symbol of human pain.

Themes and Meanings

The notes Amy Clampitt appended to "The Kingfisher" are probably the best starting point for a discussion of the poem's themes. On the face of it, her comparison of the work to a novel, episodic in form, and her mention of a "piece of cloisonné" would appear to be at odds, for one implies narrative movement, the other a static form. (Cloisonné is a technique for applying enamel to metal, as for jewelry.) However, while the poem is organized chronologically, the love affair itself does not go anywhere. As the persona points out in the sixth stanza, every meeting had the same pattern. However well it began, each encounter went wrong. Thus the love affair and the poem describing it are both more like cloisonné, with its repetition of colors and forms, than like a narrative that moves to a conclusion.

In the notes, Clampitt also amplifies her parenthetical comment on the poet Dylan Thomas, thus stressing one of the themes that is repeated in each of the four episodes, that of destruction, decay, and death. For example, the lovers walk near a convent that is in ruins and later meet in a cemetery. The male lover makes a "wreck" of Stravinsky's music and of the evening. Later, he is said to have "mourned" as one would a death, evidently over the loss of "poetry" and because he sees himself aging. The death of Thomas, which is mentioned parenthetically, occurred the same week and in the same city as the lovers' Sunday morning meeting. His death could certainly, in a sense, be considered another death of poetry.

These symbolic references reinforce what is evident throughout the poem: that however "dazzled" the lovers were, the relationship was doomed. Even that first "gaudy" evening evidently became "frantic," and the second evening depicted was wrecked by a quarrel which revealed not only dissimilarities in taste but also insensitivity or downright malice on the part of the male lover. At the zoo, the two were isolated because they used different headphones; moreover, the male lover seemed focused only on his own feelings, not hers.

The use of the kingfisher in the title and in the final stanza is therefore highly ironic. As the poet explains in her notes, the bird has long been a symbol for marital devotion and for serenity. In the story told by the Roman poet Ovid, a human couple, Ceyx and Alcyon, were so devoted that when Ceyx was drowned, his wife Alcyon plunged into the waves to join him. The sympathetic gods changed the two into kingfishers and made them immortal. Ever since, Ovid continues, there has been a period of seven successive days each year when the seas are calm, for that is the period when Alcyon is brooding over her nest as it floats on the surface of the water. From this story comes the term "halcyon days," or, in Clampitt's definition, a time of "general peace and serenity." Clampitt uses mythology not to indicate a parallel but to underline the ironic difference between what one hopes for in love and what one generally gets. With their "halcyon" hue, the peacocks seemed to forecast a happy outcome for the lovers, and even now the kingfisher looks like "felicity afire," but the reality is that there has been a death of love. The kingfisher, then, is not a symbol of serenity but of the persona's plunge through incomprehension into "uninhabitable sorrow."

Rosemary M. Canfield Reisman

LABYSHEEDY (THE SILKEN BED)

Author: Nuala Ní Dhomhnaill (1952-   )
Type of poem: Pastoral lyric
First published: 1988, as "Leaba Shíoda," in *Selected Poems*; English translation
collected in the same volume

The Poem

"Labysheedy (The Silken Bed)" is a translation by Nuala Ní Dhomhnaill from her own Irish-language poem, "Leaba Shíoda." The title refers to a small town (also identified by the spelling Labasheeda) in County Clare on the north bank of the river Shannon. The poem uses the features of the landscape as a living entity in an address to a lover, creating a mood of deep feeling and pulsing sensuality that is striking in its openness and moving in its tenderness.

The first stanza begins as a declaration of devotion, the poet speaking directly from a core of passion, describing a place of intimacy:

> I'd make a bed for you
> in Labysheedy
> in the tall grass
> under the wrestling trees
> where your skin
> would be silk upon silk
> in the darkness
> when the moths are coming down.

The physical presence of the person to whom the poem is addressed is emphasized by the focus on the body in the second stanza, which continues the tactile image of skin (metaphorically presented initially as silk), here compared to "milk being poured" so that its liquid qualities complement the sensuous textures of fine cloth. Then, in the latter part of the second stanza and the first half of the third, other attributes (hair, lips) are depicted with luscious, extravagant comparisons to the natural surroundings. In the third stanza, without pausing, the descriptive passage shifts with no change in tone to a flowing narrative of a couple walking on the banks of the river Shannon, "with honeyed breezes blowing."

The poet's adoration is exemplified in the latter part of the third stanza and the start of the fourth by a worshipful image of "fuchsias bowing down to you/ one by one" in a display of singular devotion. Then the poet returns to a direct, first-person perspective, continuing the traditional catalog of tasks that the lover would perform for the beloved:

> I would pick a pair of flowers
> as pendant earrings
> to adorn you
> like a bride in shining clothes.

The speaker then reaffirms the sentiment of the first line by repeating it with the evocative exclamation "O" preceding and the variant "in the twilight hour/ with evening falling slow" closing a quatrain with the first tight rhyme of the poem. The last stanza, another quatrain which extends and then concludes the thought of the poem's close, summarizes the spirit of the lyric; the poet anticipates the pleasure of entwined limbs wrestling "while the moths are coming down." The body consciousness of the last lines joins the couple to the physical presence of what has been described as a supportive natural setting, linking the desire of the pair to the forces that seem to govern the flow of growth and change in the world around them.

Forms and Devices

Emphasizing the importance of the Irish landscape in her work, Ní Dhomhnaill has recounted a family visit to the eastern end of the Dingle peninsula in Kerry, where her brother said "he had something special to show us." The highlight of this "special" place was a *bile*, "a sacred tree, dear to the Celts. A fairy tree. A magic tree." Ní Dhomhnaill celebrated the occasion in a poem that concludes with the query: "What will we do now without wood/ Now that the woods are laid low?"

Her personal response has been to place the features of a sacred landscape in many poems, and in "Labysheedy" the place where two lovers meet at twilight is both a figure for and a reflection of their emotions. The parenthetical title "The Silken Bed," which she added to the place name when translating the Irish into English, sets the pattern for the extended metaphor comparing feeling and geographical feature that controls the imagery in the poem. Although it is not apparent in the English version, the Irish title "Leaba Shíoda" is both a place name and a description, since the word "shíoda" means "silk." This additional meaning conveys the poet's wish to see and shape the setting so that it becomes an expression of her desires, both an inviting physical prospect and an affirmation of her admiration for the person she addresses.

The descriptive imagery that brings the place of "the silken bed" into vivid life continually connects human elements to the terrain. Skin is like silk; skin glistens like milk "poured from jugs"; the trees wrestle like human lovers; hair is likened to a "herd of goats/ moving over rolling hills" (the hills resembling the curves of the human body); lips are like "honeyed breezes." In addition, the natural world is like a chorus resonating with rhythms that parallel the emotions of the couple. The moths at darkness suggest the creatures that produce silk, and their descent echoes the lovers settling into the silken bed.

The flowers that seem to be bowing in respect to human beauty become the adornments of a bridal decoration. The gradual arrival of darkness, "the twilight hour/ with evening falling slow," suggests the building intensity of passion, and the riverside location aligns the couple with the procession of the Shannon, a traditional device to situate a human pair in concert within a poetic or symbolic life flow. The entire image pattern is augmented by the form of address, since the poet is speaking directly to the person for whom the silk bed is being prepared. The use of "I," "you," "your," then "we," and eventually "our" implies a recurring intimacy, while the attitude of reverence for the person, the place, and ultimately their joining gives the poem its mood of celebration.

Themes and Meanings

In an essay "Why I Choose to Write in Irish, the Corpse that Sits up and Talks Back," Ní Dhomhnaill mentions that "the attitude to the body enshrined in Irish remains extremely open and uncoy." It is accepted as *an nádúir*, or "in nature," and "becomes a source of repartee and laughter, rather then anything to be ashamed of." To illustrate this approach and to carry the ancient Irish tradition of regular speech as akin to song—a continuing heritage of a culture that has always admired verbal virtuosity—into the present, Ní Dhomhnaill in "Labysheedy" uses a motif common to classic folk ballads from the British Isles. To prove the truth of one's love, a person must carry out a particular series of tasks, and in "Labysheedy" these tasks are described as a means of making the body comfortable in a natural setting. The thematic thrust of the poem as the tasks are described is toward a recognition of affinities between human and natural phenomena.

The poem's other essential theme, the idea of a cultural community persisting through centuries of pressure to conform to distant (in this case, English) national standards and styles of literary expression, emerges through the depiction of the psychological mood of the poet. Against the quasi-gentile conception of proper diction for describing (or submerging) erotic impulses, the "open and uncoy" tenor of the poet's speech is offered as an appealing alternative. The calm confidence of the syntax, as the poet shifts from resolution ("I'd make") and prophecy ("your skin/ would be") to a narration in an ongoing present ("your hair is"; "we walking/ by the riverside"), then back to a projection into the future ("I would pick"), and finally to bold conjecture ("and what a pleasure it would be") is indicative of the will and volition underlying the poetic invitation.

The absence of fear, the avoidance of qualification or caution, suggests not only the self-confidence of the poet but also, by implication, a shared assumption that this type of discourse is familiar and welcome. The theme of the natural world as the true home for humanity—an understandable position in a country as beautiful as Ireland—is supported and complemented by the theme of an unfettered expression of emotion in vivid language as its most natural form of communication.

Leon Lewis

THE LACE

Author: Rainer Maria Rilke (1875-1926)
Type of poem: Lyric
First published: 1907, as "Die Spitze I-II," in *Neue Gedichte*; English translation collected in *New Poems,* 1964

The Poem

Ranier Maria Rilke wrote part I of "The Lace" in Paris, France, in the early summer of 1906, and part II in Capri, Italy, in February of 1907. In addition to varying in time and place of origin, the two parts also differ in form. Part 1 has three stanzas of five, four, and four lines, and alternating rhyme. Part 2, with its octave (in the original German) and sestet, is an Italian sonnet. The meter throughout is iambic pentameter, varied by Rilke's strongly rhythmic language. Both parts begin with abstract musings about the nature of human existence. Both parts end with a smile.

Contrary to what one might expect from the title, there is little description of the lace itself. In part I, we learn only that it is a small, densely woven piece; in part II, that it is a flowery border. Not that Rilke's knowledge of lace was limited—a passage in his novel *Die Aufzeichnungen des Malte Laurids Brigge* (1910; *The Notebooks of Malte Laurids Brigge,* 1930, 1958) displays his familiarity with various kinds of lace: Italian work, Venetian needlepoint, point d'Alençon, Valenciennes, Binche, and pillow-laces. It is the existence of the lace, though, that is central to the poem.

In *New Poems,* Rilke was placing newfound emphasis on objects, sometimes describing them in detail, other times, as in "The Lace," seeking to extract their meaning from them. German has a word for such a poem—a "Dinggedicht," or a poem about a thing. The lace is referred to as "this thing" in both parts of the poem.

Rilke's interest in objects was strengthened by his close association with contemporary artists. From 1900 to 1902, he lived in an artists' colony in Worpswede, a village north of Bremen, Germany. Among his friends were Heinrich Vogeler, who illustrated many of Rilke's first editions; Paula Modersohn-Becker, whose early death is mourned in Rilke's "Requiem"; and the sculptor Clara Westhoff, who became Rilke's wife and introduced him to the French sculptor Auguste Rodin. Not only did Rilke admire their works, he also understood their creative personalities. It is, therefore, not surprising that, in both parts of "The Lace," his focus shifts from the lace to the lace-maker, from the artwork to the artist.

The only personal glimpse Rilke provides about the lace-maker is that she eventually went blind. His first impression is that her eyes were, perhaps, too high a price to pay for a piece of lace. Then, with astonishing directness, he apostrophizes the lady: "Do you want them back?" From this changed perspective, he understands that the lace was made with joy and still contains a trace of that joy. In fact, the very soul of the lace-maker seems present in the lace, kept alive in it long after her body has perished. The poet, with new insight, smiles at its usefulness.

In part II, Rilke derives a lesson from the lace. It is a source of inspiration, an example of the perfect artistry to which humanity aspires. Well worth the effort, the finished product makes the artist smile.

Forms and Devices

According to the Germanist Käte Hamburger, Rilke's basic literary maneuver is the comparison, such as a simile or a metaphor. There is one of each in part 1 of "The Lace." The simile is in the second stanza: "is all your human joy here inside this thing/ where your huge feelings went, as between/ stem and bark, miniaturized?" There is a detailed analysis of this simile in Wolfgang Müller's study, *Rainer Maria Rilkes "Neue Gedichte"* (1971). Müller finds the comparison fitting in three ways: First, it stresses how small the lace is that has nevertheless taken on such significance—thin enough to fit between the stem and bark of a tree; second, it likens the process of lace-making to organic growth, since a tree adds new rings between the stem and the bark; third, when the bark is peeled off, a lacelike pattern is left on its dried inner side.

The metaphor is in the third stanza: "Through a tear in fate, a tiny interstice,/ you absented your soul from its own time." The verb in the original German is *entzogst*. The root of it, *ziehen*, means "to draw or pull," and the prefix *ent* means "away." Drawing something through a hole is fundamental to the art of lace-making. Rilke retains the basic gesture, but, instead of having the lace-maker absent herself from everyday activities by drawing threads through parts of her pattern, he has her transcend her own time by drawing her soul through a hole in fate. The commonplace is transformed. The image of lace-making conveys the idea of spiritual permanence.

Rilke's writing is persuasive without being polemical. His skillful use of questions in "The Lace" gently de-emphasizes a pragmatic viewpoint without denying its validity. The sober fact of the matter is that the lace-maker went blind. While being human is fraught with changing fortunes, her fate seems particularly unkind. Rilke anticipates such a comment and avoids having to refute it by phrasing it as a question. He then effectively precludes debate by suddenly asking the lace-maker herself, by accessing the only truly knowledgeable source.

The second stanza, with its striking simile, is also phrased as a question. While stated more positively, it leaves room for doubt, as if the poet is not quite sure what the lace-maker is telling him. Not until the third stanza does her soul seem so present in the lace that he is able to employ the indicative and explain how it got there.

Proceeding from the knowledge gained in part 1, part 2 opens confidently with a lengthy rhetorical question. The poet is now sure of the deeper meaning of the lace, but, by appearing to ask, he continues to engage the reader. In a subtle series of questions, he has shifted our attention from the lace-maker's ailment to her ecstasy.

Themes and Meanings

In the section of *The Notebooks of Malte Laurids Brigge* that deals with lace, looking at the family lace is something the young Malte and his mother like to do. They carefully unwind the familiar specimens from a spindle and behold their patterns with awe and wonderment yet again. By writing a second part to "The Lace" months after completing the first, Rilke is doing the same thing, taking another look at the lace, seeing something else in it, describing it in a different form.

Like any good work of art, the lace rewards repeated visits. Aesthetically pleasing, it remains the same in a changing world. It is interesting that Rilke, in part 2 of the poem, presents this permanence and perfection as particularly pleasing to adults, which has to do with his perception of the adult world as not necessarily an improvement over the world of a child, as hardly worth the effort of outgrowing "our first pair of/ shoes." Above all, adulthood seems to the poet a time of uncontrollably changing fortunes, as if we hardly get settled when something else happens to disrupt us.

As evidenced by the different locales in which Rilke wrote the two parts of the poem, he had no permanent home in his adult life. Rilke lived the life of a benign vagabond, traveled extensively to satisfy his curiosity about other cultures, and was a migrant guest of various admirers of his work. That was his chosen lifestyle. Multilingual, he felt at home in most of Europe and Russia. He also improved steadily as a writer, enjoying considerable success in his own time. Today, he is considered the most significant and influential German lyric poet of the first half of the twentieth century.

In "The Lace," the poet *par excellence* disregards his own accomplishments and is drawn instead to the product of what seems to have been an enviably settled lifestyle. The lace-maker's art was the fruit of years working with intricate patterns, striving for perfection. Lace-making is too complicated to be a casual pursuit, so it was usually done by intelligent ladies of the nobility whose secure lifestyles left them the time to embark on long-term projects.

Rilke admires, in the octet, the fact that the lace, the complex product of an intelligent, artistic adult mind, got made. In the sestet, he admires the perfection of the completed product. Art, unlike life, can, in gifted hands, conform strictly to a grand design and, when finished, can reflect the artist's vision, untainted by extraneous or random forces.

That argument, though, applies not only to works of fabric art. It applies equally well to musical compositions, dance choreography, visual arts, and literature. Rilke responds as one artist to another, as someone who understands the trials and rewards of the creative process, and who knows that each work, in its own way, contains some of the artist's soul.

Jean M. Snook

LAMENT BY THE RIVER

Author: Tu Fu (Du Fu, 712-770)
Type of poem: Ballad
First published: Written in 757; published as "Aijiang-tou," in *Jiu-jia ji-zhu Du shi*, 1181; English translation collected in *The Little Primer of Tu Fu*, 1967

The Poem

"Lament by the River" is one of the most well-known poems by Tu Fu (Du Fu). The title suggests a tragic sense aroused by scenes along the river; its function is to establish the setting and mood of the poem. The word "lament" leads naturally to the "stifled sobs" in the beginning line. The poem is written in the first person. Although "I" is never mentioned and the first person speaks through the persona of "an old rustic from Shaoling," no distinction lies between the poet and the speaker of the poem. Like most Chinese classical poets, Tu Fu attempts to capture the intense feelings of his personal experience.

The poem was written in the spring of 757, after the imperial court was usurped by the rebel An Lushan. Many loyalists believed that the fall of the emperor was caused by his concubine Yang Guifei and her relatives, who gained power and wealth through nepotism. When Emperor Xuanzong escaped from the capital he was forced to have Yang Guifei put to death because of the impending mutiny of his troops. By January, 757, An Lushan had been killed in a palace coup in Loyang and his son had become the rebel emperor. Tu Fu was absent from Chang'an at the time of its fall. He was probably taken by the rebels as a porter to the capital. It is possible that, while escaping from Chang'an, he paid his last tribute to the Serpentine River and was agonized by its plight.

The poem can be divided into four stanzas. The first stanza, with four lines, serves as the introduction. It portrays how on a spring day Tu Fu, an old country person from Shaoling, southeast of Chang'an, walks stealthily along the Serpentine River—the river is actually a constructed waterway in the main park of Chang'an. He cannot help sobbing at the sight of the abandoned palaces along the waterside. Since the palaces are deserted, "For whom are the slim willows and new rushes green?" the poet questions rhetorically. The liveliness of nature plunges the poet into his reveries of the jostling scenes that could often be seen before the emperor was banished from the capital. The second stanza, lines 5-12, vividly captures how, at that time, the park was brightened by the royal gaiety. The maids of honor, armed with bows and arrows, lead the way for the carriage of the emperor and Yang Guifei sitting side by side. Their white horses are champing at the gold bridles. Leaning back, face skyward, one maid shoots into the clouds; two birds fall to the ground transfixed by one arrow. The third stanza, lines 12-16, shifts back to the poet's sorrowful feelings with the question, "Bright eyes and white teeth, where are they now?" Tu Fu visualizes Yang Guifei's wandering soul, tainted with blood, unable to make her way back. What grieves the poet even more is the realization that there will be no way for Xuanzong, who remains alive, to communicate with his beloved Guifei, who has gone like the east-flowing water of River Wei.

It is typical of Tu Fu to return to the present world in the final stanza. Lines 17-20 observe that any human with feelings, like himself, will shed tears over the tragic fate of Xuanzong and Yang Guifei, but the flowing waters and the blooming flowers along the bank remain unmoved. The last two lines correspond to the first two lines of the ballad: At dusk, the Tartar cavalry fills the city with dust. As the poet starts to move toward the south, he gazes longingly to the north. There are various interpretations regarding the "south" and "north" of this final verse. The poet is possibly heading toward Fengxiang, where the traveling court of the new emperor Suzong, son of Xuanzong, was located. His gaze to the north conveys a loyalist's mixed feelings of nostalgia and expectancy. He longs for the emperor to return to the capital.

Forms and Devices

The form of the poem falls to the category "Xinyuefu" (new court songs) in classical Chinese poetry. It resembles the style of the Western ballad, such as Samuel Taylor Coleridge's *Ryme of the Ancient Mariner*; Arthur Cooper has observed similarities between these two works' poetic imagery. The poem, with twenty seven-syllabic lines, has a clear rhyme scheme in the original Chinese: Lines 1-4 rhyme with the sound *u*, while lines 5-20 maintain a basic rhyme pattern. A change of rhyme sets off the first four lines as an introduction. Iterations such as "qu . . . qu" (line 2), "jiang . . . jiang" (line 18), and "cheng . . . cheng" (line 20) add to the musical quality of the poem in Chinese.

Tu Fu employs two major poetic devices: contrast and indirectness. The poem is replete with binary images. The lush green of willows and rushes is in sharp contrast with the gloom of the locked palaces. Nature's constant revival in a sense ridicules the ghost of Yang Guifei, who can never return. Thus the lover who is gone can no longer communicate with the lover who remains. Their distance is like the Wei River, which carried away Yang Guifei's body, flowing eastward, while the Sword Pass, where Xuanzong remains, stands remote to the west. The final contrast between sentimental humans and indifferent nature brings the ballad to a denouement, deepening the helplessness of human sorrows.

Poetry can be quite effective in revealing truth indirectly, and Chinese poets especially cherish indirectness in poetic expression. Although Tu Fu laments the death of Yang Guifei, no explicit references to her can be found in the poem. Instead, Tu Fu writes about "the first lady of the Chaoyang Palace." This lady is historically known as Zhao Feiyan, the consort of Emperor Chengdi, who reigned from 32 to 5 B.C. Chaoyang was the name of the imperial palace during Zhou times. Although Zhao was slim and light like a flying swallow, while Yang was quite plump, their feminine charms for the ruler of the country were the same.

Tu Fu's deliberate transplantation of the first lady of the Zhou Dynasty into the capital of the Tang Dynasty adds to the reader's poetic pleasure. Similarly, "rainbow banners" allude to Yang Guifei's extravagant sisters, who display their power and richness by riding horses with gold bridles. "River Wei" refers to Yang Guifei because her body was carried away by its water, while the Sword Pass refers to Xuanzong because he traveled there after Yang's death. The line "the blood-soiled, wandering ghost cannot return" presents an interpretive enigma, as Yang Guifei was strangled to death on the Buddhist oratory in the Mawei Post Station, about thirty-eighth miles west of the capital. Such indirectness may sorely challenge today's readers' historical knowledge. However, one may discard all allusions to history and enjoy the musical sound and beautiful imagery of the poem itself.

Themes and Meanings

Like any sophisticated poem, Tu Fu's ballad allows for multiple interpretations. In spite of its autobiographical nature, it transcends personal experience and historical specifics. The universal theme of the vicissitude of human life and dynasties is enriched by Tu Fu's lamentation for Yang Guifei's tragic death and the pitiful fall of Chang'an. Tu Fu was the first in Chinese literature to address the theme of the love of Yang Guifei and Xuanzhong, which continues to attract poets, storytellers, and dramatists today. The poet begins with sobbing for the fallen capital but ends with "weeping upon his breast" for the lover who remains as well as the lover who is gone. Death can carry away the body and even soul but cannot kill love. The pain from love is infinite.

Tu Fu believed in the political function of poetry. Most of his poems contain subtle criticism of social problems. This poem shows that Tu Fu sympathized with the loyalists. He attributed the fall of Chang'an to the corruption of Yang Guifei's sisters and brothers. Their abuse of power and the squandering of wealth are indicated by the "rainbow banners" following the emperor and the "gold bridles" for their horses. Their reckless gaiety foreshadows the death of Yang Guifei and the emperor: Two birds drop downward at their laughter. Tu Fu seems to regard Yang Guifei as innocent, like the "clear water" of the River Wei. However, because it was through Guifei's tie with the emperor that her relatives gained and abused power, her soul is soiled symbolically by the blood of victims.

Tu Fu was influenced by the Taoist concept of nature; he perceived nature as indifferent and merciless. Yet humans pale by comparison with nature's powerful, reviving force and permanent beauty because their glories are transitory and they give in to emotions too easily.

Qingyun Wu

LAMENT FOR THE MAKARIS

Author: William Dunbar (c. 1460-c.1525)
Type of poem: Ballad
First published: 1508, as "I that in heill wes and gladnes," in *The Chepman and Myllar Prints*; collected in *The Poems of William Dunbar*, 1932

The Poem

"Lament for the Makaris" is a poem in twenty-five stanzas, each of four lines with a rhyme scheme of *aabb* and a recurring refrain. Although written in a ballad form, Dunbar's poem is actually a meditation on serious moral and religious issues, including what for his time would have been the most important of all, the afterlife. The poem is about mutability and transition, including the transition from life to death, and what the human response to those changes should be. Death is a central concern because, as Dunbar notes in his repeated refrain, *"Timor mortis conturbat me"*: "The fear of death confounds me."

In order to emphasize the shifting, uncertain nature of the world, Dunbar points out that the powerful and educated are subject to death. Neither position, wealth, nor learning will protect a person from the inevitable end. Dunbar then narrows his focus from the broader society to a very specialized group with whom he was familiar, the "makaris" (poets of Scotland and England) who have died. There is a further twist, for the poem's subtitle is "Quhen He Wes Sek" (when he was sick), and it has been speculated that Dunbar may have himself been very ill at the time the poem was composed. At such a time, meditation on life and, especially, death would be expected. This would be particularly true for Dunbar, who was a priest, most likely in the Franciscan order.

"Lament for the Makaris" is written in the dialect known as "Middle Scots," which was the traditional literary language of Scotland during the period from the latter half of the fifteenth century through the early part of the seventeen century. Middle Scots and English derived from essentially the same sources; their syntactic patterns are almost identical. The major differences are in vocabulary, pronunciation, and spelling, and these differences are clearly evident in "Lament for the Makaris."

Dunbar has been regarded by many scholars and critics as the finest lyric poet in the British Isles in the period between Geoffrey Chaucer and Sir Thomas Wyatt, and this work clearly displays his ability to produce a consistent, powerful, and moving poem that combines genuine sensitivity and insight with a high level of poetic technique and skill. The individual lines are relatively short, each having four main stresses, but Dunbar avoids the sense of choppiness or abruptness that readers sometimes find in a similar, nearly contemporary poet, the Englishman John Skelton.

As Dunbar constructs his poem, the central theme of mutability and death is introduced; then the topic is further considered by a roll call of famous Scots and English writers who have died; finally, Dunbar closes the poem by acknowledging that he, too, will die and noting that such is the common fate of all human beings. For that reason, he concludes, we must do our best to live proper lives.

Forms and Devices

Dunbar is an extremely skilled and competent poet, and "Lament for the Makaris" is a carefully constructed work. There are twenty-five stanzas, each of four lines of rhyming couplets with a running refrain, "*Timor mortis conturbat me.*" This pattern, which developed in earlier French court poetry and was transported to England and Scotland, is known technically as "kyrielle" verse.

The refrain is from the religious ceremony known as the Offices for the Dead, and its repetition at the end of each stanza drives home one of the poem's central points: In the midst of life we are surrounded by death and should live accordingly. For a moralizing, religious poet such as Dunbar, this point entailed opposing a *carpe diem* (seize the day) philosophy; instead of living for the moment, people should constantly and consistently behave well in order to deserve a life after death.

By using this running refrain and by restricting his verses to quatrains, Dunbar has imposed a limit on himself: He has, essentially, only three relatively short lines (four strong beats per line is his pattern) in which to present his meaning in each stanza. Further, since each stanza ends with the refrain, his rhyme scheme is limited, since line 3 must always match the "*conturbat me*" of the final line. The overall impact of the repetition and inevitable rhymes is to emphasize the repetitive and inevitable natures of change and death themselves, which constantly recur in human life.

Dunbar's syntax is simple and direct. He uses a number of parallel constructions, especially in the earlier, establishing portion of the poem. Stanza 8, for example, compares the "campion in the stour," the "capitane closit in the tour," and the "lady in bour." These three people are similar in having privileged positions in late medieval society; they are also all similar in being subject to inevitable death.

This parallelism is found elsewhere in the poem, again emphasizing the transitory nature of existence. Human beings, Dunbar notes in stanza 3, are "Now sound, now seik, now blith, now sary [sorry]/ Now dansand mery, now like to dee [die]." The language of the poem suggests that these changes occur with such speed that they may in fact seem simultaneous states: One moment we are happy and alive, and the next we are sick or even dead.

The metrical pattern of the poem reinforces this sense of inevitable change. Like the syntax, it is simple, even basic. The essential, almost unvarying, rhythmic pattern gives four strong stresses to each line — one of the oldest and most consistent metrical forms in English and Scots literature. Its presence here serves a dual purpose: to underscore the sense of inevitability and to link this specific poem with other verse from the past. This latter point becomes important during the long central section of the poem, in which Dunbar commemorates and laments the other "makaris" or poets who have died.

The rhyme pattern also helps give the poem a sense of inevitable pattern. The regularity of the *aabb* scheme encourages the reader to expect the same message to be repeated from stanza to stanza, and the recurring refrain further emphasizes this sense of continuity and human mortality.

Themes and Meanings

The themes of "Lament for the Makaris" may be found in the very pattern of the poem itself. Dunbar constructed his poem in order to examine, in logical progression, the various forms of mutability in this temporal existence, especially as they affect his fellow poets.

Stanzas 1 through 12 are concerned with mutability in general. In particular, stanzas 1 through 4 function as a sort of introduction, first telling us that the poet, once healthy and happy, is "trublit now with gret seiknes." This leads him to consider in stanza 5 how changeable the human condition is, especially in its final change, from life to death: "On to the ded gois all Estatis."

In stanzas 6 through 11 Dunbar works out in some detail how all stations and conditions of human life are subject to this iron law. The poem specifically details how knights, clerks (that is, scholars), physicians, noble women, magicians, astrologers, rhetoricians, logicians, and even theologians are not spared from death. No matter how great their position or extensive their knowledge, they all must share the common human fate.

So must poets, as Dunbar acknowledges in stanza 12: "I se that makaris," he admits, are among those who "gois to graif." For the remainder of the poem, except for a concluding stanza, he focuses on a list of twenty-four Scots and English poets who have died. He begins with three of the most prominent, whose work had an influence on his own poetry: Geoffrey Chaucer, John Lydgate, and John Gower. Although their verse is immortal, they have been devoured by death.

So have others, and the poem catalogs them, a list of the more notable "makaris" of the British Isles of the period. Although the emphasis is on Scots writers, Dunbar's cosmopolitan outlook is shown by the inclusion of a number of English writers as well. Finally, Dunbar concludes the list by bringing it up to his own time, noting that his contemporary poet, Walter Kennedy "In poynt of dede lyis veraly."

With this, the poem uses its final two stanzas to bring the work back to its underlying theme: that the transition from life to death is not to be escaped by any human being, including William Dunbar: "Sen he hes all my brether tane,/ He will nocht lat me lif alane" (Since he has all my brethern taken,/ He will not let me live alone). The only recourse is to prepare for death—to deserve salvation in the next world, since there is no permanence in this one.

Michael Witkoski

LAMENTATIONS

Author: Louise Glück (1943-   )
Type of poem: Poetic sequence
First published: 1980, in *Descending Figure*

The Poem

"Lamentations" consists of four brief lyric poem sequences in free verse. Each sequence has its own title: "The Logos," "Nocturne," "The Covenant," and "The Clearing." Individual sequences contain from three to four stanzas each. These vary from two to seven lines in length, and the lines themselves mimic the stanzas through the economy of words used.

The title of this poem, "Lamentations," suggests mourning for something irrevocably lost. It especially recalls the Old Testament's Hebrew prophets lamenting the folly of the Children of Israel and their resultant separation from Jehovah. There are also correspondences between Louise Glück's sequence titles and the New Testament gospel of Saint John. For example, the title of the first sequence, "The Logos," recalls John's story of Jesus Christ, as the gospel of John opens with the phrase, "In the beginning was the Word." One definition of "word" in this context is the Greek word *logos.* "The Logos" can be described as cosmic reason or, according to ancient Greek philosophy, as the source of world order and intelligibility. The title of "The Logos" therefore suggests a story of cosmic origins and mythical figures that echoes both Greek and Christian mythology. Indeed, the poem's first stanza describes archetypal figures of a woman—described as "mournful"—and a man. These figures in turn recall the Genesis story of the garden of Eden and the origins of humankind. The figures are not alone, according to the poem: "god was watching."

The second sequence, "Nocturne," indicates, if not a literal setting, a mood of dusk, with a landscape bathed in twilight that projects feelings of both human warmth and "panic." Here the reader begins to feel a division between the figures from the preceding sequence: There are three distinct entities, "the man, the woman, and the woman's body." The unity of "The Logos" sequence, in which there is woman with man "branching into her body," is gone. With night comes separation and fear.

The result of this fear is an attempt to procure security in the third sequence, "The Covenant": "Out of fear, they built a dwelling place." However, this attempt at unity is thwarted by the "child [who] grew between them." The division of "man" and "woman" as well as the realization of a child's dependence upon them force the figures from the first sequence to realize that they are now "mother and father." They are responsible, and like the god who watched them in "The Logos," they watch the developing "small discarded body" of their creation.

The final sequence, "The Clearing," speaks further of the separation and alienation begun in "Nocturne." Even the familiar becomes strange: "Nothing was as before," and language, the source of communication, is compared with wounds that show distinctly on the "white flesh" of humans. God, now spelled with a capital *G,* leaves the children of his creation and ascends into heaven. This final separation between the creator, God, and his children is not openly lamented; instead it is quietly described from the viewpoint of God, who, the narrator muses, must have been awestruck by the beauty of Earth when seen for that first time "from the air." There is a sense in this closing stanza of both despair at the separation of God from his Creation and wonder at the beauty of that Creation.

Forms and Devices

"Lamentations" abounds with rich mythic imagery that serves as the poem's touchstone. The four sequences recall the days of Creation that began with the word, or *logos*, and ended with night. "The Covenant" echoes the Genesis Creation story, in which God makes a covenant between himself and "the man" and "the woman." At the conclusion of six days of Creation, God rests from his work and calls it "good." "Lamentations" ends with a corresponding note with the lines, "How beautiful it must have been,/ the earth, that first time" as God saw it when He "leapt into heaven."

"Lamentations" sets archetypal figures against a backdrop of nature. The man, woman, and child are seen within a world of stripped-down imagery. Readers see the primitive beginnings of humankind, set within a natural world of flowers, beasts, day, night, and they are made aware of the minimal human needs of shelter, warmth, security, and food. The simple, direct imagery of "Nocturne" illustrates the tone of the poem with images of a "forest," "hills," "dusk," "reeds," and "leaves." Beasts, "wolves," and "the man, the woman" populated this environment. "Nocturne" concludes with a line reminding one of the moon glancing off night trees with a "moan of silver." Such mythic images are explicit metaphors for fundamental human impulses and emotions.

Glück's sparse language mirrors her use of mythic imagery. Her style in this poem is characteristically pared, chopped, and brief. Calvin Bedient, in an essay in *Parnassus* (Summer 1981), compares her style to Ezra Pound's Imagist poetry, full of "hard light, clear edges." In an essay published in the *American Poetry Review* (September/October, 1993), Glück wrote: "I am attracted to the ellipsis, to the unsaid, to suggestion, to eloquent, deliberate silence . . . they haunt because they are not whole, though wholeness is implied." Her style is exhibited in the tightly compressed sequences, stanzas, lines, and words of "Lamentations." Each of its sequences has no more than four stanzas, and no line has more than nine words. The lines themselves are also clipped, with no more than three or four stresses. Lines from the second stanza of "The Logos" illustrate these tendencies: "But god was watching,/ They felt his gold eye/ projecting flowers on the landscape."

Despite the poem's brevity, the poetic sequence suggests the entire cycle of creation, and elemental human emotions of "panic," hunger, and isolation. These themes are explored in a simple language that leaves much to the reader's imagination. Everything is reduced to a minimum, as if the poet—like the god in "The Logos"—"want[s] to be understood" but cannot adequately explain.

Themes and Meanings

The title of "Lamentations" encapsulates a central concern that is developed throughout the poem. The instant of creation in the poem occurs at the beginning, the genesis, of separation and loss. "Birth, not death, is the hard loss," Glück wrote in "Cottonmouth Country" from her first book, *Firstborn* (1969). Helen Vendler writes in *Part of Nature, Part of Us: Modern American Poets* (1980) that Glück's "parable" passes from creation "through splitting and panic to birth and authority . . . [to] language and estrangement." The lament is a moan of mourning, "a slow moan," for a time when man, woman, and child were not dissolved into distinct, separate beings whose only source of communication hinges on "words," the language which the poem compares to "wounds" on "white flesh."

The woman faces a double alienation: She is divided from the man, and the angels see that the division also includes "the woman, and the woman's body." It is from this "woman's body" that "a child grew between" her and the man. There is isolation from the nuclear family, but also from her own flesh. The child's beseeching as it "reached its hands" toward the man and woman makes them realize that they must take responsibility for their creation, as they are now the highest authority. All is built upon this premise. From the realization of authority, humanity is fully realized and the figures try to understand and imagine the god who created them.

The attempt to conceive God's view of the earth shines a ray of hope into the landscape of the poem. It portrays the capacities of humankind's imagination, and leaves a sense of wonder, "How beautiful," in the last stanza. A flicker of faith is expressed throughout the poem that the power of creative imagination can heal the wound of the alienated self and bring it into contact with the external world and other human beings. The poem projects an intense need to create meaningful language, to make the world familiar as a respite against the isolation so keenly described. Language, while being depicted as the final example of human estrangement, has the potential to redeem the divided relationships within the poem. Language attempts to express the wild beauty of human imagination so that there is, along with lamentation, elation. The poem tries, through the use of archetypal imagery, to bring the readers to a greater understanding of the world through Glück's vision, communicated by the shared medium of language.

Tiffany Werth

THE LANDSCAPE NEAR AN AERODROME

Author: Stephen Spender (1909-1995)
Type of poem: Meditation
First published: 1933, in *Poems*

The Poem

Stephen Spender's "The Landscape near an Aerodrome" is a poem of thirty lines arranged into six stanzas of five lines each. The poem is a description of the flight of an airplane and its landing at an urban airport. Such a flight would still have been a somewhat unusual event in the 1930's, and the speaker meditates upon the meaning and significance of the airplane, the landscape over which it flies, and the airport ("aerodrome" means airfield or airport) at which it arrives. The title suggests that the focus of the poem is the landscape, but in the first stanza the speaker describes the airplane. It is "More beautiful and soft than any moth/ With burring furred antennae feeling its huge/ path/ Through dusk." In the first line, therefore, Spender announces his perspective: Modern machinery surpasses the traditional beauty of nature. However, nature is not completely lacking in the description of this machine: It has "furred antennae" like the moth to guide it through the air, but it is directed toward its destination by human design rather than by instinct. Significantly, it is gliding with "shut-off engines," so there is no discordant sound of mechanical engines. Its descent is gentle, and it does not disturb the "charted currents of air."

The second stanza shifts from an appreciative description of the airplane to the perspective of its passengers, who are "lulled" by its gentle descent. The landscape over which they travel is given human attributes: It is described as "feminine" and "indulging its easy limbs/ In miles of softness." This is a landscape both natural and suburban, and its softness is attributable to the broad patterns of farms and meadows unbroken by the hard, masculine buildings and monuments of the city. As stanza 2 continues, the passengers' eyes "penetrate" the beginnings of a town where "industry shows a fraying edge." The attitude toward the industrial landscape is neutral: "Here they may see what is being done."

In the next stanza, the passengers look past the "masthead light" of the landing ground and "observe the outposts/ Of work." The chimneys are "lank black fingers" that appear "frightening and mad." These negative images are quite different from the descriptions of the airplane and the farmlands. The urban landscape is broken and mournful: The "squat buildings" look "like women's faces/ Shattered by grief," and the surrounding houses moan. The airplane then flies over a field where boys are playing. In contrast to the first stanza, Spender now sees positive value in things that are linked to nature: The shouts of joy that accompany the boys' active play are like the cries of "wild birds." However, those cries "soon are hid under the loud city." The urban world is a nightmare of sound and broken visual images, in direct contrast to the airplane that can fly high above it.

In the last stanza, the airplane finally lands. Its passengers are met by a "tolling bell/

Reaching across the landscape of hysteria." The landscape is one of madness, intensifying the nightmarish images of the previous descriptions of the city. Industry and the military are dwarfed by the mad bells of religion, "the church blocking the sun." The freedom of the airplane in the sky is now destroyed by the institutions of industry and religion.

Forms and Devices

The meter of "The Landscape near an Aerodrome" is primarily iambic with some trochaic substitutions, and the line length is hexameter with a few pentameter variations. For example, the first line is iambic pentameter, but the second shifts to iambic hexameter. The poetic purpose of these lines of uneven length is unclear, however, and seems more arbitrary or accidental than designed.

The major poetic device used to describe the airplane and the rural landscape over which it flies is personification. The farmland, for example, is described as a "feminine" landscape with "easy limbs." Metaphor and simile become the dominant figures of speech in the poem as it develops from the early contrasts between the natural and the mechanical. The airplane is metaphorically seen as a moth with fur and antennae, although it is more beautiful. Similes tend to appear later: The urban houses "remark the unhomely sense of complaint, like a dog/ Shut out and shivering at the foreign moon," and the chimneys are "like long black fingers/ Or figures, frightening and mad." The change from the playful "winking" world of the airplane to the grimy city is dramatic. In a more positive simile, the boys at play are described as being "like wild birds." Their cries, however, are "hid under the loud city." The sound images are the crucial poetic device that Spender uses to establish the contrast between the natural and the urban landscapes. The gliding airplane makes no noise, but the city is loud. The tolling bell of the oppressive church is even louder, and it is inescapable. This onerous institution is also "blocking the sun" and bringing darkness upon the land, blotting out the promise of new technology and the freedom to pass effortlessly over the seas.

Themes and Meanings

The positive treatment of a mechanical subject in the first part of the poem is typical of the poets of the 1930's (particularly those in the W. H. Auden, Stephen Spender, and Louis MacNeice group) as well as the earlier Futurists. In poems such as "The Funeral" and "The Express," Spender celebrates the machine and those who work with it. To these poets, the airplane is poetically more significant and beautiful than the objects of nature that for centuries were considered the proper subject of poetry. In contrast to such old themes, the airplane is a sign of progress, flying over the sea and carrying the passengers gracefully to their destinations. It suggests the birth of a new era that requires poets to follow advances in technology and science.

An important change in the poet's perspective occurs in the second part of the poem. The images describing factories are negative, and the children's play is drowned out by the city's noise. The machines of the city are noisy in contrast to the silent and gliding airplane. The reason for this change is at least partly related to the portrayal of the dominant church that blocks the sun and has a tolling bell louder than industry or the batteries of the military. The progress signified by the machine has been undone by the presence of a church that demands allegiance to its history and myths. The landscape that began free as the wind and "feminine" is now dominated by negative images, such as shivering dogs, mad "figures," and women's grieving or hysterical faces—the "landscape of hysteria."

The condemnation of the church and other traditional institutions that are deemed responsible for the oppression of the masses is an important part of Marxist ideology and was a staple of the work of many poets of the 1930's. They believed that it was necessary to destroy such ideologically powerful institutions in order to bring into being a new world in which there would be economic freedom for ordinary people. Auden made it clear that he believed changes in technology would lead to changes in people when he said, "New styles of architecture, a change of heart."

James Sullivan

LANDSCAPE WITH TRACTOR

Author: Henry Taylor (1942-   )
Type of poem: Lyric
First published: 1983; collected in *The Flying Change*, 1985

The Poem

Henry Taylor's "Landscape with Tractor" is a mid-length poem in free verse, written in twelve four-line stanzas. Although mildly evoking the pacing and feel of blank verse, the poem employs no formal metrical device. In terms of its carefully plotted visual arrangement and disciplined emphasis on rhythm, however, "Landscape with Tractor" establishes and maintains a sense of order and control that reinforces its principal thematic concerns.

The poem is written in the first person, with the speaker relating an apparently hypothetical event in the form of long rhetorical questions. The most unusual aspect is the fact that the speaker continually addresses his reader or listener as "you"; because the person being addressed is also the person performing the apparently hypothetical actions of the poem, the actions are also performed by "you" ("you're mowing," "you keep going," and so on). This device suggests a deliberate attempt on the part of the speaker to distance himself from the action of the poem. It also lends this startling poem its unique character, reinforcing its playful equivocation and offhanded ambiguity.

The poem begins with a rhetorical question that serves as both the formal and thematic locus of the poem. Asking the reader "How would it be if you . . . ," the speaker plunges into a surrealistic narrative reminiscent of the fictive musings of Magical Realists such as Jorge Luis Borges or Franz Kafka. The poem proposes a situation in which a man—perhaps the narrator, perhaps not—perfunctorily mows his three-acre lawn with a "bushhog" (a small tractor or mowing machine), sinking further into the numbing mundaneness of the task as the narrative progresses. Just when he seems to have completely lost himself in his work, a bizarre and unforeseen tableau presents itself in his otherwise pastoral landscape.

A dead body is lying in a yet unmowed patch of grass "maybe three swaths" from where the man is cutting. At first he offers himself some more rational, palatable explanation of this grotesque, unsettling image. "It's a clothing-store dummy, for God's sake," he consoles himself. A seeming realist, doubting to the last moment the possibility of an encounter with something so patently bizarre as a corpse, the speaker candidly dismisses the scene, musing ironically that "People/ will toss all kinds of crap from their cars." In a few more moments, however, he realizes the truth of the situation. An anonymous car "from the city" has apparently discarded a body "like a bag of beer cans." The mower's inherent connection with the obligations of the human condition—as well as his practical urge to get things done—lead him to alert the authorities; two country doctors dutifully arrive and "use pitchforks/ to turn the body, some four days dead, and ripening." The cause of death is immediately apparent; the person has been shot.

According to the narrator, weeks pass and no one "comes forward to identify the body." He repeats the question "how would it be?" only now in a redefined context. Initially the speaker regards the idea of encountering a dead body as an abstract concept to be debated. Now it becomes a reality, lending new urgency to the problem: Just how *would* it be? In the closing stanzas the speaker directly addresses a "you" that is clearly meant to be anyone claiming to be a part of humanity. You clearly wish to "go on with your life"—putting gas in the tractor, for example—but cannot easily dismiss the glimpse into mortality revealed in the vision of the "thing not quite like a face/ whose gaze blasted past you at nothing" as the decomposing corpse was gathered and taken away.

Forms and Devices

Taylor is best characterized as a narrative poet. His work is rich with the flavor of a storytelling tradition inherited from his Quaker roots. Thus many Taylor poems, "Landscape with Tractor" being no exception, are replete with the techniques and trappings of a good story—setting, character, conflict, and resolution (or at least a yearning for resolution). Taylor's meticulous attention to visual arrangement and structure reinforce a central theme of the work, the role of the artificer in the execution of his art. "Landscape with Tractor" concerns the storyteller as much as it does the story, and its appearance on the page shows the reader just how much presentation can impact interpretation. The tight, regularly arranged stanzaic pattern suggests at every moment, in an otherwise stylistically unobtrusive poem, the omnipresent hand of the artisan. Likewise, the call-and-response pattern suggested by the poem's rhetorical questions reminds the reader that poetry may be as much about the nature and practice of questioning itself as it is about providing "answers" to life's most stirring questions.

The dead body and the bushhog-steering man mowing stand out as the two images in "Landscape with Tractor" that convey the most resonance. Each suggests a wealth of interpretive possibilities, some of which have already been alluded to. For example, the corpse, as well as the man's enigmatic attraction toward it, may represent the human psyche's fascination with its own mysterious destiny. Further, the body might be said to represent the enigma of death itself. A somewhat genteel, contemporary incarnation of Everyman, the mowing man is the thoughtful but slightly jaded persona through whom the problem of this poem is viewed.

The style of Taylor's language should also be noted. A poem quite accomplished in its mastery of idiom, "Landscape with Tractor" provides in its speaker an absorbing version of the rural "gentleman farmer," although with a unique postmodern spin. This late-twentieth century man of the country is clearly exiled from "the city" by choice, not by birthright. His general attitude is revealed by the playful and slightly irreverent use of phrases such as "for God's sake" and "Christ!" At points Taylor instills a wry flippancy into his persona, a figure self-admittedly "with half [his] mind on something [he'd] rather be doing." By the final lines of the poem, however, his genial manner regarding what he has witnessed has dissolved into a disturbing sobriety brought on by the realization that the dead woman's image will remain with him, will "stay/ in that field" that houses his memory and conscience until he himself dies.

Themes and Meanings

The three primary thematic concerns of "Landscape with Tractor" are the nature of unexpected change, the contemplation of mortality, and the inexplicable connection between human beings. In his review of Taylor's *The Flying Change* for *The New York Times Review of Books* (May 1986), Peter Stitt views the first of these themes, the consequences of change and mutability, as the thematic core of the book. Stitt observes that Taylor seeks to portray the "unsettling change," the "rent in the veil of ordinary life." Clearly "Landscape with Tractor" explores this idea extensively; the speaker's unexpected encounter with a dead body awakens in him the realization that change, even extreme change, lurks clandestinely around every bend in the human journey.

Perhaps the most disquieting kind of change looming on the human landscape is one's own inevitable death. The speaker's moment of facing his own mortality, depicted in his uneasy confrontation with the "ripening" corpse, reflects Taylor's second preoccupation. Death, especially as the result of sudden and unexplained violence, is a theme that dominates much of Taylor's work, especially in memorable poems such as "Barbed Wire," from *The Flying Change*, and "A Voltage Spike," from Taylor's 1996 collection *Understanding Fiction*. In these poems violent, sudden, and seemingly meaningless deaths force both the poet and the speaker to recognize the tenuous nature of life and to examine the consequences that stem from this realization. A final thematic concern, and one that perhaps distinguishes "Landscape with Tractor" from other Taylor poems, is its concern with the inexplicable but strongly felt bond between human beings. For Taylor, an elusive but undeniable bond links all of humanity together, a bond that is unquestionable but very difficult to articulate.

Gregory D. Horn

LE MONOCLE DE MON ONCLE

Author: Wallace Stevens (1879-1955)
Type of poem: Meditation
First published: 1918; collected in *Harmonium*, 1923

The Poem

"Le Monocle de Mon Oncle" is one of the longer poems in Wallace Stevens's first collection, *Harmonium*. It consists of twelve eleven-line stanzas of flexible blank verse. Its title has multiple reverberations, as its sound play and its French title distance the poem from the author. Readers are asked to accept that they are looking through the uncle's monocle and not the poet's own eyes. The title turns the poem into a kind of dramatic monologue, except that the poem's emphasis is not on characterizing the speaker, as is generally the case in a true dramatic monologue, but on posing and answering, or attempting to answer, philosophical questions. It presents a persona who is aging, disappointed in love, and skeptical about religion. This world-weary speaker explores the nature of desire and inquires how desire translates into art.

Beginning with a mocking speech, perhaps part of a quarrel, the narrator examines his relationship with a woman, presumably his wife. He proceeds to examine the nature of the man-woman situation in general. His tone is of fatigue, disappointment, and withdrawal. He describes an apparent rejection and compares the present with the past: "The radiant bubble that she was." He is aware of how old he has become and of how he is edging toward death: "I am a man of fortune greeting heirs;/ For it has come that thus I greet the spring." The poem develops a meditation on sex and death as the speaker muses on his worn-out love, the aging of the body, and sexual confusion, and wonders how these things relate to the creation of art. Sexual "verve" is a source of poetry, but what if that fails? What is left for the artist or poet to draw on?

The speaker concludes that the waxing and waning of sexuality is not all there is. He claims, "There is a substance in us that prevails," but this "basic slate" remains undefined and not entirely satisfactory. It is true that there is another wellspring for art besides sexual longing that is longer lasting: metaphysical desire. This longing too is unsatisfiable, and the speaker discusses the lack of credibility in traditional religion and compares the two kinds of desire: "The honey of heaven may or may not come,/ But that of earth both comes and goes at once." Picturing himself and his love as "two golden gourds" overripe and ready to rot on the vine, he considers the irony of the human situation: Signs of earth's fruitfulness are in evidence, but this kind of fulfillment is not for the aging; on the other hand, metaphysical fulfillment remains beyond his grasp. He retreats into resignation, pondering what growing old has taught him and how different his perspective is now from what it was when he was young.

It is significant that this tired philosopher appears in Stevens's first collection, accompanied by Crispin of "The Comedian as the Letter C," who is also a played-out questioner but one who has been fully satisfied in sex and love—to the extent that these elements of his life took the place of art. It would seem that neither indulgence nor denial was fully effective in producing artistic creativity.

Forms and Devices

The blank verse is a suitable form for this philosophical poem; its division into twelve eleven-lines stanzas provides a sense of order and completion. The rhythm is flexible rather than metronome-like. The casual, conversational rhythm helps to develop the character of the speaker as well as to present the issues. Figurative language abounds. In fact, the poem is a series of metaphors presented and then explained self-consciously by the narrator. Since this is a poem of meditation by an invented character, the metaphors show the speaker's rather precise, pedantic way of looking at the world. They are often parables to explain the positions explored in the poem. The speaker describes angels riding mules down from the heavens, while "centurions guffaw and beat/ Their shrilling tankards on the table-boards." He then explicates: "This parable, in sense, amounts to this," the explication being the passage quoted above about the "honey of heaven" as contrasted with "that of earth." The motifs in the poem underscore its theme of mortality: fruit, ripe and rotting; a frog, suggesting the human grotesque; and a mystical tree, which, in its self-replenishment, may suggest the inexhaustibility of nature.

The images of nature suggest the limits of the individual life in contrast with the life force. Images of fluttering birds appear in the last section, and these movements may suggest the helplessness and fragility of the individual. The birds also suggest a contrast between the perceptions of youth and age:

> A blue pigeon it is, that circles the blue sky,
> On sidelong wing, around and round and round.
> A white pigeon it is, that flutters to the ground,
> Grown tired of flight . . .

The blue pigeon may suggest participation, what Stevens calls in another title "The Pleasure of Merely Circulating." The white pigeon is aware of being "tired," and circling has changed to a downward fluttering. Both the images explained by the speaker and those left for the reader to unravel express the speaker's sense of exclusion and his need to find another source of self-definition besides sexual love. The speaker is self-mocking but nevertheless serious about his predicament.

Themes and Meanings

"Le Monocle de Mon Oncle" is a poem about art as are, on one level, all of Stevens's poems. This poem explores the relationship of sexuality to art. The poem's argument is relatively direct and meanings are not hidden in symbols or allusions. Some critics hold that Stevens's disappointment in marriage resulted in this poem. Stevens's engagement was protracted because he wanted to be in a position to support his beautiful fiancé Elsie Moll before marrying her. During his long engagement, he wrote her voluminous letters that showed her role as his muse; after the marriage, it is clear from the letters that passion cooled fast. Stevens apparently needed to admire his muse from afar. To have her fail as a source of poetry may have made him raise the issue of the role of sexual love in the creative drive and may have made him look for a substitute—not only for her but also for the whole male-female procreative-creative impulse. The speaker asks: What source can bring forth art, if not that one? How can older poets write at all, if they are not impelled by the same energy that brings them to their lovers' arms? Although Stevens may have separated himself from his speaker with a French title, these are his questions too. What about metaphysical desire as the replacement for physical desire? Although metaphysical longing is powerful, it is uncertain of fulfillment. The "honey of heaven" is too vague and unreliable. Nevertheless, it is desire, whatever the object, that brings poetry into being. Unfulfilled desire is the underground stream that also feeds this poem.

Whether or not Stevens's own relationship is the basis of the poem, it examines this issue persistently and obsessively. Like so many of his other works it is elegiac in tone, perhaps regretting a remembered or imagined period of full participation in love and in life. The reward of aging—wisdom—is not sufficient to replace youthful drive, although wisdom itself contributes to art. The poetry of age has wisdom, while the poetry of youth has verve; it seems impossible to have both. This problem is one cause for the speaker's ironic resignation.

"Le Monocle de Mon Oncle" is one of several poems in which Stevens creates older, somewhat pedantic speakers to reflect on art and its relationship to life. The tone of self-mockery may seem to undercut the conclusions reached by the narrators, but even this affected self-awareness may be considered a part of the artist's perspective, especially in Stevens's early poems. The speaker of "Le Monocle de Mon Oncle" may be seen as a counterpart to T. S. Eliot's ineffective suitor in "The Love Song of J. Alfred Prufrock," except that "Mon Oncle" has the wisdom to look beyond his own insecurities in an attempt to make sense of his situation and find a valid source for his art.

Janet McCann

LEARNING EXPERIENCE

Author: Marge Piercy (1936-   )
Type of poem: Narrative
First published: 1969, in *Hard Loving*

The Poem

"Learning Experience" focuses on a boy who is about to take an examination to determine whether he will be subject to being drafted into the United States Army. The twenty-two-line poem is written in free verse that conforms to no predetermined rules and follows no particular meter. It comprises one long, unified stanza. The title of the poem is ironic. The boy, who is sitting in a classroom in Gary, Indiana, is supposed to be "learning" how "to think a little on demand," but he is bored, and the teacher's lessons on "dangling participles" are not going to teach him much about life. In the world outside he will undergo a learning experience, certainly, but one that has little to do with "French irregular verbs" and "Jacksonian democracy," with the material listed on an English or history syllabus. The speaker of the poem is a teacher who has come "out on the train from Chicago" to Gary to teach English grammar.

History forms a backdrop to Marge Piercy's poem and to the plight of the boy in the Gary classroom. In 1965 President Lyndon Johnson authorized General William Westmoreland, commander of U.S. troops in Vietnam, to commit soldiers to the battlefield. Therefore, at the time of this poem, American soldiers are fighting in Vietnam, and more young men are being drafted into the Army every day. The second crucial historical aspect is that in March, 1951, President Harry Truman had issued an executive order deferring the draft for college students of adequate scholastic standing. There would be no second chance for those who failed the college aptitude test that would permit a student deferment.

In line 11, halfway through the poem, it is revealed that "The time of tomorrow's draft exam is written on the board." This fact points to, and explains, the final line of the poem, which says that tomorrow the boy "will try and fail his license to live." Because the boy has been too bored to learn enough in school, he will fail the exam and ultimately will be drafted into "Today's Action Army," qualifying for an education in "death that hurts."

Forms and Devices

One of Piercy's primary interests in delineating history is to make the lessons of the past part of a learning experience that prevents the repetition of past horrors. History can be a kind of moral instruction. The significance of place—where the boy is, physically, socially, and politically—is crucial to the poem. A series of nine prepositional phrases using the word "in" points to where he is: "in the classroom/ in Gary, in the United States, in NATO, in SEATO/ in the thing-gorged belly of the sociobeast,/ in fluorescent light in slowly moving time/ in [thick] boredom."

In the poem's twenty-two lines, twenty-two prepositional phrases attest the weight of the preposition "in" in the poem. To be "in" something is to be contained, and perhaps, as here, trapped. He is trapped by the situation of his life, which has left him few options. Were the war not raging, he might go to work in the steel mills that "consumed his father." As it is, if he had been more interested or studied harder in school, he might be able to attend college and avoid the draft; he will not have this chance. Yet academic pursuits are shown as unappealing as well; a simile describes classroom boredom as "thick and greasy as vegetable shortening."

Marge Piercy refers to Gary, Indiana, in her first novel, *Going Down Fast* (1969). Here, early in her career, she taught English composition and questioned the merit of a learning experience such as that experienced by the boy. Piercy notes that Gary, named for a judge who acquired a reputation for hangings, was a steel-mill town "you never forget you came from" (*Going Down Fast*).

NATO and SEATO are both treaty alliances to which the United States belonged (the North Atlantic Treaty Organization and Southeast Asia Treaty Organization, respectively). Both were established largely to stop the international spread of communism. Being "in" these organizations widens the trap containing the boy far beyond Gary and even the United States. Moreover, the boy is "in the thing-gorged belly of the sociobeast"—the sociobeast emblematic of a capitalist, consumer-oriented society that has turned into a monster and begun consuming its own material and members. It may remind one of the "military-industrial complex," a term often used in the 1960's to refer to the complicity between industry and the "war machine" dedicated to fighting the Vietnam War.

Would it be better, the poem asks, to be alive in a world of scholastic obfuscation or to be drafted into the Army and sent to Vietnam, the Dominican Republic, or Guatemala? The juxtaposition of an education represented by a curriculum of lifeless facts with that of the instruction provided by the Army defines the complexity of the "learning experience" portrayed in the poem.

Themes and Meanings

The central issue in the poem is what constitutes a worthwhile education or "learning experience." The poem examines the teaching role of history, but Piercy also raises a number of points regarding education. Classroom learning often seems to have little relevance to the world outside or to what a young adult will need to know to thrive in that world. Classroom education often seems to consist of exercises such as mastering the conjugation of French irregular verbs before students have yet experienced life, but it is also an attempt to get them to "think a little on demand."

The boy in the poem, and thousands of others like him in the late 1960's, because of their lack of interest in the classroom, were literally "bored to death." Perhaps the education system, stuffing him with "lectures on small groups" in classrooms with "green boards and ivory blinds," has failed them. Piercy's interest in history and in the process of education led her to depict a learning experience in which established systems fail to preserve what Americans value in life. It could be argued that young people, like the boy in Gary, are America's finest resource and that they are of more value than steel.

What the boy is learning in the classroom has ill-prepared him for the experience of living his life. The classroom—and the Army, for that matter—may elicit learning experiences of a type, but those experiences cannot truly be equated with education. The series of prepositional phrases allied in the poem point to dead-end places: the classroom, the city of Gary, the United States of America, NATO, SEATO. All are leading the boy to "Today's Action Army." On the other hand, academic success would offer the boy a draft deferment but would give him in return a life of deathlike boredom.

Sue B. Walker

LEGAL FICTION

Author: William Empson (1906-1984)
Type of poem: Meditation
First published: 1928; collected in *Poems*, 1935

The Poem

"Legal Fiction" is a closely argued sixteen-line poem of four quatrains. A legal fiction is any point in law which is deemed to be true even though in reality it either is a nonsensical point or has no existence. The legal fiction involved here is one of property ownership. The poem explains that in buying any piece of land, the space below and above it are included in the sale, being deemed to be part of the property. That is to say, property has a three-dimensional existence rather than a two-dimensional one.

Empson links this fiction to a cosmic and mythic view of space: the space below extends logically to the center of the earth, where every radius ("long spikes") must necessarily meet. "Your rights reach down where all owners meet." Mythically, this is where hell has been placed, at least in the traditional "three-decker" universe. Similarly, the space above extends logically *ad infinitum.* Mythically again, this is where heaven is situated. From a mythical viewpoint, then, the legal fiction of property ownership states that "you own land in Heaven and Hell."

Empson then extends this fictional concept of property ownership in two ways. First, he defines the geometrical shape of this legal configuration as a cone or "growing sector," with its point at the earth's center and the top "growing" as space extends outward (or upward). Second, he considers the earth's rotation about its axis: "your spun farm's root still on that axis dwells," where "still" could mean ambiguously "continuously" or "without movement," the central point of a turning sphere being deemed not to rotate. The fact, however, is that "Earth's axis varies"; there is no still center after all, so that the whole cone is not fixed, but "wavers . . . at the end."

In this tightly argued meditation, the conclusion is built around three contradictions or paradoxes arising from this fiction. First, in putting "short stakes" around their property, owners are actually buying up rights to boundless volume: They are getting much more than they bargained for. Second, far from buying something fixed in which to settle down, a property owner is "a nomad yet," because the bought space is continuously moving. Finally, in buying something material, owners are actually buying into the mythical.

The image that Empson leaves in conclusion is that of a lighthouse whose beams penetrate the darkness of space. They form a cone, just like the shape of the property. The beam flashes "like Lucifer, through the firmament." The figure of Lucifer, traditionally a name for Satan or the devil, thus forces the theological dimension of heaven and hell into the reader's consciousness. Life is less certain, less solid, than humans suppose. They are inevitably involved with questions of ultimacy, of final judgment, and however uncertainly and tentatively, they must acknowledge the depths and heights of which human life consists.

Forms and Devices

Although he wrote during a period of modernist and experimental verse, Empson's poems remain traditional in stanza form and rhyme scheme. Here the quatrain form is used, each stanza being clearly completed by a period. The alternating rhymes are marked as clearly. The lines have a basic iambic pentameter, but the demands of Empson's density of expression typically push extra spondees into the line. Thus there is no easy rhythmical reading of the verse: It has to be read in controlled speech rhythms that move toward prose, and one must follow the punctuation carefully to retain the sense of the argument.

Both diction and imagery are interesting in the poem. The diction at first appears to be solidly legal: "law," "real estate," "flat" (apartment), "citizen," "owners," and especially "your rights." The use of "you" is typical of Empson; it challenges the reader much more directly than "we" or "they," and with "you" he is forcing the readers' rights on them. However, the materiality of this diction is constantly challenged—for example, by the oxymoron "the nomad citizen." (One may wonder how a nomad can own a "high flat," let alone overlook a piece of real estate.)

Although the "rights" mentioned here are apparently property rights rather than human rights, the two concepts merge "at earth's centre," where the separateness and exclusiveness of property rights are countered by the communality of human rights "down where all owners meet." In the end, too, "nomad" merges with the owner, since the space owned is so vast and is not actually fixed, but shifting. The stability that owning land brings is a delusion: People are still as much moving, restlessly even, whether they own property or not.

One strand of the imagery, as stated earlier, involves the traditional view of hell, earth, and heaven as three layers of existence. However, the cone image is more reminiscent of Dante's Inferno, where hell is depicted as a series of narrowing circles running from the surface of the earth down into its center. For Dante, only the worst villains are located at the lowest points, whereas Empson keeps the traditional image of the whole of hell being down there. The combination of the two schemes would seem impossible, but Empson's geometrical logic keeps the conceit powerfully alive.

The other strand of imagery transforms the cone into a beam of light, first from a lighthouse, finally reduced to a candle. A certain ambivalence lies in this light image, since the lighthouse flashes are compared to Lucifer, who, while originally an angel of light (literally the name means "light-bearer"), has become prince of darkness. In the same way, one's "central cone" is dark; one sees not the candle wavering but its shadow. What emerges from the poem is a sense of the darkness of space as well as the darkness of the earth's center: Human life only flashes or gleams intermittently in this darkness.

Themes and Meanings

Although he was still an undergraduate at Cambridge University when he wrote this poem, William Empson's poetic formulation and style were already remarkably well developed. The dense intellectualism of its style and its avoidance of direct emotional expression could easily render the poem an exercise in that mental puzzlement often devoted to crosswords. However, the sheer philosophic power behind it gives it movement and coherence. In fact, "Legal Fiction" is one of the easier poems to decipher in Empson's first volume of poetry. In reading other poems in the volume, certain themes, motifs and images emerge to help in the elucidation of any one poem.

For example, the excitement of space travel and the new theories of cosmology then current is evident, as in the poems "Camping Out" or "Dissatisfaction with Metaphysics," in which Empson writes: "New safe straight lines are finite though unbounded." As did the Metaphysical poets of the early seventeenth century, whom he much admired, he seeks to unify cosmological and other scientific discovery with metaphysics and theology through the medium of poetry. The poet thus becomes the polymath. Good examples of such poems are "This Last Pain," in which heaven and hell are featured frequently, and "The World's End," in which notions of the world's circularity are viewed cosmologically and eschatologically—no end comes to mean no purpose; everyone has to define their own.

Empson's theological interest is not that he has a religious faith—far from it—but that within literature, theology has been given mythical forms that people still need to explore mentally. As he stated in his study *The Structure of Complex Words* (1951), "myths are where incompatibles are joined." The key phrase in the poem is thus "real estate of mind." In Empson's poem "Letter 1," the cosmos becomes the typical image for inner space or being. The fear expressed in that poem is that both inner and outer space will merely be a void. In "Arachne" he writes similarly of "his gleaming bubble between void and void." In "Legal Fiction," that fear does not seem so urgent, and an allusion to a Jungian notion of a feared "shadow" self is not developed.

Throughout his life Empson conducted an argument with another intellectual poet whose imagination was cosmic, seventeenth century poet John Milton. Empson could quote Milton's epic *Paradise Lost* by heart. In his scholarly work *Milton's God* (1961), he takes issue with Milton's adherence to the traditional Christian view of heaven and hell and of God as the just, perfect Creator. For Empson they are still needed, in revised forms, as literary fictions to help people come to terms with an otherwise amoral, purposeless, though magnificent cosmos. Lucifer becomes the central ambiguous figure, as he was for William Blake and other Romantic poets.

"Legal Fiction," then, is part of Empson's attempt to remap the cosmos now that God is not there. The "contradiction and conflict" that Christopher Ricks saw as "the foundation of his poems" here is that of the human condition, in touch with and capable of acting in dimensions of good and evil, yet uncertain how to find a true and fixed place in which to own such possibilities.

David Barratt

LETTERS TO A PSYCHIATRIST

Author: May Sarton (1912-1995)
Type of poem: Poetic sequence
First published: 1972, in *A Durable Fire*

The Poem

As the title suggests, "Letters to a Psychiatrist" is a series of letters in verse. They are six in number, written to Marynia F. Farnham, the author and psychiatrist to whom *A Durable Fire*, the collection in which these poems first appeared, is dedicated. As a sequence of poems, these six letters in verse, though varied in length and form, move from Christmas, 1970, the time of the first poem, through Easter, 1971, the time of the fifth poem. The movement of the sequence is at once linear and circular. The first-person narrator, a patient of Marynia the psychiatrist, is modeled on May Sarton herself, a poet/artist who, while singing songs of praise to Marynia, moves from a state of suicidal depression to a state that is more whole, conscious, and integrated by the poem's end, an action of change made possible by the vehicle of the accepting and skilled therapist.

The eulogy to Marynia begins with "Christmas Letter, 1970." Consisting of five numbered parts, the numbers provide slight shifts to the ongoing, interior lyrical narrative, an internal dialogue from the "I" of the poem to Marynia, sometimes referred to as "she," sometimes addressed directly by name, and sometimes addressed as "you." In this first poem, Sarton establishes Marynia metaphorically as an "angel" of wisdom, someone so gifted in her profession that she allows those wounded ones, like the narrator herself, to go deeply into themselves to begin the process of healing. The second poem in the sequence, a sixteen-line poem with four stanza breaks entitled "The Fear of Angels," continues the eulogy to the psychiatrist. The poet expands the angel metaphor: The psychiatrist is described as one whose brightness and almost-divine presence allows the patient to drop her defenses in order to go deeper into herself.

"The Action of Therapy," the third poem, is similar to the first poem in structure, a long poem in verse divided, in this case, into six parts. Sarton begins this poem with a whirlwind, a dangerous time when "The psyche nearly cracked/ Under the blast," a metaphor linking the chaos of nature to the turmoil of the individual psyche. Darkness and storm, earthquake and whirlwind evoke a destructive passion that has blasted the narrator to the core. Yet the poem centers on the healer, the psychiatrist Marynia who, as the "psychic surgeon," has the angelic power to accept, give, heal, and bless. Without judgment, with "Simple acceptance/ Of things as they are," Marynia allows the patient to dig into her past, allows the patient to love her in a structured but nonthreatening and nonjudgmental atmosphere, and thereby allows the patient to break the spell her own mother had over her. To give and to receive love, to be receptive and teachable, are some of the actions of therapy. The psychiatrist is once again eulogized in glowing terms of light, transformation, and transparency—the soul's realm.

The fourth poem, entitled "I Speak of Change," is the pivotal poem in the sequence. An eighteen-line poem with no stanza or numbered breaks, it is more formally structured than those that have preceded it. Indeed, the tight structure serves to mirror the poem's content: the lesson of passion contained (a recurring theme in Sarton's poetry). The poet begins with the couplet, "Tumult as deep and formal as in dance/ Seizes me now for every scheduled hour." The tension between chaos and order, passion and detachment is resolved by merging these two seemingly opposite impulses. Here the psychiatrist and poet meet, representing, on a figurative level, the reconciliation of elements in the poet's own psyche. Indeed, reconciled opposites inform the poem: words and silence, light and darkness, distance and closeness. The narrator indicates the relationship has served growth and change and has allowed the narrator/patient/poet to become more fully and authentically herself.

The fifth poem, entitled "Easter 1971," is a celebration of the riches that have come from the patient-therapist relationship; it is also a celebration of the poet's aloneness. The narrator knows that an epiphany is near, and she celebrates the antiphonies of opposite forces, named in the poem as "fervor and detachment," two qualities that Sarton herself believes to be necessary for the poet/artist. In the last line of this poem, the narrator calls the psychiatrist-patient relationship "a structured, impersonal, and holy dance."

In "The Contemplation of Wisdom," the last poem in the sequence, the narrator speaks of the inevitable severing of the relationship with the psychiatrist and contemplates the wisdom she has gained. The narrator accepts more fully the life of one who has to live on the edge, the artist's life, and shows acceptance of her darkness and loss. Once again the narrator eulogizes the psychiatrist: "I summon up fresh courage from your courage." She ends with the acceptance of the psychiatrist's love as the key that will help her with her solitary poet/artist's life.

Forms and Devices

These poems abound with references to the natural world of plants and animals; light and dark; seasons, earth, water, and sky; and earthquakes, storms, and fire. Used as both metaphors and images that inform the poetic landscape, these references make it clear that human beings, with their capacity for suffering and joy, also belong to this natural kingdom. The personal psyche can be blasted just as a tree struck by lightening can be blasted or the earth, rent by an earthquake, can be blasted. Juxtaposed with these natural images are images of transcendence, an arena of experience belonging to both God and humans.

Sarton begins "Christmas Letter, 1970" with "These bulbs forgotten in a cellar,/ Pushing up through the dark their wan white shoots,/ Trying to live—." Used metaphorically as a part of the narrator/poet that is lost in unconsciousness, the bulbs, a symbol of potential beauty and transformation (the flower), serve as that potential for growth that is acknowledged yet "forgotten," that part of the narrator's own psyche that wants realization. Sarton, who speaks lovingly in her journals of gardening, writes, in her *Journal of a Solitude* (1973), a non-fiction journal she was writing even as she composed the poems for *A Durable Fire*, "For a long time, for years, I have carried in my mind the excruciating image of plants, bulbs, in a cellar, trying to grow without light, putting out *white* shoots that will inevitably wither. It is time I examined this image."

Juxtaposed with the natural world in these poems is the more transcendent world of angels and God, a nonetheless human world that incorporates mystery, wisdom, and rebirth as well as the great "Unknown." The movement toward reconciliation of these seemingly opposite forces contributes to the tension of this sequence. The human rises to the divine in the person of Marynia, described again and again as "an angel," one who has "superior powers." Marynia is also emblematic of a surrogate mother figure, the divine Mother, the Eternal Feminine. The divine also descends to the human in the figure of Christ, a symbol of transcendence and rebirth but also of suffering (his earthly life leading up to the Crucifixion). In the fifth part of the third poem, "The Action of Therapy," Sarton writes, "In middle age we starve/ For ascension," clearly indicating that in maturity the interior psychological drive is for transcendence, which means, for Sarton, a drive for love and connection, for earthly communion and wisdom. "The cruel ascension/ Toward loss" described in part 3 of "The Action of Therapy" epitomizes the narrator's struggle to transcend humankind's animal nature by merging into it and accepting loss and change.

The Christian holidays of Christmas and Easter are integral to the sequence and parallel the narrator's struggle. Christmas, symbolic of Christ's birth, is, in the Christian tradition, a time of joy and hope for the world. It is also, for many, a time of loneliness and depression. In part 2 of "Christmas Letter, 1970," the reader hears Marynia's voice through the interior dialogue of the narrator/patient: "'Yes,' you say, 'of course at Christmas/ Half the world is suicidal.'" Sarton also draws the parallel between vulnerable infant love, which the Christ child also represents, and the vulnerable love of the patient for the psychiatrist, a love that, in parts of the sequence, appears naïve in its ubiquitous adoration, a naïveté that is clearly a part of the process of therapy. The patient, like the vulnerable infant and the "homeless cat" mentioned in part 1 of this same poem, is "hungry" and "starving." This animal need for food, symbolic of the narrator/patient's need for love and acceptance, will be satisfied by a meeting of the divine presence, symbolized in the literal as well as figurative Marynia, one who is associated with both the human and divine mother. Words such as "food," "nourish," "restore," "save," "shelter," "provide," and "mother" surround Marynia throughout these poems as do words such as "angel," "goddess," "power," "light," "mysteries," and "blessed." The narrator/patient/poet must, like the Christ child, integrate the human and divine into herself. She does this through the meeting with the literal and figurative Marynia, who, as a psychiatrist with "superior powers," represents for the patient mother love, divine love, and transcendent love.

As Christmas connotes both joy and suffering, Easter connotes both as well. In the Christian tradition, Easter represents Christ's death and suffering as epitomized in the crucifixion; Easter also represents Christ's rebirth and resurrection. In "Easter 1971," the narrator has been, through "the action of therapy," figuratively resurrected. She writes, "I come to this Easter newly rich and free/ In all my gifts." Celebrating both the richness of her own gifts as a poet and her "winter poverty," the aloneness and detachment required for a writer, the narrator has come to a fuller acceptance of her self. Though the poet feels reborn through "the action of therapy," she nevertheless must struggle, as all humans do, with loneliness, suffering, and loss. Wisdom, the topic of the last poem, is, Sarton implies, the true meeting place that is both God-like and human, the reconciliation of the human and divine soul.

Themes and Meanings

"Letters to a Psychiatrist" is a poem about the interior journey, a theme that has occupied Sarton in her novels, fiction, and poetry. While "Letters to a Psychiatrist" explores the unique relationship between psychiatrist and patient, it also explores the human journey of suffering, pain, depression, and loss as well as the human journey of growth, love, and transcendence. Although the patient/narrator is modeled on Sarton herself, it is most important to realize that any poem, if it works at all, should not require an exhaustive search into the poet's own life and psyche to be understood, for good poetry speaks of the largesse of the human experience, however idiosyncratic the subject or even the poet may seem. However, because Sarton's life and art are so closely related, her themes can be better understood by looking at a few of her own words.

In *Journal of a Solitude*, Sarton writes, "Here in Nelson [New Hampshire] I have been close to suicide more than once, and more than once have been close to a mystical experience of unity with the universe." This preoccupation with both the realm of suffering and the realm of transcendence, the mystical realm, is what, most of all, informs these poems. Though Marynia F. Farnham was Sarton's real therapist, readers will realize, if they look at the poems themselves rather than Sarton's life, that Marynia must also be seen as a facet of Sarton herself and, by implication, as a facet of the feminine, if not the divine feminine, in every person.

Though the decision to exclude talk about the relationship between Farnham and Sarton in *Journal of a Solitude* was left to critic and editor Carolyn Heilbrun, Sarton herself argued, "There are still many people who believe that going to a psychiatrist is an admission of failure or an act of cowardice . . . I am a fruitful person with a viable life and I believe it would be helpful for people to know that I have had help and did not fear to ask for it." This quote is important because Sarton's personal life and her art are almost inseparable; yet, paradoxically, because she is an artist, her art is at once larger than her personal life.

Once again, though Marynia was a real, living person, this woman, through the action of the poems themselves, becomes much larger than a simple woman or a psychiatrist in the same way the narrator of these poems becomes much larger than Sarton the writer and poet. While the meanings and themes of this poetic sequence are based on what happened in Sarton's real life, they are also much more than what happened; they are about emotional involvement and emotional detachment (stereotypically and traditionally represented in Western culture as the feminine/masculine) as well as the human/divine nature in each person that aspires to self-knowledge, understanding, love, and wisdom. As far as the patient/narrator/poet is concerned, Sarton asks, in *Recovering: A Journal* (1980), "Is there anyone, I sometimes wonder, who is not wounded and in the process of healing?" thereby aligning each reader with her narrator.

Though some of Sarton's critics have criticized the poems in *A Durable Fire* for not confronting "the emotional issues she writes about with candor, openness, or a sufficient sense of honesty," the strength of the poems in "Letters to a Psychiatrist" is that they transcend that which is purely personal. Human beings all suffer from lack of growth and unconsciousness, like those bulbs "forgotten" in a dark cellar that begin the sequence. While on one hand "Letters to a Psychiatrist" is a eulogy to Marynia, this poetic sequence also concerns, at its core, the struggle toward integration of all the disparate parts that make people human, the struggle to integrate the feminine within themselves, the struggle to integrate the open and vulnerable child with the mature, suffering, and more cynical adult, and the struggle of the poet to integrate the passionate and emotional lover with the more rational detached artist, "those antiphonies/ Where the soul of a poet feeds and rests." Finally, this poem is about the journey of the psyche and the self toward what Sarton calls "Total awareness," toward "a new landscape" where "souls, released at last,/ Dance together/ On the simple grass."

Candace E. Andrews

THE LIAR'S PSALM: REPENTANCE

Author: Andrew Hudgins (1951-   )
Type of poem: Meditation
First published: 1984; collected in *The Never-Ending*, 1991

The Poem

"Repentance" is one of four poems which together constitute a longer work entitled "The Liar's Psalm." The epigraph that precedes "The Liar's Psalm" states the subject and sets the tone for the entire work. It is a quotation from the beast-fable, "Reynard the Fox," one of the many medieval versions of the adventures of an immoral predator who manages through cunning to avoid the punishment he deserves. The epigraph begins by pointing out that, while it takes neither "art nor cunning" to tell the truth, a skillful liar "may do wonders." Motivated by the "hope of gain only," he can rise high in the secular world or in the Church. Almost as an afterthought, the speaker adds that, though lying is indeed an "art," it inevitably ends in "misery and affliction."

With its emphasis on Reynard's accomplishments rather than his downfall, this epigraph establishes the ambivalent tone that is evident throughout "The Liar's Psalm." Andrew Hudgins, the poet, cannot but admire a creature with the artistic talent of the fox; on the other hand, Andrew Hudgins, the moralist, knows that though truth may seem dull, lies are the devil's instrument.

"Repentance" is the second segment in "The Liar's Psalm." It is preceded by "Homage to the Fox," in which the fox's gifts are praised and his worldly success emphasized, while the truth is characterized as both cowardly and unimaginative. The section that follows "Repentance" is called "Judas, Flowering." In it, the speaker says that his hero and presumably his model is Christ's betrayer Judas. Again, the deceiver is shown as being a fascinating character, unlike pedestrian truth. In the last section of "The Liar's Psalm," "treachery" is again honored; it is far more valuable, the speaker says, than "love" and "hope." There is, however, a puzzling comment in the final lines of the poem. The speaker admits that on occasion he does believe that the moon (light, good, and truth) might eliminate the darkness of the night sky, or evil, but he hastens to add that such a notion is merely proof that he can deceive even himself.

Like the other segments of "The Liar's Psalm," "Repentance" exalts fiction above fact, lies above truth. What the speaker repents is his own failure to lie. He sees truth as powerless; not only can it not keep the persona's father from dying, but it also keeps the son miserable anticipating grief. The speaker rejects logic, the supposed servant of truth, for in actuality it has "no god": it can be used to prove anything.

Having rejected both reality and logic, the speaker now vows never again to "insult" those he cares about "with the actual." He recalls and regrets the times he told the truth and hurt those he loved—his mother, his wife, a friend, his brother. From now on, he resolves, he will lie to others and believe the lies they tell him. At the end of the poem, the speaker asks forgiveness for his past skepticism, for behaving like Thomas the

Apostle, who would not believe that Christ had indeed risen from the dead until Thomas had placed his hand in Jesus's wounded side.

Forms and Devices

Though Hudgins often utilizes blank verse for his poetry, "Repentance" is written in a mixture of forms. Some of the lines are conventional blank verse—for instance, "and I repent logic, which has no god: it will do." Other lines are either shorter or longer but still regular and iambic: "So I have made this vow" and "of apple pie, a black chrysanthemum, a job—I could go on." Sometimes anapests dominate, as in "It is nothing against principalities, against powers." Occasionally the meter becomes so uncertain as the line progresses that Hudgins seems to have forgotten metrics altogether, but when that happens, he soon returns to a regular pattern, if not necessarily to iambic pentameter. For example, after "or with their densities. They are not worth their flawed kingdoms," is followed by a line which begins with three iambic feet, "And neither do I love" before veering away from regularity. However, Hudgins is a careful craftsman, and there is method in what might seem to be metrical madness. To emphasize a point, for example, he uses simple words and a simple, regular pattern, as in the first four words of the poem and in the later "So I have made this vow."

Hudgins' imagery is as varied as his metrics. Some of it is grand and abstract, such as the Miltonic "principalities" and "powers" and the references to "gods" and "kingdoms." On the other hand, much of it is taken from the everyday world. Reality, like manual labor, will "blister" his hands and "make them raw." Logic is compared to a "taxi," lies to self-indulgences like "a piece/ of apple pie," and when in the past the speaker "attacked/ with actuality," he used the "blade" of a knife.

There are often surprising juxtapositions of images in "Repentance." For example, the list of minor "gifts" to oneself (clothing, pie, a flower) ends with a matter of major significance in life, "a job." Similarly, when the speaker lists the truths that he regrets telling, he moves back and forth between moral flaws and matters of taste or appearance. Thus he appears to give the same importance to adultery and theft as to making an unfortunate choice in clothing or simply being too fat.

Often Hudgins is classified with Carson McCullers and Flannery O'Connor as a southern gothic writer. In this poem the final image is more graphic than the biblical original, for here the speaker has his finger not on, but "knuckle deep" in the wound. The earlier reference to human flesh, "sliced from my thighs," is also grotesque. In both cases, however, and throughout the poem, Hudgins places his dramatic, concrete imagery at the service of profound philosophical concepts.

Themes and Meanings

In "Homage to the Fox" and "Judas, Flowering," the speaker glorified evildoers because, as the epigraph points out, they are both interesting and successful. However, the epigraph ends by noting that evil results in "misery and affliction." Certainly it did for Judas, who committed suicide and presumably is spending eternity in Hell. It is obvious, then, that though Hudgins's persona may be deceived, the poet is not.

Instead, he is using his speaker to demonstrate how human beings are seduced by evil and specifically by lies and lying.

"Repentance" differs from the segments before and after it in that here lying is not shown as a way to worldly power but as a positive good. For example, people would be happier, the speaker argues, if they could not anticipate the deaths of those they love. The knowledge God gave humankind, then, is a burden, not a blessing. The persona then insists that it is lies, not facts, that make a person happy. For one thing, reality is limited, while the human imagination can invent possibilities "six times a second." Even if these dreams do not come true, anticipation alone can bring one great delight.

It is difficult to refute this argument, especially when one broadens it to include in the category of "lies" all the works of the imagination. If one were to divide the world on that basis, as a writer Hudgins must be on the side of lies, and so would everyone be who has chosen to read this poem. Hudgins now proceeds to another argument in favor of lies: that they are kinder than the truth. As has been noted, his examples of cruelty vary from the trivial, such as a comment about an unbecoming dress, to scathing attacks on character traits, such as "stinginess." In a peculiar reversal of Christian doctrine, then, one hopes to be "blessed" with lies, rather than being damned by telling the hurtful truth.

Having pointed out the value of lying to oneself and to others, the persona carries his argument one step further, insisting that one should also believe all the lies one is told. Since he then alludes to Thomas's encounter with the risen Christ, one might read the final lines as a suggestion that faith is a matter of believing in untruths. However, the allusion itself contradicts that implication, for Thomas felt real flesh. His doubts, therefore, were beside the point, for he did not create or imagine Christ. "The Liar's Psalm," then, is not an argument for evil, but an examination of humanity's suscepti- bility to it. Thus the speaker in the final section of the poem foolishly rethinks his brief moment of faith, while in "Repentance" the liar somehow manages to miss the important truth: that when he decides to "repent the actual," he is rejecting the God who does not lie.

Rosemary M. Canfield Reisman

LIBRETTO FOR THE REPUBLIC OF LIBERIA

Author: Melvin B. Tolson (1898-1966)
Type of poem: Epic
First published: 1953

The Poem

Melvin B. Tolson, a professor of English at Wiley College in Marshall, Texas, and author of a collection of poems entitled *Rendezvous with America* (1944), was appointed poet laureate of Liberia by that African nation's president, William V. S. Tubman, in 1947. Tolson was commissioned to compose a poem to celebrate Liberia's centennial. He spent six years at the task, and the book-length *Libretto for the Republic of Liberia* was eventually published in 1953. While he might have fulfilled this commission with a flattering poem, Tolson had a much more ambitious idea. He told an interviewer in 1965, "I, as a black poet, have absorbed the Great Ideas of the Great White World, and interpreted them in the melting-pot idiom of my people. My roots are in Africa, Europe, and America." This self-image as an intellectual synthesizer of world culture informs his poem.

Tolson produced an epic poem in the tradition of Vergil's *Aeneid* (c. 29-19 B.C.) presenting Liberia's history in terms of a grand mythology, recounting significant events, and attaching symbolic resonance to the deeds of great leaders. The poem is divided into eight sections—each given the title of one of the notes in the *do-re-mi* musical scale—which Tolson thought of as the rungs on a ladder. Each section brings the reader (and the poet) closer to attaining an overview of history. Because *Libretto for the Republic of Liberia* is intended to be an epic poem, this view of history—like Dante's in *The Divine Comedy* (c. 1320) or John Milton's in *Paradise Lost* (1667) and *Paradise Regained* (1671)—includes past, present, and future.

Section 1, "*Do,*" opens with a series of questions about the Eurocentric view of Africa as a mysterious continent, the very shape of which suggests "a question mark." The meaning of the independent black nation of Liberia is the question that Tolson must answer. He contends that Liberia's unique history makes it "A moment in the conscience of mankind." "*Re,*" the next section, presents the history of Africa before the slave trade began, citing the Songhai Empire, the great city of Timbuktu, and other precolonial centers documented in works by J. A. Rogers and in W. E. B. Du Bois's *The World and Africa* (1947). In section 3, Tolson describes the establishment of Liberia as a haven for freed slaves from the United States sponsored by the American Colonization Society. He describes these settlers as "Black Pilgrim Fathers" because their return to Africa in 1820 reverses the direction of the voyage of the Mayflower exactly two hundred years earlier. The section ends with a leap forward in time to 1942, when airfields in Liberia were a staging area for Allied bombers in World War II.

Section 4 presents images of predatory nature juxtaposed with the refrain "in the interlude of peace," symbolizing Liberia's struggle to remain independent while

European nations partitioned the rest of the continent into colonial possessions. Section 5, *"Sol,"* emphasizes that the Liberian settlers must survive perilous conditions, but in addition they are charged with the task of refuting Europe's racist judgment of African inferiority. Tolson counters such views with a series of African proverbs, beginning: "Africa is a rubber ball;/ the harder you dash it to the ground,/ the higher it will rise." The next section, *"La,"* recounts the heroic efforts of Jehudi Ashmun, the white American missionary who devoted his life to help establish the Liberian settlement.

Section 7, *"Ti,"* is a 232-line tour de force of literary allusions and intricate rhyme schemes that attacks European imperialism and the Eurocentric misreading of history that supported the exploitation of other continents. The final *"Do"* section—which rivals *"Ti"* for inventive density—is a vision of a glorious African future that will herald a new era of genuine peace and international cooperation. In this coming age, after centuries of turmoil, Tolson predicts that it will become possible for human beings to balance "the scales of Head and Heart."

Forms and Devices

In form, *Libretto for the Republic of Liberia* may be considered an irregular ode, but its eight-hundred-line length and historical subject matter also qualify it as a modernist epic comparable to Hart Crane's *The Bridge* (1930) or Ezra Pound's much longer *Cantos* (1925-1968). Tolson's poem also has some stylistic similarities to these works. However, as the title suggests, he intended *Libretto for the Republic of Liberia* to be a grand song joined by many voices.

Tolson's dividing of the poem into sections titled with notes from the musical scale indicates that each section has its own distinct tonality, allowing the poet to use a number of different poetic forms. Since a libretto is ordinarily understood to be the words for an opera, this arrangement suggests that Tolson intends the reader to understand that his words form the "meaning" of each musical note. Music is ordinarily thought of as an abstract or nonreferential art form, but there are African traditions suggesting that specific notes or musical tones have specific meanings. Indeed, the tones produced by the West African *dundun* (or "talking drum") can simulate words in a tonal language such as Yoruba. Tolson studied African proverbs extensively, and his use of them in the poem indicates his concern that *Libretto for the Republic of Liberia* would embody traditional African artistic elements.

The poetic techniques that Tolson most often employs in this poem are metaphors and highly concentrated allusions (references to other literary works). As in his earlier long poem "Rendezvous with America," he also devises different rhyme patterns for each section of the work.

Tolson's complex structure of literary allusions and historical references is similar to the juxtapositions found in Pound's *Cantos*, and he directs the reader to his sources with footnotes in the manner of T. S. Eliot's *The Waste Land* (1922). The range of references documents Tolson's own scope of knowledge and suggests a curriculum for the reader's further education. The scope of these references supports Tolson's belief that culture and knowledge are not limited by racial, geographical, or political boundaries; he cautions the reader not to ignore "the dusky peers of Roman, Greek, and Jew" in attempting to assess the progress of human civilization, to which all of the world's cultures have contributed. The dedicated reader of *Libretto for the Republic of Liberia* can seek out the specific references behind the poem's allusions and, by so doing, will gain a deeper understanding of Tolson's argument and his unique mental associations. To use a musical analogy, exploring this level of the poem is like focusing on the bass line of a familiar song; suddenly one becomes aware of a delightful new set of designs and parallel inventions. When Tolson alludes to a line from Rudyard Kipling's 1897 poem "Recessional," for example, he is leading the reader to the idea that the advent of an independent, peaceful future for African nations must necessarily also involve the recessional or retreat of the exploitative European colonialism that Kipling's poem celebrated.

Section 5 of the poem demonstrates that, while he was clearly an avid student of European literature, Tolson's approach to writing this epic poem includes the traditions of the West African *griots*, the oral historians and bards described in Tolson's footnote as "living encyclopedias." Just as those poets were responsible for memorizing the genealogies of the families in their region, Tolson's poem contains the stories of the Reverend Jehudi Ashmun, the Reverend Robert Finley of the American Colonization Society, and Liberia's first president, Joseph Jenkins Roberts. Although he employs the elevated language suitable to an epic poem, Tolson does not provide a straightforward narrative structure. The reader who consults encyclopedia entries on Liberia and the American Colonization Society can learn many of the historical details needed to follow Tolson's references.

Themes and Meanings

In vivid contrast to the beginning of *Libretto for the Republic of Liberia*, in which the shape of the African continent suggests to Tolson a question mark or a skull, the poem's concluding section presents a series of glowingly positive images. The poem's final prophetic section, the musical scale's resolving "*Do,*" is written in verse paragraphs reminiscent of the Bible or Walt Whitman's *Leaves of Grass* (1855). Here Tolson depicts the continent via the metaphor of the Futurafrique—imagined as a fast train, supersonic airplane, or ocean liner. This promise of a glorious modernistic future is followed by Tolson's vision of a Parliament of African Peoples.

Earlier in the poem, Tolson quotes (in French) the nineteenth century rationalization for slavery and the colonization of Africa based on the argument that "alone of all the continents, Africa has no history" or civilization. It is against this claim that he offers his vision of the continent's future. Rather than devoting the poem to a list of great African leaders or a chronicle of memorable precolonial achievements, Tolson refutes the myth of African inferiority with a catalog of African proverbs that testify to the wisdom and experience of the continent's peoples. Finally, Tolson presents Liberia not only as a nineteenth century refuge for American slaves, but also (as a result of its heroic survival) as a beacon of global promise, the coming fulfillment of humankind's best possibilities as reflected in the nation's motto, "The Love of Liberty Brought Us Here."

Lorenzo Thomas

THE LIE

Author: Sir Walter Ralegh (c. 1552-1618)
Type of poem: Satire
First published: 1608, in *A Poetical Rapsody*; collected in *The Poems of Sir Walter Ralegh*, 1929

The Poem

Given that "The Lie" is now Sir Walter Ralegh's best-known poem, it would be ironic if the French critic Pierre Lefranc were correct in his assertion, in *Sir Walter Ralegh, Ecrivain, L'oeuvre et les idées* (1968), that it was not written by Ralegh. The earliest known manuscripts, which date from approximately 1595, are unsigned, as is the first printed version in Francis Davison's *A Poetical Rapsody* (1608). Lefranc argues that the poem is obviously the work of a Puritan, which Ralegh emphatically was not. Lefranc further argues that the poem is too clumsy and tedious to be Ralegh's. The vast majority of English critics, however, agree that the attribution is correct, claiming that the impression of Puritan sentiment is derived from a too-literal reading of a satire and observing that the poem's rhythm, based on iambic trimeters with five initial trochaic feet, closely resembles poems that are unmistakably Ralegh's. The English critics also disagree with the contention that the poem is clumsy or tedious, although its tempo is certainly furious enough to give it a reckless quality, and it hammers home its point with a rain of blows whose quantity is suggestive of overkill.

The thirteen stanzas of "The Lie" comprise a series of instructions addressed to the soul, famously characterized as "the body's guest," demanding that it strip away the poses and pretenses with which social life is armored. Each six-line stanza concludes with an injunction that any reply should be stoutly met: The last line of each stanza (except the thirteenth) is a variant of the phrase "and give the world the lie." Following the introductory stanza, the main series moves through three phases. In the first phase (a single stanza) the soul is commanded to tell the court that "it glowes,/ and shines like rotten wood" and the Church that "it showes/ whats good, and doth no good."

In the second phase, which comprises three stanzas, the soul is instructed to address itself more generally to potentates, "men of high condition," and "them that brave it most." The potentates are gently reminded that they are "not loved unless they give"; the men of high condition are attacked far more vituperatively because "their purpose is ambition/ their practise onely hate"; the third group, by contrast, is let off more lightly than the addressees of any other stanza, it merely being said that "they beg for more by spending,/ Who in their greatest cost/ like nothing but commending." In the third and longest phase (seven stanzas), the soul is commanded to penetrate the illusion, each in its turn, of zeal, love, time, and flesh; age, honor, beauty, and favor; wit and wisdom; "Phisicke" (medicine), skill, charity, and law; fortune, nature, friendship, and justice; arts and "schooles" (philosophy); and faith, manhood, and virtue. The last stanza gives the screw of cynicism one last turn in conceding that "to give the lie,/ deserves no lesse then stabbing" but notes triumphantly that "no stab thy soule can kill."

Forms and Devices

"The Lie" is a poem about disillusionment, and its method is admirably suited to its subject, for disillusionment is a process that proceeds by inexorable degrees, stripping one layer of falsity after another until the last is gone. Ralegh employs the repetitive rhythm of the poem to build up a relentless surge that cannot be interrupted until it has taken its corrosive task to its logical end point. The suggestion of overkill that seems tedious to Lefranc is, in fact, entirely appropriate to the project.

Disillusionment is the principal stock-in-trade of satire, which was newly fashionable as a device when "The Lie" was written. The satirical method is one of contemptuous exaggeration that magnifies faults so aggressively that no half measures are tolerated. "The Lie" accepts this extremism wholeheartedly, accelerating as it moves through its phases of generality to the point at which each of the soul's addressees is condemned by a single, dismissive adjective: "Tell fortune of her blindnesse,/ tell nature of decay,/ Tell friendship of unkindnesse,/ tell justice of delay." The poet is not stating that all these things are worthless but that they are flawed. The essence of the poem's argument is that nothing is perfect—except, of course, for the soul itself, the measure of all these things that "no stab . . . can kill."

Because the form and devices of the poem are determined by its subject matter, which reflects and embodies the process and progress of disillusionment, care must be taken in evaluating the implications of its argument. In spite of its relentlessly downbeat thrust, the poem is not as nihilistic as it might appear at first glance, nor is it atheistic or puritanical as its early detractors suggested. "The Lie" is not atheistic because all its charges are directed against earthly institutions and human endeavors. It is not puritanical because it makes no distinctions and offers no policies. It is, in fact, entirely concerned with admitting and accepting the truth and not at all concerned with organizing behavior. It advises the inner being to be perceptive and suspicious of all imposture, but it advises no more than that. It is an angry poem, but its wrath is wry rather than righteous, directed inward rather than outward; although the soul is directed to do a great deal of "telling," the entities that are to be told are ideas rather than actual individuals. The soul that the author is admonishing is his own and so are the ideas; the only person who is under attack is the poet himself.

When the soul is told to "Tell Potentates they live,/ acting by others action," Ralegh undoubtedly has his former patron Queen Elizabeth in mind, just as he has the earl of Essex, the rival who replaced Ralegh as Queen Elizabeth's favorite, in mind when he refers to "men of high condition," but what he is doing is instructing himself to recognize and understand their agendas. The next stanza, addressed to "them that brave it most" (who else but Ralegh?) asks that he should also recognize and understand his own agenda and its built-in flaws. The whole composition is a matter of the poet standing aside from himself and looking back with a coldly clinical and uncompromising eye. Such an imaginative sidestep is not unprecedented, but the measure of "The Lie" as a literary work is the authority, economy, and forcefulness of the manner in which that self-analytical act is accomplished.

Themes and Meanings

No one knows exactly when "The Lie" was composed, but it surely does not belong to the 1580's when Ralegh's career was in the ascendant. When he was knighted in 1584, he was given a monopoly in the highly profitable wine trade and authorized to conquer and colonize distant lands in the queen's name; for some years thereafter, he was on top of the world, and he spent forty thousand pounds of England's taxes on exercises of bravado for which tobacco and the potato must have seemed precious little recompense. No man in that position would have written "The Lie," although the stanza that exhorts the soul to "Tell them that brave it most,/ they beg for more by spending" might well refer back to such golden days.

There is a strong temptation to assign "The Lie" to the year 1592, when Ralegh, who had been displaced from the queen's affections by Essex, was nevertheless sent to the Tower of London for making love to one of her maids of honor (Bess Throckmorton, his future wife). It is easy enough to imagine Ralegh whiling away the time of his not-entirely-just incarceration with exactly such reflections on folly and excess. If Ralegh did write "The Lie" during his first spell in the Tower, its lack of nihilistic implication is clearly demonstrated in his subsequent career. By 1595, he was out adventuring again, this time financed from his own coffers.

If Ralegh did spend his first incarceration in "giving the lie" to all the delusions to which he had formerly fallen prey, perhaps it is both entirely natural and beautifully ironic that he spent so much time thereafter manufacturing illusions to sell to others. The Scottish philosopher David Hume described Ralegh's *The Discoverie of the Large, Rich, and Bewtiful Empyre of Guiana* (1596) as "full of the greatest and most palpable lies that were ever attempted to be imposed on the credulity of mankind." After being imprisoned by King James I on suspicion of treason, he talked his way out again—though not for thirteen years—with tasty rumors of El Dorado, the fabled city of gold that he set out in search of in 1616. James eventually had him beheaded in 1618 for piracy against the Spanish (whose Princess Infanta was about to marry Prince Charles), but such was the sympathy of the people that no other victim of the royal axe is credited with quite so many stirring last words, including "What matter how the head lie, so the heart be right?" For all its froth and fury, the heart of "The Lie" is right.

Brian Stableford

LIFE IN AN ASHTRAY

Author: John Meade Haines (1924-   )
Type of poem: Lyric
First published: 1993, in *The Owl in the Mask of the Dreamer: Collected Poems*

The Poem

"Life in an Ashtray" is a free-verse poem of twenty-three lines divided into nine stanzas of no more than three lines each. The poem personifies cigarettes and follows them through their brief "lives." Written in 1970, it might be seen as an allegorical commentary on American existence at that time. The poem's tone, at first glance, seems bleak and fatalistic and probably reflects John Haines's attempt to capture the emotional aura of the country in the late 1960's and early 1970's. Known as a nature writer, Haines nevertheless found himself affected by the political and social unrest of this era. He writes, "For a time in the late 1960's I was preoccupied with events in the outside world—politics, social conflict, all that absorbed so many of us at the time . . . but on the whole I was too far from the events themselves for them to dominate my poems as convincingly as the wilderness world had up until that time."

This tight, elegant metaphor belies that statement. The poem opens with cigarettes speaking in the first-person plural. In the initial stanza, the poetic creatures describe themselves: "our thin white paper skins," "freckled collars," and "little brown shreds for bones." The second verse introduces action and the first hint of futility: "we begin with our feet in ashes,/ shaking our shoes/ in a crazy, crippling dance." The third stanza is the only one that includes a direct reference to the ashtray in the title. These lines define the ashtray as the characters' entire "world" with the cigarettes skating on its "metal rim."

The initial three stanzas of three lines each are followed by two of two lines, a move that builds urgency into the poem. It echoes the hapless burning of cigarettes toward their inevitable end with an abrupt reference to "the only people born tall,/ who shrink as they grow." Haines then returns to three verses of three lines each. In these, he elaborates on the different aspects of a cigarette's life. When the cigarette tries to speak, it produces only smoke and coughing. As it ages, the "yellow glare" of its eyes turn red, and its feet stomp to "put out the fire." The poem ends with a three-line stanza followed by one line set alone: "And always the old ones crumpling,/ crushed from above/ by enormous hands,/ the young ones beginning to burn." Poetry should speak to everyone in the same way a piece of artwork does. It can cut through barriers of culture and race and nullify questions of science, which really are only comments on the world outside the human heart. The successful poem takes a familiar subject and employs it simply, almost deceptively, to reach something deep inside its reader, something responding out of recognition in a truly visceral way. Although "Life in an Ashtray" works on many different levels, the final line evokes such a gut response. It seems to blend all of the various images into a single archetype, that of an endless cycle that concludes only to immediately repeat itself.

Forms and Devices

"Life in an Ashtray" is an extended metaphor (or even conceit) using personification and imagery. In *The Wilderness of Vision: On the Poetry of John Haines* (1996), William Studebaker explores mysticism in Haines's work. His essay asserts that Haines takes metaphor beyond its accepted definition of implied comparison into the realm of allegory and parable: "His poems are passageways, intersecting symbols, allegories to extra-ordinary consciousness as it grows and fills every silence. . . . Through metaphoric logic, he joins the preternatural and the temporal, announcing a fresh perception of reality." It is far easier in the health-conscious days that have followed the writing of this poem to link mysticism with nature (as seen in the bulk of this poet's work) than it is to discern any kind of equation between mysticism and cigarettes. However, such was not always the case. In her books, Ayn Rand likens the tiny glow of the cigarette to the campfire around which aboriginal man gathered for comfort, company, and myth-making. When Haines wrote this poem in 1970, smoking was a pervasive, acceptable part of American life. He chose to use the cigarette in this sense, then, as a common denominator for the struggle of being human. Perhaps it is only the passage of time that makes the idea of utilizing cigarettes and an ashtray as a trope for life in modern American society seem unusually fanciful and places this particular metaphoric poem in the conceit category.

The use of the first person in "Life in an Ashtray" gives the poem its sense of immediacy. How different it would read if it began "In *their* thin white paper skins." Haines chose to include the reader, thus making the fate of the poetic characters more personal and inescapable. The fact that it is a plural use of the first person widens the scope to all of society in a fatalistic, lemmings-to-destruction way. The careful reader will also notice that Haines selects verbs to reinforce the powerlessness he wishes to portray in this metaphor. The action words "shake," "skate," "shrink," "prod," "dissolve," "stomp," "crumple," and "crush" all underscore the feeling of a society caught up in something that cannot be stopped by individuals. Alliteration is applied sparingly in "Life in an Ashtray." The few examples—"shaking our shoes/ in a crazy, crippling dance"—subtly assist the narrative flow.

Themes and Meanings

Haines maintains that writing, for him, is "a necessary undertaking, a means by which I place myself in the world." Although he feels his political poetry was not as convincing as his wilderness work, "Life in an Ashtray" is strong enough to discount that belief. It is a sharp, witty, and incisive look at America in the days of flower children, protests, and the Vietnam War. Written in 1970, this poem is found under "Interim: Uncollected Poems from the 1970's" in his collection *The Owl in the Mask of the Dreamer.* Originally a homesteader in Alaska, Haines left his solitary life in 1969 and returned to live in society. In addition, he both divorced and remarried in 1970. It is a dangerous game to try looking into the mind of the poet to deduce his thoughts based on the outward appearance of his life. However, it would probably be safe to say that Haines was experiencing some major life changes at the time he wrote this poem. He also turned forty-seven in 1970. Many people have their first encounter with a slowing body during their forties, which often brings on thoughts of mortality.

Allegorical poems such as this typically display interpretations on several levels. "Life in an Ashtray" portrays, first, the excellent physical description of what happens as a cigarette burns and the careful personification of how the cigarette views life. Then the larger societal connotation emerges. Finally, the personal meaning appears, or rather two personal meanings appear: one for the poet and one for the reader. The fifth and sixth stanzas illustrate this nicely:

> Prodded by hired matches,
> we'd like to complain,
>
> but all our efforts to speak
> dissolve in smoke
> and gales of coughing.

These words create an almost literal picture of a Vietnam War-era demonstration. Uniformed personnel ("hired matches") confront marchers and reward their attempts to be heard with tear gas. More personally, the reader identifies with the poet's effort to chronicle those moments in life when thoughts and ideas go unrecognized, becoming as useless and ephemeral as smoke.

"Life in an Ashtray" again meshes three different meanings at the end. The reader easily sees the motions of a chain-smoker who grinds out a finished cigarette and lights another. Also clearly recognizable are both the worn-out oldster whose weight of years has crushed the need to fight and the fiery young protester who believes fiercely in cherished ideals. On a personal note, the meaning deepens to reflect the feelings of one approaching later years who looks back on vigorous youth with a sense of loss. Readers see a consistent return to various themes throughout Haines's career, and chief among these is his use of cycles. In this poem, the perpetual rhythm of the cigarette smoked to its end only to be replaced by another echoes the wheel of life and death, thus revealing a universal pattern. "Life in an Ashtray" chooses to leave the reader on the upbeat of that cycle rather than its necessary conclusion. Such a sense of the absolute vitality of life remains a familiar theme in Haines's work.

Sue Storm

LIKE WALKING TO THE DRUG STORE, WHEN I GET OUT

Author: Joyce Carol Oates (1938-   )
Type of poem: Epistle/letter in verse
First published: 1994; collected in *Tenderness*, 1996

The Poem

"Like Walking to the Drug Store, When I Get Out" is a letter in free verse with eight stanzas and a short, cryptic "PS." The title of the poem is also the final line in stanza 6 and is a statement of the utter nonchalance with which the writer of the "letter" regards his impulse to violence, even murder. Although initially a confusing phrase, the title becomes a nugget of clarity when it appears within the poem. The speaker is a prison inmate, a convicted child molester, who writes a letter to the "famous" author Joyce Carol Oates, threatening her (indeed all unimprisoned, free persons) with vicious murder: "I'd just grab a baseball bat and I'd beat you/ till your brains leaked out." The chilling aspect of the inmate's harangue is his insistence that he "wouldn't feel a thing." It would be "just like walking to the drug store."

The poem is written in the first person in the voice of an obviously male sociopath. Clearly obsessed, deeply paranoid, and intensely bitter, the prisoner has time on his hands and vitriol in his pen. He has written to Oates five times previously, and, although he promises this letter is the last, it is quickly clear to the reader that he is an obsessed fan. He has seen Oates's picture in the paper in Iowa City, the location of a federal penitentiary where the reader may assume the letter writer has been imprisoned for the last "6½ years." It is intriguing that, in fact, Oates the poet writes this letter/poem to herself, to Oates the famous fiction writer, in the persona of an inmate, in the ungrammatical language that an ill-educated criminal might actually use.

The letter writer of the poem is vengeful as well, despising those who have "done everything [they] want/ to [him]" and promising repayment for the insults and confinement he has suffered. He states that he has no remorse, that he feels no guilt or shame. In stanza 6, he wonders if he should not have committed mass murder—"four or five hundred people"—to make his mark on society. The reader is led to wonder if this is anguished exaggeration or monomaniacal raving. At the poem's close, the inmate insists he is not a child molester and spits out a wild accusation, calling everyone on the outside "capitalist swine" who are molesting their "own sons & daughters" with the express permission of the Constitution! The reader cannot be sure which of the freedoms guaranteed by the Constitution the prisoner is railing against, but it is clear that freedom and recognition are what he desperately wants.

The last stanza zeroes in on Oates again. The prisoner repeats that he is not a child molester, bluntly claiming that he likes grown women but that Oates is "too old" for him. The final threat is chilling indeed: "Believe me if I started murdering people/ there'd be none of you left." The reader is left feeling no doubt that the writer of the letter would make good on this promise.

The poem ends with a cryptic "PS" that is almost an epithet: "The U.S. started

World War II." Clearly, the inmate's anger goes well beyond Oates: The entire United States government (and the American people) are to blame for World War II and, more important, for his imprisonment, his tragic life, his crimes. The "you" that the prisoner addresses in the poem is Joyce Carol Oates, but it is also all other people who have shunned or ignored him. Oates so skillfully constructs this persona that readers leave the poem feeling that the prisoner holds them personally responsible for his fate.

Forms and Devices

It is ironic that a poem such as "Like Walking to the Drug Store, When I Get Out" appears in a collection of poems Oates titles *Tenderness*. The poem is the antithesis of tenderness: It sits on the edge of violence for eight stanzas, each line a taut threat spit out between the clenched teeth of the angry prisoner who writes the letter. The poem begins with the salutation of a traditional letter, "Dear Joyce Carol." The writer assumes familiarity in using Oates's first names but, interestingly, does not sign his own name at the end of the letter. The reader must conclude that something prevents his signature, perhaps latent fear or embarrassment, or that perhaps the poet omits it intentionally. It could be anyone. Through this omission, Oates may be indicating that we all experience extreme states of mind; taking responsibility for them is terribly difficult. The prisoner's bravado is not strong enough to allow him to reveal his identity. He is, like many of Oates's characters, trapped by his circumstances.

He is, quite literally, in prison, but he is also imprisoned by his unfulfilled need. The lines of the poem vibrate with his frustration that his story will not be told, that he will not "make his mark." His primary regret is not his crimes but that his crimes have not made him famous. The matter-of-fact diction, profanity, spelling errors, and awkward constructions contribute to the realism of the poem. The hyperbolic political accusations punctuate the text of the poem and contribute to the reader's impression that these are the ravings of a madman. The run-on, breathless structure of the lines ("In my whole life I burglarized a 7-11, some nickels & dimes/ & busted open a stamp machine/ & some cars & cashed a couple checks") conveys a desperate self-righteousness. The voice in the poem is unmistakable. The diction and syntax are chillingly realistic. There is nothing quite so frightening as a threatening letter, particularly when the author is a violent criminal, a convicted child molester, and an aspiring murderer. The absence of formal poetic devices such as metaphor, the loosely narrative structure, and the conversational (and occasionally profane) tone of the poem contribute to its realism. After reading the poem, one feels almost as if Oates has simply recopied an actual letter she received from a deranged fan.

Themes and Meanings

"Like Walking to the Drug Store, When I Get Out" is much more than a threatening letter. It is an embodiment, in the person of Oates's own psychotic "pen-pal," of the rage and hostility society's outcasts feel. One cannot be sure whether or not the prisoner writing the letter in the poem is a real-life or a fictional person, but Oates, like most celebrities, has been threatened several times by persons who might be considered mentally disturbed and dangerous. In a *Writers at Work* interview (1981), she recalls a time when she was not allowed to teach a large lecture class at the University of Windsor because, during the previous night, one of her students had received a phone call from an angry, distraught man who announced he intended to kill Oates. The poem is about the irrational anger the prisoner feels toward Oates and others, but it is also about the palpable terror he is able to inspire in the reader.

The reader feels victimized just as Oates must have in the above threatening situation. The end result of the poem is to make the reader feel hunted and powerless. When one is the object of a fantasy or an imagined slight or wrongdoing and the fantasy is uncontrollable (by the imaginer *or* the victim), it is truly terrifying. Oates is often asked why her writing is so violent, a question she considers insulting and sexist, as though a woman cannot explore dark, intense, violent themes successfully. Oates is particularly effective at creating the violent, vengeful, obsessive persona in "Like Walking to the Drug Store, When I Get Out." It is, perhaps, a fulfillment of traditional gender roles that the victim in the poem is female (Oates herself) and the victimizer is masculine (the prisoner). Regardless of their sex, readers are likely to be unsettled by this poem. There is an undercurrent of madness in the persona of the letter writer: He is self-absorbed, self-righteous, and self-deluding. Furthermore, his final threat is directed at the reader as well as Oates. The "you" in the poem is truly the "you" reading the poem: "Believe me, if I started murdering people/ there'd be none of you left." All of these combine to make him terrifying and terrifyingly real.

Linda Kearns Bannister

LILACS

Author: Amy Lowell (1874-1925)
Type of poem: Lyric
First published: 1925, in *What's O'Clock*

The Poem

"Lilacs" is a poem of 109 lines of free verse separated into four stanzas. The first and third stanzas are of unequal length; the first is a long stanza of fifty-two lines, and the third has twenty-seven lines. The second and fourth stanzas are fifteen lines each. Another asymmetry in the poem is that stanzas 1, 2, and 4 begin with the same five brief lines: "Lilacs,/ False blue,/ White,/ Purple,/ Colour of lilac." By contrast, the association of lilacs with New England that is mentioned briefly in stanza 1 is developed in the opening lines of stanza 3: "Maine knows you,/ Has for years and years;/ New Hampshire knows you,/ And Massachusetts/ and Vermont."

Also interesting is the change in perspective as the poem progresses. In the first three stanzas Lowell speaks to the lilacs directly, addressing them as "you." In the first stanza, she mentions the timelessness of the lilacs and lingers on their details: their heart-shaped leaves and the crooks of their branches. From precise physical detail the poem moves to the acts of lilacs, and it becomes apparent that they are more than mere flowering shrubs. She describes the effect they have on preachers, schoolboys, housewives, and clerks; typical New England figures. Wherever the lilacs occur they have a beneficial effect, as when they call to the clerks and cause them to write poetry.

Lowell refers to the Persian origin of lilacs in the second stanza, comparing their exotic beginning with the domestic attitude the shrub has adopted in New England: "A curiously clear-cut, candid flower,/ Standing beside clean doorways,/ Friendly to a house-cat and a pair of spectacles." Lowell is still speaking directly to the lilacs, but the sensibility of the speaker is clear. She has a sharp eye and a profound attachment to nature, and she is deeply grounded in the New England of the poem. Although "I" is not used yet, it is reasonable to assume that the speaker is the poet herself rather than an assumed persona.

In the third stanza, Lowell connects the lilacs to specific New England places, such as Cape Cod and Maine. She also specifies, and repeats, the time of year, May, when the lilacs are most profuse and associates the flowers with a luminous series of spring nature images. Lowell finally reveals herself fully in the fourth stanza, where "I" appears for the first time. She claims both lilac and New England as her own in a metaphor in which she becomes both the flower and the place. The poem builds to a powerful, almost triumphant ending as she "sings" the lilacs as her own.

Forms and Devices

"Lilacs" uses many of the techniques of the Imagists, a group of poets bound by similar ideas who were active roughly between 1905 and 1917. The group was first led, and perhaps defined, by poet and critic Ezra Pound with the help of another

American poet, Hilda Doolittle (H. D.). Amy Lowell became identified with the group in 1913 and displaced Pound as leader in 1915. She organized the group to carry out a publicity campaign to free poetry from the "tyranny" of rhyme, regular meter, and other traditional devices. Under Lowell's leadership the annual anthology, *Some Imagist Poets*, was published for three years and contained statements of Imagist theory. The Imagists believed in short poems structured around a single image or metaphor, clarity and concreteness of detail, economy of language, and an avoidance of abstract meaning or "message." Imagist poems generally were concerned with presenting an object or scene for the direct understanding of the reader.

The patterns of stanza openings and length first establish expectations in the readers' minds and then cause a small shock of surprise when the patterns are broken. This asymmetry affects both the eye and the ear and is characteristic of free verse, which was widely used by the Imagists.

The poem is structured around the lilacs of the title, the central image. An image refers to sensual impressions that the poem reproduces in the mind of the reader. Lowell carefully establishes the visual image of the lilacs by listing their colors and their shapes, "great puffs," at the beginning of three stanzas. She mentions the fragrance of the flowers in the first stanza and, since odors are difficult to describe, brings it to life by describing the effect the fragrance has, primarily on New England clerks in customhouses. The lilacs are personified—they acquire human characteristics. They are as active as the people: They tap the window, run beside the schoolboy, and persuade the housewife that her husband is pure gold.

Repetition is an important device in the poem. The five identical, very short lines that open stanzas 1, 2, and 4 acquire an incantatory quality, as if the colors of the lilacs have some magical power. The repetition also keeps the image fresh in readers' minds as the poem explores other aspects of the shrub in addition to its appearance. "New England," first introduced in the seventh line of the poem, is repeated several times, each time becoming more specific until it culminates in the final metaphor.

Not only are images repeated, but sentence structure tends to fall into patterns as well. In the first stanza, Lowell establishes a pattern of subject/verb when she addresses the lilacs: "You are . . ./ You were . . ." and repeats the pattern eight times. In the third stanza Lowell expands the meaning of lilacs in a series of metaphors, one of which plays on the figure used in stanza 1 that describes lilac leaves as "heart-shaped." Here she speaks of "the leaf-shapes of our hearts," an implied metaphor that connects the human and botanical world in a concise phrase. Everywhere, Lowell exhibits an economy of language. Seven lines in sequence begin with "May is . . . " and pile up images in a series of tight metaphors.

The climax of a poem occurs when a series of sentences that repeat words from previous sentences build to a high point of force or excitement. This high point occurs in the fourth stanza, when the two major images that are repeated many times in the poem are fused with the speaker when she reveals herself overtly for the first time. Lowell switches to the first person, a tradition in lyric poetry. The effect is dramatic; the poem suddenly changes from an ode to lilacs to a powerful personal statement.

Stanza 4 effectively unites all the imagery in one extended metaphor. Lowell identifies herself as the lilac with roots and leaves, and then with New England. In the lyrical line "Lilac in me because I am New England," she uses synecdoche, a type of metaphor in which a small part stands for the whole.

Themes and Meanings

Amy Lowell was descended from a distinguished colonial family that included James Russell Lowell, the nineteenth century poet and Harvard professor; her brother, Abbott Lawrence Lowell, president of Harvard University; and later the Pulitzer Prize-winning poet Robert Lowell. Amy Lowell also won the Pulitzer Prize in 1926, posthumously, for her book *What's O'Clock*. Her impassioned identification with New England is an affirmation of her life and heritage; it is difficult to separate the Lowells from the history of Massachusetts.

Although Lowell's work has been criticized for dealing too exclusively with vivid images and neglecting emotional values, when "Lilacs" is judged by the Imagist ideals that shaped it, the poem is successful. The poem is composed primarily of concrete nouns that describe the appearance of the lilacs in exquisite detail, from their individual flowers to the way they appear in the New England landscape. The concern with appearance, color, and light in the poem illustrates Imagist ideas and has led some critics to associate the movement with Impressionism, the art movement.

Perhaps the most overt expression of Imagist ideas is the absence of a deeper meaning to "Lilacs" than what is stated. There is no "message" or hidden meaning. The poem is a clear statement of what lilacs mean to the poet; she identifies lilacs with the New England of her ancestors and, finally, with herself. Significantly, the poem achieves interest not because of its meaning, which is relatively simple, but because of Lowell's technique, which communicates the meaning in a vivid and unique way.

Sheila Golburgh Johnson

LINES FOR THE PRINCE OF VENOSA

Author: Lars Gustafsson (1936-   )
Type of poem: Narrative
First published: 1972, as "Rader för Hertigen av Venosa," in *Varma rum och kalla*;
    English translation collected in *The Stillness of the World Before Bach*, 1988

The Poem

Lars Gustafsson's "Lines for the Prince of Venosa," as translated by Yvonne L. Sandstroem, is a narrative poem of approximately 875 words. The poem is written in free verse with irregular line and stanza lengths. Although the predominant configuration is two-line stanzas with occasional one-line stanzas for emphasis, the five parenthetical stanzas are more irregular, varying from one to eight lines. The unpredictable line and stanza patterns reinforce the free-flowing nature of the narrative in which the speaker describes an aimless journey through time and space. Although the poem begins in November, 1971, in Sweden, it quickly moves to an encounter with nineteenth century composers Anton Bruckner and Gustav Mahler in Egypt's Sinai desert. During the course of his travels, the speaker meets, in person and in daydream, a number of well-known historical figures, but he never encounters the poem's title character, Prince Venosa.

The narrator of "Lines for the Prince of Venosa" is clearly intended to be the poet himself. This point is made clear when the speaker, a writer, complains about a newspaper review that reads: "Gustafsson, above all, is unnecessarily *learned*." This offhand comment about Gustafsson's writing reinforces the whimsical tone of the entire narrative. The poem begins by dismissing "Robinson," apparently Daniel Defoe's Robinson Crusoe, because "he was nothing but a character in an adventure story." Next, the narrator finds himself in Gothenburg (Göteborg in Swedish), the second-largest city in Sweden, talking with people who do not "understand" him. Then he travels to the university town of Lund, where a supposedly learned professor prophesies a series of events that actually occurred years before.

Next is a trip to the Sinai with Mahler and Bruckner, who are pictured as wearing "soulful little eyeglass frames." The two composers accompany the speaker on a tour of the monastery of Saint Catherine, reputed to be the oldest inhabited Christian monastery, in Egypt's Sinai desert. The tour prompts a bizarre discussion on the distinction between the way that ordinary people are buried and the way that bishops are buried in Saint Catherine's monastery. While commoners' bones are sorted by body parts, bishops are buried with their bones intact. Bruckner theorizes that on Judgement Day the bishops must "*pull themselves together*," and Mahler agrees that they must "*get on their legs* quickly to take command."

With no clear transition, the narrator finds himself back in Sweden riding a train to Karlstad for a literary reading where he is to share the lectern with two writers of primitive verse: an old Lapp woman and a football player. During the train ride, the speaker fantasizes a meeting between Jack Kerouac, American hero of the Beat generation, and "a little psychiatrist in gold-frame glasses," apparently Sigmund Freud, who died in 1939. The narrator pictures Kerouac getting the best of Freud in their discussion concerning the differences between the definitions of neuroses and inhibitions by Kerouac's suggestion that they drop their trousers on the count of three.

During the uncomfortable literary reading, the narrator fantasizes that he spots in the audience Maria d'Avalos, the beautiful wife of the Prince of Venosa. When he meets her again at the bar of a local hotel, the speaker is so struck with Donna Maria's beauty that he blurts out a question about the young woman's husband. He remembers too late that the sixteenth century composer had ordered his wife and her lover murdered. However, Donna Maria's graceful, noncommittal reply about her husband's beautiful music shakes the narrator out of his reverie and sends him back to snowy Sweden where his dog happily welcomes him home.

Forms and Devices

In "Lines for the Prince of Venosa," Gustafsson uses two techniques that are typical of American poet T. S. Eliot. The first is the deliberate omission of transitions, a technique that forces the reader to actively participate in the poem in order to arrive at some kind of understanding. For example, Gustafsson's poem begins with a reference to a Romantic nineteenth century novel set on a tropical island and immediately shifts to late twentieth century Sweden. Gustafsson expects the reader to supply the transition.

A second Eliot-like device is the use of multiple allusions that only a widely educated reader would recognize. Even the narrator-poet jokes that reviewers complain that Gustafsson's erudition seems "unnecessary." Although place names such as "Gothenburg," "Lund," and "Värmland" would be familiar to Gustafsson's Swedish readers, other references are more obscure. While the three composers, Venosa, Mahler, and Bruckner, may also be known to the reading public, they are hardly as well known as Johann Sebastian Bach or Wolfgang Amadeus Mozart. Also, "Robinson" is mentioned with the expectation that the reader will fill in "Crusoe," and one wonders whether a Swedish audience would understand the jokes about "wholesales Whitman" and Kerouac's first-class Atlantic passage.

A third technique, one that is a distinct departure from Eliot's style, is the humor laced throughout the poem. The picture of the supposedly erudite Professor Ehrenswärd "sucking a milk carton/ as if it were a mother's nipple" while he poetically describes farmers as "proletarians of the plow" is perfectly delicious due to the juxtaposition of the professor's puerile actions and his alliterative word choices. References to "Mahler and Bruckner" as both a "congenial firm" and a logical name for a delicatessen serve as perfect counterpoints to both composers' ponderous music. In addition, the imagined argument between the freewheeling Kerouac and the stuffy Freud ends with Kerouac's scatological test of inhibitions.

Themes and Meanings

In spite of the lighthearted tone, "Lines for the Prince of Venosa" is a serious poem about what it means to be an artist. The three themes that the poem considers are the artist's need for fame and for affirmation of his or her work, the artist's needs as a human being, and the artist's search for truth. The most immediate concern is the need for affirmation of one's work. Most of the artists that Gustafsson mentions had difficulty finding popular acceptance. For example, Mahler's reputation was hampered by his unpopularity as an exacting conductor and by the fact that he was a Jew. Even though Bruckner had written three masses that were performed in Linz, Austria, he was treated in Vienna like a rustic outsider. Walt Whitman's poetry, with its disjoined lines, likewise languished in obscurity. Of himself, Gustafsson says that people in Gothenburg do not understand him "(as usual)" and that the press considers him too "*learned*." However, the narrator's own appreciation of Mahler and Bruckner is qualified by the description of their symphonies as being interminably slow and ponderous in order "to convince us that death isn't so bad after all." Whitman's disconnected rhyming catalogs are juxtaposed with the piles of disjointed body parts found in Saint Catherine's monastery. Finally, Defoe's widely read novel is dismissed because it is only "an adventure story/ that everyone's read before."

The second theme, the artist's needs as a human being, is tied to the meaning of home. For Prince Venosa, home became a place of shame rather than a place of rest and comfort. Even the Renaissance composer, who was noted for his devotional masses, did not possess faith strong enough to forgive his wife for her infidelities. In contrast, the narrator is happy to settle for a wifeless homecoming with only a bouncy dog to greet his arrival. Concerning the meaning of home, the narrator comments that one will always "find a way home," but he warns that it will not be the same safe haven that was left behind.

The most important theme is the artist's search for truth, a concept that the poet uses interchangeably with the concept of beauty. The following lines occur three times in the poem: "Yes/ beauty is the only thing that lasts." The first comment ends the pontifical professor's lecture and the third is part of Donna Maria's cocktail chatter about her husband's music. In spite of the comical contexts, the reveries that follow these lines indicate the serious purposes of the poem. The first reverie begins with a comparison of beauty to stones, both of which are not only long lasting but are also "pure and simple." Then, both the first and second reverie continue the comparison by commenting on what is inside the stone. The narrator says that certain types of quartz trap water that is "older than all the seas in our world." Furthermore, this water, never having been exposed to light, is both clean and pure. The darkness inside the stone stands in sharp contrast to the blinding but often sterile light in the mountains of the Sinai and other sterile areas of the earth. Gustafsson suggests, then, that truth is ancient, pure, and encased in darkness or in misunderstanding. Therefore, it is the task of often-misunderstood artists to release the truth, but the price that artists pay for their efforts may be high indeed.

Sandra Hanby Harris

LISTEN!

Author: Vladimir V. Mayakovsky (1893-1930)
Type of poem: Lyric
First published: 1914, as "Slushaite!"; collected in *Polnoe sobranie sochinenii*, 1955;
English translation collected in *Mayakovsky: A Poet in the Revolution*, 1973

The Poem

"Listen!" is one of several short lyric poems of existential questioning by Vladimir Mayakovsky that appeared in the first issue of *Pervyi zhurnal russkikh futuristov* (*First Journal of the Russian Futurists*) in 1914. The poem combines youthful angst about the writer's insignificance in the vast universe with a self-assured mastery of his idiom and technique. In the preceding year, Mayakovsky had published his first lyric collection and had produced and starred in an autobiographical play in verse, *Vladimir Mayakovsky*. In "Listen!" Mayakovsky entertains the possibility, somewhat perversely for a Futurist who rejected all of humankind's past beliefs, that there is a God, arguing, from the ancient position, that God must have set the stars in the sky.

Mayakovsky makes an appeal to pure intuition for proof of the existence of God: He begins three lines of his thirty-line poem with "You know" (*ved'* in Russian), a nervous, rhetorical colloquialism sometimes left untranslated and sometimes translated as "surely?" The appeal to intuition is continued in five more lines, all beginning with "That means," another nervous colloquialism that urges causality, connection, or equivalence. Thus:

> You know—if they light up the stars—
> That means—somebody needs them?
> It means—someone wants them to be there?
> It means—someone calls that spit pearls?

The irreverent and colloquial language characteristic of Mayakovsky is softened here by an almost childlike tone in his choice of words. Pure, direct rhetoric and almost conventional imagery are used to express his thoughts. The poem is particularly poignant in the context of his other works, which make clear that his childhood had ended early, even before his six months of imprisonment and solitary confinement as a sixteen-year-old Bolshevik schoolboy. The naïve tone is suitable to his final rhetorical question of whether the stars are lit up to ensure that every single evening, above the roofs of humankind, at least one star will always shine.

While the poem is sometimes ambiguous about whether the "somebody" who needs the stars is God or humankind, the central section makes clear that humans need both the stars and the God who gives them those stars. The unnamed "somebody," an uncharacteristically humble figure who replaces Mayakovsky's habitual "I," begs for stars as a pledge of good faith. "Somebody" kisses God's hand but does not ask for the father figure's love directly: The gift of stars is enough. The stars alone will rid him of fear and make him feel "all right."

In the poem that followed "Listen!" entitled "And Yet," a more mature, worldly tone reasserts itself. The anonymous "somebody" is replaced by Mayakovsky in the first person, who speaks defiantly of prostitutes who worship him. The poet predicts that God will read Mayakovsky's books and weep and will then rush about the heavens showing them to his acquaintances. "And Yet" was followed by "Petersburg Again." In this third poem of ontological questioning, the universe has become menacing, a "cannibalistic" fog blocks out the stars, and God is an absurd, distant, and rejected figure who looks down from the sky with irrelevant dignity "like Leo Tolstoy." In its structure, however, "Listen!" is by far the most innovative of the three poems.

Forms and Devices

"Listen!" is a short but complex work. Its level of technical control makes the categorization of free verse almost irrelevant, although the poem does not follow traditional rules of versification. It is divided into three parts: the introduction, the body, and the conclusion. The first and last parts mirror each other like the *aba* form of a classical sonata movement. The rhythmic structure consists of a mixture of feet and lines of varying lengths. Feet of three syllables tend to predominate, with the key word "Listen" being a dactyl in the original. However, Mayakovsky builds up tension with feet of four, then five, then six syllables, always with a stress on the final beat. He then delivers punchlines of a single word for further contrast. Trochees are also used to provide a cross-rhythm to the polysyllabic feet, as if working against them. While not perfectly regular, a structure clearly emerges from the alternation of lines of increasing length and lines of a single word.

The one-word lines acquire a lyrical, expressive prominence: "Listen," "Sobs," "Begs," "Swears," and "Yes." Each of the exceedingly long lines gives prominence to its final word, which contains the long-awaited stress. Mayakovsky is able to create a rhyme scheme that utilizes much longer jumps from rhyme to rhyme than are found in traditional poetry. His rhymes are not perfect but tend toward assonance. The word "star" (*zvezdá*) rhymes boldly with "yes" (*da*) and again with itself across cosmic gaps in space. In his advice to aspiring proletarian poets in *Kak delat' stikhi?* (1926; *How Are Verses Made?*, 1970), Mayakovsky observed: "Without rhyme (understanding the word in a wide sense) poetry falls to pieces."

Parallel constructions are underlined by the very structure of Russian and have long been prominent in Russian style. They have a strong role to play in Mayakovsky's work. With parallels at both the beginnings and the ends of lines, and with the end of the poem reflecting its beginning, this poem could scarcely be more highly structured despite its use of free verse. On the finer scale of sound, Mayakovsky's use of alliteration provides the final organizing factor. In the Russian, the sound "z" shines forth, beginning with "star" itself and echoing in the repeated words "light up" and "that means." Other alliterations deliberately restrict the poem's palette of sound, focusing meaning with impassioned intensity.

Themes and Meanings

While his formal education was interrupted early, Mayakovsky read widely and eclectically. He was aware of the far-flung origins and echoes of the themes of stars, God, and the cosmos, from the Bible to the nineteenth century Russian classics. In Russian literature, "Listen!" most nearly echoes the lyric poetry of Mikhail Lermontov, a tragic rebel who despised "the establishment," who was very partial to polysyllabic rhythms, and who was profoundly affected by the stars shining over the Caucasus, the region of Biblical grandeur and solemnity that was Mayakovsky's birthplace. Lermontov's works are filled with angels, demons, stars, clouds, and cosmic space, all conversing with one another. His cosmic imagery, inspiring a series of works by the painter Mikhail Vrubel, was very much in vogue in the years preceding the Russian Revolution of 1917. Mayakovsky had studied art while Lermontov, the self-taught amateur, could sketch. In a final, unfortunate parallel, Mayakovsky and Lermontov both wrote about the impulse to self-destruction.

Mayakovsky's persona of the street urchin, usually expressed as an impudent orphan cynical beyond his years, is tempered in "Listen!" by an unexpectedly childlike, naïvely questioning, and vulnerable voice. The child is on familiar terms with the father-God whom he importunes with his huge request for stars; the child rushes to him, trusting and hopeful, so as not to be "late" (as if to dinner) and kisses his "veiny" hand (an obligatory gesture of child to parent in prerevolutionary Russia). The possibility of a cosmic parent is left open in this poem, and all mockery is hushed. It may represent a turning point in Mayakovsky's relationship to God that hangs between the trust of a self-effacing child (a nameless "somebody" who finds comfort in faith) and the disillusionment of the youth who mocks the face of God to the skies, who wishes to set his own name everywhere and yet who proclaims that this very self-assertion, which in effect replaces the need for God, is a "tragedy."

The stars of the cosmos continued to be a key image for Mayakovsky throughout his life. The long poem *Oblako v shtanakh* (1915; *The Cloud In Trousers*, 1960) ends with the beautiful metaphor, "The universe is asleep/ its huge ear,/ star-infested,/ rests on a paw." His last lyric poem, "Past One O'Clock," from which he quoted in his suicide note, ends with the immortal lines: "Night has laid a heavy tax of stars upon the sky./ In hours like these you get up and you speak/ To the ages, to history, and to the universe."

D. Gosselin Nakeeb

A LITANY FOR SURVIVAL

Author: Audre Lorde (1934-1992)
Type of poem: Lyric
First published: 1978, in *The Black Unicorn*

The Poem

"A Litany for Survival" is a short poem in free verse containing three dense stanzas and a concluding three-line stanza. The title refers to a type of communal prayer involving alternating speakers, usually a leader and a congregation of petitioners. The form of the poem enacts the title's scene: The lead speaker begins the prayer, directly addressing the other petitioners yet speaking as if also one of the petitioners. The first two stanzas could be delivered by the leader's solitary voice as both stanzas give prolonged descriptions of the petitioners' needs and circumstances. The petitioners' multiple voices then deliver the third stanza, which proceeds in parallel phrases with succinct repetition similar to the rhythmic verses that a congregation would chant in unison. The leader's and the petitioners' voices blend together in the concluding stanza in which a resolution is given for the grave situation that has prompted the ceremony.

As in most ceremonies in which prayer is offered, the petitioners recognize their own insignificance and their defenselessness in relation to powers greater than themselves. They know that those with greater power desire to terrorize them into deathly silence—a silence that will erase their memories and extinguish their children's dreams for the future. Although the petitioners face their own obliteration, their prayer does not, as prayers normally do, request divine intervention. Engaging in the communal ceremony represented by the poem is itself a means of resisting the will of the powerful. The act of self-expression and the communal sharing of their own desires, all of which are embedded in their meditation, enable the petitioners to resist those who desire their defeat.

The vocality of the poem derives from the oral literary traditions of Africa. Audre Lorde lures the reader into a ceremony that promises to be a common prayer. After joining the ceremony, however, the readers find themselves in unfamiliar supernatural territory where the power being summoned is not the distant, omnipotent Father of Christian faith. The readers discover and the petitioners remember that the power being summoned lies within themselves in their own communal voice.

Forms and Devices

The prayer ritual is immediately signaled in the poem's opening line with the words "For those of us who . . ." This phrase, which also appears at the beginning of stanza 2, creates a solemn mood, alerting the reader that a hallowed ritual is being performed. Reverence is required of the reader as alternating voices utter a precise array of images that evoke intense emotional reactions. Stanzas 1 and 2 follow the same form and describe the petitioners' situation; therefore, these two stanzas might be uttered by the same voice, which functions as the celebrant who leads the ritual but does not assume a position of superiority over the other petitioners. The celebrant speaks not for but with the other petitioners and is clearly included in the dedication "For those of us who. . . ." The celebrant intimately describes the grave situation of the petitioners' lives in images that evoke feelings of insecurity, instability, and precariousness.

Life, for the petitioners, takes place "at the shoreline," a place of constant change where they face momentous decisions with apprehension. The celebrant envisions another time unlike the unbearable present. In the "now" of the present time, their desires must be squeezed into confined spaces "in doorways coming and going." These spaces were designed for more impersonal pursuits. In the present, they are forced to express love cautiously at inopportune times—"in the hours between dawns/ looking inward and outward/ at once before and after"—because security is not possible. The first stanza ends with a fusion of metaphor, simile, and personification, making the present animate—a living thing that must be nourished so that it can propagate the future: "seeking a now that can breed/ futures/ like bread in our children's mouths."

Stanza 2 begins by repeating the dedication "For those of us/ who. . . ." This reminds the readers that they are witnessing a ritual. The first voice then amplifies the imagery of nourishment begun in stanza 1 by superimposing maternal imagery. However, these are not the entirely soothing maternal scenes that the reader expects them to be. The customary repose one anticipates in a maternal image is subverted because the suckling ones are being fed fear along with their "mothers' milk." Because the nourishment is coming from a maternal source, the deception is nearly perfect. The mother cannot be rejected even though the nourishment she provides has been contaminated with fear, which will ultimately be lethal. The fear fed to the petitioners at their mothers' breasts is the perfect weapon designed by the "heavy-footed" people in power. Their ingenious design gives the "illusion of . . . safety" while it also engenders a paralyzing fear that results in a lifetime of terrified silence.

In the third stanza, the other voices speak, chanting phrase after phrase in unison, naming their painful life experiences in pulsating cycles. The collective voice emanating from each phrase crescendos into a mystical incantation that finally breaks through to the realization that fear has caused them to be silent—but their silence never eliminated their fear. The incantation concludes with all voices uttering the final stanza. All have summoned the courage to speak, for speech is the antidote to the censure that has proved so detrimental to self and survival: "So it is better to speak," the voices chant, "remembering/ we were never meant to survive."

Themes and Meanings

The ultimate anxiety of the petitioners is based on their awareness that the condition of their lives offers no provision for a better future for their children. The petitioners know that the future already exists in the present and that the future must be nourished in the present so that their children's existence will not be similarly distressed. Reviewing their own situation as a group and contemplating what the future holds for their children has brought the petitioners to discover the elaborate scheme perpetrated by the powerful. They realize and articulate in their prayer how daily events (the sun rising and setting, eating, indigestion) have become unexpected sites of stifling silence and unrelieved insecurity, a legacy of ruin for their children. As the ceremony continues, the petitioners recognize and echo the leader's belief that they "were never meant to survive." Through their collective ceremonial recitation, they are emerging from their silence, speaking their new understanding, dispelling the deception that has silenced them for so long, and restoring and empowering themselves.

In "A Litany for Survival" as in many of her other works, Lorde is concerned with the politics of marginalization. Knowing the devastating effects of being devalued and discarded, Lorde asks bold questions about who is chosen for such treatment and why. As an African American, feminist, and lesbian thinker, Lorde often experienced life from the position of the outsider. Much of her work is an exploration of the alienation one feels as an outsider, but Lorde does not stop there. She is also concerned with the process of reversing marginalization and restoring self-worth and belonging. To unmake systematic marginalization, Lorde concentrates on understanding how the system was made. In "A Litany for Survival," she carefully exposes the elaborate scheme that powerful and esteemed members of society use so successfully to subdue and disempower those they designate as "other." Lorde does not, in this poem, name the "others," and this opening allows all marginalized people and groups to join the ceremony and identify with the poem's petitioners. With a masterstroke, Lorde identifies the fulcrum of the devious scheme. This scheme does not rest solely on what the powerful do but on the way they enlist the "others" to carry it out: The scheme requires the complicity of the marginalized members of society; therefore, the "others" are implicated in their own marginalization. The consequences of all this for the marginalized are self-reproach and silence. Such silence seals their destiny, but it also conceals the culpability of the powerful. For the marginalized, silence leads to social death. However, Lorde's message to the marginalized is always one of hope and life. She points the way in the poem: To invigorate and preserve life, one must speak, share one's experience, name one's fear, and seek communion.

Veta Smith Tucker

LIVING ALONE

Author: Hayden Carruth (1921-   )
Type of poem: Lyric
First published: 1992, in *Collected Shorter Poems, 1946-1991*

The Poem

"Living Alone" is a fairly long poem (165 lines); it might appear at first to be in free verse, but actually it employs several types of rhyme, rhythm, and formal lineation. Excluding the epigraph and dedication, the poem is divided into seventeen sections, several of which are further divided into stanzas. The poem is dedicated to John Cheever, an American prose writer, and begins with an epigraph taken from one of Cheever's works. In this epigraph an observer on a ship sees a Ping-Pong table washed off the ship's deck because the helmsman made a miscalculation. Watching the table bobbing in the ship's wake, the observer is reminded of the plight of someone washed overboard.

The first section of the poem is a single stanza that acts as a backdrop for the melodrama that follows. The narrator of the poem sees, through the insulated window of his apartment, a solitary chrysanthemum, the last one of the season. As wind and ice tear at its head, a gull cries and hovers above it. In the second section the narrator compares his pain to that of a "snake run over." It is not until the third section that the reader learns the source of his pain and shock: He has been expelled "from her house" by his "successor" and is now living alone—thus the title of the poem. Although the reader learns that her name is Rachel and that the speaker probably knows her grandmother, he never identifies her as wife or lover. He simply states that he was "Jettisoned in one night" and that he felt as if he were "falling as a parachutist might/ in vacant air, shocked/ in the silence, nowhere."

In subsequent stanzas readers learn that, in addition to his emotional misery, the speaker is physically ill. He compares the way he feels with having a bad cold— possibly pneumonia, flu, bronchitis—while in a strange town with no one he can call and a fever that, along with the winter sunset, brings thoughts of mortality. At one point he talks about both fearing and seeking death as other men have done. He adds that women must have felt this way too, but then expresses doubt about his ability to make any judgement regarding women: "I disclaim/ whatever knowledge I thought once/ to have of them."

In the first of the two tercets that make up the fifth section of the poem the narrator expresses his belief that "Experience is unique" and implies that he will not compare his plight with others who may have suffered similar fates. In the second tercet he makes an immediate turn by crying out to François Villon, Spartacus, and others who have suffered similar indignities. As the poem progresses he sarcastically complains of the "endless joy" of housekeeping; complains of thin apartment walls that inundate him with a mother's cruelty to her child, the ubiquitous flushing of toilets, and children screaming; complains of pins, tacks, and glass in the wall-to-wall carpeting; and in general complains of the squalor and boredom of living alone in an apartment.

In the end the narrator turns his troubles and his energies toward the blues—that art form that seems specifically created as a refuge for the lonely and the spurned. Readers who know of the music of Charles Ellsworth "Pee Wee" Russell may have a special insight into the last two sections of the poem, but Carruth's faith in the power of jazz shines through regardless.

Forms and Devices

The first obvious device used in this poem is the epigraph from an unnamed work by John Cheever. It sets the tone for the entire poem. The "I" of Cheever's piece feels powerless in the face of the sea. Even the ship is out of his control, in the hands of an erring helmsman. He identifies with an inanimate object washed overboard and lost from everything that could give it meaning. The "I" of Carruth's poem exhibits similar feelings about being at the mercy of a wrong-thinking person who throws him into a veritable sea of troubles where he is at the mercy of forces he cannot understand.

Carruth uses alliteration, assonance, and a dizzying array of rhyme schemes and patterns of lineation. The single nine-line stanza of the first section uses one of the most complex mixtures of alliterations and end rhymes in the whole poem:

> Mystery. Seeds of every motion.
> See out there beyond the thermal-
> pane that last chrysanthemum
> in the frozen bed by the concrete wall
> winging wildly its lavender
> and shattered head. How fast
> the wind rises. How the mud
> elaborates in patterns of ice.
> A gull, hovering, shudders and cries.

The reader should notice that at the end of the second line the poet forces a line break in the middle of a word. The break not only provides an end rhyme with the fourth line but also enhances the alliterative effect of all the *m* sounds in the first three lines and the final "mud" of the seventh line. Carruth uses a similar and more complex effect in the first two lines with "Mystery. Seed . . . motion./ See" and in the fourth, fifth, and seventh lines with "wall/ winging wildly . . ./ . . . wind."

The second section is divided into two stanzas of four lines each with a very conventional rhyme pattern: *aabb ccdd*. The third and fourth lines of each stanza are indented, giving these two quatrains the feeling of four rhyming couplets. The second quatrain opens with an inversion that appears to have no greater purpose than to generate an end rhyme with the next line: "comfort me who will then?/ Or otherwise that time soon when." Throughout the poem, Carruth continues to use inversions like this one to gain end rhymes.

The poem's rhyming patterns change with each new section, and no two sections use the same pattern. One of the more interesting rhyme schemes comes in the tenth section. This section has only one strophe of four lines. The final word of the second line rhymes with the final word of the third line (there is nothing unusual in that). The final word of the final line rhymes, not with the final word of the first line, as one might expect, but with the first word of the first line. There is also a wonderfully playful irony in this section. This is the only place where the "I" of the poem provides the name (Rachel) of the woman who has abandoned him. He exposes himself as an unreliable narrator by saying, "Rachel, your name won't rhyme, the language itself/ has given up on you. Zilch." Then, at the end of the next sentence, the very last word of the stanza, he gives her name a rhyme, "satchel."

The variety of stanza choices is as wide as that of rhyme schemes. Carruth runs the gamut from free form to couplet, tercet, quatrain, quintain, sestet, septet, and upward. By the time the reader reaches the end of the poem the constant and rapid changing of rhyme schemes and stanza types has left little doubt that the poet is a master craftsman and that his narrator is somewhat—but not hopelessly—paranoid.

Themes and Meanings

As the title suggests, the first and most pronounced theme of "Living Alone" is isolation. It is not, however, the only major theme and is probably not the most important. That distinction falls to survival.

The "I" of the poem starts as an outcast, a person who has been suddenly and permanently ejected from what he thought of as his home, the one place where he felt safe and had some sense of security about his identity. At first he falls victim to self-pity, wallowing in his own dirge about all the different ways he was wronged. Then the ordinariness of life starts nibbling at the fabric of his lament. The voices and vulgar noises that seep through the thin walls of his apartment, the boredom and occasional drudgery of housework done alone, and the simple process of growing older each day begin to reshape his complaints until he declares, "All one can do is to achieve nakedness."

His solitude appears to have brought him down to a point at which he is able start up again. He questions whether he will return to the same place, be the same person or type of person. On the road to rebuilding (surviving), he turns to the art of music, specifically the blues. This move to the blues would suggest to a person already familiar with the work of Carruth that the poem is, at least in some part or fashion, autobiographical: Carruth has, over several decades, written extensively about jazz and the blues.

Edmund August

LOCKS

Author: Kenneth Koch (1925-   )
Type of poem: Lyric
First published: 1962, in *Thank You and Other Poems*

The Poem

"Locks," a love poem, is an extended list of locks that have brought the narrator "happiness." The twenty-eight-line poem, written in free verse, is actually one sentence long; the sixteen different locks mentioned in this catalog are separated by semicolons. The lines are lengthy, nearly half of them spilling over to a second or third line of indented text.

The single-stanza poem's first line is "These locks on doors have brought me happiness," and the list commences. The variety of locks suggests the narrator's full, vigorous life—a life replete with experience. The first happily remembered lock, for instance, is "The lock on the door of the sewing machine in the living room/ Of a tiny hut in which I was living with a mad seamstress." The next is "The lock on the filling station one night when I was drunk/ And had the idea of enjoying a nip of petroleum."

It quickly becomes clear that these locks are not only literal—although some do seem more literal than others—but also metaphoric or symbolic. "The lock inside the nose of the contemporary composer who was playing the piano and would have ruined his concert by sneezing, while I was turning pages," for instance, cannot be a hardware-store variety lock any more than "The lock in my hat when I saw her and which kept me from tipping it,/ Which she would not have liked, because she believed that naturalness was the most friendly" can.

The narrator, fully alive and alert to physical sensations, has lived in the world and enjoyed its pleasures. He has lived in a hut, ridden a camel in the desert, witnessed a "lipstick parade," and felt alert to the physical thrill of "gales of sweetness blow[ing] through me till I shuddered and shook."

The narrator presents himself as a man of the world, a man not easily shocked, a man fairly unruffled by physical danger or discomfort. This pose, however, is touchingly undermined at the end of the poem. The "locks" with which the poem concludes, presumably the locks that have brought the narrator the greatest happiness of all, are "the lock on the sailboat/ That keeps it from taking me away from you when I am asleep with you,/ And, when I am not, the lock on my sleep, that keeps me from waking and finding you are not there." The narrator's bravado comes to seem a pose, or at the least a less significant element than the reader might have supposed, of a much deeper and more rounded character. The narrator is, in fact, utterly dependent on a lover, so much so that he expresses special gratitude for the ability to sleep when they must be apart. To awaken without her by his side would be too great a horror.

Forms and Devices

Perhaps the central irony in this poem is that it is written in free verse, an open poetic form that does not rely upon traditional rhyme schemes or regular metrical patterns. It is ironic considering the title and the subject of the poem: "Locks." A lock is a kind of limiting device, something that bars the access to something else, such as a room. Similarly, strict adherence to form can be a kind of limitation for a poet, and early experimenters with free verse, such as Walt Whitman in America and Charles Baudelaire in France, consciously rebelled against the kinds of fixed forms and a slavish devotion to rhyme and meter that they viewed as limiting to the possibilities of poetic expression. There is, then, a kind of humor in the fact that Koch should write a hymn of praise to locks and use the least "locked" form, free verse, in which to do it.

To say that the poem is written in free verse, however, is not to say that Koch ignores the question of meter altogether. Koch employs the most traditional metrical line in English poetry in the poem's first line: "These locks on doors have brought me happiness" is written in iambic pentameter. The first line, however, is the only one written in such a formal, regular meter. It is almost as if, having expressed his "happiness," the narrator feels the kind of freedom from restraint that allows him to experiment more boldly with meter.

The meter of the remainder of the poem is not fixed, yet there remains a kind of music and rhythm. "Locks" benefits a good deal from being read out load. To read the poem orally or to listen to it being read is to hear how Koch builds its momentum. The first two feet (a foot is a poetic unit of two or three syllables), for twenty-one of the twenty-eight lines, for instance, consist of an iamb followed by an anapest—or at least a close variation of that pattern. (An anapest contains three syllables, the first two unstressed, the final one stressed.) Not every line approximates the iamb/anapest pattern in its first two feet, but enough of them do to help give the poem a loose kind of structure. "Locks" sounds like a poem rather than straight prose.

Readers who believe that free verse is no different from prose or that free verse is inherently disorganized or unmusical will have their ideas challenged elsewhere with "Locks." Koch uses sound devices such as assonance, or the repetition of vowel sounds, throughout the poem. Koch plays with long *o* sounds, for example, in the fragment "The nose of the contemporary composer who was playing the piano." Koch almost always writes in free verse, but it would be a mistake to assume that he has therefore forgotten that poetry has its roots in the musical tradition.

Themes and Meanings

"Unscrew the locks from the doors!/ Unscrew the doors themselves from their jambs!" wrote Walt Whitman, the American poet whose impact on the American poetic tradition has been greatest, in "Song of Myself." Whitman's sensibilities were essentially Romantic, and in these lines he is calling for a radical "unlocking" of old hierarchical political structures and old strictures governing interpersonal relations. Whitman is the great poet of democracy, hearkening back, in his thinking and writing, to the ideas of the French philosopher Jean-Jacques Rousseau, who wrote, "Man is born free, but is everywhere in chains." For Rousseau, as for Whitman, humankind is essentially free but has been corrupted by institutions of society, such as governments and churches, that create limitations to that freedom. If people are to return to their free and natural state, they must revolt against the tyranny of kings, the dogma of churches, and the conventions of social intercourse that prevent them from being free and natural with one another.

Koch is clearly the beneficiary of this Romantic tradition. Were it not for Whitman, writing approximately one hundred years earlier, free verse would probably not have developed to the point where a poem such as "Locks" would have been possible. Much of the humor in this poem lies in the fact that Koch builds upon Whitman's techniques—in his use of free verse, in his cataloging, in his lengthy lines—to sing the glories of something as "un-Whitmanic" as locks. Koch is perhaps parodying a deeply admired predecessor, much as he does in "Variations on a Theme by William Carlos Williams," a poem that appears in the same volume as "Locks."

Yet the poem is by no means pure parody with no underlying seriousness. Koch summed up some of his thoughts about his own poetics in an interview with Elizabeth Farnsworth: "I don't intend for my poetry to be mainly funny or satirical, but it seems to me that high spirits and a sort of comic view are part of being serious." In "Locks," Koch uses humor to ask his readers to consider a serious question: What kind of freedom would be possible without some kinds of limitations? Locks have given the narrator possibilities for privacy that allowed sexuality to thrive (the lock on the door of the tiny hut), have prevented him from possible bodily harm ("The lock on the family of seals, which, released, would have bitten"), and, most important, have kept him from "waking and finding you are not there" when separated from his loved one. Without the lock of blissful sleep, the narrator would be forced to confront a deep loneliness potentially more harmful than anything else an unpredictable, treacherous world might offer.

Douglas Branch

LOT'S WIFE

Author: Wisława Szymborska (1923-   )
Type of poem: Dramatic monologue
First published: 1976, as "Żona Lota," in *Wielka liczba*; English translation collected
  in *Sounds, Feelings, Thoughts: Seventy Poems by Wisława Szymborska*, 1981

The Poem

The story of the death of Lot's wife in the biblical book of Genesis has both intrigued and disturbed many readers. Angels command Lot to take his family and flee the evil cities of Sodom and Gomorrah, telling them not to look back. For disobeying this warning, Lot's wife is turned into a pillar of salt.

"Lot's Wife" features forty-three unrhymed lines of varied lengths. Its unnamed title character apparently is speaking to the reader after her death. The paradox implied by having her do this is compounded by other unusual circumstances as the poem unfolds. Although the speaker discusses her possible reasons for turning back toward Sodom and therefore perishing, she seems either unable or unwilling to reveal her true reasons for doing so. She begins noncommittally, "They say I looked back from curiosity./ But I could have had reasons other than curiosity." Nowhere does she state exactly what *did* happen; rather, she presents a variety of possibilities. She suggests reasons such as longing for a silver bowl she left behind, distraction while adjusting her sandal, and even weariness of looking at the back of her husband's neck. Mentioning that Lot would not have stopped even had she died, she adds that she may have looked back in resentment of him.

The wife also alleges fearing that someone was following them and hoping that God had decided not to destroy the cities. She states that she may have felt fatigued, lonely, or frightened at going into the wilderness. After mentioning these feelings, she suggests glancing back while setting down her bundle, or turning away in revulsion at the vermin she saw on her path. At yet another point, she claims that the crackling of the flames made her think the Sodomites were laughing at her for running, causing her to look around in anger.

After describing possible mental states, the speaker goes on to blame the difficult mountain path for her turning, claiming first that she slipped while stepping on a loose stone, then that she drew back from a chasm in her way, and finally that she slipped off a cliff and saw the burning city as she rolled down. She not only fails to state what prompted her to look back but also pictures increasingly severe events, as if repeating a bad dream that keeps getting more threatening, until the story has unraveled in absurd and contradictory claims.

Forms and Devices

Although no translation can fully communicate the sounds of the original, translators Magnus J. Krynski and Robert A. Maguire captured much of Wisława Szymborska's technique. The lines are similar in length and, as far as grammar permits, usually display the same phrasing and word order as the Polish, although minor exceptions occur. For example, where the original sixth line reads "męża mojego, Lota," the translation has "of Lot my husband," putting Lot's name before his relationship to the speaker. The translation stresses the rhythmic nature of the line, with the stressed syllable "Lot" between the unstressed "of" and "my," allowing the line to be read more fluidly than "of my husband, Lot," its literal rendering. This subtle change preserves Szymborska's original rhythm.

"Lot's Wife" uses conversational language, which, combined with the uneven lines and lack of rhyme, gives a strong impression of everyday communication. However, the apparent simplicity is deceptive. The language itself is carefully chosen. For instance, seven of the lines in English, or almost one-sixth of the poem, begin repetitively with "I looked back." (There is an eighth in the Polish.) Almost half the poem's repetition is lost in translation generally—as in lines which in Polish, but not English, begin with the same preposition. Still, the translation has rhythm and repetition enough to create a pattern in which the woman who died because she looked back at Sodom returns to her death again and again. Adding to this perception of recurrence are echoes of sound between words, as in the statement that wild animals "crept and leapt" to escape destruction. The language also suggests a confused or out-of-breath quality on the part of the narrator. For instance, some "sentences" are single words, such as "Remoteness." Such isolated words help emphasize the meaning expressed with great economy of language; they also make it seem as if Lot's wife is trying to recollect jumbled or confusing memories.

Besides the patterns of language, the images suggest imprecise thought, being organized by association of ideas. After stating that she looked back "from fear" of the animals on the path, the wife reflects that "By now it was neither the righteous nor the wicked" who fled, but "simply all living creatures/ . . . in common panic." Immediately after this, she wonders if she looked back from loneliness, as if the "living creatures" which shared nothing but fear made her realize her isolation. Many ideas contradict previous ones; the speaker's shame at "stealing away" from Sodom as if betraying it is followed immediately by her anger at the illusory Sodomites jeering at her from the walls. This stream of possible motives gives an impression of complex mental processes, helping make the speaker of the poem more than a two-dimensional icon while also rendering her puzzling.

The narrative confusion is amplified when the speaker asserts that she did not turn back by choice, as previously suggested, but rather because of a physical mishap. Moreover, she abruptly contradicts one accident story—that she slipped—with another, that she continued running and fell off the cliff. Further reminding the reader of how hard interpreting events can be, she adds that anyone watching her tumble would have thought she was dancing. Finally, underlining the absolute lack of certainty in her story, she states, "It is not ruled out that my eyes were open" as she fell, and "It could be that I fell, my face turned toward the city." The reader wonders which reconstructions, if any, are accurate and which are fantasies or falsehoods. Lot's wife may have looked back while rolling down a cliff, while fixing her sandal, or while dropping her burden to the ground, but she could not have done all three simultaneously. The monologue therefore becomes a paradox.

Themes and Meanings

Like the scriptural narrative upon which it draws, "Lot's Wife" offers much opportunity for speculation. The fate of Lot's wife is known, but neither her reasons for looking back nor her name are given in the Bible. Both her singular doom and the paucity of other information have prompted many reactions, from simple pity to elaborate speculation about her reasons for turning. Commentators have alleged motives ranging from desire for the corrupt pleasures of the doomed cities to rebellion against authority, although Genesis makes no such statement.

Szymborska's character discusses most of the less lurid motives traditionally ascribed to Lot's wife, including materialism (her desire for the silver bowl), resentment of her husband's orders, regret for the doom of Sodom, and fear. However, she confesses to no truly evil motive. If she longs for her bowl, she seems more to miss a prized keepsake than to display greed. In her shame at "stealing away" from Sodom, she displays a possibly misplaced devotion, but she does not seem the sensualist imagined by some readers of the Bible. Indeed, many of the reasons she suggests imply no fault of her own, but only misfortune. She sounds neither especially noble nor ignoble if she is attempting to be truthful, although her trustworthiness itself is questionable.

The colloquial language reinforces the impression of Lot's wife as an everyday person, probably in late middle age (she complains about having "felt old age" in her bones as she fell behind her husband and daughters). Her evident confusion about her own motives reflects not only the varied reasons ascribed to her by biblical commentators but also the confusion most people have about their own impulses, especially the soul searching they are likely to do after their actions lead to some catastrophe. The mystifying uncertainty as to whether the wife cannot remember or will not divulge what she does remember also recalls the often contradictory interpretations placed upon the scriptural story. Almost at the midpoint, as if mulling the issue over repeatedly has led her to some insight, she adds, impossibly, that she looked back for all the reasons she has considered, and probably a few of which she has not thought.

Lot's wife demonstrates how difficult motives often are to analyze. She also suggests how unsure anyone's knowledge of others is, for we cannot know fully what happened, just as the hypothetical observer would not have known whether the speaker was falling or dancing as she spun down the cliff. Lot's wife does not seem particularly wicked to the reader of this poem, although the reader depends on her for this impression and cannot be certain whether she is confused, lying, or simply playing games in offering the multiple possibilities.

Paul James Buczkowski

LYRICS OF LOWLY LIFE

Author: Paul Laurence Dunbar (1872-1906)
Type of work: Book of poems
First published: 1896

The Poems

Lyrics of Lowly Life is a collection of 115 lyric poems by African American poet Paul Laurence Dunbar. The collection contains poems written in both standard English and African American dialect. The meter of the poems follows standard iambic and trochaic patterns. Dunbar employs a variety of traditional stanza and rhyme patterns.

The first poem in *Lyrics of Lowly Life* is "Ere Sleep Comes Down to Soothe the Weary Eyes," written in standard English, on the subject of death. In the opening stanza, Dunbar describes the persona's deep weariness after a day of searching unsuccessfully for "magic gold," the goal of his waking dreams, probably material goods. He resists sleep because it brings dreams that deceive by making the world appear better than it is. This conflict between sleeping dreams and waking frustrations tortures the subject, making him desire and dread both sleep and wakefulness. In the second stanza the subject's drowsy state causes harsh memories to become "poisonous vapors." In the third stanza phantoms continue to invade the narrator's consciousness until depression deepens into "teeming gloom" and "inexplicable pain."

The poem's second half begins with lighter images about a place "Where ranges forth the spirit far and free." This hope for escape into imagined "lands unspeakable—beyond surmise" ends abruptly, when "Fancy fails and dies" of weariness. The next stanza depicts self-scrutiny, a sort of judgment time, hinting to the reader that when sleep does come it might be accompanied by death. The poet's soul moves into a state beyond the "sad world's cries," into "the last dear sleep whose soft embrace is balm," sealing forever the narrator's eyes.

In addition to standard English lyrics Dunbar wrote dialect poems. The purpose of the majority of dialect poems at this time period was to entertain readers with charming characters and a combination of lively rhythm, hyperbole, and humorous images. However, another purpose of dialect poetry was to portray African Americans as carefree and childlike. That is, dialect poetry was popular in nineteenth century America because it reflected the stereotypes of black Americans favored by prejudiced white minds. The language in these poems contains deliberate errors in usage and spelling. An example of Dunbar's dialect poetry from *Lyrics of Lowly Life* is "When Malindy Sings." The poem begins,

> G'way an quit dat noise, Miss Lucy—
> Put dat music book away;
> What's de use to keep on tryin?
> Ef you practises twell you're gray.

The poem consists of nine eight-line stanzas in which the narrator relates to "Miss Lucy" the superior singing talents of "Melindy." The tone is gay and humorous, and the poem easy to understand. In the second stanza Miss Lucy learns that she "ain't got de tu'ns an' twistin's/ Fu' to make it sweet and light." Regarding Melinda, however, the poem's speaker has nothing but praise: Melindy's warbling outdoes "Robins, la'ks, an' all dem things"; her singing silences the fiddler, converts sinners, and indeed travels to the "very gates of God," at the poem's end.

In a small number of his standard English and dialect poems Dunbar expresses the reality of the racism that shackled him as man and artist. For example, "We Wear the Mask" (a standard-English poem) reveals that the outward cheerfulness of his African American subjects in his dialect poems is a mask of cheerfulness that hides their "torn and bleeding hearts." In writing this poem Dunbar momentarily removes the mask and says bluntly that in both slavery and the oppression that came after, black people have hated wearing a mask that belies both their suffering and their human dignity. In the third stanza the poet allows the "tortured souls," now unmasked, to cry out to God the pain they suffer because of racism's power in society and art. The repetition of "We wear the mask" as the poem's last line acknowledges that the mask is still demanded of the black race living in a racist and predominantly white society.

In two other standard English lyrics Dunbar looks behind the mask another way: He portrays the humanity and nobility of two African Americans. In "The Colored Soldiers" he honors the black soldiers who fought for their own freedom as members of the Union Army during the Civil War. In "Frederick Douglass" he elegizes the great African American ex-slave and abolitionist.

Dunbar also escapes racist rules for the portrayal of black subjects in at least one dialect poem. At first "An Ante-Bellum Sermon" seems to be another portrayal of happy slaves, this time listening to a preacher's words. However, in a manner similar to the composers of spirituals, the preacher transforms a call for heavenly freedom into a call for freedom from slavery on this earth.

Forms and Devices

Certainly the most obvious device Dunbar employed was, as noted previously, the use of African American dialect in many of his poems. Although these poems were popular, they have generally not stood the test of time well. The stereotypical nature of this use of dialect seems, to put it mildly, off-putting to many modern readers. Also, as critics have pointed out, the stylized "Negro dialect," as it was called, of the nineteenth century, did not even reproduce the sounds of folk speech accurately; it had evolved its own set of conventions independent of the speech patterns and pronunciation of real African Americans.

Influential literary critic William Dean Howells, a champion of Dunbar's poetry, arranged for the publication of *Lyrics of Lowly Life*. In his introduction to the volume, Howells wrote that Dunbar's dialect poems are superior to his standard English poems and that they communicate African American life "aesthetically," "lyrically," and with humor. Howells was expressing a view of the time; today readers would agree with

Dunbar himself that the dialect poems are not his best work. Yet Dunbar did combine the dialect sound with iambic and trochaic meters to great effect, a fact that can be best appreciated when the poetry is read aloud. The following stanza from "A Negro Love Song" is meant to entertain the reader, and entertain it does:

> Seen my lady home las' night,
>> Jump back, honey, jump back.
> Hel' huh han' an' sque'z it tight,
>> Jump back, honey, jump back.
> Hyeahd huh sigh a little sigh,
> Seen a light gleam f'om huh eye,
> An' a smile go flittin' by—
>> Jump back, honey, jump back.

Dunbar himself was educated and well-read and spoke standard English, as did white writers who chose to write in dialect, such as Chandler Harris. Dunbar, as he says in "The Poet," from his *Lyrics of the Hearthside* (1899), wrote in dialect because publishers and the public wanted this kind of verse from any writer who portrayed African Americans: "the world, it turned to praise/ A jingle in a broken tongue." He wore this "mask" unwillingly, unhappy that it hid his real voice, demeaned his people, and enabled white Americans to ignore racial injustice.

Throughout *Lyrics of Lowly Life* Dunbar uses sound to great effect. In "Ere Sleep Comes Down to Soothe the Weary Eye," the title is repeated as the first and last line of each of the poem's six stanzas. The result reminds one of a lullaby, but it also sounds melancholy, with a heavy, sad beat created when the predominantly monosyllabic first line is read. The long vowel sounds in "sleep," "soothe," and "weary" add to this feeling.

Dunbar uses metaphor throughout his poetry. In "Ere Sleep Comes Down to Soothe the Weary Eye," the poet expresses the narrator's waking hope as finding the "magic gold" of material success. The poet personifies life as full of "aches," and griefs that haunt are the product of a "witch's caldron." In Dunbar's metaphors there is almost always a comforting familiarity, a clear meaning, rather than extraordinary invention and subtlety. This approach was in keeping with what readers of popular poetry in his time expected, whether the writer was Dunbar or Henry Wadsworth Longfellow, a popular European American poet of the period.

Dunbar's strongest use of metaphor occurs when he protests the need of the African American to hide their humanity behind dialect and other subterfuges in order to survive in a racist environment. In "We Wear the Mask," the mask represents this duplicity. The line "We wear the mask" is used three times: to begin the poem, to end the second stanza, and to end the third and last stanza. The poet begins the poem wearing the mask, then in the second stanza removes the mask and faces the reader without it, and finally replaces it at the poem's end. While the mask is off, the poet reveals the pain it hides, crying out even to God for an end to this "guile" and all the injustice it implies. Only in his pain does Dunbar find this powerful metaphor. "We

Wear the Mask" is the finest poem in *Lyrics of Lowly Life*, containing in its metaphor the history of a people wrapped in racism and the dilemma of an artist who must wear a mask.

Many of Dunbar's poems use images from nature or are about nature itself. In "Rising of the Storm," for example, the lake heaves with "a sob and a sigh." "Ballad" explains how a lover's loyalty brings a bright day and joy while a lover's deceit brings a dark day and sadness. In "The Lover and the Moon" a lover faces the dilemma of keeping his love faithful while he is on a journey. He prays to the moon that it keep an eye on the lover from whom he is parted. After the moon fails in its task and the lover loses his mate, he asks the sea to punish the moon, which is why in stormy weather "waves strain their awful hands on high/ To tear the false moon from the sky."

Themes and Meanings

The poems written in standard English in *Lyrics of Lowly Life* cover conventional topics, including the poet, nature in all its moods, love requited and unrequited, youth, aging, birth, and death. Dunbar's lyrics have a Romantic poet's emphasis on extremes of emotion—exhilarating joy and deep sorrow. A poem such as "Ere Sleep Comes Down to Soothe the Weary Eye" expresses a sadness that verges on the melodramatic. Other lyrics are more lighthearted. For example, in "Retort" the poet has a traditional head-versus-heart dialogue; he first doubts his love for "Phyllis" but then affirms it lest he be "worse than a fool." In "Passion and Love" a teary young girl is wooed by a passionate suitor whom she rejects and then by a more "aloof" one she accepts. Dunbar's lyric poems in standard English generally have simple themes, in keeping with the late nineteenth century American popular poetry tradition. Since "Ere Sleep Comes Down on Weary Eyes," the most complex lyric in this volume, is also first in the volume, Dunbar may well have believed that this was his most successful attempt to go beyond the conventions of the day.

Dunbar did not live long enough to witness and participate in the Harlem Renaissance of the 1920's. If he had, he would have heard his poetic descendants announce their independence from white influence and their determination to express the African American experience according to their own choice of language and form. In the achievement of these later poets the reader hears echoes of Dunbar's earlier voice.

Langston Hughes's poem "The Weary Blues," for example, is similar to Dunbar's "Ere Sleep Comes Down to Soothe the Weary Eyes" in content, but unlike Dunbar, Hughes particularizes the experience using the language and rhythms of the African American vernacular—in this case, of blues music. Hughes tells the reader about someone who (like the persona in Dunbar's poem) is near exhaustion but still awake. Hughes pictures his subject as a blues player "Droning a drowsy, syncopated tune." Though the musician is not actually dead at the poem's end, as Dunbar's subject seems to be, Hughes does picture him as one who sleeps "like a rock or a man that's dead." Significantly, Hughes affirms that the blues expresses a black man's soul, whereas Dunbar's poem does not specify the race of the poem's subject.

Likewise, Dunbar's poem "Sympathy," from the collection *Lyrics of the Hearth-*

side, is quite similar to Countée Cullen's later sonnet "Yet Do I Marvel." As Dunbar compared the poet—implicitly an African American poet—to a "caged bird," wondering why the bird keeps singing through his bars, Cullen asks the universe the reason God would "make a poet black, and bid him sing." Again, Dunbar does not explicitly identify the "caged bird" as a black poet, while Cullen does, but it is entirely reasonable to assume that Dunbar's own difficulties as an artist in a racist world formed the core of the poem.

Francine Dempsey

MALCOLM SPOKE / WHO LISTENED?

Author: Haki R. Madhubuti (Don L. Lee, 1942-   )
Type of poem: Lyric
First published: 1969, in *Don't Cry, Scream*

The Poem

Haki R. Madhubuti's "Malcolm Spoke / who listened?" is written in the black poetry style of the 1960's, a free-verse, conversational form containing altered spelling, short, explosive lines, and the rhythms of black street-corner speech. The title implies that the social and political messages of Malcolm X were not heeded by African Americans, who, for various reasons articulated in the poem, either were deceived by other spokespersons or simply adopted superficial attributes of black consciousness. The poem is a warning and somewhat of a diatribe chastising African Americans by using Malcolm X as a symbol of political integrity and identity. The poet admits that the messages are also for his own edification, suggested in the subtitle *"this poem is for my consciousness too."*

The first stanza describes outer trappings of black culture such as "garments" and "slogans" and contrasts them with a genuine commitment to certain ideals. In the second stanza, Malcolm X is portrayed as a man who discarded the negative acts of hustling and pimping to evolve from the life of a street hustler (whose physical identity was also a distortion) to a revolutionary. His odyssey is juxtaposed to the dilemmas of color identity within the black community and the transformation in the 1960's to identities that valorized natural hairstyles and dark complexions. The poet is concerned with the way light skin has been associated with class pretensions among African Americans. The poem identifies historical signifiers of color identity, inverting the "blackface" stereotype of minstrelsy to signify status in the 1960's based on darker skin color. Aware that privileging lighter skin and other aspects of bourgeois identity might be disingenuous, the poet emphasizes the new appearances (such as "nappy-black" hair) but also warns of false alliances with intellectual whites who might be insincere in their motives even though they are perceived as "authorities on "'militant'/ knee / grows." Most important, however, is the deception by black spokespersons through rhetoric that is overused and implicitly empty of true meaning.

The third stanza contrasts the pre-1960's image of the "hipster" with the black consciousness identity of the 1960's, evident in symbols of apparel. Attitudes of the 1960's are equated with African designs as opposed to Western clothing: The "double-breasted" suit is supplanted by the "dashiki," although the change in physical garb does not necessarily mean a genuine projection of black consciousness. Furthermore, there are references to higher education as a credential of 1960's activists, but the intellectual association with university training is undercut by the suggestion that the would-be black leader has majored in "physical education," an obvious criticism of academic depth. The fourth stanza uses the metaphors of "animals" and "colors" to imply that exterior signs of black identity may not necessarily be sincere. The poem projects a genocidal ending for blacks, a black holocaust in the "unitedstatesof-america's/ new/ self-cleaning ovens." The title of the poem is reprised in the ending along with the warning that African Americans need to listen to the message of Malcolm X.

Forms and Devices

The principal poetic device is the juxtaposition of pre-1960's identity symbols with those of the 1960's. These symbols are especially related to appearance versus reality, not only in physical style but also in the veracity of statements made on behalf of black identity. Because Malcolm X did not wear obvious African apparel, he is used as a measure of integrity without the possibility of deceit through physical representation. The notion of wearing "blackness" as opposed to actually living it is developed throughout. To "wear yr / blackness" connotes a superficial identity that belies one's actual political consciousness, which may be anything but black. However, the first stanza also emphasizes the hypocrisy of language if one voices "slogans" that are also indications of insincerity, mimicry, and popular positions. The popularization of black rhetoric is reflected in the metaphor of musical notoriety symbolized by the music charts. Like popular music, rhetoric can also generate a "top 10" list of statements, which suggests widespread appeal but not necessarily depth of content.

The characterization of Malcolm X is achieved through the use of language drawn from street-corner black vernacular used throughout the poem. The phrases "super-cools" and "doo-rag lovers," referring to Malcolm X's earlier life as a hustler and his conked or processed hairstyle, are linked to the image of the counterfeit black spokesman, the "revolutionary pimp," which combines both a progressive and retro-gressive identity. Black vernacular is also used to describe color: "high-yellow" is used as a signifier of class prejudice within the black community, and the term "blackface," drawn from minstrelsy, is used as a parallel to disguise and deception. These images of color are historical markers in that they are derivatives of plantation and postemancipation labels and terminology. Manipulation of language is another key device, particularly the respelling of certain words to achieve emphasis: "negroes" as "knee / grows," "your" as "yr," "black" as "blk," and "from" as "fr." The collapsing of the spelling of "United States of America" to "unitedstatesofamerica" is another example of word manipulation used to achieve the effect of seeing the word or phrase in a different linguistic configuration.

The juxtaposition of physical symbols is found in the third stanza, where the "double-breasted" suit is paralleled to the "dashiki." Both items can be used to manipulate one's identity and also to deceive, the Western attire indicating the establishment and black bourgeois sophistication, the African clothing implying black nationalism. These images suggest that transitions in attire from European to African may not represent a true development of black identity. The imagery in the fourth stanza is also based on juxtaposition, repeating notions of color used earlier. The implication is that "dark meat"—people of color—and "whi-te meat" (the spelling of white is altered to approximate the pronunciation of "whitey")—people of European descent—can both be subject to deception. The final image of the "new/ self-cleaning ovens," directly evoking the Holocaust of World War II, uses the modern appliance to further the irony of genocide.

Themes and Meanings

The primary themes of the poem involve the potential for hypocrisy and deceit within the black consciousness/black nationalist movement of the 1960's because of deceptive leaders who appear to represent the black movement but who are not genuine representatives such as the icon Malcolm X. The idea of being sold out by black leadership is the ultimate message. However, the poem also operates on a psychological level, urging the reader to question identity through appearance and language. The prevailing theme of appearance versus reality is developed not only through the mockery of black nationalist clothing but also through the criticism of black rhetoric that becomes a cliché. The use of Malcolm X as the icon of trust and integrity is supported by Malcolm X's own transition from hustler to revolutionary. Malcolm X is portrayed as having shed the outer appearances of the hustler, emerging as a conscious representation of incorruptibility; he is juxtaposed to leaders who are visibly nationalist but who maintain intraracial hierarchies that reflect color distinctions of past eras. The irony is that Malcolm X also sought certain false physical attributes inasmuch as he was known to have straightened his hair during his years as a street hustler.

Though black consciousness can be corrupted through disingenuous leadership, there is also the possibility of infiltration by Caucasians and the undermining of militancy from within. Though the poem is not completely antinationalist, its projection of the physical trappings of the black nationalist as a disguise, its mockery of the dashiki and the natural hairstyle, is a warning against being seduced by language and style rather than adhering to the teachings of Malcolm X, who did not wear the apparel of the black nationalist but who was, nevertheless, an advocate of nationalism. The transformations of the 1960's that praised natural appearance, African clothing, and black imagery might themselves be contemporary versions of prior emblems of deception such as "blackface." Distinctions based on skin color are symbols of retrogressive political consciousness as well as the historical roots of intraracial color distinctions. Preference for a certain physical appearance is viewed as a game, a manipulation of appearance for reasons of status. The physical image of African Americans through hairstyles is also used to characterize pre-1960's identity in which emulation of white appearance ("straighthair") was associated with achieving bourgeois status. Certain artifacts of 1960's popular culture are used symbolically: "air conditioned volkswagens" are associated with intellectuals, and the study of "faulkner at/ smith" ironically indicates white liberalism and a trendy connection to the black struggle.

"Malcolm Spoke / who listened?" questions whether transitions in physical style and appearance are also representative of valuable political and social transformations. Essentially pessimistic about those who have overtly made the physical transition, the poet recognizes the possibilities of the "rip-off" in cultural terms, the replacement of color and class distinctions with measures of "blackness" represented in clothing and rhetoric. Though the poem is concerned with deception, it also articulates the outcome of failing to listen to the message of Malcolm X; that is, the possibility of the annihilation of African Americans through acts of genocide that rival the Holocaust.

Joseph McLaren

THE MAN WITH NIGHT SWEATS

Author: Thom Gunn (1929-   )
Type of poem: Dramatic monologue
First published: 1987; collected in *The Man with Night Sweats*, 1992

The Poem

"The Man with Night Sweats" is one of a series of poems Thom Gunn has written about the acquired immunodeficiency syndrome (AIDS) epidemic in general and friends of his who either presently have the disease or have already died of it. The title refers to the night sweats that are one of the symptoms frequently experienced by victims of the disease. This poem is the dramatic monologue of a persona afflicted with AIDS remembering and pondering his past life and the way in which he became ill. In the first stanza, the speaker awakens in the night, sweating; the sheet has become wet and he feels cold even though he has been having erotic and passionate "dreams of heat." Now, the only residue of these dreams is the night sweat that has left his sheets wet and his body chilled. He rises from the bed to change the sheets, but he is immobilized by the remembrance and contemplation of his past sexual adventures and by a growing sense of helplessness. The second through the fifth stanzas involve his memories of these past experiences, which have resulted in his present condition. The final three stanzas return to the present as he contemplates that condition.

There are two basic tensions in the poem. The primary one is built on the contrast between the strong, masculine flesh of the speaker's body in the past and its weakened physical state in the present. When he was sexually active, he believed that he could "trust" his body, and he relished the sexual risks he took. At that time, it was as if he were shielded by his skin from harm, and when "it was gashed, it healed." In the present, however, the ill man, his protection gone, faces the pains of future physical deterioration. Because the shield that once protected him—explicitly his skin but also, by implication, a condom—has cracked at some point, his mind has been reduced "to hurry" and his flesh to a "wrecked" state.

Another element of tension is the contrast between heat and cold, in terms of both the man's physical temperature and the heat that is generated by sexual passion and erotic dreams. Ironically, although he is sweating, the speaker wakes up from his "dreams of heat" to cold, which is a marked contrast to the sexually active past, when he "Prospered through dreams of heat." The "residue" of that heat is sweat, and the need to change wet sheets is a contrast to the gratification of desire that followed sexual activity in the past.

He stands, hugging himself as though, thereby, he might be able "to shield" his body from the pains that await, as though "hands were enough" to stave off the approaching "avalanche," that is, the inevitable and overpowering progress of the disease that will sweep over him and, ultimately, destroy him. Now, his only protection is his hands, but they are incapable of performing such a task.

Forms and Devices

Despite the contemporary and even controversial concerns to which he turns his attention, Gunn has always been something of a formalist in an age in which free verse abounds. He frequently employs long-established forms of verse as well as traditional patterns of meter and rhyme, achieving, through the juxtaposition of avant-garde subject matter and classical forms, an effectively startling tone. In "The Man with Night Sweats," he alternates four quatrains with four couplets to produce a unique pattern of juxtaposition. This pattern represents a combination of traditional form and innovative alterations by the poet. The lines of both the quatrains and the couplets are iambic trimeter with several effective variations in the beats.

The rhyme scheme in the quatrains is *abab*; in the couplets it is *aa*. Many of the rhymes are full ("heat" and "sheet," "trust" and "robust," "in" and "skin"), although Gunn also employs slant rhymes, as in the third quatrain when he links "sorry" and "hurry," in the fourth quatrain in which he links "am" and "from," and in the concluding couplet, where "enough" is rhymed with "off."

The imagery of the poem centers on the sheets made wet by the night sweat and on the flesh of the speaker, which was once invulnerable but now suffers the effects of the illness. He can change the wet sheets, but he is unable to alter the condition that produced them. Among the metaphors is his comparison of his skin to a shield that once protected him but now has been pierced, resulting in flesh that is "reduced and wrecked." The "skin" is also clearly an allusion to and a metaphor for a condom, whose breaking may have resulted in the disease. In addition, the sheet might be considered, metaphorically, a kind of skin that was once dry and protective but now makes the speaker cold. The "dreams of heat" from which the persona awakens are a metaphor for the sexual passions of the past, experiences that he enjoyed and through which he "prospered" but which have now become emblematic of his physical decline. He compares the further physical deterioration that awaits him to an "avalanche" that he is not strong enough to stave off.

Themes and Meanings

"The Man with Night Sweats" is a poem about facing one's inevitable death. In this instance, the individual happens to be suffering from AIDS, but the universality of death and its effect on human beings are, nevertheless, present in the poem. As the speaker remembers the past, when he was full of life and unafraid to take sexual risks, he grieves for the good health that he will never again enjoy and for the fact that he might have been able to prevent the illness that is now racking his body. Another thematic element of the poem centers on this man's—and any human being's—helplessness in the face of physical decay.

The subject of death has always been prevalent in poetry of all ages and countries. Often, the contemplation of death is eased by the hope and consolation of eternal life, as in Alfred Lord Tennyson's "In Memoriam" and John Milton's "Lycidas," or by the deceased person's return to and absorption by nature, as in Walt Whitman's "When Lilacs Last in the Dooryard Bloomed" and Percy Shelley's "Adonais." There is, however, no such consolation offered in "The Man with Night Sweats," only grief and a sort of quiet despair for the passion of the past that will not come again, the passion that was responsible for the wasting illness the speaker experiences. While dealing with the same theme—death and its effects on the human consciousness—Dylan Thomas urged a struggle against the impending end to life in his poem "Do Not Go Gentle into That Good Night," and something of the same notion is employed here by Gunn. His speaker hugs his own body in defiance of the illness, endeavoring to shield it from the "pains that will go through me." However, the body, now weakened by the disease, is no longer the shield that it was in the past, and the concluding couplet makes it clear that there is no hope: Hands are not powerful enough to "hold an avalanche off."

Another theme emanates from the contrast between the sexual companionship that was available in the past, when the "robust" body and the mind of the persona relished the heat of passion, and the loneliness with which he must now face his own death. The memories and dreams are insufficient consolation as he imagines the further deterioration of his body from a disease of which the night sweats are only a symptom.

W. Kenneth Holditch

THE MARSHES OF GLYNN

Author: Sidney Lanier (1842-1881)
Type of poem: Lyric
First published: 1878, in *A Mask of Poets* (edited by George Parsons Lathrop); collected in *Poems of Sidney Lanier*, 1884

The Poem

"The Marshes of Glynn," consisting of 105 lines, is considered Sidney Lanier's best long poem. In this poem, he experiments with new rhythms in opposition to the old, established meters of the poetry of his time. Using a form of logaoedic verse, Lanier freely employs iambs, anapests, and dactyls as well as a wide range of patterns from rhyming couplets to single-syllable lines to achieve the desired effect. Because of his interest in both poetry and music, Lanier explores the relationship between these two disciplines in this poem. Consequently, "The Marshes of Glynn" is arranged almost orchestrally, with the elements introduced and arranged much as instruments in a symphony perform together for maximum effect.

"The Marshes of Glynn" follows its first-person narrator from the edge of the marsh into its lush and mysterious depths. Lanier's use of long, flowing sentences filled with alliteration and assonance gives a sense of lushness to the setting his narrator inhabits. As the narrator contemplates life on the outskirts of the marshes, he is inexplicably drawn "To the edge of the wood// to the forest-dark." However, the edge of the marsh, though attractive during the "noon-day sun," is not enough to satisfy the seeking narrator. He has been content to spend the daylight hours on the edge of the wood, but, as twilight approaches, he recognizes the beauty of the "sand-beach" to the east and finally acknowledges his desire to enter the marshes.

As he enters the heart of the marshes, the narrator notes the features of life near the sea and considers their beauty. Any fear he has felt about approaching the depths of the marshes disappears when he enters the wood and sees that it has been touched with the "reverent hand" of the "Lord of the land." When he sees "what is abroad in the marsh and the terminal sea," he realizes that his "soul seems suddenly free." It is while contemplating this simplicity and the freedom of the marshes that he first sees the marsh-hen and decides that, like her, he will build his "nest on the greatness of God."

As the narrator contemplates the meaning of life in the marshes, night falls and the tide rushes in. With lush and descriptive language, Lanier describes the swamp at night—the fullness and the quiet—as a place of both ecstasy and uncertainty. While the sea overwhelms the land of the marshes with the "waters of sleep," the narrator reflects on what is going on underneath the surface. Envisioning the "souls of men" under these powerful, enveloping waters, he wishes that he could understand all that is under the tide that now covers the beautiful marshland he has discovered. However, all he can do is acknowledge that though he has come into the heart of the marsh and experienced it directly, it is not possible to completely understand it.

Forms and Devices

Lanier's interest in music is effectively illustrated in "The Marshes of Glynn" through the use of alliteration and assonance as well as through the use of long and flowing sentences to describe the marshlands. In contrast, Lanier also uses short phrases to illustrate the musical aspect of his poetry (for example, the double rhyme and flowing rhythm of the lines "Emerald twilights,—/ Virginal shy lights"). The use of strong, repeated stresses to illustrate the importance of what is being said has the effect of slowing the pace of the poem, while other lines move it forward using shorter, fast-paced dactyls. Throughout the poem, these rhythms work with the poem's internal rhymes and easy flow of words and phrases to create a sense of ebb and flow that emphasizes the musical quality of the work.

Another important aspect of "The Marshes of Glynn" is Lanier's rich use of metaphor and imagery. For Lanier, the woods symbolize the kind of paradise inhabited by God. As the narrator nears the woods, he feels a sense of fear and awe common when approaching God. In addition, Lanier describes this paradise by using language suggesting religious imagery: "Closets of lone desire" and "cells for the passionate pleasure of prayer" suggest cloisters or monasteries and thus the kind of reverence and holiness reserved for God and His holy places. When Lanier writes, "I will fly in the greatness of God as the marsh-hen flies," he equates the marsh-hen with the superiority of God and nature. However, the hen also represents the narrator and his intentions—"As the marsh-hen secretly builds on the watery sod,/ Behold I will build me a nest on the greatness of God." The narrator sees in the marsh-hen a way to live life in relation to God's greatness. Similarly, Lanier uses the sea as a dual image. Again, the sea symbolizes God, who is "Here and there,/ Everywhere." At the same time, the waters of the sea eventually flood the marshland with the "waters of sleep," the tide and its flooding symbolizing both God, who overcomes humanity with His nature, and death, which covers everyone with its "sleep."

Themes and Meanings

"The Marshes of Glynn" is dense with religious imagery and meaning. By entering the woods, the narrator is cleansed from his former world outside the marsh and acquires faith, which leads him to a union with the marsh and thus God's greatness. In observing and considering the marsh and all that is in it, he reaches that point where he can begin to understand—though not fully—the true meaning of this newfound faith. "The Marshes of Glynn" is also a poem about journeys. It examines both the narrator's search to understand self and his spiritual progress toward a union with God and nature. First, Lanier explores humankind's journey into the dark depths of self. The poem follows its narrator from the very edge of self-knowledge—the woods—to the depths of the narrator's questioning soul—the marsh—to discover that self-knowledge is not really possible. The poem also illustrates another kind of journey— the universal search for God and the ultimate truth of life through nature. The narrator desires to "fly in the greatness of God." By the poem's end, he has discovered that "from the Vast of the Lord will the waters of sleep/ Roll in on the souls of men." In this case, the sea represents God, whose tide envelops the marshes or the human soul. As in the narrator's search for self, he discovers that true knowledge of God and nature is impossible. In both cases, it is during the night in the marshes that the narrator comes to terms with the unknowable and, though it is unknowable, nevertheless gains peace.

The narrator's journey begins at "noon-day." At first, it is a journey of fear and hesitancy. This person does not want to leave the warmth of the comfortable world outside the "dim sweet woods." By twilight, however, he has left behind the comfort he has felt during the day and is drawn by these "dear dark woods" into the midst of all he fears. The unknown presents him with a land beyond his expectations, and he soon comes to prefer the freedom he discovers within the "world of marsh that borders a world of sea." Ultimately, he must face the night and the tide. Once again, faced with the unknown and unknowable, he must come to terms with the meaning of human existence: "But who will reveal to our waking ken/ The forms that swim and the shapes that creep/ Under the waters of sleep?" Though the narrator never finds the answer to this question, he accepts both this lack of knowledge and, ultimately, the inevitability of death. Like Lanier, the narrator searches for God's ultimate truth through nature and finds a peace that, though couched in uncertainty, is an answer he can accept.

Kimberley H. Kidd

MEDITATION ON A MEMOIR

Author: J. V. Cunningham (1911-1985)
Type of poem: Meditation
First published: 1945; collected in *The Judge Is Fury*, 1947

The Poem

"Meditation on a Memoir" is a brief poem of sixteen lines that are arranged in four stanzas of four lines each. The meter is iambic dimeter, a very short and unusual metrical line. The first stanza contains three questions, the next two stanzas respond to those questions, and the final stanza resolves the poem with another question. The title announces both the approach (meditation) and the subject (memoir). To meditate is to think deeply on the significance of a subject, and it is not the usual poetic mode in J. V. Cunningham's work. "Memoir" is a word that Cunningham uses a number of times in his poetry, and it requires some commentary. For Cunningham, a memoir is the revelation of all of the intimate details in a person's life. Another poem by Cunningham, "Memoir," makes clear what type of revelations are involved: "Now that he's famous fame will not elude me:/ For $14.95 read how he screwed me." The first line of "Meditation on a Memoir" immediately calls such revelations into question: "Who knows his will?" Does anyone truly know himself or herself well enough to reveal all in a memoir?

The second stanza continues to undermine the claim that anyone can know his or her "will" well enough to confess all in a memoir. People's lives consist of the "Surf of illusion," and they can find peace in sleep only by "skilled delusion." This is framed syntactically as an answer to the questions of the first stanza. "Illusion" and "delusion" seem closely related to each other, but they make up two very different worlds: awareness and sleep. Both of these are guided or determined by the error of illusion or willed delusion. Therefore, one cannot truly know one's own will; any pretense to knowledge is mere illusion.

The third stanza shifts the perspective from the questioning speaker to an observer of the inner life of the memoir writer. At that moment, "silence hears/ In its delight/ The tide of tears/ In the salt night." One reveals one's inner self not in the words of a memoir but in the "silence" where "the tide of tears" is released. This is in direct opposition to the illusion and delusion of stanza 2. Silence is delighted by the breaking of illusion into the inevitable tears. Silence is also the opposite of the audience that is hungry for the truth of a person's life that a memoir represents.

The last stanza completes the poem by coming back to the questions with which it began. The questions are the appropriate answer to the pretense of self-knowledge that a memoir assumes. Now, after piercing the "skilled delusion" that protects such false knowledge and having heard the tears, the speaker announces the final estimation: "Who knows what themes,/ What lunar senses,/ Compel his dreams?" The dreams and themes that make up a memoir are controlled not by the self but by a tidal and lunar force. The dreams that are supposed to be the most personal part of an individual are not one's own; rather, they are compelled and controlled. The poem attacks the Romantic assurance of self-revelation and calls self-knowledge into question.

Forms and Devices

The poem is unusual in its use of very regular iambic dimeter. The effects of such a short poetic line are significant. The short and regular lines are gnomic and epigrammatic as they sort out large and general principles in human affairs. In addition, the lines in the first and last stanzas are end-stopped, while those of the second and third stanzas are run on. This follows the syntactic form of question and answer. The rhymes of the poem are also of interest. The rhymes of the first stanza promise certainty, as "will" is related to "fulfill" and "mood" to "conclude." The rhymes of the second stanza undo any claim to completion in the conjunction of "illusion" and "delusion." In addition, the subjects of a memoir are paired in the rhyme of "themes" and "dreams."

Cunningham often uses personification in his poems. Here "silence" is portrayed as a human figure who listens with "delight" to the tears that are released. Cunningham tends to use personification rather than images, since the poems deal with general principles instead of particular occurrences. However, there are a few images in the poem. For example, in the second stanza, the image of surf suggests a swirling of illusion that destroys any stability. However, surf that "Spins from the deep" is connected to a sustained metaphor that controls the structure of the poem: the moon that controls the tides of all of the oceans and seas. The movement of the moon controls the "tide of tears" and the surf of the second stanza. Humankind is tossed about by some unknown, greater power just as the seas are tossed about by the moon. The question of the first line of the poem is answered by the metaphor that concludes the poem: "What lunar senses, / Compel his dreams?" People do not control or know their wills; their themes are only dreams and they are compelled by something other than human will. The pride of people in both knowing and revealing their wills is reduced at the end to a creature who is moved back and forth at the will or whim of another uncontrollable force.

Themes and Meanings

There are a number of significant themes in "Meditation on a Memoir." First, the memoir is a common theme for Cunningham. In "To a Student," he distinguishes memoirs from fiction: "Fiction is fiction: its one theme/ Is its allegiance to its scheme./ Memoir is memoir: there your heart/ Awaits the judgment of your heart." Fiction is an imaginative creation that is true to its "scheme" or art. Memoirs subordinate art and design to one's "heart." Fiction is a classical form, while a memoir is a Romantic form.

Will is another important theme. Cunningham uses will in the Shakespearean sense: It represents people's untrammeled desires that must be controlled by reason and conscience. Cunningham wrote a critical essay on a phrase by Hamlet to his mother: "Reason panders wills." In this example, reason should guide but instead gives license to the will to act. It is clearly an important theme to Cunningham as a Shakespearean scholar and a poet. The average reader may not realize what is at stake with the seemingly innocent first line: "Who knows his will?" Cunningham has a classical perspective on art and morality; the will should be controlled rather than exercised or revealed.

The controlling metaphor of the poem is also directly related to the theme. The poem begins by questioning people's abilities to know and then reveal their wills and moves to an obliteration of any control by them. They are tossed around at the will of a greater power that they are not even aware of, the "lunar senses" that "compel" their dreams. Cunningham seems to use "senses" in this passage in a very precise way. Once again it is a personification: The lunar force acts out of its own instinctual senses and, therefore, negates the will of humankind. The use of silence in the third stanza is another thematic reversal. Silence is filled with "delight" to hear people break down and reveal their tears. This contrasts to the earlier claim to will and fulfillment. There is none of that now, only frustrated tears that are heard by silence rather than published in the revealing words of memoirs.

Humankind's dreams and themes also have thematic implications. One's dreams are not one's own but are determined and controlled by the "lunar senses." The themes expected in a memoir are not one's own but are compelled by an outside force. The end result is a mockery of any pretense to a true memoir. Most of the poems of J. V. Cunningham are very brief, and "Meditation on a Memoir" is a more detailed and expansive poem than Cunningham's usual epigrams. It is a poem that deals with philosophical as well as aesthetic issues. People's claims to be transcendent beings who are in control of their destinies or even their concepts of themselves and their wills are undermined, and a memoir is seen as either an illegitimate or impossible form or art.

James Sullivan

MEETING AT NIGHT

Author: Robert Browning (1812-1889)
Type of poem: Lyric
First published: 1845, as "Night and Morning," in *Bells and Pomegranates, No. VII: Dramatic Romances and Lyrics*; as "Meeting at Night," in *Poems*, 1849

The Poem

"Meeting at Night" is a short poem divided into two parts, each consisting of a single six-line stanza. The poem was originally entitled "Night and Morning" and included a third stanza that described the speaker's departure; Browning later separated the concluding stanza and retitled the two poems "Meeting at Night" and "Parting at Morning." Although "Meeting at Night" is written in the first person, Browning rarely directly identified himself with his speakers. When asked about this poem and "Parting at Morning," Browning indicated that the poems' speaker was male.

As the title suggests, "Meeting at Night" describes the speaker's nighttime journey to meet his lover. The poem focuses on the speaker's anticipation of the meeting and the stages of his journey. Although by the poem's end the purpose of the journey is made clear to the reader, the speaker does not explain where he is going or why and never gives any details about his relationship with the person he is meeting. Given that the meeting takes place at night and at a remote location, it may be an illicit rendezvous.

In the first stanza, Browning takes advantage of the nighttime setting to create a contrast between the energetic speaker and the inert and featureless landscape. The reader is not provided with a narrative but is offered a series of images and details that suggest the speaker's state of mind. The speaker, who is traveling by boat, begins by presenting a spare, camera-like representation of the sea, sky, and land. In the first two lines the speaker's minimalist descriptions of the "gray sea," "long black land," and "yellow half-moon" emphasize the darkness of the night, which makes it difficult for the speaker to see what is around him. At the same time, the speaker's response indicates that he is not interested in his surroundings but is instead focused on arriving at his destination. The remainder of the stanza emphasizes the speaker's eagerness to reach land. The effect of the speaker's vigorous rowing on the water is conveyed through a vivid metaphor in which "startled little waves" form "fiery ringlets" as they are awakened from "sleep." Browning allows the speaker's personification of the waves to parallel and foreshadow the end of the second part of the poem, in which the speaker is reunited with (and perhaps awakens) his lover. The speaker's lover is thus identified with nature (the waves). The link between the speaker's lover and the natural world is also important in the last lines of the poem, in which the image of the boat's "pushing prow" coming to rest in the "slushy sand" takes on sexual overtones. By the end of the first stanza, the male speaker is identified as active and dominant over nature, which is identified as passive and female.

In the second stanza, readers learn that the speaker's journey is by no means over: He must still walk a mile on the beach and cross three fields before he will arrive at his lover's farm. The first stanza's pattern of moving toward and finally arriving at a destination is thus repeated. Since the speaker is still traveling in darkness, his description of his reunion with his lover is related almost entirely through his sense of sound: his tap at the window, the sound of his lover striking a match, the sound of a voice, and in the last line, the sound of their two hearts beating. The sounds the speaker relates are in themselves commonplace, but here they take on intense meaning and enhance the mystery and excitement of the speaker's reunion. When the speaker's lover lights the match, one realizes that the darkness of the speaker's journey is finally over, both in the literal and the figurative sense. The poem ends with the speaker's implied claim that the lovers' reunion is a kind of epiphany that blots out the "joys and fears" of everyday life.

Forms and Devices

The poem is written in iambic tetrameter, but many of the lines include anapestic feet that hurry its pace. Browning's use of a traditional yet somewhat irregular meter seems appropriate for this speaker, who is both in control and in a hurry. Browning uses the rhyme scheme to insert a subtle contradiction of the poem's implicit assertion that love is the speaker's ultimate goal. Each stanza follows the same pattern: *abccba*. In this rhyme scheme, the last three lines (*cba*) reverse the sequence of the first three (*abc*), and the last line rhymes with the first. Thus, while each stanza moves forward toward a goal (the beach, the lover), the rhyme scheme moves backward, signalling that the speaker cannot remain with his lover indefinitely.

As indicated above, Browning also uses imagery and figurative language to convey the speaker's situation and attitude. The poem's opening lines present the bleak and almost colorless setting of the speaker's journey: "grey" sea, "black" land, and a "yellow" half-moon. The poem's tone seems to shift when the speaker personifies the waves, which "leap" to form "fiery ringlets": Suddenly the water is full of motion and color, but only in response to the speaker's actions and preoccupations. The speaker's first use of "I" takes place in the fifth line—"I gain the cove"—as if to reinforce the notion that he is in control of his environment. Browning uses personification not to enhance the role of nature in the poem but to emphasize the speaker's sense of dominance.

In the second part of the poem, Browning's images shift as the speaker reaches land and nears his goal. Although a mile of beach still separates him from his lover, the beach, unlike the bleak and cold water, is "warm" and "sea-scented." As discussed earlier, the imagery from this point on is predominantly aural, with the exception of the "blue spurt" of the match. The flash of light recalls the "fiery" appearance of the waves in the first stanza and strengthens the connection between the waves and the speaker's lover.

At the end of the poem, the speaker uses figurative language again, this time hyperbole, when he claims that the lovers' hearts are louder than a human voice; at

Masterplots II

the same time he downplays the importance of the "voice" and its "joys and fears" by not telling us whose voice it is (it could be his or his lover's). The speaker's hyperbole attempts to bestow permanence upon the ecstatic moment, in which the heart, emotion, and union take precedence over the head, reason, and separation.

Themes and Meanings

The poem both asserts and questions the idea that passionate emotion, especially love, is not only powerful but also enduring and vital. The speaker argues for the power of love by insisting upon his ability to conquer all that separates him from his lover. Time, distance, and even the lovers' "joys and fears" cannot stand in his way and are not important once the two are together. Displaying characteristic Victorian optimism, the speaker believes firmly in his ability to achieve his goals and ends the poem at the precise moment when he has done so.

At the same time, the speaker's own words amply demonstrate the difficulty of attaining the kind of experience that he exalts. Most of the poem's few lines are devoted to recounting the distance that the speaker must travel and the obstacles he must overcome. The fact that the speaker must travel a considerable distance to reach his lover's farm is especially important. The speaker says nothing about his day-to-day life, but he obviously lives far from the rural setting that his lover inhabits. The physical distance between the lovers points to other ways in which they, as a man and a woman, are different and irrevocably separate. Both before and after marriage, Victorian men and women lived within separate social spheres; men were increasingly called upon to identify themselves with work and with the world outside the home, while women were encouraged to participate primarily in domestic activities and to nurture the emotional and spiritual life of the family. It is therefore significant that the meeting takes place within the female lover's home, because the experience itself is nonrational and belongs within the domestic and private women's sphere.

The speaker must eventually leave the farm, along with the realm of female experience and emotion, to return to the male world (which he does in the four-line "Parting at Morning"). The journey depicted in "Meeting at Night" is thus in part a journey from the male world to the female; this accounts for the long distance that the speaker must travel and for his need to separate himself from the passivity he associates with nature and the female realm. Although the speaker's intense emotion causes him to represent the moment of reunion as all-powerful, the distance between the speaker and his lover remains, like the distance between the social worlds of men and women, and this distance marks the reunion as a rare and transitory event.

Maura Ives

MEETING-HOUSE HILL

Author: Amy Lowell (1874-1925)
Type of poem: Lyric
First published: 1920; collected in *What's O'Clock*, 1925

The Poem

A short poem in free verse, "Meeting-House Hill" contains a single stanza composed of twenty-five lines. Although the title may be taken literally because Amy Lowell is describing the scene of an actual meeting house at the top of a hill, it also serves as a metaphor for the convergence of two cultures. The poem is written in the first person. As the speaker of the poem, Lowell addresses the reader directly, sharing her experience of observing the beauty of two vividly described scenes, one real and one imagined.

The first fifteen lines focus on the scene immediately before Lowell: the blue bay, the church in the city square, the spire reaching toward the sky. In line 16 this perspective changes as Lowell imagines seeing a clipper ship in the distance. The final nine lines describe the imaginary ship in as much detail as the actual scene that lies before her.

Lowell shows that the simple charm of an ordinary New England church matches the more exotic beauty of a "tea-clipper" returning from China. In so doing she moves the reader from the familiar reality of the meeting house to the imagined enchantment of the ship with its cargo of "green and blue porcelain." Focusing her attention on the ship and the "Chinese coolie" on its deck, she seems to wonder how the church would appear to him as he gazes at it from the ship. As Lowell reflects on the beauty of the two scenes, she shares with the reader the intense emotion she experiences when she perceives the blending of the two cultures into one image of spiritual beauty.

Coming from the wealthy and distinguished Lowell family of New England, Lowell traveled extensively in foreign countries. In contrasting the familiar loveliness of the church with the beauty of a tea-clipper just back from Canton, China, she reveals her fascination with ships and ocean travel and her appreciation for the beauty of foreign scenes. The poem reflects her lifelong interest in the Far East. In collaboration with Florence Ayscough, she published a collection of translations of ancient Chinese poetry. Fir Flower Tablets, in 1921. Her work was also influenced by her study of the concise haiku form of Japanese poetry, which is devoted to some aspect of nature. With its visual images, concern with shapes and moods of nature, and suggestion of a divine presence, "Meeting-House Hill" reflects the major qualities of the haiku.

Forms and Devices

In "Meeting-House Hill" Lowell employs a technique that became her trademark: word painting. The visual images provide an impression of reality that approximates the style used by Impressionist painters of the nineteenth century. Impressionist painting was characterized by short brush strokes, bright colors, and the play of light on objects. Lowell provides a word picture of the church through direct observation of the natural elements. Through her powers of intuition she extends the emotional experience to include the depiction of the ship that exists only in her mind.

Alliteration is the poem's most obvious poetic device. Lowell employs a variety of alliterative techniques to achieve a harmonious effect. In the phrases "blue bay beyond" and "shrill and sweet to me like the sudden springing of a tune," repetition of the initial consonant sound occurs in words within the same line. A more subtle form of alliteration occurs in the poem's first three lines, each of which ends with a word beginning with the letter *t*: "I must be mad, or very tired,/ When the curve of a blue bay beyond a railroad track/ Is shrill and sweet to me like the sudden springing of a tune."

In other instances alliteration comes from repetition of initial consonant sounds from previous lines. The following passage, for example, compares the church to the ancient Parthenon of Greece and later refers to the "pillars of its portico": "Amazes my eyes as though it were the Parthenon./ Clear, reticent, superbly final,/ With the pillars of its portico refined to a cautious elegance." Lowell enhances the alliterative effect by repeating the initial *r* sound of "rising" in the second syllable of "unresisting" in "Rising into an unresisting sky." These variations imbue the words with a melodious quality and create a sense of balance in the form of the poem.

Lowell is known as an Imagist, one who stresses clarity and succinctness in presenting poetic images. Sensuous imagery and precise economy of words characterize her poem. In describing the scenes she uses images of color. The whiteness of the church that "amazes" her eyes suggests purity. The green and blue colors of the porcelain in the hold of the imagined ship represent the sea and sky, as well as the beauty of East Asian art. In the phrase "curve of a blue bay," color combines with shape to create a vivid image.

In addition to the sight images, Lowell includes sounds engaging the aural sense and atmospheric images that appeal to the thermal sense. The light, high sounds coming "shrill and sweet" like the "sudden springing of a tune," capture her attention even before she sees the church. Atmospheric images add to the sensory impression. The church spire is "cool," and the ship's sails are "straining before a two-reef breeze."

The poem does not follow a set metrical pattern; instead it intertwines lines as long as sixteen to eighteen syllables with lines of only five to six syllables. Like the brush strokes of an Impressionist painting, short lines containing only one- or two-syllable words strengthen Lowell's imagery.

Themes and Meanings

Lowell was a dominant force in the Imagist movement founded by Ezra Pound. Imagists advocated the use of free verse, concrete images, and concise language. With its realistic sense impressions, simple language, and free verse form, Lowell's "Meeting-House Hill" typifies Imagist poetry. *What's O'Clock* (1925), a collection of

Lowell's best later work and the first volume of her poems published posthumously, was awarded the Pulitzer Prize in poetry in 1926. This volume included "Meeting-House Hill" along with poems about landscapes and seasons, including one of her most famous poems, "Lilacs." The central theme of both poems is the discovery of the unity that lies beneath the surface of diverse forms.

Lowell lived in two worlds. The first included the room from which she wrote and the familiar landmarks and gardens of her New England heritage. The other embraced the culture and poetry of the Far East, with its exotic beauty and serenity. "Meeting-House Hill" expresses the sense of oneness she experienced when images of both worlds met on that hill in New England. By juxtaposing the gritty reality of railroad tracks, a city square, and thin trees with the "clear, reticent, superbly final" Parthenon, Lowell's poem helps the reader see beyond the immediate, everyday world to catch a glimpse of something higher. The contrast is even more obvious when she compares the "pillars of its [the Parthenon's] portico refined to a cautious elegance" with "weak trees" and "a squalid hilltop." Vivid images convey a clear impression of the beauty of a familiar scene, as it suddenly stands out against the sky. Lowell describes the imagined scene in equally brilliant images as she explores the sense of unity represented by two diverse settings.

As Lowell perceives the harmony existing in the beauty of a New England church as well as in the face of a Chinese man on a ship, she describes her physical reactions to show the impact of her vision. She "must be," she writes, "mad, or very tired" when the sight of a church "amazes" her eyes. She feels "dizzy with the movement of the sky." Whether a church in New England, the Parthenon in Greece, or a ship returning from China, a sense of unity transcends the physical limits of one particular place. Her poem is her attempt to share the feeling of harmony she experiences when the diverse images blend.

Judith Barton Williamson

MEN AT FORTY

Author: Donald Justice (1925-   )
Type of poem: Lyric
First published: 1966; collected in *Night Light*, 1967

The Poem

"Men at Forty" is a short poem in free verse, its twenty lines divided into five stanzas. The meditative lyric both expresses how it can feel to be at the midstage of one's life and reflects on the condition of being middle-aged. Although Donald Justice was himself in his forties when he wrote it, the poem is in the third person, the poet wanting to convey an impression not so much of his personal experience as of the way things are. This is characteristic of Justice, although it is not characteristic of the dominant American poetry of the 1960's, which came to be called "confessional." As Justice said, in an interview collected in his book *Platonic Scripts* (1984), he "conscientiously effaced" his self in his poetry.

The poem's five declarative sentences affirm different facts about the situation of men at forty, all of which have to do with a sense of time passing. The men, one reads, "Learn to close softly/ The doors to rooms they will not be/ Coming back to." The rooms are metaphoric; they are the rooms of one's past which adults learn to leave behind—not with a boisterously youthful slam of the door, but with a quiet, perhaps wistful, close. In the poem's second sentence the men feel the landing of a stair moving beneath them "like the deck of a ship." Again the image seems not literal but rather to be a way of referring to the impression one has in middle age of being carried along on a voyage. Common human experience is that children take little note of time, whereas it seems to pass more and more swiftly as one ages. Thus, Justice's poem implies both that one does not have the impression in youth of being carried along (the men at forty feel the movement "now") and that the gentle swell one feels in middle age may become rougher later on.

The sense of time passing is again suggested in the poem's third sentence, which notes that men at forty see in mirrors a blend of the present and the remembered past: Deep in his own features the middle-aged man detects the face of the boy he was as well as that of his own father as a middle-aged man. In the only sentence which takes a single line, the speaker states that men at forty "are more fathers than sons." In this condition, belonging more to the world of the adult than to that of the child, men at forty are being filled, the poem's fifth sentence mysteriously declares. What fills the men is never made explicit, but the fifth sentence provides a powerful simile which describes it as being like the sound of "the crickets, immense,/ Filling the woods at the foot of the slope."

Forms and Devices

Many of Justice's poems are gracefully expressed within the constraints of traditional forms, but "Men at Forty" proves that he could skillfully write free verse as well. When asked what determines a line in unmetered verse, Justice observed (in *Platonic Scripts*) that it seems to be whim but that the poet should enforce the whim so that it comes close to being a perceptible principle. In "Men at Forty" meaning becomes the principle governing when lines are end-stopped and when they are enjambed. The enjambment in stanza 2, for example ("They feel it moving/ Beneath them now like the deck of a ship"), mimics the gentle swell being described, and the enjambment between stanzas 4 and 5, and between the first two lines of stanza 5 ("something// That is like the twilight sound/ Of the crickets"), creates a sense of flow appropriate to the pouring into and filling of the men which is being discussed.

Another principle seems at work when one notices that most lines end on an unstressed syllable. In part this fits the poem's quiet tone, which mentions doors closing "softly," a "gentle" swell, and such intimate moments as a boy secretly practicing "tying/ His father's tie" and the father's face being "warm with the mystery of lather." Such a tone is consistent with the elegantly restrained and self-effacing voice of the poet who once said he "would prefer quiet to loud any day" (*Chattahoochie Review*, Summer, 1989). The poem's quietness also provides a contrast to the last stanza's dramatic aural image of crickets, its three lines ending on stressed syllables. The understatement of the poem's next and final line ("Behind their mortgaged houses"), achieved by its ending on another unstressed syllable, and by its being an offhand prepositional phrase, makes the line all the more piercing.

Justice's skill with language lies not only in his ability to fashion a well-shaped verbal construct and to create a distinctive and dignified voice, but also in the beauty, clarity, and power of his images. They involve not only sight, but also perceived motion (the stair landing), remembered warmth (the father's face), and sound (the crickets). Cannily, Justice tightens his poem's unity by tying its elements together— by the rhyming of "father" with "lather," for example—and by establishing a list of activities in the poem's first half: closing doors, standing on a stair landing, looking into mirrors. The poem's second half is tied together by the motif of secrets running through the stages of childhood, adulthood, and old age. The boy wishes to be like his father and so "practices tying/ His father's tie . . . in secret"; the father is privy to adult rituals such as shaving, with its "mystery of lather"; and, later in life, men will arrive at the ultimate enigma, symbolized in the poem by the sound of crickets.

Themes and Meanings

Mutability and loss are recurrent themes in Justice's poetry, and "Men at Forty" is no exception. Doors closing, a stair landing in motion, a father's features becoming discernible in his son's face, and men being filled with something like the sound of crickets all become intimations of mortality.

Subtly and with originality Justice touches on traditional ways of imagining the human life span: the journey metaphor, for example, was invoked by Dante Alighieri in the opening words of *The Divine Comedy* (c. 1320), which translate as "in the middle of the journey of our life." It is also implicit in poems by Robert Frost ("The Road Not Taken" 1916, "Stopping by Woods on a Snowy Evening" 1923) and many others. In "Men at Forty," as has been noted, it is as if men first notice they have embarked on a voyage after they have passed the midpoint of the biblical life span of three score years and ten. The trope of a stage of life being expressed as a time of day, found in Shakespeare's Sonnet 73 (1609) when the aging speaker says, "In me thou seest the twilight of such day," becomes, in "Men at Forty," the aural metaphor of the "twilight sound" of crickets. The commonplace conception of human life as an arc, rising and falling, which is part of a double entendre in the title of Gerard Manley Hopkins's poem "Spring and Fall: To a Young Child" (1918), is in Justice's poem suggested by the men at midlife being situated in houses at the top of a slope.

What destination awaits people at the end of their journey through life? The last stanza of "Men at Forty" presents a mystery followed by a certainty. The sound of the crickets is "immense," as will be the change from life to death, but the poem is ambiguous as to whether that immensity represents something positive or negative. The chirping of crickets can strike one as festive; many people in Japan keep crickets in cages as pets. It could, however, be experienced as frightening—the insect world taking over, as one imagines it does after the body decays. Perhaps to some the chirping simply sounds eerie. One cannot say, on the basis of this enigmatic aural image, that the poem either suggests an afterlife or rules it out.

Yet whatever lies beyond, if anything, the fact of death is certain, and its certainty is symbolized in the poem's last image—"mortgaged houses." People have their bodies, as it were, only on loan: They must be given up at death. When questioned about the last line of "Men at Forty," Justice replied, "the houses become, I'd like to think, almost an image for their bodies, the men themselves, extensions" (*Platonic Scripts*). Verbal technician that he is, Justice chose the precise adjective, for "mortgage" is, etymologically, "dead pledge."

Jack V. Barbera

THE MIND-READER

Author: Richard Wilbur (1921-   )
Type of poem: Dramatic monologue
First published: 1972; collected in *The Mind-Reader*, 1976

The Poem

Richard Wilbur's "The Mind-Reader," a dramatic monologue of 151 lines, unveils the inner world of a fortune-teller. Although Wilbur leaves gender unspecified, out of convention the reader may regard the aged figure as a woman. The reader cannot rely on convention, however, when it comes to judging her psychic talents. While not able to see the future, she can see past appearances. She can read minds and has a special talent for finding lost items by probing people's memories. Nothing put into a mind is ever truly lost: "What can be wiped from memory?" she asks, adding that "Nothing can be forgotten, as I am not/ Permitted to forget."

Unnamed in the poem, the mind-reader begins her monologue by ruminating on loss. Things that no one sees disappear are "truly lost," she says. She imagines a hat that slips over a cliff. "The sun-hat falls,/ With what free flirts and stoops you can imagine,/ Down through that reeling vista or another,/ Unseen by any, even by you or me." She likewise imagines a "pipe-wrench, catapulted/ From the jounced back of a pick-up truck," and a book sliding from beneath the chair of a reader on the deck of a ship, into the "printless sea."

The mind-reader then tells of her childhood, when her talent was used for finding missing objects. She likens exploring a mind to exploring a landscape: "you would come/ At once upon dilapidated cairns,/ Abraded moss, and half-healed blazes leading/ To where, around the turning of a fear,/ The lost thing shone." Her youthful experience led to her lowly profession: "It was not far/ From that to this—this corner café table" where she sits and drinks "at the receipt of custom." She describes the people who come to her, ranging from those who put faith in her talent to those who outwardly scoff but seek her nonetheless. Skeptics arrive, too, "bent on proving me a fraud."

She describes how she performs for customers. She hands them writing materials, turns away, and smokes. Then she touches their hands and engages in the "trumpery" that her audience expects. She recognizes her own showmanship and explains that she obtains the information she needs through her natural ability: It gives her the thoughts of her customers. Within herself, she sees those thoughts unfold "Like paper flowers in a water-glass." She rues that when her talent fails her she is thought a "charlatan." Of actual fortune-telling, she says, "I have no answers." Yet her customers leave satisfied; "It makes no difference that my lies are bald/ And my evasions casual."

The mind-reader concludes with a brief revery, wondering about the existence of a divine level of intelligence: "Is there some huge attention, do you think,/ Which suffers us and is inviolate . . . ?" She then notes that she distracts herself from the burdens of her talent by fleshly concerns. Yet she still yearns for the place where "the wrench beds in mud, the sun-hat hangs/ In densest branches, and the book is drowned." The one who can find lost things wishes, above all, to lose herself.

Forms and Devices

"The Mind-Reader" is in the form of a dramatic monologue, a poetic form in which the poet assumes and speaks through the identity of another. (Nineteenth century poet Robert Browning is known for refining the dramatic monologue into a unique way of examining character and human nature and of producing unexpected or ironic revelations.) Within this framework, Wilbur achieves many of his poetic effects through introducing richly imaginative details that dovetail unexpectedly with metaphor. The reader, by the end of the first stanza, for instance, has vividly seen a sun-hat "plunge down/ Through mica shimmer to a moss of pines/ Amidst which, here or there, a half-seen river/ Lobs up a blink of light," as well as a catapulted pipe-wrench, and the book lost to sea. As concrete and factual as these objects and events seem, by poem's end they have come to represent an unattainable and immaterial goal: oblivion.

Metaphors serve the mind-reader well in describing her own mind and the minds of others. Finding lost objects becomes a search through strange landscapes with their paths and "dried-up stream-beds." She describes a lost thing as someone waiting at a railway platform, where long cars with fogged windows arrive. There is "a young woman standing amidst her luggage,/ Expecting to be met by you, a stranger." Elsewhere she describes her own talent, her "sixth/ And never-resting sense," as "a cheap room/ Black with the anger of insomnia,/ Whose wall-boards vibrate with the mutters, plaints/ And flushings of the race."

Wilbur composed "The Mind-Reader" in blank verse. Although many of the lines fall within a strict pattern of iambic pentameter, Wilbur freely adds syllables, sometimes resulting in hexameter passages. In the lines set in regular pentameter, he frequently employs elision, as in the following example: "See how she turns her head, the eyes engaging." The vowels in "the eyes" elide to make a single syllable, making this line a regular ten-syllable, or five-foot, line.

Themes and Meanings

Speakers and listeners interact on several levels in "The Mind-Reader." As the mind-reader speaks, she makes it clear that she is talking to a privileged listener. In speaking of "truly lost" things, she mentions that such things are "Unseen by any, even by you or me." The "you," the "professore" who is finally addressed directly at poem's end, is not specifically identified. Presumably she addresses the poet, who then transfers the monologue to the reader. Yet the possibility exists that she addresses another poetic persona, who may or may not be the poet. Moreover, her words make clear that, in this poem, speaker and listener are linked in the activity indicated by the title. Both "read" minds.

She refers to this directly only at the end of the poem, in a joking manner. After mentioning that she is "drinking studiously until my thought/ Is a blind lowered almost to the sill," she responds to her listener: "Ah, you have read my mind. One more, perhaps . . ./ A mezzo-litro. Grazie, professore." This ending pair of lines is the only suggestion that the "professore" has said anything at all. He may in fact have said nothing verbally, since he knew he was dealing with a mind-reader. He may have simply conceived the thought of buying her a drink, a thought which she then "read." Earlier she spoke of the "professore" as being understanding of her situation. Presumably, as a mind-reader, she could accurately appraise her listeners. To what kind of person, then, would she entrust her true story? Quite possibly the listener is another mind-reader. "I tell you this/ Because you know that I have the gift, the burden," she says. The listener knows, and the mind-reader knows of the listener's knowledge. If the listener is also a mind-reader, the entire monologue might be unspoken, with speaker and listener reading each other's minds.

On the other hand, since the "professore" may be the poet himself, the reader begins to see that Wilbur may be talking about himself as a poet or about poets in general. In writing a poem such as this, the poet throws herself or himself into the mind of another. The poet divines the truth about another person without words, even though words are the final result. Even the charlatan act may be consistent with the poet: "I lay/ My hand on theirs and go into my frenzy,/ Raising my eyes to heaven, snorting smoke,/ Lolling my head as in the fumes of Delphi,/ And then, with shaken, spirit-guided fingers,/ Set down the oracle." The mind-reader writes fortunes on paper, even as the poet does poems; both feel pressure from their audience, who expect the miraculous on demand.

If both fortune-teller and poet set "mind" down on paper, moreover, what does this suggest of the reader? In reading the monologue, all become, in a sense, the subject of the poem. The reader is reading a mind. The identification of poet with mind-reader allows Wilbur to speak about the poet as the one who gives voice to a silent multitude. The fortune-teller says of her customers, "It contents them/ Not to have spoken, yet to have been heard." Wilbur may well be speaking about readers, who encounter in poetry feelings felt but never expressed and thoughts thought but never spoken.

Mark Rich

MR. COGITO LOOKS AT HIS FACE IN THE MIRROR

Author: Zbigniew Herbert (1924-1998)

Type of poem: Meditation

First published: 1974, as "Pan Cogito obserwuje w lustrze swoją twarz," in *Pan Cogito*; English translation collected in *Mr. Cogito*, 1993

The Poem

The title of this brief six-stanza, twenty-eight-line poem in free verse recalls the seventeenth century Dutch paintings that Zbigniew Herbert greatly admires and strikes a note at once contemplative and pictorial. Narrated in the first person, it takes an unusual approach to a commonplace occurrence: a person looking at himself in the mirror. Instead of remarking how much he has changed over the years, Cogito questions who "wrote" his face. The question suggests that Cogito conceives of himself less in individual terms than in collective or historical terms—which is to say, less as a unique person and more as a cultural product, even a text (the one written rather than the one writing).

Contemplating himself synecdochically in the mirror, Cogito comes to see his face as a mirror reflecting the ways that history, including heredity, has shaped or mis-shaped him. He begins with the chicken pox, which wrote "its 'o' with calligraphic pen" upon his skin, and moves on to the ancestors from whom he inherited the protruding ears and close-set eyes that worked to their advantage in the age of mastodons and marauders but that now make Cogito look comical. In the third stanza, this line of thought swerves in a more troubling direction as Cogito contemplates his low forehead filled with "very few thoughts," the result of centuries of subservience to aristocratic rule during which "the prince" did the thinking for Cogito's ancestors.

In the fourth stanza, the poem returns to the trope introduced in the first stanza: Cogito as a failed, or at least an imperfect, work of art. The "powders ointments mixtures" he has purchased "in salons" and applied to improve himself "for nobility" are not unlike the art he has seen, the music he has heard, and the "old books" he has read. Instead of being paths to enlightenment and understanding, Cogito implies that they have been little more than ornaments or mere ointments as he contemplates a face, a self, in ruins. In a startling and characteristically self-deprecating turn of phrase (made all the more effective by its unusualness in a poem of otherwise surprising simplicity), Cogito compares "the inherited face" he observes in the mirror to "old meats fermenting in a bag." Gluttonous ancestors, with their "medieval sins" and "paleolithic hunger and fear," are the ones responsible for his double chin, the outward and visible sign of the thwarted hopes of his soul, which "yearned for asceticism." According to the poem's final line, "this is how [Cogito] lost the tournament with [his] face."

Forms and Devices

The question Herbert and other Polish poets of his generation face is how to find a language and a syntax that can adequately reflect recent experience. Herbert's answer is to strip his poetry of virtually all punctuation ("Mr. Cogito Looks at His Face in the Mirror" contains only one dash and one pair of inverted commas) and all signs of poetic convention and ornamentation. Herbert does not begin new lines with upper-case letters; he eschews rhythm, rhyme, and regular stanzaic structure; and he prefers the synecdochies and metonymies of realist writing to the metaphors upon which poetry, particularly Romantic poetry, usually depends. As Herbert writes in "Mr. Cogito on the Imagination,"

> Mr. Cogito never trusted
> tricks of the imagination
> the piano at the top of the Alps
> played false concerts for him
>
> . . . .
> he loved the flat horizon
> a straight line
> the gravity of the earth.

Cogito prefers "to remain faithful to uncertain clarity" and to use the imagination as an "instrument of compassion." The prosaic quality of Herbert's poetry is deceptive (as are the clean lines stripped of punctuation, which require more, not less, effort and involvement on the reader's part), as is proven by comparison with Herbert's numerous prose poems and essays.

The seeming simplicity of Herbert's Cogito poems (many of his other works are more openly allusive in their treatment of myth and history) contrasts sharply with the more lyrical (and somewhat more conventional) work of Poland's best-known postwar poet, Czesław Miłosz. They also differ from the poems of Wisława Szymborska (like Miłosz, a winner of the Nobel Prize in literature), which, though usually even briefer, are equally modest in appearance but much less ascetic in their pursuit of what Herbert calls "the nonheroic subject." Herbert's terseness, his crystalline and austere style, his modest expression and subdued, level voice play their parts in creating the poetic equivalent of the portraits and still lifes of the seventeenth century Dutch painters, practitioners of a sober, somber art devoid of the tricks of the imagination. Like their paintings, Herbert's poems are both pictorial and narrative, little vignettes to which he adds a wryly ironic and, at times, sardonic note. Equally important, Herbert, like the Dutch painters, also positions his art in public terms rather than narrowly personal terms. As a result, what may prove most startling to American readers of Herbert's poetry is the absence of the highly personal, confessional style of his transatlantic contemporaries such as Robert Lowell and Sylvia Plath.

Themes and Meanings

As the poet and critic A. Alvarez has pointed out, "The tension between the ideal and the real is the backbone on which all [Herbert's] work depends." This "incurable duality," as Harvard professor Stanisław Barańczak calls it, is especially pronounced in the recurrent figure or persona of Cogito, the title figure of the collection *Pan Cogito* (*Mr. Cogito*) who reappears in twelve of the poems in *Raport z oblężonego miasta i inne wiersze* (1983; *Report from the Besieged City and Other Poems*, 1985). Cogito is a tragicomic figure, as comically absurd as Charlie Chaplin's Little Tramp, as attenuated as an Alberto Giacometti sculpture, and as existentially bereft and bewildered as any of Samuel Beckett's tramps and disembodied voices. His name indicates his and modern Western philosophy's origins in René Descartes's famous dictum *Cogito, ergo sum*. However, the synecdochic nature of the name of this strangely representative character also suggests his predicament. He is consciousness cut off from bodily existence, thought cut off from meaningful action, existence in the form of alienated awareness, unless one believes, as Barańczak more optimistically does, that what Cogito represents is the healthy reversal of Descartes, not "I think therefore I am" but "I am therefore I think."

At worst, Cogito evidences a capacity for an unwise and typically Cartesian dualism of mind separated from body ("old meats fermenting in a bag"). There is something ridiculous in Cogito's attempts to improve himself with "powders ointments mixtures" no less than with the art he apes ("I applied the marble greenness of Veronese to my eyes"), the music (synecdochically "Mozart") to which he listens, and the "fragrance" of the "old books" he reads. There is, however, also something sobering, even deeply affecting, in his recognition of "the body linked to the chain of species," which is to say linked genetically, culturally, and historically to something other than oneself, a self considered in the narrowest biological and psychological terms. At the same time, there is also something decidedly comical in Cogito asking who gave him his "double chin" when his soul "yearned for asceticism." However, this is comedy touched by pathos, a combination even more problematically present in the poem's final line (which is also the poem's final stanza): "this is how I lost the tournament with my face." The word "tournament" underscores the possibility of Cogito's ridiculousness, his inflated, romantic notion of himself, unless there is for Cogito, as there certainly is for Herbert, some saving irony (Cogito beating the reader to the punch as it were). Even without the trace of irony, there is certainly the regret of one committed, in his own decidedly nonheroic way, to trying to answer the question that is at the heart of Herbert's poetry: namely, how to live this life. With this regret there is also recognition of the risks run by someone like Cogito: resignation on the one hand and mere romantic yearning on the other. To his credit, Cogito heeds the warning implicit in all of Herbert's poems and most simply stated in the "The Envoy of Mr. Cogito" with which the 1974 collection appropriately concludes: "beware of unnecessary pride/ keep looking at your clown's face in the mirror."

Robert A. Morace

MR. COGITO ON THE NEED FOR PRECISION

Author: Zbigniew Herbert (1924-1998)
Type of poem: Meditation
First published: 1983, as "Pan Cogito o potrzebie scislosci," in *Raport z oblężonego miasta i inne wiersze*; English translation collected in *Report from the Besieged City and Other Poems*, 1985

The Poem

"Mr. Cogito on the Need for Precision" is one of twelve "Cogito" poems published in Zbigniew Herbert's *Report from the Besieged City and Other Poems*. These twelve poems supplement the forty that Herbert collected earlier in *Pan Cogito* (1974; *Mr. Cogito*, 1995). The present poem, one of Herbert's longest, contains 131 lines divided into three parts, which are subdivided into stanzas of from one to eight lines each. Most stanzas contain two to four lines; the shortest, with one line, and the two longest stanzas, of seven and eight lines, appear in the final stanza.

The poem is written in the third person, with Mr. Cogito as a character rather than the narrator of the poem. Herbert uses a stiff, slightly pedantic language to create an aura of pseudo-scientific objectivity. This he deploys ironically to underscore the distance between detached treatment and human subject. The poem begins: "Mr. Cogito/ is alarmed by a problem/ in the domain of applied mathematics/ the difficulties we encounter/ with operations of simple arithmetic."

At one extreme, there is the child's sense of addition and subtraction, "pulsat[ing] with a safe warmth"; at the other, there are physicists who have succeeded in weighing atoms and heavenly bodies with extraordinary accuracy. "[O]nly in human affairs/ inexcusable carelessness reigns supreme." Only here does one find a "lack of precise information."

For the German socialist theorists Karl Marx and Friedrich Engels, the specter haunting Europe in the mid-nineteenth century was communism. For Cogito it is "the specter of indefiniteness," which haunts not merely these horrifically Chaplinesque modern times but "the immensity of history." There follows a brief, illustrative allusion to battles from ancient Troy through Agincourt and Kutno, and of terrors identified only by "colors innocent colors": white, red, and brown. Cogito is alarmed by his and our ignorance of how many died in each battle and during each reign of terror. He is also alarmed by our willingness to remain ignorant by accepting "sensible explanations." What "evades numbers," he rightly, and achingly, contends, "loses human dimension." To restore this human dimension necessitates both correcting "a fatal defect in our tools" and atoning for "a sin of memory."

The second part of the poem offers "a few simple examples/ from the accounting of victims." In contrast to history's war, airline passenger lists make accounting for the victims of plane crashes relatively easy. Train accidents are more difficult because they often require reassembly of mangled bodies. Worse still are "elemental catastrophes," such as earthquakes and hurricanes, in which the simple arithmetic of the living and the dead is complicated by a third category, those ambiguously "missing."

In the third part of the poem, "Mr. Cogito/ climbs/ to the highest tottering/ step of indefiniteness." The poem then alludes to the immense difficulty of accounting for, of actually naming, "of all those who perished/ in the struggle with inhuman power." Neither official statistics, nor eyewitness, nor "accidental observers" can be trusted, each for different reasons. Despite the difficulty, Cogito argues, no one must be allowed to disappear "in abysmal cellars/ of huge police buildings" or in "doubtful figures/ accompanied by the shameful/ word 'about.'" "[A]ccuracy is essential/ we must not be wrong/ even by a single one," he admonishes, because "we are despite everything/ the guardians of our brothers/ ignorance about those who have disappeared/ undermines the realty of the world." Thus our need to count, to account for, to name, and therefore to know, if we are to be truly human.

Forms and Devices

Herbert was a member of a generation of Polish writers who came of age during and immediately after World War II. Their wartime experiences made them feel it necessary to devise new poetic forms and syntaxes appropriate to life as they had just experienced it. For Herbert this meant stripping away virtually all punctuation. He also avoids what he calls, in another poem, "tricks of the imagination": all merely ornamental language including rhythm and rhyme, even metaphors. Herbert prefers the device of synecdoche—the naming of the part to stand for the whole.

Herbert's vocabulary is generally simple; his tone matter-of-fact, almost prosaic; his lines and stanzas brief, starkly seen against the otherwise blank page. Nevertheless, his poetry is carefully connected to the larger historical, philosophical, and cultural contexts. This he achieves through allusions, either directly presented (Troy, Agincourt, Leipzig, Kutno), or indirectly (the red, white, and brown terrors). His Cogito poems are generally less allusive than his other poems.

For all its cool detachment and prosaic accessibility, Herbert's poetry is surprisingly, and subtly, varied. The formality of the opening stanzas of "Mr. Cogito on the Need for Precision" gives way to colloquialism, which becomes especially evident at the end of the second part. The register changes again in part three, which opens with a cartoonish image, then changes into lines of great moral passion and power, before ending with language more resonant than any before it. The final lines are no less realistic than what precedes, but they are realistic in a different way. Instead of the earlier positivism, Herbert offers up the verbal equivalent of one of the seventeenth century Dutch still-life paintings he so greatly admires: "in a bowl of clay/ millet poppy seeds/ a bone comb/ arrowheads/ and a ring of faithfulness/ amulets."

The poem's subject matter lends itself to the sentimentalism of the film version of *Schindler's List* (1994), but its kitchiness, however well intentioned, is precisely what Herbert's seemingly straightforward but in fact understated, deeply ironic, and blackly humorous poem deftly avoids. The lucidity (or what Herbert elsewhere calls "uncertain clarity") of the writing underscores, by means of contrast, the grimness and horror of Herbert's vision. His, and Cogito's, pose or stance of cool detachment serves as a disguise beneath which the reader can detect the author's barely but brilliantly controlled pain and outrage. It is the immense and purposeful gap separating simple observations, such as "we don't know" or "somewhere there must be an error," and the passion that drove Herbert to write this poem and others like it that gives the poem the extraordinary moral force that enables Herbert to use the imagination as an "instrument of compassion."

Themes and Meanings

"Mr. Cogito on the Need for Precision" is one of the many poems in *Report from the Besieged City* bearing witness to the injustice and inhumanity of life in Poland under the martial law imposed by General Wojciech Jaruzelski in 1981, the year Herbert chose to return to his native land. The government crackdowns, reprisals, arrests, interrogations, torture and killings that led Herbert to write the poem do not limit it, the fate of so many topical literary works. Even as it gives voice to Herbert's dismay and anger, it reveals his desire to use his poetry "to bestow a broader dimension on the specific, individual, experienced situation" to "show its deeper, general perspective." This broader dimension extends beyond Poland's borders to include the political situation in many other countries during the same period, in Eastern Europe, as well as in Latin America and South Africa. In this sense the poem anticipates the necessity for the many "truth commissions" established in Poland and elsewhere only a few years later.

"Mr. Cogito on the Need for Precision" functions, as does the collection's title poem, as a report from a besieged city where not only is there "a lack of precise information" but where "sensible explanations" are offered and apparently accepted by all but the Cogitos of the world, and where "inexcusable carelessness reigns supreme." The poem's Cogito is like the first-person narrator, the I-, or eye-witness of "Report from the Besieged City" who accepts the part he has been assigned, "the inferior role of chronicler" (or in Cogito's case, the role of accountant, one not so much assigned as chosen). "Keeping a tight rein on my emotions, I write about the facts," Herbert's chronicler reports before ending his litany of betrayals with the words, "and only our dreams have not been humiliated."

To the extent that the title figure of "Mr. Cogito on the Need for Precision" and the eleven other Cogito poems in the collection resemble "Report's" eyewitness, he differs from the central figure of Herbert's earlier *Pan Cogito*. Less comically Chaplinesque, this later Cogito seems closer to Herbert himself in his commitment to this life and how one's life should be lived and measured. In a related poem in the same collection, "Mr. Cogito Thinks About Blood," Herbert sardonically notes that science's discovery of how little blood the human body actually contains does not mean that that blood—and the human life it synechdocically represents—is now seen as precious and therefore shed any less abundantly than before. In "Mr. Cogito on the Need for Precision," the reader finds a similarly horrific sense of humor and sense of helplessness along with the determination, Cogito's no less than Herbert's, to bear witness to that most absurdly humane of principles "in the struggle with inhuman power," namely our own accountability: the fact that "we must not be wrong even by a single one."

Robert A. Morace

MR. COGITO TELLS OF THE TEMPTATION OF SPINOZA

Author: Zbigniew Herbert (1924-1998)
Type of poem: Dramatic monologue
First published: 1974, as "Pan Cogito opowiada o kuszenia Spinozy," in *Pan Cogito*;
English translation collected in *Mr. Cogito*, 1993

The Poem

At sixty-five lines, "Mr. Cogito Tells of the Temptation of Spinoza" is one of the longest of the forty poems of *Pan Cogito* (*Mr. Cogito*). The sense of fullness and completion that such length implies is, however, offset by Zbigniew Herbert's division of the sixty-five lines into twenty-seven stanzas, some just a single line long (and none more than six). All the lines are short, and several are just one word long ("think," "calm," "Great"). At once whole and fragmentary, "Mr. Cogito Tells of the Temptation of Spinoza," with its disconcertingly long and decidedly unpoetic title, seems less a poem in any conventional sense than a vignette with dialogue, a kind of philosophical comedy only loosely tied (and then only by title) to the dramatic monologue form.

The poem's ostensible subject is the seventeenth century Dutch philosopher Baruch Spinoza. Known as "the God-intoxicated man," Spinoza was a fiercely independent person who supported himself by grinding lenses and who frequently moved from one lodging to another in Amsterdam. His dedication to freedom of thought and speech led him to turn down a faculty position at the University of Heidelberg and to refuse a pension from French king Louis XIV because it required him to dedicate a work to the king.

The formal, stilted, and at times clichéd quality of the first three stanzas (nearly one-fifth of the poem) does not so much set the overall tone of the poem (unless the astute reader, familiar with other Herbert poems, detects the carefully controlled irony) as it sets up the reader and Spinoza for what follows. "Seized by a desire to reach God," Spinoza, in his attic, "pierce[s] a curtain" and stands "face to face" with Him. Speaking at length and finding his mind enlarged, Spinoza asks questions "about the nature of man." What follows this rather dramatic opening is a series of one- and two-line stanzas in which readers see Spinoza earnestly inquiring into first and last causes while God acts bored and looks off "into infinity," merely biding his time as he waits his turn to speak.

When God finally does speak, he does not sound like a distant, divine voice coming from a burning bush. Instead, He sounds avuncular, albeit something of a Dutch uncle. He starts by praising Spinoza for his "geometric Latin," "clear syntax," and symmetrical arguments before going on to speak not of first and last causes but of "Things Truly Great." God reproves Spinoza for not taking better care of himself and advises him to settle down, buy a house, be more forgiving and more compromising, and look after his income even if it means dedicating a work to the king ("he won't read it anyway"). Spinoza should, God says, "calm/ the rational fury" and "think/ about the woman/ who will give [him] a child." God's final words prove to be his most

self-revealing (another curtain "pierced"), but it is a revelation that, in effect, repudi-
ates Spinoza's intellectual pursuit of God and truth: "I want to be loved," God tells
him, "by the uneducated and the violent" because "they are the only ones/ who really
hunger for me." The vignette ends much the same way it begins, with a more or less
conventional scene. The curtain that was pierced only moments before falls, leaving
Spinoza alone in the darkness hearing "the creaking of the stairs/ footsteps going
down." He has been tempted, but in what sense, to what end, and by whom?

Forms and Devices

Like virtually all the Cogito poems and many of Herbert's other poems, the simple
language and form of "Mr. Cogito Tells of the Temptation of Spinoza" is both inviting
and deceptive, a deliberate attempt on the part of Herbert and other Polish poets of his
generation to devise a poetry appropriate to their experiences during and immediately
after World War II. In Herbert's case, this effort involves stripping away punctuation
(the only punctuation in "Mr. Cogito Tells of the Temptation of Spinoza" is a single
set of parentheses and a number of dashes to introduce most of the stanzas in which
God speaks directly to Spinoza). The dearth of punctuation marks, the absence of
uppercase letters at the beginning of lines, and the extreme brevity of lines and stanzas
make the words look especially bare, almost vulnerable on the page. Herbert also
strips away much of the ornamental language that makes poetry poetic for many
readers: not only the rhythm and rhyme jettisoned by earlier practitioners of free verse
but also metaphors other than those deployed ironically in order to deflate pretensions
(for example, "seized by a desire to reach God," "pierced a curtain," and "his mind
enlarged"). Instead of the metaphors so closely associated with the Romantic poets,
Herbert prefers synecdoches (parts for wholes, wholes for parts) drawn chiefly from
everyday experience.

Herbert also avoids the lyrical impulse and, with it, the intensely and at times
self-indulgently personal nature of so much Romantic and contemporary poetry: thus
the appeal and the usefulness of a persona such as Cogito who, though usually the
focus of Herbert's attention, whether in first or third person, serves here solely as
narrator whose presence the reader hardly feels. Refusing both lyrical intensity and
epic sweep, Herbert adopts a narrative mode better suited to his simple, austere,
almost ascetic style. His "modest expression" and "level voice" provide an anecdotal
glimpse, a truncated scene rather than a five-act drama not unlike the pictorial style
of Spinoza's contemporaries, the seventeenth century Dutch painters whose portraits
and still lifes Herbert so greatly admires for both their style and their choice of
nonheroic subjects. The title "Mr. Cogito Tells of the Temptation of Spinoza"—indeed
the titles of most of the Cogito poems—strongly suggests Herbert's affinity with these
same Dutch painters whose realistic representations of commonplace subjects often
possessed a carefully but unobtrusively coded allegorical intent. In Herbert's case,
however, both title and Cogito also clearly suggest a truly contemporary perspective
rather similar to the skeptical retelling of Christian myths and legends in Ted Hughes's
poetry collection *Crow* (1970).

Themes and Meanings

It is precisely this deflating of all that is elevated, poetic language as well as philosophical pretension, that is so noticeable in Herbert's poem. The high-minded diction of the opening lines is put in perspective and in its place by God's colloquial speech, and Spinoza's single-minded pursuit of God is offset, even undermined, by God's unadorned advice on getting ahead and on "Things Truly Great" (though those uppercase letters should give the reader pause). There is something incongruous and therefore comical in someone advising a philosopher of Spinoza's stature to buy a house even if that someone is God, but there is wisdom, not just humor, in reminding Spinoza that pleasure is not in itself a vice and in admonishing him to "forgive the Venetian mirrors/ that they repeat surfaces," for what those mirrors accomplish is rather similar to what the seventeenth century Dutch painters did in so faithfully rendering their commonplace subjects. However, the same title that links Herbert's poem to their paintings also suggests that even if Spinoza is wrong not to heed God's advice, he is right to resist the temptation to abandon or compromise his principles by colluding with those in power (for example, dedicating a treatise to the king who "won't read it anyway").

The poem, with its ambiguous depiction of the nature of both God, who may be the devil, and a temptation that is a reversal of the Faustian bargain and not without its own saving grace, illustrates perfectly "the tension between the ideal and the real" that is, as poet and critic A. Alvarez has astutely noted, "the backbone on which all [Herbert's] work depends." This "incurable duality," as Harvard professor Stanisław Barańczak calls it, leads to a "threshold situation," the point where a Spinoza or a Cogito must make a choice, a point Herbert usually takes the reader to but not beyond. Spinoza's choice can be inferred from his career and writings even if not from the poem per se. Spinoza's regret, on the other hand, can only be inferred from the "uncertain clarity" of Herbert's poem, a meditation on the pursuit of the principled life that will take on added ambiguity in Herbert's "Spinoza's Bed" in *Marta natura z wedzidlem* (1993; *Still Life with a Bridle: Essays and Apocryphas*, 1991) and added urgency in his later, more overtly political collection *Raport z obleżonego miasta i inne wiersze* (1983; *Report from the Besieged City and Other Poems*, 1985).

Robert A. Morace

MONTAGE OF DISASTERS

Author: Amy Gerstler (1956-   )
Type of poem: Narrative
First published: 1997, in *Crown of Weeds*

The Poem

"Montage of Disasters" begins with an italicized query: *"Where's the eloquence in all this?"* The question is followed by, as the title indicates, a montage of disasters—train wrecks, fires, earthquakes, bombs, viruses, biblical plagues, mutant spiders, and sinking ships. The poem is like a series of newsreels spliced together in a random fashion or a collage of cover stories from old newspapers, a few copies of *The Star* and *The National Enquirer* thrown in with *The New York Times*. The narrative begins with the train wreck: "The train lurched, shuddered, and snapped in two." However, the train story is abandoned there, and other disconnected scenes follow: "No one knew for sure how the fire started./ Then the virus got into the milk supply." As cataclysm is piled on cataclysm, the report becomes oddly and blackly humorous as reality merges with fiction and nightmare blends with horror story. After bombs destroy the zoo, setting the animals free, "grinning crocodiles new orphans watched/ slither into fountains by the ruined library."

The poem begins in the third person. However, somewhere around the middle the first-person point of view finds its way into what was hitherto a report by an unidentified narrator: a meteorite is described as crashing through the window and turning "my side/ of the bed to a tidy pile of cinders." Once the first person surfaces it remains until the end of the poem, and the events become continually more bizarre and absurd. Murders and scenes from science fiction horror films are slipped into the mishmash of natural disasters. The dog keeps lunging at the trash barrel until "he tipped it over and out fell/ this manicured hand." Typical film monsters are produced by radiation, which causes "tarantulas in the basin/ to grow hundred of times their normal size." The effect is of fireworks of terror shooting off in rapid succession and then all at once; at the end, "the dead bodies" begin to "glow, bluely" and looters begin to "work the ruins." The final scene changes the "I" to "we" as it invokes the last scene in so many horror movies in which the heroic couple is left over in the debris at the end of the nightmare after the monsters have been killed. The city is still aflame, but the fires are dying:

> . . . We first met
> oh, it seems lifetimes ago, staggering
> through fog banks, dodging columns of oily
> smoke, wandering the city in singed pajamas.

This last scene summarizes the conclusion of all the horrors, real and imagined. At the beginning, the poem asks: What kind of eloquence, what kind of verbal beauty, can appear in such a bizarre sequence? There is no answer, only the strange pileup of odd miseries that suggests the collection of disasters chronicled by Voltaire in *Candide* (1759). The poem has a Voltairean kind of humor throughout. "Montage of Disasters" is similar in tone to Amy Gerstler's other work in her 1997 collection, *Crown of Weeds*. Gerstler's poetry is known for its eccentric jumps, weirdly on-target associations, and oddball personas. Her works tend to begin with startling announcements or scraps of hair-raising action. This poem is another of her thrill-ride narratives. Riding the edge of surrealism, "Montage of Disasters" makes the reader question the smooth surface of the ordinary. It also demonstrates that terror has its own clichés.

Forms and Devices

"Montage of Disasters" is a forty-four-line poem in blank verse. The tone is relaxed and conversational. Most of the lines have three to five accented syllables, or six to eight words, which give a vague uniformity to the poem's slightly ragged rectangular appearance on the page. There is, however, no clear pattern of rhythm, and there is no obvious reason for the positions of the line breaks except to maintain the overall appearance. The enjambed lines are not pulling against an underlying rhythm, and this informality enhances the flat, reporter-style tone of the poem. The flatness of style is also emphasized by the lack of simile and metaphor. Language is simple and direct, with some colloquialisms and some deliberately vague expressions that create the impression of casual understatement: "The women/ caused an awful lot of trouble/ in the lifeboats that night." There is a preponderance of short words, even monosyllables. The sentence structure is intentionally unvaried, with verb predictably following subject. The reader has a sense of being given "just the facts," although the facts themselves are strange and shocking and combine the improbable or mythical with the ordinary: "Nuns poured stiff jolts of whiskey/ into paper cups for sooty rescue crews./ Later, it rained frogs." When the ordinary is consistently and repeatedly combined with the peculiar, the reader tends to blur them after a while, and this blurring contributes to the effectiveness of the poem. Traces of postmodern technique appear in this superficially coherent, though bizarre, narrative. As does much post-modern work, the poem effaces boundaries, allowing material from one world to flow into another. Here the immediately obvious violated boundary is between fact and fiction, but there are others—dream and experience, self and other, night and day, human and animal. The picture is finally something like Pieter Brueghel the Younger's paintings of hell, but this hell is painted with tongue in cheek.

What is most compelling about Gerstler's style is the distinctive voice. The reporter style challenges assumptions about observation and reporting. The reader can almost hear the voice of a newscaster describing horrific events in a determinedly cheery timbre and with a certain standard rhetoric. The mismatch between tone and content becomes even more obvious when the first person enters the story: The speaker exhibits only mild curiosity about the untoward events she is witnessing, and perhaps now and then a certain satisfaction creeps into her own observations, such as when she sees "a tidy pile of cinders."

The way the disasters merge and overlap allows them to lead off in all directions from the central narrative, posing unanswered questions. The montage form itself, in its piecing together of parts of things, has both a limited surface and a wider implication beneath the surface as each piece also implies the rest of the picture. Scraps torn from other complete pictures have been stuck together to create a new shape, the shape of this narrative.

Themes and Meanings

Gerstler's themes in "Montage of Disasters" are similar to those in the other poems of *Crown of Weeds*, which continues strains of thematic concern found in her earlier books. "Montage of Disasters" implies that the conscious and the unconscious are more connected than people think. The surreal narrative, with its clips from nightmares, horror films, and newsreels, may suggest that there is an unconscious, shared script for the disasters people fear and that this script, cribbed from the same sources she uses, is filled with clichés.

In any case, the wild flinging together of disparate images in "Montage of Disasters" asks that readers revise their concept of what is ordinary and expected. In Gerstler's poetry, the unexpected is the expected, and anything may follow from, or cause, anything else. The strange is so close to the surface that it may poke through at any point. Nothing is predictable or reliable, but everything is reported as though it were. "One lesson we learned was this:/ you cannot cut corners when building a dam." Gerstler's poetry often has a social dimension that comes from her emphasis on offbeat characters; although in this poem it is really situations rather than characters that are eccentric, the poem may telegraph a message of egalitarianism through its equivalence of all disaster scenes and all social upheavals. In this surreal landscape of disaster, all are equally victims. The world falls away beneath the feet of humankind.

"Montage of Disasters" is also memorable for its sheer narrative pyrotechnics. Several reviewers have referred to Gerstler's style as "acrobatic," and there is skill in her narrative leaps and loops. As the story jumps from one scene to another, it seems to deconstruct itself. Humor replaces horror. The humor has a sting; the reader is complicit in laughing at all these exaggerated horrors, but what does this say about the reader? The conclusion has a hint of euphoria as the couple wanders through the ruins, having survived and reported upon all these natural and supernatural events. Influenced but not overwhelmed by postmodernism, "Montage of Disasters" is a superficially simple poem, but underneath it is subtle and teasing and defies closure.

Janet McCann

THE MONUMENT

Author: Elizabeth Bishop (1911-1979)
Type of poem: Lyric
First published: 1946, in *North & South*

The Poem

Elizabeth Bishop's poem "The Monument" is written in seventy-eight lines of free verse with a few significant breaks for verse paragraphs. The title is important in that it defines the object that is being described and discussed by the poet. The poem is narrated by a knowledgeable and perceptive speaker who describes the monument and tells the naïve reader, an otherwise undefined "you," how to see it and read it. This speaker asks, "can you see the monument?" with some interest and urgency. It is of prime importance that readers see what is immediately before their eyes, that they understand what it is and what it does.

The word "monument" suggests a memorial or sacred object that holds special significance to a group of people or a nation. The word will acquire other connotations and denotations as the poem proceeds. The monument is made "of wood/ built somewhat like a box." Immediately, there is a clash between readers' expectations about the object and the material of which it is made: One expects a monument to be made of marble rather than wood. The poet-speaker then describes its shape and size. It is not stately but seems to be jerry-built "like several boxes in descending sizes/ one above the other." It does, however, have a form: It has four sides, and four "warped poles" hang from it like "jig-saw work." The speaker then shifts to the monument's context. It is "one-third set against/ a sea; two-thirds against a sky." The perspective is also significant: "we are far away within the view." The sea that it is set against is also a human-made object: It is made of "narrow, horizontal boards."

At this point, the person who is being instructed objects: "Why does that strange sea make no sound?" It is not natural to the naïve reader, who asks if "we're far away." The tone of the poet-speaker changes at this point. She more directly insists on the monument's nature and significance. It is from "an ancient principality" with an "artist-prince" who might have intended it to be a tomb or boundary. The naïve reader is still not satisfied: "It's like a stage-set; it is all so flat!" It does not meet the reader's predetermined and limited expectations of art and nature. The poet-speaker becomes even more insistent. She points to its existential nature: "It is the monument." However, the naïve speaker continues to object and asks, "what can it prove?" Apparently this speaker wants art to be useful and to do something.

The poet-speaker has the final word. She says, "It is an artifact," not a thing of nature. It is organic: "It chose that way to grow and not to move." Its uniqueness "give[s] it away as having life." It is not limited by intention or one meaning; it may be one thing or another. What is inside, perhaps its meaning, "cannot have been intended to be seen." Its existence, rather than any meaning ascribed to it, is what is significant. The poet finally defines the monument as a work of art: "It is the beginning of a painting,/ a piece of sculpture, or poem, or monument,/ and all of wood. Watch it closely." The poem begins with the demand that readers see the work and ends with it becoming active and alive, something that must be watched closely.

Forms and Devices

Bishop is a poet noted for her use of description, and, in "The Monument," this technique is especially important. Description, in her poetry, tends to replace the use of such traditional poetic methods as metaphor. The poem is a detailed description of an object that acquires significance as the poem develops. It is written in free verse with many run-on lines, very few lines that end with a period or semicolon, and sentences that are long and meandering. This construction mirrors the indirect nature of the argument that Bishop constructs in the poem.

The diction and tone of the poem are especially interesting since it has two very distinct speakers who use very different language. The naïve speaker's sentences are all questions, while the poet-speaker uses direct declarative and imperative sentences. The tone of the naïve speaker is querulous and complaining, while the poet-speaker's tone becomes more insistent, demanding that readers see the monument and see what is significant about it. There are also some important juxtapositions of words in the poem. There is, for example, the clash between "artist" and "prince" in "artist-prince." Furthermore, the monument is always described as an object made of wood while readers and the naïve speaker expect it to be made of marble or granite.

There is a good deal of imagery in the poem, although much of it is set against readers' expectations and the connotations of the monument. There is a lot of wood imagery: "grains," "splintery," and "whittled." In contrast, there are a number of images associated with artifice: The monument is a stage-set and, most important, an artifact. There are also the very different images of light and growth at the end of the poem. There is no specific use of metaphor; however, the monument becomes, through the detailed description, a metaphor or symbol for a work of art. The poet-speaker insists that readers be aware of the nature and existence of that work of art and to see what significance it does and does not contain. To do this, the poet must show readers what a work of art is not: It is not a thing of nature, and it does not prove anything. Bishop's approach is indirect, but the poem begins to grow from mere description into an exemplification and definition of the nature of art.

Themes and Meanings

"The Monument" is about the nature and existence of a work of art. On that theme, Bishop has surprising things to say. For example, the material of the monument is wood rather than the expected granite or marble. This suggests that art is made of everyday material and experience rather than great matter that is wrought into a fixed position. The monument also has an unexpected and irregular shape. For Bishop, one definition of a work of art might be that which defeats expectations and grows out of ordinary material into a shape that is very much its own.

A work of art is also very different from nature. The naïve speaker complains of the artifice of the monument and wants it to be more like nature, to mirror the form of natural elements rather than becoming a thing in itself. One source for Bishop's view is Wallace Stevens's poem "Anecdote of a Jar." Stevens's jar and Bishop's monument are unmoving. They do not ape nature but dominate it, although they are connected to it by analogy. "The Monument" also insists that a work of art does not prove anything or make a statement. Any meanings it may have seem to be accidental or to grow out of its nature. What is inside is not intended to be seen. "The Monument" seems to embody the famous dictum of Archibald MacLeish's "Ars Poetica": "A poem should not mean but be." "The Monument" also suggests that a work of art cannot be limited to one reading or interpretation. The words "might" and "may" recur several times in the poem. To fix the work is exactly what the naïve speaker is trying and failing to do.

The poet-speaker makes clear what the monument stands for at the end of the poem: "It is the beginning of a painting,/ a piece of sculpture, or poem." It represents any work of art. Significantly, it is only the beginning of that work. It cannot come into existence unless a reader becomes aware of its nature and brings it into being. Readers must understand any work of art on its terms rather than on their own. That is why the reader is urged at the end of the poem to "Watch it closely." By giving oneself up to the work of art, the reader can watch it come into being.

James Sullivan

THE MORNING OF THE POEM

Author: James Schuyler (1923-1991)
Type of poem: Lyric
First published: 1980, in *The Morning of the Poem*

The Poem

"The Morning of the Poem," James Schuyler's longest poem, extends to forty-four pages and is the title poem of the book for which the author won the Pulitzer Prize in literature in 1981. The lines, except those in a few short sections, are long, and the appearance of those lines is nearly uniform, most extending to a second line of indented text. The poem is written mostly in free verse.

The event that has propelled the poem into being is Schuyler's awakening one morning, in July, 1976, at his mother's home in rural East Aurora, New York. Domestic pleasures and comforts abound, nature provides opportunities for reverie and entertainment, and the poet's mother is not overly intrusive: "Then to the kitchen to make coffee and toast with jam and see out/ The window two blue jays ripping something white while from my mother's/ Room the radio purls." Schuyler, however, misses New York City, where his life is centered and where his friends are. The painter Darragh Park, to whom the poem is dedicated, is especially on Schuyler's mind; the "you" addressed in the poem is often Park, whose relationship with Schuyler seems ambiguous. The two appear not to be lovers, exactly, but they are probably more than good friends: "How easily I could be in love with you, who do not like to be touched,/ And yet I do not want to be in love with you, nor you with me," Schuyler writes.

By the conclusion, July has slipped seamlessly into August, and Schuyler is anticipating his return to New York City. There has been very little action, but the reader has learned much about Schuyler. In this poem, which closely resembles a personal journal, Schuyler records quotidian events such as trips to the toilet and petty squabbles with his mother; reminisces about erotic encounters, which occur less frequently as he drifts into later middle age; thinks fondly of his friends, most of whom, such as the painter Fairfield Porter and the poet John Ashbery, were or are closely connected with the New York art world; and delights in both the beneficence and occasional cruelties of the natural world. (It should be noted that Schuyler, Ashbery, Kenneth Koch, and Frank O'Hara constitute the nexus of the "New York School" poets, all of whom have in common, to varying degrees, an involvement with the work of New York-centered artists of the middle of the twentieth century such as Willem de Kooning and Jackson Pollock.)

The structure of the poem is loose. Schuyler's impressions of the physical world, memories from childhood, thoughts of friends, and occasional travel notes ("in New York City you almost cannot buy a bowl/ Of oatmeal: I know, I've tried") do not occur in any clear order but are noted in a stream of consciousness. The poem's beginning and ending, with vivid descriptions of the poet urinating, constitute the most concrete elements of traditional structure. As critic Stephen Yenser notes, "He seems to mock the notion of aesthetic unity by virtually framing the poem with trips to the john." Schuyler is much concerned with the ordinary, the mundane, the flotsam and jetsam of daily life, but he also addresses issues many readers may consider more serious: Deaths of friends, especially of Porter, and more ominously, his own death, which may lie in the not-too-distant future, are a constant refrain.

Forms and Devices

Schuyler laments the dearth of good poets. The problem is that most have "No innate love of/ Words, no sense of/ How the thing said/ Is in the words, how/ The words are themselves/ The thing said . . .// A word, that's the poem./ A blackish-red nasturtium." Schuyler is perhaps echoing the American poet William Carlos Williams, whose dictum "No ideas but in things" influenced later generations of American poets.

"The Morning of the Poem" employs few poetic devices such as simile, metaphor, or symbol. For Schuyler, the "thing said" is interesting enough in itself, and there is little need to obfuscate through abstraction. As *The Diary of James Schuyler* (1997) reveals, Schuyler was drawn to the writings of naturalists and diarists, often from the previous century, whose appeal rests much in their powers of observation. Roses can never be roses for Schuyler. They are, instead, "Bunches of roses on/ The dining table, Georg Arends, big and silver-pink with sharply/ Bent-back petals so the petals make a point . . ./ or Variegata di Bologna, streaked and freaked in raspberries and cream." The poetry is both in the description of the rose and the name of the rose; it is in a similar spirit of collecting and recording that Schuyler reproduces a shopping list or recounts a childhood erotic experience. However, words are not important in simply their power to name or describe. "How the words are themselves/ The thing said" refers as well to the sounds of words. The following lines illustrate:

> . . . the pigs were big and
> to be kept away from: they
> were mean: on the back porch was the separator,
> milk and cream, luxurious
> Ice cream, the best, the very best, and on the
> front porch stood a spinet
> Whose ivory keys had turned pale pink: why? . . .

Schuyler employs a number of poetic sound devices in this selection. The reader notices the internal rhyme in "pigs/big" turning into assonance, or near assonance, and consonance in "milk/spinet/pink." Similarly, the reader may appreciate how the repeated long *e* and *m* sounds in "mean" and "cream" (twice) carry into "ivory," repeating the long *e*, losing the *m,* and picking up "cream's" *r*. There is a certain resolution in "keys," again repeating the long *e* and also the *k* sound established in words such as "kept," "back," "milk," and "luxurious." The plaintive question "why?" is given poignancy by Schuyler's preparing the reader, in terms of sound, by the long *i* assonance in "ice" and "ivory."

The passage quoted above is not unique in the poem. The careful reader, noticing Schuyler's complex use of sound devices, may avoid the error of reading the work as a disorganized compendium of sense impressions and memories but may instead appreciate how Schuyler's art, while appearing, upon casual inspection, to lack the kind of linguistic artifice people may associate with poetry, is, in its own subdued way, wrought with great subtlety.

Themes and Meanings

Readers might explore the larger ideas in "The Morning of the Poem" through the prism of Schuyler's homosexuality, which he writes of freely. In this, it is tempting to see Schuyler as an heir of Walt Whitman, whom Schuyler names in the poem and who wrote of homoerotic desire in *Leaves of Grass* (first published in 1855, revised a number of times) in a manner that nineteenth century readers and even some twentieth century readers found shocking. Whitman was compelled to keep his homosexuality under a veil in ways that Schuyler is not. Thus, Schuyler's description of his attempt to pick up a man in the grocery store and not obscuring real curiosity about the man's body ("trying to get a front view of him and see how he was/ Hung and what his face was like") may be read as a sign of poetic kinship with perhaps American poetry's most important figure.

Yet for Schuyler's relative openness about his sexuality, a certain covertness and a certain sadness remain. Schuyler, born in 1923, was fairly entrenched in middle age by the time of the gay liberation movement. Thus Schuyler, with all the importance he places on naming things and people (a love of naming, too, with roots in Whitman), only very rarely names boyfriends or lovers. In this respect, it seems rather sad that Schuyler cannot actually name "the one who mattered most," presumably a lover. Schuyler echoes the experiences of a generation of gay men whose characters were shaped both by the repression of the 1940's and 1950's and the greater freedom of the 1960's and 1970's.

Schuyler's homosexuality might account for many of the poem's tensions. The poet's relationship with his mother, for instance, appears not altogether loveless but remote. Occasional references to the sanitarium, Anabuse (a drug used to aid recovering alcoholics), and psychiatrists remind the reader of the narrator's bouts with substance abuse and schizophrenia, problems associated with societal pressures a homosexual of Schuyler's generation might have faced. Such scattered references, coupled with the fact that "The Morning of the Poem" follows, in its printed form, Schuyler's "The Payne Whitney Poems" (short poems about one of Schuyler's stays in a psychiatric hospital) make the reader wonder whether the visit to East Aurora was planned to aid the poet's recovery. Finally, Schuyler's state of near homelessness underlines a certain deep loneliness the reader senses. Although Schuyler has a mother in East Aurora and friends in New York City, he lacks a true home with a committed, lifelong companion. The reader is left wondering if, when Schuyler returns to his apartment "back to Chelsea, my room that faces south," he will find anything resembling fulfillment. The poem's open-endedness ("Tomorrow: New York: in blue, in green, in white, East Aurora goodbye") is liberating insofar as a man weighed down by little may experience life as a series of endless possibilities. However, this sense of freedom is also disquieting: If a man has nothing to weigh him down, what remains?

Douglas Branch

MORNING SONG

Author: Sylvia Plath (1932-1963)
Type of poem: Lyric
First published: 1965, in *Ariel*

The Poem

Sylvia Plath had recently given birth to her daughter Frieda when she wrote "Morning Song" in February, 1961. This eighteen-line lyric is structured in three-line stanzas or tercets. Although the title promises a song, the only song the reader gets is a baby's cry. Plath may be experimenting with a traditional form of love poem called an *aubade* in French or *alba* in Provençal. Both refer to a lyric about dawn or for a morning serenade. In such poems, the lover, usually in bed with a beloved, laments the dawn because it signals their inevitable parting. Plath's poem mentions love only in the first line: "Love set you going like a fat gold watch"; that is, the love of the parents gave birth to the baby. The mother love that the speaker is expected to feel is strangely absent in this poem. Instead, the mother-speaker moves from a strange alienation from this new being to a kind of instinctive awakening to the child's presence, her connection to it, and her appreciation for its "handful of notes."

Once the reader grasps the situation of the poem—the birth of a child—the remainder of the poem is reasonably clear. Although the emotional interest of the poem focuses on the new mother, both parents are mentioned: "Our voices echo" and "your nakedness/ Shadows our safety. We stand round." Plath startles the reader with line 7: "I'm no more your mother." Maternal feelings do not automatically occur. Plath is extremely honest to admit such strong feelings of alienation and separation in her poem. In the last three stanzas, the emotional estrangement of the speaker changes. She is compelled to listen to the sound of her child as it sleeps. She seems attuned to that "moth-breath" and says, "I wake to listen." When she hears her baby cry, she gets up to feed it: "cow-heavy and floral/ In my Victorian nightgown." As she breast-feeds her child she observes the coming dawn as the light changes outside the window.

Plath closes with a reference to the sounds the child makes, probably not a cry of need since it has just been fed. The "Morning Song" of the title turns out to be the baby's "handful of notes;/ The clear vowels rise like balloons." Plath makes a definite contrast between the "dull stars" of the morning and the "clear vowels" of the baby. The speaker praises her baby and appears much less alienated than at the poem's beginning.

Forms and Devices

Plath is known for her striking images and her metaphors and similes. In this poem, there is a surreal quality about some of her imagery. In its attempts to express the workings of the subconscious, surreal art employs fantastic imagery and incongruous juxtaposition of subject matter. To compare a child to a "fat gold watch" is surreal. The child is animate while a watch is inanimate. Love is engaging while winding up a watch is a mechanical act. What the simile suggests is the great distance between the act of love and the fact of the baby. What does this baby—this thing with its own existence—have to do with the emotions that engendered it? By raising this question about what most people consider a most "natural" phenomenon—the birth of a child—Plath helps the reader see something very old (childbirth) as something quite strange, new, and unsettling. The disorienting effect of Plath's style is typical of Surrealism.

Plath emphasizes the child's strangeness—its thingness—by referring to its cry as "bald." Her choice of adjective is odd. The baby's head may be "bald," but by describing its cry this way, Plath seems to emphasize the nonhuman quality of this new being/thing that does not take its place among other humans but "among the elements." Stanza 2 reinforces the nonhuman quality of the baby as perceived by its parents. The child is a "new statue." The parents are pictured as gazing at it "in a drafty museum." In other words, they cannot help staring at the child, but they feel vulnerable and inadequate: "We stand round blankly as walls." With the child as a statue and the parents as walls, not much communication occurs. Plath's surreal images underline the parents' feelings of alienation and strangeness in this new (to them) situation.

Stanza 3 contains not only the most striking line ("I'm no more your mother") but also the most puzzling image: "Than the cloud that distills a mirror to reflect its own slow/ Effacement at the wind's hand." First, clouds do not distill mirrors. The shadow cast by a cloud reflects it; when the wind moves the cloud along, both cloud and shadow disperse. The bond this mother feels to her baby is just as insubstantial and fleeting. Plath's image is convoluted and perhaps deliberately inexact. She suggests the tenuous relationship between mother and child, cloud and mirror. It is as if the birth of the child were external to the mother rather than part of her. Fortunately, the speaker discovers she is wrong. Maternal instincts arise in her.

She is attentive to the breathing sounds her child makes. The imagery animates those sounds: They are like "moth-breath," suggesting how quiet and subtle they are. It is as if she can see the moth as it "flickers among the flat pink roses," suggesting the patterns on wallpaper or fabric. Otherwise, the roses would not be "flat." The contrast signifies the aliveness and motion of the moth-breath versus the less vibrant roses. The new mother, listening to her child's breath-in-sleep, uses the image "A far sea moves in my ear" as if she were holding a shell to her ear and capturing the sounds of the ocean. The child's delicate moth-breath suggests something more ponderous—new life and new possibilities.

The child's mouth is "clean as a cat's," with the emphasis on "clean": This new being is untarnished. Plath uses this word again in "Nick and the Candlestick" to describe her son: "The blood blooms clean/ In you, ruby." It is a word of praise. No longer a statue, the child's presence takes on more spirited animation through the animal imagery. The speaker's lack of feeling for her child gradually transforms into appreciation and wonder, particularly at its sounds—not a "bald cry" any longer but something shaped, "a handful of notes." The child enters the human world when the speaker perceives its attempts at language: "The clear vowels rise like balloons." The poem closes on this image of ascension, a typical Plath strategy. "Morning Song" records how the speaker's perception of her baby changes; her intimacy with her child grants her the vision of its animated being.

Themes and Meanings

The dominant theme in "Morning Song" is alienation and the process by which it is overcome. A woman's poem, it deals with maternal instinct and its awakening. Plath avoids sentimentality in taking up a subject—becoming a mother—that is too often treated in our culture in a fluffy way. A woman—certainly an ambitious poet such as Plath—does not come to motherhood merely by giving birth. New behavior is learned. The being of the mother is as new as the being of the child. Readers can appreciate Plath's honesty in dealing with her subject. It also takes a certain amount of courage to admit to a colossal lack: "I'm no more your mother/ Than the cloud." The alienation in the poem is overcome by such acute delineation of the feelings. Instinct has a role to play as well: The speaker finds herself listening to the child's sounds. This is not self-willed or under her control. She follows her instinct: "One cry, and I stumble from bed." In the end, she is rewarded. Alienation is overcome in her connection to her baby. Her own child serenades her with a "morning song" and a bond is formed through language, the quintessential human act.

The third tercet, with its convoluted imagery, introduces a secondary theme: the speaker's awareness of her child as potentially marking her insignificance, her erasure as a poet: "I'm no more your mother/ Than the cloud that distills a mirror to reflect its own slow/ Effacement at the wind's hand." Can a woman be both mother and famous poet? Plath, writing in 1961, had few predecessors who managed to achieve both. In engaging this theme, she is dealing with one of the major issues that faced women poets in the twentieth century. If mothering absorbed her attention, would she still be the poet-artist she longed to be? This superb poem answers her implied question. Further, the joyous ending proclaims the arrival of both a new singer on the scene and a mother proud of her child's vocal bravura.

Claire J. Keyes

MOTHER IRELAND

Author: Eavan Boland (1944-   )
Type of poem: Dramatic monologue
First published: 1995; collected in *The Lost Land*, 1998

The Poem

"Mother Ireland" is a short poem in free verse in which the speaker is Mother Ireland. The poem repeatedly reminds the reader of the speaker's presence: every sixth word, on average, is a first-person pronoun ("I," "me," "my"). The poem is difficult to classify. It has some qualities of the lyric, with the author speaking through a persona. It sketches the outlines of a story (hence is a narrative), and the story's scale has epic proportions, though the poem (at only thirty-six lines, 142 words) is obviously not an epic. It might be considered a parable, but that term identifies a type of story, not a type of poem.

Mother Ireland tells her story: Once passive, unselfconscious, blind, and voiceless, she became active, self-conscious, sighted, and articulate. At first, she says, she was the land [of Ireland] itself, unable to see, only seen by others. The season early in the poem is winter: "I was a hill/ under freezing stars."

The transformation began because "words fell on me" continually, she says. They were others' words (she calls them by different names: "Seeds. Raindrops./ Chips of frost."), and she was but their passive recipient. From one of these words, in the poem's pivotal lines, she says,

> I learned my name.
> I rose up. I remembered it.
> Now I could tell my story.
> It was different
> from the story told about me.

Knowing her own name empowers her, and the change in her is immediately followed by a change of seasons, to spring. Having arisen, Mother Ireland distances herself from and gains perspective on the physical landscape. Once she "was land"; now, having "travelled west," she looks lovingly "at every field// and at the gorse-/ bright distances." However, she "looked with so much love" that those things she gazed upon "misunderstood me./ *Come back to us/* they said/ *Trust me* I whispered. Thus the poem ends with what appear to be Mother Ireland's first words spoken aloud. The reader, trusting Mother Ireland, has faith that the change, though wrenching, is for the good.

Certain puzzles remain in this enigmatic poem. Were the words that fell on passive Mother Ireland those of generations of Irish bards and poets (mostly male)? May we assume that the "wound . . . left/ in the land by [Mother Ireland's] leaving it" is not a physical, but a psychic, wound? Is Mother Ireland's journey west a movement toward roots, toward an older, truer, Irish-speaking (and possibly less patriarchal) Ireland?

What, crucially, does the transformation which Mother Ireland undergoes represent? If this is a parable, its lesson seems mysterious.

Forms and Devices

"Mother Ireland" is not divided into stanzas, as most of Boland's poems are; it is, however, broken up on the page, its lines indented irregularly. The lines of no other Boland poem are so scattered across the page, and their scattered appearance reinforces a reader's sense of the disruption caused by Mother Ireland's separation from the land.

The poem has no regular rhyme scheme, yet patterns of consonant and vowel sounds resonate in it. The last syllable in three-fourths of the lines, for example, contains at least one (and often more than one) of the following sounds: *d*, *r*, *s*, and *t*. Lines vary in length, unpredictably, between two and nine syllables; meter is irregular, but 80 percent of the poem's metrical feet are anapests or (more often) iambs. If free verse, as Robert Frost said, is like playing tennis with the net down, this is carefully controlled free verse: The ball is as precisely stroked, so to speak, as if the net were still there.

Beginning with inarticulateness and ending with Mother Ireland's first whispered words, the poem also progresses from simple to more complex, verbally and syntactically. The first six lines contain only words of one syllable, twenty-four of them in a row, and almost all words of more than one syllable come after Mother Ireland has learned her name and arisen. Similarly, sentences in the first half of the poem are much shorter, on average, than those in the second. Early sentences tend to be terse ("I did not see./ I was seen."), but the speaker's voice grows relaxed, even faintly eloquent, especially in its second to last sentence, which stretches unhurriedly for one-fourth of the poem's length.

Throughout, the language of the poem tends to be basic, elemental. "Yes," a reader thinks, "this is how the land would sound if it (she) could speak." One of every four words in the poem is a verb or verb form—a high proportion. (In language, nothing is more basic than verbs.) Another one of every four words is a pronoun. There are only the simplest adverbs *(now, also, so)* and few adjectives, especially in the first half of the poem. In the long sentence toward the end, a phrase such as "the gorse-/ bright distances" stands out by contrast. The elemental quality of the language seems appropriate to the epic scope of the poem's story.

The poem's basic figure of speech is Ireland personified as a woman. The image does not originate with Eavan Boland but has a long history in the literature of Ireland. In her prose book, *Object Lessons: The Life of the Woman and the Poet in Our Time* (1995), Boland is highly critical of what she calls "The nationalization of the feminine, the feminization of the national," by male Irish writers, traditionally. Boland's use of the figure is original in several respects. Her Mother Ireland is not merely a representation of Ireland in female form; she is the land itself, its very topography (Mother Earth/Ireland), as well as the spirit or personality which, acquiring name and self-awareness, emerges from the land. This emergence represents Boland's boldest innovation: the liberation of Mother Ireland.

Themes and Meanings

A 1988 documentary film, also entitled *Mother Ireland* (directed by Anne Crilly, produced by Derry Film and Video), provides background to Boland's poem. The film explores the diverse array of female personifications of Ireland: in literature, in nineteenth century political cartoons, in songs such as "Ireland, Mother Ireland." It demonstrates that, depending upon time and circumstances and the eye of the beholder, Mother Ireland can be a powerful symbol of Irish nationalism or the Sorrowful Mother, either a strong nurturing protector or a pathetic victim of oppression. Eleven Irish women interviewed in the film offer a variety of perceptions of, and a variety of feelings about, the concept and the persona of Mother Ireland. Eavan Boland is not mentioned in the film, and her poem does not allude to it, yet hers could be considered a twelfth voice, extending the film's discourse.

Mother Ireland's progress, over the course of the poem, closely parallels the progress that Boland describes Irish women, especially writers (including herself), undergoing in *Object Lessons*. In the past, she says, the female figure in Irish literature (written by men) "was utterly passive. She was Ireland or Hibernia. . . . She was invoked, addressed, remembered, loved, regretted. . . . And she had no speaking part." She became a "projection of a national idea" and in the process was oversimplified, misrepresented, her true story untold. During Boland's lifetime, however, "women have moved from being the objects of Irish poems to being the authors of them"

The themes of "Mother Ireland" connect with those of earlier Boland poems from the late 1980's and early 1990's—other poems that speak of, for example, "the silences in which are our beginnings" ("The Journey," 1986). From being part of a national mythology, Irish women, in Boland's view, are moving "out of myth into history" ("Outside History," 1989). "[M]yth is the wound we leave/ in the time we have," she writes in "The Making of an Irish Goddess" (1989). Lines 47 to 64 of the poem "Anna Liffey" (1994) provide the most sustained poetic parallel to "Mother Ireland." This section begins, "I came here in a cold winter.// I did not know the name for my own life"; it ends with the poet "Becoming a figure" in her own poem, "Usurping a name and a theme." Mother Ireland also usurps a name, claims a theme, tells her story.

Something of Mother Ireland's own story, "different/ from the story told about me," is suggested by what she looked at lovingly. The "rusted wheel" and the frame of a baby carriage seem to be the domestic debris of a depopulated area. The fields in which they have been discarded are not under cultivation, nor is the land in the distance, though it is beautiful to look at, covered with yellow gorse (a spiky furze). Part of Mother Ireland's story, then, appears to be the ongoing migration, particularly during the nineteenth and twentieth centuries, from the rural west of Ireland to cities (especially Dublin) and abroad, to England, North America, Australia, and so on.

When at the end of the poem the fields entreat Mother Ireland to "*Come back to us*," her refusal is tacit and gentle, but firm. She will not return to her cold, mute, insensate, helpless former condition. "Mother Ireland," written during the transformative term in office of Mary Robinson, Ireland's first woman president, is a parable about a changing Ireland, changing as—and because—its women and their roles are changing; there is no going back.

Richard Bizot

MOTHER LOVE

Author: Rita Dove (1952-   )
Type of poem: Lyric
First published: 1993; collected in *Mother Love*, 1995

The Poem

The title poem "Mother Love" appears in the second of seven sections of Rita Dove's collection *Mother Love*. Like all the poems in the collection, "Mother Love" examines a dramatic story from Greek mythology, the story of Demeter, goddess of grain and agriculture, and her beautiful daughter Persephone. It is, in Dove's words, "a tale of a violated world," simultaneously ancient and modern.

A summary of the myth is important for this poem. With almost no witnesses and with the permission of her father Zeus, the supreme Olympian deity, Persephone has been abducted and raped by Hades, the ruler of the underworld and her uncle, who subsequently makes her his queen. Unable to find her daughter, an angry and inconsolable Demeter wanders among mortals, disguised as an elderly woman. She comes to Eleusis, where she meets the four lovely daughters of Celeus, king of Eleusis, and his wife Metaneira. Demeter, at Metaneira's urging, becomes nurse to the couple's only son, the infant Demophoön. Determined to make the boy immortal, each night Demeter secretly places him in the fire. One night Metaneira discovers this and screams in terror, thus thwarting Demeter's plans. An angry, radiant goddess reveals herself and disappears, but not before ordering the people of Eleusis to build a temple and altar in her honor and promising to teach them rites that became known as the Eleusinian Mysteries.

It is the episode of Demeter and the young son of Celeus and Metaneira that Dove addresses in the poem "Mother Love" and that precedes the rest of the myth: Still inconsolable, Demeter lets the crops die and refuses solace from the other Olympian gods and goddesses. Eventually Zeus agrees to return Persephone, but because she has eaten pomegranate seeds offered by Hades, she must spend fall and winter with her husband and spring and summer with her mother, thus ensuring the seasons, agriculture, and partial consolations.

Demeter's first-person voice dominates the poem, which is divided into two stanzas of twelve and sixteen lines. These twenty-eight lines suggest a subtle doubling of the traditional fourteen lines of a sonnet, a form that preoccupies Dove throughout the collection. The poem is, in fact, a sort of double mothering and a double mourning. In the three sentences that make up the first stanza, Demeter reflects on maternal instincts that combine deep comforts and fears. Tracing in her mind the nurture and natural maturation of children, she voices parents' universal worries as their children "rise, primed/ for Love or Glory" and as their daughters' youthful myopia blinds them to advancing perils.

The poet then makes a shift between the two stanzas, moving from generalizations to specifics. Demeter recalls "this kind woman" (Metaneira), "her bouquet of daughters," and her young son. Demeter will not stop those daughters from being scattered and taken in marriage, but she decides to save the "noisy and ordinary" boy who, if "cured to perfection," could become immortal. This attempt is not simple. She wants to make Demophoön invulnerable, but Metaneira's terrified screams end all that and force Demeter to remember her own screams and her vulnerable, lost daughter. She thus answers the rhetorical question with which she begins the poem: "Who can forget the attitude of mothering?"

Forms and Devices

In drawing from mythology for this poem's structure and themes, Dove joins a long line of writers, artists, musicians, and choreographers. Her awareness of this shows throughout the collection *Mother Love* in epigraphs taken from works by writers such as H. D. (Hilda Doolittle), Muriel Rukeyser, James Hillman, Jamaica Kincaid, John Milton, Kadia Molodowsky, and even Mother Goose. It shows more deeply in her combined preoccupation with mythology and the sonnet form, a combination she acknowledges as an "homage" and "counterpoint" to *Die Sonette an Orpheus* (1923; *Sonnets to Orpheus*, 1923) by German poet Rainer Maria Rilke.

"Mother Love," like many of the collection's poems, reflects no ordinary approach to traditional sonnet forms with their set meters, rhyme schemes, and stanza lengths. Still, the sonnet form is a stubborn and surprising presence in the poem. For example, unlike the final two rhyming lines (a couplet) with which any Shakespearean or English sonnet ends, Dove begins "Mother Love" with a couplet (rhyming "mothering" with "bothering") that does not create a closure. The second line of the couplet uses enjambment (no end stop) to continue directly on to subsequent lines and irregular end rhymes throughout the two stanzas. (The second stanza, for instance, is filled with end and internal rhymes of "er" and "ur" syllables.) Furthermore, the poet reverses and doubles the stanza patterns of a Petrarchan or Italian sonnet, which begins with an eight-line stanza (an octet) and concludes with six lines (a sestet). "Mother Love" thus begins with a twelve-line stanza and concludes with sixteen lines. These sonnet cues and reversals are powerful. It is as if, like Demeter's daughter, the revered sonnet forms have been taken underground. Like Demeter's response to Demophoön, the absence of the primary form heightens the reader's awareness of that form and its replacement.

Despite such changes, Dove follows the thematic development scheme of a Petrarchan sonnet. "Mother Love" begins with an exposition of the theme, then elaborates on that theme. The poet then creates the traditional turn between the two stanzas by shifting to a specific example of the theme before moving, in the final two lines, to the theme's conclusion. The reader is certainly more conscious of the poem's voice and language than its nuanced structure. Dove achieves this by giving Demeter highly accessible language and informal, conversational speech rhythms; equally important, each of her six sentences is a natural breath unit. As a result, the reader, drawn effortlessly into Demeter's voice, focuses on the unfolding narrative and the poet's arresting images and diction.

Themes and Meanings

The title of the poem "Mother Love" announces its purpose: to explore Demeter's fierce maternal love and grief. In this exploration, particularly in the poem's second stanza, Dove closely follows one of the episodes included in the ancient Greek "Homeric Hymn to Demeter." However, the poet's complicated treatment of Demeter opens up the larger subjects of the collection *Mother Love*: the complex nature of maternal love and the even more complex nature of relations between mothers and daughters.

The description of Dove's portrayal of Demeter as complex is not based on the poem's horrifying simile: "a baby sizzling on a spit/ as neat as a Virginia ham." It is important to remember (as several critics have not) that the account of the Demeter-Demophoön episode in the "Homeric Hymn to Demeter" does not end with the baby being roasted alive but with an angry Demeter promising that since she was not allowed to make him immortal, the child will, at least, receive "imperishable honor" as a man. The knotty qualities of Dove's Demeter surface in the last three lines of stanza 1: Demeter's pride in her maternal skills and her delight in children give way to an intense denigration of adolescent maturation (girls with their immature "one-way mirrors" of romance and boys as "fledgling heroes") and sexuality ("the smoky battlefield"). That the goddess-mother will not face either this natural cycle or Persephone's sexual awakening becomes clear in the change of subject in stanza 2. By this abrupt shift, the poet underscores the extremity of Demeter's repressive mental state. Her denial and repression of memory are acted out without a single mention of her daughter: Since Persephone was taken from her, she will take another's child—a son rather than a daughter who might remind Demeter of her own; because Persephone was violated by the underworld of death (Hades), she will make sure that this surrogate child is made impervious to death and destruction.

In Demeter's foiled substitution and in the searing understatement of her final sentence, the poet accentuates the open-endedness of Demeter's dilemma: To remember her daughter the child and her daughter the vulnerable, sexual, autonomous adult is to be forced back into an ambiguous, even ruthless circle of love and life. As the poem, young Demophoön, and Demeter demonstrate, this is a place that cannot be "cured to perfection." Nevertheless, this is the charged circle into which the Pulitzer Prize-winning poet Rita Dove places herself and this collection; her dedication in *Mother Love* makes that clear from the start: "FOR *my mother* TO *my daughter*."

Alma Bennett

MY CAT, JEOFFRY

Author: Christopher Smart (1722-1771)
Type of poem: Meditation
First published: Written c. 1759; published in 1939, in *Rejoice in the Lamb: A Song from Bedlam* (William Force Stead, ed.)

The Poem

One of the most delightful and best-known poems in praise of a house cat, Christopher Smart's "My Cat, Jeoffry" is actually one section of a much more complex and difficult work entitled *Jubilate Agno* (Latin for "Rejoice in the Lamb"), composed while the poet was locked in a private madhouse because of religious mania in 1759 or 1760. Despite the bad reputation of eighteenth century hospitals for the insane (which Bedlam, for instance, deserves), Smart's institution was liberal and his time there not totally unpleasant. Already a well-known writer, he was allowed pen and paper, a garden in which to work, privacy, social visits—and the company of his cat. The separate title later given this section comes from its first line, "For I will consider my Cat, Jeoffry."

Smart combines naturalistic, careful observation of feline behavior with religious interpretation. The result is that Jeoffry carries the symbolic weight without losing his vivid individuality, and Smart conveys love of his pet without becoming too precious or sentimental. The first image is of Jeoffry, "the servant of the living God," worshipping "in his way," "wreathing his body seven times round with elegant quickness," and then leaping up after "musk" (probably a scented, catniplike plant), "which is the blessing of God upon his prayer." Anyone can see a house cat in these motions, chasing its tail and then leaping up for catnip; Smart's artistry is such that the reader is also able to see it as a kind of worship.

The first third of the poem outlines Jeoffry's daily habits just as Smart had his own habits, which included writing some lines of *Jubilate Agno* every day. After worship, Jeoffry "begins to consider himself." Again the actions are both characteristic and endearing: The cat "looks upon his forepaws to see if they are clean," "sharpens his paws by wood," and "fleas himself, that he may not be interrupted." In this sequence of actions, Jeoffry is both an individual and every cat. The poet also anthropomorphizes Jeoffry, although the human motives attributed to him never jar with his feline nature: "For having considered God and himself he will consider his neighbor./ For if he meets another cat he will kiss her in kindness." Smart artfully combines the image of cats sniffing each other with the idea that it shows courtesy.

The other two-thirds of the poem celebrate the many virtues of Jeoffry and cats in general, often with strong religious associations. That "one mouse in seven escapes by his dallying" is a sign of his mercy; to Smart, it also implies biblical uses of seven, such as the seventh day being the Sabbath. Smart writes that the Children of Israel took cats with them when they left Egypt. There is even humor, as when Smart praises the cat as "an instrument for the children to learn benevolence on" or says of his cat's voice, "it has in purity what it wants in music."

The last third of the poem describes Jeoffry's activities and "varieties of his movements." Again and again, one can imagine the friskiness of Jeoffry and how much it means to Smart. "For he counteracts the Devil, who is death, by brisking about the life," Smart writes. Jeoffry has learned many tricks that show his "patience" and walks to the rhythm of music. Moreover, his motions form a microcosm of all animals: He swims, creeps, and, "though he cannot fly, he is an excellent clamberer." Interestingly—and in keeping with the scientific interest Smart shows elsewhere in *Jubilate Agno*—the poet has discovered the static electricity from stroking a cat: He sees this "fire" as both protection against "the powers of darkness by his electrical skin" and "the spiritual substance that God sends from heaven to sustain the bodies both of man and beast." Jeoffry's character admirably mixes opposites. As Smart writes, "For there is nothing sweeter than his peace when at rest./ For there is nothing brisker than his life when in motion." Also "he is a mixture of gravity and waggery." At one point, Smart interrupts himself with "Poor Jeoffry! poor Jeoffry! the rat has bit thy throat./ For I bless the name of the Lord that Jeoffry is better." Smart may well have seen himself in the incident, blessed by God but beset by adversity.

Forms and Devices

Jubilate Agno is composed of numerous fragments. Critics debate the relationships among them or even if they form a poem rather than a daybook collection of notes in poetic form. Except for the first two lines, every line in the poem begins with either "Let" or "For" (one view holds that these lines are to be read antiphonally—that is, one "Let" line read with a "For" line read in response). Some fragments do not have sections of both kinds, although the section containing the lines about Jeoffry does. Generally, the "For" sections are more personal; "My Cat, Jeoffry" begins each line with "For." In this structure and counterpoint, Smart was influenced by Anglican liturgy and biblical literature such as the Psalms and the Prophets. Specifically, Smart owes much to Robert Lowth's *De Sacra Poesi Hebraeorum* (1753; *Lectures on the Sacred Poetry of the Hebrews*, 1787).

The poem is written without traditional rhyme and meter. Smart relies on similarity of structure and sometimes similar length for unity between lines. Above all, Smart's extreme sensitivity to the sound of words both enriches his work and provide patterns to tie it together. He is especially fond of alliteration, as in Jeoffry "duly and daily" serving God or "at his first glance of the glory of God." Smart also coins new words or adopts old ones, again sensitive to sound, as when he onomatopoeically describes the cat's play as "spraggle upon waggle" (as a noun "sprag" is an archaic term meaning "a lively young fellow"). Humanizing metaphor is basic to the work; Smart's genius is that the religious and anthropomorphic levels do not obscure the literal level. Smart also excels in sharp, visual metaphors as when he writes that Jeoffry "camels his back," an apt description of a cat arching in anger. Elsewhere in *Jubilate Agno*, Smart explains his theory of art in terms of "punching," in which the impact of the words on his readers' eyes convey the visual impression that Smart intended. *Jubilate Agno*, while not composed for publication, is central to Smart's career. Through its experimentation, he went from traditional eighteenth century verse to something much more personal and, in many ways, modern. Some critics feel it anticipates William Blake's poetry in both the idiosyncratic form and the deeply personal theology conveyed in multiple ways.

Themes and Meanings

According to Smart, *Jubilate Agno* is (and he was aware of the pun) a *magnificat*, a song of praise by all of creation to glorify God. Smart's interest in plants and animals—including unusual or little-valued ones—combines with a theology that finds spiritual significance in everything. This is not pantheism, since creation is decidedly secondary to God, but a vision of all creation as one whole united in God down to its smallest component. The view that nature reveals God in its design spurred Smart's interest in natural history, just as it informed his careful observation of his cat Jeoffry.

Unlike the theory, popular at the time, that human minds are *tabula rasa*—blank pages at birth and written on by experience—Smart's theology adopts the Platonic or Neoplatonic idea that all selves contain knowledge of God, which must be remembered and lived out. In the Jeoffry section, his cat becomes an example of this, not a lesser creature but almost a role model. Jeoffry's natural religion is also reciprocated: As Jeoffry adores God, he is supported by and brought closer to God. Other sections of *Jubilate Agno* explore numerology, semikabbalistic interpretations of the English and Hebrew alphabets, and other hidden sources of understanding. Smart's insight is clearer and stronger when the message is wrought from Jeoffry's life and interpreted through Smart's own.

Jubilate Agno differs from Smart's other religious poetry (some, such as "The Song of David," much better as poetry) in its intensely personal nature. Smart interweaves biblical names with those from the newspaper of his day, and conveys—sometimes cryptically and sometimes more clearly—his own adversities and small triumphs. At times, the style approaches that of a modern confessional poem. "I have neither money nor human friends," Smart writes, ever mindful of his feline friend. On another level, the entire poem is an act of Smart coming to terms with his situation and identity, examining himself in relation to God and those around him. Ultimately, perhaps Smart does not distinguish the personal from the public any more than he divides animals or even plants from people because it is all the same in God's creation.

Bernadette Lynn Bosky

MY DARK MASTER

Author: Nuala Ní Dhomhnaill (1952-   )
Type of poem: Meditation
First published: 1995, as "Mo Mháistir Dorcha / My Dark Master"

The Poem

Written originally in Irish, Nuala Ní Dhomhnaill's "My Dark Master" is a short poem of ten four-line stanzas that loosely follow an *abab* rhyme scheme. Ní Dhomhnaill, a leading voice among Ireland's women writers, was born in Lancashire, England, but grew up in the Dingle Gaeltacht in County Kerry (an area of Ireland that still speaks Irish as its primary language) and in Nenagh, County Tipperary. She has been the recipient of numerous poetry awards, including the Irish American Foundation Award (1988) and the American Ireland Fund Literature Prize (1991).

As the title suggests, "My Dark Master" focuses on the relationship between a dominant figure, the unnamed dark master, and the subordinate speaker. The poem opens with the speaker striking a bargain with "death" to spend time with him. The identity of the dark master is not made clear at first. Instead, the initial stanzas detail the agreement they strike, as the speaker spits in her palm before shaking the dark master's hand (a traditional symbol of a solemn pact) and signs a contract to become "indentured on the spot." In the third stanza, readers learn that the speaker was only nineteen years old at the time, suggesting that her youthfulness contributed to her naiveté about the relationship, which she called "a stroke of luck." However, the optimism underlying Ní Dhomhnaill's initial tone shifts to a more ominous note as she describes falling "into his clutches." The poet makes it clear, however, that she entered into this arrangement willingly and that she was not "meddled with or molested" in any way. Nevertheless, she is clearly subservient to her master, and although she describes their relationship as amicable, it is not a partnership of equals.

In the fifth stanza, Ní Dhomhnaill incorporates traditional pastoral elements into the poem. The movement of "walking out" with her master is extended to herding his cattle across the Irish countryside. Descriptions of the pastures and "hills faraway and green" lend an idyllic air to the poem as she romanticizes her subordinate position as a field hand. The poem's narrator leads the cattle to Lough (lake) Duff, where they find sustenance, but again the poem's tone darkens as the poet's wanderings take her "through the valleys of loneliness." While the cattle appear content in this environment, Ní Dhomhnaill finds no security or comfort from the land. At the top of a hill, she pauses to survey her master's realm and is dizzied by the recognition of how small she is in comparison to it. Her master, she grasps, possesses "riches that are untold," and she can harbor no hopes of rising above the status of shepherdess.

The poem concludes with Ní Dhomhnaill lamenting that she hired herself out to death, and she worries that she will never be able to void that contract. Although earlier she considered herself indentured, suggesting that an ultimate release from her obligation was possible, now she foresees a future filled with the "sough-sighs/ of suffering souls." Despite her efforts to forge an equal partnership, she is not sure what she will gain from her servitude; even having as little as three hot meals a day and a place to sleep seems unlikely. The final line leaves her wondering whether her own autonomy, her voice, will ultimately be subsumed by her master.

Forms and Devices

That "My Dark Master" was originally written in Irish is significant for several reasons. On one level, it serves as a bridge between contemporary poets and Ireland's ancient literary history. Ní Dhomhnaill explains that writing in Irish "is the oldest continuous literary activity in Western Europe, starting in the fifth century and flourishing in a rich and varied manuscript tradition right down through the Middle Ages." She began writing poetry in English as a little girl, but Irish seemed the more natural language to use to express herself. She believes that poetry must come from deep within the individual where native culture lies, and so the poet's search for meaning in life mimics an archaeologist seeking to unlock history from layers of cultural sediment. One of the omnipresent themes in Irish literature is the search for a national identity, and to this Ní Dhomhnaill adds the woman poet's search for artistic identity. Working in Irish provides the poet with a stronger connection to the past and thus helps create an artistic genealogy that male writers have enjoyed all along; it also serves as a reminder that Ireland must reestablish an inclusive literature.

In addition to its political implications, composing in Irish allows Ní Dhomhnaill access to "a language of enormous elasticity and emotional sensitivity, of quick hilarious banter, and a welter of references both historical and mythological." Her soul is Irish, and so she writes in Irish, not so much as an act of rebellion, but to find the best expression for her art. The popularity of Ní Dhomhnaill's poetry reflects a resurgence of national interest in Irish as a language. Until the late nineteenth century, a majority of citizens used Irish for their daily speech, but the mass emigrations following the Great Famine (1845-1848) and the steady urbanization of the rural western counties where Irish was most frequently spoken has dramatically reduced the number of speakers. In the Irish Republic, an estimated 20,000 to 100,000 people still use Irish as their primary language, and an additional 150,000 are estimated to use it in the six counties of Northern Ireland (although many speakers are bilingual).

Themes and Meanings

Despite Ní Dhomhnaill's statement that death is her master, it is clear that death in this case is a metaphor for the condition of women writers in Ireland. She claims that women have been largely excluded from the Irish literary cannon, and so, on one level, the master she serves is Irish literary patriarchy. The females in Irish poetry were, in the words of Irish poet Evan Boland, "fictive queens and national sibyls." Rather than be allowed to write a literature of their own or to take on roles of substance, women were reduced to playing stereotypical roles such as earth mother, goddess, and hag. In the masculine poetry tradition, Ní Dhomhnaill says that "it has been a long and tedious struggle for us women writing in Irish to get even a precarious toehold in visibility." Accordingly, the poem's narrator wanders about the symbolic Irish countryside without a sense of direction or belonging; it is ironic that she is uncomfortable in a land most often described in feminine language. The theme of the writer in isolation or exile within her own country is common among Irish women poets. By exploring this theme in her poetry, Ní Dhomhnaill is reclaiming a past that was lost in traditional Irish patriarchy, and the poem itself is her poetic search for the voice she cannot seem to find in the final stanza.

While symbolizing the cultural and creative forces repressing her voice, the dark master also represents Ní Dhomhnaill's personal muse or poetic inspiration. Commonly, muses are given feminine personas; however, she believes hers is male and sees herself following in a long history of women writers with masculine muses. She describes her muse as "all or nothing action: killing yourself, walking out of a relationship, black or white, right or wrong . . . [and] he's allied with society against you, against your deeper levels of femininity, because he's male." Instead of struggling against the muse, she surrenders to its control and is lead to realizations that she could not have uncovered consciously. Ní Dhomhnaill considers writing poetry a reflective act, and so, as with a journey, the poet cannot know what is ahead until the experience has passed and can be reflected upon. In this reflection, the poet matures and must continue to "break through into deeper levels" to discover new creative directions.

With this interpretation of "The Dark Master," the narrator's reaction to the vastness of her master's possessions is not a response to the limited creative space male writers have left her but to the seemingly limitless scope of her muse's artistic vision. He possesses an overwhelming store of subject matter, the "jewels and gems" of life about which she can write. Her anxiety, then, arises from the daunting task of doing justice to what he has shown her. Since for Ní Dhomhnaill writing relies so heavily on the subconscious and meditation, she is unsure of what the final product will eventually turn out to be or whether she will maintain any control over what she writes.

Thomas F. Suggs

NAMING OF PARTS

Author: Henry Reed (1914-1986)
Type of poem: Lyric
First published: 1946, in *A Map of Verona*

The Poem

"Naming of Parts" is a thirty-line lyric poem divided into five stanzas. The poem depicts a group of infantry recruits receiving a familiarization lecture on their rifles. The title reflects the practical, if prosaic, necessity of knowing the proper term for each of the rifle's parts. Readers hear two distinctive voices in the poem—that of the insensitive, boorish drill instructor giving the lecture and that of a sensitive, young recruit whose mind is wandering during this mind-numbing discourse on rifle terminology. The key to understanding the poem is realizing that roughly the first three-and-a-half lines of each stanza present what the young recruit is literally hearing and enduring while the remaining lines suggest what he is thinking and noticing as his instructor lectures about rifle parts.

The first stanza opens with an overview of the week's training schedule. As the first lines make clear, this day's class will be devoted to learning the names of the rifle's parts. The recruit's mind, however, is elsewhere. He notices the Japonica shrubs blooming in neighboring gardens, a detail that establishes the season as spring. In the second stanza, the instructor is calling the group's attention to the rifle's "swivels" that are fastened to the weapon's wooden frame or "stock." The missing "piling swivel," a part the military deems inessential, inspires the recruit's sudden notice of the branches described in lines 4 and 5. In marked contrast to his present situation, he finds the natural scene to be complete and whole in and of itself. The third stanza concerns the rifle's "safety catch," which functions to prevent unintentional firing. The sudden mention of blossoms at the end of the fourth line once again indicates that the recruit is dividing his attention between the lecture and the springtime scene. He is struck by how the blooms of flowers simply exist. Despite their fragility, they need not learn safety procedures nor must they comply with any arbitrary strictures.

With the next stanza, the instructor has moved on to the principal moving part of the rifle: the bolt. In an effort to demonstrate how the rifle operates, the instructor is mimicking the firing process, using the bolt handle to move the spring-operated bolt back and forth. The military jargon for this procedure is "easing the spring." Witnessing the local bees engaged in the process of pollination, however, inspires the young soldier to reinterpret this phrase in a sexually suggestive sense. As the initial repetition of the phrase "easing the Spring" indicates, the fifth and final stanza functions as a sort of reprise of both the lecture and the recruit's reactions to it. He has obviously seized upon two phrases from the lecture, the "cocking-piece" and the "point of balance." The rifle's "cocking-piece" functions as a fitting symbol of sexual tension, once more suggesting the "release" he and his fellow soldiers are being denied. The rifle's "point of balance" leads the young soldier to reflect on how their present situation has thrown their lives out of balance.

Forms and Devices

Reed divides the poem into five six-line stanzas, each of which follows the alternating pattern already explained. Within the stanzas, the principal poetic devices are imagery and wordplay calculated to evoke connotations at odds with the denotations of the instructor's words and phrases. The effect is to illustrate what Reed sees as the inherent contrast between the world of nature and the world of war. In the first stanza, for instance, the image of Japonica plants glistening "like coral in all of the neighboring gardens" stands in stark opposition to the rifle imagery in the first three-and-a-half lines. The second stanza turns on the image of the missing "piling swivel"; contrary to this image, the tree branches mentioned in the fourth and fifth lines bespeak a peaceful, harmonious, and integral relation with nature. The phrase "silent, eloquent gestures" sets up a thematic opposition to the third stanza in which the soldiers are being admonished to release the safety catches of their rifles with their thumbs. This clumsy gesture further contrasts with the serenity of the "fragile and motionless" blossoms, and the corresponding reiteration of the phrase "using their finger" evokes a sexual connotation the instructor hardly intends.

The fourth stanza juxtaposes the image of "easing the [rifle's] spring" with that of bees "assaulting and fumbling the flowers." The imagery and the connotation are again sexual, with the flowers likened to passive victims and bees to sexual predators. The principal play on words is the repetition of the phrase "easing the Spring"—now with an uppercase *s*. The young recruit is thinking of the sexual release symbolized by the bees pollinating flowers. The last stanza serves as a summation: The first few lines are once more devoted to the instructor's phrases, but this time they are taken out of context. As a consequence of what has come before, the phrases and images come home to the reader in the full force of their associated sexual implications. Juxtaposing these once again with the natural images repeated in the fourth and fifth lines heightens the reader's sense of what these young soldiers do and do not have.

Themes and Meanings

"Naming of Parts" addresses an issue philosophers and military historians have long termed "the problem of war." In its simplest terms, this problem is whether war is an aberration or a perennial part of the human condition. Reed's poem posits at least a partial answer. The fact that spring, the season of renewal and rebirth, still unfolds quite heedless of this group's commitment to the mechanistic processes of war and death carries the main weight of the theme. Reed obviously views militarism and war as distinctly unnatural. Reed's choice of the red-flowered Japonica in the first stanza, for instance, is significant. As its name implies, Japonica, or "Japanese quince," is native to Japan—one of the Axis powers against which England and America were allied in World War II. (Reed, an Englishman, served in World War II, the ostensible period during which the poem is set.) The effect is to suggest that nature transcends both national borders and human notions of loyalty and enmity.

In the third stanza, the criticism becomes personal and specific. In marked contrast to the instructor's affected anxiety about operating the "safety-catch" correctly, the young soldier is struck by the serenity of the spring blooms all around him. Reed's inspiration may well have been the biblical Sermon on the Mount in which Christ urges his followers to heed the example of the "lilies of the field" that neither toil nor spin (Matthew 6:28). Trapped in the unnatural world of war, this young soldier feels no such confidence about his basic needs being met. By applying the instructor's admonition against using one's finger to floral blossoms, the soldier evokes the sexual connotation of the phrase and betrays his present anxiety. In biological terms, flowers are essentially feminine receptacles and therefore have long been recognized as symbols of female receptiveness. This young man, the reader should realize, is confined to a sexually segregated training camp in the springtime. Sex is clearly on his mind.

The soldier's sexual frustration becomes particularly evident in the fifth and sixth stanzas. The rapid back-and-forth movement of the instructor's rifle bolt calls to mind the corresponding motion of the sexual act, an image this soldier connects to the bees in the process of "assaulting and fumbling the flowers." The connotations and imagery are implicitly sexual, expressing the soldier's frustrated yearning for sexual release. The introduction of two new elements, the phrase "point of balance" and the alluring "almond-blossom" image, is perhaps meant as an ironic evocation of the *carpe diem* tradition that counsels complete surrender to the life-affirming lures of beauty and love. Reed's point seems to be that the enforced segregation of military life precludes striking a wholesome balance between self-indulgence and disciplined abstinence.

In terms of tone, "Naming of Parts" stands in a long line of poetic responses to war ranging from the satiric to the elegiac. It is certainly not a reverent acknowledgment of noble sacrifice in the manner of John McCrae's "In Flanders Fields," nor is it a cavalier endorsement of the traditional martial virtues of courage and honor such as Richard Lovelace's "To Lucasta, Going to the Wars." It is also not an unsentimental depiction of death in the manner of Wilfred Owen's "*Dulce et Decorum Est*" or Randall Jarrell's "The Death of the Ball Turret Gunner." Reed's "Naming of Parts" reflects an earlier modernist mood of "irony and pity," to borrow Hemingway's phrase, and not the bitterness and despair characteristic of the later postmodern movement in literature. A tone of pessimistic resignation rather than a true antiwar sentiment informs the poem. The real problem with war, Reed seems to be suggesting, is that people have long deplored modern mass warfare as dehumanizing and unnatural, as a perverse human superimposition upon the world of nature, yet they find themselves as impotent in the face of this insanity as they would be confronting a force of nature.

Edward F. Palm

NICODEMUS

Author: Howard Nemerov (1920-1991)
Type of poem: Dramatic monologue
First published: 1950, in *Guide to the Ruins*

The Poem

"Nicodemus" is a fifty-five-line poem divided into six stanzas and three parts. The dramatic monologue is an imaginative rendition of the New Testament Nicodemus's response to Jesus's statement that no man sees the kingdom of God without being born of water and spirit (in John 3). "Nicodemus" is the priest's account to an unknown audience of his and Jesus's encounter. Written in the persona of Nicodemus, the poem depicts the spiritual seeker as a lonely, bitter man who, although he seeks the company of Jesus, cannot or will not understand his words.

Part I of the poem follows the biblical account closely. John 3:1 states that Nicodemus was a pharisee who visited Jesus at night—undoubtedly to avoid controversy, although this is not stated in the gospel. The poem opens with Nicodemus's admission that he went down back alleys, not because he was ashamed, but from a "natural discretion." As the pharisee made his way to Jesus, he saw a couple embracing against a white wall and hastened to turn his eyes away, no doubt to follow the Pharisaic tradition of avoiding "impure" thoughts. Although he quickly averted his eyes, he confesses to whomever he is speaking that at the sight of the lovers he was shaken. He tries to analyze whether his agitation was from the aridity of his mind or from the lovers' hot blood. Nicodemus recalls the howling of a dog in a stone corner right after seeing the lovers—a parallel to his solitary state.

Part II also begins by paraphrasing John 3, "How is a man born, being old?" and then shifts to Nicodemus's central philosophical stance, that life is miserable and empty and that nothing can ever be known. He argues against the concept that a man can be reborn, then says that even if he could, he himself would not be born again. Nicodemus views life as being forced on humankind and implies that it is a blessing that it can be forced only once. He recounts the illnesses, sadnesses, and indignities of childhood, especially that of being forced to study despite eyestrain. He cites as particularly distasteful the obedience demanded despite a child's lack of understanding. The next stanza expresses bitterness at having trusted to the learning and conforming process so as to establish a suitable adult identity. Despite his long study, he finds that he has achieved no real knowledge or enlightenment. Nicodemus is puzzled that even though he has earned enough accolades to be called a master, he is still as ignorant as a child.

Part III continues in this pessimistic vein. Nicodemus argues with Jesus, saying that although the rest of nature "flowers again," a man does not. From intellectual debate, Nicodemus shifts to an encapsulization of his life as a profound disappointment. His parents have been sorrow and humiliation, he says, and he has never been swept up in fleshly or spiritual concerns, no doubt a response to Jesus's declaration that "What is born of the flesh is flesh, and what is born of the spirit is spirit" (John 3:6). After his confession that he has been engrossed in neither realm, Nicodemus again expresses bewilderment that he is "exalted in Israel" for "all I do not know." He has no answer to Jesus's question, "Are you a teacher of Israel, and yet you do not understand these things?" (John 3:10).

The next stanza intensifies Nicodemus's despair as he states that "the end of [his] desire is death." His life contrasts sharply with that of his foremother Sarah, who laughed during her life and just before her death—first with a mocking laughter at God's promise to cure her barrenness, then with a delighted laughter at God's fulfillment of that promise. Nicodemus proclaims that not only will he not laugh but that he will produce no new word because of "the dryness" of his mouth.

The final stanza moves from unmitigated gloom into asking Jesus to let him go to the ancient burial ground and cave of Abraham and Sarah. In this wish, the old priest echoes Genesis 23, which recounts how Abraham struck the first land claim of Israel when he bought a field which contained a cave in which he buried Sarah.

Forms and Devices

"Nicodemus" has a conversational tone yet also contains the stately, formal rhythms befitting a prestigious old man. The metrics are lavishly iambic but are so varied that the poem must be classified as free verse. Its slow, long lines support the often slowed speech of age and the deliberate manner in which Nicodemus tells his story. The heavy use of vowels in internal rhyme creates a mournful tone: "howled," "once," "stone" (line 23); "forced," "only," "one" (line 46); and "nor," "not," "born" (line 46). Juxtaposed against the dirgelike internal rhymes are sharp consonant alliterations which not only quicken the tempo but also support Nicodemus's negative statements: "dryness," "driving," (line 9); "book," "burning,"(line 20), "bitter," "bewilderment" (line 30), "cold," "cave" (line 55). Nemerov alternates harsh alliteration with soft *s* sounds when he mentions positive aspects of life, such as lilacs, honey, and the laughter of Sarah.

The poem makes use of images to heighten the contrast between life and Nicodemus's spiritual death. Images of dryness—Nicodemus's mind, mouth, and burning eyes—support the portrayal of Nicodemus as a dried-up intellectual who is bitter because his earnest studies have not brought him definite knowledge or understanding. Nicodemus' death-thrust is also illustrated by images of cold. He wants to end in a "cold cave" where even Abraham's seed is "cold." The dog's howl in a stone corner as Nicodemus travels to visit Jesus prefigures his lost, lonely wish to be buried in a cold cave. Other striking parallels are Nicodemus's declaring sorrow and humiliation to be his parents but wishing to return to the parents of Judaism, Abraham and Sarah—once vital but now cold and dead. A subtle device is that the first two-thirds of the poem "answer" Jesus, although Jesus is never directly quoted. The effect of leaving out Jesus's comments is powerful, for it suggests that Nicodemus assumes his audience knows the details of the encounter or that he is too troubled to fill in missing parts. This omission also adds to Nicodemus self-justification, possibly to his colleagues, who would approve of his desire to go back to his Old Testament roots.

Themes and Meanings

"Nicodemus" is about an old man who will not take chances on a new way of living or on anything he cannot understand. His modus operandi of understanding is intellectual, and he will not brook the possibility of any other knowledge. Like many old people, he looks backward instead of forward—to the glorious foundation of Israel, which even Nicodemus himself knows is now "cold."

It is not simply age which causes Nicodemus to reject the possibility of rebirth or perhaps even rebirth itself, but Nicodemus' assessment of life as essentially suffering and disillusionment. His intellectual attainment produced respect from the people but emptiness in himself. He trusted that study would produce answers, but it failed him, and he admits to knowing nothing. In answer to Jesus's declaration about life in the flesh or life in the spirit, Nicodemus states that he has attached himself to neither, thereby revealing another reason for his emptiness. His bitterness is enhanced by what he implies is his community's stupidity for exalting him. To Nicodemus, life is a bad joke. Therefore, he clings to his belief that a "man may not flower again," principally because he himself does not want to flower again.

In a painful summing up, Nicodemus states that he has had nothing to laugh over and that unlike Sarah, who produced an heir in her old age, he will produce no new word of truth or knowledge. Instead he is confounded by Jesus's words and wants to return to the source of his roots, however cold and dead. Ironically, if Nicodemus had immersed himself in aspects beside the intellectual, he might not have become dry and might have found life worthwhile enough at least to delight in some of its incongruities. Although Nicodemus is honest in his admission that study has taught him nothing, he remains convinced that he is right rather than admit that his lifelong perceptions might be wrong. Nicodemus visits Jesus because he has a hunger for knowledge, but when he is presented with something he does not understand, he rejects further learning. In the last analysis, he will not again be the child who must endure the "malady of being always ruled to ends he does not see or understand" (lines 22-23). Despite Nicodemus's rejection of Jesus's teaching, he treats Jesus as an authority. He asks permission not to enter the kingdom of God but to go back to his cold "home" to die. Although Nicodemus ends his story on a proper political note, his reverence of Jesus reveals the subversiveness that first brought him to visit under "cover of night."

Mary Hanford Bruce

MCMXIV

Author: Philip Larkin (1922-1985)
Type of poem: Meditation
First published: 1964, in *The Whitsun Weddings*

The Poem

"MCMXIV," like many of Philip Larkin's poems, is a meditation. This poetic form, modeled on John Donne's prose *Meditations*, begins with a description of an object, a place, or an event. The description leads directly into a response or a consideration of the issues, problems, and complexities suggested by the object; this consideration then leads to a conclusion or resolution. In "MCMXIV" the object is a 1914 photograph of British volunteers lined up in front of an army recruiting office after England entered World War I. By extension the poem considers the prewar British society that those men represent. The poem itself does not overtly indicate that the photograph is the object of meditation; rather, the title (Roman numerals for 1914) and the description provide that context. While readers can not know whether Larkin was contemplating a particular photograph, there are examples of this type of picture in most illustrated histories of World War I.

The first three stanzas of the four-stanza poem offer an interpretive description of the scene in the photograph. The men stand patiently in line, as they might wait to gain admission to a sporting event or an "August Bank Holiday lark." (In England a bank holiday is a legal holiday when the banks are ordered closed.) This holiday is in August, since August 4, 1914, was the date England declared war on the Central Powers. The scene Larkin describes is holiday-like: The shops are closed, but the pubs are open. Children are playing; the men in line are grinning. No one yet suspects the horrors that World War I will bring.

Stanza 3 moves beyond the photo of the men in line at the recruiting office to include the countryside. In the poetry, novels, and memoirs of World War I, idyllic, pastoral prewar England is often contrasted with the horrors of European trench warfare. Therefore Larkin's meditation on innocence includes such pastoral references. Significantly, the grass and wheat fields cover place names and property lines, much like they would later cover the graves and names of the five million Allied casualties of the war.

Also recalled as background to the photograph and the war experience is the orderly class structure of prewar England: "The differently-dressed servants/ With tiny rooms in huge houses." Many authors, such as Ford Madox Ford in his *Parade's End* novels (1924-1928), wrote about men from all social classes, content in their separation before the war, who suddenly found themselves fighting side by side in the trenches. The belief in the inevitability and morality of the class structure was part of the "innocence" lost during the war.

"Never such innocence" is the poet's interpretative conclusion. The prewar world "changed itself to past" and could never be recaptured. The photograph shows a large crowd of men willingly, happily volunteering for the war. They were doing their duty as well as heading off for an adventure, never imagining the misery and destruction ahead of them. While the poem does not describe the battlefields, the idea of lost innocence brings into the poem World War I as described by those who experienced it. The trenches, mud, rats, barbed wire, tanks, snipers, poison gas, grenades, and air attacks (vividly described, for example, in Wilfred Owen's poetry) were a yet unimagined horror. The war destroyed all fantasies of war as a glorious, heroic adventure played out on orderly battlefields by gentlemen: "Never such innocence again."

Forms and Devices

"MCMXIV," like all of Larkin's poems, is characterized by clear, straightforward, unadorned language. Larkin is the best-known and most successful of a group of British poets from the 1950's known as "The Movement" (other Movement poets include Robert Conquest, Kingsley Amis, and Donald Davie). All these poets used a direct, plain language which was deliberately chosen in rejection of the rich, melodic, metaphoric language of Dylan Thomas and the dense, allusive, intellectual language of T. S. Eliot. It was an appropriate language for the skeptical, unsentimental, sometimes hopeless worldview of their poems. Larkin, like other Movement authors, worked within a narrow emotional range, ironically noting the pain and dreariness of everyday experience that must be accepted.

When Larkin departs from his usual plain language, the effect is striking. In stanza 3, describing rural fields, he refers to "Domesday lines": These are the boundaries between property first defined in 1086 by William the Conqueror and recorded in the *Domesday Book*. The historical reference is a jarring pun, since the *Domesday Book* is also known as the *Doomsday Book*. The men in Larkin's photograph were taking their first step toward their doom.

That Larkin's language is generally plain does not mean that he eschews metaphor entirely. The lines of men waiting to enlist in the British Army are like lines waiting to see a cricket match at the Oval in London. The atmosphere on the day war was declared was like a bank holiday. The rural fields are, in their description at least, like the war cemeteries of Europe. Most significantly, the men, in their eagerness to go to war and with their belief that nothing will be changed when they come back, are a metaphor and a symbol for innocence that was lost.

The images of the poem, like the language, are clear and straightforward. They move in an ever-expanding pattern. The first stanza limits itself to the actual content of the photograph: the appearance of the men standing in line. Stanza 2 moves just outside the picture itself to provide details about the neighborhood of the recruiting office. One sees the advertisements in shop windows, the children playing, the pubs. Next one moves outside the city to the fields and the manor houses. All of England is drawn into the picture. Finally, in the last stanza, the larger significance of the scene is stated; at the same time, the poem returns to the individual men in the photograph, each with his own tidy garden and marriage.

Themes and Meanings

World War I was a highly literary war—it was unusual in the number of soldiers who wrote poems, novels, and memoirs about their experience. Wilfred Owen, Siegfried Sassoon, Rupert Brooke, Ford Madox Ford, Robert Graves, and David Jones are but a few of the authors to write major works about the war experience. So important is World War I as a subject in modern British literature that it is in no way unusual to see Larkin returning to it nearly fifty years after the event. With "MCMXIV" he places himself in a significant literary tradition.

He also restates for his time the major literary interpretation of the war. His conclusion that innocence was lost as a result of the horrors of war is consistent with the reading of the experience given by his predecessors. In fact, this reading has reached the status of myth or master narrative—a coherent story which claims to explain a major social phenomenon. In this myth, prewar England is seen as idyllic. The social order was fixed and secure: Each class knew its role and strove only to succeed in that role. The country shared adherence to the Church of England. Science assured an unbroken path of progress, promising that life would continue to get better and better. All was orderly, civil, and decorous. In fact, in an ironic contrast, the summer of 1914, the months immediately before the war, were warm and sunny, the most beautiful summer anyone could remember.

The decorous and orderly men who lined up patiently to enlist in August of 1914 were to have their faith in order (even their faith in God) seriously shaken in the trenches of Europe. Those who were not killed by bombs or snipers might face excruciatingly painful deaths from poison gas or entrapment in barbed wire. Those who survived had to live in dirt trenches containing a foot or two of collected rainwater, sharing the space with rats. They were changed, according to the story, by the experience; when the war was over, nothing could be the same. Their world had changed, and romanticism gave way to cynicism and despair. The lower classes were no longer content; the Church of England lost its influence; those who had seen the bestiality of the war could no longer believe in progress: "Never such innocence again."

The myth of World War I has resonance beyond twentieth century experience. It has literary parallels in John Milton's *Paradise Lost* (1667) and William Blake's *Songs of Innocence and Experience* (1794). Through them it repeats one of the fundamental narratives of Christianity, the fall from innocence in the Garden of Eden, and a basic psychological pattern of maturing from naïve childhood to disillusioned adulthood. From his meditation on an old photograph of men waiting to enlist in World War I, Larkin recapitulates one of the most enduring stories of Western culture, the story of the inevitable movement from idyllic naïveté to disappointed experience.

Bruce H. Leland

NINETEEN HUNDRED AND NINETEEN

Author: William Butler Yeats (1865-1939)
Type of poem: Meditation
First published: 1921; collected in *The Tower*, 1928

The Poem

William Butler Yeats's "Nineteen Hundred and Nineteen," from the 1928 collection *The Tower*, is not the most accessible of his poems, but it encompasses many of the themes, motifs, and techniques of his mature poetry. It is probably best understood and best enjoyed in the greater context of his work. Written in six parts of unequal length, the poem uses, as its focal point, the bloody retribution of British soldiers against the Irish citizenry during the time of the Sinn Féin rebellion (1919-1921). Although rooted in the Irish Home Rule struggle, it is more than a political poem, examining the fluctuating relationship between time and understanding, reality and illusion, and nature and artifice. What seems clear at one point in time can easily be thrown into flux by the events of a later time, perpetuating an ascending series—a metaphysical "tower"—of transformation and reappraisal. Woven together with the poet's private pantheon of symbols are allusions to contemporary, historical, and classical events, challenging the reader to follow the byways of Yeats's visionary landscape.

The first section introduces all the threads that will appear, in ways reminiscent of a fugue, throughout the poem. In the first two stanzas, Yeats takes pains to emphasize the difference between appearance and reality. "Things" that seemed miraculous and "protected" have vanished; laws and opinions—presumably immutable—have changed; most tragically, the assumption that the "worst rogues and rascals had died out" has been proven wrong.

Readers familiar with Yeats's frequently anthologized poem "Sailing to Byzantium" (1928) will recognize the same world of artifice in the "famous ivories" and "golden grasshoppers" of the first stanza. By stanza 4, however, Yeats plunges back into the writhing physical world of Ireland in 1919: "Now days are dragon-ridden." Here is the kernel of the poem, the events that inspire this reflection. Here, as well, are the poem's most vivid and most horrific images: the slain mother in her blood juxtaposed against the murdering, drunken soldiers who escape. The visual impact of these verses is all the greater given the contrast with the philosophical musings that have preceded them.

By the sixth stanza, the last in the first section, Yeats poses the question that is preeminent in his work: "Man is in love and loves what vanishes,/ What more is there to say?" Love and loss are the twins who inhabit every cranny of Yeats's poetic territory. His strongest work, poems such as "Crazy Jane Talks with the Bishop" (1933) and "The Circus Animals' Desertion" (1939), affirm the necessity and, indeed, the inevitability of love, even in the face of change and disintegration. In this context, it is significant that it is a mother, not simply a woman, who is killed, since mother-hood is emblematic of both love and renewal.

The second section amplifies the theme of the recurrence of change, while at the same time emphasizing its ultimate superficiality. The poem mentions Loie Fuller, a dancer who was a contemporary of Yates and who specialized in dramatic spectacle and illusion; the grisly image of the dragon in the first section has been trans-formed—and tamed—into an artificial "dragon of air" in the hands of a dance troupe. In a reversal of the anticipated, the Platonic Year brings in nothing new but rather what is old. Nothing has been learned from history, no real or lasting achievements have been made. Over the courses of time, humankind still participates in the same "dance," but, ominously, the gong that sounds the music is "barbarous."

In the third section, Yeats concentrates on classical allusions, returning to the philosophizing of the early part of the poem. The dominant image is that of the swan, or the soul, as conceived by some earlier voice. Yeats is deliberately vague about whom this might be, a "moralist or mythological poet." History has tricked him of any personal fame. This swan later comes to life, as it were, leaping into "the desolate heaven." The theme continues to be one of loss.

In the fourth and shortest section, the swan has disappeared, and Yeats takes up an earlier image, that of the weasel. The cynical fifth section invites the reader to "mock at" the great, the good, and the wise for their inefficacies, and finally to mock the mockers. Both poet and reader are implicated in all those who "Traffic in mockery."

In the final section, Yeats unleashes a whirlwind of visual scenes, hurling pell-mell on one another, a veritable "tumult of images." Confusion reigns; "all are blind," the poet affirms. In this maelstrom of bleakness, the final image is of misguided love bestowed on an object unworthy and "stupid."

Forms and Devices

For effect, "Nineteen Hundred and Nineteen" relies heavily on allusion: classical (Platonism, the Athenian sculptor Phidias), biblical (Herodias), historical (the four-teenth century Robert Artisson), and contemporary (Loie Fuller). It is not as important to identify each and every reference, however, as it is to understand that the poet's disillusionment over any real human progress dates from earliest history and perme-ates subsequent ages of time. The range of allusions serves to emphasize the essential sameness of history and to connect the present with the past.

These connections are reinforced by the language and the structure of the poem. Each section has its own regular rhyme scheme, but Yeats intensifies the internal pattern by frequent repetitions. Commonly, he will use a word several times in quick succession: "thought" three times in two lines in the second stanza, "dancers" three times in the second section. The fifth section turns on the word "mock" and its cognates. In addition, sections are joined by such repetitions: The short fourth section appears to exist solely to reintroduce the weasel image from the first. In the last section, none of the symbols are as important as the sheer accumulation of the language of despair: "violence" (twice in one line), "evil," "crazy," "angry," "blind," "stupid," "insolent," "fiend."

Themes and Meanings

"Nineteen Hundred and Nineteen" is a poem that explores the contradictions of the human condition. In a world filled with change, where the things most precious are irretrievably lost, what remains constant is a propensity toward violence and the inevitable loss that follows in its wake. The loss is twofold, at least: the loss of confidence in one's understanding—whereby the accomplishments of humans (art, philosophy, laws) are reduced to "pretty toys"—and the actual loss of those "toys." Time alters everything, not the least of which is perception. Additionally, the weight of the poem suggests these illusions are also delusions and diminishments, the "great army" unveiled as a "showy thing," the towering statue by Phidias eroded to "that stump on the Acropolis." The best that humankind can do is seen as paltry if it cannot rid the world of the "worst rogues" who slay mothers.

For all the universality of Yeats's poetry, he remains very much an Irish bard, and it would be a mistake to overlook the Irish heart of this poem. Like "Easter 1916" (1916) and "The Second Coming" (1920), "Nineteen Hundred and Nineteen" is political, and it is a memorial to the troubles of Ireland immediately following World War I. Irish patriots, many of whom were connected intimately with Yeats, had hoped that, with England's attention focused on Europe, the time would be propitious for freeing their country from the English yoke. Should any reader be tempted to overlook the specific and particular historical events that infuse this poem, Yeats keeps them in strong focus with his title. All Irish readers (presumably) would understand the context; all others would be expected to discover it.

"Nineteen Hundred and Nineteen" is a dense and tightly connected poem, but it also contains verses of great simplicity, such as "Violence upon the roads: violence of horses." Herein is Yeats's "natural world"—the world of real people and their real pain. Within the intricate structure of his many symbols and allusions, Yeats maintains the balance between direct and ornate language and keeps the poem from sliding into purely idiosyncratic or private images. It is no accident that the most spare and simple language is usually reserved for contemporary events, the ones with most urgency.

The verses more laden with symbols belong either to the world of the mind or the world of history (usually the ancient kingdoms of Greece, Rome, or Byzantium). These historical references often function as other manifestations of the creative domain. The "ingenious lovely things" of the first stanza are exemplified by "Phidias' famous ivories" and an "ancient image made of olive wood." When, in the second stanza, he speaks of "habits that made old wrong/ Melt down, as it were wax in the sun's rays," one hears echoes of the fall of Icarus, flying too close to the sun. In the bitter vision of this poem, all the golden ingenuity of humankind lies naked to the ravages of the weasel.

Linda Turzynski

1929

Author: W. H. Auden (1907-1973)
Type of poem: Narrative
First published: 1930, in *Poems*

The Poem

W. H. Auden spent part of the year 1929 in Berlin, hoping to get away from the stultifying atmosphere of the more socially conservative London. Thus began his most political period, when he got caught up in antifascist movements and, eventually, went to Spain during their civil war. In the late 1920's, Berlin was becoming a battleground between conflicting political factions. Auden and his English contemporaries often blamed older generations for the destruction of World War I, concluded only ten years earlier. They also saw, or thought they saw, the early indications of the next war. Political demonstrations often turned violent. Clashes between the police and demonstrators were common, as were brawls between communists and fascists. This political situation, which Adolf Hitler used to his advantage when he came to power in 1933, eventually lead to World War II, the outbreak of which Auden marked with the poem "September 1, 1939."

The poem known as "1929" was included in Auden's first book of poetry, *Poems* (1930). The poem is often printed without a title, but Auden also published it in a slightly revised version in his *Collected Shorter Poems, 1927-1957* (1966), giving the year of its composition as its title. It is a composite of four segments—dated April 1929, May 1929, August 1929, and October 1929—taken from four separate poems. It has a fractured autobiographical narrative to match its fractured syntax. Some of the fragments were written while the poet was living in Germany (the public garden in which the poet walks is the *Tiergarten* in Berlin), and the whole thing was most likely compiled in England in late 1929 or 1930.

The first and last sections are narratively connected but separated by the poet's meditations, very personal and somewhat obscure, about his development as an intellectual in a time of social unrest. The poem starts with seasonal imagery but departs sharply at the beginning of the second stanza, when the poet's attention turns to thoughts of death and failure. Describing his own personal situation and that of his friends, Auden shifts to a more general description of life in Berlin.

Section 2 describes his engagement with friends discussing political events. The poet appears to be both engaged in the situation and an observer of it, saying that he is pleased, while he is really feeling angry at both sides. As an observer, the poet considers the development of people as individuals in whom he can see "fear of other" and a basic inability to forgive. The poet, however, can see the goodness in life and feel peace.

Part 3 describes Auden's return to England and to his mother's house. The poet shifts from his own development to a general process of growth and individuation experienced by young people who take their first steps away from home, falter, and eventually come to appreciate home. Although this section is dated August, there is a growing awareness of winter. Here, winter is an earthly indication of death, arranged so that one will be familiar with death when it comes. In both sections 2 and 3, Auden shifts from the personal to the general, indicating that the development of the individual parallels the development of a culture. As the individual grows to fear others, so too do societies; as the individual grows through an awareness of death, so too do nations.

The final segment returns to the idea of error with a strong statement: "It is time for the destruction of error." This section describes autumn in England, when furniture is brought in from the garden, and makes the analogy between the end of an era in England, the dawn of a new age in Europe, and the hope for a more honest life in the new decade (eventually termed, by Auden, a "low dishonest" one). In a poem so infused with the idea of death, the last stanza offers hope. The poet and his companion are aware of the needs of love, "more than the admiring excitement of union," and they know of the necessity of death for rebirth.

Forms and Devices

The poem mixes observation and meditation. As the line "Tiny observer of enormous world" indicates, the poet is interested in describing what he sees as well as the effect his observations have on himself. The world tends to make him feel insignificant, like a cog in a machine. In fact, the monuments of modern life, machinery, factories, and industry, figure prominently in the political landscape of "Auden country," as scholar Samuel Hynes dubbed it in the 1970's. With his contemporary Stephen Spender, Auden brought the reality of contemporary England and Europe into English poetry. The poem "1929" is rife with images of ordinary life and the materials of that life, such as buses, bicycles, and the "strict beauty of locomotive."

In a similar move, Auden adds intensity to the poem by using a specialized kind of language, that of the postcard or telegram written with an urgency that may sacrifice clarity. The poem is noticeably lacking in definite and indefinite articles; that is, Auden leaves out "the" and "a" ("solitary man" rather than "a solitary man," for example). In his preface to *Collected Shorter Poems, 1927-57*, Auden attributes this style to "some very slovenly verbal habits. The definite article is always a headache to any poet writing in English, but my addiction to German usages became a disease."

Aside from the issue of articles, however, the diction in this poem has a quality that a reader might see as similar to that of American writer Gertrude Stein. Employing repetition and variation, the poet gives the impression that he enjoys his words. For example, section 2 opens with the lines, "Coming out of me living is always thinking,/ Thinking changing and changing living,/ Am feeling as it was seeing—". Like other writers in the early half of the twentieth century, Auden was also very interested in psychoanalysis, especially the work of Sigmund Freud and his followers, and so the idea that "thinking is always living" becomes the basis for the deliberate archaism of the poem and the imitation of the language of the "primitive man" in the fourth stanza of section 2: "Is first baby, warm in mother."

Another, perhaps stronger, influence is Irish writer James Joyce, whose *Portrait of the Artist as a Young Man* (1915) is written from the perspective of Stephen Daedalus. The famous first chapter begins when Stephen is a young boy: "Once upon a time and a very good time it was there was a moocow coming down along the road." Writing in the voice of the very young, Auden uses a similar technique in the line, "Is first baby, warm in mother." It is Auden's attempt to write not only in a prebirth voice but also from a preverbal state, as if from the point of view of an uncivilized man. He does this to describe what he sees as the primeval fears and drives of humankind.

Themes and Meanings

Perhaps the first idea the reader notices in this poem is that of death, which seems to permeate it from beginning to end. The opening line identifies Easter as the day on which the poet takes his walk, and Auden immediately signals the dual themes of death and rebirth. Easter is, after all, the celebration of Christ's resurrection, his death a "necessary condition" of his rebirth into something greater than his earthly being. Yet, for a poem that starts out sounding so hopeful, with its "emphasis on new names, on the arm/ A fresh hand," the shift to a discussion of death can be disconcerting.

The subject of death, however, is constantly mingled with images of natural life, such as the colony of ducks, and with the poet's appreciation of the human life he sees around him (the hymns he hears in the village square, for example). So it is the combination of death and life that intrigues him and that he sees as necessary. In order to fully love life, one needs a knowledge of death.

The truly strong man, as he calls his friend Gerhardt Meyer, recognizes this idea and acts accordingly. For Auden and his friend Christopher Isherwood (the novelist to whom Auden dedicated his *Poems* of 1930), the truly strong man is the anti-heroic hero. Unlike traditional ideas of male strength—a glorious, risk-taking hero—Auden and Isherwood see the truly strong man as one who possesses inner security and self-confidence, who does not need to prove himself to anyone, and whose actions are, consequently, pure in heart. The truly strong man is able to resolve traditional dichotomies, such as public/private, inner/outer, and, as in this poem, life/death, to achieve peace within himself. Auden develops this idea in "The Orators" (1931) as does Isherwood in *Lions and Shadows* (1938).

The final image of the "lolling bridegroom, beautiful, there" may leave the reader a bit perplexed. It is a variation on the Lady of the Lake of Arthurian legend, who gives the sword, Excalibur, to Arthur. The mysticism implicit in the image connects back to the image of the risen Christ, for the figure in the lake will eventually rise, be reborn, and bring a new power of good to the world.

James J. Berg

NINETIETH BIRTHDAY

Author: R. S. Thomas (1913-   )
Type of poem: Meditation
First published: 1961, in *Tares*

The Poem

R. S. Thomas's "Ninetieth Birthday" is a poem of two stanzas of unequal length written in free verse. The second stanza is further divided for emphasis, the seventh line beginning immediately below the end of the sixth line rather than at the left margin as do the other lines. The poem is written in the second person; though the speaker seems to be addressing another person, it is possible to read the poem as the speaker's own memories or thoughts about an event. The poem describes a person going to visit an old woman, perhaps a mother or grandmother, on the occasion of her ninetieth birthday. The first stanza describes a walk up a steep hill on a midsummer day and does not indicate where the person is going or why the person is going up the hill. Instead, the stanza portrays the landscape: a road, probably dirt, on which it is better to walk than drive, a rocky hillside where trees give way to bracken, a distant view of the sea, and a small stream. The description is similar to those in other poems by Thomas set in the mountainous areas of Wales.

The second stanza moves from a description of the landscape to the description of an old woman waiting for her visitor at the top of the hill. The old woman "Waits for the news of the lost village/ She thinks she knows, a place that exists/ In her memory only," which indicates that she rarely, if ever, leaves her farm and that the world has changed in ways of which she has no knowledge. This point is emphasized later in the second half of the stanza: "Yet no bridge joins her own/ World with yours." The poem concludes with a description of the visitor listening to the old woman but with the sense that what she has to say has no relevance to the present.

The movement from the first stanza to the second is a movement from the external to the internal; although the second stanza contains descriptive elements as well, it makes judgments about the characters and their worlds while the first stanza sets the place. The poem does not contain a description of the visitor's world; the first stanza's precise images bring the reader into the poem and provide the sense that the visitor is familiar with but not part of the landscape. The second stanza reinforces this, implying not only that the visitor is removed enough from the landscape to notice it but also that the visitor can never become part of that landscape. Even the landscape does not serve as a bridge between the two worlds.

Forms and Devices

"Ninetieth Birthday" is written in very plain language with sentences that are long but not syntactically difficult. It uses neither rhyme nor formal meter, and there are very few metaphors or other figures of speech. Thomas does not usually dress up his poems, particularly the earlier ones, with many adjectives or long words, and this poem is typical in its plainness. In the first stanza, the only word of more than two syllables is "history," and his few adjectives are simple and ordinary: "green," "warm," and "far," for example. Such simple language is particularly effective in describing the landscape; it is precise enough for the reader to visualize it clearly, and it gives the poem a quiet and thoughtful tone.

The second stanza differs from the first in that it contains more metaphors, and the metaphors are used more to create a complex emotion that to clarify an image. For example, the first stanza uses the metaphor of lichen "That writes history on the page/ Of the grey rock," which strengthens the mental picture of lichen on a stone, covering it like words on a page or hieroglyphs on a clay tablet. It also creates a sense of the mountain's age. In the second stanza, however, the metaphor of "time's knife shaving the bone" does not provide a useful visual image if one tries to picture it literally. While it does functions as a description of the physical diminution that comes with aging, it is more effective when read as an account of the old woman's life. Each year there is a little less. She is slowly dying. The stanza's other metaphors, "bridge" and "abyss," both function on a conceptual rather than visual level. There is no physical abyss between the old woman's world and the visitor's world, but there is a vast cultural and social difference.

Formally, one of the more interesting aspects of the poem is the use of the second person. While the second person is not unusual for poetry, there is often a clear sense that the speaker is addressing another person. In "Ninetieth Birthday," however, the quiet and sad tone as well as the privacy of the moment—only the visitor and the old woman are present—imply that the poem could well be the speaker's own thoughts or memories. While it is certainly possible that the speaker is addressing a close friend, the speaker might also be using the second person to feel more detached when describing a painful experience. The phrase "all you can do" near the end of the poem expresses feelings of futility and helplessness, emotions from which the speaker might well want to be somewhat distant. The visitor is glad that the old woman is still alive, but her old age and solitude are deeply sorrowful to the visitor. In using the second person, the speaker lessens some of the immediacy of the sad feeling. Yet, powerfully, the distance increases the reader's sense of the depth of the sadness. The distance between the speaker or reader and the visitor gives a greater idea of the distance between the visitor and the old woman.

Themes and Meanings

"Ninetieth Birthday" is not a particular complex poem thematically; it reveals the cultural difference between people of earlier and later generations. Such a difference is not stated; rather, it is implied by the phrases such as "lost village," "a place that exists/ In her memory only," and "words that were once wise." When one steps outside the poem to look at its author and the time of its writing, however, other related meanings emerge. Thomas is Welsh, and many of his poems are about the changes in Welsh culture, language, and history. Thomas's poem "Welsh History" presents an image of Wales trapped in the past, the people, having lost their language, confined by their own history of poverty and violence. In the poem "Expatriates," Thomas describes Welsh people leaving the mountains for the city and leaving their language behind. When one reads "Ninetieth Birthday" with an awareness of the changes in Welsh culture, the old woman's separation from the visitor is even stronger.

"Ninetieth Birthday" was published in the volume *Tares* in 1961. If the poem is supposed to be taking place at the time of publication, the old woman would have been born in 1871. In 1871, many Welsh people did not speak English, a condition that had changed by 1961; furthermore, the number of people who spoke Welsh decreased substantially over the same period. With increases in technology, cars replaced horses and tractors replaced the old horse-drawn ploughs. The old woman's farm seems to be a farm caught in the nineteenth century, her words of wisdom applying to a time that is long gone. The second line of the poem describes the track as one "That will take a car, but is best walked"; the modern world and the old woman's farm do not connect. The visitor's sadness is not only about the old woman's aging but also about how the world has changed so that the old woman no longer fits in with it. What has been lost is a culture, a way of living, perhaps even a language. The "history" in the first stanza becomes, in the second, a history that encompasses loss and alienation: Time cannot be reversed to counter aging, and it cannot be reversed to alter changes in a culture.

Elisabeth Anne Leonard

A NOCTURNAL UPON ST. LUCY'S DAY

Author: John Donne (1572-1631)
Type of poem: Lyric
First published: 1633, as "A nocturnall upon S. *Lucies* day,/ Being the shortest day,"
in *Poems, by J. D.: With Elegies on the Authors Death*

The Poem

"A Nocturnal upon St. Lucy's Day" is characteristic of John Donne's art: It is
compressed verse full of tightly woven images and concepts, it is rapid, and its metrics
and shape are atypical of traditional verse. The rhythmic diversity suggests speech and
debate. The act of reading the poem is rather like that of deciphering a cryptogram or
solving a puzzle while riding over a bumpy road. In sum, it is difficult to imagine
anyone but Donne writing this poem.

It begins with a time reference, namely to the shortest day of the year—the winter
solstice (December 12 in the Julian calendar)—and more specifically to the dying
moments of the year. The speaker contemplates this day while (fictionally) writing the
poem on the previous evening. He deploys this strategy as a way to explain by
comparison that his condition is more dire than is the death of the earthly year: "yet
all these seem to laugh/ Compar'd with me." The reader is left to wonder what has
brought him to this calamitous, exaggerated grief.

In the second stanza, the speaker enjoins the readers (who are lovers, or will be
lovers in the next spring) to study him in order to learn how love transformed him. In
this arrangement, love is a personified being who miraculously produces a restorative
substance ("quintessence," and later "elixir") from the speaker's destruction. Thus the
lovers are offered a cautionary story of the transitory nature of humankind, but a story
that also hints at potential good as a result.

The third stanza continues the regenerative concept by contrasting love's treatment
of him with how good is normally produced. He again emphasizes that he has been
reduced to nothing. In the middle of the stanza the subject shifts. The speaker
considers how he and an implied lover have produced cataclysmic effects: floods,
chaos, and zombies, or carcasses without souls. The effects of their love have been
great, superhuman if not supernatural, suggesting a power consistent with that which
might affect time.

The occasion for the grief expressed in the poem is presented at the outset of the
fourth stanza. Here readers learn that the speaker's lover has died. Her death has
resulted in his return to a primordial nothingness, and it troubles him that he loses his
identity in the process. He realizes that her death has transformed him into a being that
is no longer easily classified.

He begins the last stanza by arguing that he is none of the possibilities listed in the
previous stanza—man, beast, or ordinary body. He invites the lovers to enjoy their
time together, including an implied reference to sexual activity ("the Goat is run/ To
fetch new lust"). While they are thus occupied, he asks to be allowed to offer devotion

to his dead as both tribute and means to a kind of resurrection. The poem then ends with the recurrent image of the death of the year.

"A Nocturnal upon St. Lucy's Day" is said by many critics to be one of Donne's most complex poems. Some believe that Donne is too obscure most of the time and conclude that this poem in particular is impenetrable. Another objection that has been voiced concerns the extreme expression of grief, especially in the first stanza, with some critics considering it overblown bombast.

Forms and Devices

"A Nocturnal upon St. Lucy's Day" consists of five nine-line stanzas following the unusual rhyme pattern *abbacccdd* over a total of forty-five lines. The rhymed units cohere to form an initial discursive block of four lines, followed by a recursive or appositive group of three lines, followed by a concluding couplet. This pattern encourages a narrowing or a distilling of thought. It also reflects some of the characteristics of both the rime royal and Spenserian stanzaic forms, most notably in the sense of completion caused by the comparatively longer last line.

The metering and rhythm are irregular, somewhat echoing patterns of speech. In general, the lines of each stanza initially tend to favor a tetrameter length (in mixed iambic and anapestic feet), leading up to the stanza's iambic trimeter fifth line. This pattern produces a necessary pause and a heightened emphasis on that fifth line. The halting cadences of the sixth through eighth lines lead to a greater balance in the stanzas' concluding pentameter lines. Donne adds to this scheme an inventive use of the caesura to create more frequent pauses and shifting emphases. Though Donne's habit of engaging in metric irregularity occasioned Ben Jonson's remark that Donne "should be hung for not keeping accent" (meter), in this poem the effect is consistent with the wracking grief the persona expresses throughout his song.

Most compelling as evidence of Donne's artistic control is the poem's symmetrical structure. The poem offers a precise midpoint, the middle of the middle line of the middle stanza (line 22 in stanza 3). This line consists of four syncopated feet. The second foot is broken. This is the only line in all the stanzas that engages an end-stop caesura in the middle of a line—in this case, a period—and the beginning of a new sentence after that second foot. This occurs immediately after the word "nothing," which in Donne's time would most probably have been pronounced as two separate words: "no thing." It is clear that this is a thematically significant division, for it further emphasizes both the speaker's devastation and the potential generative ambiguity.

The question of resulting substance, positive or negative, depends upon this pattern of alchemical and generative imagery. Donne's word choice suggests careful arrangement, especially in how the liver's death produces an elixir that is related to images of growth and continuation. The images simultaneously occupy spiritual and material domains, suggesting a tension often noted in Donne's writing.

Themes and Meanings

Donne intertwines the sacred and profane in this poem. At once readers have the physical death and subsequent mourning, and the spiritual celebration and rebirth of the year. Readers can sense Donne pondering the paradox of these as simultaneous events, forcing them to ask how they could coexist.

Though few of Donne's *Songs and Sonnets* are datable with any precision, ample evidence supports the claim that Donne contrived "A Nocturnal upon St. Lucy's Day" after the death of his wife, Ann, in 1617. Some scholars find such biographical implications to be distractions and prey to fallacious interpretative logic. Others attempt to blend historical material into various interpretative stances. It is certainly hard to deny the power of the poem if one imagines the poet's personal grief. It is even more fitting when one considers that Ann died after an ill-advised twelfth childbirth. It has been suggested that her sacrifice in marital fruition was similar to Saint Lucy's martyrdom—both died unswerving in their manifest faith.

Interpretation of this poem often takes one of two positions: that the poem is an anguished expression of grief and ends in despair, or that it encourages faith in restoration and ends in hope. Either camp must clarify how one should interpret the nulls, zeroes, absences, and no-things that pervade the work. One interpretation involves accepting a sexual representation of the word "thing" as standing for the penis, apparently a common slang usage in Donne's time. This approach presents readers with the implication of emasculation or, in a bawdier sense, a lack of erection: The speaker is reduced to "no thing." Some critics reject such physical punning as inconsistent with the decorum necessitated by the mourning expressed in the poem; others find the correlation between sex and death, consistent with Freudian concepts, to be psychologically appealing.

Further irony may be found in the contrast between the lack of light emphasized in the long-night, short-day positioning, and the fact that celebrations of Saint Lucy often involved emphasis on light and vision. The name "Lucy" is itself cognate with the Latin *lux*. Much of the poem plays off this loss of light, Donne's loss of his wife as loss of the sun (or son). Such verbal punning is regularly found in Donne's writing, and his sermons often focused on the emanations and explications of key scriptural words.

Beyond these themes is the fact—the existence—of the poem itself. It is something produced from a death, and in several instances the poem calls attention to itself. Further, the speaker enjoins the reader to "study me then," which must refer as much to the study of the poem as to the study of the speaker. Since the speaker has indicated that he has become the couple's epitaph, reading the poem is tantamount to reading or studying the speaker. To read the poem is thus both to see the folly of temporal love and to see the restoration that is possible if one has sufficient eternal faith (in the beloved, in God, and perhaps in the poem).

Scott D. Vander Ploeg

NOTES TOWARD A SUPREME FICTION

Author: Wallace Stevens (1879-1955)
Type of poem: Meditation
First published: 1942

The Poem

Notes Toward a Supreme Fiction, considered by many to be Wallace Stevens's most important poem, did not receive much critical attention until the 1980's. Considered long and unwieldy, the poem was overlooked in favor of shorter and more easily accessible poems until critics became aware that much current theory has its parallel in Stevens's *Notes Toward a Supreme Fiction*. Contemporary notions of historicity, aesthetics, and even chaos theory can be read from this work.

The notion of the "supreme fiction" was a major preoccupation of Stevens, who, in the early 1940's when this poem was written, was attempting to find a stronger justification for poetry in times of war and social disintegration. Poetry was not to be accused of escapism or irrelevance. Rather, the poet was to assume a heroic role in attempting to find meaning in chaos and to articulate the human myth. Indeed, this long, philosophical poem gives a relatively complete discussion of Stevens's later aesthetic and can be used to gloss his other work. *Notes Toward a Supreme Fiction* was first published in 1942 and then collected in the 1947 book *Transport to Summer*. It is prefaced by a dedication and an eight-line introduction that addresses the fiction itself. The poem is organized formally, with three sections of ten sets of seven three-line stanzas, each developing a subtopic (or a single "note") of the main theme, and a concluding set of seven tercets. The three subtopics are "It Must Be Abstract," "It Must Change," and "It Must Give Pleasure" ("It" in each case refers to the supreme fiction). The last group of tercets does not have a title, but it is an address to a soldier that attempts to make poetry and poetry writing relevant to war. When the poem was first published in 1942, Stevens wished to have the "soldier" lines emphasized. He claimed at one point to have planned a fourth section titled "It Must Be Human"; although this fourth part was never written, the humanity of the supreme fiction is assumed or asserted throughout the poem. The dedication ("To Henry Church") is confusing; the reader is likely to connect it with the introduction to the poem, which begins, "And for what, except for you, do I feel love?" However, the dedication was a last-minute addition, and the opening likes are actually addressed not to his friend Church but to the fiction, an entity that seems as much creator as created. It is the fiction that is the ultimate object of desire.

The first section of the poem considers the process and nature of abstraction, one of the three essentials of Stevens's supreme fiction. Abstraction is equated with seeing in "the first idea"—the poet must strip perception of accumulated interpretations in order to restore the freshness of the first-time vision. The speaker addresses an "ephebe," or pupil/apprentice, whom he instructs in the art of abstraction. The goal of such rigorous stripping is to get back to the uninterpreted base of reality. The sun, to be seen in the first idea, must "bear no name . . . but be/ In the difficulty of what it is to be." "Do not use the rotted names," Stevens says elsewhere, and this instruction is at the bottom of his concept of abstraction. The supreme fiction cannot be another perfunctory statement of what has been previously thought and said—it must be fresh, and the revitalization of reality calls for stripping it. Abstraction is not easy, as the rest of this section explains. Reality is not merely a human thing: "There was a myth before the myth began" in the "muddy centre" of prehuman history. The world humans know is not theirs, and its foreignness both causes and complicates poetry. However, the creators of present fictions are human, although they have a superhuman task. After describing the meaning and process of abstraction, the poem turns to the figure of the poet. Who is the poet, and what is the result of this attempt to abstract not only the indifferent world but also humankind itself? A series of images is proposed, and the final and lasting one is an old clown, a Charlie Chaplin type who will create and who will be the subject of the ultimate poem.

The second essential characteristic of the supreme fiction is explored in "It Must Change." This part of the poem is filled with images of fruition and change, creating a picture reminiscent of the bountiful earth described in Stevens's more famous poem "Sunday Morning." These nature images are contrasted with a statue of the General Du Puy that does not change and therefore belies nature. (This poem is really about the process of creation rather than about the product, but it is clear that the speaker, here indistinguishable from the poet, believes following his directions for creation would provide the best art.) The speaker describes the meeting of opposites and the resulting births and speaks of the pleasure brought by change and the delight that comes from the natural cycle of birth, ripeness, and decline. The cycles of nature allow for renewal and refreshment whereas art that turns flesh to bronze is deadening.

"It Must Change" is closely linked to the third part, "It Must Give Pleasure." In the second section, the poet establishes that change produces delight while in the third he examines the relationship between pleasure and art. It contains a long parable of the Canon Aspirin and his sister that explores the differences in their perceptions of the world. She is more of a bare minimalist while he is a creator of order; neither one is able to create ideal art because neither strikes the right chord of the relationship between reality and the imagination. In the most difficult sections of this poem, the speaker tries to define what this relationship might be. The Canon imposes order, but the true poet must be able to discover rather than impose. It must be possible, the speaker muses, "To find the real,/ To be stripped of every fiction except one,/ The fiction of an absolute." This point, at which invention becomes discovery, would be the locus of the supreme fiction. The speaker then retreats from his assertion that the poet can find this point of conjunction. (Stevens often retreats from positions he explores, as though unwilling to make any absolute statement.) However, the poem concludes with the possibility of a conjunction between mind and world that encompasses all his essentials: abstraction, change, and delight. The last group of tercets is addressed to a soldier and shows the connection between poetry and war, which is seen in the perspective of the human myth: "The soldier is poor without the poet's lines." Poetry gives meaning to the soldier's life and sacrifice.

Forms and Devices

The three-line stanzas are appropriate for a long, meditative poem and may evoke the spirit of Italian poet Dante Alighieri, who seems to be a ghostly presence in the poem (Stevens saw Dante as the creator of a powerful but now historical fiction that continues to haunt today's would-be fiction maker). Stevens's late work frequently uses the tercet together with a relaxed blank verse in extended explorations of poetics. The result is a kind of essay in verse enhanced by poetic devices such as alliteration, consonance, metaphor, and a variety of rhetorical devices.

The images and metaphors, mostly from art, nature, or art and nature combined, attempt to demonstrate the facets of the supreme fiction: abstraction, changeability, and capacity to delight. Each section is very different in tone and metaphor because the three characteristics differ, although the second and third sections are more closely allied than is the first with either of the others. Images of nature and art in the first section tend to serve as illustrations of abstraction or as analogies that demonstrate how the poet sees. Images of animals show the process of mythologizing, while art is wedded to nature in passages illustrative of how perception turns to art: "Weather by Franz Hals,/ Brushed up by brushy winds in brushy clouds." The interpretation has been welded to the perception so that metaphor becomes equivalence, with art and nature mirroring each other. At the end of part 1, a sustained metaphor illustrates the notion that "The major abstraction is the idea of man." This concept is further defined: "The major abstraction is the commonal,/ The inanimate, difficult visage. Who is it?" The figure that emerges is the old clown, the Charlie Chaplin type in "slouching pantaloons" seen "Looking for what was, where it used to be." This is the basis for the image that must serve as the "final elegance."

Images crowd together and change rapidly in "It Must Change." The sequence of images of nature in flux (bees, apples, and pigeons, among others) is in stark contrast with the "great statue of General Du Puy" that is not subject to change and therefore not reflective of reality. There follow images of mystic marriages that represent the thesis, antithesis, and synthesis that constantly create new versions of reality. Part 2 also contains what may be an appealing reprise of one of Stevens's early poems, "The Comedian as the Letter C," which details the adventures of Crispin as he tries and discards different types of art only to completely succumb to the life of the world at last, becoming a cabin-dwelling farmer instead of a poet. In *Notes Toward a Supreme Fiction*, the "planter," by yielding to reality rather than attempting to impose order on it, has not lost out on anything.

"It Must Give Pleasure" uses images of music, a beautiful woman, and angels in its argument that pleasure is an essential ingredient of the supreme fiction. The complex concluding image of this poem is teasing and inconclusive. It is another scene of sexual attraction. The speaker addresses a woman who is identified with the earth, with the real: "Fat girl, terrestrial, my summer, my night/ How is it I find you in difference . . . ?" He is compelled by her, just as the imagination is compelled by the real; what he wants to do because of her attractiveness is to name her. This naming is the act of poetry and the act of love: "this unprovoked sensation requires/ That I should name you flatly, waste no words." He concludes that the supreme fiction is "the more than rational distortion,/ The fiction that results from feeling." Thus, images of mind and world merge with the male and female lovers: "I call you by name, my green, my fluent mundo./ You will have stopped revolving except in crystal." The mind's embrace of the world is the same as a lovers' embrace. As in a lovers' embrace, both mind and world are participants.

The last section, the seven-tercet address to the soldier, uses images of the soldier's life in a comparison between the real war and the poet's war in an attempt to justify the ways of poetry to the war-torn present. This section was not a part of Stevens's original project. For many readers, the triumphant meeting of poet and world at the end of "It Must Give Pleasure" is the high point of the poem and its true conclusion.

Themes and Meanings

Stevens expressed in letters his desire to define a role for the poet similar to the role of the priest. This poem is an effort to exalt poetry and to explore its possibilities as a replacement for religion or perhaps as a religion in itself. In one letter, Stevens commented, "In principle there appear to be certain characteristics of a supreme fiction *and the NOTES is confined to a statement of a few of those characteristics. . . .* In trying to create something as valid as the idea of God has been, and for that matter remains, the first necessity seems to be breadth." The varied themes of *Notes Toward a Supreme Fiction* bind into one strand leading toward such an exalted definition of the supreme fiction. Interestingly, Stevens said to one correspondent that the supreme fiction was, of course, poetry—but to another correspondent, after he had immersed himself fully in the project, he claimed that he did not want to be so limiting. The concept had begun to widen and to transcend itself.

Stevens was preoccupied throughout his life with the way art becomes dated so quickly, and, in "The Noble Rider and the Sound of Words" (a paper first given at Princeton in 1942 and later published, in his essay collection *The Necessary Angel*, in 1951), he described how some well-known statues reflected their culture and were incomprehensible if divorced by time or space from that culture. His long poem looks at the possibility of setting poetry or art or even the creative act itself free from the limits of time and circumstance. He suggests that this be done by altering the way the artist looks at the world. Creative perception requires all of the perceiver's resources. It involves stripping away the accretions of the past to look at the real world as if through Adam's eyes, accepting change as the basis for all art, and opening art itself to change. It also involves being aware of the pleasure that comes from both the world and the artistic act, thus allowing the work, in a sense, to celebrate itself. Thus the ideal fiction as described in this poem is not time-bound because it is abstract, changeable, and pleasurable. It is the one love object worthy of the poet's desire. It is both subject and object, creator and created. To be abstract, the reality on which the fiction rests must be stripped of the perceptions of others and the fictions of previous perceivers. It must be of both humankind and the alien world. The poet and his human subject are to be realistic rather than aggrandized or presented as a caricature. To be changeable, the fiction must be based on nature's cycles rather than being a prison for nature. Statues of generals or anything "set in stone" cannot be the truest form of art. To produce delight, the poem must be an energetic search for the real in which the mind approaches the world like a lover. This poem is Stevens's sustained effort to create, as a poem, a poetics that demonstrates itself in the lines that describe it.

Janet McCann

O CARIB ISLE!

Author: Hart Crane (1899-1932)
Type of poem: Lyric
First published: 1927; collected in *The Collected Poems of Hart Crane*, 1933

The Poem

"O Carib Isle!" is a lyric poem of thirty-four lines divided into seven irregular stanzas with intermittent rhyme. The stanzas are further grouped into two sections followed by a concluding four-line stanza. The poem presents a beach scene in which a Caribbean island teeming with nonhuman life is associated with death in the mind of the speaker, the poet Hart Crane himself rather than an imaginary persona. In the first stanza, the poem describes the foot end of a grave in white sand where lilies have been laid and a tarantula rustles among the dry flower stalks. Crabs scuttling sideways seem to rearrange the letters of the name of the dead written in the sand. However, nothing in nature seems to mourn except a partly withered eucalyptus plant.

In the second and third stanzas, the speaker sees the seashells littering the sand as mother-of-pearl "frames of tropic death." Empty of the bodies that once gave them life, the shells themselves are reminders of death. The shells also seem to the speaker to mark off graves in squared patterns in the sand. If the speaker can count these shells, then he may "speak a name" that the names of the living and dying trees and flowers near the beach contradict. The name may be death, or it may be God. The "brittle crypt" suggests shells and bones in which the dead are encrypted. A wind mounting toward hurricane force also suggests the poet's withdrawn breath. The breathless silence evokes the atmosphere before a storm begins and represents the speaker's emotional and creative deadness.

The second major section, subdivided into two parts, asks who is in charge of this deserted island where a pirate captain may have buried gold doubloons. The island is "Without a turnstile" such as one might find at an airport or a train station because no one wants to be there, and there is no obvious escape. Only the crabs occupy the land, patrolling the infertile underbrush. The absent captain or commissioner has created the complexity of what the speaker sees through sun-baked eyes. Called into question, this captain stands for a God whose "Carib mathematics" reminds readers of the shell count in the first stanza. The second subdivision of the second part of the poem represents a prayer to let the speaker's ghost be "Sieved upward" until it meets the "comedian" who "hosts" the blue sky. This ascension is preferable to being left on earth where he can look around on the beach and see the "slow evisceration" of his body, dying like terrapins turned on their backs and helpless to return to their element, the sea. The final stanza is a four-line coda. Left in the wake of the hurricane hinted at earlier, the speaker admits that he has only the dry fragments of shell rather than the soul he hoped for, his own mortal body the "carbonic amulet" on the necklace of shells littering the beach.

Forms and Devices

"O Carib Isle!" comprises two groupings of fifteen lines, each ending with a rhymed couplet. (Metrically, the seventh line is a single line that is divided to indicate a paragraph break.) These two groupings are followed by a four-line concluding stanza. Crane uses rhyme sparingly to define the poem's overall structure and to emphasize key points. In spite of the loose and, at first glance, haphazard placement of rhyme, a careful reading reveals that the poem actually falls neatly into three parts with its major division marked by rhymed couplets as well as spaces on the page.

"O Carib Isle!" is characterized by complex meter rather than free verse. Iambic pentameter and end rhyme provide a foundation for the lines that depart from the regular pattern. For example, the divided line "In wrinkled shadows—mourns./ And yet suppose" is perfectly even metrically: ten syllables with stresses on the second, fourth, sixth, eighth, and tenth syllables. The opening line further illustrates the poem's metrical complexity. The first line has twelve syllables rather than the ten expected in a perfect iambic pentameter line. After the definite article, an unstressed syllable, Crane begins boldly with a four-syllable word ("tarantula"), which is two iambs, then finishes the line with four iambs starting with the accented first syllable of "rattling." The effect of the very word "tarantula" is to make the line heavy with syllables like the big spider's legs moving slowly at the stalk of the lily. The line is at once busy and slow moving, very much the effect a tarantula might have on an observer.

Throughout the poem, Crane plays longer and shorter lines against the basic five-stress line. For example, line 20 ("Is Commissioner of mildew throughout the ambushed senses") has fifteen syllables but only five strong accents (on the third, tenth, twelfth, and fourteenth syllables). That long line comes right after a line of only four syllables ("What man, or What") that has two strong accents (on "man" and on the second "What"). The fact that this is the shortest line in the poem calls attention to it. Inside the line, the repetition of "What" further focuses the reader's attention on that syllable. The first "What" does not receive a stress; the second does. The repetition and the end stress arguably make the second "What" the central note of the poem—the unknown force that created the grim scene the speaker surveys.

Crane tries to force his inspiration with a visual rhyme: "senses" and "lenses." However, the sound is not quite right. Should readers trust their eyes or their ears, their "ambushed senses" or the "baked lenses" of their eyes? The end couplet of the second grouping of fifteen lines again offers a visual rhyme, "strain" and "again," which may or may not be a sound rhyme depending on how one pronounces "again." At the end of the first fifteen-line section of the poem, "Death" and "breath" is an easy and tired rhyme, at first glance surprisingly amateurish in the work of a poet as skillful as Crane. "Death" also ends line 8. However, the technically lazy rhyme suggests the very thing the poet is describing: a failure of inspiration and a spiritual weariness. A lack of inspiration is both a lack of breath and a lack of spirit.

Themes and Meanings

As is often the case in Crane's poetry, "O Carib Isle!" relies on images and word associations to release its emotional energy. Sensuous description of a hot, dry Caribbean island stands as an extended metaphor for the dry, desolate state of the speaker's consciousness. Ironically, it is a beautifully realized poem about the failure of poetic inspiration. The poem expresses the poet's exhausted sensibility and spiritual pessimism but creates in the poem itself a belief in something beyond himself, if only in Satan. Actually, Satan is no more present in the poem than the absent "Captain" (God). However, the depressed and weary speaker is more inclined to believe in the hot, desolate landscape of the island as hell rather than paradise.

Poetry also begins with the process of naming. However, although "name" or "names" appears four times in the first section, these appearances are in the context of generalities ("tree," "flower," "a name") rather than the specific eucalyptus of poinciana named elsewhere in the poem. Furthermore, Crane chooses his specific names carefully: For example, the poinciana, a red-flowered plant, was named for a former governor of the French West Indies, M. de Poinci. The landscape is torpid, dead, or inhuman, and in some cases all three. The scuttling crabs "anagrammatize" an unstated name, thereby obliterating a specific identity and reminding the poet that any naming of the mystery of life is conditional and temporary—written in sand, to use the familiar cliché. (It has been observed that "crab" is a rearranging of the letters of "carib" with the *I*, or identity, deleted.) Counting shells is a way of giving order to a mind at least temporarily incapable of the richer possibilities of naming that are the beginnings of poetry. In a later and more hopeful poem, Crane seeks a transcendent "name for all."

Although the speaker seems depressed and doubtful of transcendence, he retains some faith in his poetic powers. Many of Crane's poems are written in four-line stanzas. "O Carib Isle!" has only one clearly delineated quatrain, whose position at the end of the poem oddly suggests a return to confidence and to a sense of himself. The richly alliterative last line, "Sere of the sun exploded in the sea," which describes a sunless world in which human life is either nonexistent or powerless, is, perhaps ironically, a tour-de-force conclusion. Offering such triumph as sound and verbal grandeur can provide, it reads against the grim description in the rest of the poem.

Thomas Lisk

ODE ON A DISTANT PROSPECT OF ETON COLLEGE

Author: Thomas Gray (1716-1771)
Type of poem: Ode
First published: 1747; collected in *Six Poems by Mr. T. Gray*, 1753

The Poem

The three elements of the title prepare the reader to understand the poem. First, it is an ode, a lyric poem on a serious subject conveyed in dignified language. Second, it focuses on "a distant prospect." This distance is both in place—Thomas Gray's view of Eton, his old school, from across the Thames River—and in time—the years since the poet's graduation from Eton. Furthermore, the prospect is a literal view of the campus as well as an imaginative vision of what the future will hold for the boys now on the campus. Third, Eton College refers not only to Gray's school but also to one of England's oldest and greatest preparatory schools for boys, the alma mater of many of England's leaders and writers.

The epigraph, "I am a man, reason enough for being miserable," a quotation from the Greek playwright Menander, crisply states the poem's theme: the ultimate trouble and unhappiness of human life. Gray's use of an ancient quotation also suggests the timelessness of the theme.

The Eton College ode represents, for Gray, a homecoming to his old school as he reflects on his time there as a boy and on what the future will bring to the present students.

In the opening stanza, Gray, standing alone, describes the campus—its spires and towers, Windsor Castle in the background, the surrounding groves, lawns, and meadows, and the shade trees and flowers along the winding Thames River. His references to Henry (King Henry VI, founder of the school in 1440), whose "shade" (or spirit) presides, and to the "shade" of the old trees affirm the harmony of history and nature at the school—and they hint at the "shade" of death that awaits everyone.

Stanza 2 conveys a refreshing wistfulness as Gray remembers the playing fields, "beloved in vain," on which he showed little athletic promise and observes "careless childhood" now at play. His memories of youth are "gales" that bring a fleeting joy, a "momentary bliss" to him.

The third and fourth stanzas show Gray apostrophizing (directly addressing) Father Thames, spirit of the river and rural nature, who has seen centuries of boys ("a sprightly race") at the school. Poetic diction (language that seems either artificial or archaic) marks these stanzas as Gray depicts the boys' activities: "Disporting on thy margent green" (playing on the green riverbanks), cleaving "thy glassy wave" (swimming in the river), chasing "the rolling circle's speed" (chasing a hoop), and urging "the flying ball" (playing cricket). All of the boys find their playtime more sweet because school rules and study are the "graver hours" that limit their fun. Other boys explore the campus and even wander, against the rules, off school grounds. Aware of their disobedience, they imagine that the wind reprimands them, tempering their forbidden joy with fear.

In stanza 5, Gray reflects that hope is driven only by unrealistic imagination: "Gay hope is theirs by fancy fed." Because he sees typical childhood as a blend of brief disappointments, enthusiasm, health, wit and invention, and vigor, its days are carefree, its nights restful, its mornings bright. Gray thinks that children imagine, unrealistically, that their good times will last forever.

However, in line 51 of the sixth stanza, the very middle of the poem, the ode's tone and direction change. The nostalgic tone of the first part becomes melancholy; the childlike hope of the fifth stanza now becomes doom: "Alas, regardless of their doom,/ The little victims play!" Now, instead of describing the boys' joyful present, Gray foresees their fateful future. Because they are "regardless of their doom," he wishes to "tell them they are men," that is, that they are subject to all the troubles and mortality of human beings.

Stanzas 7-9 are a catalog of the troubles of adult life. Furthermore, because Gray thinks them to be typical, he personifies (depicts an abstraction as human) them. Stanzas 7 and 8 reveal these "fury Passions" that accompany adulthood, including "Shame that skulks," "pining Love," "Grim-visaged comfortless Despair," "The stings of Falsehood," and "moody Madness laughing wild."

The ninth stanza presents "A grisly troop . . ./ The painful family of Death" whose "hideous . . . queen" is Persephone, Greek goddess of death and the underworld. This "death" group consists of racking pain, numbing poverty, and degenerative aging, all personifications of human mortality.

Gray's conclusion in the final stanza is that while suffering is the human lot, there is no point in preaching that lesson to children, for such a "Thought would destroy their paradise." Rather, "where ignorance is bliss,/ 'Tis folly to be wise."

The paradox of "foolish wisdom" shows both Gray's insight and virtue, for if he knows that happiness is fleeting and cannot be realized, then letting the boys enjoy their brief "paradise" is, indeed, the virtue of kindness.

Forms and Devices

The poem's ten stanzas, each consisting of ten alternating iambic tetrameter and trimeter lines, is a fine version of the Horatian ode, developed by the Roman poet Horace, which is noted for its restraint and the regular similarity of its stanzas in length, meter, and rhyme.

Gray's Eton College ode is constructed in a perfect symmetry with an exact balance between the first fifty lines and the last fifty lines. This symmetry is seen in the contrasts between each part that, together, unify the poem: the joys of youth versus the ills of age, childlike innocence versus adult experience, hope versus despair, the Thames valley versus the "vale of years," wit versus madness, health versus sickness, Gray's past (and the boys' present) versus Gray's present (and the boys' future), a tone of wistfulness versus one of melancholy doom, boys at play versus a man in reflection.

A further symmetry is evident in the end rhymes of the fifth and sixth verses that link the two parts of each stanza.

Assonance (repeated vowel sounds) is a device that enhances the ode's tone, particularly the number of long, low "o" and "a" vowels that echo the nostalgia of the poem's first half and the melancholy of the second.

Two other devices, thought to be old-fashioned, are explainable. The first, poetic diction, was, in Gray's time, considered proper for the ode, which demanded elevated, traditional words. According to eighteenth century reasoning, since a poem is artificial—a work of art and not of nature—its proper diction should likewise be artificial. Thus, phrases such as "margent green," "enthrall," and "the rolling circle's speed" are the proper materials with which to build a well-constructed ode. Another device, personification, also seems dated, but, in the eighteenth century, it was valued as a way to express a universal truth. Gray's personifications are not flat; rather, he brings them to life with telling verbs or modifiers: "Shame that skulks," "grinning Infamy," and "moody Madness laughing wild." These and others grant a vividness to his generalizations.

Themes and Meanings

Two themes play through Gray's "Ode on a Distant Prospect of Eton College." The major theme is the inevitability of suffering, death, and unhappiness for humankind. Sad though the theme is, Gray tempers it with his own fatherlike concern in keeping this knowledge from the children. Because he knows that the "paradise" of their youth is brief, he tenderly allows them to enjoy it.

Related to this theme is a minor biblical one, the key to which is again paradise: the state of happiness before the Fall. As Gray watches the boys at Eton, he notes their health, hope, and joy. However, he reveals neither a desire to return to youth nor a disgust with adulthood. To Gray, the children are happy but deluded, and their delusions keep them happy until their growth to knowledge unveils the hardships and sadness of life. Both themes evolve from Gray's philosophy of stoicism: that all life must be endured with fortitude, self-control, and restraint of feelings.

Gray's concern with children, rural description, reflective imagination, and melancholy are tendencies that made him a forerunner of the English Romantic movement. Writing in the mid-eighteenth century, however, Gray was also one of the last English Augustan or neoclassic poets who used balanced poetic architecture, poetic diction and personification, and classical poetic types, and who tended toward the ethical and the didactic. Along with his great *Elegy Written in a Country Churchyard* (1751), the Eton College ode reveals Thomas Gray's poetry as an important, strong, and beautiful bridge between two very different periods of English literature.

H. George Hahn

ODE TO AN ARTICHOKE

Author: Pablo Neruda (Neftalí Ricardo Reyes Basoalto, 1904-1973)
Type of poem: Ode
First published: 1954, as "Oda a una alcachofa," in *Odas elementales*; English translation collected in *The Elementary Odes*, 1961

The Poem

"Ode to an Artichoke" (it has also been translated under the title "Artichoke") is a short poem consisting of thirty-three lines of free verse. The poem establishes the poet's connection to the elemental or basic qualities of objects that surround everyone in daily life—here, common food items or vegetables. Pablo Neruda imagines the relationship that an artichoke may have to the rest of the members of the vegetable kingdom and, in the broadest terms, to reality itself. The artichoke is described as being "of delicate heart" yet dressed for battle inside its small "cupola" (a rounded vault that forms a roof). It keeps itself isolated and protected under its scales. This humble member of the food chain is surrounded by less prudent inhabitants of nature's botanical kingdom. Wild, even crazy, vegetables bristle, raising their backs as if to engage in battle. At the same time, the carrot sleeps under the soil and the cabbage busies itself trying on a skirt. The spicy oregano perfumes the rest of the world while the artichoke, armed for a battle, stays quietly in its garden plot, burnished and proud like a pomegranate.

The poem presents a vision of the natural world, of grape vines and common vegetables come to life, conscious of their place in the scheme of nature and able to make choices about the ways in which they live their lives. Like humans, they can either be calm or belligerent; they can be showy and pretentious or stoic and independent. In the poem Neruda takes an approach quite different from that of many Latin American modernists, such as Rubén Darío, who express a vision of human life in terms of a so-called "poetical" reality. Rather, Neruda utilizes mundane objects as a springboard for his divagations on the nature of human life and the role of the poet in the midst of the flux of history.

Forms and Devices

The poem's references to plant life establish a basic and obvious metaphor for the various modalities of human life. The poem's style is spare and abrupt; the ode begins with a direct naming of Neruda's center of interest, the artichoke, without any fanfare. Neruda's personification of the vegetables does not stop with the artichoke itself but continues throughout the work. The poem has an effect something like a Disneyized cartoon in which the plants and flowers suddenly come to life to adopt human emotions and act in human relationships.

The artichoke protects itself within its "cupola," Neruda's way of describing the green fibers that protect the central part of this plant. Rather than indulging in myriad adjectives to describe a humanized scale of emotions, the poet uses simple action verbs such as " perfume," "try on," "bristle," and "sleeps." He consciously refrains from interjecting personal reactions or emotions into the goings-on of the various members of the botanical kingdom.

The short, even terse, lines of the poem—sometimes limited to only two syllables—contribute to the starkly direct effect that this work has. The ideas are generated by broken syntax in lines of poetry which are most often incomplete in themselves. They must be read in groups of two or three to understand their basic meaning. The result is a choppy, brusque, poetic expression that may be seen as a linguistic corollary to the prosaic and "antipoetic" nature of the subject itself.

Certainly Neruda's choice of the artichoke to be his vehicle for an allegory on certain aspects of human life is original and deceptively simple. Casual readers may read this as just one more poetic description of a garden as can be seen in traditional ballads or in the more saccharine productions of late Romantic and Victorian poetry. The depiction is mundane to the point of being prosaic. It clearly avoids the pitfalls of clichés that often spring up around the poetry of gardens. It is simplistic to the degree that it would be easy to find this a one-dimensional poem in which the author indulges his well-known affinity for the sights and sounds of immediate reality without engaging a deeper level of literary meaning.

Themes and Meanings

Neruda refers to the artichoke as having a tender heart, and he extends the metaphor of the poet—a tender-hearted artichoke—to himself. The poet must find ways of accommodating his sensitivity to his life and to the world in order to survive. Here the artichoke-poet is stoic in his courageous defiance of the madness that surrounds him. He digs deep into his own cupola, the ecclesiastical connotations of this domelike structure suggesting that this protectionism becomes his religion. It is his way of reaching transcendence or is at least his path to survival as he readies himself to do battle with the forces of reality that surround him.

Somehow he manages to keep calm, "impermeable bajo sus escamas" (untouchable under his scales). Other plants, such as the carrot, prefer simply to stay asleep, while the vines in the orchard expose themselves to the dangers of the strong rays of sunlight and wither and die. The cabbage is pretentious and aspires to physical beauty, while the oregano seeks sublimity through the piquant aroma that it gives off. Through all this the humble artichoke, dour and prosaic, does not aspire either to sublime beauty or to the popularity that a spicy oregano enjoys because of its aroma. It remains quiet and calm, always ready to do battle but stoically unmoved by the pretention of the other plants. It is sure in its own identity and proud of its ability to give pleasure in and on its own terms.

Clearly Pablo Neruda is alluding to his own existence—to the poet's place in the world and to his willingness to acknowledge his gifts as well as his limitations in the vast panorama of human life. He is sure that he will have to do battle, like the Romantics and the modernists before him, against the crassness of the profane modern world, but he is also sure that his art and the strength of his poetic gift can shield him to a certain degree from the blight of that reality.

The poet appears to be content to be himself, to adopt a stoic and slightly bemused view of the contours of the society in which he finds himself. Yet Neruda's vision is also one of praise. The poem is an ode to the beauty that he finds in the commonplace, in the sensuous world, full of its own secret poetic meaning and special beauty.

Arthur A. Natella, Jr.

ODE TO WALT WHITMAN

Author: Federico García Lorca (1898-1936)
Type of poem: Ode
First published: 1940, as "Oda a Walt Whitman," in *Poeta en Nueva York*, 1940;
English translation collected in *Poet in New York*, 1955

The Poem

The Spanish poet and dramatist Federico García Lorca wrote his famous "Oda a Walt Whitman" ("Ode to Walt Whitman") in 1930 while completing a year of study at Columbia University. The poem did not appear in its entirety, however, until it was collected in the first two editions of *Poeta en Nueva York* in 1940, more than three years after the poet was executed by Generalissimo Francisco Franco's fascist troops during the Spanish Civil War. From the outset this emotionally charged piece, translated by Ben Belitt in *Poet in New York* (1955), subsumes the confusing onslaught of city images that bombarded the non-English-speaking García Lorca during his first ever trip abroad in the wake of the disastrous stock market crash of 1929. The irregular stanzas and varying lengths of the poem's 137 free-verse lines accurately reflect the bustling, chaotic character of this major metropolitan center. In addition, the poem implicitly contrasts the city's arduous striving for economic recovery through local industry with the splendors of its half-concealed natural beauty. Thus the poem's speaker can address "filthy New York" as the city of "cables and death" while musing in the very next line, "What angel do you carry, concealed in your cheek?"

García Lorca uses the ode, a celebratory lyric form, to praise the charitable nature of the influential American poet Walt Whitman (1812-1892), a writer closely associated with New York City, where Whitman published his landmark collection of verse, *Leaves of Grass*, in 1855. Some see in the style and structure of "Ode to Walt Whitman" García Lorca's attempt to emulate the lilting cadences of Whitman's long, rhythmic lines, his spontaneous, lush diction, sincere outpouring of feeling, and fluid, highly personal voice. García Lorca undoubtedly admired Whitman's verse for embodying America's democratic ideals and elevating the genuine decency of the common man to a more exalted plane. Yet in all likelihood García Lorca harbored a more immediate reason for choosing Whitman as the subject of his poetic paean.

Both García Lorca and Whitman were homosexual, and both deplored their societies' moralistic intolerance of same-sex love. "Ode to Walt Whitman" repeatedly distinguishes the (assumed) purity and sincerity of Whitman's sexual predilections from its own cold-eyed depiction of the largely self-gratifying, sometimes violent, even depraved aspects of urban homosexual relations. To the poem's speaker, Whitman is nothing less than a "blood-brother," a "lone man in a sea," a "comely old man" who is an "old friend," while the "perverts" around him are "so much meat for the whiplash,/ for the boot or the bite of the animal-tamers." Whitman's easy relation to what little of nature remains visible amid the hardscrabble cityscape of New York may be viewed in stanzas such as this one:

You looked for a nude that could be like a river,
the bull and the dream that could merge, like seaweed and wheel,
sire of your agony, your mortality's camellia,
to cry in the flames of your secret equator.

Clearly, the speaker of the ode finds the scenario of two people sharing a love akin to transcendent bonding infinitely preferable to seeking fleeting and sordid sexual encounters, "looking for the scar on the eye,/ or the overcast swamp where the boys are submerged."

Forms and Devices

Throughout "Ode to Walt Whitman," García Lorca uses the richly evocative, highly figurative, and elusively metaphorical language that is a hallmark of both his lyric and dramatic work. In writing a poem about male love during the early part of the twentieth century, García Lorca would have felt compelled to approach his subject with linguistic indirection. So, while the ode opens with the obviously homoerotic image of young men "singing, baring their waists,/ with the wheel and the leather, the hammer, the oil," it phrases an ensuing (imagined) sexual fantasy of Whitman's obliquely as "your dream/ where the playfellow munches your apple." Similarly, one of the first images describing Whitman refers to him suggestively as a "bird/ whose sex is transfixed by a needle."

In making allusions to both classical and biblical antiquity, the poem reminds the reader of the grandeur of times past, to which the "fallen" present of New York City (as well as other European and Latin American cities) compares unfavorably. The ode mentions, for example, the "faun of the river"; Whitman is conceived as having "chaste, Apollonion thighs" and as being the "satyr's antagonist," an "Adam" whose authenticity in seeking a communion in love will prepare the way for greater sincerity between sexual partners in the future. Both the hopeful evocation of natural images and capitalization in the following lines attest this possibility: "Tomorrow our passion is rock, and Time,/ a wind come to sleep in the branches." As it stands in the poem's present, though, "life is not noble, or wholesome, or holy."

The greatest tension in the ode concerns the opposition of human-made reality (often mechanical) and the marginalized realm of nature that survives on the outskirts of the city in animal life and, more important, in the East River mentioned in the very first line. What should be a beautiful, pristine "moon-rise" in the fifth stanza is marred: "the block and the tackle will veer and startle the sky." The figure of Whitman, introduced in the twenty-ninth line after a lengthy preamble, promises a return to nature and the natural love lacking in grimy, industrial New York, as García Lorca's speaker declares: "Not for one moment . . ./ have I ceased to envision your beard full of butterflies." Throughout the poem, Whitman is associated with the natural world, especially with the eternal, purifying force of the river. The speaker wonders, using still more natural imagery, "What ineffable voice will speak the truths of the wheat?"

Themes and Meanings

The vituperative stance of the poem's speaker regarding urban homosexuals, called "perverts of the cities" and "mothers of filthiness," implies a certain distance between the speaker and García Lorca himself. These wanton carriers of disease who "bestow upon boys/ the foul drop of death with wormwood of venom" disgust the speaker with their base disregard for the feelings of their sexual partners and the studied artifice of their appearance.

Midway through the ode, these "toadies of women" and "dressing-room bitches" improbably try to claim Whitman as one of their own, pointing him out publicly with the "taint of their fingernails." Their obvious antagonism to the natural world, though, precludes this possibility. Indeed, even when described in natural terms as animals, these raffish urban homosexuals appear in a negative light as "catlike and serpentine" and are later pronounced "dove-killers." After all, sexual desire need not manifest itself so vilely; in contrast to the primarily physical and self-indulgent encounters of the city, the speaker reminds men that "we might, if we would, lead our appetite on/ through the vein of the coral or the heaven-sent nude."

Having suitably praised Whitman for the sincerity of his motivations, the speaker unhesitatingly goes on to group his poetic forebear with those homosexuals whose honest embracing of their identity is reason for admiration. Addressing Whitman directly, as he does throughout much of the ode, the speaker explains that he does not denounce all urban homosexuals, such as "the boy who inscribes/ a girl's name on his pillow," or "the young man who dresses himself like a bride/ in the dark of the clothes-closet," or "the stags of the dance-hall/ who drink at the waters of whoredom and sicken." These men suffer unjustly because of who they are, and they harm no one (except, in some cases, themselves) as they poignantly attempt to come to grips with their confusing sexual stirrings. The speaker sympathizes with their plight and hopes that "the pure, the bewildered,/ the illustrious, classic, and suppliant/ shut the festival doors" in the face of their less genuine and more selfish counterparts.

In dire contrast to the "perverts," then, Whitman, the poet so in tune with nature that he is dubbed a "patriarch, comely as mist," emerges as the only figure in the ode to exist in spiritual harmony with New York City's East River. "Nobody slept/ or wished to be: river," the ode recounts of the single-minded workers in the first stanza. Of Whitman, again addressed directly by the speaker, the reader learns: "you dreamed yourself river, and slept like a river." While "America drowns under engines and tears," the poem closes with Whitman "on the shores of the Hudson . . . asleep," García Lorca's ode having again reiterated the poet's enduring promise of love as peaceful, supernal coupling:

> It is fitting that no man should seek
> in another day's thickets of blood for his pleasure.
> Heaven has shores for our flights out of life,
> and the corpse need not make itself over at dawn.

The poem's final striking image takes another step toward this ideal union of men by heralding the arrival of a phallic reign of nature in which "a black boy declares to the gold-getting white/ kingdom come in a tassel of corn."

Gregary J. Racz

THE OLD AND THE NEW MASTERS

Author: Randall Jarrell (1917-1965)
Type of poem: Lyric
First published: 1965, in *The Lost World*

The Poem

In order to understand Randall Jarrell's "The Old and the New Masters," one must look first to English poet W. H. Auden's "Musée de Beaux Arts," which begins: "About suffering they were never wrong,/ The Old Masters." Auden's poem claims that the master painters—his primary exemplar is mid-sixteenth century Dutch painter Pieter Brueghel—recognized and depicted humankind's callous indifference to the suffering of others. Their depictions are endorsed by Auden, not as the way things should be but as the way they are, and the title implies that art at its best presents this view. In "The Old and the New Masters," Jarrell initially challenges this assertion by means of example, a series of paintings elaborately and lovingly described. As readers move through his argument, they see that in order to dispute Auden's glib characterization of the old masters, Jarrell has created a gallery of his own, made up of other artists for whom the suffering in the world is the single most important fact of human existence.

Jarrell has little interest in formalistic constraints on his poetry. He intends for the subject and the dramatic occasion to determine the shape of the verse. This sixty-one line poem is constructed of three parts. The first section sounds the Auden echo and posits Jarrell's own poem as response. It goes on to describe French Renaissance painter George de La Tour's *Saint Sebastian Mourned by Saint Irene* in such a way that the martyr's pain and the witnesses' responses to it are connected to the agony of Christ. The second part moves chronologically backward in art history to Belgian Renaissance painter Hugo van der Goes's *Nativity* from the "Portinari Altarpiece." Jarrell notes the way in which the painting manipulates time so that "everything/ That was or will be in the world is fixed/ On its small, helpless, human center." The brief third section advances to the "new masters" who "paint a subject as they please." These artists are contrasted with Italian Renaissance painter Paolo Veronese and a description of his *Feast in the House of Levi.* The poet reminds readers of how the Inquisition challenged the painter's overly realistic depiction of Christ sitting at the feast with dogs playing about his feet. Jarrell bemoans the "abstract understanding" of the "new masters," how they diminish the human element. The final image of the poem becomes both a jab at Auden and a lament for art in which Earth itself is that "small radioactive planet" off in the corner of the canvas.

One of Jarrell's foremost critics, Suzanne Ferguson, has described him not as a born poet but as a born teacher, and in a poem such as "The Old and the New Masters" that desire to instruct comes through forcefully. Just as strong as the desire to instruct is the desire to correct: Jarrell sees a mistake with dire consequences in Auden's assumptions about art, and he sets about putting it right.

Forms and Devices

This poem is fueled by allusion, and to grasp the full import of this device readers should remember that an allusion does not merely force another text into their consciousness; rather, it borrows a mood, announces a debt, calls up another context that no longer exists, reminds the reader of an absence, and interjects a tone of pity for the reader's loss. Another term for this effect is "intertextuality," the acknowledgement that no text can be read outside its relations to other, already existing texts. In this case, the poem begins by calling to mind another poem (therefore another poet) that, by its title, declares as its subject the whole realm of fine arts. Jarrell then follows Auden's lead in calling forth the exemplary works that will make his case. His careful choice of examples—religious subjects, emphatically Christian—brings into his poem the very elements that Jarrell fears are disappearing for more contemporary art: respect for the human being and for human suffering. Through such depictions of an art with a "human center," Jarrell points beyond the poetry and beyond the painting to the world of spiritual and moral value.

In Jarrell's poetry, the sentence is often more important than the line, and the sentences in this poem are built upon simple declaratives that are then embellished and extended by additional details, all connected by semicolons. By means of such sentences, the poet focuses the readers' attention on a central point of the examined canvas and then, in what seem like concentric circles, moves their eyes to a wider and wider comprehension of the total picture. To some degree that comprehension is vital. Jarrell tries not to call attention to himself or to his language by the showy employment of metaphors and other tropes (figures of speech). His similes, when he uses them, are functional rather than exploratory, as when he speaks of all the elements in a painting being pointed "like the needle of a compass." For his poem, like the paintings he so admires, the human center is the crux.

However, even though he spurns a densely figurative idiom, Jarrell's voice might be considered the other dominant device in the poem; at times its tone is that of a guide or instructor, loving, passionate and, in the words of author Joseph Conrad, determined "to make you see." Just as the paintings are themselves focused on the perception of suffering, on attention being paid, Jarrell's carefully modulated descriptions of the painters' visions direct and sharpen readers' recognition of what is important. To this purpose, the voice is itself a rhetorical strategy, foregrounding the poet's awareness of his audience: "far off in the rocks/ You can see Mary and Joseph and their donkey/ coming to Bethlehem." By speaking to the readers directly, Jarrell involves them in the dynamic that these paintings establish: "everything/ That was or will be in the world is fixed/ On its small, helpless, human center."

Themes and Meanings

In "The Old and the New Masters," Jarrell declares that art is meant to confront and acknowledge human suffering. Through all his poems depicting the victimization of soldiers, women, and children by the great forces of what he calls "Necessity," he has staked out an aesthetic based upon the perception of suffering as a defining act for the human being. It is a kind of adoration, the kind that can be seen in versions of the Nativity. To attend to the hurt and the helpless is a human's finest expression of a godlike capacity. The alternatives to such attention become evident in the curious final stanza. Jarrell is not lamenting the disappearance of an overtly religious perspective in modern art; rather, he pleads for a humanistic, overarching sympathy and projects dire consequences in the final passage of the poem:

> Later Christ disappears, the dogs disappear: in abstract
> Understanding, without adoration, the last master puts
> Colors on canvas, a picture of the universe
> In which a bright spot somewhere in the corner
> Is the small radioactive planet men called Earth.

With the telescopic power of art to bring past, present, and future into synchronous alignment, the poem itself composes this picture with which it ends, a "painting" that seems the logical extreme of the art Auden depicts in "Musée de Beaux Arts":

> In Brueghel's *Icarus*, for instance: how everything turns away
> Quite leisurely from the disaster; the ploughman may
> Have heard the splash, the forsaken cry,
> But for him it was not an important failure . . .

It is likely that Jarrell has seen Auden's position as posturing, as a grimly stoic pose. He mockingly calls up the older poet's interpretation and shows how such an attitude makes possible far greater disaster. Auden's "Old Masters" are Jarrell's new ones. The Cold War, an imminent threat when "The Old and the New Masters" was composed, looms over the meticulous re-creations of Renaissance painting within the poem, upping the stakes. At risk here, Jarrell implies, is not a point of aesthetic interpretation but humankind's very survival. It does not seem too outlandish to read that "abstract understanding" as a version of what Jarrell sees around him in the daily discourse of print journalism and television news: Civilian deaths become "collateral damage," millions of lives cindered in seconds become "acceptable losses," and the escalation of nuclear arms development and deployment becomes a policy of "deterrence." All this abstraction threatens to displace the "human center"; the result is a small radioactive planet off in the corner of the canvas. The "last master," according to the terms of the poem, is no longer an artist at all but a dictatorial ego far gone into the realms of power for its own sake, and Jarrell subtly juxtaposes the master with a "subject" to reinforce this notion.

Nelson Hathcock

OMEROS

Author: Derek Walcott (1930-   )
Type of poem: Epic
First published: 1990

The Poem

Omeros is a searching, evocative 325-page modern epic poem. It is searching in the sense that it has a mission: to right the wrongs of history by illuminating shadowed chapters of events in the lives of ignored or victimized races and individuals. It is evocative in the sense that it is sophisticated, multilayered, complexly symbolic, and artfully musical. It is also vigorous human drama. Largely on the basis of its publication—but also in recognition of earlier published poetry and drama—its mixed-race author, born on the Caribbean island of St. Lucia and teaching at Boston University, was awarded the Nobel Prize in Literature on December 10, 1992.

Literally, *Omeros* gives the impression of being loosely chronological, set on St. Lucia and spanning one day—from sunrise, when fishermen are felling laurel trees to fashion into canoes, to sunset and then a full moon on the sea after a successful day of mackerel fishing. Figuratively, however, the poem is far more complicated, spanning as much as three hundred years in its many time-warp flashbacks. Walcott tells several different stories, parts of which are embedded in other stories, so that to begin to make sense of the poem the reader must attend carefully to the identity of the narrator, or rather, narrators, who are often unidentified.

The cast of characters in *Omeros* is one of simple Caribbean fishing people with derivative Greek names—Hector, Achille, Helen, Philoctete—who swill white rum, swear in French patois, bounce to Bob Marley reggae in a blockorama dance, and play out their lusts and feuds in the hot sun. There are also a pair of long-married, decent colonialist settlers, Irish homebody Maud Plunkett and former British soldier Dennis Plunkett, who have moved to St. Lucia to retire. Maud dies and is buried during the course of the poem. For a time the seductive black beauty Helen is employed in the Plunkett household, though she is dismissed for her arrogance and for stealing clothing items. Though Maud gives Helen some money out of pity for her unborn child, she refuses to reinstate her. Helen is the object of jealousy between brawny fishermen Achille and Hector, and she is uncertain which man has impregnated her. Hector gives up the sea to drive tourists around the island in his transport van. After he dies in a crash, Helen moves in with Achille to raise her baby, though the couple cannot agree on what the child should be named.

One of the poem's few non-Caribbean episodes takes place at the Standing Rock Indian Reservation right before the massacre at Wounded Knee, focusing on a minor but intriguing historical figure. Catherine Weldon, a well-heeled East Coast widow, in 1889 decided to travel west with her adolescent son under the auspices of the National Indian Defense Association. She worked for a time in Buffalo Bill Cody's touring Wild West Show, actively protested the government mistreatment of the Sioux, and served as personal helpmeet to Chief Sitting Bull. Her story, occupying fewer than twenty pages of the poem, culminates with her pitiable, solitary death on a winter night in her rocking chair, her finances depleted, her son having died of tetanus, the Sioux bent on ignoring her pleas to keep peace with the government by refusing to participate in the Ghost Dance.

The most intriguing and elusive character in the poem is the shape-shifting narrator, who suffers many things and spellbinds the reader with his protean nature. The poem is named for this figure, which is also place, sound, and object:

> *O* was the conch-shell's invocation, *mer* was
> both mother and sea in our Antillean patois,
> *os*, a grey bone, and the white surf as it crashes
> and spreads its sibilant collar on a lace shore.
> Omeros was the crunch of dry leaves, and the washes
> that echoed from a cave-mouth when the tide has ebbed.

This chameleon figure becomes, by turns of page, the ancient Greek poet Homer, an inanimate carved white marble bust, a blind old man named Seven Seas who keeps a khaki dog, Omeros the salt-sea life-force and inspiration, and Walcott the poet, who visits his mother in a nursing home, who is jilted by a promiscuous Greek lover named Antigone (whom he fruitlessly pursues throughout Boston), and who experiences a profoundly liberating sea-change that ends his midlife crisis. This transformation in poet Walcott is brought about when he follows another character, named Dante, through the St. Lucian sulfur pits known as Maleboge, a difficult, purgative journey that liberates him to own, to verbalize, and to celebrate the history and identity of his native people. They come to symbolize the dispossessed, displaced, and discriminated against peoples of all time.

Forms and Devices

Omeros is divided into seven books and sixty-four chapters, each with three parts or movements. The first book is the longest, having thirteen chapters, and the fourth book, with four chapters, is the shortest. There is an identifiable theme to each book, which is introduced near the end of the previous book. The first book, appropriately, introduces all the important characters and hints at all the major themes. Near the end of book 2, Achille is on a fishing trip and follows a sea-swift, an action that provides a segue into an important dream vision and reunion with his now-dead father in Africa in book 3. The poet narrator visits his elderly mother at the end of book 3, which sets the course for book 4, with its angst-filled present-day wanderings of the poet and the historical tragedy of the Sioux Indians right before the Battle of Wounded Knee. Book 5, even as it continues the anguished tale of the Sioux and the Ghost Dance, widens the voyages to Portugal, Spain, England, and Ireland, glimpsing black slaves, Greek slaves, and a Polish waitress in Canada, all shadows of diaspora and exodus.

Book 6 brings the narrator and the focus of the story back "home," to the island and characters of St. Lucia. It ends in an African ritual dance in the capital city of Castries.

This location sets the stage for the purgation and catharsis of the final book, in which Dennis Plunkett sees a loving vision of his dead wife in a seance, the poet reaches his inner vision and peace through a trial by fire, the sea-swift figuratively stitches up wounds in the soul of the world by joining two hemispheres together (the old world and the new), and the supremacy and eternity of the sea is affirmed and celebrated. The poem ends with the phrase "the sea was still going on," and the past progressive verb suggests that past hopes, dreams, fears, and realities will continue intentionally into the present and the future. Now and ever, the salt sea, the origin of life, offers blessing and renewed and invigorated life for those who intuit and accept it. The source of all salves for the wounds of all of the characters is, directly or indirectly, the sea.

Omeros is written in eight thousand lines of terza rima stanzas. Its meter is irregular. The rhyme scheme is often unpredictable, unlike that of traditional epics, which tend to maintain a very strict rhyme scheme and meter. Walcott's poem is full of exquisite and uncommon versification. It is an ambitious enterprise and a technical masterpiece, with rhymes varying from *rime riche* (rhyming words with identical sounds but different meanings, such as "stair" and "stare") to assonance and eye-rhyme. Walcott seems to be showing off his artistry, giving readers a catalog of all the varieties of rhyming possibilities. Yet nowhere is the language strained: It is fluid, musical, and even simple, and where appropriate it follows rhythms of conversation or evokes sounds of ocean waves.

Walcott's lines are visually, though not metrically, the same length, and the number of lines in a stanza (three) seems to be fixed, with one notable exception—an anguished passage of thirty-four lines of tetrameter couplets at the very center of the poem, where the loveless poet narrator contemplates his empty house. The form uses couplets, but the poet himself is sadly solitary. The section begins, "House of umbrage, house of fear,/ house of multiplying air/ House of memories that grow/ like shadows out of Allan Poe." This section details the heartbreak of a failed marriage and the pangs of loneliness. The poet feels trapped and cursed, his house is "unlucky," and he would "uncurse" it "by rites of genuflecting verse." He wishes that he could "unhouse" his house because it is such a hard, cold place, and the only guests are "fears." The placement of this section in the heart of the poem reveals the tragedy within the poet's heart, his anguish and angst. It is fall, a time of dying things, and the section follows episodes of various losses, abandonments, disappearances, "castaways," and "dead-end[s] of love." Following this section the poet expresses a more general nostalgia for transitory things, which is preparatory to the Catherine Weldon and Sioux Indians section.

Omeros is an epic poem that, in many significant aspects, reverses epic convention. The very writing of an epic in the late twentieth century is unusual; the long narrative form flourished with Homer, Vergil, Dante, and Johann Wolfgang von Goethe. While traditional epics begin with an invocation, *Omeros* ends with one that is both a salutation and a leave-taking:

I sang of quiet Achille, Afolabe's son,

. . . .

who had no passport, since the horizon needs none,

. . . .%0

whose end, when it comes, will be a death by water

. . . .%0

. . . I sang the only slaughter

that brought him delight, and that from necessity—

of fish, sang the channels of his back in the sun.

I sang our wide country, the Caribbean Sea.

The passage continues, "but now the idyll dies . . .// . . . let the deep hymn/ of the Caribbean continue my epilogue."

While epics usually chronicle a journey or a quest, *Omeros* is fabricated of many diverse voyages—some highly charged, others slight—that are means to a more important end: gaining meaningful insight into what matters the most—first for self, then for the world. Walcott explores why traditional historical accounts are problematic and seeks to flesh out incompleteness and inaccuracies. This is, finally, the poet-narrator's means to coming to terms with himself, to owning up to his mixed identity.

Themes and Meanings

Omeros is about memory, history, and identity, and these issues are explored from both a personal and a global perspective. An intriguing aspect of Walcott's art is his merging of elements of personal biography with global history. For example, the invalid mother whom the poem's narrator visits refers to "Roddy" and "Pam" (Walcott's siblings in real life) in speaking with him and calls him "Warwick's son" (Warwick is the actual name of Walcott's father). An important thread in the poem is the poet trying to solve a midlife crisis that is rooted both in living in an empty house and in experiencing writer's block. *Omeros* celebrates the hard-won discovery of the subject best suited to the poet's individual expression: his own island people of St. Lucia. The affirmation of parental and ancestral ties is connected with this personal and ethnic exploration. It is explored, for example, in the beginning of book 3, where Achille figuratively goes back to Africa and spends time with his father, Afolabe. Their anguished discussion of naming and identity resonates hauntingly with black slaves enduring the Middle Passage. A slave was customarily renamed by his owner at the time of purchase.

The narrator-poet tells readers that he has "stitched" wounds into his characters because "affliction is one theme/ of this work." The biggest wound of all is the most obvious: a weeping, starfish-shaped sore on Philoctetes's shin that he incurred from a rusty anchor and that he moans about throughout the entire poem. For a dollar he will display it to tourists so they can photograph it. In despair, he drinks himself into daily oblivion at the No Pain Cafe and tears out tender white yams from his own garden by the roots in frustration. Finally, blessedly, he is healed by a voodoo woman named Ma Kilman, owner of the No Pain Cafe, who bathes his leg with tincture of an elusive ill-smelling herb that she has gleaned in the forest, having followed a line of ants in her search. Significantly, the seed of the healing herb originated in Africa and was carried to St. Lucia in the beak of a sea-swift.

Bird imagery is very important in the poem: flight, crossings and criss-crossings, building bridges and connections between hemispheres, races, and generations. Maud Plunkett, who is homesick for Ireland, stitches an elaborate quilt that displays the rich variety of birds that inhabit St. Lucia, many of which have immigrated just as she has:

> The African swallow, the finch from India
> now spoke the white language of a tea-sipping tern
> with the Chinese nightingales on a shantung screen,
>
> while the Persian falcon, whose cry leaves a scar
> on the sky till it closes, saw the sand turn green,
> the dunes to sea, understudying the man-o'-war,
>
> talking the marine dialect of the Caribbean
> with nightjars, finches, and swallows, each origin
> enriching the islands to which their cries were sewn.

Maud's quilt, symbol of cultural diversity and harmony, becomes her shroud in death.

Cultural blending and melding is a central theme that infuses almost every aspect of *Omeros*. The simple Caribbean fishermen's names connect them with Greek gods. Black Helen is as beautiful and desired as her Greek counterpart who ignited a war; the poem compares them—"one marble, one ebony"—and seems to prefer the one who is "here and alive." Helen's identity as a woman is also merged with the island of St. Lucia; Walcott finds connections in the entomology of their names: "the island was once/ named Helen." Helen's promiscuous vacillation between Hector and Achille is compared with the island's having changed hands fourteen times between the French and the English before it gained its independence in 1979. The narrator-poet, of mixed racial heritage, seeks to re-enter his "reversible world," aware that his "disembodied trunk [is] split/ along the same line of reflection that halved Achille." Connecting essential halves is both method and message of the poem.

Jill B. Gidmark

ON A VIEW OF PASADENA FROM THE HILLS

Author: Yvor Winters (1900-1968)
Type of poem: Lyric
First published: 1931, in *The Journey, and Other Poems*

The Poem

"On a View of Pasadena from the Hills" is made up of seven stanzas of varying length written in heroic couplets (units of two lines of rhymed iambic pentameter that are self-contained in meaning and terminate in a full stop). The physical setting is the home of the poet's father, a man in late middle age. The speaker may be identified as a version of the poet, a man in his early thirties. As the poem begins, the poet notes the subtlety of the transition from night to day at dawn: "No light appears, though dark has mostly gone." There are no sharp distinctions between one stage and the other, yet there are boundaries and divisions. The garden is arranged in terraces supported by concrete. The poet's mind shifts to the past as he notices what is not there. The palms of his childhood have disappeared, and this observation gives rise to a vivid memory of walking in this area before the changes. However, images of "powdered ash, the sift of age" suggest that impermanence and mortality had their place in the design of things even then.

In the fifth stanza, the place is specifically identified and the poet's father is situated in that place, his home, his "phantasy of Paradise." He is also situated in time. He is approaching the last stages of a life that has included some success but has been ultimately unfulfilling, each "step . . . gained" matched by a "loss of heart," at least in the eyes of his grown son. The poet's father is also situated within his generation, his friends who "With tired ironic faces wait for death." Even at home, the father is held within limits: He is "Forbidden . . . to climb." For his part, the poet holds himself, at least to some extent, apart from the scene, knowing as he does that he will never live here. This is his father's home, not his.

In the sixth stanza, Pasadena, the California city named in the title, finally appears. Or does it? It is concealed by mist. Yet the poet senses its presence at dawn on the edge of sleep—that is, on the edge of waking. The poet also notes in the neighboring hills the evidence of the automobile culture that for some passes for progress and others revile as decline. Of such issues he has nothing to say. The poem ends neither in celebration of progress nor in nostalgia for an irretrievable past; rather, the closing lines include the marks of modernity in the larger setting, as much natural as it is anything else. The poet sees not a war between nature and civilization but a whole containing both.

The reader senses the poet's willingness to be poised on the edge between sleep and waking, night and day, past and present, nature and civilization, father and son, and life and death. His position allows him to hold these opposites in a delicate balance, acknowledging both difference and continuity. He feels no need to move to a higher level where all opposites can be reconciled and the many can finally be perceived as one. In both his poetry and his criticism, Yvor Winters has turned away from the Romantic tradition in poetry. In the resolution of this poem, he rejects a strategy of transcendence characteristic of that tradition.

Forms and Devices

The heroic couplet, the verse form adopted by Winters for "On a View of Pasadena from the Hills," dominated English poetry in the late seventeenth and eighteenth centuries, the period often referred to as the neoclassical age in English literature. It largely fell out of favor in the course of the nineteenth century, although it was still occasionally and effectively employed. By the 1930's, when Winters wrote this poem, the form had been largely abandoned as tied inextricably to the ideologies of earlier eras. Thus Winters went against the grain of contemporary poetic practice, a move he was never unwilling to make. In its days of dominance, the heroic couplet was often put to satirical or didactic use by poets such as John Dryden and Alexander Pope, its most revered masters. Winters's application of the form, however, is more reminiscent of the practice of George Crabbe, who emphasized the form's descriptive and expository possibilities. Robert Bridges, one of the few poets of the nineteenth century who excelled in couplets and a poet Winters greatly admired, may also have served as a model.

One of the attractions the heroic couplet may have for a poet is the discipline it imposes on the expression of feeling. Another is the possibility it affords for subtlety. Because the rules are so rigorous, the slightest variation can assume expressive power. For Winters, the poet must match emotion precisely to motive, to the event or occasion that gives rise to the emotion. Rhythm is an essential component of that precision, and working with and against the restraints imposed by the couplet's conventions can create the finest of rhythmic nuances. To take just one example, note the force in the first stanza of one of the poet's few deviations from the practice of ending each couplet with a full stop: "The hills/ Lie naked but not light. The darkness spills/ Down the remoter gulleys." Rhythm and darkness spill together. Furthermore, as Winters knew from the examples provided by poets who had gone before him, the closed couplet allows a cadence not dissimilar to that of the speaking voice while at the same time imposing the formality of artifice. In turning to what others might have regarded as an obsolete form, Winters escaped the vernacular of a particular time and place without abandoning the sense of actual speech.

Of the many critical utterances of Winters, perhaps none has been quoted more often, whether in agreement or disagreement, than his observation that a poem is a statement about a human experience. His adversaries have zeroed in especially on the word "statement," suggesting that it is scarcely adequate to the intensity and variety of poetry. It should be noted, therefore, that "On a View of Pasadena from the Hills," while it contains statements, is in no sense the poetry of statement. Rather, it resolutely evades any final summarizing statement, finding its resolution in a rich and ultimately ambiguous image.

Themes and Meanings

In acknowledging the artifice of terraces as "bastions of our pastorals," Winters affirms a tension. In one sense, the pastoral is readily associated with the natural, and bastions, the work of human hands, are restraints. To a certain kind of Romantic temperament, the imposition of restraints on nature is unnatural, and "unnatural" is the strongest possible term of condemnation. For Winters's classical temperament, no such issue arises. The cultivation of nature, inevitably involving some measure of restraint, is simply one of the things that human beings do. The gardener arranges the garden in terraces supported by concrete, and the poet organizes the stuff of human emotion into the twenty syllables, regular stresses, and recurrent rhymes of the couplet. Moreover, in these activities poet and gardener imitate a quality of nature that Romantic temperaments sometimes overlook: the regularity suggested in the "metronomic" pulsing of fish's mouths. This, says the poet, uttering what may be his strongest term of approbation, is "true."

Winters, then, refuses to perceive life in the sentimental terms of a corrupt Romanticism. If what lies before the poet is not a vernal wood but a mowed lawn, the poet's work is to observe that lawn so closely that he finds the life in it as Winters does here. "On a View of Pasadena from the Hills" implies a deep recognition and acceptance of limits as a part of life. The ultimately defining limit is death, awaited by the poet's father and his friends and, after all, by the rest of humanity as well. This implies that even the closest human relationships, between parent and child for example, do not and should not exclude boundaries. Winters is exquisitely aware that he shares with his father all that belongs to the human condition, but he recognizes as well that he is not his father. In the light of that knowledge, he views his father's circumstances with a sympathy that is not less honest or authentic because it is disillusioned.

As for Pasadena, the poet finally does not view it because it is concealed by mist. Yet it is nonetheless there, and a view of Pasadena concealed remains at some level a view of Pasadena. This is, the reader may feel, very much a poem about boundaries, limits, the edge, and the place between. It is not, however, a poem about uncertainty. To recognize the individual reality of whatever is on either side of the boundary is not, for this poet, to surrender to relativism. If this poem is listened to properly, it is possible to hear in it the affirmation of a man so little a slave to fashion that he was proud, in the middle of the twentieth century, to declare himself an absolutist.

W. P. Kenney

ON ALL THAT GLIDES IN THE AIR

Author: Lars Gustafsson (1936-   )
Type of poem: Lyric
First published: 1984, as "Om allt som ännu svävar," in *Fåglarna, och andra dikter*;
    English translation collected in *The Stillness of the World Before Bach*, 1988

The Poem

"On All That Glides in the Air" is a short lyric poem of forty-two lines divided into three unequal stanzas originally written in Swedish. The title of the poem suggests a casual meditation on the joys of floating through the air. When a bird in flight appears to be resting, it is considered to be "gliding," an apparently effortless motion. However, a closer examination of the poem's three stanzas suggests that "gliding" has multiple meanings, many of which are not as benign as they appear on the surface.

The first line in the first stanza implies that the narrator is expecting to die soon because he says, "My grave is still nowhere to be seen." With no clear resting place, the narrator is forced to continue searching and gliding. He is joined in the latter activity by other beings: companion gliders, companions at rest, and even those who are already dead. The image is of a vast landscape in which all beings, both dead and alive, join together in one continuous motion. Although the speaker admits that there is no word to express the image that he sees in his mind's eye, he compares this gliding to the sailing of a balloonist through the sky in an "ocean of air." The speaker abruptly shifts to the second-person point of view in a warning to the reader: "this ocean of air is yourself." In one quick turn of phrase, the speaker moves from a dreamy, peaceful image of a hot air balloon floating through exterior space to a chilling reference to the loneliness of interior space.

In the second stanza, the narrator contemplates the precarious border between life and death as he recalls an early-morning experience in a diving pool. The view from the high dive is both exhilarating and terrifying. Looking at the deep, clear water gives the sensation of floating through the air, but there is also an awareness that an uncontrolled fall so far from the water would mean almost certain death. In this context, the speaker thinks of gliding as a multilayered experience whereby one falls and glides at the same time, the fall turning into a glide that is somehow aided by an unknown force. However, there is no assurance that the fall will be broken, so exhilaration becomes inseparably mixed with fear. The recollection of the view through the swimmer's goggles reminds the speaker of another way of seeing, the way that observers see a two-dimensional Renaissance canvas. Because of the technique of linear perspective, the canvas appears to create a three-dimensional world. Not surprisingly, it is the depiction of birds in flight that most interests the speaker. He says that the birds come alive precisely because they are placed in a kind of in-between state, "between earth and air, between light and shade,/ between water and land." The birds, looking "like reckless punctuation marks," are not unlike human beings struggling to discover their interior existence that they can never see or completely understand.

In the last stanza, the narrator continues contrasting images of positive and negative with "signs" gliding over "white pages" and "rooks" (black birds of prey) gliding over "snow." However, at issue is more than just a comparison of good and evil. The narrator returns to the landscape image where "everything" is both gliding and standing "as the angels stand/ in an unthinkable motion," just as the world itself, although it appears to be immobile, is actually in continual rotation.

Forms and Devices

In "On All That Glides in the Air," Lars Gustafsson's most obvious technique is the repetition of words and phrases. For example, the word "glide" is used six times, "glides" is used twice, and "gliding" is used four times. Another repetition is the phrase "ocean of air," which is used three times. These are important images that lead to the poem's central concept. Another device is counterpoint, which, in music, refers to the combination of two or more independent melodies into a single harmonic texture. Gustafsson uses words and word variations to create a kind of rhythm. For example, "swimming becomes gliding" and "living with all that lives" are variations of sound that contribute to the poem's central paradox that humans are all parts of one whole. Another poetic technique is the use of simile, which the speaker uses to compare his movement through the air to the motion of a hot air balloon through the sky. In still another image, Gustafsson likens the apparent flight of birds in a Renaissance painting to "reckless punctuation marks." Finally, the motion of all humanity is compared to the nameless "flight of the world."

What makes the poem intriguing and gives it tension is the use of irony or the contrast between expectation and fulfillment. The first stanza begins with a familiar description—the soaring motion of birds as they move through the sky—and ends with a suggestion that the great expanse is actually interior rather than exterior. In the second stanza, the narrator suggests that the *trompe l'oeil* (trick of the eye) that painters use to create linear perspective is also a trick that humans use to fool themselves about the true nature of existence. The third stanza, which begins with yet another gliding image, ends with a haunting pun on "flight" to suggest that the world both glides and escapes humans in the same motion.

Themes and Meanings

"On All That Glides in the Air" is a poem in the Romantic tradition that considers the immediate, emotional impact of an experience to be closer to a real understanding of truth than the logical, reasoned reaction to the same experience. For a Romantic writer, the images of floating, gliding, and soaring represent a release from the natural, pragmatic world and are therefore closer to nature, to God, or to previously unknowable truths. The Romantic sensibility is further reinforced by Gustafsson's reference to the super-analytical Renaissance painters' re-creation of the visual world not as a work of beauty but as a "childish trick." However, "All That Glides in the Air" is far from a Romantic poem because the predominant images are not positive and optimistic but neutral and unsettling, particularly at the end of stanzas 1 and 2 where the physical freedom of open spaces turns inward to subjugate the human psyche.

In the passage comparing swimming and gliding, the feeling of uncertainty is reinforced by the recognition of the close relationship between life and death. One false step on the diving board could cause a fatal fall, but even that free fall might change to a glide "by something invisible." The suggestion that free-falling and gliding are intertwined is strengthened by the image of the painted birds that are frozen in their landscapes between the juxtaposed "earth and air," "light and shade," and "water and land." Just as perspective in a painting is more than the technique of drawing straightedge lines directly to a single vanishing point, the truth of existence is more than simply living and dying or motion and stasis. It is in the passage on art that the narrator shifts from the first person "I" to the more inclusive "we," which suggests that the contrasting experiences are universal; at the same time, however, it is up to all humans to discover "the interior/ of their own picture." Unfortunately, there are no clear rules or maps for such an exploration.

The most problematic passage occurs in the last stanza in which the narrator comments that "signs glide over the white pages." At first glance, the word "signs" appears to refer to symbols or letters on a piece of paper. However, "sign" can also mean "emblem," "mark," or "omen." The latter seems to fit best in the light of the next image in which birds of prey glide over white snow. Next, the birds of prey are juxtaposed with another type of flying being: angels. The paradoxical comment that all beings both glide and stand "as the angels stand/ in an unthinkable motion" suggests that all motion, like existence itself, is both contradictory and indescribable. There is "no name" for either mortal existence or for the existence of the world. Gustafsson, then, uses varied images of gliding to suggest the complex, paradoxical nature of existence not only for humankind but also for all living things.

Sandra Hanby Harris

ON INHABITING AN ORANGE

Author: Josephine Miles (1911-1985)
Type of poem: Meditation
First published: 1935; collected in *Lines at Intersection*, 1939

The Poem

"On Inhabiting an Orange" is a short, low-key poem about the discrepancy between hopes and actuality. It briefly, dryly, and precisely notes that travelers never arrive anywhere near their exalted destinations but rather follow the route defined by the shape of the globe on which they walk. Like other poems in Josephine Miles's first major collection, *Lines at Intersection*, "On Inhabiting an Orange" makes use of geometrical imagery. In this poem, Miles makes an extended metaphor of a geometrical puzzle. Miles's early work is preoccupied with shapes and figures and sometimes plays with multiple meanings of geometrical terms. This approach led some of her early critics to criticize her work for lack of passion; because the emotion in a Miles poem is never on the surface, they claim that her poetry is more interesting than moving. However, this philosophical poem does have feeling that is not expressed directly but is carefully confined within the imagery.

"On Inhabiting an Orange" takes as its basis the paradox that one cannot walk straight (in a theoretical sense) upon a sphere. The curved surface of the earth disrupts the projected straight line, drawing the walker's path toward its origin. Because the earth is a sphere, humans "inhabit an orange." At first glance, the title might suggest living within a sphere, but this is not what is intended. The earth dwellers live on the surface of the orange, forced by its shape to travel paths unimagined by the walker. The poem speaks in the first person plural, using a casual editorial "we" that includes the whole human race: "All our roads go nowhere." Because humans are on the surface of the sphere, their roads do not, in fact, go anywhere beyond that surface—maps are "curled" like a piece of paper around an orange to make the streets conform to the curved surface. The demands of this geography make all trips intended to go somewhere simply fall back against the roundness. Instead of the "metric advance" people intend and expect from forward motion, their footsteps "lapse into arcs." The circumstances of gravity and geography prevent advance. Journeys forward toward space cannot be undertaken—the physical conditions simply prohibit their progress: "All our journeys nearing Space/ Skirt it with care,/ Shying at the distances/ Present in air."

Travelers, of course, intend to follow the imaginary lines their minds envision, and they thus set forth "blithely" with the goal of some kind of exalted arrival; they do not learn from their experiences. Although they are "travel-stained and worn," they remain "Erect and sure," their attitudes untouched by the reality they experience. They do not ever realize that they cannot follow their hearts out into the distances and that they are constantly forced to make "down the roads of Earth/ Endless detour." That the lines in their heads do not correspond with their footpaths does not faze or discourage them. The contrast between ideal and real, straight and curved, what is expected and what happens, creates the central irony of the poem.

Forms and Devices

"On Inhabiting an Orange" is a seventeen-line poem with an idiosyncratic form: The second and fourth lines of the first three four-line stanzas are rhymed, while the last stanza has five lines and rhymes *abccb*. The first and third lines of each stanza are longer, while the second and last lines of each, the rhyming lines, contain only two stressed syllables. There are many trochaic feet (single syllables followed by unstressed syllables); this falling rhythm seems particularly appropriate to the content. The last stanza contains the extra longer line but otherwise follows the pattern.

This is a straightforward poem consisting of an extended metaphor announced in the title and developed throughout the poem. It is similar to the Metaphysical poetry of John Donne, George Herbert, and others in the use of the extended metaphor or conceit, although Miles's conceits are much simpler. Miles, who was greatly influenced by the poetry of Donne, liked her poetry to have the fine-tuned precision that the Metaphysical poets found in the detailed comparison of apparently dissimilar objects and thoughts. Indeed, the comparison in "On Inhabiting an Orange" recalls the drawing compass image that concludes Donne's "A Valediction Forbidding Mourning," in which the central pole of the woman's love perfects the path of the speaker, who is joined to her as the two halves of the compass are joined. However, the circle of the inhabitants of the orange is not a happy circle; their deflection from their hoped path is made by circumstance, not love. Even the bumpy figure of the orange contrasts with Donne's perfect circle.

The rhythms tend to suggest falling short of high hopes or noble goals. The lines tend to curve back like the footsteps of the frustrated travelers who really wish to leave where they are and arrive somewhere else but cannot because their roads go "nowhere." The short lines seem to fall short, to be pulled back from a high enterprise. The additional line in the last stanza adds a meditative tone and adds to the sense of closure ironically provided by the final deliberately inconclusive image of "endless detour." Though some critics scoff at the notion of imitative form, the poem may be seen to reflect the progress of someone attempting to travel in a straight line, constantly pulled by gravity away from this goal.

Themes and Meanings

"On Inhabiting an Orange" is a playfully ironic poem. It uses common terms and concepts of geometry in an attempt to describe human disappointment in its failure to attain goals. While this poem is not very passionate in tone, it does neatly describe the irony of the human failure to recognize limitations (in the metaphor, the inability of straight walkers to see the curves that control their direction and prevent them from making any real progress). Thus the walkers always have high hopes, and, even though they should know better, their minds follow the stars while their feet follow the curve of the earth. The attitude expressed in the poem is of resignation and regret.

The realization that the environment is not made for human aspirations has been treated by many other writers and poets. One of the most vocal of these was Stephen Crane, whose poetry and prose on the subject ("The Open Boat" and "A man said to the universe") is widely known, but Miles's attitude is less bitter. She presents the problem as universal. The failure of the world to conform to human desires is simply accepted as how things are.

The poem also invites the reader to play with its meanings and explore its implications. To be earthbound means to always walk in circles, to make endless detours away from a goal that is not earthbound. The figure of Donne and his ideal circle lurks in the background, providing a subtle, ironic contrast to the tired and unproductive circles walked in this poem. Other geometrical issues arise: What happens to parallel lines if they are traced on a sphere? What is the poem's concept of dimensionality? What is angularity if there are no straight lines? What is the true difference between the two-dimensional map and the three-dimensional world?

The image of the earth as an orange is also provocative. An orange is a fruit meant to be eaten, its peel discarded. Is the outside shape of the orange the only factor to be considered in this metaphor? Besides being perishable, the orange is an imperfect sphere, and it sometimes has shades and shadows on its skin that resemble those on a globe. Is this relevant? The simplicity of the poem invites examination of its terms. The pleasure of this poem is in how it engages the reader. The easily grasped and appropriate geometric metaphor attracts the reader's attention, and then the delight of the intellectual game takes over as the reader attempts to push the comparison into other areas besides those specifically noted. The spareness of the poem contributes to its effect as a puzzle designed to entertain as well as present a well-known perspective on the human situation. In "On Inhabiting an Orange," Miles provides an extended metaphor not unlike those of the Metaphysical poets but without the difficulty of Donne and the others and with more room for individual interpretation and intellectual play.

Janet McCann

ON LOOKING INTO SYLVIA PLATH'S COPY OF
GOETHE'S *FAUST*

Author: Diane Ackerman (1948-   )
Type of poem: Elegy
First published: 1985; collected in *Jaguar of Sweet Laughter: New and Selected Poems*, 1991

The Poem

"On Looking into Sylvia Plath's Copy of Goethe's *Faust*" is a short poem in free verse with one stanza of nineteen lines and a second stanza with fourteen lines. The title of the poem makes two allusions that are expanded and explored throughout the rest of the poem. In the title, Diane Ackerman refers to Sylvia Plath, the promising young American poet who committed suicide in 1963 at age thirty. She also refers to Johann Wolfgang von Goethe's play *Faust: Eine Tragödie* (1808; *The Tragedy of Faust*, 1823).

The first stanza is a direct address by the poet to Plath: "You underlined the 'jugglery of flame'/ with ink sinewy and black as an ocelot." Ackerman identifies Plath with Faust, a medieval alchemist whose story has been retold most notably by the English playwright Christopher Marlowe and later by Goethe. Faust's tragic flaw was his insatiable desire to know the unmediated truth of the universe. Like Faust, Plath explored the natural world for authentic experience. In the first stanza, Ackerman portrays Plath as "keen for Faust's appetite, not Helen's beauty." Plath looked to the natural world for answers, dissecting each part of life with words. Ackerman details Plath's transformation into "the doll of insight . . ./ to whom nearly all lady poets write." According to Ackerman, Plath was alternately angry and wistful. Within the characterization of Plath, however, are chilling references to her own self-destructiveness: "You wanted to unlock the weather system/ in your cells, and one day you did."

The second stanza shifts focus to the speaker. Whereas the first stanza has four lines beginning with the word "you," the second stanza has three lines beginning with the word "I." In shifting the focus, Ackerman connects herself to Plath as naturalist and poet. Ackerman, whose writings include several long prose works on natural science, seems to identify with Plath's "nomad curiosity." What Ackerman admires most about Plath is not her pain but her ability to see and report on the world with "cautionless ease." In line 25, Ackerman reveals her mistaken thoughts about Plath: She had thought that Plath had come to terms with her existence. Line 31, however, returns to Faustian imagery in order to correct Ackerman's mistaken assumptions: "But you were your own demonology,/ balancing terror's knife on one finger,/ until you numbed, and the edge fell free."

Forms and Devices

An elegy is a meditation, often one that mourns the death of another individual. Although Ackerman does not follow the rules of meter and rhyme common to classic elegy, she does employ a number of devices to give her poem a decidedly elegiac tone. Through the use of apostrophe, Ackerman turns away from her audience and addresses the dead poet directly, speaking to her as "you." She uses images from the natural world to draw her picture of Plath: The ink Plath uses to underline the text is "sinewy and black as an ocelot," and her cells contain "a weather system." Furthermore, Ackerman describes the pleasures Plath took in life, including collecting bees, cooking, and dressing simply. She also identifies Plath's talents and her tragic flaws. Finally, Ackerman reveals that she does not mourn Plath for the pain she "wore as a shroud" but for her "keen naturalist's eye." It is Plath's talent as a poet, not her tragic life, that ranks highest in Ackerman's estimation, a stance that differentiates Ackerman from other "lady poets."

Another device that Ackerman uses effectively in this poem is the pairing of oppositions; by doing so, she emphasizes the paradoxes of Plath's life and helps explain Plath's inevitable suicide. For example, early in the poem she opposes "Faust's appetite" and "Helen's beauty," suggesting the mind/body split with which Plath struggled. Immediately after describing Plath as "armed and dangerous," she describes her as "the doll of insight." Dolls are without passion and without power; they are the creation of someone else and are certainly not armed and dangerous. In addition, Ackerman uses the strange image of "a morbid Santa Claus who could die on cue." It would seem that the gift Plath gives to "lady poets" is her death; that is, it is her suicide, not her poetry, that offers inspiration to would-be poets. In the second stanza, Ackerman continues the use of oppositions. In lines 23 and 24, Ackerman opposes mind and body by portraying Plath's mind as something like a knife sliding "into the soft flesh of an idea." Finally, Ackerman opposes "a hot image" with "cool words." This opposition is at the heart of Ackerman's notion of poetics: Authentic experience must be rendered intelligible to a reader through words.

Themes and Meanings

"On Looking Into Sylvia Plath's Copy of Goethe's *Faust*" is more than an elegy for Plath. It is also an exploration of two poets, Plath and Ackerman, and their notions of poetry. Through the use of allusion, Ackerman expands and widens the scope of her poem; however, in order for readers to understand the poem, they must know something about Plath's life, work, and death, and about Goethe's *The Tragedy of Faust*. Plath, a graduate of Smith College in Massachusetts, had her first poem published when she was a child. After that, she wrote hundreds of poems. She married the English poet Ted Hughes and the couple had two children. In the semiautobiographical novel *The Bell Jar* (1963), she chronicles her own struggle with depression and attempted suicide. On February 11, 1963, alone and ill in a London flat, her marriage in ruins, Plath killed herself by sticking her head into the oven and turning on the gas.

The recognition of Plath's talent as a poet has grown in the years since her death, and Ackerman's careful characterization of Plath reveals close attention to her poetry. For example, Ackerman writes that Plath "undressed the flesh/ in word mirrors." This line alludes to the poem "Mirror," in which Plath, speaking as the mirror, writes, "A woman bends over me/ Searching my reaches for what she really is." This line suggests that words can somehow mirror reality in such a way that a reader can find truth in poetry. Likewise, Ackerman writes that Plath "wanted/ to be a word on the lips of the abyss," a reference to the creation story according to the Gospel of John: "In the beginning was the Word." This reference speaks the belief that words can create worlds *ex nihilo* just as God created the world out of the abyss.

In the most important allusion in the poem, Ackerman links Plath with *The Tragedy of Faust*, a play about a medieval scholar who makes a pact with the devil in order to obtain knowledge, wealth, and power. Faust's deal requires Mephistopheles to give him whatever he wants of earthly pleasures, but Faust will forfeit his life and soul if he ever stops striving to experience more, if he ever becomes satisfied with what he has. In the poem, "Faust's appetite" refers to his longing to know the world directly, something Ackerman also attributes to Plath.

It would be a mistake, however, to suggest that this poem is only about Plath. Ackerman is known for her intense curiosity and her sensory appetite. She longs to explore the natural world and lay its secrets bare. Consequently, some of the same images and allusions she associates with Plath appear in other poems Ackerman has written. For example, the ocelot image from line 2 surfaces in another poem from *Jaguar of Sweet Laughter*: In "Dinner at the Waldorf," Ackerman writes, "Unleash me and I am an ocelot/ all appetite and fur." Even more telling, Ackerman's earlier collection of poems is called *Lady Faustus* (1983). In the title poem she writes, "I rage to know/ what beings like me, stymied by death/ and leached by wonder, hug those campfires night allows,/ aching to know the fate of us all." This is the theme of much of her work: the desire to know the natural world directly and to learn the truth of existence. Thus when Ackerman writes that she thought Plath had "found serenity in the plunge/ of a hot image into cool words" and that she thought that Plath had taken "the pledge/ that sunlight makes to living things," it seems likely that she is writing to herself, for this certainly describes how Ackerman has come to terms with her overwhelming desire to know. For Ackerman, the tragedy of Plath's life is not her suicide but rather her numbness, her growing inability to experience life's terror and joy.

Diane Andrews Henningfeld

ON MR. MILTON'S "PARADISE LOST"

Author: Andrew Marvell (1621-1678)
Type of poem: Lyric
First published: 1674, in the second edition of *Paradise Lost*

The Poem

Andrew Marvell's poem chronicles his reactions to the artistic merit of John Milton's *Paradise Lost* (1667) in seven verse paragraphs of fifty-four rhymed iambic pentameter lines. The opening sentence forms a grammatical unit of ten lines. The remaining lines, marked with a grammatical pause at the end of each couplet, follow the poetic practice of end-stopped couplets.

Initially, Marvell contrasts Milton's "slender Book" with its "vast Design," its Christian topic of salvation history and its cosmic scope of infinite time and space. He fears that Milton will mar or disfigure "sacred Truths" by expressing them through, or by confining them within, the devices of an epic poem, a pagan or nonbiblical art form. Also, Marvell deals bluntly with Milton's blindness, mentioning it in the first line as well as in lines 9-10 and lines 43-44. Milton had become blind at least fourteen years prior to the first publication of *Paradise Lost* in 1667. Marvell assumes that Milton's blindness may have had something to do with his choice of a biblical "Argument" or subject. Tentatively, he questions Milton's "Intent," comparing Milton's motives in writing the poem to those of the biblical Samson, who sought "to revenge his sight."

As Marvell then begins to reflect upon his experience of reading, he grows "less severe." He favors the poet's "Project," but he fears that Milton will not succeed, given the inherent difficulty of the subject matter. Milton's poem concerns truths beyond physical nature and beyond human comprehension. He might, for example, leave his readers "perplex'd" with matters of thought and faith, doctrines involving paradoxes and simplicities. In addition, Marvell associates Milton's epic with the contemporary literary scene. He imagines that someone less skillful will imitate Milton's poem by writing a play based upon it. He seems to refer to John Dryden, who had recently written a dramatic version of *Paradise Lost* in rhymed verse entitled *The State of Innocence, and Fall of Man* (1677).

In his next paragraph, Marvell unexpectedly addresses Milton directly, speaking with deep respect and sympathy. He now realizes that a view of the poem as a whole demonstrates its artistic perfection. Consequently, he apologizes to Milton for his "causeless" doubts or speculations. He believes that Milton's artistic achievement is so great that other writers will have to work within the frame of reference Milton has laid down, even though *Paradise Lost* will demonstrate "their Ignorance or Theft." Also, Marvell praises the "Majesty" of Milton's poem, which "Draws the Devout, deterring the Profane." He believes that Milton's handling of religious truths within the medium of a pagan epic leaves those truths as well as Milton himself "inviolate." Moreover, Milton's sustained elevation of style and his ability to handle large and fearsome truths leave his readers awed and delighted because he sings "with so much gravity and ease."

Marvell specifically commends Milton's powers of mind and determination. Earlier in the poem, he had called Milton "blind, yet bold," as well as "strong." Blindness had not diminished Milton's poetic ambition, daring, or capability. In the sixth paragraph, Marvell asserts that "Heav'n" must have offset Milton's loss of physical sight with the power of prophecy. In the last paragraph, Marvell defends Milton's decision to reject rhyme at a time when the popular taste called for it. Other poets, such as Marvell himself have used rhyme as ornament or fashion. Rhyme, however, seems trivial next to the unrhymed grandeur of *Paradise Lost*. Milton's blank verse is as sublime as his theme; it does not need the support of rhyme.

Forms and Devices

As Marvell recounts the way *Paradise Lost* unfolded itself to him, his thoughts evolve dramatically from doubt to resolution. He begins by addressing readers and ends by addressing Milton himself. Although a personal friend of Milton and a professional colleague in the Cromwellian government, Marvell takes a detached, agile, skeptical, and reflective stance toward Milton's poem. As a critic seeking to illuminate Milton's epic for himself and for other readers, he maintains his integrity and a sense of perspective. He reads the poem carefully, assimilates the overall meaning, and describes, analyzes, and evaluates both substance and style. He candidly expresses his fears regarding the main features of *Paradise Lost* and Milton's own motivation in writing it.

In addition, Marvell maintains his independence as a poet. For example, he knows that Milton virtually created a new poetic medium of narrative blank verse and acknowledges its superiority to rhyme. Nevertheless, he does not abandon rhyme in praising Milton's unrhymed verse. Instead, with gentle irony he asks Milton to overlook his rhyme. Once he has grasped the poem as a whole, Marvell realizes that his doubts, though well intended, are "causeless." He does not, however, explain the exact reasons for his change of mind. He conveys his conclusions through assertion and through a change of attitude or tone. He demonstrates the assurance that grows out of wide literary knowledge and a principled, independent stance. His praise of Milton communicates itself as accurate and sincere, rendered by someone qualified to give it.

Marvell uses blind heroic figures of the past to convey his transition from doubt to certainty. For example, when Marvell compares Milton's poetic strength to Samson's physical strength, he suggests that Milton might have misused his abilities, perhaps to bring down and not build up the "sacred Truths" of Christianity. Marvell's mention of Samson is of biographical, political, and literary significance. Milton had published *Samson Agonistes* in 1671. In this lyrical drama, Milton's Samson becomes a heroic deliverer who brings God great glory. Marvell's reference to Samson may not be entirely negative. In lines 44 and 45, Marvell follows Milton's own comparison of himself to Tiresias in *Paradise Lost*. Tiresias, a blind man from Greek mythology, was rewarded with prophecy. Marvell suggests that Milton is similar to Samson but is perhaps more similar to Tiresias (even though Tiresias was not a biblical figure) because he exemplifies heroic achievement in the service of heaven. *Paradise Lost* results from divine influence working through an extraordinary individual. Marvell has no doubts about the purity of Milton's motives or his intent.

Themes and Meanings

Marvell's poem concerns fundamental questions of whether or not Milton can artistically combine the "sacred Truths" of Christianity with the devices of a pagan epic. Marvell recognizes Milton's imaginative, intellectual, and moral challenges, which stagger the mind. For example, as with all his major poems, Milton's epic is a form of biblical explanation. It involves "*Messiah* Crown'd, God's Reconcil'd Decree,/ Rebelling Angels, the Forbidden Tree." Milton cannot redefine biblical meanings, put strains upon the text of scripture, or inject personal, unwarranted, or offensive elements. He must impress Christian beliefs into the mind and memory of his readers without violating the letter or spirit of scripture. Faith, however, guides the apprehension of religious truths. Marvell fears that a presentation of Christian mysteries in poetic terms may confuse matters of thought and faith or that the attempt to do so may be vain. In addition, the restrictions of the ancient epic form might lower "sacred Truths" to the level of a "Fable and an old Song," an amusement or curiosity in which the moral content is not well integrated into the work itself. Furthermore, Milton outdoes all previous epic poets in the cosmic setting of his poem. The poem develops against a background of "Heav'n, Hell, Earth, Chaos, All"—all the regions and all the time known to human imagination and experience as well as regions and time beyond human conceptual range. Milton must describe both natural and supernatural environments and the characters who inhabit them or who are shaped by them. Marvell has good reason to question Milton's intent; too many factors must combine to make the poem successful. Milton could easily lose artistic control of his material.

Nevertheless, after considering the imaginative challenges Milton faced and his response to them, Marvell fully approves of Milton's artistry: "Thou hast not miss'd one thought that could be fit,/ And all that was improper dost omit." The "Majesty" that reigns through Milton's poem indicates that Milton had maintained the decorum required by his subject matter and the epic genre. Marvell wonders how Milton could have stretched his mind sufficiently to express truths and situations beyond direct human experience. He uses the word "sublime" to describe the elevated nature of Milton's poem and its grand subject matter, a term critics have associated with it ever since. Marvell's poem is one of the first responses to *Paradise Lost* and one of the first critical recognitions of an individual English literary work.

Timothy C. Miller

ON SHAKESPEARE

Author: John Milton (1608-1674)
Type of poem: Lyric
First published: 1632, as "An Epitaph on the Admirable Dramaticke Poet, W. Shake-speare," in *Mr. William Shakespeare's Comedies, Histories, and Tragedies*; collected in *Poems of Mr. John Milton*, 1645

The Poem

"On Shakespeare" is a sixteen-line epitaph written in iambic pentameter or heroic couplets, an unusual meter for John Milton's poetry. In English verse, the heroic couplet was not a smoothly honed stanza until after Milton's poetic career had concluded. The poem was originally published under the title "An Epitaph on the Admirable Dramaticke Poet, W. Shakespeare," though the title Milton used in the 1645 edition of his lyric poems has been accepted ever since. The epitaph is related to the classical epigram, a brief lyric that includes pithy wit and polished verses. An epitaph, usually a brief poem, deals with a serious or philosophical subject in a witty manner. The poems were often written on the occasion of a death, as in Milton's "An Epitaph on the Marchioness of Winchester." The genre designation suggests a tombstone inscription, though few known poetic epitaphs actually served that purpose. William Shakespeare's own four-line epitaph, inscribed on his gravestone in Stratford's Holy Trinity Church, represents a notable exception. In Milton's lengthy epitaph on the marchioness of Winchester, he describes her family background, details the circumstances surrounding her death, and proclaims her heavenly reward for suffering. However, since Shakespeare's death occurred fourteen years before the composition date, Milton makes no allusion to death and mourning in the poem commemorating him. Instead he centers upon the immortality that art offers.

An occasional lyric (one written for a specific event), "On Shakespeare" was composed in 1630 to appear among the many poems prefatory to the second folio of Shakespeare's *Works*. In all likelihood, Milton was invited to contribute to the collection, possibly by his friend Henry Lawes. Commendatory poems were designed to set a tone of celebration for the event and to praise the author for his artistic achievement. Appropriately, the poem assumes an audience of readers rather than theatergoers. Like other contributors to the collection, Milton celebrates the power of poetry and the fame it brings its creators by endowing them with a form of immortality.

The opening six lines pose questions concerning Shakespeare's need for a monument. Initially, the poem implies that "my Shakespeare" needs no conventional monument such as a pyramid. Laboriously piled stones and pyramids, Milton proclaims, are not needed to cover or house Shakespeare's "hallowed relics." The usual monuments, however elaborate, can offer only "weak witness" of Shakespeare's name, whereas his works make him a "son of memory" and "heir of fame." Still, these exaggerated images of elaborate memorials are fictional, and Milton would have known that Shakespeare's actual grave was below ground, covered by a marble slab bearing a modest inscription. Milton's second question implies that Shakespeare is preserved through memory and fame, and the imagery of relics and the hint of succession distance the poem from the poet's death.

Shakespeare's works are responsible for the immortality that assures undying fame. The second portion of the poem (lines 7-14) opens with the ambiguous line "Thou in our wonder and astonishment," whose meaning is clarified within the context of subsequent lines. Initially, it would appear to mean that the bard has created his own monument to arouse the "wonder" of readers. However, "astonishment" is proleptic, foreshadowing the idea that the works affect the readers and thus create Shakespeare's genuine monument. Before the works' effect can be celebrated, however, the poem praises the creative power of the author. Milton asserts that the bard has surpassed "slow endeavoring art" to produce the fluent, easy numbers of genius. This achievement places him in a class above that of ordinary writers.

Having characterized the seeming ease of Shakespeare's art, the poem shifts its focus to concentrate on the effects of poetry on the audience. Shakespeare's art, it asserts, leaves an impression on hearts like that of an engraving on marble. Readers are so deeply impressed by the works, the "unvalued [invaluable] book," that their imaginations are suspended as if rapt in meditation. The effect has been a kind of ecstasy that suspends all thoughts and transforms them into marble. This power to move the emotions and overwhelm the imagination ("fancy") represents the important monument and Shakespeare's lasting achievement. Through art, Shakespeare has attained the ability to move or transform his audience, a feat associated from antiquity with divine power. In effect, his art has become the poet's monument, and this outcome is of greater significance than sepulchral pomp. In a witty, paradoxical conclusion (lines 15-16), the poem proclaims this ability so rare that, for a similar monument, even kings would wish to die.

Forms and Devices

In a poem concerned with fame and immortality, Milton appropriately employs an impressive number of images relating to death and monuments: "bones," "relics," "pyramids," "monument," "stones," and "marble." Thus the images create a sense of tangible durability associated with lasting parts of the person ("relics" and "bones"), with the materials that form monuments ("stones" and "marble"), and with the monuments themselves. They fittingly remove the tone from the immediacy of death to focus on posthumous fame. The concrete images, however, subtly shift to metaphor when the poem attributes everlasting qualities to Shakespeare's works and their effects, denying the view that fame rests upon tangible objects. The enduring "monument" created by Shakespeare consists of his works. Thus the imagery reinforces Milton's early denial of the need for conventional aids to fame. By contrasting the concrete images of fame to the metaphors that suggest a greater fame, the poem asserts that the more important kind of monument assures memory through successive generations.

The achievement is reinforced through an allusion to Greek "Delphic lines" (line 12), intimating that Shakespeare's artistry rivals that of the Greek classics. The allusion may well hark back to Milton's earlier epithet "great heir of fame," suggesting that the bard either writes in the immortal tradition of the classics or that he merits the respect accorded classical poets. At the very least, Milton recognizes that Shakespeare, like the ancients, has staying power. For any contemporary poet, this was high praise indeed. Furthermore, references to "pomp" and "kings" in the final lines accord Shakespeare a magisterial place among poets.

The subdued point of view moves from first person singular to the plurals "our" and "us" as the poem shifts to the effects of reading the poetry. By identifying himself with others, the poem's persona effectively becomes a spokesman for numerous readers. By the same token, through limiting and subordinating the role of the speaker, Milton achieves a tone of assurance and majesty appropriate to the power he celebrates in the subject.

Themes and Meanings

"On Shakespeare" develops the primary theme of immortality through artistic creation. A commonplace idea in Renaissance and seventeenth century poetry, it is pervasive in Shakespeare's sonnets, which celebrate a poet's power to endow the subject with immortality. The theme also commonly appears in the poems prefatory to various folio editions of Shakespeare's poetic works. Its widespread use, however, does not mean that it lacked special meaning for Milton. From his student days at Cambridge University, Milton made fame through art a motif in his lyric poetry, and he later introduced the theme into his prose works as well. As one who sought fame through poetic achievement, he found it congenial to proclaim that Shakespeare had already attained it. However, Milton surpasses the conventional treatment of the theme by adding another minor but pervasive motif in Renaissance poetry, that of metamorphosis or transformation. Evidence of Shakespeare's genius is to be found in the bard's ability to transform readers, to take them out of themselves with wonder and admiration and, metaphorically, render them marble. Milton realized that the power of transformation traditionally represented a divine attribute and a source of inspiration.

A further significant theme emerges from Milton's characterization of Shakespeare's creative imagination. Though his references to Shakespeare are limited, Milton became an early proponent of the view that Shakespeare was a naturally gifted genius, more a product of nature than of art. At its extreme, it depicted the bard as a pure and unlearned genius surpassing all the dicta of art. As applied to Shakespeare, the point of view can be traced to the writings of Shakespeare's contemporary Ben Jonson, though Jonson, the consummate artist, suggests in *Timber: Or Discoveries Made upon Men and Matter* (1641) that Shakespeare's ignorance of the classics and canons of art is a flaw. With Milton, however, there is no hint of disapproval. Milton celebrates Shakespeare's "easy numbers" and, in "L'Allegro," refers to Shakespeare as "Fancy's child" who warbles "his native woodnotes wild." In the epitaph, Milton draws a sharp contrast between art and nature: "For whilst to th' shame of slow-endeavoring art/ Thy easy numbers flow" (lines 9-10). Shakespeare thus achieves the effects of ease while ignoring the canons of art.

Stanley Archer

ON THINKING ABOUT HELL

Author: Bertolt Brecht (1898–1956)
Type of poem: Meditation
First published: 1964, as "Nachdenkend über die Hölle," in *Gedichte*, vol. 6; English
 translation collected in *Bertolt Brecht: Poems, 1913–1956*, 1976

The Poem

"On Thinking About Hell" is a relatively short poem written in free verse without
rhymes. It consists of twenty-one lines divided into three stanzas, each of which is a
different length. The words of the title also form the beginning of the first stanza and
are repeated in its fifth line. They set the tone of the poem, which is a reflection, a
meditation on the earthly representation of hell. The word "Hell," capitalized in the
English translation of the poem, thus emphasizing the biblical allusion, is repeated in
the first line of each stanza; each repetition, however, hints at a different aspect of
Bertolt Brecht's vision of hell. The poem is written in the first person, which poets
often use to speak through a persona whose outlook and experiences may be quite
different from their own. Here, however, no distinction is implied between Brecht the
poet and the speaker of the poem. The poet reflects on his own impressions of Los
Angeles, where he lived during part of his exile from Nazi Germany (from 1940 until
1945). To Brecht, the city appears strangely suspended in time and place. Attractive
at first glance, its illusive nature quickly becomes apparent under his scrutiny, and Los
Angeles turns into a repulsive urban sprawl.

In the first stanza Brecht declares his kinship with the British poet Percy Bysshe
Shelley, who had likened the city of London, England, to the place of human
damnation. The speaker of the poem, however, feels that Los Angeles is more like hell
than London. The second stanza elaborates on this theme and deepens the contradictory feelings of superficial lure and deeply felt disgust. It is a study of the slow
destruction of illusions fostered by the appearance of abundance and an easy life.
However, this semblance of natural wealth in Los Angeles is superficial. The second
stanza ends with the notion of aimlessness and emptiness that neither the unceasing
movement of automobiles nor the "jolly-looking people" can mask. The first line
of the third stanza continues the theme of beauty in hell, albeit in its negative form
("not . . . ugly.") The last three lines of the poem talk about the specter of homelessness
that lurks behind the mask of affluence and security. Brecht leaves the reader to
imagine the various reasons for being thrown out into the streets, a fate that can catch
up with the inhabitants of villas as well as with those of the shanty towns.

Forms and Devices

Present participle constructions (such as "on thinking" in the English translation)
abound in the original German version of the poem. This linguistic construction
depicts an action suspended in the present tense. It is found six times in the poem and
underlines the mood as it describes a state of unchanging sameness and immutable

but ongoing monotony that holds the poem in limbo. This stasis consists of contrasts that hold the structure of the poem and its content in a precarious balance. Brecht uses exaggerations and contrasts to emphasize his point, a device that can also be found in other poems about his experience of exile in the United States. Even the lines of the second stanza are symbolic of this exuberance: They are so long that they must be printed on two lines.

"On Thinking About Hell" describes "flowers as big as trees" brought forth by the wasteful use of expensive water. There are "fruit markets/ With great heaps of fruit" that have "Neither smell nor taste," their appearance promising delectable delights that they cannot keep. Furthermore, the reader sees an endless procession of cars moving "faster than/ Mad thought" without any destination. To Brecht, the artificial growth and constant movement signify stasis rather than change and development. The passengers of the cars, however, keep up a jolly appearance. Coming from nowhere and going nowhere, they are caught in the vicious cycle of an adopted lifestyle that they are unable to change.

The hiatus of the juxtapositions is found in lines 16 and 17: "And houses, built for happy people, therefore standing empty/ Even when lived in." These lines hint at a past during which life still had meaning and provided contentment while the people who now live in Los Angeles can no longer fill space with life because they are no longer happy. Just as the fruit of the overgrown plants has no flavor, their houses remain hollow. In the last four lines, Brecht attempts to break any illusions that the reader might still hold about this washed-out paradise: The word "Hell" is now complemented by the adjective "ugly" and the nouns "fear" and "shanty town." The illusions and lures that masked the reality of life in the fast lane are ripped away. The poem ends by depicting psychological hell—the fear of homelessness—and thus comes full circle: The reflections at the beginning have been realized, and they will foster more thoughts and continue the cycle.

Themes and Meanings

Brecht and other refugees from Nazi Germany—authors, composers, and art-ists—moved to Los Angeles because of its reputation as a safe haven. Despite this positive, lifesaving function of the city, the poem conveys Brecht's feelings of dislike for this sprawling metropolis on the West Coast of the United States. According to a published note on Shelley, Brecht felt akin to the British poet in his awareness of the plight of the lower classes. Brecht expands this notion to include people of all social strata. Taking up Shelley's theme of the modern city as a manifestation of hell, Brecht believes that Los Angeles provides a more appropriate model of hell than London because it is no longer the smoky (yet productive) city of the Industrial Revolution that was hell mainly to the workers. Instead, the lush, overripe city of Los Angeles alienates people of all classes. The semblance of riches, of nature blown out of proportion, of houses that are empty shells, and of people apparently pursuing an idle life merely signify decadence that hovers on the edge of decay. The individual no longer plays a meaningful part in the life of the city but is swept through it as an isolated being, engulfed by the raging river of the masses. The American tendency to "keep smiling," exemplified by the "jolly-looking people" in their cars, is no longer a sign of happiness but rather of emptiness. Society's goal is no longer the contentment of people occupied with purposeful work. On the contrary, it appears to Brecht that its hectic movement is reduced to complete idleness that continues moving only to serve itself. Without its unabating motion, symbolized in the poem by "the endless procession of cars/ Lighter than their own shadows, faster than/ Mad thoughts," society might collapse. However, it would be mad to think about change. In the original German version, the word for "mad" is *töricht*, which carries the meaning of folly rather than of madness. *Töricht* implies that entertaining thoughts of changing the cycle would have disastrous effects: Once questioned in its function, this nonstop movement might collapse into itself, leaving behind a ghost town that is already envisioned in the empty houses.

In the last stanza, Brecht shatters all appearances by hinting at reality in the form of social conscience. The fear of being thrown out into the street carries with it the association of economic hardship, a logical contrast to the villas and the abundance described in the previous stanza. Brecht is probably also alluding to the experience of having been driven out of his home by the ruling powers in Germany. After all, he had to flee from the persecutions of the Third Reich, which stopped at neither villas nor shanty towns.

Karin Schestokat

ORCHARD

Author: H. D. (Hilda Doolittle, 1886-1961)
Type of poem: Lyric
First published: 1912, as "Priapus"; collected in *Sea Garden* as "Orchard," 1916

The Poem

First published under the title "Priapus" and often referred to as "Spare us from Loveliness," "Orchard" is a short poem. Containing thirty-one lines, it is written in free verse and divided into four stanzas of unequal length. As its title suggests, its setting and focal point is an orchard in autumn, replete with epicurean treasures that inspire both awe and apprehension in the first-person narrator.

Unlike many poems in which orchard or garden imagery is used simply to suggest fecundity, fertility, or abundance, for this narrator the splendor of the orchard sets up a dilemma. This dilemma is the source of conflict within the poem: The orchard contains hazelnuts, figs, quinces, and "berries dripping with their wine"; however, like many people with puritan sensibilities, the narrator is wary of being seduced by its aesthetic and sensual appeal and leaves it "untouched."

On entering the orchard, the narrator is profoundly moved by its opulence. A falling pear serves as a reminder of the resplendent blossoms that preceded it, and the narrator is overcome with emotion and reverence. Because of the seemingly unbearable beauty of the orchard, the narrator falls to the ground and begs for mercy, wishing to be spared its intoxicating effects. In contrast to the bees who take no notice, the narrator feels vulnerable to the allure of the orchard, and must struggle to overcome its aesthetic appeal. However, the narrator feels obliged to reject the orchard's beauty for reasons ranging from veneration to disdain. Rather than taking pleasure in its gifts, the narrator repeatedly entreats the god of the orchard to "spare us from loveliness."

In comparison to the orchard, the god appears coarse. He looks on impassively. Like the bees, he is unimpressed by the surroundings. But his plain appearance and indifferent demeanor make him a less threatening, more deserving, object of adoration. By making an offering of the orchard's treasures, the narrator subordinates the aesthetic appeal of the orchard to authority of the "unbeautiful" (and therefore less suspect) deity. By using the immoderate bounty to supplicate a more meaningful ideal, the narrator satisfies both the impulse to revere the fruit of the orchard and the compulsion to reject it. By taking pleasure in the fruit by proxy, the narrator minimizes the risk of falling under its intoxicating spell.

Forms and Devices

Probably the most conspicuous form in "Orchard" is that associated with a style H. D. is credited with helping to invent: Imagism. Tenets of this literary movement included a propensity for short, concrete descriptions of naturalistic scenes, as well as an inclination to focus on images in and of themselves, rather than more elusive or enigmatic meanings. Much of this poem's meaning depends on its success in depicting images in unfamiliar ways, attributing characteristics to objects with which they are not normally associated. For example, instead of picturing pear blossoms as delicate, white, fragile, or ethereal, the poem implies that they are cruel, flaying observers with their beauty. Bees, instead of their familiar buzzing, "thundered their song."

By rejecting conventional portrayals, H. D. forces readers to reconsider the effect and meaning of everyday objects. However, the objects themselves are less important than the relationships among them. The narrator competes with the bees, realizing too late that they do not share her interest in the wonder of the orchard. The god of the orchard becomes more remarkable for his unpolished simplicity because he presides over a place of aesthetic enchantment. By juxtaposing disparate elements, H. D. calls attention to how contexts can determine how situations are likely to be interpreted.

Another way that H. D. brings attention to selected elements within the poem is by reducing them to their characteristics instead of referring to them directly. Thus, the bees become "golden-banded" and "honey-seeking." This technique serves a number of purposes. It allows the poet to direct readers toward the characteristics she feels are most important. In this case, the bees' stinging ability is less significant than how they follow sweet scents that lead them to flowers and fruit. Moreover, her reducing of the bees to a certain familiar activities invites associations that might otherwise be overlooked. Human visitors to an orchard may well find little in common with the insects flying about them; however "honey-seeking" may be an activity with which they have something in common.

H. D. also uses other devices to portray the scene in ways at once selective and complete. Repetition highlights the most significant occurrences in the poem: The pear falls, the narrator falls, the hazelnuts have already fallen, marking a succession of descents. The narrator flounders, then remains prostrate, symbolizing humility as well as a misstep. The narrator repeats the plea, "spare us from loveliness," drawing attention to the ongoing struggle that occurs throughout the poem. In each instance the significance of the event is stressed through repetition, and the repetitive elements increase in importance exponentially.

Themes and Meanings

The poem's central theme is the tension, most often associated with Puritan ideology, between that which is beautiful, pleasurable, or sensual and that which is moral, ethical, or "good." The questionable nature of the orchard's bounty is addressed throughout the poem, from the opening lines in which the pear falls, through the last stanza, in which the narrator makes an "offering" of the succulent fruit, rather than enjoying it in a more self-indulgent way. Is earthly pleasure inherently immoral? For the actors in "Orchard," the answer seems to be a qualified "yes."

The god of the orchard is, presumably, above the kind of corporeal temptation that plagues the narrator. For the bees, "honey-seeking" represents not joy, but gainful activity, rendering it unproblematic for them as well. However, what about the orchard's human visitors? Certainly the narrator of "Orchard" feels compelled to reject the orchard's gifts; less certain is whether the poem suggests that readers should follow suit. There is little to suggest that H. D. meant to offer advice; however, the narrator does seem to offer a warning to those who place material loveliness above moral or spiritual goodness: Be careful, cautions the narrator, the beautiful pear blossoms have the power to distract, to enchant, to render one helpless.

The appreciation that the narrator feels upon entering the orchard makes it all the more difficult to steel oneself against the impressiveness of the physical surroundings. Indeed, although the narrator succeeds in avoiding the sinful pleasures of the orchard, ceasing to desire them is another matter. This raises another question: Is it more virtuous to renounce worldly pleasures completely, or does true virtue depend on denying those things that tempt oneself? In this poem, rather than lessening, the temptation of the orchard seem to increase, as evidenced by the thick description of the tempting verdure that occurs in the last stanza. Even while resolving to dedicate the fruit to the god of the orchard, the narrator describes the offerings in appreciative detail, envisioning the wine that might flow from the grapes, and the auspicious disrobing of the hazelnuts. Even as it is consecrated, the treasure of the orchard is secretly idolized by the narrator, who can renounce but not completely free herself from its allure. In this case, when the narrator repeats the phrase "I bring you an offering," the repetition is an essential part of mustering the resolve necessary to complete the sacrifice.

Like many of H. D.'s poems, "Orchard" observes a microcosm more complicated than a casual examination might suggest. It contains a multilayered interplay among the various elements of the poem, allowing readers a polychromatic glimpse of the carefully depicted imagery within. The question of whether we should be suspicious of earthly enjoyments is one that might now appear dated or irrelevant; however, in view of the extent to which Puritan ethics inform modern American Judeo-Christian beliefs, perhaps the question posed by the poem is more topical than it seems. Certainly because it is one of the underpinnings of our belief systems, the role that aesthetic pleasure, and the rejection of it, plays in our life deserves a thoughtful reexamination.

T. A. Fishman

PARSLEY

Author: Rita Dove (1952-   )
Type of poem: Narrative
First published: 1982; collected in *Museum*, 1983

The Poem

"Parsley" revisits a horrific moment in Caribbean history and, in doing so, high-lights the manner in which language and ideology can combine to produce political violence. The poem dramatizes the slaughter of thousands of migrant Haitian sugar-cane workers by troops following orders from Dominican Republican dictator General Rafael Trujillo on October 2, 1937. (Rita Dove's notes to the poem erroneously indicate the date of the massacre as October 2, 1957.) In Dove's poem, the Haitians are killed because they could not pronounce the letter *r* in *perejil*, the Spanish word for "parsley." They are slaughtered at the behest of a dictator who, as historical documents show, was obsessed with removing influences of neighboring Haiti from Dominican culture. The first section, a villanelle titled "The Cane Fields," is narrated in the voices of Haitian workers as they are murdered. The second section, titled "The Palace," takes as its subject the psychological and sociological dimensions of Trujillo's motivations. The narration in this section shifts from first person to third person as Trujillo arrives at the decision to murder the cane workers because of the way they speak.

The poem opens with a contrast of original and unoriginal modes of language. The general's parrot, with its "parsley green" feathers, offers the first articulations of the poem by imitating human language and human convention but signalling, through this imitation, the appearance of nothing new. This section establishes Trujillo's absolute authority and the Haitians' unmitigated oppression. The sugarcane, a dominant image for the livelihood of the Haitians and the economic power of Trujillo's government, appears ghostly, an image of the blood sacrifice demanded by the general. Dove pivots the villanelle on repeated lines that emphasize the conjunction of unoriginal language and bloody violence: "there is a parrot imitating spring// Out of the swamp the cane appears."

Section 2 portrays how Trujillo's murderous decree finds its origin in his psychological equation of desire and death. As section 2 progresses, it becomes clear that Trujillo's desire to "purify" the workers' Spanish is linked to his desire to resurrect his dead mother. He keeps his parrot in his mother's old room and feeds it elaborate sweets, memorials to his mother who collapsed and died one day while preparing pastries for the Day of the Dead, an Aztec festival assimilated into contemporary Dominican culture. "Cane" again serves as a dominant image in this section, as it does in section 1. Yet the phantasmal sugarcane of section 1 becomes, in section 2, the mother's walking cane "planted" by Trujillo at her grave and perceived by him to flower every spring. When Trujillo hears the workers mispronouncing "Katarina," a local mountain, as "Katalina," he perceives this as an affront to his dead mother, who, he says, "was no stupid woman" and "could roll an R like a queen." Remembering the parsley sprigs that the men of his village wore to signify newborn sons, the general closes his equation of desire and death begun when the parrot opened the poem: He orders the Haitians "to be killed/ for a single, beautiful word."

Forms and Devices

The villanelle is one of the most complex forms in English poetry; therefore, it is ironic that Dove chooses this form for the Haitians' voices, since the general considers their speech inferior to his Spanish. The dancelike circularity of a villanelle pivots on five tercets that lead to a final quatrain. The first line of the opening tercet is repeated as the final line of the second and fourth tercets; the third line of the opening tercet is repeated as the last line of the third and fifth tercets. These two repeated lines form the last two lines of a villanelle. In section 1, this complex, rigorous repetition contrasts with the empty repetition of the general's parrot. While the Haitians work the cane fields, they are denigrated by the general, who lavishes luxury upon his parrot in the palace. The Haitians speak a rough Spanish wholly their own; the general, however, privileges the imitative repetitions of his parrot over the original hybrid tongue of the workers. In this upside down version of linguistic authority in which the imitative is privileged over the original, the general "searches for a word" that will signify that "he is all the world/ there is." As the section closes, the blood of the Haitians is framed by the "parrot imitating spring."

Personification dominates the narrative of section 2 as, for example, the workers personify the mountain in their songs while they hack at the fields. The dominant image of the sugarcane becomes the sugared pastries that spoil the parrot, which is the general's replacement for his dead mother. Trujillo sees his mother's walking cane in the sugarcane, the parrot resides in the mother's former room in the palace, and the parrot imitates even the voice of his mother. Desire and death are linked in those images. Symbols of life and creativity are twisted in this section: The original song of the Haitians inspires Trujillo to kill them, he corrupts the life force of his mother into an occasion for massacre, and his memory of artillery fire is dramatized as a song of war in his flashback to the violence of his military career.

Themes and Meanings

Like many poems situated at the crossroads of politics and culture, "Parsley" assumes that political ideology and cultural practice intersect most vividly in language. Dove's poem exposes the violence inherent in attempts to control the dynamic, creative changes that transform all languages over time. Trujillo understands his language to be authentic. Yet at the same time, the most important speaker in his life is a parrot that only imitates language. Trujillo's parrot merely repeats and does not create. In contrast, the Haitian workers re-create language (in this case, the Spanish language) to reflect their dual cultural position as migrant workers. As much as their language might seem to be an unauthentic derivative of "pure" Spanish, Dove makes sure to cast their voices in the elite form of the villanelle. The parrot's imitations evoke the wounds of the mother's death to the point of even imitating the voice of the mother. The Haitians create a new language but suffer death at the hands of a dictator who believes that the imitative language of his parrot is more authentic. Trujillo declares, "Even/ a parrot can roll an R!"

These issues of authenticity, language, and violence are enacted against a ritualistic background that fuses love and death. From the beginning, the parrot's language is described as "imitating spring," which stands in direct contrast to autumn, the season of the mother's death. The parrot's language is part of an endless circularity that, for Trujillo, brings the mother back to life in the same way that spring cyclically revives the natural world. The cane, too, is part of such a cycle: The Haitians are killed cutting cane in the fall, but the walking cane planted at the mother's grave "blossoms" for the general each spring.

As much as the poem seems to partake of the impersonal verity of seasonal change, the violence of the poem instead is occasioned by the general's personal stake in such change. Trujillo's "thoughts turn/ to love and death" in the fall. The Haitians are the innocent victims of Trujillo's violent fusion of desire and domination and his location of this violent fusion in language itself. As a child, Trujillo was nicknamed *chapita*, Spanish for "bottle cap," because he was a fervent collector of bottle caps. When he became dictator, he banished *chapita* from the language. "Parsley" describes Trujillo's attempt to extend such political control to the cycles of nature itself. His parrot can only imitate spring, but Trujillo orders a slaughter in October to reenact spring. His slaughter of the innocent workers is an attempt to "purify" the language of outside influence and cleanse autumn of its associations with his mother's death.

Usually, ritual is evoked in culture to revive authenticity. Rituals are meant to reacquaint a culture with the epic memory of its past. Yet in "Parsley," rituals such as the yearly cane harvest, the cycles of nature, national holidays (the Day of the Dead), and childbirth are reduced to images of individual obsession and mass murder. Most of all, the cyclic pattern of the villanelle, which evokes ritual in its creative circularity, is understood by the general as a threat to authenticity. Dove dramatizes Trujillo's motivation in the form of the poem itself; the shift from villanelle (section 1) to free-verse narration (section 2) portrays Trujillo's purification strategy as a misreading of language. Trujillo prefers individual memory to cultural verity and thereby produces a series of misreadings in the poem: He elevates imitative language over original language, free-verse narration over the centuries-old villanelle, and the parsley colors of his parrot over the greenery of spring.

Tony Trigilio

PATROCLEIA

Author: Christopher Logue (1926-   )
Type of poem: Epic
First published: 1962; revised and collected in *War Music: An Account of Books 16 to 19 of Homer's Iliad*, 1981

The Poem

"Patrocleia" is a free adaptation of book 16 of Homer's epic poem about the siege of Troy (c. ninth century B.C., first transcribed in the sixth century B.C.) by the Greeks after the Trojan prince, Paris, seduced Helen, the wife of Menelaus, one of the Greek chieftains, and fled with her to Troy (the fortress kingdom of his father, King Priam).

The Greeks and their allies have had limited success in attacking Troy; the war has gone on for more than nine years, and their efforts have not been helped by the fact that their finest warrior, Achilles, has quarrelled with Agamemnon, the king of Mycenae, the leader of the expedition, and now refuses to fight. In addition, difficulties for both sides lie in the intrusion of several gods of varying powers and eccentric inclinations. Achilles (whose mother is a deity) has asked the gods to deter the Greeks so long as he is at odds with Agamemnon. His absence has led to the Trojans being more successful in battle: The Greeks are backed up to the shore, where they are hard pressed to protect their ships.

Patroclus, Achilles' closest friend (Logue uses his name as a basis for the title of this section of the poem), chides Achilles for his stubborn inaction and suggests that if Achilles will not fight, he should at least allow his troops, the Myrmidons, to go into battle. Patroclus offers to lead them; to ensure their success, he suggests that he be allowed to wear Achilles' distinctive armor to frighten the Trojans. Achilles consents, but only on the condition that once Patroclus has driven the Trojans back he will stop his advance. Only Achilles is to have the glory of finally defeating the Trojans.

Patroclus agrees, and the attack on the Trojans is so successful that in the confrontation several leading Trojan warriors are killed. Patroclus is elated. He ignores Achilles' instruction and presses the attack on Troy itself. This action enrages the god Apollo, who stuns Patroclus with a godly blow. Patroclus is then wounded by a Trojan soldier. Disabled, he is caught and killed by Prince Hector, the greatest of the Trojan fighters. The section ends with Patroclus, in his dying moments, warning Hector not to rejoice, since it took the attacks of others to slow him down before Hector could strike the fatal blow. He predicts that Achilles will avenge his death, and a surly Hector acknowledges that possibility. This section is the turning point of *The Iliad*. The death of Patroclus devastates Achilles, who returns to the battle and kills Hector. Hector's death ultimately leads to the destruction of Troy.

Forms and Devices

Perhaps the best way to consider this work is to remember that it is only one part of an adaptation of a major poem and is best read with an accurate translation of

Homer's original *Iliad* at hand. Logue has no ambition simply to translate the poem, but to filter parts of it through his twentieth century artistic sensibility. He makes use of motifs common to all epics, but with the difference that metaphor, narrative, language in general, and, perhaps most significantly, the facts of the original, are artistically, morally, and psychologically influenced by his own time and place.

The poem is laconic, the tone is cool, the voice of the third-party narrator distanced and uncommitted. The free verse is sometimes hardly verse at all, but informal, conversational, often little more than a kind of shorthand aside. The romance and the excitement of triumphant male endeavor, however deadly and cruel it may be, is celebrated in the Homeric work. The same events happen in Logue's poem, but the victories are sour, and poetic expansiveness and rhetorical flourish are avoided. The epic similes, so wide-ranging and poetically extravagant in the original, are rarer and shorter. Patroclus attacks a terrified warrior, cowering in his chariot: "And gracefully as men in oilskins cast/ Fake insects over trout, he speared the bog,/ And with his hip his pivot, prised Thestor up and out/ As easily as later men detach/ A sardine from an opened tin."

Logue does not set the action in the present, but he often uses language that would not—could not—have been used in the original. "Cut to the Fleet," for example, comes from instruction in a film script. The poem is closer to the modern short story than to the epic in structure, tone, and its ambiguous ending.

Themes and Meanings

The elements of the original that Logue abandons in his version give some indication of how he wants the poem to be read. There is considerably less spiritual meddling in the poem, save for the rescue of Sarpedon's corpse and Apollo's attack on Patroclus late in the work. Logue focuses the poem on the conduct of the men without having the constant diversion of the gods manipulating the action. The same desire to narrow the field of vision is behind the tendency in the poem to abandon the very long poetic passages of description and involved, detailed accounts of the battles. In the original much is made of the other warriors and their struggles; here the Patroclus tale is really the only story being told. For instance, little is made of Hector's desertion from the battle and his later return in Logue's version, since he does not want the story to wander, and the narrative is sharply cut back to concentrate on the Achilles-Patroclus-Hector triangle of mutual destruction.

Logue is primarily interested in the ironic nature of how men make their own fate, whereas the Homer poem makes more of how much they are the playthings of the gods. The heroes of the original are Achilles and Hector, who set the standard of heroism for their respective societies. Logue's poem shows how little power they have over their destinies. Patroclus takes the place and costume of Achilles, and in such is killed by Hector, who strips him of the armor that he should not be wearing—and is not worthy of wearing. Hector in turn will be killed by Achilles for so doing, and Achilles, in turn, will die young, since his fate has already been decided by the gods.

This sense of inevitability and disdain for military prowess is peculiar to the late twentieth century. Logue turns the Homer poem upside down, stripping it of its triumphs in the face of the grim reality of mindless slaughter and the waste of life occasioned by the male enthusiasm for egotistical, deadly conduct. Logue seems to suggest that even at their best, the men are there to kill and be killed. People of the twentieth century, with its loss of spiritual connection, cannot blame the gods for their bloody conduct.

Charles Pullen

PATTERNS

Author: Amy Lowell (1874-1925)
Type of poem: Dramatic monologue
First published: 1915; collected in *Men, Women and Ghosts*, 1916

The Poem

An eighteenth century Englishwoman walks through an elegantly patterned garden. The carefully arranged garden paths and flower beds cause her to reflect that her society has similarly arranged her, seeing to it that she will passively endure her stiff, brocaded gown, her powdered hair, and a jewelled fan after the fashion of the day. Although her pink and silver gown and high-heeled ribboned shoes are decorative, the woman feels imprisoned, sealed off from the softness and passion of her heart, her true self.

At first she feels that both she and the flowers are locked into rigid patterns, but she begins to realize that her situation is mocked by the wider liberty of nature. Inspired by the greater freedom of the flowers and trees, she passes a marble fountain and sees herself bathing nude in the basin, all the while imagining that her lover is hiding in the nearby hedge, observing her. Continuing the fantasy, she imagines the water sliding over her body as would her lover's hand. The sensuality of summer makes her wish to shed her restrictive, conventionally feminine clothing for a newly liberated body whose nudity expresses a more desirable combination of pink and silver.

She imagines herself running fluidly through the maze of paths, laughing, pursued by her lover, who will eventually catch and embrace her, the buttons of his military uniform pressing sensuously against her flesh, allowing her to achieve the erotic release she has been seeking. Her desire is to be free and, by exposing and then contrasting her nude body to his military uniform, to free him as well. In reality, the woman's body is still in its heavy, fussy clothing, and she can release herself only in dream and wishful thinking.

Her sense of frustration is explained more fully when the reader learns that in her bosom is a letter brought that morning which informs her that her lover, Lord Hartwell, has died in action while serving under his commander, the duke, in Flanders. This revelation further explains the entrapment and despair she has felt while walking in a seemingly beautiful and tranquil garden. Although in another month they would have been man and wife, the woman now regards the future as a meaningless cycle of seasons in which, winter or summer, she will pace her manicured garden forlornly, her body stiffened by the stays, bones, and buttons of her repressive clothing. In addition to the constraints of her patterned garden and of her clothing, which reflect her society's regulation of her sexuality and personal freedom, she realizes that the business of war is an even more crushing pattern that has intruded into her life. Reflecting on war's official and socially sanctioned pattern of aggression, the woman reaches a catharsis by taking the name of Christ in vain. This daring profanity is followed by a defiant questioning of the meaning of all the societal patterns that have controlled her life and shaped her destiny.

Forms and Devices

"Patterns" is a poem composed in the light of the Imagist movement in modern poetry, for which Amy Lowell had great sympathy. She eventually became one of its major proponents and leaders. Imagists sought to break with the traditional forms of poetry, preferring unrhymed and unmetered ("free") verse and a more colloquial, economical diction closer to prose or to the rhythms of speech. In "Patterns," her best-known poem, Lowell used an irregular rhyme scheme to suggest that expression must follow the movement of the natural speaking voice rather than customary poetic diction. The lack of formal constraints in "Patterns" creates a free-flowing style that passes effortlessly from verse to prose and back again, according to the mood or emotional needs of the narrative voice.

Although Lowell employs recognizable poetic devices, she is also using her poem as a way to tell a story—complete with a heroine and a supporting set of characters—as a piece of prose would. This story of a woman in crisis is facilitated through the technique of dramatic monologue, which allows the poet to explore the psychology of her narrator. In addition, dramatic monologue reinforces Lowell's conviction that poetry is an oral art that should be heard to be completely understood. The woman's unaffected but impassioned human cry of pain at the end suggests a speaking voice breaking out in anguished spontaneity.

The lack of a formal rhyme scheme in "Patterns" does not mean that Lowell is simply writing a form of cut-up prose. While not following a strict meter, the lines in "Patterns" can be defined as loosely iambic and as having from two to four accents a line with varying numbers of syllables. More important, the poem is composed of interweaving sound patterns that establish a musical or cadenced rhythm. This musicality is one of the attributes of "Patterns" that distinguishes it from that of a prose narrative. In addition, Lowell uses such formal poetic devices as internal rhymes (quills, daffodils), end rhymes (brocade, shade), assonance (paths, patterned, daffodils), and consonance (gown, fan). It is this interplay between formal devices and freer verse that is also germane to the poem's theme of the necessary balance between freedom and constraint.

A final important aspect of "Patterns" is Lowell's selection of vivid images. Readers must draw their own inferences from her images, however—she feels no need to supply an extended explanatory commentary. When the narrator is brought the letter announcing the death of her lover, for example, the letters on the page are compared to writhing snakes. This image may call to mind the serpent in the Garden of Eden, bringing sin and death, but Lowell does not provide this interpretation herself, instead letting the image resonate in its own way for each reader. The poem's economical but sensuous images especially concern the garden and the gown, and when these images are carried from stanza to stanza, one begins to understand that they are also being deployed as symbols. For instance, the imagery of the woman's gown, with its stiffness and its stays, develops into a symbol of society's cruel repression of healthy instinct.

Themes and Meanings

"Patterns" centers on the unmet needs of a love-starved woman. While the woman in the poem yearns for an ecstatic eroticism, her civilization has denied her a sexually responsive identity. Her unbearably constricted clothing articulates the theme of a world that has instituted a set of social controls that do not accommodate or recognize female sexuality. She is trapped in a system that has deprived her of her inmost identity as a passionate, sensual, and free-spirited young woman. Psychologically, her emotional state suggests suppressed hysteria, the result of a society that requires female passivity and affords few opportunities for spontaneous expression of feeling. A corollary of this theme is that of the female body. Although her social mask is that of a decorous product of her society, the socially constructed femininity represented by her gown and the formal garden acts as a prison for her body, which yearns to be free. This awareness of her own body is an inherently enlivening one, leading her to think of the fulfilling experience of sexual love.

Like her garden, which is perfectly pruned and arranged after the custom of the day, the lady is likewise beautifully organized. However, as she paces along the mazelike patterns of her garden, she feels imprisoned in a social system and in a false identity that denies her what she truly wants. A woman's capacity for passion and its cruel restriction become a figure for yet another theme—the general denial of personal freedom in a repressive society. Just as the form of the poem contains both free flowing elements and formal poetic devices, the image of the woman's nude body pressed against her lover in uniform indicates an eroticism based on the balanced interplay of nature and cultural order. It is the one-sided, overly masculine and puritanical dominance over both the natural world and women's lives that is the problem; the poem suggests that it is necessary to permit the sense of freedom and guilt-free sensuality, associated here with the female body, to act as a welcome counterpoise to the claims of civilization.

The final theme in the poem is of war. The sharp cry of pain that concludes the poem can be interpreted not only as a defiance of conventional morality but also as a protest against the inhumanity of war. The woman becomes a tragic figure, victimized by male-dominated modes of aggression that leave her languishing in an unvisited garden. The profane invocation of the deity at the end is not only a protest against war—it is also an opposition of the war by connecting the women's passions with what is truly sacred. It is her celebration of the body and its erotic life that preserves what is holy in the face of the misguided patterns of her culture.

Margaret Boe Birns

PERSEPHONE IN HELL

Author: Rita Dove (1952-   )
Type of poem: Poetic sequence
First published: 1995, in *Mother Love*

The Poem

"Persephone in Hell," a sequence of seven poems, forms the third of seven sections in Dove's collection *Mother Love*. The sequence and the collection explore the Greek myth of Demeter: With almost no witnesses and with the permission of her father Zeus, the supreme Olympian deity, Persephone has been abducted and raped by Hades, the ruler of the underworld and her uncle, who subsequently makes her his queen. Unable to find her daughter, an angry and inconsolable Demeter wanders among mortals, disguised as an elderly woman. She comes to Eleusis, where she meets the four lovely daughters of Celeus, king of Eleusis, and his wife Metaneira. Demeter, at Metaneira's urging, becomes nurse to the couple's only son, the infant Demophoön. Determined to make the boy immortal, each night Demeter secretly places him in the fire. One night Metaneira discovers this and screams in terror, thus thwarting Demeter's plans. An angry, radiant goddess reveals herself and disappears, but not before ordering the people of Eleusis to build a temple and altar in her honor and promising to teach them rites that became known as the Eleusinian Mysteries. Still inconsolable, Demeter lets the crops die and refuses solace from the other Olympian gods and goddesses. Eventually Zeus agrees to return Persephone, but because she has eaten pomegranate seeds offered by Hades, she must spend fall and winter with her husband and spring and summer with her mother, thus ensuring the seasons, agriculture, and partial consolations.

The focus of "Persephone in Hell" is the riveting episode with which the ancient account of the myth, the "Homeric Hymn to Demeter," begins: the abduction and rape of Persephone by Hades. Dove's treatment of this episode is innovative and complex. The former U. S. poet laureate (1993-1995) announces its complexity in the section's epigraph by American expatriate poet H. D. (Hilda Doolittle): "Who can escape life, fever,/ the darkness of the abyss?/ lost, lost, lost . . ." In the sequence's opening poem, radical innovations appear, including a modern Persephone, a nineteen-year-old American "Girded . . . with youth and good tennis shoes." Her first-person voice ushers the reader into the sequence's setting: Hell is a bone-chilling October in Paris, the City of Lights; the city, Persephone notes, of detritus and neon-lit underground sewers; and the city of Our Lady (Notre Dame Cathedral) to whose heavy presence, like the mental presence of her mother Demeter, Persephone keeps turning her back. In the fifth poem, another innovation appears: Hades is a sardonic, older Frenchman, a habitual seducer whose character borders on caricature.

The mood of the sequence's first six poems combines ennui and irritation. Both underscore the detachment with which Persephone thinks of her mother who "with her frilly ideals// . . . couldn't know what [Persephone] was feeling;// . . . I was doing everything and feeling nothing." Ennui characterizes the way in which Persephone and Hades individually assess their surroundings and people. Both are especially irritated by ineffectual artists and intellectuals, whom Hades compares metaphorically to a "noisy zoo"; Persephone responds, "let this party/ swing without me." Within this dissatisfaction, Dove reconstructs their encounter.

The sequence is crafted as a three-stage rite of passage for Persephone: fledgling initiatives/waiting, the contact, the life-defining initiation. In the first four poems, Persephone experiments with sexual and social relationships, which remain superficial. She is curious but detached, a young woman who knows only "seven words of French," the language of Hell and adulthood. The one who will teach Persephone that language appears in the fifth poem, a monologue delivered by a bored Hades whose "*divertissement*" (Persephone, as it turns out) will be a matter of chance: "The next one through that gate,/ woman or boy, will get/ the full-court press of my ennui." The sixth poem captures Persephone and Hades's first meeting and conversation. Both realize that Persephone does not belong there, but, as she inadvertently points out, the "Midnight./ The zero hour" of their encounter has arrived. In the sequence's final poem, Dove alternates their voices as each approaches their pivotal sexual encounter. Persephone, for example, recognizes that a part of her "had been waiting," to which Hades counters, "I am waiting/ you are on your way."

Forms and Devices

The "Persephone in Hell" sequence is linked by theme rather than form. Dove gives each of the seven poems a distinctive format, using the varied forms, lines, quotations, and typography for crucial purposes. They identify multiple voices and personas that move in and out of the poems. They also intensify a driving sense of order that moves below the seemingly random surface of Persephone's experiences and responses. The result is an intense unit. While none of the seven poems of "Persephone in Hell" is in the sonnet form, the closely linked thematic unit suggests that Dove may have had in mind a seven-poem form known as a "crown of sonnets." Whatever the case, "Persephone in Hell" ends with Persephone being claimed sexually as the queen of the underworld.

Surprising appearances of formal language in the dominant informality of the sequence support its unsettling effect. In addition, although Dove occasionally uses irregular end or internal rhymes, most of the lines are unrhymed. This decision, as well as the poet's mixtures of other devices, emphasizes the poems' nuanced informality. For example, Dove frequently sets up terse catalogs of details. Just as often, she uses a consonant emphasis, such as *s*, to carry a barrage of details and partial and irregular rhymes: "Through the gutters, dry rivers/ of the season's detritus./ Wind soughing the plane trees./ I command my knees to ignore the season/ as I scuttle over stones." Similes, used sparingly but strategically, combine tension and details. Typical examples include Persephone's description of Paris's sewer system ("like some demented plumber's diagram/ of a sinner's soul") and her initial impression of Hades ("He inclines his head, rather massive,/ like a cynical parrot.") A more important device is

Dove's repetitions of images and emphases. To trace, for example, her use of Africans, "way," light/dark, Mother/Our Lady, food and drinks, and autumnal references is to study the poet's craft and the poems' themes.

Themes and Meanings

The "Homeric Hymn to Demeter," even in its disturbing account of Persephone's rape, gives the starring role to the goddess of agriculture. Dove expands Demeter's role, adding psychological layers to the goddess-mother's love and loss. The poet, however, also develops Persephone's and Hades's characters, giving them prominent first-person voices throughout the collection. These revisions of the myth serve Dove's thematic purposes. With this triad, the poet can emphasize contradictions in and pressures on maternal love, mother-daughter relationships, and adulthood.

One such contradiction, the narcissism of all three characters, is Dove's covert psychological gesture to the account in the "Homeric Hymn to Demeter" in which a narcissus flower attracts first Persephone and then Hades to Persephone. Certainly, Demeter's maternal pride matches the self-absorption of both Persephone and Hades. The result is a triangle of willfulness, uneasiness, and power struggles. Demeter, for example, will not accept her daughter's sexuality or autonomy. The goddess is also a chronic worrier. Persephone, even as she gains independence and tries to shake off her mother's worry, is bored and numb. The latter problem also characterizes Hades and the detachment with which Hades and Persephone approach each other. In fact, all three characters in this sequence reflect numbed states of waiting: *"It's an old drama, waiting./ One grows into it,/ enough to fill the boredom . . ./ it's a treacherous fit."*

Finding a way out of this treacherous, three-way fit is the goal of Dove's account of the myth. Dove allows Persephone to articulate that difficulty: "For a moment I forgot which way to turn"; *"Which way is bluer?"*; and *"And if I refuse this being/ which way then?"* The quest is for light and enlightenment, and, ironically, Persephone approaches it when she raises to Hades the glass of chartreuse that he compares to *"un mirage,"* which she coyly translates as "a trick of light." As their sexual encounter begins, she reflects confusion in whispered questions to herself ("if I whispered to the moon,/ if I whispered to the olive/ which would hear me?"), which are patterned on the opening line of German poet Rainer Maria Rilke's 1923 *Duineser Elegien* (*Duino Elegies*, 1930): "Who, if I cried out, would hear me among the angelic orders?")

By invoking (in whispers, not screams) the virgin goddesses of the moon (Artemis) and the olive (Athena)—both with contradictory roles, both cruel when offended—Persephone confirms her divided mind. Still, in her charged last question—"who has lost me?"—she moves toward an unexpected nexus where selfhood, sexuality, an adult relationship, and her mother's advice ("be still she whispers/ and light will enter") meet and where understanding can begin.

Persephone is on her way to becoming the perennial traveler-mediator between darkness and light, fragmentation and harmony, and interior and exterior worlds. However, she must begin with an interior journey. As Dove explained in a 1996 interview, "I would like to remind people that we *have* an interior life . . . and without that interior life, we are shells, we are nothing." The "Persephone in Hell" poems demonstrate Dove's wise advice. The reader is pulled into a modern interior of the Demeter myth, into its underworld of change, chance, sexuality, grief, willfulness, violence, and love. It is only within the interior that poetry and myth reveal their secret: The underworld teaches the reader the way back to the seasons of life, seasons transformed by the journey.

Alma Bennett

PERSIMMONS

Author: Li-Young Lee (1957-   )
Type of poem: Narrative
First published: 1981; collected in *Rose*, 1986

The Poem

"Persimmons" consists of eighty-eight lines of free verse. The speaker is clearly Li-Young Lee himself, who immigrated to the United States from China as a small boy. The poem begins with Lee in trouble with his sixth-grade teacher because he cannot hear the difference between the words "persimmon" and "precision." This scene is the first of several episodes Lee recalls in "Persimmons," each of which involves a verbal ambiguity, misconception, or blunder of some sort. In the course of the poem these encounters involve Lee and four other people: Mrs. Walker (the teacher), Lee's wife Donna, his mother, and his father.

After recalling his punishment in school, Lee jumps ahead many years to a scene in the backyard, where he and his wife are making love. Here, too, words seem to fail the poet; he can teach Donna the Chinese for crickets, but cannot remember the words for dew and naked. He does, however, "remember to tell her/ she is as beautiful as the moon." The love between them quickly eliminates the awkwardness Lee feels.

Next he recounts other words "that got me into trouble" as a boy, "wren and yarn" most poignantly. His mother seems to have contributed to his confusion, but she also helped him to see the underlying unity of things: "Wrens are soft as yarn./ My mother made birds out of yarn." She also made a rabbit and "a wee man" as Li-Young watched, toys for her child, acts of love that taught him to see how rich words might be if they were not tied too tightly to single meanings. From his mother the toymaker, Lee takes the reader back to Mrs. Walker. She has brought a persimmon to class "and cut it up/ so everyone could taste/ a Chinese apple." The boy can see that the fruit is not ripe, but he says nothing and only watches the faces of his classmates.

Two brief verse paragraphs follow in which the poet describes the persimmon more fully and compares it with the cardinal on his windowsill, which sings to him, "The sun, the sun." The remainder of the poem focuses on Lee's father, who has gone blind. His relationship with the persimmon is the most complex and has the most to teach the poet.

Forms and Devices

"Persimmons" opens with the scene in Mrs. Walker's sixth-grade class. The incident is recounted in the flat language of simple narrative, but the stage is set for a more complex, stream-of-consciousness account of the poet's coming of age, both as a poet and as a man. "Persimmon" itself constitutes the strongest current in that stream: The sound of the word, the taste, feel, and appearance of the fruit, and the symbolic significance it has for the poet and his parents all contribute to the design of the poem.

"Persimmon" and "precision" may not sound much alike to a native English speaker, but that same speaker may also lack the "precision" Lee has learned from his Chinese mother in distinguishing ripe from unripe fruit, a difference he can trace as he watches the faces of his classmates as they sample pieces of an unripe persimmon Mrs. Walker has imprecisely chosen in the market. This kind of wordplay is the dominant poetic device Lee employs in "Persimmons," a kind of play that continues with wren and yarn and fight and fright. In each instance, the poet finds in the memories of his childhood something that connects the words with each other.

It is not only the sound of these words that engages Lee's attention but also the sense impressions they evoke. Lee uses imagery of taste and touch as well as sight and sound, among them rich images like the touch of a wolftail brush on silk, the sounds of crickets and the feel of dew in the yard where Lee and his wife lie naked in the moonlight, and especially the taste of a genuinely ripe persimmon. (The sense of taste is something of a Li-Young Lee trademark; see especially "Eating Alone" and "Eating Together," collected in *Rose*, the volume in which "Persimmons" appears.) Lee's imagery often employs synesthesia, whereby one sense is described by evoking another; thus, the persimmon tastes like sunlight, and the backyard shivers with the sound of crickets.

The persimmon also carries a kind of symbolic weight for the poet and his family. When Mrs. Walker calls the fruit a "Chinese apple," she points to a meaning of which she is almost certainly unaware. Lee's father is a political refugee whose pursuers have driven his family far from home. They can never go back, it would seem, but they have brought knowledge of the persimmon with them; what is exotic to the American teacher and her students is familiar to Lee's family. Further, the more his mother and father tell him about the fruit, the more mysteriously potent it becomes: It has a sun inside, it is "heavy as sadness/ and sweet as love." Lee has been granted a kind of power through knowing the secrets of the persimmon.

Other objects carry similar weight in the poem. Lee finds three of his father's paintings: "Hibiscus leaf and a white flower/ Two cats preening./ Two persimmons, so full they want to drop from the cloth." All of these subjects seem to have been ones that Dr. Lee could still paint after going blind, suggesting that blindness and vision are no more remote from each other than wren and yarn. This stress on the thing rather than an idea links Lee to older modern poets such as Wallace Stevens and William Carlos Williams.

One more point should be made about the structure of "Persimmons." Until near the end, the poem moves from episode to episode as sounds and images carry the poet from one place in time to another. When he asks his father the "stupid question" about his blindness, however, the nature of the movement changes. With his painting of the persimmons in hand, Dr. Lee takes over. He describes painting blind, with the physical sense of brush in hand and the strength and "precision" in the wrist substituting for sight. The last episode is narrated not by the son, but by the father, who at this point sees more effectively, even though he is blind. This situation is an ironic twist familiar to readers of Sophocles and John Milton, but it seems less painful here, as Dr. Lee emphasizes how much remains to him.

Themes and Meanings

"Persimmons" is a poem about ways of knowing and of expressing what one knows. The most obvious form of expression for a poet is words, but Li-Young Lee learned early that words can mean very different things and that without love, including the kind of love a patient teacher might display toward a slow student, words may carry more confusion than understanding.

Lee's experience as an immigrant provides him with a novel perspective on this familiar theme. Because English was not his first language as a child, he readily confused one word with another in ways a native speaker could hardly imagine. To his teacher, he simply seemed stupid, and she punished him. There was no love between them and therefore no understanding. Later in the poem, when she brings a persimmon for the class to share, Lee merely watches the faces of his classmates as they bite into the unpalatable fruit. Neither student nor teacher is prepared to teach or to learn from the other.

In contrast, when Lee tries to share the language of his childhood with his American wife, he finds that much of the understanding between them is nonverbal. It does not really matter that he cannot think of particular Chinese words because they share a complex set of physical and emotional sensations. Love, which is in part a deep sharing of such experience, creates and maintains understanding in the absence of the exact word.

Similarly, his relationship with his mother is also charged with love. Although the confusion between wren and yarn got him into trouble with his teacher, he was learning a new way to look at the relationships between word and thing and between one thing and another. The yarn can become a wren in the hands of the knitter or in the language of the poet. For both kinds of artist, reality is more fluid, the possibilities more creative, than a literalist such as Mrs. Walker could ever imagine.

This is the point the poet's father makes. Dr. Lee can still paint even though he is blind because he has never lost certain sensations: the taste of a persimmon, the scent of a lover's hair. Seeing, feeling, hearing, tasting, loving, imagining, by the end of the poem, the persimmon comes to stand for all these things.

William T. Hamilton

PEYOTE POEM

Author: Michael McClure (1932-   )
Type of poem: Meditation
First published: 1958; collected in *Hymns to St. Geryon and Other Poems*, 1959

The Poem

   Peyote Poem is a long serial poem of 242 lines divided into three major parts. The three numbered parts are further divided into stanzas or sections. Part 1 consists of seven sections of various lengths, part 2 is divided into two sections, and part 3 into seven. None of the sections or stanzas are numbered but are separated from each other by long, horizontal lines. The poem is written in the first person. The occasion of the poem is a record of Michael McClure's first experimentation with the hallucinatory drug peyote, a form of mescaline used by some North American Indian tribes in religious ceremonies. The mystic painter/photographer Wallace Berman, who was an active member of a small cult of peyote eaters in the San Francisco Bay area, was McClure's guide during his first peyote experience in 1957. McClure considered this experiment to be one of several alchemical tools that he used to explore the boundaries of consciousness. McClure, who is both a Beat poet and a member of the San Francisco Renaissance group, treated the use of such drugs as a serious vehicle for developing and expanding spiritual states. McClure and some other poets made these experiences the content of some of their poetry.

   The setting of part 1 is the living room of McClure's home in San Francisco, and the poem records what he experiences as he looks out of the window. After ingesting the drug, he becomes acutely award of pain in his stomach, a recurring image that becomes a metaphor for what Buddhists consider the center of consciousness. The stomach ache recurs over twenty times during the course of this twelve-page poem. The first revelation of his peyote experience is that there is no time, only space; he also realizes that he is "separate." Throughout the poem, the speaker defines his fall as a fall into the knowledge that there are only two facts of existence (consciousness and empty space) and that they are connected only by the speaker's imagination. This traumatic cleavage becomes the cause of his "!STOM-ACHE!" as he views the world from his window. The window becomes a metaphor for the separation of the artist from a world he can only view from the outside; he can never participate in it. At the conclusion of part 1, he has a terrifying vision of a frozen osprey, an echo of a feathered Satan in Dante Alighieri's *Inferno* (c. 1320; English translation, 1802).

   In part 2 the osprey, which is a bird of prey (a fish hawk), glares at the speaker ominously, an act that brings him into the full realization of the nature of reality: "I have entered the essential-barrenness/ . . . I face the facts of emptiness." The osprey grows more gigantic and fierce and terrifies the speaker into an even deeper awareness that he is utterly alone: "The fact of my division is simple I am a spirit/ of flesh in the cold air . . ./ . . . I am separate, distinct." Part 3 documents the speaker's increasing sense of isolation but further intensifies the pain in his belly by the growing discovery that "There is nothing but forms/ in emptiness." That sense of terror overwhelms him from within: "I AM AT THE POINT OF ALL HUGENESS AND MEANING," a foreboding that spreads from his stomach to the rest of his body. From this knowledge, he realizes in the poem's climactic section that his peyote trip has reduced him to "a bulk/ in the air" in a world devoid of categories, justifications, and, therefore, meaning.

Forms and Devices

The formal requirements of the serial poem dictate to some degree the structure of this long, complex poem. However, the movement of the poem comes not from intellectual analysis but rather from information that his senses, especially his stomach (that is, his literal "gut" feelings), reveal to him. The persistent metaphor of the stomach as the center of consciousness pervades all three parts of the poem. The peyote's effect is to clarify the speaker's perceptions to such a degree that mere sight is transformed into cosmic revelation (that is, visionary experience). The recurring motif of stomach pain signals the next development in the speaker's expanding awareness of the emptiness of existence, which is embodied in the repetition of the word "space."

A result of the speaker's knowledge of the world's emptiness (another recurring image throughout the poem) is his deeply disturbing discovery that he is separate and distinct from it. Another revelation in part 1 is that time is an illusion created by the imagination, and without time the cosmos literally has no point or reason. Empty space is transformed into a dragon surrounded by clouds, mists, and vapors out of which emerges the principal image of part 2, the dragonlike figure of "an osprey frozen skyhigh/ to challenge me," a metaphor more than a little reminiscent of Satan in Dante's *Inferno* and French Symbolist poet Stéphane Mallarmé's recurring "frozen swan" motif.

Many of the images running throughout the poem (aching stomach, space, emptiness, timelessness, and separateness) culminate in the controlling metaphor for the whole poem: the fall into consciousness. However, that knowledge creates only weariness, a sense of ennui best expressed in one of Mallarmé's most brilliant lines: "Alas, the Flesh is sad/ And I've read all the books." Many of the poem's images attest McClure's familiarity with the work of the French Symbolist poets of the nineteenth century, such as Mallarmé, Arthur Rimbaud, and especially Charles Baudelaire, whose influences are evident throughout the poem.

In part 2, the metaphor of the stomach as knowledge and the seat of consciousness nears the bursting point: The speaker says, "MY STOMACH IS SWOLLEN AND NUMB!" as he realizes that "measurement is arbitrary" and that metamorphosis and transmutation are spiritually alchemical processes that are irrelevant in the "essential-barrenness" of the world. In part 3, however, McClure juxtaposes the brutal images of empty meaninglessness with images of memory, warmth, and love that are centered in his voice: "The answer to love/ is my voice" and "I am caught in reveries of love." Though experience is intractably solipsistic, the speaker finds some consolation in the knowledge that though his experience is private, it does, nonetheless, belong to him. That knowledge momentarily assuages the pain of ennui and isolation: "My stomach is gentle love, gentle love."

Themes and Meanings

Peyote Poem is about discovering that the cosmos is essentially empty and meaningless without the structuring capacity of the human imagination. However, McClure came to that knowledge only with insight gained from his peyote experience. As one of the principal Beat and San Francisco Renaissance poets, he recognized that there were very few avenues for transcendence available to artists and poets in the spiritually empty and excessively materialistic United States of the 1950's. He also realized that he could not attain a clear vision of reality that was not distorted and conditioned by cultural and societal preconceptions. By taking part in the rituals of a small peyote cult in the San Francisco Bay area, he hoped that the hallucinatory visions of peyote might somehow expand his consciousness beyond the mundane world of mere time and space. Linguistic philosophers such as Ludwig Wittgenstein and Ferdinand de Saussure, as well as phenomenologist Edmund Husserl, had been addressing similar problems earlier in the century. They all found it virtually impossible to get beyond the conditioning nets of perception and language. McClure and his fellow peyote eaters utilized the pre-Columbian religious practices of some American Indians, who attained spiritual transcendence through drug-induced visions, but only within the regulating contexts of ritual.

What McClure discovers in his peyote vision is not a unified, harmonic vision of the cosmos but rather the opposite. He discovers that time is arbitrary and is the product of the imagination, and he is left with only space: "I have entered the essential-barrenness/ . . . I face the facts/ of emptiness." Concurrent with the "facts of emptiness" comes the corollary proposition: "The fact of my division is simple I am a spirit/ of flesh in the cold air . . ./ . . . I am separate, distinct." From his discovery that he is alone and utterly unconnected to anything, he also begins to understand the true nature of the universe: "There is nothing but forms/ in emptiness." The poet has descended into Hades, his own "dark night of the soul," similar to those experienced by earlier visionary poets such as Dante, Saint John of the Cross, and Saint Teresa of Avila. Though his response to the essential emptiness of the cosmos gives him little cause for celebratory ecstasy, the dark vision does produce feelings that authenticate his existence: "I KNOW ALL THAT THERE IS TO KNOW/ feel all that there is to feel."

The final revelation of *Peyote Poem* produces a mixture of despair and hope because the poet has found within the painful recognition of the world's emptiness and meaninglessness that he must rely on the only evidence available: "My feelings real to me. Solid/ as walls.—I see the meaning/ of walls—divisions of space,/ backgrounds of color./ HEAVEN AND HELL THIS IS REACHABLE." He had earlier discovered that "The answer to love" is his voice. What the speaker understands after his nightmarish vision is that "The room is empty of all but visible things./ THERE ARE

NO CATEGORIES! OR JUSTIFICATIONS!" The cosmos is, then, the product of his imagination and, as a poet and painter, McClure has redeemed the emptiness of the cosmos with the power of his imagination to define himself with utter precision: "I am sure of my movements I am a bulk/ in the air." The recognition that the cosmos does not possess any inherent categories, justifications, and, therefore, meaning, releases him to celebrate the fact that the world is inexorably his own solipsistic world. However, that evidence is authenticated solely by his deepest feelings.

Patrick Meanor

PITCH PINES

Author: Brendan Galvin (1938-   )
Type of poem: Lyric
First published: 1980, in *Atlantic Flyway*

The Poem

Brendan Galvin's "Pitch Pines" is a forty-four-line poem divided into nine stanzas of four to six lines each. Each stanza presents a series of images that culminate in the stanza's final image. In stanza 1, for example, the trees are described as assaulted by winds and other natural forces; they are bent and twisted. In the final line of the stanza, readers see the trees as a jumble, leaning in all different directions. Stanza 4 gathers images of sourness and acidity until the final line states that the pines' pollen "curdles water." The cumulative effect is one of harshness, of forces constantly attacking the pitch pines and the pines barely able to withstand the attack.

Although the predominant images in the poem are those of assault and death, the overall impression crafted by Galvin is one of awe and respect. Despite the inhospitable environment and indifferent treatment by nature (storms and fires), the harvesting of forests for human needs, and the pitch pines' own sometimes thwarted efforts to survive (they pollinate windows and water), they do survive. While other varieties of trees—cedar, birch, elm, beech, and oak—are harvested for specific purposes, the lowly pitch pine stands neglected; it may be knocked down by accident or as a matter of course. Nevertheless, they have developed ways to hold on. The poet is as interested in looking at previous generations of trees as he is in the trees standing in front of him.

In Galvin's landscape, trees are nearly anthropomorphized; they perform deliberate, though treelike, actions: They "loft their heads," "rattle maroon clusters," and "pollinate windows." However, the poet stops short of personification. The trees do not whine, weep, or stretch; rather, they do what trees do, only more deliberately. In this way they begin to people the reader's world.

The poem encompasses a sweeping historical panorama. From a present-day vantage point, the reader is moved back in time to the specific historical moment when the forest was first being "civilized" and its natural abundance was being gathered to build ships and meeting houses, to make shingles, and to build fires for smelting and other activities that required huge amounts of concentrated heat and energy. Images of industrious human endeavor predominate, but the unspoken reaction of the poet is one of wonder at how, amid unthinking industry and human activity, anything of the natural world survived. Galvin does not dwell on the sins of the past, however; he is fascinated by how the trees have evolved and learned to adapt. The poem concludes: "the grandfathers/ of these pines held on until/ heat popped their seeds/ to the charred ground."

With that closing image, the poem moves outward to encompass not only the sturdy, common pitch pine but also the early colonists who settled in the New World. They too were common stock, and many fell to storms, fires, and the vagaries of nature.

What has survived best in the New World, Galvin reminds readers, is not the exotic or the rich and high born, but the common, dependable, and adaptable.

Forms and Devices

Galvin does not depend on conventional devices such as rhyme and meter to shape and control his poems. Readers must look for subtle devices that are closely tied to the subject matter and the cadence of the lines. He writes in vernacular English at its best, firmly in control of the words and how they will be read. The conversational tone of the poem holds readers' attention as they await the next phrase, the next image. The brief lines waste no syllables. Each contains three or four stressed syllables in conversational rhythms. The no-nonsense lines and clear images command attention. Powerful, sometimes unexpected, verbs propel the lines along: Winds are "salted out of the northeast," old branches are "knotted" and "mingle . . . and rot," a shower of pollen "curdles water," and the cape is "timbered to its shores."

The diction that shapes the terse lines and stanzas is also forceful. Repeatedly in Galvin's work, poetic structures gather power from the transforming power of nature. In this poem a particular "[verb] to [noun]" structure is used no less than a half dozen times; it propels action and emphasizes the transformation and use of the elements involved. Three examples are "limbs flaking and dying/ to ribs," "a shower/ that curdles water to golden scum," and "hardwood that fell to keels." In these very brief, consistent structures, massive natural and artificial forces are shown at work. Like much that is American, there is little time for the decorative—the elaboration of phrase, the prettification of an image or action.

Unlike the landscape that is clear-cut in the process of harvest, unlike the gigantic wastefulness that Galvin depicts, the poem itself is economical. The poet demonstrates, without explicitly lecturing his readers, that the best approach for humans is to conserve, to trim—in a sense, to edit their actions. Just as humans have the power to "[boil] the Atlantic to its salts," they have the power to reduce and concentrate their efforts when it comes to nature. Galvin subtly advises his readers to see how the pitch pines have learned to hold on, to clutch their threatened seeds inside cones.

Themes and Meanings

"Pitch Pines" celebrates all forms of life that exhibit the will and the tenacity to survive even when the odds are stacked against them. Just as the common, yet sturdy, pitch pine has survived all that nature and humankind have hurled at it, so have the people who inhabit the pines' native ground. The unheralded American ancestor appears through these images. It was from these early generations that America emerged and continues to emerge. The image of the seed-bearing cone is also the image of the seed of America grasped tight in the minds and wombs of colonists and pioneers.

Galvin's poems in general contain an elaborate and powerful sense of respect for nature, its objects and its forces. Galvin, along with a handful of other contemporary poets, has been an environmentalist since long before it was fashionable to be one.

These poets are cut more from the cloth of Aldo Leopold and Henry Beston than from that of Robert Frost. Frost certainly knew nature intimately, but he ultimately rejected its calling. The environmentalist poets, Galvin significant among them, engage as well as respect nature. Natural objects are beheld, not from a distance, but through the intimate closeness of eye and hand, nose and ear. One need not anthropomorphize the natural world in order to make it interesting: Closely observed, all things in nature may be seen to do the unexpected, the wonder-causing, the awe-inspiring.

"Pitch Pines" does not attempt to elevate the common tree above its station; it merely seeks to observe and fix it in its natural place. For the poet, respect for nature arises from the act of recognizing the dignity of the thing, beholding it, and setting it down in words. "Pitch Pines" contains an understated sense of wonder and even something very akin to joy in the illustration of the beaten and threatened marshaling against indifferent nature, uncaring humankind.

H. A. Maxson

POEM ABOUT MY RIGHTS

Author: June Jordan (1936-   )
Type of poem: Narrative
First published: 1980, in *Passion: New Poems, 1979-1980*

The Poem

"Poem About My Rights," written in free verse, juxtaposes the personal odyssey of one black woman facing oppression in the United States with the political struggle of nations against oppression in southern Africa. The poem's title is ironic, as the narrator chronicles the "wrongs" that exist within the person she is as well as the external conditions that impact her. Society's edicts infringe upon and impede any rights that author June Jordan feels are hers. She is a product of her people's heritage and, as such, must live according to contemporary cultural suppositions.

Using first person throughout, Jordan details the wrongs that she perceives in herself: wrong color, wrong sex, and living on the wrong continent. She is the potential victim of any man who would physically force himself on her. The rape victim becomes the wrongdoer because the law assumes implied consent in cases of rape and brutality. Burden of proof is also left to the victim in order for justice to be served. Personal, consensual rape is then transferred to the broader area of southern Africa: South Africa's forced penetration into Namibia and Namibia's subsequent penetration into Angola are detailed.

Jordan then shifts the scene of "Poem About My Rights" back to the United States and cites both national and personal wrongs. She highlights the use of power by the government and the Central Intelligence Agency (CIA), the killing of black leaders, and the treatment of blacks on college campuses. The poet was even rejected by her parents, who wanted to alter both her behavior and her physical appearance. The latter third of the poem culminates in the poet's realization that she is very familiar with all of the problems elucidated: "the problems/ turn out to be/ me/ I am the history of rape/ I am the history of the rejection of who I am/ I am the history of the terrorized incarceration of/ my self." She is also the "problem everyone seeks to eliminate" by forced penetration. In a dramatic ending, Jordan avows that this poem is not her consent to anyone: "*Wrong is not my name/l. . .* my resistance/ my simple and daily and nightly self-determination/ may very well cost you your life."

"Poem About My Rights" is a pessimistic poem. However, the work ends on a somewhat hopeful and optimistic note. Throughout the poem, the individual is seen as a victim of society. Near the beginning of the work, Jordan asks, "who in the hell set things up/ like this?" The phrase is repeated again near the end of the poem as Jordan calls on the reader to resist and to take an active stance in order to guarantee individual freedom and rights. The poem is reflective of the storytelling tradition. Readers feel as if they are at the scene with Jordan as she shares her thoughts and beliefs and implores them to comprehend her situation from her point of view.

Forms and Devices

The individual human condition is juxtaposed with national and global conditions. Victimization of the black female by society is compared to the victimization of African countries by more powerful African countries. Jordan has said that when she writes a poem, she searches for the most harrowing or superlative way to express her feelings and get her point across. The rape image in "Poem About My Rights" reflects this practice. The poem's shocking and violent images are used to make comparisons among individual, national, and global situations. The forced gang rape of an unconsenting female in France is deemed by law as consent since male penetration did not include ejaculation, and therefore there is no proof. It is determined that the individual is wrong because of who and where she is at the time of the incident. To Jordan, this is analogous to the penetration of African nations by more powerful countries. Jordan also applies the rape image to her current situation as a black female: "I am the history of rape"; "I have been raped because I have been wrong"; "I have been the meaning of rape"; and "I have been the problem everyone seeks to/ eliminate by forced/ penetration with or without the evidence."

In Lauren Muller's *June Jordan's Poetry for the People* (1995), Jordan defines poetry as "a political action undertaken for the sake of information and the exorcism that telling the truth makes possible." She goes on to say that poetry should achieve a maximum impact with a minimum of words. Punctuation should be omitted. Vertical rhythm may be used to move the reader from one line to the next. Jordan also notes that a poem should not depend solely on the distribution of stressed and unstressed syllables but should incorporate musical qualities such as assonance and dissonance. Written in free verse, "Poem About My Rights" has little punctuation but is divided into four segments. In the first segment, Jordan's personal situation and viewpoint are introduced. The section ends with the word "silence" and a colon. In the second segment, the rape images of both the individual and the globe are presented. The idea of implied consent by the victim and a semicolon end this section. The third section is introduced with the capitalized comment "Do You Follow Me." This section recounts the wrongs inflicted upon blacks and upon Jordan by her parents, the government, and the world. Jordan is at the same time the product of her history and a member of current society. It is in this section that Jordan states, "I do not consent." The final section, briefer than the first three, is set off by the italicized words "*I am not wrong: Wrong is not my name.*" It is here that Jordan becomes an active and self-determined resister. She becomes proactive rather than reactive.

The ending of the poem is unsettling. Jordan writes that her "self-determination/ may very well cost you your life." The poem concludes on a dramatic and implied violent note without punctuation. The poem begins with the tranquil notion of taking a walk so the poet can clear her head and think. This calm setting gradually fades as images of oppression, brutality, and loss of freedom emerge. Rather than reverting back to the calm beginning, the ending portends more violence as the oppressed begin to take action.

Themes and Meanings

Violence toward and oppression of individual African Americans and countries in southern Africa are the overriding themes of "Poem About My Rights." This treatment is inflicted by those with power who choose to abuse that power. The misuse of power by those who are now empowered and the need to take a stand by those who are seemingly without power are themes to which Jordan repeatedly returns. The American culture as perceived by Jordan is antifemale, antiblack, and cruelly and unfairly violent. Victimization and oppression are unavoidable in Jordan's everyday life. This is also true of the victimization of Third World countries by neighboring countries. Both individually and globally, burden of proof is essential. In an essay in *I Know What the Red Clay Looks Like* (1994), Jordan decries this practice of blaming the victim.

"Poem About My Rights" is a passionate, emotional, and personal poem. Jordan's view of the world serves as a mandate for change. A bleak and violent society's condition becomes a vehicle for change both by the individual and by society. "Rights and wrongs" and "right and wrong" are subjects of the poem despite the fact that the words "right" or "rights" are never mentioned except in the title. Jordan is never right and never has rights in the narrative, but, by the poem's end, at least she is no longer wrong. She is her own person, ready to act. To Jordan, consent is not equivalent to having rights, and she consents to no one: not to family, not to school, and not to the country's bureaucracy.

"Poem About My Rights" serves as a testament to the belief that the individual can make a difference even though doing so requires an ongoing struggle. Near the end of the poem, Jordan avows, "my name is my own my own my own." The strength to meet challenges head-on is evident. The ending, however, portends violence: Individual action may cost participants their lives. While people do have the power to alter the course of oppression and correct the loss of rights, they must take action to make a difference. Indeed, this proactive position is the only hope for altering the current scenario.

Lynn Sager

POEM ABOUT PEOPLE

Author: Robert Pinsky (1940-   )
Type of poem: Lyric
First published: 1974; collected in *Sadness and Happiness*, 1975

The Poem

"Poem About People" is composed of thirteen unrhymed quatrains with no imme-diately obvious metrical pattern. Its title establishes its subject; written in the first person, the poem is the speaker's quiet meditation on what people are in appearance and in actuality and how they relate to one another.

It opens with the "I" speaking of the people he sees at grocery stores. In particular, he notes apparently middle-class, middle-aged, but still attractive women, and polite, fattish young men. Although they are all strangers to the speaker, they are people whom he believes he could like. Indeed, he says, one could "feel briefly like Jesus," referring to the New Testament (as well as Old Testament) command "to love thy neighbor as thyself."

The first three quatrains are concrete and almost cheerful; by suggestion, it is broad daylight. As the fourth quatrain opens, the tone and the images begin to change. The speaker feels "a gust of diffuse tenderness" that seems to link him with these people, but this gust is "crossing the dark spaces" between him and them. The poem is no longer about the sunlit world of people at the market, about human relationships; it moves within and is now about what the speaker is seeing and remembering, there where "the dry self burrows."

The remainder of the poem is given over to showing how people do not connect with one another despite this "gust." The third line of the fifth stanza begins with a "but" that signals the change. The speaker says that "love falters and flags" whenever a person is asked to face squarely another person in need. The poem now develops both by discursive statements and by two expanded images.

The people at the grocery store were strangers, easy to love in the abstract or to reject, but now the speaker remembers a friend. This friend, divorced and alone, hangs up the pictures he had painted; his wife had kept them hidden in a closet. He says, ruefully, that she was probably right, yet he puts them up. He asks too much of others, asks for their approval and their love. Then the speaker presents an image drawn from movies that depict the development of love and its triumph over hatred. It is a rather obvious story of a young Jewish soldier attempting to save the "anti-Semitic bully" drowning in a river as they are raked by "nazi fire." The image represents the type of symbol that modern culture provides when attempting to teach forgiveness and love.

The first of these two images shows an actuality: The divorce itself suggests that love can come to an end, and the man's situation shows how the fact of being alone makes one more needy. The second image, the movie scene, sentimentally depicts how love and forgiveness (and, therefore, connection) between seemingly irreconcil-able people win out. Movies are not actualities, however, so this image becomes deeply ironic. The last three stanzas, in a way, shift the scene again, for, although the reader is still in the mind of the speaker, the speaker gives a description of the external world again—this time of a world of full night and rain-filled wind. The images have progressed from bright, calm day to black stormy night, from images of possible love to the recognition that people's own desperate selves keep them from one another.

Forms and Devices

The critic Ian Hamilton, in the *Oxford Companion to Twentieth Century Poetry*, calls Pinsky a discursive poet—that is, one who is more likely to deal with statements and abstractions than with images. This is true in that Pinsky's subject matter is usually more than expressions of mood or feelings: His poems are also explorations of ideas. "Poem About People," however, is filled with images and subtly metaphoric language, as, for instance, those that bring out human commonalities with animals—animals that are, in the end, alone. The young men have a "porky walk," and "the dry self burrows." More important, these deep selves are connected by a simile (a comparison using "like") to the robin on the lawn and then evolutionarily back to the robin's "lizard" ancestry. The only other simile in the poem is the moment when the speaker speaks of momentarily feeling "like Jesus." These two similes are opposites, with the second one, leading from self to robin to lizard, cancelling out the first, which speaks of love.

Sound is very important to Pinsky and to this poem. Sound is an essential element in the meaning. Although the poem lacks an obvious meter, most of the lines are built on three- or four-beat measures and are so arranged that the poem continually hesitates on the edge of becoming iambic tetrameter. In short, there is a traditional music in the background, but there is also a tension between the finely rhythmical beat that is actually there and the understood, traditional meter. The structural contrast reinforces the thematic contrasts of the poem's ideas, the otherness of others.

Equally important, Pinsky makes extensive use of alliteration, repeating the beginning sounds of words to emphasize those words. Examples include the related *b*'s and *p*'s of the second and third stanzas in the description of the young men. The last *p* and *b* in the third stanza are in the line "possible/ To feel briefly like Jesus," and so connect the young men with the idea of love. One more alliteration (of *f*) signals the change in the fifth stanza of the poem, for as the images change, the speaker tells how "love falters and flags."

This alliteration also emphasizes the language of the poem. The language is almost solidly drawn from Old English roots and has many single-syllable words. The sound itself comes at times close to the emphatic beat of Old English alliterative verse. Such a beat hammers home the statements of the poem. More subtly, Pinsky uses contrast in language roots that also adds to the emphases: "my friend/ In his divorced schoolteacher/ Apartment" has two words, "divorced" and " apartment," derived from French, separated by the Germanic "schoolteacher." There is also the strange uses of "divorced schoolteacher" as a kind of compound Old English adjective for "apartment," which calls the reader's attention to the oddness and separateness of the friend.

Themes and Meanings

The major thematic concern of the poem is, as previously noted, that people are separate from one another, but that they need one another. This need is deeply egoistic and destructive. The people whom the speaker describes in the first lines are, by implication, not too different from the speaker himself, the point being that he should be able to relate to them if one can relate to others at all. Pinsky is, by using these people and this speaker, emphasizing the difficulty. "Only connect," the English novelist E. M. Forster wrote, suggesting that individuals, by coming truly together, could perhaps create a better world. Pinsky's poem questions whether this coming together is possible.

Even the title emphasizes this theme in stating that the poem is "about" people. It is not a lyric effusion about one person, not a communication to a particular person. Rather, it stands outside people, even when the reader seems to be inside the mind of the speaker. The poem is saying that people cannot quite leap the gulf that separates them, one from the other. They cannot because people are all essentially egoistic, incapable of real love for others: *"Hate my whole kind,* but me,/ Love me for myself." People want to be loved simply because they are "selves," not because they are human beings.

Human beings have thought of themselves as different from other species because humans are supposed to be capable of altruism—selflessly loving others. Yet humans are animals, concerned primarily if not exclusively with themselves. At the end of the poem, the speaker says that we can only "dream" of the gust of wind that connects us, for it has become a "dark wind." These words are set against the earlier reference to a "gust of diffuse tenderness." Perhaps the dark wind can cross "the wide spaces between us," but those spaces are indeed wide. Oddly, the poem is in the end not entirely pessimistic. The speaker regrets that people do not, perhaps cannot, love one another, yet such a regret suggests that at least they can try. In addition, a poem about a failure to connect is paradoxically a way of connecting, for art is one way that human beings do communicate beyond simply presenting facts.

L. L. Lee

POEM FOR AN ANNIVERSARY

Author: Cecil Day Lewis (1904-1972)
Type of poem: Meditation
First published: 1935, in *A Time to Dance and Other Poems*

The Poem

"Poem for an Anniversary" is a brief poem of twenty-four lines divided into four sestets. Each stanza is made up of a pattern of short and long lines; the first and last lines are terse and repeat a sentencelike format, and each stanza is, in itself, a complete thought. The poem gives the reader a command ("admit then and be glad") at the onset of each stanza, and each order is reminiscent of an action associated with an anniversary celebration: admit, remember, admire, and survey.

The anniversary of the title is never specifically indicated, yet the reader is left with a sense of worldwide chronology. There are references to boiling lava, storms, and "giant lightning" that evoke images of the beginning of time. In fact, the beginning of the poem notes the end of a prehistoric age: "Our volcanic age is over." The second and third stanzas introduce ages "made for peace" in which religious and philosophical thought exists. These lines eschew former times, times in which "foul" love existed, times of evil, thoughtless procreation. The final stanza leads the reader through a new world with a balmy climate in which plants and people flourish. This new world is "Love's best," a fecund place and time with fields of grain harvested by a community of people with "linked lives." These inhabitants are the survivors of fire and storm. They know the value of the rain clouds for engendering fertility and growth rather than causing havoc and wanton destruction. Each anniversary, each harvest, is important because it marks the continuance of stability.

Forms and Devices

The first two stanzas contain striking imagery of violent earthquakes, tidal waves, and "terrible lava" flows. Then clouds appear that reflect "the fire below," and "Shuddering electric storms" unleash a cooling water that tames the lava's deep furrows with peaceful streams. This rather pedantic, at times frightening, picture is broken up by Cecil Day Lewis's use of alliteration. Much like an Old English poet, he makes use of a repetition of sounds to reinforce the imitating message in each stanza. Thus the reader is dually instructed to "admit then and be glad" that the pre-Jurassic period, with its "bedrock boiling," has come to a close. Similarly, the fire storms that form the earth's cooling crust are to be remembered without regret as a necessary evil, a coupling of "foul or fair" nature that destroys as it creates.

In the second half of the poem, the countryside becomes a place to admire. Plants provide shade, and dangerous boulders lie at rest, providing "landmarks" for travelers. The earth's vista is no longer a fearful place but rather a "contour fine" ready for the plow and the seed. This is an area where the waterways go "Hotfoot to havoc" to provide an aquifer for future fields where before only "the lava went." Finally, the earth has "grain to grow," tilled by the "linked lives" of those who have taught the "lightning to lie low." Yet the author also uses puns and personification to allow the poem a little laughter amid its serious story. The "rent" the earth must pay for its fertility is its own destruction. Initially, seas leap from the ocean floor, clouds dream, and storms "shudder," but finally lightning crouches in obedience to humankind.

There is a curious rhyme scheme in the poem: The third and sixth lines of each stanza end with an *o* sound. This does not seem particularly significant until it is observed in relation to the overall subject of the poem: the destruction and re-creation of "The little O, th' earth" (William Shakespeare's *Antony and Cleopatra*, 1606-1607). With its repeating *o* sounds, the poem reverberates with the message that the resurrection of society is a continuous process, one that must be endured if humankind is to advance rather than decay. Indeed, that image is echoed in the choice of *o*-rhyming words. In the first stanza, the earth is shaken "from head to toe," but only temporarily. The poem goes on to assure the reader that this tremor did not last. The second section is a reminder of the "fire below" that all "used to know" but that is no longer evident. In fact, where there was once fire and molten rock, now "Cooler rivers flow." By the close of the poem, the awful discord on earth has lain "low," leaving time and space for a harvest to "grow."

Themes and Meanings

Echoing the dominant images of fire and fertility, "Poem for an Anniversary" is an anthem of destruction and creation. Espoused by his politically leftist comrades, Day Lewis promotes in this poem the paradox of total dismemberment of a state in order to rebuild it under a new regime. The persistent vision of volcano and fire reinforces an image of the phoenix of a new government rising from the ashes of the complete destruction of the old order. The volcano itself is a symbol of both debacle and miracle. Its eruption and the resultant lava and spume of ash set the earth aflame and choke out all life; but it is that same volcanic action that creates midocean atolls, providing a resting place for birds and animals that eventually settle on them to create an island of life where before there were only seas.

Images of living and mating are evident throughout the poem, except in the opening stanza in which the seas leap "from their beds" and the "World's bedrock" is deemed "terrible" in the light of the abundance of lava. Yet the persona assures readers that "Now it is not so." Soon there is a "mating in air" that is evaluated as neither "foul" nor "fair" love but rather as a natural phenomenon. Soon, however, prayers are raised, perhaps signifying the onset of enlightened thought and action. An "us" appears, the advent of rational life, and soon humanity experiences "Love's best," resulting in their "linked lives," a people joined in tending the new crop of ideas in a fine and cogent climate. Even though these changes are wrought under violent circumstances, the reader is instructed to admire, not fear, the incipience. They may seem terrifying at the beginning, but they should be remembered for their reproductive qualities, much like the farmer who burns his field, not to destroy it but to make way for the next year's crop.

Jennifer L. Wyatt

POEM OF THE END

Author: Marina Tsvetayeva (1892-1942)
Type of poem: Poetic sequence
First published: 1925, as "Poema kontsa"; collected in *Izbrannye proizvedeniya*, 1965; English translation collected in *Selected Poems of Marina Tsvetayeva*, 1971

The Poem

"Poem of the End," composed in 1924, is a poetic sequence of fourteen lyrics describing the end of an affair between the poet, Marina Tsvetayeva, and her lover Konstantin Rodzevitch. Although the poem is autobiographical, it is not necessary to know much about the relationship to understand the poem, which is universal in the intensity of its emotion. As the lovers meet, walk along a river, and pass places they once frequented, the poet struggles with her lover's decision to break off the relationship, and the structure of the poem reflects this struggle. Much of the poem is written in first person, and the "I" functions as referent to both the poet and the persona. It is often difficult to tell who is speaking, the poet or her lover, indicating that the parting is difficult for both; the two are still very much in love, but the lover is driven away by the intensity of the poet. The ambiguity of the speaker's voice, however, also suggests that their conversations may be imagined or remembered.

In the opening lyric, the lovers meet, and the poet becomes suspicious of her lover's demeanor, the "menace at the edges of his/ eyes." When the lover suggests going to a movie, the poet insists on going home, but, in the second poem, "home" turns into "houses/ collapsing in the one word: home," and the lover's house on the hill appears to burst into flame as the poet finds her love self-destructing. The third lyric provides a contrast in imagery as the couple walks along the river and the poet notes her affinity for water, in which she will not drown because she was "born naiad," a reference to the poet's given name (Marina). The fourth poem presents a striking shift in tone and structure; in this segment, Tsvetayeva imitates a popular ballad form to ridicule ordinary people going about their daily activities, "snout-deep in the feathers of some/ business arrangement." The poet reveals both a disrespect for common people and her sense of alienation as a poet, a theme that recurs in the twelfth lyric as the pair walks through the Jewish ghetto of Prague: "In this most Christian of worlds/ all poets are Jews." In the fifth poem, the lovers begin a painful discussion of their relationship, and the awkwardness of their conversation is reflected in the spacing between words, the speech interrupted by parenthetical remarks and abrupt shifts indicated by dashes.

There is little action after the fifth poem, and the remaining segments explore the poet's inner thoughts. The poet grapples with her emotions; she is angry at her lover's cowardice in making a clean break and at his superficial gestures—he has offered her a ring as a symbol of parting rather than commitment; still, she does not want to leave and determines to cling more tightly in order to force her lover into a violent separation: "I bite in like a tick/ you must tear out my roots to be rid of me." Finally, the lover is reduced to tears and is ridiculed by a trio of prostitutes passing by. The poet marks the contrast between the intimacy of her affair and the casual, commercial sexual exchanges of the laughing women, but the cycle ends on a somber, pessimistic note as "without trace—in silence—/ something sinks like a ship."

Forms and Devices

"Poem of the End" is not easily translated because Russian is an inflected language and because Tsvetayeva uses many innovations that cannot be rendered into English. Russian, unlike English, employs case endings so that meaning is more independent of placement than in English, in which objects regularly follow verbs that are preceded by subjects. Tsvetayeva takes advantage of Russian inflection, deviating from standard word order, a feature that cannot be translated. English translations cannot adhere to the rhyme schemes and metrical patterns of the original either. Therefore, some of the power and innovation of the poem are lost in translation.

Structurally, "Poem of the End" is very complex. Tsvetayeva employs a stream-of-consciousness technique to take the reader into the poet's psyche. Her style is characterized by dashes, refrains, spaces between words, odd line breaks, and enjambment (run-on lines) to create new, jolting meters. For example, in the sixth section, she imitates the struggle to control her tears with the lines "So now must be no/ so now must be no/ must be no crying" and continues to repeat "without crying" in the next six stanzas. Although she does not repeat the phrase in the final stanza of the section, the reader expects to hear the phrase and is invited to supply it. Such refrains connect the poetry yet provide a contrast to the pervasive ellipses of her style. Additionally, Tsvetayeva varies the meter from section to section to show mood swings and shifts in focus. Such stylistic contrasts and variations maintain both syntactic and semantic tension throughout the work.

Tsvetayeva's metaphors contribute to this tension, jolting the reader from one image to another, as in the following line, which begins as a rhetorical question but ends with a startling comparison: "who shall I tell my sorrow/ my horror greener than ice?" She frequently shifts between colloquial and formal diction, between classical allusions and description of her surroundings, often ending with a disturbing image. In the third section, for example, she alludes to the lush hanging gardens of the Assyrian princess Semiramis, then describes the river along which she and her lover walk as "a strip as colourless/ as a slab for corpses."

Themes and Meanings

On the surface, "Poem of the End" is a journey, a simple walk along a river in Prague, but it is also a psychological journey, and this is where the meaning of the poem resides. For Tsvetayeva, who believes the poet holds an exalted position, ordinary life means death; she is incapable of conventional emotion, and it is her intensity that has caused the break with her lover. The end to which the poem refers is both the ending of the affair and the poet's rejection of ordinary life. As the cycle moves between detailed descriptions of Tsvetayeva's physical surroundings and her mental landscape, these endings become apparent.

The poem reveals its meaning through images of banality and death, which are introduced in the first poem. In the opening line, the poet waits for her lover beneath a sign, "a point of rusting/ tin in the sky," and when her lover arrives, he is as "on time as death is." In the seventh stanza, these images combine: "life is/ at death point." This repetition of the word "point" suggests that the rusting tin signifies not just a shabby café but death as well. In the third and fourth segments of the cycle, Tsvetayeva again juxtaposes themes of death and tawdriness, this time using separate poems for each. In the third poem, the river, traditionally a symbol of life, is described as "a slab for corpses," and references to death recur throughout the third lyric. In the next poem, the locale shifts abruptly to a café, perhaps a flashback to the café where the lovers met; here the poet examines the banality of ordinary people. She returns to this juxtaposition in the twelfth poem, saying "Life is only a suburb" and, four stanzas later, "Life is a place where it's forbidden/ to live." The poet goes on to identify herself with the Jews: As a poet she is an alien, an outsider, and to live she must exile herself from ordinary life and its ordinary affairs. Her love must fail because she is a poet, someone too intensely emotional to succeed at conventional love.

Tsvetayeva's break with the conventional is reflected throughout "Poem of the End" in her innovative structure, which also functions thematically. In order to rise above the deathlike river and the deadly towns and suburbs, she must not follow "a path for/ sheep." Instead, she must soar beyond traditional modes of expression. By employing stream of consciousness, using unconventional punctuation and line breaks, and varying the meter, Tsvetayeva demonstrates that she has rejected the conventional: ordinary love, ordinary life, ordinary verse.

In spite of the poet's commitment to existing on a higher plane, the poem ends somberly: "And into the hollow waves of/ darkness—hunched and level—/ without trace—in silence—/ something sinks like a ship." This final stanza suggests that the poet fears failure, that her voice will not be heard, that she herself will disappear in silence without a trace. In fact, when "Poem of the End" was first circulated, it was not well received by critics, perhaps because of its stylistic innovation. However, it has since come to be considered one of Russia's finest psychological poems and the best example of Tsvetayeva's mature style.

K Edgington

REFERENCE